The Blue De

A History of the 88th Infantry Division in World War II

•

By JOHN P. DELANEY

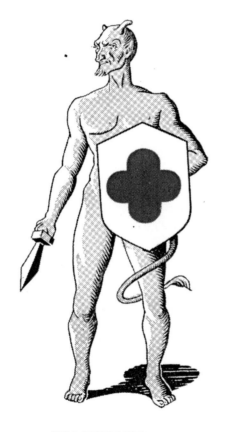

WASHINGTON
INFANTRY JOURNAL PRESS

FIRST EDITION

TO
ALL THE BLUE DEVILS
WHO NEVER CAME BACK

CONTENTS

FOREWORD ix

INTRODUCTION xi

ACKNOWLEDGMENTS xiii

WHY I FIGHT! xiv

THE INFANTRY DIVISION xvi

THE UNITS xvii

END OF A LONG ROAD xxi

ACTIVATION 1
    The New 88th 8

TRAINING 12
    The Cookson Hills 12
    Louisiana Maneuvers 25
    Is This the Army? 28
    Liberty Ships 31
    What Kept You? 33
    Playing for Keeps 37

THE QUIET WAR 42
    Cassino 44
    Minturno 47
    The Buildup 58

THE FIRST TEST 62

ROME 89

DUST AND MINES 105

THE GOTHIC LINE 126

THE WINTER LINE 164

THE PO VALLEY 186

POW COMMAND 225
    No Vacations 234
    Redeployment 239
    Information and Education 242

OCCUPATION 249

BATTLE CASUALTIES 279

DECORATIONS AND AWARDS 295

BATTLE HONORS 357

OUTLINE OF POW COMMAND ACTIVITIES 359

MAPS

ROUTE OF THE BLUE DEVILS xx
THE JUMPOFF 64
THE ROAD TO ROME 80
TO THE ARNO 106
THROUGH THE GOTHIC LINE 128
INTO THE PO VALLEY 188
OCCUPATION FORCE IN VENEZIA-GIULIA 250

Major General John E. Sloan.
He built the 88th, led it from Camp Gruber to the Arno River.

FOREWORD

This history, made by the officers and men of the "Blue Devil" Division, is an accomplishment in which each can take just pride and pass on to his children with a feeling of deep satisfaction. A duty has been well done—a duty to our country, to our civilization, to our God.

Today I feel deeply the honor that was mine as your general, working with you, fighting with you and sharing your hardships. We older men are approaching the culmination of our careers, but many of you, in your youth and strength, have many active years ahead. Not forgetting the past, you will maintain the high standards of courage, unselfishness and devotion to duty which have been displayed so frequently on the field of battle by you and even unto death by those who now rest in peace. Let us keep these things ever before us. This—*your* history—will be a constant reminder.

In recording our history, I feel that we would be ungrateful if we did not give full credit to those who made our success possible : our fathers, mothers, wives, sweethearts and many, many loyal friends in Muskogee, San Antonio and elsewhere. They all assisted us, believed in us, encouraged us, and now take pride in our deeds. Many of them suffered with us, they are part of us, Blue Devils all.

If we are to be fair to those who follow us and to those whom we laid to rest in foreign lands, we will not let our history stop here in these pages. We must direct our efforts toward assuring that the lessons we have learned from our experiences shall be so applied as to benefit future generations. Without submerging sentiment, we must be realists, factual in our thinking since we are living in a world where greed, enmity, corruption and selfishness exist. We must safeguard the next generation from loose thinking and overconfidence in idealisms; there must be no more Hitlers, Mussolinis, Tojos, Pearl Harbors nor Bataans. Wishful thinking alone will not assure this; we who know, we who have learned the hard way, must instill action in those who do not know, must put steel in the souls of those who are hesitant.

As we go our separate ways, I feel that we are better men for the associations we have experienced in the 88th. As the years pass, those associations will become more and more dear to us. Let us enshrine them in our hearts with memories of our comrades who did not come back, and draw on these two inspirations to march on in the tradition of the Blue Devil Division.

With utmost trust in you and our America, I am, your oldest Blue Devil,

JOHN E. SLOAN
Major General, USA

INTRODUCTION

The 88th Division played a major role in the battle of Italy, where it was rated by the Germans after the summer of 1944 as the best American division in Italy. Because of the outstanding job it did in Italy, the 88th contributed its share to the winning of the war. It was the first of the draft infantry divisions to enter combat on any front in World War II and it was among the top divisions in the American Army. It won its share of territory and honors durings its 344 days of combat. It paid dearly for all that it won—it lost 15,173 officers and men killed, wounded and missing in action. Only thirteen other divisions in the U. S. Army suffered heavier losses.

The 88th fought its battles on what was called "a forgotten front." Some day history will appraise the true worth of the Italian campaign in the over-all war picture. Military historians will analyze and sift and publish detailed volumes on the operational contribution of the 88th in the battle for Italy.

This book is not a history, in the true sense of the word. It is not intended to be such.

It is rather the story of a combat division from its beginning to its end. It is a story compiled both from official journals and from the personal experiences of the citizen-soldiers who made up its squads and platoons. It is a story which never can be told in every complete detail. For every one of the incidents related here, a reader can remember scores that are not found in these pages. There are not enough words, or paper, to list them all. The incidents related are considered to be representative of the experiences of the majority of 88th men.

What then, is the purpose of this book? The purpose is simply to record as much of the story of the 88th as it is possible to do while it is still comparatively fresh, so that in years to come the men and the families of the men who fought with it can read of some of their exploits. When Junior asks, "Where were you in the war, Daddy?" the ex-Blue Devil can hand him the book and reply, "I was there, with the 88th!"

Of necessity, the story will concern itself with the front-line riflemen, for theirs was the toughest and dirtiest job. No one will deny that. But all ranks and branches of the 88th served with distinction and all teamed to make the 88th what it was. There is glory enough in the record for all.

For every name mentioned in this book, a score of names could be substituted. In the long drive up the peninsula, every man had experiences in combat similar to the incidents described in the book. All the men who served with the 88th in any capacity added their bit to its unit success.

Some few men failed themselves, their buddies, and the Division. Since no man knows another man well enough to question his courage, the failures are not mentioned or considered as such. In the heat of battle, there is no explaining—or accounting—for an individual's reactions. No man is qualified to cast the first stone.

There is no leading character in this book. The only real hero is the 88th Infantry Division.

As Blue Devils, the men of the 88th fought to win a war, to preserve the ideals of freedom, justice and security. As civilians, the former Blue Devils must continue that fight on the home front. They must preserve those ideals, or they will lose the peace they fought so hard to attain.

It was an honor to have served with the 88th. It is a privilege to tell its story.

JACK DELANEY

ACKNOWLEDGMENTS

Sincere thanks for their help in furnishing material and suggestions for this book are in order to: Paul J. LeVine, William M. Ragan Jr., Milton B. Dolinger, Edward J. Zink, Gerald S. Root, Lynwood C. Walton—killed in action—Edwin M. Mortensen, Paul L. Pappas, J. B. Culwell, Col. R. J. McBride, Col. J. C. Fry and Lt. Col. W. J. Skelly, who wrote the rough draft of the Occupation chapter. Also: The Associated Press, The United Press, International News Service, *The Stars and Stripes Mediterranean, Yank: The Army Weekly, The Muskogee* (Oklahoma) *Daily Phoenix* and *The Standard-Times,* New Bedford, Massachusetts. Unless otherwise indicated, all photos were taken by the Signal Corps, U. S. Army. Maps are based on original sketches by Franklin P. Sayles.

WHY I FIGHT!

Why does a soldier fight? Why does a doughboy keep going in the face of enemy fire until death or wounds bring him down? Why does any man endure the horror and fear and pain and the ever present shadow of death? What is it that keeps him going? What impels him to get up out of the comparative safety of a foxhole and charge into what he knows may be his eternity? The greatest authors, the most learned teachers have tried, and failed, to answer. The best answer, and the most sincere, came from S/Sgt. Aubrey B. Sally of the 349th. His answer could well represent the collective opinion of the entire 88th Division.

"Why do I fight? I don't know. I just don't know!

"I don't know, unless it's because I feel that I must, and I must because I'm expected to. If I should fail to do what is asked of me, I would betray the trust of the men fighting with me. And if I betrayed this trust, not only do I feel that I would become a traitor both to my fellow fighters everywhere and to all that I hold dear at home, but also in my own eyes I believe I would become so despicable that no longer would I feel worthy of the comradeship of men.

"It is difficult to put into words the feeling that impels a man to advance when he knows that his next breath may be his last, when he knows that his next step may set off a foot mine, when he expects at any moment to feel the blast of a Jerry machine-gun and feel himself smashed to the ground by the impact of many bullets even before he can pull the trigger.

"But it seems that there is an urge inside me that compels me to go with my buddies when they attack and to sweat it out with them in defense, something that makes me go with them on seemingly useless patrols and come back to endure seemingly useless privations, all to what may be a useless end.

"In my reasons for fighting I don't believe I stand alone. Instead, I believe that all fighters fight for much the same reasons.

"So you see that which makes me fight is neither bravery nor anger, nor is it fear or hatred. I believe that I fight because something within me, something that I am at a loss to understand, tells me that I must fight so long as there is need to."

Our army is no better than its infantry, and victory will come only when and as our infantry gains it; the price will be predominantly what the infantry pays. These days the entire nation is following operations on its war maps. It is to be noted that the front lines of these maps are simply where the infantryman is. It is true that he is supported magnificently by artillery and air, but this support is behind and above him. There is nothing in front of him but the enemy.

LT. GEN. LESLEY J. MCNAIR
COMMANDING GENERAL, ARMY GROUND FORCES.
KILLED IN ACTION 25 JULY 1944.

THE INFANTRY DIVISION

A brief note on the organization of an infantry division may be helpful to the non-military reader.

A modern infantry division has approximately 14,000 men. About 60 per cent are infantrymen; the rest are artillerymen, engineers, medics, signalmen, reconnaissance troops, quartermasters and ordnancemen. A division is a well balanced fighting unit.

In addition, special units, such as tanks, tank destroyers, antiaircraft or long-range artillery may be attached to the division for specific missions. These units function as an integral part of the division as long as they are with it.

In battle a division generally operates under an organizational setup known as combat teams. A combat team is composed of one regiment of infantry, a battalion of artillery and the necessary attachments of signal, medical, engineer and reconnaissance troops. There are three combat teams in a division. Each combat team may be likened to a miniature division.

For special missions to be accomplished by the division, it is sometimes necessary to form what is known as a task force. A task force may consist of infantry mounted on tanks, for example, with the mission of exploiting a breakthrough or racing on ahead of the main body of the division to seize an important bridge, road junction or town. The task force operates as an independent unit under its own designated commander until the special mission has been accomplished.

Below the division level the units are:

Regiment. Three infantry regiments and the division artillery of four battalions are the main units of the division. A regiment has approximately 3,000 men. An artillery battalion has about 500 men.

Battalion. Three battalions and four separate companies make up one regiment. A battalion has approximately 850 men.

Company. Five companies make up one battalion. The companies include three rifle companies, one heavy-weapons company, and one headquarters company. A company has approximately 180 men.

Battery. In the artillery, the battery corresponds to the company in the infantry, but a battery has only approximately 100 men.

Platoon. Four platoons make up one company. A platoon has approximately 40 men.

Squad. Three squads make up one platoon. A squad has 12 men.

Above the division level the units are:

Corps. Two or more divisions may make up one corps.

Army. Two or more corps may make up one army.

Army Group. Two or more armies may make up one army group.

THE UNITS

349th Infantry Regiment
350th Infantry Regiment
351st Infantry Regiment
337th Field Artillery Battalion
338th Field Artillery Battalion
339th Field Artillery Battalion
913th Field Artillery Battalion
313th Engineer (Combat) Battalion
313th Medical Battalion
88th Reconnaissance Troop
88th Signal Company
88th Quartermaster Company
788th Ordnance (LM) Company
Division Headquarters
Division Headquarters Company
Headquarters and Headquarters Battery,
    Division Artillery
88th Division Band
88th Division Military Police Platoon

★

ROME–ARNO
January 22 to September 9, 1944

★

NORTH APENNINES
September 10, 1944 to April 4, 1945

★

PO VALLEY
April 5 to May 8, 1945

THE BLUE DEVILS IN ITALY

Route of the Blue Devils.

END OF A LONG ROAD

The silence was loud.

Here, high in the Italian Alps, suddenly, there no longer was the shuddering crash of artillery, the steady chatter of machine guns or the irregular blurt of rifles. There was no sound. There would never again be the sound of a shell screaming in.

The war was over.

You had to say that several times before it made any sense—you had to listen hard to hear nothing—you had to breathe deeply to inhale the sweet night air.

You didn't quite believe it—the war was over and you had made it—alive. You had gambled and won where you figured to lose. You were alive, and the war was over, and you had all the rest of your life to get used to the wonderful idea of peace.

But you were tired, too dog-tired to celebrate, too weary to do anything or want anything but sleep. The war was over, but its end was nothing like the movies, just as its beginning and its whole bloody length had not been anything like the movies.

You were tired; you'd come a long way for this moment; you'd come all the way—in battle—from Cassino to the Brenner Pass. And never really, during all the days and nights, deep down where you admitted it only to yourself, had you expected to make it all the way. Now that you had, and realization came slowly, now that the tight knot of fear in your stomach was finally beginning to loosen, you needed sleep more than anything.

It had been a long grind and a long fight. And a lot of good men had died all along the route to help push you up and through to the end. At Cassino and Minturno, Rome and the Arno, the Gothic Line and across the Po Valley, a lot of buddies were resting easier tonight because, although their war had ended months and years before, the jobs they had died doing had finally paid off.

Right now, in the first minutes of peace, their names and faces and deeds were hazy. You remembered them dimly. You thanked them. And you thanked Whoever you called God for bringing you through. Sleep you needed more than anything. It was difficult going back and remembering; there were all the peaceful days ahead to use and to remember the war days just finished, to remember back to the beginning when all of the 88th's recruits had started off on the longest way home.

At that "beginning," they were untried, untested and unknown. They were just a bunch of draftees, those 88th recruits; a bunch of draftees at an army camp as new and as raw as they were.

At the end they were old and hard and tired, as battle-wise and combat-weary as only Italian mud and mountains and combat could make an outfit.

They'd been tried and tested many times; they were no longer unknown. Individually and collectively, they'd won their share of territory and honors the hard way. They'd slugged their way through that misnamed and often cursed "soft underbelly of Europe." It was called "soft" by men who never had been there.

To the Army, they were the men and units of the 88th Infantry Division. To the Germans, who tried and failed to stop them, they were the "Blue Devils"—blue for the color of their cloverleaf insignia and "devils" for the way they'd fought since their first kickoff in May 1944.

In their combat time, 344 full and official days of it, they had answered all the questions raised by themselves and by others. They had proved they were good.

They were better than good.

They were, as Major General Schulz of the 1st Parachute Division, the pride of the German Wehrmacht, told his interrogators, "The best we have ever fought against."

The glory of the colors never will be sullied as long as one man of the 88th Division still lives.

MAJ. GEN. JOHN E. SLOAN

Colors are lowered at Division Headquarters.

ACTIVATION

The Air Corps "pulverizes" and "obliterates" targets; the artillery "blasts" enemy installations, and the tankers "smash through" stone walls of opposition. That's the way it is always done. But despite the preparatory assaults, and the glowing adjectives, the infantryman in any battle is the deciding factor.

To the infantryman falls the toughest job. When the bombers have finished their runs and the artillery has dumped its shells, the infantryman must rise out of his foxhole, charge the contested position, clear out the remaining opposition, take and hold the ground. He seeks out the enemy in his hiding place and with rifle, bayonet, hand grenade or bare hands wrings final surrender from the enemy soldier.

In the final stages, the infantryman goes alone. He does the job by himself; succeeds or fails by his own efforts. It is a man-to-man, kill-or-be-killed proposition. He moves in and takes the ground. If he fails, then the Air Corps and the artillery and the tankers fail. If he succeeds, all other arms succeed and another little patch of ground, another pillbox, another hill is added to the sum total of victory.

War is never on a grand scale. It is a composite of little battles for bridges, road junctions, houses and even single machine-gun emplacements. To the men engaged in these individual struggles, these little battles are the most important of all for their lives are at stake in the outcome. The foxhole occupied by one doughboy is the most important hole in the world, because he is in it. The successes or failures in all the little battles, added up, mean victory or defeat in the final analysis. Without the infantry all other arms and services would be useless. In back of the infantryman are all the support weapons and supplies so necessary for war. In front of him there is "nothing but the enemy."

War is never glamorous.

War is a dirty, filthy business. It is life lived under the most miserable conditions. It is death suffered under the most horrible circumstances. It is fought on lonely hillsides, in rubbled towns, in ditches and sewers and cellars, in rain, and snow and mud, in pain and fear.

War is training and marching, privation and lack of individual privacy, work and sweat and loneliness, periods of long waiting, short battles, endless patrolling, enemy planes that strafe highways, the whistle of enemy shells, cold rations and foot blisters, life stripped to its barest essentials.

War is dead men in the hot sun, dying men screaming in pain, wrecked men in hospitals with plates in their skulls, sightless eyes, stumps of legs and arms, men fed through tubes or with their insides held together by wire.

War is men with shattered minds in padded cells.

War is men who wake up in the middle of the night, shaking and screaming, and then realize they're waking from a dream.

War is people saying endless goodbyes—is women waiting, and some not waiting—is men returning and telegrams which read that "The War Department regrets . . ."—is "Welcome Home" or "I don't want you."

War is something that never should happen, but does. War is the most awful, the most unforgettable experience a man could have.

War, in the infantry, is all that and more. There is "no glamour in the infantry. You learn how much blood you have to pay for fifty-odd yards of battle-scarred mud. In the infantry, there are no crash helmets, no fancy wings for the girl back home to wear. You're just a guy with a gun, and a job to do!"

For the second time in a generation, a job to do was handed to Americans when the Japanese attacked Pearl Harbor on December 7, 1941. For the second time in recent history, "greetings from the President" were sent to millions of men throughout the country. Scores of divisions were activated at old and new cantonments. One of the divisions was the 88th Infantry, formed for the second time to defend a nation at war.

The 88th was not a brand-new outfit. It was created during World War I and served with such distinction in that conflict that its colors had been decorated by General John J. Pershing.

The first 88th Division was activated on September 4, 1917, at Camp Dodge, Iowa, under command of Maj. Gen. Edward H. Plummer. Training began immediately, but hardly had the recruits been put through the rudiments of military drill when thousands of them were transferred out to other units. So long did this transfer policy continue that most of the officers came to believe that the 88th was to be merely a replacement division. More than 45,000 replacements were furnished by that first 88th to other units overseas. However, in February 1918, gloom was dispelled when men of the 163rd Depot Brigade at Camp Dodge, who originally had been earmarked for transfer to other divisions, were ordered transferred to the 88th. From then on, training progressed rapidly. In July, the Division was shipped to a POE and landed in France in late August and early September of 1918.

Meanwhile, General Plummer, the original Division commander, had been relieved of command because of physical disability and he was succeeded by Maj. Gen. William Weigel on September 10, 1918. Under General Weigel's leadership the Division gave a good account of itself and on conclusion of its service in France, its own colors and the colors of its regiments were decorated by General Pershing.

In France the Division quickly was sent to a training area in the beautiful and historic Côte-d'Or region, where it stayed until orders came for a hurried trip to the front. On September 14 this move began and the Division displaced forward into the Haute-Saône area. Official records give the date of entry of the 88th Division into the line as October 12, 1918, the date on which French front-line battalions were relieved by 88th battalions. The trenches occupied by the Division were in the center sector of Haute-Alsace. The sector was a quiet one although it had seen fierce fighting earlier in the war. The area was in bad shape with trenches partly filled with water, revetments caved in, shell holes and old barbed-wire entanglements. Engineers of the 88th immediately were assigned to rehabilitate and strengthen that part of the old trench system included in the Division's plan of defense.

During its occupation of the Haute-Alsace sector the 88th participated in four raids. The Germans were of the opinion that the Allies were preparing for large-scale attack on the important city of Mulhouse which lay a short distance to the northeast. Arrival of the 88th had lent color to this belief and the enemy maintained constant air observation of front and rear areas. First division casualties came on the night of October 12–13 when the enemy launched a raid on 2d Battalion, 350th Infantry, resulting in the death of one soldier and wounds to 18 others. One officer and four enlisted men were awarded the Croix de Guerre by the French for gallant conduct in repelling the raid. Official report of the engagement made to headquarters was as follows:

On the night of October 12–13, 1918, two working parties were sent out from the 350th Infantry under command of Capt. Safford and Capt. House, respectively; their mission being to connect the advance line with the first German trench at Ammertzwiller. Ammertzwiller and other towns were not held in their entirety nor continually occupied by enemy forces, and French Seventh Army commander had directed that such portions of territory be taken over. Hostile salient at Ammertzwiller particularly favored seizure and consolidation into our own lines. The 2d Bn. 350th Infantry was preparing to effect this plan when the raid occurred. These two detachments were each to be protected by French covering detachments provided by reconnaissance parties which included a number of officers and NCOs. It was reported that these covering parties were late in arriving and the reconnaissance parties were cut off by a Minenwerfer barrage in advance of our front lines. This was at 1900 hours, at the same time our own barrage was laid down by the French artillery in support. The reconnaissance party took shelter in old shell holes and dugouts. When the hostile barrage moved back, they were trapped by a German raiding party which followed its own barrage. The entire party was taken captive with the exception of one French lieutenant, one machine gun officer and one 2d lieutenant of the 2d Battalion, 350th Infantry. The working party in which Capt. Brethorst and several of his men were killed was near the

Air view of Camp Gruber, Oklahoma

entrance of Balschwiller and was caught by the German barrage as it moved back.

On the following day, October 14, the second action took place. The 350th advanced in its sector and Company D penetrated into Ammertzwiller undiscovered by the enemy and established outposts. Company H occupied the hostile front line in Enschingen. At daybreak the outposts in Ammertzwiller were discovered and attacked. Although outnumbered, the six outposts held off the initial attack and gradually withdrew into some old trenches, remained until night and then withdrew, by order, under cover of darkness. None were killed or wounded and only one was captured. It was this action for which the four Croix de Guerre, mentioned earlier, were awarded. The attacking party from the 2d Battalion remained undiscovered in the enemy lines in Enschinger for several hours after 1st Battalion outposts had fallen back, and began to consolidate, but were later ordered to withdraw.

The third event of importance in the Division sector took place on October 18 when the enemy attempted a raid on the 351st Infantry in Schönholz Woods. Schönholz Woods formed an extreme salient in the center of the Division sector. Located on a steep hill sloping toward the German lines with the communicating trenches visible to the enemy, it

4

st toward the Cookson Hills.

was one of the most difficult parts of the entire terrain to hold or support. Lines were very close together, and being in the same woods, observation was mutually difficult, and it was almost impossible to ward off surprise. The Germans habitually raided this point to capture prisoners at least once or twice a month.

Company I of 351st Infantry was given the task of first defending the salient and was the first element of the Division to repulse a raid there. On the morning of October 18 during a heavy fog, a German raiding party, strength unknown, was sighted. After about twenty minutes they were compelled to withdraw under cover of a smoke screen. This raid was made on October 18. On the 31st they attempted another. The salient was held at that time by Company I, 352d Infantry. It opened with an artillery barrage lasting twenty minutes, about thirty shells of which fell in the M Company sector, at which point was located a machine gun that they unsuccessfully tried to knock out. This was followed by an attack which was successfully repulsed.

No further combat occurred during the Division's tour in this sector. The enemy had acquired a healthy conception of its fighting qualities, for after the first week's period of duty in the Haute Alsace sector, the Germans had assumed an attitude almost entirely defensive. Patrols from the division crossed No Man's Land at will and penetrated the German lines at practically every point without opposition. In this tour the Division had demonstrated to the satisfaction of both French and American high commands that it was ready to take part in major offensive operations. Morale was high, fighting qualities had been amply shown in the four raids, and the command was ready to assume its full share in any offensive for which it might be selected. The tour in the Haute Alsace sector was its last as a front-line division. After relief there it was sent to the Toul Sector where it was to become corps reserve for the IV Corps, a part of the American Second Army. The Armistice brought about the cessation of hostilities before the entire Division reached the new assembly area in vicinity of Lagney northwest of Toul.

After the Armistice time was taken up in training, schools, and other activities. Finally, on May 8, 1919, the Division started the homeward movement, with the 349th Infantry the first to sail for the U.S. The 88th, less engineers and artillery, was together as a unit for the last time on May 15. Upon arrival in this country the unit was broken up, officers and men were sent to Camp Dodge, the original home of the division, for discharge. Others were sent to other camps throughout the country.

It was during the time immediately following the Armistice that the Division insignia was adopted. The Division was known as the "Cloverleaf Division" because its insignia is based on the cloverleaf idea. Actually, the design adopted was two solid figures 8 crossed at right angles which gives somewhat the appearance of a Maltese cross made with loops, or a four-leaved clover.

During the years of the Division's existence as an organized reserve unit, thousands of reserve officers had been assigned to it. The regimental units supervised and directed the training of thousands of CMTC students at Fort Snelling, Minnesota, and Fort Des Moines, Iowa. In those peacetime years Division Headquarters was maintained at Minneapolis, Minnesota, with headquarters of its several units in Iowa, Minnesota, and the Dakotas.

To sum up, the 88th Division, although not sent to France until August 1918, trained and sent 45,000 men to France to represent it gloriously there. Immediately on arrival in France it was rushed into the line in a quiet sector. Without transportation, without equipment, the Division gave a splendid account of itself in the Haute-Alsace sector. By its activity there it prevented the Germans from withdrawing troops on the

Maj. Gen. John E. Sloan and John S. Quigley, 88th Veterans Association of World War I, on conclusion of formal Activation Day ceremonies.

south to be sent against American forces in the Meuse–Argonne Offensive. By its activity in Haute-Alsace, and by its presence later as American IV Corps and Second Army reserve, it permitted other American divisions to be used directly with the First Army in the Argonne Forest and along the Meuse.

An interesting sidelight on the Division is the fact that the 88th is the real founder of the American Legion. The idea of the American Legion originated at a conference between Lt. Col. Bennett C. Clark, AC of S, G-1, Major Eric Fisher Wood, AC of S, G-2, of the 88th Division, and Lt. Col. Theodore Roosevelt. Colonel Roosevelt was named temporary Chairman, and Major Wood, temporary Secretary. Later Colonel Roosevelt was ordered home and Lt. Colonel Clark was appointed Chairman while Major Wood was made Secretary at a later meeting in St. Louis, Missouri.

Only a comparative handful of troops was present for Activation Day ceremonies.

THE NEW 88TH

After twenty-three years of existence as a "paper" outfit, the dim embers of the old 88th were fanned into fitful flame early in 1942 by the winds of Mars blowing from Europe and Japan. The War Department had decided to reactivate the Division and appointed Maj. Gen. John E. Sloan of Greenville, South Carolina, a veteran of thirty-one years in the Field and Coast Artillery, to command the new outfit. Assigned to assist him were Brig. Gen. Stonewall Jackson of Plattsburg, New York, as Assistant Division Commander, and Brig. Gen. Guy O. Kurtz of Alhambra, California, as Division Artillery Commander.

Camp Gruber, Oklahoma, eighteen miles up the winding mountain road from Muskogee, was designated as the training camp. Located deep in the Cookson Hills, long-time hideout of Oklahoma's bad-men and the nation's public enemies, Camp Gruber was one of the largest of the new training camps.

While the General and Special Staffs were training at staff and command schools and draft boards were scooping up thousands of candidates, General Jackson journeyed to Fort Bragg, North Carolina, and there personally interviewed and selected an enlisted cadre from the crack 9th Infantry Division. Other cadre men came from the Infantry Replacement Training Center at Camp Wheeler, Georgia, and from Camp Wolters, Texas, laced with a sprinkling of National Guard and Reserve officers. Converging on Camp Gruber, the officer and enlisted cadre underwent special training there, set up regimental and battalion headquarters, and made preparations to receive the thousands of draftees then still enjoying their last few days and weeks as civilians. The 88th, primarily, was an all-draftee outfit.

There were but a few hundred men in the formation called for the official flag-raising ceremonies at Division Headquarters on July 4, 1942, when General Sloan hoisted the national colors. The ranks were swelled

8

First selectees for the 88th arrive at the Braggs railroad siding.

somewhat on July 15 at formal activation ceremonies when new members and a handful of civilian and soldier veterans of the old 88th watched their regimental colors catch the faint breeze.

Lt. Col. Martin H. Burckes of Waltham, Massachusetts, Adjutant General and a veteran of Pearl Harbor, read the official orders of activation. Chaplain Alpha E. Kenna of Fort Leavenworth, Kansas, 88th Division chaplain during World War I, in his Invocation asked God to "enable these men to do a better job than we were able to do."

A plea and a pledge were made on that Activation Day. In a brief address, graying Capt. John S. Quigley of Des Moines, Iowa, president of the 88th Division Veterans Association, challenged the new soldiers to "take up the job we didn't get done" in World War I.

That was the plea.

General Sloan accepted "the torch passed on to us by the men of the old 88th," and promised that "their faith will be sustained, their record maintained and the glory of the colors never will be sullied as long as one man of the 88th still lives."

That was the pledge.

It was a large order, and the majority of the men who would have to make it good had no knowledge of what had been promised in their name.

Activation ceremonies were of special significance to several officers present, officers who had served with the Division during World War I and who had returned to lead some of its units again. Col. Charles P. Lynch, commanding officer of the 350th Infantry Regiment, took command of the regiment in which he had served as a lieutenant in G Company during 1917–18. Officers who served with the 88th in its paper days between 1920–42 were Lt. Col. Loyd D. Bunting, commanding the 1st Battalion, 351st Infantry Regiment; Major Marion D. Avery, Executive Officer of the 913th Field Artillery Battalion; Major E. C. Sanders, Assistant AC of S, G-2; Major Martin H. Otto, Assistant AC of S, G-3, and Lt. William H. Unsderfer, Executive Officer of A Battery, 339th Field Artillery Battalion.

There were some dry throats and high hopes that day of activation in 1942 when the 173rd Field Artillery Band from Camp Livingston, Louisiana, struck up the National Anthem. The new 88th was born. Its growing pains were yet to come.

But the new men, with no memories of anything but civilian life and pleasures, stood at attention, tried to look interested, muttered about the heat and hoped the PX wouldn't run dry before they got there.

We are a real division now . . . our training is nearing its end.

MAJ. GEN. JOHN E. SLOAN

TRAINING

Although they didn't know it, draft boards in the East were selecting some pretty tough fighting men for the 88th. To be sure, the men who were hearing their numbers called up were busboys and mechanics, waiters and insurance salesmen, dress designers and typists, farmers and soda jerkers, clerks and engineers, cab drivers and department store buyers. None of them was a soldier; few ever had heard a gun go off. They all were just draftees and almost 15,000 of them were slated for the 88th. Hustled through induction stations and reception centers, large groups of them were started on the long ride to Oklahoma. Tired, dirty, confused but still able to muster a laugh or a wisecrack, the draftees began pouring off the trains from the East in the days immediately following activation. Fresh from Fort Devens, Massachusetts; Camp Upton, Pine Camp, and Fort Niagara, New York; or Camp Dix, New Jersey, half of them didn't know where they were—the other half didn't care.

They came, those draftees, from all parts of the United States as more troop trains arrived to supplement the initial increments from the New England and Middle Atlantic States. Their names and families were indicative of the history of the nation they were training to defend.

From the backwoods of Maine to Florida's resort cities, from Louisiana's bayous to Michigan's lakes and from the ranches of Texas and the movie lots of Hollywood they came—by the thousands. Of necessity, their lives and habits were molded from the start into a regular pattern—they learned what GI meant—but no Army regulation or bulletin directed their thoughts and feelings.

Met at the Braggs siding by cadremen, the recruits were transported through the still-growing camp to processing areas. There, after the inevitable physical, they were assigned to units. The regiments—the 349th, 350th and 351st—took most of them, but the artillery battalions—the 337th, 338th, 339th and 913th—claimed their share, as did the Special Troop units.

It would be nice to say that the men were full of zeal and patriotism from their very first day at Gruber. It would be nice, but it wouldn't be true. The 88th to them was still just a number—the war was far away—the immediate problems were how to beat details and to make up for the natural loneliness and homesickness they felt those first weeks in a new and impersonal life.

The Cookson Hills

Formal basic training for the division got under way on August 3, and the recruits experienced more difficulty from the blazing sun and dust

12

Some of the barracks-bag set just in from an induction center.

of Oklahoma than from the stripes and leather-lungs of the noncoms and drillmasters. The preliminary process of becoming soldiers was not easy. They learned how to make a bed, how to sweep and mop a floor, and how to police an area, picking up "everything that don't grow." They learned what "goldbrick" meant, and how to practice the art, and never to volunteer for anything. Well, almost anything. They learned too, the meaning of the mystic letters "KP." They learned close-order drill—how to stand at attention and to march. They learned field sanitation, courtesy and discipline, basic first aid, military organization, and the difference between stripes and bars.

On conclusion of close-order drill, the extended-order phase was taken up. Here came the first problems in the field, map reading, night compass marches, obstacle courses—most of them apparently designed by a lunatic—hikes, gas-mask drills, dry runs, firing on the ranges and pouring .30 caliber slugs from M–1s through the bulls as they shot for record. And here they discovered that "Maggie's Drawers" did not pertain to feminine wearing apparel. It was all done "by the numbers" and it was all part of the tedious process of breaking them in, the Army way.

Basic training for the first increment of recruits, drawn mainly from the First and Second Corps Areas of New England and New York–New Jersey–Delaware, respectively, was concluded on November 30, 1942.

During October and early November, the second increment began arriving. It comprised several thousand men from the Midwestern States, from Texas and the Far West, causing the 88th to lose some of its early strict Yankee makeup and assume a more cosmopolitan complexion.

While drill grounds were pounded into shape by marching feet, paper work at Headquarters listed more and more plans for the 88th. Under Col. Wayland B. Augur, Chief of Staff, members of the General and Special Staffs perfected their various departments and carried on the work so essential to the Division. Personnel matters were in the hands of Lt. Col. William A. Maloney, AC of S, G-1; intelligence under Lt. Col. George B. Hudson, AC of S, G-2, whom intimates dared to call "Breezy"; plans and training under Lt. Col. Robert J. McBride, AC of S, G-3, and supply under Lt. Col. William J. Jones, AC of S, G-4.

Visiting the camp and Division on inspection tours had been Lt. Gen. Walter Krueger, Commanding General of the Third Army; Maj. Gen. Richard Donovan, Commanding General of the Eighth Service Command; Maj. Gen. Courtney H. Hodges, Commanding General of X Corps, and Lt. Gen. Lesley J. McNair, Commanding General of Army Ground Forces.

From the new battlefields of North Africa came combat-experienced officers and men to pass on valuable tips and battle methods to the men of the 88th.

All were satisfied with what they saw and all praised the progress made in such a short time by the new 88th. All were pleased with the 88th except the men who made up its units.

A strange attitude began to grow throughout the Division. It was an attitude which continued to grow until the 88th's first combat attack. The subject never has been treated openly before but if the full story of the 88th is to be told, this attitude must be discussed in its proper place.

Briefly, the 88th was a hero to everyone but itself. Outsiders, inspectors and observers were lavish in their praise of this new outfit. For some reason, the men in it didn't agree. They thought they were over-rated, thought the Division was "snafued" from the start and that it never would go any place. In bull sessions, the various units were criticized and the men took pleasure in recalling incidents where things hadn't gone as planned. Individual or unit mistakes were magnified all out of proportion and the men adopted a defeatist attitude toward their own outfits.

Why this attitude developed is difficult, if not impossible, to explain. In the way of training and equipment, the 88th had everything. Its progress had been satisfactory. Its members were as good, if not a little better, than the average run of infantrymen. Its top commanders were hand-picked men and its cadre had been chosen from one of the best divisions in the Army.

Yet the word spread, quietly, insidiously. The whispering campaign went on and new arrivals were told that "this outfit can't get out of its own way."

General Sloan, a strict disciplinarian and a stickler for minute details, was everywhere during those early days when his Division was taking shape. Mess sergeants found him poking around their kitchens, supply sergeants discovered him checking their equipment, motor-pool mechanics were quizzed as they greased their vehicles, young lieutenants got nervous as they drilled their platoons with the General an interested spectator.

The General drove his men hard, insisted on the observance of rules and methods of procedure which at the time appeared more "chicken" than necessary. He was unsparing in his criticism of a job poorly or sloppily done. Colonels and privates shared equally in his wrath, but the privates unfortunately did not know this and General Sloan began to build a "hard-man" reputation among his men. Frankly, he was feared and respected but he was not popular nor well liked. The General knew this and knew too that his method of training was one that would some day pay off in battle performance and lives saved. He took the short-term unpopularity, gambling with himself that at some future date his men would learn the truth and understand what he had done for them.

Civilians in the section of Oklahoma near Camp Gruber were curious as to what had been transpiring in the Cookson Hills since the day of activation. They'd heard artillery firing on night problems, seen columns of dusty men marching along hill and mountain roads, had thousands of soldiers swarming through Muskogee and Tulsa on weekend passes. They got two formal glimpses of the 88th; the first from October 4–12 when 88th men staged exhibitions and demonstrations of military equipment at the Oklahoma Free State Fair in Muskogee and again on November 11 when detachments marched in Armistice Day parades in Tulsa and Muskogee.

The civilian reception of 88th men in cities and towns near Gruber had much to do with the building of the 88th as it finally was built. Anxious and eager to do what they could to make pleasant the leisure hours of their new neighbors, Oklahomans, especially those in Muskogee and Tulsa, opened their homes and hearts to the troops. Never was a welcome so sincere or so complete. Nothing was too good or too much for the soldiers. And the men themselves, at first amazed at the warmth of their welcome, responded by considering Muskogee and Tulsa as alternate home towns. It was lonely in barracks and dayrooms, and PXs and service clubs could

not fill the need and desire for companionship and home atmosphere. The civilians more than filled the gap by their adoption of the men from the East.

Unit training was begun on December 1, 1942, and carried through to February 28, 1943. During this phase, the men learned to work together, to coordinate all they had been taught as individuals and to operate efficiently as squads, platoons and companies. Artillery batteries hurled tons of shells at the mythical enemy in the impact area.

The Division acquired a new nickname about this time. It had been known as the Cloverleaf Division, because of the shape of the insignia. Desiring to honor the memory of U. S. Rangers who had died in the raid on Dieppe, France, General Sloan directed that the 88th be called the "Ranger" Division. As nicknames go, it never went and the men never quite accepted it. They used it but it did little or nothing for morale.

Early in December, on completion of basic training, first furloughs were granted to those men of the initial increment who were eligible. An

ng in review at Camp Gruber.

insignia new to civilians, the blue Cloverleaf of the 88th, was sported in cities and towns throughout America by men who had left home as civilians and returned bearing the outward appearance of soldiers.

For those of the second increment who had come during October and November, mainly from Michigan and the Midwestern States, there were no furloughs and the prospect of Christmas away from home was a bleak one—was, until Muskogee mothers and families pitched in to help. These kindly women obtained the names of all soldiers at camp who were without families and then prepared boxes of gifts for them. Other soldiers were invited to Christmas dinners in Muskogee and Tulsa. No man was forgotten.

Mess sergeants at camp forgot ration allowances and loaded the tables with all they could hold while service clubs and recreation rooms put on special shows and parties. Gaily decorated Christmas trees and holly festooned the otherwise grim barracks and buildings throughout the Division area and special religious services were held in every chapel.

Colonel Robert J. McBride
As Chief of Staff from December 1942 to August 1946, he went all the way from
Camp Gruber to Venezia-Giulia.

That first Christmas at Gruber was one to remember.

Turning the year into 1943, the tempo of training picked up considerably. Foxholes and slit trenches became SOP every time a unit moved out of camp and some of the wearier line soldiers insisted that they dug foxholes in their sleep from sheer force of habit.

On January 9, in the first federal court ever held outside a courthouse in the history of Oklahoma, 29 alien soldiers were sworn in as citizens of the United States at impressive ceremonies held before Division Headquarters with more than 3,000 troops in attendance.

Succeeding Colonel Augur as Chief of Staff, Lt. Colonel McBride, G-3, was promoted to colonel on January 7 and General Sloan pinned the silver eagles of rank on his new "Chief." During his subsequent career with the 88th, Colonel McBride served as Chief of Staff to four Division commanders.

On February 8, the first cadre from the 88th left Camp Gruber for Camp Mackall, North Carolina, to activate the 11th Airborne Division. This division later saw action in the Pacific, especially in the invasion of the Philippines. Departure of the cadre gave rise to new rumors con-

Brigadier General Stonewall Jackson
Assistant Division Commander from activation until his transfer to command of the
84th Infantry Division in February 1943.

cerning the 88th. Chief story going the rounds was that the new 88th would follow the cadre trail of the old one; "this outfit is just a replacement division—it'll never leave Gruber."

Outside recognition came to men of the 88th on February 13 when the Muskogee *Daily Phoenix* editorially praised the troops for their "exemplary" conduct and behavior while on pass or leave in town. Other comments supplemented those of the editorial, one man remarking that "you can tell an 88th soldier anywhere. It's not just his soldierly appearance, excellent carriage, bearing and snappy salutes but it's just something about him that marks him as belonging to the 88th. No matter where you see him, whether or not his blue patch is showing, you know at a glance that he's one of Sloan's men."

The lessons were being learned, and learned well.

With officials realizing there was more to building a good soldier than merely developing muscles and brawn, close attention was paid to his mental development as well. Latest training films, captured motion pictures sent back from battle zones, new advances in weapons and tactics, orientation courses, news digests and frequent lectures on history and the background for war were included in the schedule. If the men were to fight—and they were—the "why" as well as the "how" was considered a necessary part of their training.

Provisions were made for recreation also with athletic competitions and other sports programs occupying off-duty hours. Post dances at service clubs, company parties, traveling stage shows and movie stars prevented Jack from becoming the otherwise stereotyped dull lad. Weekends in town helped also with Muskogee and Tulsa the happy hunting grounds of this new generation of adopted braves. Names like Cain's, Bishop's, Huber and the Mayo became old landmarks to 88th men who played, at times, as hard as they worked.

Shift of the first general officer came in late February when General Jackson, Assistant Division Commander, was transferred to command of the 84th Infantry Division at Camp Howze, Texas, and promoted to major general. Though naturally pleased at his advancement, Division personnel regretted losing an officer and gentleman of his caliber and many a private in the ranks, who at one time during his training had received a fatherly word of advice or encouragement from "Stoney," realized that a real friend had gone away. Col. Paul W. Kendall, DSC, Chief of Staff of the XV Corps, succeeded General Jackson on March 5 and received his appointment to brigadier general on March 21.

The combined-training period, during which the three combat teams were formed and operated as such, began on March 1, 1943, and continued until May 22. This phase saw the triangular 88th—in World War I the 88th was a square division with four infantry regiments—taking to the field and maneuvering for the first time as a division, and brought the realization to officers and men that the preliminaries were about over. There was plenty of work yet to be done however and Army Day that year was "business as usual" for the 88th with General Sloan maintaining that parades in cities and towns could be "postponed until the victory march on Rome, Berlin and Tokyo."

The first full Division review was held on April 10 with the 349th Infantry Regiment heading the line of march. Other reviews were held during the week following and a suspicion grew that the 88th was being prepared for something big. That "something big" suspicion was crystallized further on April 16 when a reviewing stand with special auto ramp was constructed on the west side of the main parade ground and orders went out calling all men to report back to camp not later than noon of Sunday, April 18.

Telephone lines to town were cut off, all civilian personnel moved off the post and armed guards were placed along all roads, in buildings and

Trainees enter the gas chamber to test masks.

other installations while troops from the 102d Infantry Division of Camp Maxey, Texas, guarded bridges, highways and rail lines from Braggs to Tulsa and on to Camp Robinson, Arkansas. At 1700 hours, a special train pulled into the Camp Gruber siding and General Sloan and Col. Harry C. Luck, camp commander, greeted their Commander-in-Chief, President Franklin D. Roosevelt.

Driven through camp streets lined with troops of the Third Army, Eighth Service Command, X Corps and the station complement, the President was taken to his reviewing stand as the 88th stood stiffly at attention on the parade ground. The President stood formal retreat with this part of his command, following which the 88th passed in review for the Chief Executive. Mr. Roosevelt told General Sloan it was the first time he ever had seen a full division pass in review as on other occasions he had trooped the line himself.

On conclusion of formal ceremonies the President and his party were taken to a messhall in the south end of camp near Division Headquarters where they had Sunday-night chow with General Sloan, Colonel Luck, Generals Kendall and Kurtz and 208 outstanding enlisted men of the Division. Mr. Roosevelt spent the night aboard his train at Gruber and moved on next day to Tulsa for a tour of the bomber plant before proceeding to Mexico and a visit with its President.

21

President Roosevelt and General Sloan during the Presidential review in April 1943.

The training continued, with combat team and CP exercises preceding the Division series problems. In six D problems, during which all units of the 88th moved into the field with air support, the Division demonstrated why and how it had come to be considered the most advanced division in the entire X Corps. During the series of attacks and withdrawals, at times with a simulated enemy and again with a combat team detached and operating as the Reds, the Division was visited by observers from the 84th, 86th and 102d Infantry Divisions, all of whom were lavish in their praise. Corps officials summed it up neatly when they said that "the morale and spirit of this division could well be emulated by any other infantry division now training in the United States."

The period May 10–27 saw some units of the Division put to a real test. Between those dates the Arkansas and Grand Rivers sent record flood crests roaring downstream smashing all existing records in two devastating floods which left thousands homeless, took the lives of more than twoscore civilians and soldiers and caused building, plant and crop damage estimated at more than fifty million dollars—more than ten million dollars alone in the area between Muskogee and Fort Gibson. Torrential rains over a four-day period sent the rivers up for the first time on May 8–9. On the morning of the 10th, when it became apparent that a major crisis was imminent, General Sloan ordered the 313th Engineer Battalion, with the 508th and 509th Engineer Light Ponton Companies attached, to evacuate civilians in the Webbers Falls–Gore area.

Under command of Lt. Col. S. A. Armogida, Division Engineer, assisted by Major James H. Green, Executive Officer, the engineers snatched from flood waters more than 1,200 civilians and their ponton

22

boats cruised the flooded countryside about Webbers Falls, Gore, Blaine, Saylor, Haskell and Sallisaw bottoms and on to Fort Smith, Arkansas. Six men of the 508th were drowned when their assault boat, caught in the swift current, crashed into a bridge pier over Highway 59 near Sallisaw at 2130 hours May 11 as they were making their last trip with rescued civilians. Flood refugees were fed at temporary quarters in Gore as water-purification units, a detachment of the 313th Medical Battalion, A Company, and other soldier details worked unceasingly to prevent the spread of disease.

As in anything where soldiers are concerned, the flood had its humorous side. With Highway 62 from Muskogee closed because of high water, more than 1,200 officers and men of the Division tacked an extra four days on to an already big weekend when they were stranded in Muskogee, Tulsa, Warner, and other cities and towns throughout Oklahoma. One lad claimed a minor record when he stretched his "stranded" plea the limit and reported back to camp twelve days later. Red Cross units and civilian volunteers swung into action to feed and house the men and recreational facilities were provided until receding waters made a return to camp possible on May 14.

Again on May 23 the rivers went on a rampage, fed by cloudbursts upstate. At the first signs of another flood, all personnel were restricted to camp. Engineer and quartermaster trucks evacuated civilians from Webbers Falls and Fort Gibson when warnings were issued that this flood probably would exceed any other in history. Rising waters closed Highway 62 east of the bridge and Highway 10 at Manard Bayou, flooded the water and filtration plants, cut off Gruber's water and light service and disrupted phone communications. The entire area of lowlands from the Arkansas River to Manard Bayou and Muskogee to Fort Gibson was under water—fourteen feet deep over the highway—as the highest crest ever recorded, 49.50 feet, swept down river and hit Muskogee at 0230 hours May 24.

Prepared this time, the 88th rode it out at Gruber and shared emergency rations with more than 1,700 civilians. News service was furnished the camp by the G-2 office and Division Artillery planes ferried mail over the flood zone. Sgt. Thomas O'Keefe, of New York City and the Division APO, went the Pony Express one better when he walked, rode, swam and rowed a boat for the 36-mile round trip to town for a load of mail. Power facilities were restored to Camp on May 26 and normal water supply on the 27th. Highways were cleared and opened on the same day and all restrictions lifted.

Commendation for "the soldierly manner in which all officers and men

Air view of Webbers Falls during the flood in May 1943.

bore the inconveniences occasioned by the flood" was given his command by General Sloan. The city of Muskogee voted an official citation for the 313th Engineers in recognition of their excellent work during the crisis.

All officers and noncoms were addressed by General Sloan during the week of May 25–29 in critiques on the D series, following which he outlined various problems to be faced during the maneuvers scheduled for June, July and August in Louisiana. The critiques were held "so that you might get to know me better, that I might get to know more of you, and all of you can get better acquainted with one another. We are a real division now—our training is nearing its end. We've been here about ten months. Before another ten months have passed we will have been under fire many times." That was General Sloan's promise.

Staff changes during the past few months had resulted in a new lineup of Gs. Lt. Col. Frank W. LaMotte had succeeded Lt. Col. Ben Jacobs as G-1. Other new faces were those of Major George L. Walker, G-2; Major Martin H. Otto, G-3, and the almost legendary Lt. Col. Helmuth E. Beine, G-4, whose record of eighteen years as a lieutenant occasioned profane verbal outbursts on his part over the rapidity of promotions to young officers in the rapidly expanding Army.

Proclaiming May 29 as "Muskogee and Eastern Oklahoma Day," General Sloan and the 88th held open house with civilians invited to inspect the Division and the cantonment. Chief feature of the elaborate military program, the 88th's formal farewell to Oklahoma, was a full division review on the main parade ground followed by day-long displays and demonstrations of military equipment. As the General put it, "the show is mainly for you people out here who have been entertaining us for such a long time and who have made us feel more than welcome in our new but temporary home."

Air-ground tests, troop schools and additional range firing occupied most of the final two weeks at Gruber. On June 13 the movement to Louisiana began, and by midnight of the 14th the last vehicles of the second convoy had cleared the main gate, maneuver-bound. The wise lads who had claimed the 88th would never leave Gruber had to change their tune.

Louisiana Maneuvers

Preceded by an excellent reputation, the 88th traveled south in two columns to Louisiana where on June 16 the last units closed in an administrative bivouac area near the town of Boyce. From the 16th to the 28th, the men learned that the tall tales told them by maneuver veterans were not tall enough and that no words could describe the bugs and snakes and chiggers and hogs and dust that were the Louisiana maneuver area and that made Louisiana a "good place to be from."

Play of maneuvers opened officially on June 28 with a series of flag problems and the 88th spent more than a week dry-running problems in preparation for the day it took the field in competition with such major units as the maneuver-wise 31st Infantry Division, 95th Infantry Division and the 11th Armored. From June 28 to August 22, operating alternately as the Reds or Blues and with the odds at times more than three to one against it, the 88th fought through central and western Louisiana and the east central part of Texas near the Sabine River.

From the outset, the 88th clearly was the best in the field and its performance evoked high praise from other commanders and from higher headquarters. Even though cut-and-dried problem plans called for the Division to retreat at times, the men preferred to ignore the plans and to fight out the mock battles on their own lines and terms. Although no personalities were supposed to be involved, the 88th rapidly came to regard the 31st as its own personal enemy. The feeling was mutual and members of both outfits refought and finished many a problem in town during the breaks between problems. Attack, night movements, defense of fortified positions, river crossings, assaults by armored forces, all were included in the major engagements. Each man waged his own personal battle with the chiggers and ticks, and mosquitoes "so big they dragged a guy right out of his pup tent."

First anniversary of the Division was celebrated near Flatwoods, Louisiana, during a break between problems and the watermelons and beer were "on the house."

The summer was long, and hot, and dusty, but the 88th worked doggedly on and piled up commendation after commendation. Visits by General McNair and various Mexican and British Army observers kept the outfit on the ball. One outstanding record was made by the 351st Infantry Regiment, Col. Arthur S. Champeny, commanding. With full gear, the regiment marched 62 miles in 42 hours—29 hours actual march time—with every man going the full distance. This record march brought official and personal praise from General George C. Marshall, Chief of Staff, and from Ground Forces, Army and Corps commanders.

Another, but less publicized, feat was the stunt pulled by a radio team from the 88th Reconnaissance Troop during the first of the river-crossing problems. Ordered to defend a river line, the 88th pulled back into Texas as the 31st, 95th and 11th Armored moved up for the attack. Left behind in Louisiana and dug in right in the enemy's backyard was a Recon radio team which stayed there throughout the problem, spotting Red

Artillerymen moving into Fort Sam Houston after the Louisiana Maneuvers.

movements and reporting regularly to the Division G-2. With such an excellent intelligence setup, it was a relatively simple matter for the Division to deploy against the Red assaults it had been warned to expect.

"We had a lot of fun over there with the Reds," said T/5 Norman Nash of Seaford, Long Island, a Recon observer during that problem. "They got rather sore when they realized something like that was up and got madder yet when they couldn't find us. We didn't get peeved until we started running out of food and water right after we heard they'd gone and extended the problem."

Two problems more and maneuvers ended in a blaze of blank artillery and rifle fire which, for once, was loud enough to scare Louisiana's wild hogs away from the Division's mess tents and kitchens and out of the general's tent. Concentrating in administrative bivouac near Merryville, Louisiana, the Division proceeded to clean up and primp for its next movement. Critiques ironed out maneuver arguments and problems and one corps commander summed up the general opinion when he told General Sloan, "Your division has been mentioned favorably for the fine handling of its artillery, the marching power and control of its infantry and the fine teamwork of its component elements." Almost in spite of itself, the lessons had been learned so well that the 88th couldn't help being good.

As a reward for its maneuver record, the 88th drew Fort Sam Houston, at San Antonio, Texas, as its new home. Advance parties sent

27

back glowing, almost unbelievable reports, and the 88th grew increasingly anxious to take off on its three-day convoy to deep in the heart of Texas. Before the departure, a solid week of orientation lectures was given the men to prepare them for their return to the bright lights after a summer in the woods.

Is This The Army?

Fort Sam Houston, one of the choicest spots in the Army, was all they'd said it was, and more. With memories of the maneuver area only slightly dimmed, the first sight of Fort Sam was like a Hollywood version of Army life to the truckloads of 88th men who rolled through its gates in late August and early September.

It was Hollywoodish, but better yet it was true. The huge brick barracks, grassy lawns, swimming pools, theaters, tennis courts, garden PXs, restaurants and streamlined buses were real, and not Off Limits. However, it was not all peaches and cream. Hardly settled in their new quarters, the men learned they'd be training on alternate weeks at Camp Bullis, an adjacent training site only one notch above maneuvers. But with Fort Sam an open post, with no passes necessary to enter and leave the main gate and with MPs behaving like personal guides instead of MPs, the linemen figured they'd found a home and proceeded to take Bullis and training in stride.

On September 10, the 88th held its first full review since arriving at its new station, with Brig. Gen. Charles K. Nulsen, Commanding General of Fort Sam Houston, and Brig. Gen. John A. Porter, Commanding General of the San Antonio Service Forces Depot, taking the honors. The 88th had a tough handicap to overcome—the handicap of the 2d Infantry Division which had been stationed at Fort Sam Houston more than a decade and which had been adopted as Fort Sam's own by post residents and civilians. Station complement officers and enlisted men joined Army-wise and parade-conscious San Antonio civilians along the ropes at Arthur MacArthur Field to get their first good look at the 88th. Aware of the spot they were in, men of the 88th came through in top fashion and when the last ordered ranks had swung briskly past the reviewing stand the spectators realized they'd seen some of the finest.

But the real novelty punch was yet to come. As the crowd started to break for home, nine artillery Cub planes in single file swooped down over the parade ground, dipped wings to the reviewing stand as the observers in each threw salutes to General Sloan, who just as snappily returned each one as though it were an everyday occurrence. That did it—the 88th was in!

Despite the intensive training program launched immediately after arrival, the 88th found time to explore historic San Antonio and Texas and created favorable comment wherever the men went. All except the one character who stepped from a bus at Alamo Square on his first visit to town and asked a native, as he pointed in the general direction of the famous memorial, "the name of that torn-down building." Furloughs were granted between September 6 and October 24, 15 days to those living east of the Mississippi or west of the Rockies with 10 days to those residing within those boundaries.

Screen stars and the 88th teamed on September 22 to give San Antonio one of its biggest days since Texas decided to come into the Union. High lighting the local Third War Loan drive, units of the 88th's finest vied with 17 of Hollywood's fairest and handsomest in a parade which drew thousands to downtown streets. Under command of Lt. Col. Walter E. Bare, Jr., of Muskogee, Oklahoma, escorting units included his 1st Battalion, 350th Infantry; the Division Band; Antitank Company, 350th; A Battery, 338th Field Artillery Battalion, and the 2d Platoon of the Reconnaissance Troop.

Quietly but none the less fervently, the 88th observed the 25th anniversary of its first combat action in World War I with informal ceremonies on October 12, underscored by a promise from General Sloan to "accomplish that which will uphold the name and honor of the old 88th."

A shocked and sorrowing Division learned on October 14 of the death of popular and beloved Maj. Gen. Stonewall Jackson, former Assistant Division Commander. Injured seriously in the crash of his light artillery observation plane near Florien, Louisiana, while watching progress of his troops on their first maneuver problem, General Jackson died at Camp Polk station hospital and was buried several days later in Arlington Cemetery, Virginia.

With a speedup in training activities and a shortening of furlough time, rumors began circulating throughout the Division regarding overseas movement. It soon became pretty much of an open secret that the outfit was headed for action. Under-strength units were filled up with replacements from the 84th and 86th Divisions. New equipment was issued. Old men and physically unfit were weeded out. There were still a couple of diehards who insisted that "this outfit never will leave the States." Rumors became fact on October 25 with departure of the advance party for Camp Patrick Henry, Virginia, and from then on the rest of the Division made preparations to sail with "showdowns" and "short-arms" scheduled almost daily.

Many seasick soldiers crossed the Atlantic by "rail."

LIBERTY SHIPS

It was nothing like the movies, that trip overseas, and many a GI hung weakly over a rail and cursed the day he ever saw the Army or a Liberty ship.

From the Patrick Henry staging area on November 2, an advance party of ten officers led by General Kendall left by plane for North Africa. Flying by way of Miami, Florida, Belem and Natal, Brazil, the group landed at Dakar on November 8, General Kendall being the first member of the new 88th to set foot on foreign soil. Another brief stop was made at Marrakech, French Morocco, on November 9, and the following day the advance party landed in Algiers. Three days later, November 13, Division Headquarters overseas was established at 18 Boulevard Clemenceau, Oran. With General Kendall in the advance party were Major Frank J. Wallis, Division Artillery; Major James E. Henderson, 349th Infantry Regiment; Major James A. Stach, Assistant AC of S, G-4; Major James H. Green, 313th Engineers; Major Elmore D. Beggs, Assistant AC of S, G-3; Capt. Frederick V. Harris, G-3 office; Capt. Louis A. Collier, 350th Infantry Regiment; Major John A. Mavrakos, 351st Infantry Regiment; and Lt. Carlos M. Teran, 313th Medical Battalion.

As preparations were being made in North Africa to receive the Division, increments were funneling through the staging area at Camp Patrick Henry following a large advance party which sailed from Newport News on November 3. Packed in the holds of Liberty ships, the 351st Infantry Regiment started across in slow convoy under command of Colonel Champeny. This first increment was passed on the high seas by the *Empress of Scotland* carrying General Sloan and a picked group of twelve officers and enlisted men, majority of the latter from the AG office. The *Empress,* a former Japanese luxury liner named the *Empress of Japan* before its seizure by the British, cleared port November 19 and docked at Casablanca November 27.

The second increment, comprising the 350th Infantry Regiment, Quartermaster Company, 313th Engineer Battalion, Division Headquarters Company main body plus various signal and medical detachments, sailed from Newport News on November 23 with Col. Charles P. Lynch, 350th CO, in charge of the slow Liberty ship convoy. Artillery Battalions, the 337th, 338th, 339th and 913th, under Lt. Col. George T. Powers, III left the States in convoy on December 7, second anniversary of the Jap raid on Pearl Harbor.

The 349th Infantry Regiment, plus attachments, and the Division Headquarters staff took the *Empress of Scotland* on her second run,

There was always room for one more in the holds of those Liberty ships.

sailing December 17 from Newport News and landing at Casablanca on Christmas Day. Original plans had called for the 349th to proceed directly to Italy and disembark at Naples but these orders were changed en route. Left behind in the States was a man the 349th hated to lose— Col. J. A. Landreth, the regimental commander who had built them from a handful of recruits to a trained and poised striking force. Transferred because of poor health, Colonel Landreth was replaced by Col. Hiram G. Fry. Sickness which broke out at Patrick Henry hospitalized approximately 500 officer and enlisted personnel. This group was the last to come over, under CWO Henry J. Foner, landing December 27.

All crossings were made without incident and not a man of the Division was lost due to enemy action. However, stacked five high in the fetid holds of lumbering Liberty ships, scrambling for two meals a day and then fighting to keep them down, without recreation facilities and locked below decks from sunset to sunrise, the men did anything but enjoy the trip, especially since Merchant Marine crew food and accommodations were so superior to their own. KP became a privilege instead of a task on many boats since it was the only way a man could be certain of getting enough to eat. Master sergeants pulled their rank on lesser grades in order to make the KP list.

Bad as it was, the men still were able to muster enough wind for a song or two and Sgt. Thomas Lucid of Jersey City, New Jersey, and Pvt. Edward Conn of Arverne, New York, aboard the SS *James Turner,*

came up with a parody of "Thanks For The Memories" which led the
troop-ship hit parade. Entitled "Memories of a Voyage," the parody
gave:

Thanks for the memories
Of pills of atabrine, that leaky old latrine,
We've had KP and smokes for free and meals that left us lean,
Oh thank you, so much.
Thanks for the memories,
Those naval terms we learned, like aft and bow and stern.
We fire-drilled with canteens filled
And for journey's end we yearned,
Oh thank you, so much.
We left our hearts deep in Texas,
Allotted our raise to the old folks,
The rest of our dough went for warm cokes,
For short haircuts and four-cent butts.
Oh thanks for the memories,
Of a cowboy's sad guitar, one note to a bar,
Salt water shaves don't merit raves
For they have left their scar,
Oh thank you, so much.
We soon learned the life of a sailor,
At first rushed to chow with devotion,
Then heaved it all up in the ocean,
On the deck, the rail, in the hold, a pail.
Oh thanks for the memories,
Of training on the way, of decks that swing and sway,
Of thieves and crabs and bayonet stabs
And a swell Thanksgiving Day—
Oh thank you, so much.

WHAT KEPT YOU?

First enlisted men staggered ashore at Casablanca, French Morocco,
on November 21 and went into bivouac at Camp Don B. Passage, a few
miles outside the city. Military security regulations had been such that
for months 88th men had not been allowed to mention the names or
numbers of their units. It had been drilled into them so thoroughly that
they'd almost forgotten the actual designation of their outfit. On landing
in Africa however, they discovered that arrival of the 88th had been the
chief topic of conversation for months and that even the Arab dock por-
ters knew about the Rangers. Camp Passage was merely a stop-over
where troops lingered long enough to get a couple of decent meals—decent
in comparison to boat fare—see a movie, and witness the sunrise parades
of the GI prisoners on Music Hill, a daily spectacle which served at once
to put the fear of God into various sharp operators and impressed the

The 88th advance party overseas.

majority with the idea that the Army played much rougher overseas with its own than it did in the States.

On the social side, if it could be called that, the troops sampled the sidewalk cafés at Casablanca, stared fascinated at Arab camel caravans, looked longingly at the off-limits Medina section, and saw their first closeups of war in the wrecked French battleships and cruisers in Casablanca harbor. Veiled Arab women came in for their share of attention but the easy days of Muskogee and Tulsa were gone forever.

Soon the men were on the move again, this time bound for Oran. Who can forget those back-breaking and disillusioning days and nights aboard those infamous French boxcars, the 40-and-8 of World War I vintage but without the horses? Cold C rations, one blanket, and in the center of each car a Lyster bag which after a couple of hours of bouncing and jerking had dumped most of its contents over the forty occupants, especially the poor devil who slept directly under it and who in many cases had to be pumped out at regular intervals. The scenery up through the Atlas Mountains was beautiful, it said in the book, but the struggle for a bit of comfort was so occupying that few men bothered to look out the doors or through the cracks in the sides of their boxcar homes.

When the troops arrived in Oran, the muddy staging area near Lion Mountain looked like the Promised Land after those boxcars. Over in

34

Direction signs in Casablanca.

Headquarters area, the theme song became "It Ain't As Bad As Trinidad," a cheerful little ditty dedicated to the CO who had put his foot in it by an attempt at comparative discomforts the day his men sloshed through the mud to their pyramidals. He never lived it down. In Staging Area No. 2, some brave soul decided that a few truckloads of cinders carefully scattered around would improve the ground surface. Whoever he was, he overestimated a bit and PBS sent 442 truckloads of cinders, gravel and fine sand to the area. Every man in the company was turned out on an unloading detail as trucks kept rolling in through the days and nights for seventy-two awful hours. Tent floors, company streets, drill grounds, latrine approaches—every conceivable foot of ground was paved with the cinder, gravel and sand combination. And still the piles left over looked like miniature Lion Mountains. A colonel from PBS checked in on the third day, took one startled look at the convoys and the squads of men unloading the cargoes with entrenching tools, and fled. Less than twenty-four hours after the last truck was cleared, the outfit moved. Two weeks later, just to round out the story, the trucks came back, collected all the sand, gravel and cinders and moved them to God knows where.

Plans to close in the entire Division at the Oran staging area were changed with the arrival of General Sloan and it was decided to move the units to a larger training area approximately four miles south of Magenta, Algeria. Division Headquarters in the field was set up here and as the various increments landed at Casablanca and Oran they were routed to the new area. Here a rigid training program was instituted with em-

35

Brigadier General Guy O. Kurtz.
Division Artillery Commander from activation until January 1945.

phasis on mountain climbing, demolitions, mines, marksmanship, physical hardening and the operations of small units at night. In the cold, rocky hills the regiments hiked and climbed and fought mock battles. On the plains near Bedeau, artillery units used the ranges of the famous French Foreign Legion for dry runs and practice barrages. The pressure was on. Favorite Division sport in Africa, which also came under the head of training, was the almost daily Arab roundup conducted by MPs and infantrymen to clear bivouac sites of the peddlers and camp followers infesting the Division area.

Training however, was not the only activity. For one thing there were parties and celebrations on New Year's Eve—lacking the color and glamour of a Times Square blowoff but nonetheless noisy and moist. In the Division Headquarters area, officers and men crowded into the Special Troops assembly tent to listen with dubious ears as General Sloan told them they "were going, not only to Rome and Berlin, but all the way around to Tokyo. We'll fight our way around the world and prove that the 88th is the best division in the entire Army. This year will see new history made—we are lucky to be in on the making." That night, introduced by the General, the Division met its smallest and newest unit, a quartet of Red Cross Clubmobile workers assigned and attached to the 88th for morale and doughnut-making. The girls, Fanny Beaty, director, Rosamond Myers, Virginia Crawford and Corlin Cullen, promptly stole the show.

No matter what the book said, Africa was cold. It was cold sleeping on the ground in those puptents and the men started supplementing gasoline fires with internal warmth in the form of a French drink wistfully named *Eau de Vie,* a highly volatile beverage which burned like kerosene when thrown on an open flame. It tasted like it too.

In a few puptents, unconvincing voices insisted that the 88th would remain in Africa to police up. Another latrine rumor had it that the whole Division was to be converted to MPs. But with the Fifth Army in Italy begging for replacements and with the 88th the first fresh division to come over since the invasion of Italy, most men realized the score and knew that time was running out.

PLAYING FOR KEEPS

For some of the Division, training days ended with the old year.

An advance party of officers and men left the Magenta–Bedeau area on December 26 and flew to Italy, under command of General Kendall, to serve as observers with the 3d, 34th and 36th Infantry Divisions and the British 5th, 46th and 56th Divisions, Fifth Army. On the night of January 3–4, 1944, the first representatives of the new 88th went into the line with the Fifth Army and on that basis, the 88th was in action at last. First Division battle casualty came even before the observer groups had completed final moves to the front. On the afternoon of January 3, on his first day in a combat zone, Sgt. William A. Streuli of Paterson, New Jersey, was killed by enemy air bombardment two miles west of Venafro.

Sergeant Streuli, member of the Division since its activation and chief of a gun section in B Battery, 339th Field Artillery Battalion, had been ordered to report for observer duty with the 185th Field Artillery Battalion, 34th Infantry Division. Accompanied by 2d Lt. Elwin A. Ricketts, Executive Officer of B Battery, and others of the observer group attached to the 34th, Streuli had just arrived at the 34th QM area and was preparing to unload his equipment when the German planes struck.

"Sergeant Streuli had started to run for a foxhole when the planes came over but tripped on a tree root in the peaceful olive grove, fell face forward and lost his helmet during the fall. Before he could recover the helmet and while he was on his hands and knees in the process of getting up, a bomb exploded about 10 feet in front of him and fragments entered his skull," said the official report. Lieutenant Ricketts was wounded by the same blast but nevertheless went to the aid of other casualties in the area, helping to get them into ambulances for evacuation. Sergeant Streuli was dead on arrival at the 16th Evacuation Hospital. Ricketts underwent an operation at the 38th Evacuation Hospital and later returned to duty with his outfit.

General Kendall, holder of several firsts, made another first the hard way when he won the Silver Star for gallantry in action despite a wound during the Rapido River crossing. Attached to the 36th Division as an observer, he accompanied assault elements of the 143d Infantry Regiment on the night of January 20–21 in the vicinity of San Angelo. The citation said he "actively aided, directed and energized the attack across the Rapido River." Presented by Maj. Gen. Fred L. Walker, commanding general of the 36th, the award to General Kendall was the first given to a member of the 88th in World War II.

Following a second advance observer party, Generals Sloan and Kurtz flew to Naples on January 27 for conferences with Lt. Gen. Jacob L. Devers, newly appointed commander of American forces in the Mediterranean, and Lt. Gen. Mark W. Clark, Fifth Army commander.

On February 1, the Division once again was on the move, this time on the last water lap of its long journey from training camp to combat zone and action. Under command of Col. Charles W. Jacobsen, Executive Officer of Division Artillery, Companies I, K, L, M, and Cannon Company of the 349th, the 337th, 338th, 339th and Headquarters Battery, plus medical attachments, and the 804th Tank Destroyer Battalion, sailed from Oran aboard the *Neuralia, City of Canterbury,* and the *James Hoban.* This slow convoy was attacked by Nazi planes, the only convoy in all the moves of the 88th to report enemy action. The raid came on the night of February 1–2 just outside the harbor of Oran. One ship in another group was sunk but none of the vessels carrying 88th personnel was hit during the raid. The convoy, proceeding by way of eastern Sicily, made port at Naples on February 12.

Location of the first 88th Division CP at Piedimonte d'Alife, Italy.

The second increment, under Col. McBride, consisting of Division Headquarters Staff and Company, most of the 349th, parts of the 351st, 313th Engineers, 313th Medics, Signal, Ordnance and Quartermaster Companies, the 913th Field and various detachments of other units, sailed from Oran on February 3 and docked at Naples on the 6th. Vessels used were the *Llangibby Castle, Lancashire, Champolion, Forbes, John Walker, Ashe, Pike, Crawford*—the latter three being freighters—and the *Highland Chieftain*. The *Chief* made a second trip with the 88th and in company with two freighters brought across most of the 350th, the ARC unit and a skeleton staff which had been left behind to operate the Headquarters in Oran.

All vessels used in the movement from North Africa were English-owned and staffed except the *Champolion,* which was French. On landing at Naples, units bivouacked for the night at the Italian Collegio Constanza Ciano, which had been used as a German staff headquarters prior to the fall of Naples. In truck convoys the outfits moved up next day and concentrated in the area generally southeast of the village of Piedimonte d'Alife where Division Headquarters had been established February 7 in a former Italian agricultural college. Artillery Headquarters drew the Grand Hotel and privates began calling for room service.

In transit since October 25, 1943, the 88th was together again as a complete division when the last units pitched puptents in their respective areas on February 21, 1944, and members of the various observer groups reported back to their outfits. After four months, the Division had arrived in its first combat zone; 14,261 officers and men had been ferried more than 8,000 miles across half of two continents and two oceans without the loss of a single man, in transit, through enemy action.

And more, had scored a notable "first" by becoming *the first of the new, or all-Selective Service infantry divisions to come overseas in World War II.*

There still were a few holdouts who muttered rather wistfully that "this outfit never will see action." There were others who knew it would but wondered if the Division could live up to its advance notices.

I promise you it will be soon!

Lt. Gen. Mark W. Clark

THE QUIET WAR

To tired, desperate men of the Fifth Army, the arrival of the 88th in Italy was a much-needed shot in the arm. These battle veterans had been in action since Salerno's bloody beaches, some since Sicily, and some as far back as Africa. They needed relief. They'd needed relief for a long time. But relief, for a long time, had been only a dream, then a promise. There had been no replacements, no fresh reserves to call upon. The original invaders had to keep going—on nerve, on a dream, a promise.

The promise had been the 88th. The grapevine had signalled its arrival in Africa. Its landing in Italy, months later when the men who had hoped for immediate relief had grown impatient and bitter at the unexplained delay, was duly noted. The 88th was the first fresh division sent to the Mediterranean Theater since Salerno. Its assignment to a rear assembly area was added gall to the exhausted infantrymen dug in before Cassino, stopped for the first time since the invasion by strong enemy defensive positions, by weather and by their own decimated ranks.

Within sound of the guns at the front, 88th bivouac areas and puptents buzzed with speculation as to when the Division was scheduled to move up. But if the enlisted men speculated and wondered, high officers did also, for plans and orders for employment of the 88th were contradictory and confusing in those first days. Attached to II Corps on February 23, the 88th went on with its training but grew impatient for some definite word.

It was cold in Italy, and raw and rainy. Even if there had been time, there was not much to do in the way of sightseeing, for the war had surged through this area leaving the usual rubble and devastation in its wake. The 88th men were seeing these results of war for the first time, the physical destruction of a country. They also were seeing the other results of war, the spiritual and moral destruction of a people reflected in the long lines of Italian civilians come to stand patiently around messhalls, hoping to pick up scraps and leftovers of food. Young children scrambled about in garbage pits and sumps looking for food. It was hard to obey orders to keep them out of unit areas—at mealtime, no matter where one looked, a pair of young or old but always hungry and sad eyes watched as you spooned the food from your messkit. These were people who were not officially enemies; not officially friends. They had no official status. They were people who had made a mistake, who had listened too long and too attentively to a dictator who lied and who now saw the country they owned being used as a battleground by the Allies and the Germans to decide a war which they themselves had lost. But above all, they were hungry people.

The usual crop of latrine rumors furnished material for nightly bull

Italians were hungry.

sessions. One rumor, that a GI in town had overheard an Italian giving a chap with a German accent a detailed description of a bivouac area was so convincing that officers feared it might result in a bombing raid. While G-2 and CIC personnel checked the story, the entire 339th Field Artillery Battalion was ordered out on a night march to evacuate the area and prevent heavy casualties should the rumor prove correct. Nothing happened.

At night faint flashes over the mountains beyond Piedimonte d'Alife indicated the direction of the front and the battleground that was the Purple Heart Valley and Cassino. The men watched those flashes, listened to the distant rumble of the guns, and wondered. Even though they knew they were needed, no one exactly relished going into the lines for the first time. This was no movie. Those were real guns and this war was the real thing. But all of them wondered, and some of them spoke like Pvt. Frank Cacciatore of the 350th who admitted "I'm nervous—sure I am—we've waited an awful long time for this. And we're still waiting."

Or like Cpl. George R. Benson who said "This waiting is killing, and that's no baloney."

Or like Sgt. Joe Judd who was "Very happy to go to the front and take a chance on the things I have in mind. I am happy to have an opportunity to do something. The Germans are as rotten as they come—I hate them."

But most of the waiting and wondering doughboys felt pretty much like Sgt. Delphia E. Garris and agreed with him: "This is just something that has got to be done. We have got to lick those bastards in order to get out of the Army. That's our main thought—to get rid of the Germans in order to get out of the Army."

Those were the feelings and those were some of the comments. No heroics, no movie talk. Just simple statements of fact from average guys who were waiting to go up for the first time.

The first indication of possible action came with orders to send the 351st Combat Team to the Anzio beachhead. Launched on January 22, the beachhead attack had scored an initial success but in a matter of days had bogged down. At this time it was under heavy attack by some ten Nazi divisions. The 351st got as far as Naples, was outfitted, equipped and set to move to the beachhead when orders were changed. After what had been a dry run, the regiment came back to its old area.

CASSINO

Since employment seemed a distant thing, plans were made to indoctrinate the men by attaching infantry battalions to the weary 34th and 36th Divisions in the Cassino sector. Before these plans could be completed the 34th and 36th began pulling out of the line for rest and re-

The Benedictine Monastery at Monte Cassino was the target for Allied bombers in February 1944.

organization and II Corps followed to the rear within a few days. Their sectors were taken over by a New Zealand corps on the left and a French corps on the right. The French were spread too thin in their sector because the main body of the corps still was in transit from Africa. Seizing the opportunity for battle training, General Sloan arranged for the 2d Battalion of the 351st to go into the line near Cervaro.

The battalion, under command of Lt. Col. Raymond E. Kendall, Manchester, New Hampshire, plus the 1st Platoon of C Company, 313th Engineers; C Company and one platoon of D Company, 313th Medical Battalion, went into the line on Hill 706 on February 27, 1944. Relief of the 141st Infantry was begun at 0300 hours with F Company the first unit to move into position, followed by G and E Companies. The relief was completed by 0830 hours that same day and the 2d Battalion, 351st Infantry Regiment, plus attachments, became the first organization of the 88th to be committed for front-line combat in World War II, exactly one year, seven months and twelve days after activation.

First patrol sent out was from E Company with 2d Lt. Herbert Wadopian in command. It checked out on a recon mission at 0030 hours February 28 and returned at 0230 hours with "nothing to report." At 2030 hours that night E Company scored another first when a Kraut patrol penetrated the company area but was driven out by rifle fire. The men were learning.

45

To the 913th Field Artillery Battalion, Lt. Col. Franklin P. Miller of Carmel, California, commanding, went the honor of firing the round which boomed the entrance of the 88th Division Artillery into the war. Ordered to support the French Expeditionary Corps in defense of Castellone and the New Zealand corps in operation against Cassino, the 913th relieved the 131st Field Artillery Battalion of the 36th Division at 2213 hours, February 27.

Through luck of the draw, C Battery was the first to adjust and the selected check point for registration was the southeast corner of the Abbey of Monte Cassino. The Abbey had been blasted for the first time a few days previously by the Air Corps after months of Allied indecision during which time the Germans had capitalized on our hesitancy in bombing a religious monument and had used the Abbey as an artillery observation point. Data were computed and with Colonel Miller yanking the lanyard of the No. 2 howitzer, the first artillery shell was on its way at 0727 hours, February 28. It was a direct hit.

Commanding the gun crew was Sgt. Ferdinand Cheon of Paterson, New Jersey, and his crew included Cpl. Clyde W. Loftus, South Charleston, West Virginia; Pfc. John J. Selepnik, New Hyde Park, New York; Pfc. Dominick W. Hurrell, Hudson, New York; Pfc. Andy J. Gray, Dardanelle, Alabama; Pvt. Joseph Dragon, Buffalo, New York; Pvt. Charles S. Lindsey, Richmond, Virginia; Pfc. Joseph Pagano, Astoria, New York; Pvt. Forrest L. Dunbar, Palestine, West Virginia; Pvt. Albert Aao, Providence, Rhode Island; Cpl. David Murray, South Bethlehem, New York, and Pvt. Robert C. Owings, Spartanburg, South Carolina.

During its first two days in the sector the 913th pumped more than two thousand rounds after that first shell. Propaganda shells were mixed with high explosive and the Krauts got script and shrapnel. The 2d Battalion, 351st, of necessity confined its activity to heavy patroling and a holding action. Though barely begun, further unit indoctrination plans came to an abrupt end on February 27 when orders came for the Division to move to the southern flank of the main Fifth Army line, relieving the British 5th Division in the Minturno area.

By combat teams the Division began its movement as outlined in Field Order No. 4. The forward command group established Division Headquarters and forward CP in the village of Carano and the rear echelon occupied the village of Casanova. At 1000 hours, March 5, command of the sector passed from the British 5th to the 88th Division, the only American division along the entire Fifth Army southern front and the first all-Selective Service infantry division to enter combat on any front in World War II. On the same date the 88th was detached from II Corps and attached to the British 10 Corps, Lt. Gen. Sir Richard L. Mc-Creery, commanding.

MINTURNO

Maintaining a three-regiment front, the 350th was assigned the left flank on the seacoast, the 351st—delayed a few days pending relief of its battalion at Cervaro—took over the center sector and the 349th moved in on the right flank. With its left flank anchored on the Gulf of Gaeta below Scauri, the 88th held a 10,000-yard bridgehead front rising from the seacoast to the heights of Damiano, near Castelforte. Opposing the 88th and dug in on a line running generally north and east from Scauri to Castĕlforte astride the Ausente River were elements of the German 94th and 71st Infantry Divisions. The American-held terrain north of the Garigliano River below Minturno comprised some flat country, what little there was in that part of Italy, up to the Nazi-held foothills.

To confuse the Germans and keep them ignorant of the arrival of the American outfit, 88th troops moving up were equipped with British helmets, the tin hats of World War I. On completion of the relief the doughboys once again sported their familiar wash-bucket headgear. So efficiently was the relief effected that all who witnessed it were "amazed by the business-like manner in which the units took over their respective sectors." And so many were the comments that Brig. Gen. L. L. Lemnitzer, Deputy Chief of Staff, Allied Central Mediterranean Force, wrote a letter of commendation to General Sloan.

Main action along the Fifth Army front at that time was the drive for Cassino with the objective of smashing through that point to the central Italian highway to Rome and consequently forcing a German retreat on both ends of the line to prevent a complete breakthrough and turning of both flanks. To the northeast the battle for Cassino raged stubbornly but despite fierce ground attacks by New Zealanders and steady plastering by bombers of the AAF, that Nazi bastion held. The primary mission of the 88th in its bridgehead was a holding and harassing action and although artillery fire was constant and heavy, ground troops engaged mainly in patrolling and feeling out the enemy. It was not done without cost and by month's end, the casualties totaled 99 dead, 252 wounded, 36 missing.

To the correspondents and rear-echelon personnel who didn't have to do the dirty work, this phase of the Italian campaign became known as "the quiet war." Compared to the previous action at Salerno, Naples and the Volturno, this stretch was dull and boring. The war correspondents came up from their headquarters to look over this new outfit. They com-

"On target. Fire for effect!"

plained of the lack of news along this quiet front, looked over the "spit-and-polish 88th" and speculated as to what would happen, how the men would stand up when things really got rough. The doughboys, once they got to know their way around the front, grew pretty cocky and to hear them talk in rear rest areas a stranger would think their combat time was measured in years instead of days. But General Sloan was pleased as he toured front-line units for his men "were getting the taste of it and getting it slowly and completely and the right way."

Intelligence units methodically piled up information on German troops opposing the 88th. Prisoners taken by 88th patrols talked freely and refugees from Gaeta furnished valuable information on German movements and installations about that town. PW interrogators quickly discovered that the best way to make the Krauts talk was to threaten to turn them over to Russian interrogators who were supposed to be in Naples. Coast patrols searched and handled Italian refugees but even so, the 88th

CIC detachment captured eight German spies attempting to make their way behind our lines during that first month.

Artillery batteries dug in along the beach, after a direct hit on one gun of the 339th the first day in action, and proceeded to build *de luxe* dugouts, some of them a cross between a pirate den and a museum. Castles at Tufo and Minturno were relieved of chairs, tables and beds—anything to brighten up a foxhole. At times the Krauts objected to this casual souvenir-hunting under their very noses and sent a couple of shells or a patrol into Minturno to back up their objections. But the cannoneers carried on, and out, everything movable including a grand piano which took them two days and nights to get out of a Minturno window. Units in the lines set up rest camps in buildings close to the front, some so close that German mortar fire hit mess tents and German patrols practically dropped in for coffee at night. Company barbers cut hair in OPs and the Recon Troop and Engineers played football near their wrecked villas across the Garigliano River with Axis Sally of Berlin warning almost nightly that someday she'd break up the games with a couple of rounds of heavy stuff.

Saturday night specials were a feature on one section of the front with Pvt. Henry D. Nicollet of Bridgeport, Connecticut, and Pvt. Aubert Coleman of Harmon, Virginia, dishing up baths for everyone from colonels to the lowest dogface. Wine casks cut in half made six tubs and Coleman, who worked in a bathhouse in the States, reported that about 12 men an hour could wash. Each man was allowed five gallons of water heated in two huge kettles in a fireplace.

Line troops in the 3d Battalion, 349th, were able to keep up with Division standards regarding haircuts and shaves thanks to company barbers who practised their trade undismayed by flying bullets and shells. Two of the front-line hair-snippers were Pfc. Gilbert E. Benton of Live Oak, California, and Pfc. Frederick Bublewitz of Burlington, New Jersey, who laid aside his normal duties as a gunner to go out to the artillery OPs after dark to trim the shaggy locks of the observers.

Engineers used mine detectors to clear possible patrol routes but Pvt. Arthur Pierron of Southport, Connecticut, discovered a new use for the detector. Pierron claimed he used one to detect wine. He insisted he'd uncovered about two hundred gallons of the buried *vino*—one of his best efforts being the discovery of fifty gallons buried near the company CP.

Buried *vino* was not the only treasure found. Sgt. Calvin Timmons of Dearborn, Michigan, was puzzled at contents of 170 packing cases he discovered in a castle at Minturno. He brought Capt. Allan J. Oppenheim of San Francisco, and Lt. Vincent H. Naramore of Orewell, Vermont, to the spot. After a quick check, the officers ascertained that the packing cases contained rare books and manuscripts worth millions of dollars and represented loot taken by the Germans from the University of Naples.

Line troops were accused of becoming a bit trigger-happy as they crouched up front and waited for enemy patrols to come their way. Whether or not the accusation was true, Sgt. Elden Riley, a sharpshooter from Hazard, Kentucky, insisted it wasn't bad shooting after one night of heavy firing. "I heard a rustling noise during the night," Riley said. "I threw three grenades in the general direction. There was silence for a few minutes. Then I heard the rustling noise again and fired a few rounds with the machine gun. This time there was no further noise." Next morning Riley found two very dead rats in front of his position.

In addition to fairly comfortable foxholes, some of the fur-lined foxhole set had struck it rich for a brief stretch when Artillery Headquarters moved into the Grand Hotel. "The night we moved into it," said Cpl. Lloyd A. McCormack of Barre, Vermont, "it reminded me of *Wuthering Heights.*" Marble staircases, modern plumbing, rooms with beds and outside balconies and terrace gardens and a fairly well stocked wine cellar were among the comforts enjoyed briefly by Divarty men. Riding their luck while it lasted were, among others, S/Sgt. Silvio A. Minoli, also of Barre, and Cpl. Charles A. Jones, McMinnville, Tennessee; Sgt. Sam Fiduccio, Auburn, New York; Sgt. Thomas A. Fisher, New York City; T/Sgt. Lloyd W. Quinby, Bloomfield, New Jersey; Pfc. Leonard Harris, Danville, Arkansas; Cpl. Pat H. Benson, Memphis, Tennessee; and Cpl. Charles Bailey, Lumberton, New Jersey.

Shortly after taking over in the Minturno sector, the 88th was introduced to the pack-train system. Getting rations and supplies to forward elements was a problem because of the terrain and several pack-mule outfits were attached to the Division. To supplement the Italian handlers, the Division was screened for mule-skinners. Many of those chosen were without previous experience in the art of bossing mules but there were some who could make the mules understand "Gee" and "Haw" in any language. One of these old hands was Pvt. Harold M. Metcalf of Lydonville, New York, who transferred experience gained in Panama to the Italian front as he bossed a train of 125 mules, 50 Italian helpers and 5 American skinners. Running a mule-train over mountain trails under fire was no cinch and the Krauts delighted in catching mule-trains in artillery barrages or ambushing them with patrols. But despite the odds, Metcalf and his squad got the rations through. The squad included Privates Russel G. Creasy of Surgoinsville, Tennessee; Raymond A. Brockman of Knifely, Kentucky; Harold C. Kelly, Burns, Mississippi; Charles A. Long, Lincoln Park, Michigan; and Nicholas Leone of Newark, N. J.

Pvt. Leo Witwer of the 349th achieved passing fame when he got lost delivering a message to the 349th CP and wandered up the main street of German-held Castelforte. Rescued by a British officer who had crept into the town a few hours before on a recon mission, Witwer's only comment after return to his outfit was that "Ma will be pretty sore if she hears about this."

Some officers and men grew impatient at this sit-down war. One CO grew so impatient that he scheduled a full regimental attack, an attack which would have been suicidal if allowed to go through. When Division heard of his plan, he was ordered to call off the abortive push and hold his section of the line as per original orders. Later the CO was relieved of command.

It was a quiet sector, but men died there. And some men became heroes.

Col. Arthur S. Champeny in the 351st set the pace for patrols when he put out a special bulletin criticizing some of his officers for "poor leadership" and pointing out that there "is no objection on my part to using company commanders as patrol leaders."

There was Pvt. John Flores of Los Angeles, California, and the 349th, who heard a funny noise in a house while he was on a daylight patrol. Investigating, Flores burst in upon a Kraut officer writing a letter. Taking a couple of deep breaths and mustering as many "cuss words as I knew," Flores ordered the officer outside. He nearly fainted when 14 more Krauts paraded meekly from another room and joined the party. He felt worse after he'd goose-stepped the supermen to a PW cage and then discovered that his rifle had been locked all during the performance. Flores was put in for a Silver Star for his exploit but instead he received a court-martial on complaint of a warrant officer who said that Flores had laughed at him when told to put on his helmet. Many months later, Flores was awarded the Bronze Star for his "heroic achievement" in volunteering to use a tower near the Arno River to observe German movements. The Krauts spotted him, turned artillery on the observation post and reduced it to rubble. Flores was sent to a base hospital with severe wounds.

There were Lt. Jasper D. Parks of Oklahoma City, and Sgt. W. A. Trapp of Wagoner, Oklahoma, both of the 350th who rescued two soldiers after the wounded men had spent six days and nights in a wrecked building in No Man's Land. Medics called to treat the wounded men were mildly astonished to find them intoxicated. The wounded, with no food or water, had existed by drinking wine found in their wrecked prison.

There were 1st Sgt. Chester W. Pastuszynski of Buffalo, New York, and Cpl. Archie A. Berry of Cincinnati, Ohio, who made the term "field

Lobbing mortar shells into enemy lines.

expedient" more than just a phrase in a manual. Kraut artillery had blown up the ammo dump of the 350th heavy-weapons company. Counter-fire was essential but the only ammo available was British mortar shells which required a larger firing pin than that of an American mortar. Fashioning a firing pin extension with three copper pennies and a nail, the pair discarded it when they became convinced it wouldn't stand up. Finally, over the protests of the company cooks, they acquired the gas jet from a field range, filed it down and soon had their mortars lobbing the British shells into German lines.

Heavy patrolling was the order of the day, and night, and while most patrols suffered relatively few casualties there were exceptions. There was one three-man patrol from the 1st Battalion, 349th, which went out at 0300 hours one day on a 24-hour mission to spot Kraut gun emplacements. The men carried a radio. After directing fire on several emplacements the patrol took refuge in a house when dawn came. They hadn't been there long when one of the men looked around quickly and saw a Kraut perched on a ladder, looking into the third-floor room. Before the Yank could fire, the German scrambled down. This was reported back to the CP. Twenty minutes later came another message: "Germans have occupied two floors below us." That was the last message sent.

Among the unusual patrol tasks was the house-wrecking assignment handed to Lt. Harry Baughman of Findlay, Ohio. It was thought that Germans were using certain buildings in a section of No Man's Land as observation posts. Windows and doors in the buildings, however, prevented 88th observers from being able to see when the buildings were being used by the enemy. Baughman and his patrol set out to knock off the doors and windows. The first four houses were given the works, but while the fifth was being taken apart, a Kraut patrol passed nearby. There were a few anxious moments as the house-wreckers took a ten-minute break. When the German patrol went on without investigating, the crew wrecked five more houses for a day's total of nine.

It was so peaceful in No Man's Land one afternoon that Pfc. George Zelinsky of Curtisville, Pennsylvania, decided to "take ten" and sat down by a big cactus plant. The first time he heard cans clanking together he thought it was just his nerves. But then came a second clanking. Zelinsky made a quick check and then discovered "I was sitting on top of some Krauts—and they weren't dead." Zelinsky moved off the dugout and brought up the rest of the patrol—Lt. Henry L. Liel of Chicago; Pfc. Frank Demers of West Sayville, New York, and Sgt. Harley Strickland of Mackay, Indiana. Lieutenant Liel, who knew Polish, said: "Anyone in there speak Polish?" There was no answer. "Come out," he yelled, and four Krauts came tumbling out. They tried to make a break for it but Zelinsky put a quick stop to that with a couple of bullets in their path.

Pfc. Marvin Blake of Mt. Morris, Michigan, crowded enough action into fifteen minutes to hold him for a long time. In that short stretch, Blake had a rifle shot out of his hands, his helmet dented by a machine-gun bullet and the seat of his pants set ablaze by a phosphorus shell. Blake said that after he had been knocked down by a shot which struck his helmet, he started to get up and another bullet carried away his rifle. "I jumped for the nearest shell crater," he said, "but a phosphorus shell beat me to it and somehow started the seat of my pants burning. I hopped into another crater and beat out the fire before it did any real harm." Five minutes later, as he prepared to re-enter action, an incoming shell hit nearby and the concussion knocked him down again. "Fifteen minutes may be a short time," Blake said, "but it sure seemed like a century to me."

Two DSCs were won during this quiet war.

The first went to 2nd Lt. John T. Lamb of Irwin, Tennessee. Leading a five-man patrol near Tufo on March 30, Lamb was wounded by machine-gun fire which opened up when the patrol reached a Kraut outpost. Withdrawing his men, Lamb silenced the position by radio-directed cannon and mortar fire. The patrol continued on and encountered 15

Krauts occupying a house. Lamb rushed this position himself and with grenades and rifle fire forced them into the open. In the ensuing fire fight, seven Germans were killed. One patrol member was wounded and Lamb carried him to safety. He later provided covering fire as the rest of the patrol withdrew when the Krauts brought up reinforcements. Every member of the patrol was wounded but all managed to make their way back to friendly lines because of Lamb's covering fire.

The second DSC went to 2nd Lt. John A. Liebenstein of Monona, Iowa—young, stocky and known in K Company, 349th, for his quick-witted good humor. Ordered to take prisoners for information purposes, Lieutenant Liebenstein and his men—Cpl. Allen L. Marsh of Covina, California, Pfc. Ralph C. Wells of Sevierville, Tennessee, and Pfc. Sidney L. Collins of Maquoketa, Iowa—crept to within a short distance of German lines on Mt. Ceracoli. Shouting "Iowa" as the code word for the attack, the quartet assaulted a machine-gun position, the officer's gun jamming as he reached the nest through a hail of fire. Undaunted, he thrust the muzzle of his useless weapon into the emplacement and ordered the one German occupying it to come out; reached in and dragged him out when the scared Kraut refused to move. The mission completed, the quartet started for its own lines. On the way, Liebenstein hit the trip wire of a German booby trap. There was an explosion and the young officer clutched his middle and fell into the arms of Corporal Marsh. The Germans, now stirred to new activity, sent mortar and artillery shells crashing into the draw. Marsh tried to carry the officer but his efforts only increased the pain and Liebenstein ordered the men to abandon him and save themselves. When medics returned to the spot later with a litter, Liebenstein was nowhere to be found.

Yes it was a quiet war—for those people who didn't have to fight it.

In mid-March, the 339th Infantry Regiment of the 85th Division came across from North Africa, landed at Naples during a Nazi harbor and dock raid. Attached to the 88th, this regiment moved immediately to the front and went into the line on March 17 to relieve the 349th which moved back to a rest area in the vicinity of Casanova. During the rest period a switch in regimental commanders was made. Assigned to take over the 349th was Lt. Col. Joseph B. Crawford of Humboldt, Kansas, thrice-wounded veteran of North Africa, Sicily and Anzio, and winner of the DSC and Silver Star. Tagged with the nickname of "Krautkiller" by the Germans for his exploits while serving on the beachhead with the 3d Division, Colonel Crawford swiftly reorganized the 349th. He built up a new pride in the outfit and shook the men out of a lethargy which had lasted for months. The 349th took "Krautkillers" for its nickname.

Other major command changes had assigned Lt. Col. James R. Davidson of Tiffin, Ohio, as AC of S, G-3, and Lt. Col. Peter L. Topic as AC of S, G-4, the latter succeeding Colonel Beine, transferred to Third Army Headquarters when the 88th left the States. Lt. Col. Martin H. Otto, former G-3, had been left behind in Africa with a new assignment to a base section unit. To command rear installations, Brig. Gen. Thoburn K. Brown was attached to the 88th following inactivation of his cavalry outfit.

While holding its own on the main front, the 88th also took part in the Anzio beachhead battle with 88th Quartermaster Company personnel trucking supplies and equipment to troops on the "pool table" via ship from Naples.

Days dragged into weeks. It was still a quiet war.

But the white crosses in the Division cemetery at Carano increased each day.

The first Easter Day in the lines was a novel one. Artillery chaplains held services in gun pits and infantry units took time out to kneel and pray in forward positions. In the 349th sector, the most unusual service ever held was staged within a few hundred yards of enemy lines on Hill 411 near Castelforte. Moving equipment and an altar up the hill by pack-mule under cover of darkness, regimental chaplains were ready shortly after dawn to bring the message of Easter to their own troops and to the Germans across No Man's Land by means of loudspeakers. After an explanation in German of what was to take place, Chaplain Oscar L. Reinboth of Seward, Nebraska, invited the enemy to take part in the services in their own fashion from their side of the lines. The big guns fell silent along the Garigliano and their thunder of death and destruction was replaced by the eternal and peaceful message of Easter.

No signs of movement were visible in German lines—their guns had not spoken since the initial words of Chaplain Reinboth. The doughboys had been told to lie low in their foxholes but now in the sudden lull of battle they came forward to gather about the small altar. A nurse, 1st Lt. Charlotte Johnson of Painesville, Ohio, sang a hymn and the music rang out sweet and clear in the still morning air. An address in German by Chaplain Reinboth was followed with English services by Protestant Chaplain Earl Hayes of Clyde, Texas, and a Catholic Mass celebrated by Chaplain Leo Crowley of Syracuse, New York.

Still and motion picture cameras in the hands of a battery of photographers clicked and ground to record the ceremony and a score of war correspondents covered the services in the uncanny stillness. In less than an hour it was over. The hill side on which the altar rested became military

Chaplain Gregory R. Kennedy saying Easter Mass for artillerymen near Minturno.

objective No. 411. The troops went back to their foxholes. A few minutes later the guns roared. The war was on again.

April stretched into May and the 88th sector narrowed to a two-regiment front with the arrival of the rest of the 85th Division, which went into the line on the left flank coastal area. The forward CP moved out into tents, cleared for battle operation. Heavy artillery units arrived to reinforce the units already in place. Front-bound traffic stepped up as huge stock piles of ammo and supplies grew. Squadrons of heavy bombers roared north every day.

But outwardly the quiet war went on. With a touch of humor now and then which served to spice the routine.

One such touch was supplied by Division Artillery Cubs, doubling as heavy bombers. Annoyed by glowing Air Corps reports of damage which always described targets as "obliterated" and areas "devastated," Cub pilots decided to dream up a few communiqués of their own. Loaded with five-gallon tins of gasoline, the Cubs hovered over Mt. Ceracoli until an artillery preparation of white phosphorus had blanketed German positions, then dove and dumped the gasoline. The results were not too good. An enemy-held tree burst into brief flame, a pillar of smoke soared all of three feet into the air.

The Krauts got sore at the gasoline bath; took pot shots at the Cubs. Lt. Arley Wilson of Marshallton, Ohio, got sore also; dove his plane and strafed the startled ground troops with his .45 pistol. Back at the airstrip, Wilson's airmen burlesqued the glamorous fighter pilots, gesturing with their hands to indicate dives and half-rolls. "Somebody above nearly hit me with one of those cans," complained a sergeant. "Please, gentlemen, let us refer to those cans as bombs," corrected a lieutenant. "We should all get the Air Medal," said S/Sgt. Edward Cooper, who described the attack as "epic, colossal, history-making. It is the only one in recent months not made by mighty swarms of four-engined bombers. We failed to shoot down 120 enemy planes. We did not obliterate the target, and despite flak which was not thick enough to walk on, we did not start fires visible for 80 miles." Apart from the burlesque, the gasoline bombing actually was the forerunner of something new in warfare. US scientists were working then on the perfection and production of gasoline jelly firebombs, a weapon which a year later was to help pave the way for an 88th attack.

A shift in regimental commanders gave the 350th a new CO. He was Col. James C. Fry of Washington, D. C., and Sandpoint, Idaho. A West Point graduate and former assistant to Generals MacArthur and Eisenhower in Hawaii and the Philippines, Colonel Fry had been assistant military attaché in Turkey when war broke with Japan. Later stationed in Egypt in the same capacity, he served after that as commander of the 69th Armored Regiment in the States prior to his request for overseas assignment. Colonel Fry replaced Col. Charles P. Lynch, whose subsequent return to the States ended one of the Army's unique father-son relationships. Colonel Lynch's son, Lt. Charles P. Lynch, Jr., remained with the regiment in command of the same company with which his father had served during World War I.

A frequent visitor to the Division, Lt. Gen. Mark W. Clark, Fifth Army commander, spoke to more than 5,500 troops in a rear area on May 3 when he made formal presentation to the Division's first DSC winner, Lieutenant Lamb of the 351st. Formally welcoming the 88th to the Fifth Army and praising General Sloan, who once had been his instructor in tactics, General Clark told the men they were ready to go places. "I promise you it will be soon," he said.

The Buildup

As May days lengthened, it was almost a cinch bet that the Big Push was coming—but soon. The 351st moved back into the line in the Minturno–Tufo area. On its right was the 350th and protecting the Division and Corps right flank, the 88th Recon Troop, dismounted. French troops took up positions before Castelforte. The 349th went into Division reserve. Engineers stepped up their mine probing, cleared areas near the mouth of the Ausente River valley and along assault routes that the doughboys would have to use. Medics completed evacuation plans and procedures for handling wounded. Signalmen strung hundreds of miles of wire to maintain communications. Extra rations and ammo and supplies of all kinds piled up in the dumps.

The Germans grew jittery, sensed that something was in the wind. They knew, because of their dominating positions and excellent observation, of the increased traffic along front roads. Enemy artillery barrages along our main supply route increased. MPs and bandsmen, accustomed to ducking shells at the constantly smoked Minturno bridge and at other hot spots along the supply roads and trails, reported they were ducking faster and more often. Despite all our efforts at maintaining military secrecy, the Germans knew what divisions faced them. A PW carried a late April edition of the German 71st Division newspaper which featured a blue cloverleaf insignia on its front page with cut-lines identifying the 88th as being in the line opposite them and having been partly relieved at various times by "another division in the 80 series." Further interrogation of the PW disclosed that the Germans had a pretty accurate idea of

German 88s coming in.

the units composing the 88th, of its Stateside training record and the identity of some of the top commanders. Axis Sally in her nightly broadcasts frequently mentioned the 88th—several nights gave the correct password—warned the Recon Troop that Kraut gunners had the range on their makeshift football field and "will open up some day when you're not expecting it."

Abandoning its circus layout near Carano, Division Headquarters moved up into a quarry south of Minturno, the farthest forward CP of any division in the line. Field Order No. 6, complete except for date and time of D-day and H-hour, went out to the units and commanders learned that II Corps was to attack west with divisions abreast—88th on the right, 85th on the left—with the ultimate objective of cutting the Itri–Pico road west of Itri.

Heavy artillery, tanks, tank destroyers and engineer bridging and sapper units moved by night into positions across the Garigliano.

The tension mounted.

The Division Commander made last spot checks of his units; commanders were briefed; men drew extra bandoleers of ammunition; wrote last letters to loved ones at home, telling them, in an effort to ease worry, that their jobs were easy, that the war was so far away from them that they never even heard the report of a gun.

Artillery maintained normal firing schedules; patrols from the 85th Division screened our front and probed nightly, reporting the enemy be-

59

coming increasingly sensitive to our movements. At Division CP, the plans and orders completed, officers and men simply went through the motions as they waited for the kickoff.

Up in the lines, the doughboy, with nothing ahead of him but the enemy, sat tight and sweated it out. Whether he realized it or not, all the plans and hopes of the highest commanders would be carried out by him and him alone. Success or failure of the entire campaign rested upon him. He surveyed the seemingly impassable mountains over which he soon would have to fight and climb—gave his rifle an extra check and got ready to start climbing, and fighting.

The war correspondents checked in with G-2 for a last briefing and then fanned out to positions along the line. To them, the 88th was one of the top question marks of the war. It had come up to the firing line as a guinea pig for several untested theories. The correspondents wanted to know how this division of draftees would perform in battle as compared with Regular Army or National Guard outfits.

The War Department wanted to know that too, and also wanted to learn how a system of replacing casualties as they occurred would work, as compared to the established practice of leaving units in the line until they were so badly battered they had to be replaced with completely new units.

There was another question, one which existed in the minds of the doughboys themselves. In the States, they'd been told they were good, that the 88th was one of the best outfits. But all the speeches hadn't quite sold the 88th to itself, to the men who wore its patch, to the men who soon were to go into their first attack and start playing for keeps up where bullets, and not words, settled the arguments. This was their first attack coming up—defensive war was over and the time was rapidly approaching when they'd have to carry the fight to the enemy. Would they go through that line or would they be thrown back?

It took time—and blood—to answer those questions.

In the 351st, Frederick Faust (Max Brand), correspondent for *Harper's Magazine,* who had been living with the regiment for weeks gathering background material for a book, requested and obtained permission to accompany assault units in the attack. And gave as his reason: "The only way I can get the feel and reactions of men in battle is to go into battle myself."

Finally everything was set. There was nothing more to do but wait for the hour. The 88th was ready.

There was no one left now who still maintained that "this division never will see action."

We did not expect you so soon . . . you fight like devils!
A German PW.

THE FIRST TEST

It was a quiet, lazy spring day. The date was May 11 but outwardly it was no different from any other day on that front. Fields of scarlet poppies nodded and bobbed in a faint sea breeze; smoke pots at the Minturno Bridge drifted the acrid haze across the valley; an incoming shell punctuated the stillness now and then with a muttering crash. South of Minturno, the men of the Vampire Platoon—so named because it had bivouacked in a cemetery, sleeping by day and gliding about the front by night —made last checks of their equipment, slept a little, wrote letters or talked idly about the job ahead of them. There was not much to say. Even the trite phrase "This is it!" had lost its original humor, for this really was it. And no joking about it.

Daylight faded and dancing stars winked across a clear sky. A dog howled somewhere, its cry echoing over the silent valley. Mimosa drenched the night air with a nostalgic perfume.

The minutes crept on. It was 2230. And then 2245—2255. It was 2300 —H-hour of D-day. Attack!

A solid, leaping sheet of flame shattered the stillness of the night as the greatest artillery concentration since El Alamein roared sudden death out of the darkness into German lines. From coast to coast along that long-dormant front, uncounted tons of steel spat from the throats of roaring American, English, French, Canadian and Polish guns. This was the spring push.

Silently, quickly, from their sangars and dugouts the men of the 88th took their first few steps on what was to be a long and bloody and bitter trail, began doing the job for which they had been trained so well, began making battle history. Part of the strategy to keep the Germans ignorant of the push until the last possible minute called for no advance artillery preparation. Shells and men moved at the same instant with the men following the savage barrage as closely as possible.

Stunned at first by the ferocity of the barrage which came hurling at them from the once deceptively quiet Garigliano River flats, the Germans nevertheless were quick to react. They poured a murderous hail of mortar and small-arms fire down the slopes at the advancing doughboys who were battering at their sector of the Gustav Line. Front-line units passed the word back to rear headquarters that this attack was the big one. German heavy batteries at Gaeta turned their guns inshore and tried for the Minturno Bridge to cut what they knew was our main supply route.

The Krauts fought back but there was no stopping our initial surge. In less than fifty-one minutes Mt. Damiano, key to the defenses of Castelforte and a height which General Clark had boasted could be taken when-

Screaming Meemies.

ever the 88th desired, had fallen to the 350th Infantry Regiment. Capture of Damiano, or Cianelli as it also was called, passed almost unnoticed in news dispatches at the time but it was described later as one of the most outstanding operations in the initial assault on the Gustav Line. Its seizure covered the flank of the French Corps and enabled the French to crack through the bottleneck that was Castelforte, nicknamed "Little Cassino" by its conquerors.

Individual exploits were numerous in that first clash and out of the smoke and flame came a young Irish lad who was destined to become the first man in the Division to merit the Medal of Honor. The lad was S/Sgt. Charles W. (Red) Shea of The Bronx, New York, and the 350th, a one-time peanut butcher at Yankee Stadium. While going over the crest of Damiano shortly after dawn, Shea's platoon leader was killed and his platoon sergeant was wounded. Taking cover from enemy artillery, Shea spotted two trip wires at his head and feet; realized he was in the middle of a minefield.

A Kraut machine gun opened up on the men trapped in the field. Shea realized it had to be silenced. Without hesitation he rose and started for the gun. As he approached the position, some sixth sense warned him to turn. He whirled about to see a German emerging from another machine-gun position and pointing a machine pistol at him. Shea leveled his rifle and the Kraut surrendered. Four other Germans emerged from the position. One refused to come out. Motioning with his rifle, Shea directed the PWs to return to the rear—one died when he stepped on a mine. The last

63

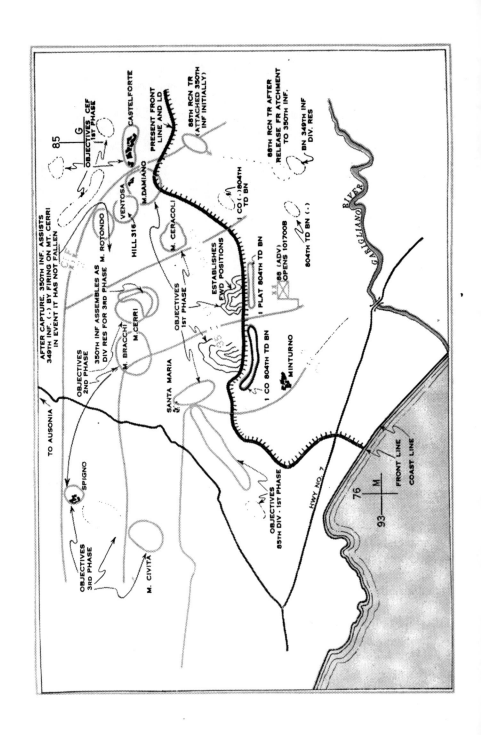

THE JUMPOFF

The Fifth Army on the left of the Allied line in Italy held a front along the precipitous mountain crests north of the Garigliano River and consisted of the II Corps (85th and 88th Divisions) near the Tyrrhenian Sea, the French Expeditionary Corps, and the Polish Corps. The 88th Division occupied the right of the II Corps front extending from Minturno to the valley east of Mt. Damiano and south of Castelforte.

The plan of attack called for the 350th Infantry to reduce Mt. Damiano, Hill 316, Ceracoli and to capture Rotondo, at the same time assisting the French force on the right. The 351st Infantry on the left was given the grim mission of taking Santa Maria Infante, the high ground beyond, and of opening the way into the valley of the Ausente. The 349th Infantry was at the outset required to support the action by fire and to be in readiness to attack on call within its zone of action. The final objective of the Division was Mt. San Angelo west of Spigno.

Staff Sergeant Charles W. Shea, 350th Infantry.

Kraut in the position rose to toss a grenade at an officer leading another platoon and Shea got him with one shot.

Maneuvering now to keep out of range of the gunner he'd started out to get, Shea suddenly found himself directly beneath another machine-gun nest, "so close I could have reached up and touched the barrel." He captured two more Krauts in this emplacement. The remaining Jerry was now the only problem. Suddenly this Kraut stood upright and fired eight shots from a P38 at Shea from less than fifteen yards—and missed. Shea pulled off eight rounds from his rifle, and also missed. Both Yank and Kraut ducked for cover. Shea waited, another clip in his rifle. He spotted the German a few moments later, blood streaming down one side of his face as he rose to toss a grenade. Shea fired. Dying, the Kraut heaved his potato-masher but it was his last, futile gesture.

Things were rougher on the left side of the line. As the 350th mopped up on Damiano, the 351st butted against the stone wall that was Santa Maria Infante, pivotal point in the Gustav Line left flank. With tanks, which knocked out 21 German machine guns in the first few hours, the 351st jumped off for Santa Maria with the 2d Battalion in the lead. A hell of small-arms, machine-gun and mortar fire caught the doughboys as they started up the rocky slopes.

E Company led the assault on the right, F Company took the left and G Company was held in reserve. Early on May 12 F overcame resistance from Hill 130 and continued its advance up the terrain feature known as "The Tits," pulling abreast of E. Its commander wounded, E was held up on the spur. When Colonel Kendall's radio was knocked out by shell fire, he moved up to determine the cause of the delay and assumed command of E on arrival. Spotting two machine guns, Colonel Kendall led an attack on one of the pillboxes. This gun was knocked out and Kendall then swung the company to the right under heavy mortar and machine-gun fire. Moving up to the right of "The Tits," the outfit was stopped again by machine guns firing from the flanks and front.

Again Colonel Kendall took off, this time with a squad from the 2d Platoon, and started for a gun which was firing from a position in a stone house to the right. First building up all the fire power possible and joining in the fire fight himself with a carbine, bazooka, BAR and M1 with anti-tank grenades, Kendall then led the final assault on the house. As he pulled the pin on a hand grenade preparatory to throwing it, he was hit by machine-gun bullets from the left flank, receiving mortal wounds. Unable to throw the grenade, he held it to his stomach and fell with it to prevent injury to his men. The first of the original 88th battalion commanders was gone.

The rubble heap that was Santa Maria Infante.

An artillery liaison officer, 1st Lt. Pat G. Combs of the 913th, assumed command of the company after the death of Kendall and personally led the doughboys as they attacked and silenced three machine guns. He then ordered part of the unit to dig in while he and the remainder drove forward to capture the spur. During the battle Lieutenant Combs maintained radio communication with his artillery and conducted effective supporting fire. When reinforcements moved up the Texan exposed himself to fire from both sides to identify his troops to the new outfit.

E Company then pushed on into Santa Maria but was driven back by a strong counterattack. F forged ahead on the left and reached a position near Tame. Supporting tanks were unable to get through because of mines and enemy SP guns. Some tanks which tried the crowned road leading up to Santa Maria were picked off like sitting ducks by SPs.

At 0415 hours May 12 the 3d Battalion, commanded by youthful Major Charles P. Furr of Rock Hill, South Carolina, was ordered to pass through the 2d to keep the attack moving. The 3d jumped off at 0730 hours for Hill 172, was held up for a time by fire from Hill 103 but continued a slow advance. Tanks rumbling up in support continued to take punishing fire from SPs.

Another German counterattack forced E Company to withdraw and F Company quickly was isolated and surrounded. Attempts to reach it failed. Going forward to check on the supply situation, Capt. Charles H. Heitman, Jr., Fort Myers, Florida, found E and G practically disorganized, badly cut up and with E minus its commander. Taking over E Captain Heitman outlined a plan of attack with 1st Lt. Theodore N. Noon, Jr., of Belmont, Massachusetts, G Company commander, who insisted on sticking despite wounds. To complete coordination with the 85th Division on the left, the attack was delayed until 1700 hours May 13. Noon had been wounded earlier in both arms but knocked out a machine-gun nest despite the injuries. Later, while making a personal reconnaissance, he was wounded by shell fragments in both legs but refused to be evacuated for treatment.

When E and G kicked off at 1700 hours, Noon had recovered sufficiently to lead his men. Hours later, and then only on direct orders, he turned himself in for hospital treatment. Heitman, with the 1st Platoon of E, moved up on two machine guns. In a struggle which lasted almost two hours, Heitman killed four grenade-throwing Krauts and knocked out two guns before being wounded himself.

With no word from the surrounded F Company in twenty-four hours, Colonel Champeny gave it up for lost and ordered a new F Company to be formed from the remaining companies of the 2d Battalion.

Col. Arthur S. Champeny, Lt.Col. Walter B. Yeager, and Major Victor Hobson.

And Santa Maria still held. The Krauts, penned up in this rubbled village which had been only a name on a map, stood off a regiment. The news spread along the front and men in other 88th units wondered if the outfit could take it; wondered if the 88th would fail in this, its first real fight. The name Santa Maria hung in the air like a dark cloud.

In the 351st, they were too busy to do much wondering about success or failure. The 1st Battalion, ordered to attack at 1600 hours May 13, was taken over by Colonel Champeny when the battalion commander was separated from the unit while on reconnaissance. And stern, graying Colonel Champeny proved himself to his men as they lay pinned down under a barrage. Standing erect, apparently unmindful of the shells falling in his vicinity, the colonel calmly directed operations—shouted words of encouragement to his bewildered doughboys.

"It was magnificent," said Larry Newman, International News Service correspondent, who had been traveling with the 351st since the jumpoff. "We wanted to lie down and stay there, but with the Old Man standing up like a rock you couldn't stay down. Something about him just brought you right up to your feet. The guys saw him, too. They figured if the Old Man could do it so could they. And when the time came they got up off the ground and started on again to Santa Maria."

Early on the 14th the 1st Battalion took Hill 109 after considerable resistance which included traversing an extensive minefield and beating off
a strong enemy counterattack. Its flank wide open because Hill 131 was
not taken on schedule, the battalion left the regimental zone and took 131
itself. During the actions of the morning Colonel Champeny spotted a
Kraut artillery battery in position about four hundred yards from the
crest of a hill. Under fire, he moved to a company position. Inspired by
the Colonel, who again stood upright in the face of enemy machine-gun
fire, the men left the cover they previously had sought and overran the
battery, killing and capturing a hundred Krauts.

Opposition now was in its final stages. The relentless attack of the 351st
had been too much even for the toughest defenders and the line began to
crack. One more heave did it. The 2d Battalion moved on Santa Maria
from the right and the 3d Battalion drove up the Minturno–Santa Maria
road. The town was occupied by 1000 hours and engineers followed
, on the heels of the infantry, clearing rubble from the streets with bull-
dozers.

On arrival of the 351st in force, the mystery of what had happened
to the missing F Company was solved when Pfc. Frank Cimini of
Northampton, Massachusetts, and two other men emerged from a culvert
in the vicinity of Tame where they had been forced to hide for more
than two days to avoid capture. Cimini told the story. F Company in the
first attack had advanced so rapidly that it soon was far out in front of
regimental lines. Cut off when the Krauts counterattacked and forced E
to withdraw, the men of F though surrounded held out for more than
thirty hours, Cimini related.

Finally the Krauts resorted to an old trick but it worked. Several
Krauts stumbled down the hill towards the company lines, hands in the
air and shouting *"Kamerad!"* As the men of F rose to capture them,
other Germans closed in from the rear and flanks. Five officers and fifty
enlisted men were taken—only three men escaped and lived to tell the
story.

Firing direct support for the 351st at Santa Maria, the 913th Field
pumped out more than 4,700 rounds in the first twenty-four hours; later
was joined at various stages of the critical battle by massed Division and
Corps artillery as well as dive bombers which pounded German gun installations at Spigno. Two American destroyers in the Gulf of Gaeta also
added their fire power to the final punch.

In the first days of the push, the Recon Troop made its bid for glory
with capture of Mt. Cerri by a 13-man patrol. During the months of the
quiet war, Recon patrols up the Ausente Valley always had met fire and

resistance from Cerri and 2d Lt. Laurence (Cookie) Bowers of Grand Island, Nebraska, swore that some day he'd "get the Krauts on that damned hill." Shortly after 0200 hours May 14, he and his little group of dismounted cavalrymen snipped the concertina wire at the base of the hill and crawled over a booby-trap wire.

"We made it," said Sgt. Leonard L. Juby of Boonville, New York, "but a couple of hours later some of the fellows tripped it. Three of them were killed." Once over that obstacle, the men worked up a draw toward the Kraut machine gun covering the wire, found the position empty but could hear the two Nazis talking as they went ahead of the Yanks up the hill.

"Then we had to scale some cliffs just like infantry," said Cpl. Vito V. Zaliagiris of Detroit, Michigan, "and when we got to the top in regular squad formation the artillery was bursting all around us and the Krauts were scrambling down the other side. Me and Evaristo Alvarado just hugged the ground and prayed." While they were praying, Cookie sent Wayne W. Mills of Henderson, Texas, and Cpl. Orval Barrett of Venita, Oklahoma—Barret bagged five prisoners during the night—back down the hill to bring up the rest of the gang. By dawn the 350th had occupied and garrisoned the hill and the Recons withdrew.

Others in that memorable patrol included Cpl. Otis A. Smith of East Tawas, Michigan; Cpl. Manuel F. Blinn of Fall River, Massachusetts; Pfc. Carl A. Nordell, Belmar, New Jersey; Pfc. John C. Johnson, Gleason, Wisconsin; and Pvts. Samuel Tucker, Crosswicks, New Jersey; Robert E. Vass, Hinton, West Virginia; Gordon W. Speegle, Clarksville, Texas; and Cecil E. Barter of Isle au Haut, Maine. The Recons were justifiably proud, and just a bit smug, about capturing what had been listed as a battalion objective.

Action in the 350th sector had been favorable. The advance was swift and resistance was quickly overcome. By morning of the 13th, both Hill 316 and Mt. Ceracoli were taken, and at 1320 hours General Kendall, who was directing operations of all units in the Damiano area, reported that Ventosa had fallen to complete the action in the first phase by the 350th. One of the highlights came when an entire German battalion was caught in an assembly area by TOT (Time on Target) fire from the 337th, 338th, 339th and 913th Field Artillery Battalions. The shoot was such a success that observers later said there was no describing the scene of carnage that had been the Kraut assembly area.

The 349th, held back as a reserve striking force, sent its 1st Battalion to occupy first phase objectives. These positions, involving a limited advance, were occupied at 0030 hours May 12 and the regiment awaited

Captured German troops were dazed at the savagery of the 88th's first attack.

further orders. On the afternoon of the 14th, the 1st Battalion jumped off for Mt. Bracchi and occupied it with A and B Companies by nightfall.

But with Santa Maria fallen, the German Gustav Line was smashed, ripped wide open. The Nazis, fighting desperately for time, began a general withdrawal, the beginning of a retreat which did not stop completely until the Krauts had back-pedalled to their Gothic Line high in the Apennines. German prisoners, stumbling through the rubble heaps that had been their "impregnable" Gustav Line fortifications, were dazed and bewildered and glad to be alive; amazed at the savagery of the attacks hurled at them so suddenly out of the night. They had expected a spring drive—it was inevitable that there would be one. But they had not expected it so soon. Their commanders had told them that May 24 was the Fifth Army D-day. That day had come thirteen days too soon for them.

They told PW interrogators that Yank troops—88th troops—who swarmed in on their positions were on top of them within seconds after the artillery lifted. And they said that those men, those bearded, dirty, tired, angry, charging men with the blue Cloverleaf insignia, "fought like devils." Many of those men did not live to hear that tribute from a beaten enemy—many of them had been dazed and bewildered and frightened also in the first hours of hell that marked their first attack.

73

Looking back toward Minturno and the Garigliano River after breaking through the Gustav Line.

But they took all that the Krauts could throw at them and kept on going, until wounds or death had stopped their individual advance.

Magnificently they had met and passed their first real combat test. But the doughboys didn't know what they had done or how good they really were. They thought, as did one lad who lost a hand and sobbed bitterly with rage as he stumbled back to an aid station, "we got the hell kicked out of us."

But the correspondents who had seen a lot of outfits and who were watching this fresh one with jaundiced eyes, admitted that this driving spirit of the 88th was something new. They knew how good the outfit was and they said so. Frederick C. Painton of *The Saturday Evening Post* and *The Reader's Digest,* said that "the 88th was such a standout the first time under fire that it was mentioned in orders by Lt. Gen. Mark W. Clark. I myself have never seen such calm purposefulness anywhere, except in the battle-toughened divisions in Sicily."

The nodding poppy fields added new patches and splashes of red to their scarlet blankets. The new red was blood. The breeze still carried the sweet fragrance of mimosa but along with that odor was a new scent, the unforgettable smell of the dead. The smoke pots at the Minturno Bridge no longer covered the valley with haze. Once again a man could walk upright, in broad daylight, across the Garigliano.

And back in the Division Cemetery at Carano where the cost of the push was counted in new white crosses, his notes for a book lay in the new grave with Frederick Faust, killed in the first hour of the push with many of the men he had wanted to write about at Santa Maria.

That was the Gustav Line. That was the first test.

Once through that Gustav Line, there were mountains and more mountains. Off the main highway, except when it swung back out of the hills to take Spigno, Itri and Fondi—there it broke the Adolf Hitler Line—the 88th walked and ached and fought across more mountains than it ever thought existed. It chased the Krauts through those hills, fought and killed them when they elected to stand and fight, moved fast and untiringly.

A General Staff officer, attached to the 88th as an observer at his own request "since that was one outfit that had its feet on the ground," reported to the War Department on that mountain thrust. "The French Goums," he said, "are supposed to excel as mountain fighters and it was quite a shock to them to find that this American division could fight through the mountains just as well as they did."

The 88th learned its mountain fighting lessons the hard way. It was not a specially trained mountain division although practically all its com-

Moving up through the hills toward Itri.

bat life was destined to be spent in the hills. It had no special equipment for crag-hopping. No writer ever compared any of its mountain feats to that of Wolfe at Quebec. It was just an infantry division whose chief weapons were the rifles and feet and guts of the doughboys who made up its squads and platoons. Their feet carried it forward; their guns and guts held the ground it took.

In that push above the Gustav Line to just below Rome, the officers and men threw away the book and fought an improvised battle. They had to. Except for what could be called rear-guard battles, the Krauts were running. It's not fair to the men who fought to dismiss their effort by casually referring to it as a rear-guard scrap. But the truth is that the Krauts were running, trying desperately to hold us off until their main body could get to a point previously prepared for a do-or-die stand. That point, although we did not know it at the time, was high in the Apennine Mountains north of Florence and called the Gothic Line. It was the line that they originally had decided to defend as their Intelligence had expected our invasion of Italy to be made somewhere between Rome and Leghorn. When we came in at Salerno they came down the peninsula to meet us, secretly delighted that the Allies had elected to push up the peninsula over natural obstacles of terrain with crack German divisions contesting for every inch of the way. All the advantages of height and observation were in their favor.

Some military writers have claimed that the original intent of the Allies was simply to capture Naples. Others take the plan a step farther and say that the high command wanted only to take Rome, for its political and psychological significance, to lop off one-third of the Rome–Berlin–Tokyo Axis. Whatever the truth of the matter, the fact remains that our armies in Italy went all the way, clear up to the Brenner Pass and junction with forces driving down from Europe. If Italy was intended to be only a sideshow in the war, fighting men of both sides thought it was the biggest show of all. Which it was, as their lives were personally involved. The Germans gave nothing freely—even when they were running, we paid for every foot that we chased them.

Pressing on after the retreating enemy, the 349th Krautkillers bypassed the 351st at the rubble heap that had been Santa Maria, took the Capo d'Aqua and at 2045 hours May 14 reported that its 2d and 3d Battalions were advancing up Mt. La Civita from the rear while the 1st Battalion drove up the forward slopes. To the northwest of Civita, the 1st Battalion, 351st, took Mt. Passasera and wiped out a German pack artillery train in the process. Continuing its drive, the regiment headed northeast and moved to cut off the Krauts withdrawing from Spigno, then under direct assault by the 350th, on May 15.

The road to Spigno was mined heavily but after personal reconnaissance by Major James H. Green, Lt. Col. S. A. Armogida, and 1st Lt. Richard T. St. Sauver, the engineers cleared the vital supply route and opened it for use by the 350th and the French. By 0830 hours on the 15th, Spigno fell to the 1st Battalion, 350th, with General Kendall accompanying the troops into town where they met a patrol from 1st Battalion, 351st, in just a few minutes before. After the fall of Spigno the 350th became Division reserve and the 351st continued its attack to the west, captured Sant'Angelo and on the 17th had occupied Mt. Ruazzo. The 349th Combat Team, attached to the 85th Division as of May 15, assisted the 85th in its drive on Castellonorata.

Punching across the mountains, the 351st stabbed to within eight hundred yards east of the Itri–Pico road before it was stopped by heavy Nazi tank, SP and machine-gun fire. Casualties were high and ammo and water ran low. Because of the terrain, artillery could not displace far enough forward to take the enemy tanks and guns under fire. Artillery Cubs dropped medical supplies, radios, rations and maps to the 351st, forced to set up on Mt. Peretta and reorganize. Corps artillery finally got the range and silenced the Kraut tanks. Later the 601st Pack Artillery arrived and went into position to support the regiment.

Detached from the 85th on May 18, the 349th was ordered to drive for Itri. At 1500 hours May 19, the 1st Battalion moved into the wrecked town behind General Sloan and Lt. Col. Walter B. Yeager, clearing the buildings and streets of snipers and small rear-guard groups. The advance was so swift that the 313th Engineers, hacking out a supply road from Marinola to Itri, were only half finished when word came to drop the project. Previously the engineers had cut jeep trails through rugged country from Spigno to Marinola and from Guanello to Route 7. In Itri itself, General Sloan gathered several companies of doughfeet who had just taken the town and held an informal critique in the town square while civilians straggled down from the surrounding hills and wondered at the kind of army that won a battle and then stopped to discuss its mistakes and successes.

Recovered from pneumonia which had hospitalized him for months, Brig. Gen. Guy O. Kurtz returned on the 19th to reassume command of Division Artillery. And arrived in time to learn of the 338th's firing-from-the-hip technique. While displacing forward on the road about one mile east of Itri the 338th was warned that the Battalion air OP had picked up considerable activity on the west side of Itri. Immediately, B Battery, with Capt. John G. Tillman commanding, dropped trails on two guns and started to fire through a fire direction center established on the hood of a jeep. Other batteries went into position on both sides of the road and remained in their improvised setup until late next morning, their fire accounting for one Kraut tank, a 170mm gun and more than twoscore Krauts.

In general, the artillery situation in this phase of the campaign became rather hectic and not at all as outlined in the manual. The doughboys, with a full head of steam up, were chasing the Krauts so rapidly that it was difficult for artillery to keep the enemy in range. Outfits would displace, locate in a new area and then find that the doughfeet again had outdistanced them. The Krauts were disorganized and wandered in small groups all over the hills, bypassed by the infantry. They were so mixed up that 1st Lt. John F. Curry of Bloomington, Indiana, convinced twenty of them who had captured him that they were surrounded and succeeded in leading the enemy group back to his unit's outpost line and surrender.

Artillery batteries met sniper fire and cannoneers became expert at patrol work. On several occasions, new areas first had to be combed and cleared of snipers before the guns could go into position. Forward observers frequently found themselves doubling in brass and leading infantry platoons and companies. Air OPs flew missions not only to spot targets but also to dump food, supplies and maps to advanced infantry elements far ahead of their ration trains. Strictly speaking and for a time at least, artillery could not be classed as rear echelon as it generally was considered by front-line riflemen.

Because of the mountainous terrain, pack mules were used extensively by the Division for supply purposes and despite several ambushes and sudden enemy raids, the 1,400 mules and more than four hundred soldier and Italian muleskinners slogged doggedly across the peaks with their precious loads.

Sally of Berlin was on the air almost constantly as the 88th battled up from the south. She grew increasingly annoyed at the doughboys and as her harassed countrymen lost more and more ground she aired a plaintive complaint that the 88th soldiers were "a bunch of bloodthirsty cutthroats" and "did not fight like gentlemen." Later the hysterical voice added a couple of hearty cuss words as descriptive adjectives and finally stuck to calling them "those blue devils."

Restless after several days of enforced inactivity at Division CP, General Kendall took off front-ward. This time he traveled on horseback, startling soldiers and war correspondents alike as he galloped after or with the fast-traveling infantrymen. Impatient at any delay and with his usual fine disregard of any detail which he considered unimportant, "The Bull" shocked the Recon Troop at one point when he told a platoon leader to move out against German armor and pretend that his scout cars were tanks.

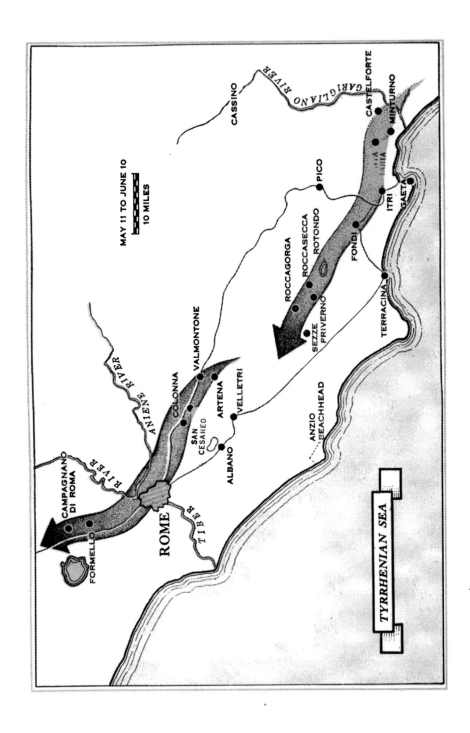

MAY 11 TO JUNE 10

10 MILES

CASSINO

GARIGLIANO RIVER

CASTELFORTE
MINTURNO
GAETA
ITRI
VIA APPIA
FONDI
PICO
ROCCASECCA
ROTONDO
ROCCAGORGA
PRIVERNO
SEZZE
TERRACINA

ANZIO
BEACHHEAD

VALMONTONE
COLONNA
SAN CESAREO
ARTENA
VELLETRI
ALBANO

ANIENE RIVER

TIBER RIVER

CAMPAGNANO
DI ROMA

FORMELLO

ROME

TYRRHENIAN SEA

THE ROAD TO ROME

Once the Gustav Line was broken, tentative plans for pursuit of the enemy were transmitted piecemeal to the various commanders. When Spigno fell orders were received for the 88th Division to pursue the enemy through the mountains with the mission of cutting the Itri–Pico road, even while the 85th Division on the left was still fighting to reduce Gaeta.

Beyond Itri lay Fondi. After its capture, and the bitter fight at San Biaggio, the 349th and 350th Infantry Regiments were ordered across the mountains to cut the enemy supply road between Roccasecca and Roccagorga. When this had been accomplished pursuit in this zone was relinquished to the French Expeditionary Corps and the Blue Devils moved by truck via Anzio to resume the offensive near Valmontone.

The 88th Division then became one of several with the mission of capturing Rome. The Blue Devils outdistanced all others and were the first of the Allied armies to enter the Eternal City on the morning of June 4. They secured crossings of the Tiber next morning and continued the pursuit to the north.

Private James Delazzaro, 349th Infantry, "takes ten" near Castellonorato.

Scauri, Gaeta and Formia fell, and the 85th drove for Terracina. Cassino and the pulverized mass that had been the Abbey and which had become a symbol throughout the world, finally was enveloped by the Poles. On the right flank of the 88th some ten thousand Goums—held back until Castelforte and surrounding heights were cleared—poured through the hills in delirious pursuit of the Krauts, shooting them by day and by night striking terror into their hearts as they slipped quietly among the enemy for a little knife work, at which they were experts.

Slugging north from Itri, leading elements of the 349th were fighting in the southern outskirts of Fondi, key point in the Hitler Line, on the afternoon of May 20, with the 350th following closely in their wake. With the capture of Fondi at 2200 hours, the 349th drove on for Mt. Passignano, took it and assembled in that area on the morning of the 21st. The loss of Fondi was a bitter blow to the Germans who had trumpeted that it was a pivotal strongpoint in their Hitler Line. After its fall, with perhaps some idea of not injuring the name of the Führer, the German radio denied that the defense system even had borne his name.

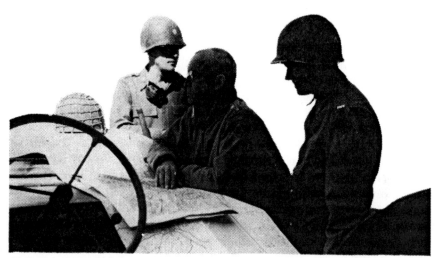

Maj. Gen. John E. Sloan plans future operations with staff members in Fondi shortly after its capture.

Back near Itri K Company of the 351st was running into heavy machine-gun fire west of that town. One squad was pinned down by machine guns firing from both flanks when Pfc. Ivan D. Black of Pearcy, Arkansas, charged one of the emplacements. Hit by an enemy grenade, Black lost his left hand and foot. Disregarding the agony of his wounds he crawled to a more exposed position to obtain a better field of fire. Then, with one hand, he fired his BAR so accurately and tellingly that an enemy attack was broken up and the Krauts were forced to withdraw from their positions. K Company was able to advance. Black died there in his exposed position but he had done his job.

Another of the heroes that day was T/5 Leland C. Grohman of the Recon Troop, a Texan from San Antonio. His platoon engaged in a fire fight and the contact point vehicles were knocked out with the surviving personnel wounded and pinned down. Grohman swung his armored car under direct observation to bring his 37mm on the Krauts. This move lifted attention and fire from the point men, who crawled to safety, but a 20mm shell scored a direct hit on Grohman's car, severing his left arm. The wounded trooper made no attempt to pull back until all the men had been evacuated and during the fray he assisted the gunner with his one good hand. When finally convinced that all his buddies were back out of fire, Grohman moved the car to the rear and then passed out.

The 350th, moving through Fondi, attacked to the northwest at dawn on May 21. The 1st and 2d Battalions were committed in the drive against Mt. Casareccio and Mt. Martino, both of which were taken late on the 21st. The 351st jumped off from its assembly area near Mt. Grande and by morning of the 21st had seized Mt. Valletonda. German planes were

83

active in this phase and on the 24th the 788th Ordnance Company was bombed and strafed heavily, resulting in the death of three men and wounds to fourteen others. The night before the Ordnance raid, the Division Rear Echelon at Casanova suffered its first casualty when seven bombs were dropped on the outskirts of town. Bomb fragments ripped through a tent and killed one member of the APO staff.

While we drove up from the south, the thorn in the side of the German Army, the Anzio beachhead, had been growing and bulging with reinforcements in preparation for a deeper thrust. On May 23 the beachhead forces kicked off, striking in on the flanks of the Krauts attempting to escape our frontal thrust. Opening of the beachhead drive was joyful news to tired doughboys of the 88th and the junction of the southern Fifth Army front with the beachhead on May 25 was a terrific morale booster. German commanders now saw themselves in danger of being caught in the jaws of a giant nutcracker of Allied troops.

Although not officially in on the junction with the beachhead, the 88th was represented after a fashion when Capt. James A. Flanagan, Assistant G-2; Lt. Milton A. Blum, G-2 office, and Lt. Wolfgang Lehman, PW interrogator, took off in a jeep piloted by Sgt. Edgar Clark, correspondent for the Mediterranean edition of *Stars and Stripes*. On the former beachhead the quartet had tea—that's what they said—with the commanding general of the British 5th Division, the outfit the 88th relieved when it first went into the Minturno sector. After a round of pleasantries the quartet made the return trip to the CP where they tried to explain their unauthorized absence to an irritated and skeptical Chief of Staff by relaying congratulatory messages from the 5th.

After regrouping in the Monsicardi–Delmonte area, the 349th continued its advance northwest, taking Mt. Rotondo and later Mt. Alto and Mt. della Salere. The 350th jumped off for Roccasecca dei Volsci. In the drive for Roccasecca, the 2d Battalion ran into stiff resistance in the valley south of San Biaggio where the Krauts poured in heavy fire from the surrounding hills.

An advance radio team with the leading elements advancing toward Roccasecca gave a magnificent example of courage when they sacrificed themselves to save their outfit. The four men—Cpl. Leonard Deinlein of Northampton, Massachusetts, Pfc. Walter Kaleka of Brooklyn, New York, Pvt. Norman Fagan of Buffalo, New York, and Pvt. Edward S. Wilbur of Detroit, Michigan, all of Headquarters Company, 350th— had volunteered to operate a radio relay station. After sending back several messages regarding enemy strength in the vicinity, they radioed that the Krauts had spotted them and were starting to close in. Aware of the absolute necessity of their job, the quartet remained calm in the

All thoughts are of Rome as 88th troops move through ruined Fondi.

face of imminent and violent death and continued sending their reports. The Krauts knew what they were doing and desperately wanted to stop it. Deinlein reported the Krauts were "on the slope of the hill," later that they "were coming up," and minutes later that "we are surrounded and must discontinue. . . ." That was the last message received. A grateful Division voted each man the Silver Star Medal, three posthumously.

On the 24th the 1st Battalion, 350th, occupied Roccasecca dei Volsci, at that point more than ten miles ahead of Fifth Army lines, and the 3d garrisoned the high ground overlooking the town. "If we had had sufficient forces and artillery support in that spot, we could have ended the war in Italy right there," said Captain Ritts. "Up there we overlooked a valley in which was the conversion of all the major routes of escape for the retreating German Army. From this point we looked down on a network of roads leading to Littoria and Rome and Cassino. We sat up there for two days watching the main strength of the German Army making its getaway and we couldn't do a thing about it.

"If we had had enough artillery support, we could have knocked out hundreds of vehicles. With enough support we could have ended the war in Italy. The biggest guns we had with us were 60mm mortars until a heavy-weapons company brought up an 81mm mortar. We hit 'em with everything we had but it just wasn't enough," said Ritts.

Whether or not the war could have been ended there, it's an interesting sidelight. Others in that little group on the heights who had to stand helplessly by and watch the Germans escape included 2d Lt. Charles Eggers of Essington, Pennsylvania, and Pvts. Clarence Keefer, Tyrone, Pennsylvania; Armand DeRosiers, Fall River, Massachusetts; Albert A. Gomez, Port Arthur, Texas; Joe Duffy, Clinton, Massachusetts; Leon-

85

ard D. Hoerath, St. Joseph, Missouri, and Jacob Brown, Grand Rapids, Michigan.

On May 27 the 2d Battalion, 349th, was advancing northwest towards its objective of Mt. San Martino and as security sent F Company, its leading element, to establish a roadblock on the road running north from Maenza, a small town to the west of the battalion objective. F Company, commanded by Lt. Paul R. Behnke, encountered a German panzer company retreating from the town. The Krautkillers swung into action and shot up three enemy half-tracks, ten cycles and two jeeps before running out of ammunition. F held its position during the night and regained contact with the battalion next day.

Ordered to clear the Amaseno River Line, the 88th accomplished the task late on the 28th and subsequently was attached to IV Corps. Shortly thereafter, its front pinched out by the French and by the beachhead troops, the Division prepared to move on the 31st to the II Corps sector in the vicinity of Anzio.

Released finally by Army press censors for identification in news dispatches, the 88th was praised for its magnificent record by newspapers throughout the United States. *The New York Times* summed up the tributes with its own accolade that "the blue cloverleaf shoulder patch has become a badge of honor to be worn proudly" by all who are, or were, members of the 88th.

Fed on victories, 88th men came up with a new battle cry. "Rome and home" was the popular chant. And Rome was just up the road.

We made it—and first!

S/SGT. JOHN T. REILLY

88th troops were first into Rome.

ROME

Of all the Allied units that were engaged in the final drive for Rome, the honor of being the first element to enter the Holy City fell to a unit of the 88th Division. Higher headquarters policy in not announcing immediately the identity of the first troops into Rome resulted in a petty squabble among Fifth Army units and the publishing of a host of conflicting stories, most of them pure press-agent fiction. They're still arguing about it but as far as the 88th is concerned, there's no argument. The 88th was first into Rome, and official Fifth Army operations reports published more than a month after the fall of the Italian capital confirms that claim.

Apart from the purely personal satisfaction attained, the capture of Rome was important in a military, political and psychological sense. From a military standpoint, Fifth Army men had performed a feat never before accomplished in the history of the peninsula : they had taken Rome by an attack from the south. In the process they had dealt punishing blows to the German Tenth and Fourteenth Armies and had convinced the Nazi high command that they were fighting men to be feared. Politically, the capture of Rome represented a lopping off of one-third of the Rome–Berlin–Tokyo Axis. Psychologically, the liberation of the Eternal City gave new hope to Italians and to subject peoples throughout the world that the sun of freedom would eventually break through the nightmare clouds of Fascism. The first ray was Rome.

Bivouacked in the former beachhead area after breaking down out of the mountains, the doughboys' half-hopes for a rest were ended with the news that the Fifth Army had all but completed mop-up operations and was ready to shoot the works for Rome, the first Axis capital to come within range of Allied forces. From Maj. Gen. Geoffrey Keyes, II Corps commander, came word to the 88th that it had been honored by a new assignment in the final drive and the Corps commander was confident it would be the first to attain the objective.

On June 2 the 88th moved back into the line with the 3d Division on the right and the 85th on the left. The 88th attacked to the northwest with the mission of cutting Highway 6 and then turning to drive for the eastern entrance to Rome. The 349th Infantry Regiment, minus one battalion, was attached to the 3d Division in this operation and the remaining battalion was sent with Howze Task Force. The 351st was directed to push northwest, protect Division flanks and maintain contact with neighboring divisions and with the 350th Infantry until that unit had advanced abreast of the 351st. In support of the 351st was the 752d Tank Battalion. ·

89

Fanning out rapidly to widen an initially narrow sector, 2d and 3d Battalions of the 351st cleared the towns of Carchitta and San Cesareo and at 1360 hours on the 2d, Highway 6 was cut. After the units had reorganized, roadblocks were established on Highway 6 and parallel routes. In the assault on San Cesareo, the 1st Platoon of G Company which had been acting as advanced guard for the 2d Battalion, ran into heavy enemy resistance. During the action, a tow-headed youngster from Virginia had a field day when he made seven bazooka rockets count for as many German vehicles and upwards of sixty Nazis.

The youngster was Pfc. Asa Farmer of Isom, Virginia, who was at the head of his platoon column when the fleeing Nazi vehicles were spotted. He'd never fired a bazooka before but when someone yelled "let 'em have it!" he swung into action and scored a direct hit with his first shot. Targets loomed in quick succession at the roadblock, but calmly and accurately Farmer and his bazooka paced the platoon. When it was all over a tally revealed that Farmer himself had knocked out two half-tracks, a light tank and four German jeeps; the platoon as a unit bagged twenty-two Kraut conveyances before sundown.

Another Virginian, 1st Sgt. Paul N. Eddy of Crewe, Virginia, distinguished himself near Monte Proziocatini when he killed five and captured eight of the vaunted Hermann Goering Division, put three enemy machine guns out of commission and neutralized an enemy mortar and crew, thereby enabling his company to advance.

Enemy air braved the skies over rear areas in futile attempts to cut 88th supply lines and block reinforcements as Nazi foot soldiers struggled to get away. And as usual the Kraut pilots were not too fussy as to what they hit. The 313th Medical Battalion clearing station was a target for six bombs and several strafing runs the night of June 1–2; a direct hit on an admission tent killed nine and wounded others.

Moving now astride Highway 6 on a 3,000-yard front, the 351st drove for vital bridges over the Aniene River. The town of Colonna was partially bypassed by the 3d Battalion. The regimental staff, with a portion of the I & R Platoon, officially "captured" the town and were treated to a preview of a Rome welcome when civilians broke out hidden stores of wine for the dusty, tired men of the Spearhead. Everybody got into the act. Eight division MPs who wanted action took off with Lt. Walter R. Glass of Dexter, Kansas, on a combat patrol and bagged eighteen German soldiers before calling it a day. With Glass on his roundup were Cpl. William A. Stewart, Pvt. Ronald Ware, Navasota, Texas; Sgt. Sidney Gabin, Bayonne, New Jersey; Sgt. Carmine Romano, Bronx, New York; Pvt. Jesse Brown, Memphis, Tennessee; Pvt. Xenophon Simitacolos, Canton, Ohio; Pvt. Robert Mahaffey, Rudolph, Ohio; and Pvt. Emanuel Holtzman, Brooklyn, New York.

After securing the bridges over the Aniene River, the 351st was ordered to halt in place. Dawn's light on the 4th disclosed the unscarred buildings of Rome some four thousand yards away. The net was tightening.

In its final stages, the drive for Rome developed into pretty much of a rat race. The II Corps—including the 88th, 85th and 3d Divisions, and the 1st Special Service Force as its major components—was moving up in the Highway 6 area. To the west, the IV Corps cleaned up what was left of the opposition and drove on Rome from that direction. In back of the line troops, jammed bumper to bumper, came all the rear echelon units from as far back as Naples. Rome was the ripest plum in Italy in the way of civilization and fancy billets and no one wanted to be left out. For months before the May jumpoff headquarters and rear outfits had pored over street and building maps picking the choice spots in the city for new quarters. Some far-sighted brass even had selected apartment sites and villas as their main objectives in their own personal drives. Now that the city was almost in our hands, every vehicle that could roll was loaded with office supplies and equipment and headed up Highway 6. For some it was a pleasant drive through the country with a glimpse of war-shattered towns to give the tour added zest. For others it was the first time they ever had been so near to the front and the distant rumble of artillery or the flares from enemy planes at night inspired many a letter masterpiece to the folks back home describing how tough a war could be. On that Sunday the traffic jam on Highway 6 began a couple of miles below Rome and must have extended almost clear back to Naples.

But the doughboys still had to take the city before the sightseers could move in. And there were some nasty bits of fighting still to be done. In the 88th the final footrace got under way. The 350th had been directed to overtake the 351st, pass through it and continue the attack. Regardless of how sound the plan was, the commanding officer of the 351st didn't like it. Everybody wanted the honor of being first into Rome. Loath to be overtaken with his goal so near, Colonel Champeny had pressed on. While not exactly disobeying orders, he nevertheless saw to it that his doughs hit a pace fast enough to outdistance the 350th. Early on the 4th when no word of a junction between the 350th and the 351st had been received, General Sloan ordered the 351st to push forward at once with one motorized battalion along Highway 101, enter Rome, and seize important bridges over the Tiber River.

Before the takeoff, however, word came that a six-man patrol from the

Tank-riding doughboys passing a street sign at the city limits of the Italian capital.

3d Platoon of the 88th Reconnaissance Troop had entered Rome at 0715 hours June 4 on Highway 6. This patrol later was credited, officially, by Fifth Army Headquarters as being the first Allied troop element to enter Rome. This credit still stands, with all due respect to the host of other units engaged in the struggle and despite the claims of *Stars and Stripes* and *Yank* correspondents who rode in later with other outfits. The patrol's story is best told in the official report of S/Sgt. John T. Reilly of Watervliet, New York, the patrol leader.

"On 3 June the troop had been operating as a screening element to insure the advance of the Division towards its objective, Rome. The 3d Platoon was operating on Highway 6 and the 1st and 2d Platoons were working to the north and east on Highway 5. On June 4 at 0600 hours a mission was received from Lt. John M. Berent, platoon leader, to work a jeep patrol as far forward on Highway 6 as possible, to make a main effort to enter Rome and to withdraw if our personal safety demanded same. At approximately 0630 hours the 1st and 2d Platoons met strong resistance just on the outskirts of the city.

"My patrol, consisting of two jeeps with Cpl. Emidio Mazzetti, Sgt. Cassie W. Kriemin, Sgt. Richard A. Robbins, T/5 Roy Q. Cuttler and Pfc. Samuel B. Baird, entered the city at approximately 0715 hours. Due to self-propelled and artillery fire we were unable to withdraw. We remained in concealment and observed enemy activity until the supporting elements of the tanks entered and together we assisted the 1st Special Service Force who by this time had entered the city," Reilly reported.

When word was flashed back to Division CP, staff officers turned handsprings and General Sloan beamed proudly. His men had made it—and first! But the struggle was not yet over. Although the Krauts had declared it an open city with the intent of denying us the network of roads, and some war correspondents wrote that the troops entered without opposition, there were sharp and bitter engagements in the city's outskirts.

Spearing up Highway 101, paced by a Recon platoon, the regimental I & R Platoon and C Company, motorized, the 351st ran into considerable German resistance from a strongpoint about one mile east of the city and just north of the suburb of Centocelle. Detrucking, the doughboys deployed and took up the challenge. In the ensuing action, Lt. Trevlyn L. McClure, I & R Platoon leader from Greensboro, North Carolina was wounded several times but continued to lead his men until caught and killed by cross-firing Nazi machine guns. Less than twenty-four hours before, McClure had led the platoon in routing 50 Germans from a strongpoint, killing 16, wounding 6 and capturing 4, and shortly after had captured an enemy tank and an ammo truck, exploits for which a DSC, posthumous, was awarded. Overcoming the last-ditch resistance, the 1st Battalion plus several TDs and three tanks swept on into Rome at 1530 hours and reported itself as the first infantry in force to make it.

Some doughs had spice added to their entrance in the form of an Italian wedding. A jeep patrol came upon the wedding party on the outskirts of town heading for a small church, both bride and groom oblivious to the fighting which raged in fields on either side. The patrol tried to convince the bridal party that the ceremony had best be delayed until the battle was over but the bride was a firm woman and told them it was now or never; she'd waited a long time for this day and nothing like a war was going to prevent the ceremony. And nothing did. The entire group arrived at the church, the doughboys taking up positions in the rear with rifles and tommy guns. To the strains of a creaking organ and the crash and chatter of artillery and machine guns, the *pacsanos* were married, feeling quite honored that Yank soldiers were among the guests.

Toiling along up Highway 6, a motorized battalion of the 350th, one battery of the 338th Field Artillery, one company of the 313th Engineers and a provisional battery of six 105mm self-propelled guns from the 752d Tank Battalion, all under command of Lt. Col. Walter E. Bare, Jr., of Muskogee, Oklahoma, battered through Nazi rear guards and crossed the city limits on the Via Palestrina shortly before 1730 hours. Once in, this outfit was joined by Italian partisans who aided the doughboys in cleaning out snipers from buildings along the route.

The civilian welcome was tremendous as Rome, the city with a halo, let her hair down. There were plenty of Fascists who joined the welcoming crowds. There were many ex-Nazis and there were many who

All Rome turned out to celebrate the "liberation."

were glad to see us come for purely selfish reasons, many who expected we'd pour out money and food and gifts from our alleged horns of plenty. But for each phony there were a hundred ordinary Roman citizens who were sincerely and uncontrollably overjoyed. They had, as they said, waited so long for us to come and now that we actually were there, in their streets and *piazzas,* they couldn't quite believe it. Despite the German censorship, they'd known about our landings at Salerno. They'd heard of Cassino and the Volturno, and the Anzio beachhead. The night before the city fell they'd heard our artillery blasting the retreating Nazi columns and on that Sunday morning they'd seen the German troops shuffle dispiritedly off to the north. And now, here we were. Old men and women just stood there in the streets and cried as the Yanks went by. Mothers and fathers lifted their small children high above the crowds to see the *Americanos.* Young people ran along beside the jeeps and trucks and marching men with wine and flags and flowers.

The welcome was like nothing the soldiers ever had expected or experienced. The Italians called us the liberators that first night, and they meant it. For them, or so they thought, a new era was at hand, an era based on this thing called democracy and in their minds we were the people who had come to bring it to them. In the suburbs, civilians poured out of their homes to greet the first troops. They milled about the vehicles, ig-

94

nored the sniper and return fire which whizzed about their heads, cheered when a German tank was hit, groaned when a Yank vehicle went out of action, cried, whistled, smiled, shouted, danced, sang, tossed flowers, poured wine and champagne and finally by their sheer exuberance succeeded in doing what the Krauts hadn't been able to do since the kickoff—temporarily stopped the Blue Devils cold in their tracks with their royal welcome. It was fantastic, it was unbelievable, but it was Rome that first night.

If the civilians were glad to see the soldiers, the doughboys were just as glad to see them. They were seeing for the first time in Italy something that reminded them of and looked like home. There were splendid buildings, street lights, sidewalks, well stocked shop windows, prosperous-appearing civilians, clean looking children and beautiful girls—beautiful girls in bright, gay spring dresses with lipstick and face powder and wearing shoes. And not at all bashful. Rome, and anything in it, was theirs that first night without the asking. And many a doughboy got "lost" in the crowd and wound up as the honored guest of some Roman family with food and wine and a real bed with sheets. The soldier-civilian honeymoon couldn't, and didn't, last forever, but the change from joy to bitterness on the part of the civilians was not the fault of the liberators. America had everything in the way of friendship and goodwill those first days in Rome, and whether by accident or design, completely and thoroughly threw it all away in a matter of weeks. The Italians threw flowers at us that first night—in a couple of weeks or months they'd be throwing rocks, and with good cause. But the fighting doughboys weren't to blame and didn't know then or care what was to come. Their job was to take the city and pursue the Germans, and they continued to do both.

Artillery units, which had been fired on by Kraut small arms and machine guns—B Battery of the 339th was pinned down while moving into position outside of Rome; Division Artillery headquarters found itself in the midst of a fire fight and surprised cannoneers of the 913th rounded up fifteen Kraut PWs—rumbled into the city, the redlegs a defiant, proud lot as they hauled their guns into new firing positions. The 913th was the first artillery battalion to fire from Rome after occupying positions in the Pincio Gardens early on June 5, followed shortly by the 338th, the 339th and the 337th. Division Artillery advanced CP moved to the Villa Borghese at 0800 hours on the 5th but later that day General Kurtz moved the CP to the Ministry of War Finance Building on the Piazza d'Armi near the Milvio Bridge. Division Headquarters and the CP of the 349th Infantry also set up in the building. Kraut artillery tossed a barrage at the area in mid-afternoon, scored hits on a jeep and an apartment house across the street.

"Grazie, Liberatori!"

In the Pincio Gardens it looked like Circus Day. Stripped to the waist, and the center of an admiring circle of *signorinas,* the artillerymen were never in better form as they pumped shells at enemy columns and vehicles across the Tiber fleeing north on Highway 2. The civilians came out as though to a picnic and stayed to watch the *Americanos* in action. The Romans cheered every round. youngsters fought for still-smoking shell cases as souvenirs, wary parents eyed their daughters who, in turn, eyed the artillerymen, who—well, there still was a war on. Signalmen held open house for the civilians in their area on the Piazza d'Armi and a bewildered CO finally muttered he "didn't care what happened as long as they kept the lines in." Quartermaster truck drivers had a field day in town as they shuttled troops to new locations. One driver embarrassed an entire regiment of the 3d Division as he pulled into its assembly area outside of town and blandly inquired the way to the rear echelon.

Weary doughboys plodded through crowd-jammed streets, their rifles and helmets decked in flags and flowers. To the majority of them, the wild welcome was just a passing show for the weary business of war still ground on. They slept on sidewalks and doorways during short breaks, snatched what fun they could and then secured their bridge and road objectives. With these missions accomplished, new orders came down to press on over the river and up Highway 2 after an enemy they were unable to catch or to make stand and fight. As one tired dough described it: "We slug 'em until they pull out and run, then we chase 'em until we can catch 'em and slug 'em again. We ain't ever satisfied to just get 'em running and leave 'em go." The 349th, held in place south of Rome after being pinched out by the French, rode and marched through Rome on the 5th, detrucked and deployed across the river to take up the pursuit again.

There were some who neither rode nor marched through Rome. They were the men who died on the outskirts, in the suburbs and in the center of Rome itself from enemy rear-guard sniper fire and who lay crumpled and twisted in the pathetic shapes that the newly dead assume. Over their silent heads, the delirious welcome celebration roared on unabated. Around their bodies, small groups of silent civilians stood watch until the GRO details took over. And from the bar of the Grand Hotel, one war correspondent so forgot the men who had died to make possible his entry into Rome, that he filed a first-day story to the States describing how pleasant it was to have his favorite bartender remember him and his favorite drink after all the long years of occupation. The dead from Salerno to Rome should have read that story.

Lt. Gen. Mark W. Clark, Fifth Army commander, officially entered the city on the morning of the 5th. Accompanied by Maj. Gen. Alfred M. Gruenther, Chief of Staff; Maj. Gen. Geoffrey Keyes, II Corps commander; and Maj. Gen. Lucian K. Truscott, Jr., VI Corps commander, General Clark's appearance touched off the celebration again as the party toured city streets.

The official parade was not without its lighter side. The comic relief was amply provided by a grimy, slightly befuddled GI who brought up the rear in a decrepit wagon hauled by an equally decrepit horse about whose neck hung a withered garland of flowers. This modern edition of Ben-Hur drove his sagging chariot at the rear of the bestarred generals' column and the delighted crowds gave him more of a hand than they did all the stars up front. Another un-GI vehicle toured Rome's streets that day, piloted by Pvt. Lloyd C. Thunberg of Fargo, North Dakota, and the 313th Medics. It was a huge bus with placards along both sides which read "Rome–Berlin–Tokyo Express" and Thunberg had no trouble picking up civilian and GI passengers as he wheeled through the crowds. The bus later was refitted as a traveling office for executive officers of the outfit but eventually fell apart and was discarded.

In attempting to describe the Rome welcome, Pfc. Sam Petralia of Lawrence, Massachusetts, went lyrical and came up with the words and music to a ditty entitled "Hey, Paesano!" As head skinner for a 150-mule train during the push from the Garigliano River, Petralia got the idea for the song as he sat atop a mule when the train plodded through Rome. Best rendition was the one by Italian muleskinners who sang it with gusto even if they didn't understand the English words they were carolling. "Hey, Paesano!" went like this:

> On June the Fourth of nineteen forty-four
> Through streets of Rome the Yanks began to pour;
> They came on truck and tank with men of every rank;
> That welcome they remember evermore.
> They kept on coming all throughout the day,
> The crowds no longer they could keep away;
> They climbed on truck and tank no matter what the rank,
> And amid the cheers the Yanks would shout and say:
>
> Hey, *Paesano!* Have you gotta the *vino?*
> I gotta the chocolate, cigarette, *caramelle;*
> *Signorina, tu sei molta bella,*
> I gotta the chocolate, cigarette, *caramelle.*
> As the boys go marching by you can hear those Romans cry:
> Maria, chocolate! Giuseppe, cigarette! *bambini, caramelle!*
> *Si! Si! Si!*
> Hey, *Paesano!* Have you gotta the *vino?*
> I gotta the chocolate, cigarette, *caramelle.*

For all of its glamor and its military, political and psychological significance, the capture of Rome swiftly was overshadowed by another and more important military venture. As press wires were flooded with news from the Italian capital, a flash came from London announcing the invasion of France. All other fronts and all other war news immediately took a minor place, blotted out by the opening of the long-heralded and awaited second front. The end was still a long way off, but it was the beginning of the end. News of the invasion of France was the climax—the first flash brought smiles to the faces of exhausted 88th doughboys and a new jag to an already happiness-saturated Rome.

The 3d Infantry Division drew the apparently choice assignment to garrison and guard Rome. To the north the 88th was still driving and the Kraut was still running, turning now and again for short, bitter fights to enable his main body to get away. Action was particularly sharp about the town of Monterosi, where the Germans used tanks. On June 7 Pfc. Alfred D. Crox of I Company, 351st, and Camden, New Jersey, spotted a Mark IV and a Mark VI tank. Firing antitank grenades, Crox scored two direct hits, destroying one tank and forcing the other to withdraw. At this point, an enemy machine gun opened up on his left but Crox silenced it with grenades, capturing two Krauts who scrambled out of the

A camouflaged 105mm howitzer firing from the Pincio Gardens in Rome at fleeing Krauts across the Tiber River.

hole. Attempting to withdraw with his prisoners, Crox was killed by machine-gun fire from another enemy tank which had come up during the skirmish.

Two days later a bold bluff saved the 3d Battalion from what might have been a disastrous flanking attack. As the battalion forged ahead against stiffening resistance, 1st Lt. Stanton D. Richart of Reynoldsburg, Ohio, and three enlisted men were ordered to bring the reserve company forward. Rounding a turn in the road, the quartette came upon a Kraut infantry company of 6 officers and 74 men marching toward them. Pvt. Lyle Rust of Cabool, Mississippi, driver, swerved his jeep across the road and manned a .50-caliber machine gun to cover the enemy. Pfc. Walter D. Deay of Lawrence, Kansas, jumped for the ditch and covered the flank with his tommy gun to prevent the column from breaking into the field. Pvt. Kurt Freisinger of New York City, speaking German, advanced to the leading enemy officer with Lieutenant Richart and told the Kraut leader that he and his men were surrounded and that they had the doubtful choice of surrender or death. It was a bluff for the reserve company was far to the rear, but it was a bluff that worked. The Krauts surrendered.

Still pressing, the 88th Division was relieved on June 10, culminating an offensive advance of 109 airline miles in 31 days from Minturno, including the rapid dash through Rome and across the Tiber from the vicinity of Roccamassima to the vicinity of Bassanelio, a distance of 56 miles in eight days. After a total of a hundred straight days in the line the Blue

99

88th Troops had little time for sightseeing as they moved rapidly through Rome to continue the fight.

Devils put down their guns, capped their mythical horns and headed back over the long trail they had won, headed for Lake Albano and rest.

There was rest at Albano, individual and unit honors and passes to Rome for the doughboys who had obtained only a brief glimpse of the capital they had taken after a lightning stab through the mountains. And taken with relatively light casualties according to a G-1 report which listed 134 officers and 1,844 enlisted men as killed, wounded or missing in action. The report indicated that German losses had been much heavier, based on the PW total which credited the 88th with bagging 30 officers and 1,942 enlisted men, members of more than six German divisions which had failed to stop the drive. German casualty totals were not available but they must have been heavy in view of the numbers captured.

There was work at Albano, too. Ever the perfectionist, General Sloan was afraid the men would rest on their laurels, grow stale. He toured unit areas and many companies were gigged and restricted for what appeared to be minor things. The complaints from the men were long and loud, but despite the gripes, the realization was growing slowly among all ranks that General Sloan's harping on minor things and his insistence on perfection had resulted in a battle performance that was all the smoother because many things were done from force of habit. The men began to realize that it was the little things that paid off, and in battle the payoff was life or death. There was no middle ground. Even though in many cases it might have been grudging, the men came around to giving credit to "Johnny Eager" for bringing them through. With men from other divisions they bragged about how tough he was, but the stories they told to illustrate his toughness were not bitter. They were, in fact, almost proud tales as if the men gloried in building up the general as a friendly tyrant. Months later, they were to be more outspoken in their praise.

In that push to Rome the 88th had answered some questions, had fought itself out of the unknown class. The papers in the United States sang its praises. But there was little time for the men of the Division to read the stories being written about them and their drive. Stories such as the article in the Baltimore, Maryland, *Sun,* in which Price Day, a correspondent who had been with it all the way, wound up his battle review by saying that "if proof were needed that well trained draftees under good staff officers can fight as well as any troops in the Army, these men have provided it." Or the Washington, D. C., *Evening Star* editorial which said "they have already run up a record that speaks volumes for what democracy can do when it is called upon to defend itself and when its young men are democratically chosen to bear arms." From official circles came satisfied statements that the new replacement system was a success, that the steady feeding of men into the 88th as it drove up the peninsula had been a primary factor in its record, had enabled it to keep going always at full strength no matter what the battle losses.

There was one tribute the men of the 88th knew, one which came from the Germans they'd beaten back, came from the PWs who were captured, came from the Berlin propaganda radio. That tribute was the nickname of "Blue Devils." They liked that. They'd proved their stuff to others—they were starting to prove it to themselves as well.

There were individual honors—the Distinguished Service Medal to General Sloan from Gen. George C. Marshall during a tour of the battle areas, and the Legion of Honor from Gen. Charles de Gaulle. A total of 114 awards, decorations and commendations was presented to members of his command after the Division was alerted and moved to Tarquinia to keep pace with the Fifth Army drive sweeping on far to the north. The 88th at the time was in Army reserve and Albano was deemed too far south to be practical if the going got rough and the 88th was needed in a hurry.

Turning the month into July, training and reorganization stepped up as the old, and generally reliable, rumors began making the rounds that the Division was scheduled for more action. Word from the front indicated the drive was slowing up, German resistance was increasing and that several Fifth Army units were in a bad way. On July 4 verbal orders were received by phone to bring up the 88th at once. On the 5th and 6th the 349th and 350th Combat Teams moved up to forward assembly areas near Pomerance, the 351st remaining at Tarquinia.

Next day Secretary of War Henry L. Stimson and Lt. Gen. Mark W. Clark made formal inspection of the 351st as it stood at attention on the Tarquinia airfield and Stimson told the men that "I have come a long way to tell you that we have not forgotten you at home. We are all proud of divisions such as those which went into action for the first time in Italy and performed like veterans. You have shown that under able leadership American soldiers are the equal of any in the world. I tell you that the thrill of victory is in the air."

*We know we'll probably lose the battle of the Arno River
. . . but you'll pay for every inch!*

A German PW

Secretary of War Henry L. Stimson inspects the 351st at Tarquinia.

DUST AND MINES

There were other questions hurled at the 88th as it took off for the Arno River, questions asked by veteran outfits who felt that this new division was perhaps just a flash in the pan. Those old soldiers weren't convinced. They thought the 88th had been given too much publicity, that its men were too headline conscious. They wanted to know what the 88th would do when the Germans stopped running, stood their ground and fought. They said the Blue Devils hadn't really had it rough, yet.

They got their answers in the Arno drive. They were answered at Laiatico, where the Germans held for four days before their positions were overrun. They were answered at Bloody Ridge, where counter-attacks were hurled back with heavy losses to the attackers. They were told at Volterra and San Miniato and Monte Foscoli, amid the dust and mines and counterartillery and tanks and more enemy resistance than the 88th doughboys had believed the Krauts were capable of offering. For here, with their backs to the Arno River, the Krauts turned, and stood and tried to slug it out. The 88th took it, shook off the punches and beat a stubborn enemy at his own game.

Concentrated near Pomerance where it relieved the 1st Armored Division, the 88th planned its drive for the Arno. The prospect ahead was not pleasant. The terrain in front of the Division was low and rolling and practically devoid of cover. The Germans had massed artillery of all types and were using it more extensively than at any other time. Enemy minefields practically overlapped one another. Enemy morale was good and enemy commanders were determined to hold as long as possible in a delaying action to protect the south and west approaches to the city of Florence (Firenze) and to give the main body of the German armies time to retreat safely across the Arno River without being encircled and trapped. To the east, the French and British drove for Florence. To the west, American units headed for Leghorn (Livorno) and Pisa. In the center sector, the 88th had a mean job to do.

The ancient Etruscan stronghold of Volterra was the first main objective. From observation points in the high, walled city, the Krauts commanded a 15-mile view in all directions and for the sake of the entire Division mission, Volterra's capture was essential. Assigned to take it were the 349th and the 350th, with the 351st held in reserve. Plans called for the 349th to flank the mountain city on the right, the 350th on the left, with both outfits then scheduled to cut in behind the stronghold and seize high ground to the north.

Clearing mines ahead of infantry outposts, Cpl. Orval Sullivan of Ontario, California, and 1st Lt. John P. Tucei of Biloxi, Mississippi, both of

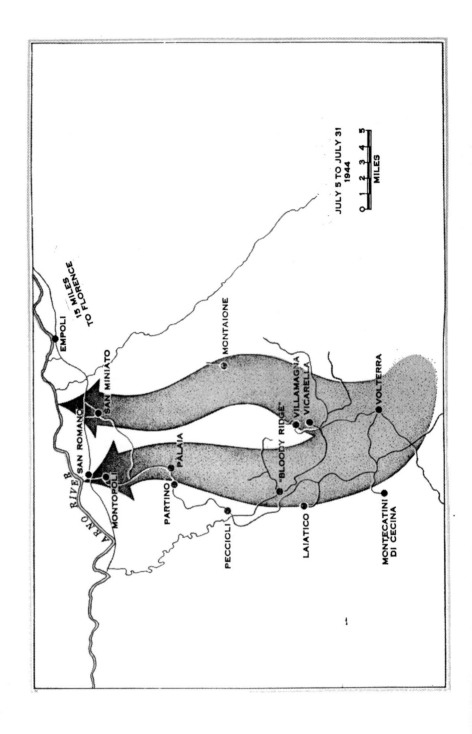

EMPOLI

15 MILES
TO FLORENCE

SAN MINIATO

ARNO RIVER

SAN ROMANO

MONTOPOLI

PARTINO

PALAIA

PECCIOLI

MONTAIONE

BLOODY RIDGE

VILLAMAGNA
VICARELLA

LAIATICO

VOLTERRA

MONTECATINI
DI CECINA

JULY 5 TO JULY 31
1944

0 1 2 3 4 5
MILES

TO THE ARNO

On July 5 the 88th Division was alerted from its training area in the vicinity of Tarquinia and rushed forward to supplement the Fifth Army assault which had bogged down south of Volterra. The plan for the Division called for a passage of lines through the 1st Armored Division and a frontal attack against the formidable hill mass crowned by the ancient city of Volterra. In the Division attack the 349th and 350th Infantry Regiments abreast (350th on the left) executed a double envelopment of the ancient Etruscan stronghold and were, upon completion of that mission, scheduled to drive the enemy before them toward the Arno River. The 351st Infantry, in reserve at the outset, was ordered to follow the Division boundary and to protect the right of the Division. Supplementary orders carried the Division forward in the formation of regiments abreast, the 351st eventually pulling abreast of the other two regiments.

Laiatico required an all-out assault by the 351st, proving to be an unexpected enemy stronghold. Twenty days later the Division ground to a halt on the high ground overlooking the Arno. The enemy in the zone of action had been destroyed or driven northward.

"Krautkillers" enter the hilltop stronghold of Volterra.

the 313th Engineers, were taken under fire by enemy 88s and SPs. More than four hundred yards of the minefield were yet to be searched. Taking cover from the first shells, Sullivan and Tucei boldly decided to make the enemy shells work for them, risking their lives in the process. Leaving their cover, the pair of them went back to work using the dust of the exploding shells to shield them from enemy observers. Working two or three minutes at a time and taking slow, twelve-inch steps, the pair calmly swept the entire area. Every time a shell came in, they hit the dirt. Immediately after the explosion they went back to work, hiding in the dust clouds. Both were awarded the Silver Star for this act.

With the mines finally out of the way and with Division Artillery pounding zone targets and the 337th dropping smoke west and southeast of Volterra, the regiments jumped off at 0500 hours on the 8th over gently rolling terrain with poor cover. The 349th had a rough scrap at the approach town of Roncolla and the 350th promptly met counterattacks in its zone. At one point, G Company of the 349th slugged its way out past the battalion line. When the CO took off to attempt to make contact with the unit on his right, T/Sgt. Frank F. Barone, of New York City, took over the three rifle platoons and organized them in beating off a counterattack. He then directed artillery fire on the retreating Krauts.

By 2200 hours the regiments had reached their objectives and the 349th sent strong patrols to block entrances and occupy the city itself. The former German prize was ours.

Hitting for Laiatico, the 351st encountered stubborn opposition, checked several strong German counterattacks but by dawn of the 11th found its 1st Battalion pinned down in the open on the west slopes of the Laiatico hill mass under direct observation and heavy enemy artillery fire. The 2d Battalion also reported itself in similar trouble.

An acting squad leader, Pfc. Benjamin Barela of G Company and San Rafael, New Mexico, worked himself forward to the top of the hill from which Kraut fire was coming. With a rifle and a little bayonet work, Barela killed seven and wounded two machine gunners, took one prisoner and worked on him until the Kraut revealed enemy positions. Barela then directed mortar fire to soften up the positions. He then led his squad in an assault which captured forty and enabled his company to move up.

T/Sgt. Frank McCormick of Caldwell, New Jersey, machine-gun platoon sergeant in H Company, dug in his guns south of Laiatico and then went forward on reconnaissance. Fire from a cave entrance killed one officer as three riflemen continued to approach unaware of the trap. McCormick ran 35 yards to the cave entrance, threw a couple of carbine shots into it and demanded the surrender of its occupants. A hail of bullets was his answer. McCormick went to work and when he stopped his fire and clamor 52 Krauts filed out and dropped their weapons.

Things got rougher for the 351st. At one point, Colonel Champeny relieved a battalion commander. On the 12th, all battalions reorganized and prepared to follow new attack orders. General Kendall arrived at the 351st CP at about 2100 hours with orders for the 2d Battalion to attack from the west, the 3d from the east, and the 1st to be held as potential reserve.

The attack was launched on time. And the doughs, tired of being used as sitting ducks by Kraut artillery, jumped off with a new anger. The 3d drove forward in column of companies under command of Capt. Harold B. Ayres of New Orleans, Louisiana, executive officer who had taken over when the CO was wounded and evacuated. Following about one hundred yards behind its supporting artillery barrage, the 3d knifed into enemy defensive positions along the ridge running east from Laiatico, penetrating as far as the CP of the 1st Battalion, 1060th Panzergrenadier Regiment. Killing the German CO by grenades tossed into his headquarters, the men of the 3d rounded up more than 420 live Krauts and killed over 250 before they resumed their advance up the ridge. Meantime, the 2d Battalion had taken Hills 212 and 166 and reached the northern part of the town by daylight. With break of day, both units were caught in fierce artillery barrages. Despite them, the 2d managed to push on about eight hundred yards beyond Laiatico when orders came to dig in. At 2400 hours the attack was resumed and both the 2d and 3d took the ridge running north and south from Laiatico by 0300 hours on the 13th.

For its outstanding performance at Laiatico, the 3d Battalion later received the Distinguished Unit Citation, the first unit in the Division to win such an award.

Near Laiatico a battalion of the 349th was caught under a heavy mortar and artillery barrage. Casualties ran high and litter crews were killed or wounded attempting to evacuate the injured. Chaplain Oscar H. Reinboth restored some measure of confidence to the almost panic-stricken unit as he moved about on the barren slopes in full view of the enemy and under direct fire. Chaplain Reinboth located the more than 85 wounded men, separated them from the dead, administered first aid and removed the casualties to points of safety.

Attempting to exploit its capture of Laiatico, the 351st was checked by stiff opposition. In its sector, the 350th stood off a strong tank and infantry attack as the 339th Field Artillery destroyed four enemy gun batteries during the encounter. On the 13th, the 349th and 350th were able to move forward abreast to limited objectives, meeting only scattered resistance. Later in the day their progress was slowed. The Krauts weren't giving anything away free.

As it battered slowly ahead, a new name was born in the 349th as a symbol of hell on earth, the name of Bloody Ridge. Pinpointed on operational maps as Hills 184 and 188, the dual objective gave the 2d Battalion some of its toughest going of the campaign before the Krautkillers rooted the fanatical Germans out of their emplacements and secured the knobs.

With his battalion hard hit and many of his aid men wounded or killed, Capt. Edson R. Rodgers of the 349th Medics went forward from his aid station to the front lines. Moving under constant enemy fire he treated the wounded strewn over the barren slopes. When a litter team was cut down by artillery, he carried the team and the original patient to safety. Returning to the action he repeatedly crossed open terrain despite heavy mortar and artillery fire and gave first aid to more than fifty men, carrying many others to safety for further treatment. One of his patients later said of him: "He's a bit too GI when guys are off the lines. But up on the front he'll go anywhere to take care of the guys and his face doesn't even change expression when he's out in the thick of it. There are probably more medics like him though I've not seen them. It's a privilege to shake that guy's hand."

Scouting the area about Villamagna, the 3d Platoon of the Recon Troop took the town itself at 1222 hours on the 13th. Later a Fifth Army G-3 report credited the 3d with capture of Villamagna, adding that "it was taken by the same unit which was first in Rome." Official confirmation at last of one of the 88th proudest boasts. At 0030 on the 14th the 3d Battalion, 349th, occupied and secured Villamagna as directed by Division.

Belvedere and adjacent high ground fell to the 1st and 2d Battalions, 351st, and all units continued the advance with the 351st moving through Monte Foscoli early on the 16th. The advance picked up speed during the morning with indications pointing to an enemy withdrawal during the night. The back of the Kraut resistance in this sector apparently had been broken and all units were directed to push forward swiftly to maintain contact with the Krauts. By morning of the 17th the situation maps disclosed that the 351st had captured Partino and was continuing north; the 349th was driving for Palaia and the 350th had taken the high ground in the vicinity of La Fornace and maintained its northward thrust. Shortly after daybreak however, the enemy began fighting back with renewed strength, increasing his use of tanks and covering the entire front with severe mortar and artillery concentrations. One PW told his interrogators, "We know we'll probably lose the battle of the Arno but when we go down we'll take as many of you with us as we possibly can—you'll pay for every inch."

Division plans to drive on to the Arno were changed and the units were directed to seize commanding terrain in their particular zones and maintain aggressive patrolling to the river. At 1900 hours, the 349th took Palaia and the heights to the north. During the battle for the heights, 1st Lt. Kenneth W. Gray of Fayetteville, West Virginia, personally knocked out an ambushing Kraut machine gun, then led his company as advance scout, reorganizing the unit twice under deadly fire to beat off savage counterattacks before he fell wounded—an exploit for which he was awarded the DSC.

When the leading platoon of F Company was pinned down near Palaia, S/Sgt. Cesaro L. Lombardi of Canastota, New York, went forward in the face of enemy machine-gun fire pouring down on the troops from an emplacement about two hundred feet above leading elements. Exposing himself again and again in order to organize the squad and lay out a base of fire, Lombardi then directed rifle, BAR and rocket fire on the Kraut machine gun and house. When enemy return fire killed 3 and wounded 33, Lombardi somehow managed to reorganize the platoon and to stop a counterattack which swirled to within forty feet of him. The company then went on to take its objective.

Arno dust.

Next day, S/Sgt. Herbert L. Redfield of Newark, New Jersey, and Headquarters Company, 3d Battalion, went to the aid of a medic group trapped on the wrong side of a minefield by Kraut machine guns. After taping a path through the field by probing with his bayonet, Redfield had reached the medic group and was leading it back when the Krauts got the range again. Redfield worked his way to the base of a knoll, pitched two grenades to silence one gun and then charged the second, forcing the crew to surrender. The aid group continued on its interrupted mission of mercy.

At 1000 hours on the 18th, the 1st Battalion, 351st, attached to Task Force Ramey, captured Montaione. Enemy opposition diminished during the night with artillery reported practically ceased. All units dug in on the 19th, established all-around security and pushed combat patrols to the Arno to learn that the enemy apparently had succeeded in getting his main body across the muddy stream.

Three days of quiet preceded one of the 349th's bitterest small-unit battles. Driving for San Miniato, an officer and 40 enlisted men of G Company got lost and took cover from small-arms fire in a house about one thousand yards east of San Miniato. Counterattacks raged along the entire regimental front. The Krauts moved in on the house. Under attack by Krauts in near-battalion strength, the small group bottled up in the house at Calenzano hurled back eight enemy charges during one of which the Krauts tried, and failed, to blow in the door with dynamite. During the attacks, T/Sgt. Carmine Tavalaro shuttled from window to window on the second floor, killing 8 and wounding 11 enemy.

Finally, with the Krauts pounding on the door with rifle butts, firing into the windows and hurling grenades through holes in the wall, Capt. James P. Lyons of Spokane, Washington, battalion executive officer who was with the embattled unit, called for direct artillery fire and the 337th Field dumped 3,500 rounds in, near and on the house during the struggle. At noon the 337th ran out of ammunition but artillery continued to pour into Nazi ranks as the 913th, one battery of the 339th and a six-gun group from the 760th Tank Battalion all fired for G Company and the gallant little group holding out in the house. Our own shells burst on the roof and around the walls of the building. The attacking Germans pressed in relentlessly until the rumble of tanks was heard and I Company broke through to relieve the Krautkillers, at that point down to a mere handful of ammunition and two antitank grenades.

G Company moved into San Miniato that night and found one of the first large-scale examples of Nazi atrocity. The enemy had withdrawn earlier. To cover his retreat he had salted the houses and streets with mines and booby-traps. During the mining, the civilians had been locked up in the church to prevent their seeing the locations of the mines and warning us when we came in. As a last gesture, the Krauts had wheeled two tanks up to the church and fired point-blank into the stunned and frightened group of civilians. The slaughter was terrific. Our first troops into San Miniato, more than accustomed to the horrors of war, nevertheless were sickened at the frightful sight that met their eyes.

Medics again took the heroism spotlight near Tojano on the 18th when I Company, 350th, found itself trapped deep in a minefield. Men in both front and rear of the column were wounded seriously and the rest of the company was near panic when Pfc. Raymond E. Platt of Hubbard, Ohio, and T/5 Russell W. Redfern of Saginaw, Michigan, moved into the minefield to aid them. The medics went from man to man without showing the slightest fear although both knew that at any moment they too might step on a mine. The leader of a litter squad tripped a mine at the edge of the field and the rest of the squad refused to move. Platt and Redfern calmly took over the job of evacuating the casualties, Platt later setting up an aid station in a house where he gave plasma to the seriously wounded and treated the others. Reassured by the example of courage on the part of the medics, the doughfeet calmed down and eventually worked themselves out of the difficult spot.

The Krauts showed no mercy to medics and frequently took advantage of Geneva Convention rules to advance infantrymen under the protection of Red Cross insignia and armbands. "One time I was trying to reach a wounded man and a sniper kept firing at me," reported Pfc. Alfred Tavares of New Bedford, Massachusetts. "Every time I moved, he'd fire. I couldn't get to the wounded man and couldn't shoot back since medics are unarmed. Finally a lieutenant crawled up behind me, located the sniper and shot him. As soon as he was hit, the German came out with his hands up and surrendered, begging for the same mercy he had refused to show our wounded. Some of the guys wanted to kill him anyway, but they let him live.

"Yes, they shot at medics and they shot to kill," Tavares continued. "I had some friends killed and they were shot right in the head—right through the center of the Red Cross insignia painted on their helmets. On the other hand, the Germans never missed a chance to take advantage of American respect for the medical code. There were countless incidents along this line. One I recall especially was the time four Germans under a Red Cross flag approached a lead rifle company, carrying a litter on which was an apparently wounded man. Our troops held their fire. The Germans tenderly carried the litter nearer and nearer—suddenly jumped into a

Blowing the Santa Trinita bridge over the Arno River at Florence.

ditch, whipped off the blankets and disclosed the wounded man to be a machine gun which cut down several of our men before return fire killed the Kraut quartette."

San Romano and Buche, a small town to the north, were cleared and occupied by the 351st on the 25th. Activity from then on was limited to aggressive patrolling to the river and limited recon patrolling across the Arno with both the 349th and 350th outposting the rail line along the south bank. The majority of the Krauts had gotten safely across. A new American division, the 91st, came up to take over the sector. To screen the relief, the 88th Signal Company maintained its radio net and filled the air with dummy messages to prevent Kraut monitors from learning of the presence of a new outfit. The 88th pulled back to the vicinity of Volterra for a period of specialized training in river crossing operations for the dreaded and expected frontal assault on the Arno.

During its twenty-three days in the line, the Blue Devils had met the German at his best, had met a German who had stopped running, who clung tenaciously to every foot of ground and who fought vicious delaying actions when his planned lines of defense had been pierced, a German who was supported by heretofore unseen masses of heavy and long-range artillery. During the push the Blue Devils had cracked through four German defense lines and had driven the enemy from Volterra to the north bank of the Arno River.

In England, Drew Middleton, in an appraisal of the enemy written

115

Another town falls to the 88th.

for *The New York Times,* said that "even the best remaining German troops are inferior to the 1st, 3d, 9th and 88th American infantry divisions. . . ." It had cost heavily in blood and death for those words, and many of the 88th never got to read them. It cost 142 officers and 2,257 enlisted men killed, wounded and missing to help earn that tribute. Those who did read it, those who were left, knew for certain that the outfit was good; forgot all the old questions which once were in their own minds and gained a new pride in themselves and in their outfit.

Rest, rumors, the inevitable training and almost daily changes in plans for the expected assault on the Arno marked the month of August. With the fall of Florence to the British, it was clear at last that the dreaded frontal attack across the river would not have to be made. The 88th licked its wounds and prepared for whatever else might be in prospect. There were the usual rumors about peace and the company pools on war's end in Europe where American armies racing across France had optimists betting that the Germans would be finished before the 88th went back into the line again.

Bivouac-area bull sessions featured some tall tales from the drive just finished. Tales like the one about the Kraut who was captured by a Blue Devil with a table fork. Cpl. John J. Burns of Dorchester, Massachusetts, was eating chow when a German walked up to him and said he wanted to give up. Burns pointed the fork at him and yelled for a rifle. The Jerry had a couple of anxious moments until he learned the rifle was just a matter of form and that they didn't intend to kill him. But that Kraut couldn't have been any more startled than was Pvt. Steve Walker of Kennedy, Texas, who took the surrender of a German officer and then learned he had captured the brother of one of his back-home neighbors. Seeing the letters TEXAS proudly displayed on Walker's helmet, the Nazi lieutenant said that his brother was a Texas rancher. When they traded names, Walker discovered he was acquainted with the rancher's son. Then there was the yarn about the soldier who leaped into a slit trench during an artillery barrage and promptly was blown out of it by the concussion of a shell. Scrambling to another slit trench a few yards away, he was blown out of this hole by a second shell. "Make up your mind," he screamed toward the German lines. "Which hole do you want me in?"

At mail call one day, Lt. Herman Yezak of Bremond, Texas, a liaison officer, received official word that the folks back home had not forgotten him. The letter was notification that while he had been fighting in Italy, voters at home had nominated him to the Texas legislature. Pvt. Alvin J. Buckinger of Seattle, Washington, also had a letter one day at mail

Going out!

call. The missive was from his draft board. A bewildered Buckinger, who had been in the Army since November 1942, learned on a hot day in 1944 that his draft board had voted to defer him from service. Down in Rome on a pass, 1st Sgt. Carl E. Sabo of Youngstown, Ohio, achieved minor fame when he devoured the one millionth meal to be served in a GI restaurant in Rome operated by the Rome Area Allied Command. The millionth meal was just like all the ones preceding : meat-loaf, string beans, asparagus, salad, bread and butter and coffee. But better than C rations, any day. Another lad on a pass, Pfc. Vincent Visco, of Philadelphia, took off for Florence to look up relatives. Unable to find them at the given address, Visco told his CO and requested a couple more days. The CO did even better and organized scouting parties which soon came to be known as "Vince's family-searching parties" as they scoured the country-side looking for the missing relatives. It wasn't long before the patrols made contact and the *signorina,* the lovely niece and various smaller Viscos were throwing their collective arms around Vincent, the CO and the searching patrols and inviting one and all to remain for a family wedding celebration.

In Italy, after the fall of Florence and the occupation of the section of Pisa south of the Arno, a strange lull settled down on the line. For the first time since the jumpoff on May 11, the Fifth Army went on the defensive. It was beautiful fighting weather—if any weather can be called that—with warm, clear days and crisp, cool nights. One reason for the lull was the projected Southern France invasion. For this operation, Fifth Army had been stripped of three divisions, the 3d, 36th and 45th, as well as a host of artillery and engineer outfits, to form the Seventh Army in preparation for the invasion. This was a heavy loss in fighting personnel. Arrival of the 91st Infantry Division was not enough to make up the difference as the 91st was new and untried and represented a sub-stitution of one for three. Fifth Army's remaining divisions were tired and mauled; the replacement situation was critical as the bulk of every-thing was given to the Seventh Army. That perhaps was the paramount reason for the lull in operations. But months later in the midst of the rainy season, with the replacement system no better and with units dogged by mud and rain and mountains as they tried to slug through the long-prepared defenses of the Gothic Line, those seven weeks of idleness by the Arno River were cursed by exhausted doughboys. Those were the weeks to attack, they said, instead of at the height of the rainy season. And since the British were in top command and more familiar with Italian weather and terrain than the Americans, the British were blamed by the doughboy who had to do the dirty work for, to say the very least, a case of bad timing and judgment.

The Seventh Army invasion of Southern France was one of the worst-kept secrets of the war. When units were pulled out of Fifth Army and sent south to training areas near Naples, everyone knew why they were sent there. The invasion date was the chief topic of conversation throughout Italy. Soldiers on leave from the staging areas talked freely about preparations for departure. Civilian waiters in restaurants, the man on the street in Leghorn and Rome and Florence seemed to know when the fleet was to sail. Even farmers in out-of-the-way country towns speculated fairly accurately on the D-day for the invasion. There was so much talk about it, and accurate talk, that when the first assault waves went ashore in Southern France on August 15 and the first flash came over news wires and radios, the general reaction was, "So what?" The only surprising thing about that invasion was the fact that the Germans did not try to repel it with any great strength for with all the talk in Italy about it, spies certainly must have been able to relay accurate information to Nazi heaquarters about the Seventh Army and the date it was due to arrive.

Back in the 88th sector, triple award ceremonies gave convincing proof that the training-rest could not last forever. Presiding at regimental ceremonies, Generals Kurtz and Kendall reviewed Division accomplishments to date and General Sloan, speaking to several thousand at special religious and memorial services told Special Troops that "complete destruction of the Boche is our objective, not how many mountains and rivers we cross." And once again, General Sloan reminded his men that even if the war in Europe should end suddenly, there still was the enemy in the Pacific to be considered.

"We in the 88th have much for which to be thankful. We were fortunate in our training, in our movement overseas and especially in our battle indoctrination. We missed many of the hardships suffered by other American divisions. In our campaigns here in Italy, you men have proved to the world that you have the stuff. It is fitting that as we pay tribute to the brave men whose deeds helped to make this success possible, we give thanks to the God Who watched over all of us and brought us safely through the difficult days. With His continued guidance and protection, we shall achieve greater success in our future actions," General Sloan said. Although no one knew it, 88th men who heard that address were hearing General Sloan's valedictory to the men he had trained and led into battle.

Command changes sent Lt. Col. Walter B. Yeager from 3d Battalion, 349th, to the 351st as executive officer and the Krautkillers who had followed him through Itri and Fondi and a score of other hot spots hated to see him go. Lt. Col. James R. Davidson, G-3, who had been hospitalized

Medics give first aid to a wounded French soldier.

for more than a month, was succeeded by Major Elmore D. Beggs, later
promoted to lieutenant colonel. The greatest change however, and one
which affected the entire Division, came when General Sloan relinquished
command of the outfit he had built from a handful of raw recruits and
entered the hospital at Leghorn to undergo treatment for an annoying
and puzzling skin condition which had bothered him for more than a
month.

The 88th without General Sloan was a prospect no dough liked to con-
sider. Even his loudest critics realized that the General's insistence on
training and discipline had been primary factors in building the 88th to its
place as one of the best in the Army. They knew his bark often had been
much worse than his bite. And they knew that *he* was the 88th, that his
driving spirit had been infused into the Division so that the entire unit
operated almost as one man and reflected in its operations the work and
ability and courage of its commander. Without General Sloan, the 88th
didn't seem quite like the old outfit. All hoped and expected that he would
be back. Weeks later, it came as an unpleasant shock to learn that General
Sloan was on his way to the United States for further treatment and that
his fighting days were over.

There was no great surprise when the new Division Commander was

121

Major General Paul W. Kendall.
He took the 88th from the Arno River to final victory.

*"You are all familiar with our glorious accomplishments in the Italian campaign.
We have grieved together, albeit silently, over lost comrades. We have cemented
enduring friendships in the blood and strife of battle.*

*We believe that we fought a good fight and that we have kept the faith as a truly
representative American division. Our place in the history of our country is secure
—we did our part in preserving our country's safety.*

*Always remember with pride that you belonged—that you still belong—to the 88th,
For although men may come and go, the Division lives on—lives in your hearts and
in the heart and soul of your country, the United States of America.*

To all members of the 88th, living and dead, God speed you on your journey."

A good soldier—or his pet—never misses chow.

announced. It was a natural choice. General Kendall, Assistant Division Commander, was designated by Fifth Army as the new Commanding General of the 88th. Named assistant was Brig. Gen. Rufus T. Ramey. The doughs knew General Kendall; they'd seen him in training days at Gruber, on maneuvers in Louisiana, and they'd had him roaming the front lines with them from Minturno to the Arno. They knew he had courage, a taste for the dramatic and the flamboyant. They figured he was capable, and they knew he was stepping into a tough spot. And like all doughboys, they had a special nickname for him. Irreverently, they called him "The Bull." They didn't know it, but he knew what they called him.

New individual honors came to the 88th from the French. General Alphonse Juin, commander of the French Corps which had served with the Fifth Army and with which the 88th had battled through the southern mountains, awarded the Croix de Guerre to General Sloan, General Kendall, General Kurtz, Col. R. J. McBride, Chief of Staff; regimental commanders Col. Arthur S. Champeny, 351st, Col. James C. Fry, 350th, and Col. Joseph B. Crawford, 349th; Colonel Beggs, Lt. Col. John S. Winslow, Colonel Davidson, Capt. Hugh E. Quigley and Capt. Newell J. Ward, Jr. Released for publication by Army press censors were the battle records of the 349th and 351st, and thousands of individual stories were sent by regimental correspondents to home-town newspapers of every officer and enlisted man in both regiments.

Exchanges in personnel were made by the 88th and the newly arrived Brazilian Expeditionary Force. Selected officers, noncoms and enlisted

123

men from the various units were sent to the BEF to give the newcomers benefit of battle experience while a small group of officers and noncoms from the BEF was attached to the 88th for training. In addition to high Army brass, important visitors during the month included Cardinal (then Archbishop) Francis J. Spellman of New York, on a tour of European battle zones, and Lt. Eve Curie, who did a series of articles for the New York *Herald Tribune* on the 88th's combat record.

The weather was hot and dry and beautiful for attack but the Army lines moved forward only in local line-straightening operations. No strategists, but simply the men who would have to do the fighting when the time came, the doughboys wondered at the delay, thought ahead to the fall rainy season and shuddered at the prospect. Late in the month the 350th was sent to Leghorn as IV Corps reserve and shortly after, the 349th moved to the vicinity of Florence to back up the 442nd Regimental Combat Team which had been attached to the 88th and had made a limited thrust across the Arno River. The 351st remained in the division area near Volterra.

By month's end it was apparent that the 88th was due for action again. The regiments were pulled back and the Division bivouacked in the Scandicci area southwest of Florence. Training continued and since the possibility existed that the 88th might go into the line in any one of three different sectors, staff officers made daily trips to the 34th, 85th and 91st Divisions to keep abreast of the daily situation.

The rainy season started. Time was running out. Another D-day and II-hour were approaching for the 88th.

Perhaps more noteworthy than the actual capture of these features was the will of our troops to hold them against some of the fiercest counterattacks yet encountered.

MAJ. GEN. PAUL W. KENDALL

THE GOTHIC LINE

Worst of all 88th combat time came in those hellish days and nights that have gone down in military history as the Gothic Line–Apennines Campaign. In that pre-Bologna drive the 88th fought its roughest battles, suffered its heaviest casualties, battled a Kraut who had suddenly become desperate as the Blue Devils slugged across mountains and through concrete defenses he'd thought were impregnable. The Kraut struck back savagely and fanatically as the 88th forged ahead in its sector, outdistanced other units and fought with its flanks wide open as it caught hell from three sides in the raw, rainy fall of 1944.

At Gesso, Mt. Acuto, Mt. la Fine, Castel del Rio, San Clemente, Mt. Grande, Belvedere, Mt. Cuccoli, the 88th stood off the worst the enemy could throw at it and then forged ahead to take its objectives. Untrained in many of the tricks of mountain fighting, the 88th learned its technique the hardest way. And added a few bold innovations of its own as it battled for every muddy foot of the route. It answered its questioners at all those spots but it answered them loudest on Mt. Battaglia where its doughboys held during seven days and nights of German counterattacks to retain the prized peak and left about a battalion of its own dead and wounded on the rocky crag before it finally was relieved. Through the worst of terrain and weather, hurling back elements of nine German divisions thrown in against it at various times, the 88th pushed on toward the Po Valley—pushed forward until, riddled by casualties and stymied by open flanks it was impossible to close, it was ordered to hold up and dig in.

Wherever and whenever 88th men gather in the years to come, the inevitable bull sessions will swing to that Gothic Line drive. Each veteran and survivor has his own personal tale of horror, his own nightmare of those forty-four days and nights which blended together in one long drawn-out hell. It has been said that "all the mornings were dark, all the days were just different colors of gray and all the nights were black." And all the time up in those mountains north of Florence was just borrowed time. The terrain was so rough the Germans figured that no troops in the world could get through the few heavily defended mountain passes. But the Blue Devils made it, through the passes or over the mountain tops. The weather was so bad that the Germans thought no foot soldiers or vehicles could possibly operate in the mud and slime. But the Blue Devils walked and rode through the worst of it. The defenses and concrete, mined emplacements were so formidable that the Germans estimated they were impregnable. But the Blue Devils stormed and shattered the biggest and the best of them. Another factor operated in the defenders' favor. The area in which the Gothic Line, as such, was located

The Radicosa Pass.

had for years been the maneuver ground for Italian and Nazi troops who had won every problem against mythical invaders. The Blue Devils, no mythical invaders, no Supermen but just trained draftees, learned the ground as they progressed and beat the odds, and the defenders, on their own ground and at their own game.

The 88th fought under conditions seldom, if ever, experienced in the history of warfare. At times, the Division fought all alone, cut off from supporting units and supplies and sustained by no man knows what. To the front-line riflemen, as always, fell the toughest and dirtiest jobs. But no branch of the Division had any easy task. The artillerymen, wrestling their big guns along cliff roads and into firing positions a tactician would have shuddered at, caught their share of hell. Engineers, whose job it was to keep open the trails which passed for roads, performed magnificent feats of construction and maintenance. Signalmen threw away the book and improvised new systems as they labored to keep communication lines in operation and the various units of the Division in touch with each other. Supplies and ammunition were kept moving to the front in steady streams despite all obstacles as the men and drivers of the Quartermaster Company met the needs of those who depended upon them. And Ordnance, as usual, called on their mechanical skills and ingenuity to keep the Division's guns and vehicles in repair and operation. More than anything, that Gothic Line drive showed what a man could do of his own will and determination and inner strength.

127

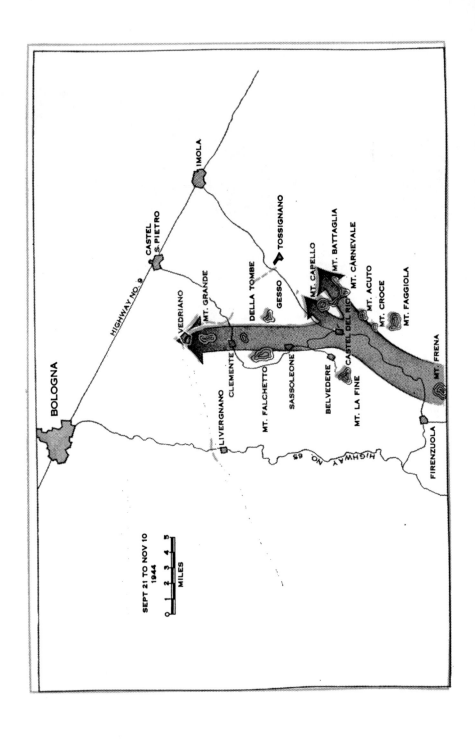

THROUGH THE GOTHIC LINE

On September 15 the Fifth Army renewed its assault on the Axis with an all-out blow against the formidable Gothic Line. The main effort was concentrated in the area immediately north of Florence with II Corps having the mission of driving through the mountains by the shortest route which was via Castel del Rio to Imola and Castel San Pietro. At the outset, the 88th Division was in reserve. The original plan called for the reduction of Firenzuola in the valley beyond Futa Pass before the Blue Devils were committed.

The artillery barrage which supported the beginning of this offensive was the greatest ever fired in Italy. The forest, which hid the mountain pass, was practically leveled by our artillery and still the Germans clung desperately to their positions in the rocks. On September 20, the 88th Division was given the task of opening a hole in the line.

The plan of attack committed the 349th and 350th Infantry Regiments abreast, 350th on the line along the mountain ridges and 349th driving through the valley along the highway. The British 1st Division was on the right of the 88th.

Forty-four days of combat followed and 6,000 casualties mark spots such as Mts. La Fine, Acuto, Carnevale, Battaglia, Castel del Rio, Capello, Falchetto, Della Tombe, Grande and Vedriano. When the offensive ground to a halt the Blue Devils held the terrain farthest forward of the entire Allied line—they could look down into the Valley of the Po but few who originally formed part of the assault regiments were left to enjoy the sight. The offensive, designed to break into the Po Valley, had failed.

Moving up.

Placed in II Corps reserve, the 88th was not committed in the initial attack on the Gothic Line—launched in the midst of the rainy season after six weeks of clear weather had been allowed to slip by—but held itself ready to pass through wherever it might be most needed. The Germans had been given precious time to get set in their mountain defenses in the Line, the line to which they had been retreating since before the fall of Rome. Despite the somewhat rosy and optimistic press releases handed out by higher headquarters which prematurely announced that the Line had been pierced, the men on the ground knew that only the barest preliminaries had been accomplished and that the toughest job lay ahead to be done without benefit of fanfare or headlines.

With the 91st, 85th and 34th Divisions cutting through the Line in the Futa Pass sector on Highway 65—described by some as the hardest link in the main chain of prepared defenses—it was not until September 17 that the 88th was alerted and warned that it probably would go in before another forty-eight hours had passed. Moving up, the Blue Devils concentrated in the San Piero area north of the Sieve River and prepared to go in on the Corps right flank, on the right of the 85th and passing through units of that division. The 349th and 350th went into assault positions during the night of September 20–21 and kicked off against the Gothic Line at dawn on the 21st. The 351st was held in reserve.

Mt. Frena was one of the first objectives. It was strongly held and

130

frontal approaches were impassable. The 349th called on the engineers who blasted a mountain trail into a jeep and supply route. With this route open, the 349th executed a brilliant flanking movement and the Germans found themselves enveloped from behind. Resistance stiffened as the day and advance progressed. Early on the 22d, disaster struck the 88th when the command post of the 1st Battalion, 350th, was raided and Lt. Col. Walter E. Bare, Jr., and all of his staff except the S-2 were taken prisoner along with top-secret operations maps, battle plans and journals. There was no time, due to the complexity of the operation, to change plans or directions and although it was evident that the Germans were now aware of our strength and our objectives, it was decided to push on as originally scheduled. Strangely enough, the loss of the battle plans did not materially hamper the advance and other favorable gains were made during the morning.

By 1700 hours on the 23d, the 349th had taken Mt. la Fine, a commanding terrain feature, and beaten off three Kraut counterattacks, one of which was of two-battalion strength and was forming in a valley until spotted and smashed by accurate and heavy 337th and corps artillery concentrations. At 1900 hours, the 351st jumped off in the center sector of the Division area and soon the three regiments were moving abreast, the 350th and 351st making the main effort, with the 349th garrisoning La Fine. Next day the enemy opposition increased and when the 3d Battalion, 350th, moved from its position on Mt. della Croce and attacked toward Mt. Acuto some 1,200 yards away, the battalion was counterattacked fiercely. It beat off the first, shortly after withstood a second and moved ahead through the night. By 0830 hours of the 25th it had scaled Acuto, stood off two more counterattacks and secured the strategic height.

In the assault, Capt. Thomas L. Cussans of Flint, Michigan, S-3, took command of a company which had become disorganized when its CO was killed and the unit suffered heavy casualties. Nailing the first three Krauts who rushed him, Cussans rallied the company, led it in a charge up the height in the face of heavy machine-gun and pistol fire, a charge which broke through tight lines and routed German defenders and a charge for which he later was awarded the DSC. Lt. George H. Carpenter of Malvern, Arkansas, led his company in standing off two enemy attacks. A third was launched. Carpenter, seeing the positions were about to be overrun, ordered every man out of his foxhole in a countercharge. He got several Krauts himself before an enemy bullet killed him. His company went on to rout the attackers. A medic, Pvt. Robert B. Langmier of Cincinnati, Ohio, was busy patching up L Company wounded near Acuto when the Krauts took back some lost ground. Langmier continued to treat

Flash floods turned dry streambeds into torrents.

his patients in what now was enemy territory, dressed their wounds and carried them to a house. A few hours later, L regained the lost ground and the enemy withdrew leaving his wounded and ours. Langmier, unperturbed, took care of and evacuated all of them.

The 88th's drive by now had become a bitter, hill-to-hill slugging match with the Krauts defending every mud puddle and counterattacking again and again, inflicting heavy casualties on our troops. The right flank of the Division was supposed to be covered by a British division. It was not. Failure of this unit to keep pace with the 88th's progress left our right flank wide open and enabled the Krauts to pour artillery at the Blue Devils from three sides. There were no rear areas. Every last reserve and various attached units were rushed in to serve as flank guards to prevent counterthrusts from snapping Division life and supply lines. Fog, rain and mud blocked observation, washed away at morale and hampered supply trains. Engineers hacked new trails and routes across mountains and strove to keep open what few inadequate routes there were. While building a by-pass over the Santerno River, engineers were driven off by enemy artillery, machine guns and mortar fire. T/4 Raymond L. Ashe of B Company and Baltimore, Maryland, although he was unable to hear the warning whistle of incoming shells over the roar of his motor, worked an angledozer for two hours as the construction party ducked the shells. The dozer was hit several times but Ashe kept plowing the mud until the job was done.

Early on the 25th it became apparent that Mt. Pratolungo, Mt. Carnevale and Mt. Battaglia would have to be captured before any further advances could be made. The 349th immediately took off for Pratolungo and had the height before darkness that same day. Throughout the 26th slight advances were made, and on the 27th the 351st, hitting the town from the east, west and south, captured Castel del Rio and won commendations from the Corps and Army commanders.

In the assault on Castel del Rio, the 88th lost one of its few remaining original battalion commanders, Major Charles P. Furr, twenty-eight, of Rock Hill, North Carolina, 3d Battalion CO. Youthful Major Furr, leading his outfit along a ridge, stepped off to the left of the path. As he did, a Kraut rose from hiding and tossed a grenade—the grenade went off as it hit Furr in the left temple and he died instantly. A rifleman, Cpl. Leroy Rickenbach of K Company, was near Furr and picked off three Krauts crawling in toward them. Hit in the leg by a sniper, he fell over an embankment but crawled up again and killed nine more of the enemy. When Furr was killed and Rickenbach saw the situation was desperate he crawled back from ledge to ledge under machine-gun fire to report the situation to his CO so that the battalion could be rallied. As an enemy attack developed, 1st Lt. Donald E. Muston of Detroit, Michigan, moved his platoon forward. He killed snipers to his left and right and then led his platoon in a charge. After a bitter scrap during which he accounted for four more Krauts, Muston led his platoon in taking the battalion objective. S/Sgt. Drew Mike of Mono Lake, California, won the plaudits of his buddies of B Company, 350th, near Castel del Rio when he led his squad through a hail of fire to a point where they could outflank the oncoming Krauts. Deploying his men, Mike fired clip after clip from his tommy gun in a standing position. Severely wounded, he fell to the ground but continued firing .at the enemy almost until the moment he died. His inspired men continued the fight until the charge was repelled.

New objectives for the 351st were designated as Mt. Guasteto and Mt. Capello, the latter resulting in one of the four bitterest battles of the entire drive for the Po Valley.

The battle for Capello, which lasted two days, was a struggle between German soldiers who would not withdraw and American troops who would not be stopped. The attack was launched at 0845 hours and by 1355 hours the 2d Battalion had reached a draw about eight hundred yards southeast of Capello. Fighting raged here for several hours. During the action, T/Sgt. Clyde A. Vaughn of Bexter, Missouri, and F Company, volunteered to lead a platoon which had been badly hit. The enemy had resorted to tracer bullets because of poor visibility and Vaughn made the

An engineer tankdozer clearing the rubble in Firenzuola.

tracers work for him. By back-tracking on the tracer paths, he knocked out three machine guns with grenades, killing seven. Although wounded, he kept on until he collapsed from exhaustion and loss of blood. An artillery liaison agent, Sgt. Lester Downing of Peoria, Illinois, and the 913th, left the heavily shelled battalion CP and spotted the Kraut OP about 150 yards away. Crawling to within less than fifty yards of the house, Downing lugged his radio and brought destructive artillery fire on Kraut mortars. The enemy saw him at about this time but despite a hail of grenades, Downing skillfully called for the fire of a single 105mm, drawing it back slowly up the ridge until three direct hits neutralized the strongpoint and the OP.

Fighting grew so fierce that the 1st Battalion was sent to aid, moving in on the right and hitting the Germans from the flank. During the night, forward elements inched ahead and reached a point about fifty yards from the summit by dawn. That was too close for the Germans. They counterattacked in deployed squads with three machine guns on the flank of each squad. The Krauts held here and stopped the men of the 1st. The 2d also was tied down and as casualties mounted, Headquarters Company personnel were pulled in as riflemen. All morning the two battalions hammered away in the face of heavy mortar and small-arms fire. At 1250 hours came the first encouraging news from Colonel Yeager, twice wounded here, that "we are proceeding slowly." For three more hours the fighting swirled undiminished until at 1536 hours came the message, "Mt. Capello taken by 1st and 2d Battalions."

During the final hours on Capello, S/Sgt. Sam McGowan of Clemson, South Carolina, won the DSC when he volunteered to lead a platoon in breaking up a German counterattack which was forming near a house on the forward slope. With fixed bayonets his platoon charged a group of 100 Germans, McGowan knocking out two machine guns on the way, killing three enemy and capturing six. Forcing one of the PWs to load an enemy gun, McGowan turned it on the Germans in a draw to the rear of the house, killing 12 and scattering the rest. Wounded in the leg, he went on with the platoon for the mop-up and refused to be evacuated until he'd organized the newly won position for all-around defense.

That was Capello, won with bayonet and blood and guts.

And then there was Mt. Battaglia, occupied almost without opposition by the 350th but held during seven days and nights of German counter-attacks in an epic stand which ranks with any in Division and Fifth Army history. Battaglia—a towering, Y-shaped height some 11 miles southeast of Bologna—dominated the terrain and road net in the entire area. Translated from the Italian, its name meant "battle." To the Fifth Army command, Mt. Battaglia meant an objective of the greatest military im-portance. It meant the same thing to the German high command, but Marshal "Smiling Albert" Kesselring was a trifle slow in getting his troops to the spot. As a matter of record, although censors prohibited its disclosure at the time, Italian Partisan troops operating between the lines in that sector were the first to occupy Battaglia, and they held it until American forces arrived.

The 350th received its orders to take Battaglia on September 25 when the regiment just had won Mt. Acuto and Mt. Alto. The message read: "The Corps commander states it is vital to Fifth Army to secure Mt. Carnevale and Mt. Battaglia. General Kendall directs you to take them as soon as possible." Those were the orders which started a week of battle which is practically beyond description.

In mere words, you can write that on the following day the 1st Bat-talion captured Mt. del Puntale. With his 3d Battalion combat team, Major Vincent M. Witter of Berlin, New Hampshire, moved forward through the hills south of Vallamaggiore. On the morning of the 27th, two days after the order was received, Lt. Col. Corbett Williamson of Macon, Georgia, led his 2d Battalion to Mt. Carnevale and drove the enemy, still in the process of digging in, from this Corps objective. Dur-ing that afternoon, Colonel Williamson's battalion moved to Battaglia, at that time the foremost point in the entire Fifth Army line. The im-

"Battle Mountain."

Mules **were** better than trucks in the Gothic Line push.

portant peak was taken without a struggle but that situation was to undergo a violent change. On the evening of the first night on "Battle Mountain," Colonel Fry received an official message of congratulations from the Corps commander for the prompt capture of the important objective. The Germans were planning messages of their own.

You can relate in words how dawn of the 28th found the 2d Battalion in position on the peak with G Company, commanded by Capt. Robert E. Roeder of Summit Station, Pennsylvania, as the base company; how every man with a rifle in battalion headquarters company was sent up to defend the left flank, where they remained for three days; how heavy-weapons companies equipped with light machine guns instead of their heavies were sent up to the crest of the peak with the riflemen to build up the greatest possible amount of fire power on the hill; how the rain, and mud, and cold, and fog and the fanatical and continuous enemy charges cut into the ranks of the 2d Battalion until the 1st went up to help it out; and how the men of the 1st fought and died in such numbers also that finally the entire regiment was up on the peak beating off the attacks which came with monotonous and terrifying regularity.

But what words can describe men like S/Sgt. Rocco Cotoia of New Haven, Connecticut, who saw his machine-gun section dwindle to four men, then went 1,000 yards to the rear, rounded up 19 more gunners and brought them back up on the hill to form a second platoon? Or Capt. Thomas S. Cussans of Flint, Michigan, who brought down mortar fire only 25 yards from his own troops in order to break up one counterattack?

They weren't the only heroes. There were others, like Sgt. Leo Beddow of Detroit, Michigan, blinded by a mortar burst after he single-handedly wiped out a group of Germans who had penetrated into the castle CP on the peak. And 1st Lt. Edmund D. Maher of Providence, Rhode Island, who with rifle, bazooka and bayonet knocked out a mortar crew, led a platoon in repelling an attack then dashed to the castle and bayoneted four Nazi paratroopers as they reached the doorway. Or Pfc. Felix B. Mestas of Laveta, Colorado, who manned a position on the forward slope for three days and with his BAR mowed the enemy down like grass as they vainly tried to get past him. On his last day in the most forward position, Mestas ordered his assistant gunner to leave, then killed 24 of them before they overran his position, giving his buddies time to re-form and beat off the attack. Mestas died doing that.

There were men like T/Sgt. Beni Mazzarella of Woonsocket, Rhode Island, who saw the strongest Kraut attack of all overwhelm the castle on the crest. Without waiting for orders, he picked up a handful of grenades and charged the castle, pitching grenades like apples and killing six and wounding more. When those ran out he used a machine gun, firing as he charged alone at the remaining Krauts who broke and ran as he came out of the fog. And 1st Lt. Walter W. Scott of Jackson, Mississippi, who potted six as he moved among his men pointing out targets and then when the attack seemed about to overrun the company took a dead man's rifle and led his men in a countercharge which stopped the Kraut attack cold. How can words do justice to the heroism of S/Sgt. Lewis R. Hamm of Olney, Texas, whom the enemy tried to get with a flamethrower, pushing it close enough to inflict severe facial burns? In agony from the seared flesh, Hamm stuck it out, killed the flamethrower operator and his assistant, took a bullet wound in the hand but managed to kill three more Krauts before he finally was evacuated.

During the seventh German counterattack—those game GIs actually kept box score—a lad named Pfc. Cleo Peek of Center, Colorado, was assistant gunner on a BAR which jammed. Peek held off the enemy with his M1, killing four, while the gunner worked frantically on the BAR. When his M1 jammed, Peek threw grenades. Those ran out. Then he resorted to the only weapon at hand, rocks, and hurled them at the enemy with such effect that they were stopped less than 25 yards from his position. And there was a soldier named Pfc. Jose D. Sandoval of Santa Fé, New Mexico, who fired his BAR until it heated and jammed. When that happened, he ran to a near-by machine gun whose crew was dead, unlocked it from its tripod and fired it from his hip, killing an unestimated number of the enemy. Can your imagination picture Sgt. Alfred E. Cassidy of Cincinnati, Ohio, who used his rifle like a mortar? Cassidy crept up on a machine gun, got it with a rifle grenade, then switched his fire to get two more. At this point, the Krauts saw and rushed him. He dashed back 50 yards, picked up a full box of grenades, returned to his old position and pumped out rifle grenades like he was operating a mortar. The Krauts couldn't take that.

In the movies they'd probably doubt the feat of S/Sgt. Raymond O. Gregory of Kings Mountain, North Carolina. His ammo and grenades gone, Gregory crawled to the crest and then savagely played "King of the Mountain" as he rolled huge boulders down the hill into confused enemy ranks. And the unselfish heroism of T/Sgt. Manuel V. Mendoza of Phoenix, Arizona, was one of the reasons why the 350th refused to be shoved off that peak. During one counterattack, Mendoza opened up with a tommy gun on 200 Jerries charging up the forward slope. Ten of them died where they fell, others lay wounded, but the rest came on. Mendoza, now using a carbine, emptied his entire ammo supply of five clips into their ranks. A flamethrower licked out at him but he killed the

Artillery dug in for high-angle fire.

operator with a pistol shot. Jumping into a machine-gun pit and pushing aside the dead gunner, Mendoza sprayed the surviving attackers until the gun jammed, then pitched hand grenades until the Krauts withdrew. Severely wounded himself by now, he nevertheless ran down the forward slope, retrieved enemy weapons lying there, captured a wounded Kraut and returned to consolidate his platoon positions.

Our wounded—and there were plenty—despite the constant enemy barrages which blasted the hill were treated by medics like Sgt. John J. Regan of Waterbury, Connecticut, and B Company, 313th Medics. Wounded himself during a barrage which fell on an infantry column moving up, Regan treated five of the doughboys and patched up two members of his litter squad. Removing them to a building, Regan made them as comfortable as possible before he started back to get help from his collecting station. It took him fifteen hours to make the hellish trip but he made it, giving directions and instructions to litter squads going up to evacuate the casualties he'd promised to bring out. Then he collapsed. And Capt. Williard Stoner of Chagrin Falls, Ohio, 2d Battalion surgeon, whose aid station was sheared to a single room by enemy shells but who kept on with his mercy task of treating the casualties which streamed in. And T/4 Joseph E. Silva, who saved countless lives as he worked

Night march to new positions.

doggedly on, shifting his patients from room to room as Kraut shells burst through the walls. Trails leading down off Battaglia were under observation and fire and Kraut snipers tried to pick off aid men and litter bearers as they struggled to bring out the wounded. One litter party of fifteen wounded men was caught in a mortar barrage. Ten of the wounded got up off their stretchers and staggered to cover. Litter hauls stretched anywhere from five to fifteen miles, but the medics somehow managed to get their precious burdens through the mud and fire to rear aid stations, ambulance points and hospitals.

There were a couple of GIs named T/Sgt. Roscoe A. Webb of Columbus, Ohio, and Pfc. George O. Porter of Boston, Massachusetts, who sweated out rifle grenades, flamethrowers and even pole charges as they consistently picked off enemy attackers during one bitter brawl. Or Major Erwin B. Jones of Brighton, Alabama, who assumed command of a battalion point when Kraut artillery wounded all members of the point and cut them off from the main unit. Jones directed artillery fire on the attackers and personally killed 19 of them before relief came up.

The citation for 2d Lt. Nicholas M. Vergot of the 338th Field and Steelton, Pennsylvania, credited him with voluntarily manning his OP for two days after being wounded on Battaglia. When a heavy fog began closing in on the third day, Vergot moved to another spot about sixty yards away. During the move, he was caught in a Kraut attack and his

142

radio operator killed. Vergot picked up his radio, and aided in beating off the attack by directing effective artillery fire on enemy concentrations. Another wounded artilleryman, Capt. Lewis B. O'Hara of the 338th and Arlington, Virginia, remained in exposed positions for two days spotting and relaying fire missions for two battalions.

A daybreak attack on the 30th temporarily drove the Blue Devils from the castle. After sending down for more grenades, flamethrowers, blankets, ammunition and dry socks, the men of the 350th slugged their way back up again to the castle and the crest of Battle Mountain. When the last officer in his rifle company became a casualty, T/Sgt. Ralph N. Grippo of Union City, New Jersey, a platoon leader, took command of the company and led the men in defense of the peak. To stem the attack, those doughs stood up in their foxholes and fired every weapon at hand. When one weapon failed or ammo was expended, they picked up the weapons of fallen comrades and continued to fire. In the heat of the battle, Pvt. Russell P. Glass of Akron, Ohio, and Sgt. John McKenzie of Lowell, Massachusetts, took time out to replace a firing pin in their machine gun, McKenzie covering with a tommy gun while Glass performed the repair job.

As the days and nights dragged by, Battle Mountain became a symbol of resistance. Those GIs had decided they were there to stay even if it took every last man to hang on. The Krauts apparently had decided they'd take that hill, even if the whole Army were expended in the effort. On headquarters situation and battle maps, the blue arrow designating the 350th stood out like a spearhead toward the Po Valley, its tip unblunted. In every headquarters throughout Italy, that spearhead was watched closely by higher commanders who knew that the comparative handful of doughboys on that peak held the fate of the Apennines drive, and of the Fifth Army, in their collective hearts and trigger fingers. Day after day they watched that map, watched that spearhead that never moved.

On the fifth day of the defense of the hill, the enemy again came up in the dense fog behind a heavy artillery concentration. Mud clogged automatic weapons but the attacking "Green Devil" paratroopers were beaten off again by rifle fire, grenades and supporting artillery. Litter bearers worked night and day to evacuate the wounded. Despite the hazards, packmule trains toiled up the trails under shell fire to bring needed supplies.

The fantastic situation couldn't continue much longer. Someone had to give, one way or the other. There is no telling just which unsuccessful attack convinced the Germans, made them realize that all their efforts were in vain. The attacks began to slow up, both in numbers and in ferocity. That was good news to our doughs; better news came in the form of

Captain Robert E. Roeder, 350th Infantry.

orders for relief. On the night of October 2, the first of the tired, drenched, gaunt men of the 350th came down off Battle Mountain. At midnight two days later the last company was relieved by British troops. As a unit, the regiment had suffered 50 per cent casualties—reported every company commander but one killed or wounded in the defense. Colonel Fry, who had actively directed the regiment during its stand on Battaglia, was praised by the Corps Commander for his work and the same message hailed the courage and tenacity of the 350th in taking and holding the key position, citing the accomplishment as a tribute to the 88th Division. General Clark visited the CP of the 350th and personally presented the Distinguished Service Cross to Colonel Fry for his "outstanding heroism and unfaltering courage" on Mt. Battaglia. General Clark told Colonel Fry he was proud to have him in his Army. The doughs of the 350th were proud of Fry also and to express this pride they tagged him with a new nickname. They called him "Fearless Fosdick."

Scores of medal award recommendations were started through channels for the gallant men of the 350th, who, exposed on three sides, denied air and ground observation, under terrific artillery and mortar barrages and hampered by bad weather which made supply nearly impossible, stood off all attacks to hold Battaglia. From Battle Mountain the 350th took its regimental nickname. And for its stand there, the 2d Battalion was awarded the Distinguished Unit Citation.

Every man who fought on that peak was a hero in every sense of the word. But there was one man whose "magnificent courage and intrepid leadership" so outshone all the rest that he was awarded the Medal of Honor. That man, an officer, gentleman and leader—in the finest meaning of those words—during his career with the 88th, was Capt. Robert E. Roeder, G Company, 350th, and Summit Station, Pennsylvania, who took the first unit up on the height and never came down. Roeder was CO of G Company, the base company in the defense. He was all over the hill, checking his men, pointing out targets, outlining new strategy, never sleeping or resting. In one of the enemy attacks in the bleak dawn and fog, Roeder was wounded by fragments and knocked unconscious by a shell burst. He was removed to his CP where he came to. Refusing medical treatment, he dragged himself to the doorway of the building. Here he braced himself against a wall, picked up a dead soldier's rifle and began firing at the still approaching enemy, meantime shouting orders and encouragement to his men. He fought on until a mortar shell burst a few feet away. That was the end. There are a hundred or more stories all attesting to his courage but the citation recommendation summed them up neatly with this tribute: "Of all the men present on this field of valor, it

Artificial moonlight off Highway 65.

was solely through Captain Roeder's leadership that his men held Mt. Battaglia."

By now the entire front was a nightmare of mud and fog. Days were hardly distinguishable from nights. Companies were low on personnel and replacements were slow in coming up. Not only were they slow in coming up, but they were hard to get. Rear-echelon units in the theater weeded out their able-bodied clerks and typists, gave them rifles and sent them up to the front. Inexperienced and untrained, many of these replacements were killed in their first few hours of action. Many died without even knowing what company or regiment they had been assigned to. It was rough, but it was necessary. Front-line units needed men and they had to be found some place. Old and young, they were sent up. Replacement depots were squeezed dry and still the calls came for more men. Several thousand were flown in from France, others from England, to bolster Fifth Army and 88th ranks. The GIs continued to give all they had but the Po Valley still lay many miles, and mountains, away.

Switching its direction of attack from northeast to north, the 88th threatened Highway 9, the vital German road from Rimini to Bologna, and the Germans reacted to this threat by throwing in no less than nine divisions against the Blue Devils at various times in a vain effort to halt the slow, but steady, advance. Among the enemy units committed were two of his best—the 1st Parachute Division and the 90th Light Division. And Italian Fascist troops also discovered, the hard way, that they couldn't stop the Blue Devils. Continuous and driving rains swelled streams to river size and the 313th Engineers doubled their tremendous efforts to keep open the lines of supply. In several places they strung high lines over washouts and flash floods by means of which supplies and ammo were sent to forward troops. Moving into Castel del Rio, the Division CP itself took a pounding from German artillery which resulted in the death of four enlisted men and wounds to one officer and six men. Among the dead was Sgt. John T. Lowenthal of Lafayette, Indiana, a soldier of German extraction who had enlisted to fight the Nazis for the liberty and freedom he had found in America. A PW interrogator, he was killed by a direct hit as he questioned four new prisoners.

Struggling along toward its key objective of Mt. Grande, the 349th dug the Krauts out of the tiny village of Belvedere. When the fight was over they were paid the supreme tribute by a captured Nazi officer who said that "in nine years of service I have fought in Poland, Russia and Italy—never have I seen such spirit. I would be the proudest man in the world if I could command a unit such as the one which took Belvedere."

Some of the men who won that tribute for the 349th were GIs like

An 88th pack-mule train bringing in supplies and rations.

A German Gothic Line defensive position.

Pfc. Ralph W. Foreman of C Company and Danville, Illinois. When enemy machine guns pinned down the lead elements, Foreman opened up with a BAR and killed the crews of two guns. He then moved to the flank, picked off three Krauts, wounded four and captured two as he plastered a house with BAR fire while his buddies moved up. A GI, Pfc. John S. Barron of Lane Coty, Texas, was one of the first to reach the ridge and took position near the corner of a house to cover his squad's approach. He was blazing away when a Kraut sniper got him in the leg. With only one round left, Barron butt-stroked a Kraut who rushed him, then smashed his rifle over the head of a German officer who tried to get in the act.

B Company now attacked the ridge, which was defended by three machine guns, snipers in four houses, seven Krauts with machine pistols and riflemen outposts. T/Sgt. Carlton H. Hand of Rio Grande, New Jersey, was the second man up on the ridge, lugging a radio he'd taken from a dead buddy to call down artillery fire. Hand dropped the radio, borrowed some grenades and went to work on the house snipers. He'd gotten two in the first one when he saw the Krauts next door trying to escape. He got three on the run. The Krauts still cooped up inside dropped grenades on

At the Firenzuola landing strip a patient is carried from an ambulance to a plane which will take him to Florence.

him but Hand picked them up and tossed them at a machine gun. With that out of the way, Hand charged into the building and the two surviving Krauts gave up.

When 5 were killed and 20 wounded as he led his company up the hill, Capt. John J. King of New York City got sore. Before he calmed down, he'd charged past a whole line of pillboxes, killed 6 Krauts in a house and from this vantage point proceeded to pick off Krauts in other emplacements until the survivors pulled out. King then brought up his company and secured the hill. En route to Belvedere at the head of his squad, Sgt. Hector M. Flores of Denver, Colorado, put three machine guns out of action and took five prisoners after a hand-to-hand scuffle with one Kraut who succumbed to a belt on the head from a tommy gun.

Driving on, the 349th took Sassaleone, cut the Sassaleone–Castel del Rio road and despite intense opposition advanced north of Falchetto after consolidating its positions on the Falchetto hill mass. In the push to Sassaleone, 1st Lt. Richard P. Walker of Coleman Falls, Virginia, won the DSC, awarded posthumously, when he put four German machine guns out of business and was killed a short time later as he led his platoon against the battalion objective. Another DSC, also posthumous, went to T/Sgt. Romeo M. Ramirez of Saticoy, California, who with a small band of 16 men clung through a bitter night to a half-wrecked and burning house. Ramirez and his group were surrounded and cut off after the house had been taken. Ramirez posted his men at doors and windows and they gave battle. The Krauts finally set fire to the house with incendiaries and although further resistance seemed useless, Ramirez induced his men to hold out. Through the night the fighting raged and when help arrived at dawn the box score showed 22 Krauts dead and 5 prisoners, with 4 dead and 10 wounded out of the 17 who had clung to the battered, half-burned building.

150

In a one-man assault near Pezzola, T/Sgt. Brance Jackson of Three Oaks, Michigan, raked the area with mortar fire, then went after the scattering Krauts. Before he was through, he'd killed 3 and captured 21. Pfc. Harry J. Brondyke of Muskegon, Michigan, killed the crews of two machine guns which had pinned down his company and then, although shot in the side, he still had enough strength left to carry his wounded squad leader some eight hundred yards to an aid station. Left alone in a flank machine-gun position while his crew went for ammo, Pfc. Thurmon B. Robertson of Cooksville, Tennessee, killed five Krauts who tried to sneak near enough to get him with grenades and then cut a haystack to chaff as he silenced an enemy mortar behind it.

Pvt. John J. Walkiewicz of Hartford, Connecticut, had a field day during a daylight patrol on Falchetto. Walkiewicz took an enemy artillery OP and from this point he spotted a series of Kraut machine-gun emplacements along the ridge. He led his men in capturing one, then took a second. Turning this gun on the other positions he called on the Krauts to surrender. A total of 75 Germans put their hands up and called it a war. In another raid, 1st Lt. Fred C. Galliart of Larned, Kansas, also bagged Krauts by the score. Galliart was manning an OP and spotted a large group of enemy moving up on a 349th patrol which just had taken some prisoners. Galliart raced to the patrol, took command from its wounded leader and led the Krautkillers in an attack. The Jerries called up mortar fire and prepared a counter assault. Before it could get under way, Galliart grabbed a Kraut machine gun and sprayed the bewildered enemy who soon began surrendering in droves to Galliart and a few men who had followed him all the way. More than 75 Krauts were taken prisoner by these few.

By 0630 hours on the 10th the 351st had passed through the 349th and slugged its way into Gesso, despite constant counterattacks in which the enemy used flamethrowers. The 351st was shoved out of Gesso. Late on the 11th, after a heavy artillery preparation, the 3d Battalion went back into Gesso and this time stayed there, routing out German flamethrowers from the church and bagging more than 140 Krauts in all. That same day the 350th managed to overcome stubborn resistance and succeeded in capturing most of Mt. della Tombe before it was relieved by part of the 351st. Near Gesso, three Spearheaders teamed up to give the Krauts a bad time. While moving his squad against Hill 462, Sgt. William J. Schnorbus of Trenton, New Jersey, took a small patrol to investigate a house. In the approach one man tripped a mine and enemy fire came down on the patrol. Schnorbus made it alone to a small shed and then rushed the house where he took 30 prisoners. Meantime, Pfc. John C. McFarland

"— — — — — — — — — — —!"

of Welch, West Virginia, and Pfc. Donald G. Taylor of Salisbury, Maryland, aided the mine victim and when Schnorbus returned to the squad to post the men, the three of them manned a sightless mortar. Pumping out six rounds, they knocked out the last Jerry machine gun between them and their objective and before the brawl was over had killed 20 and captured 58. The equivalent of another Kraut platoon was rounded up near Gesso by 1st Lt. Herbert F. Mutschler of Jamestown, North Dakota. Mutschler took 17 men to attack a house. In the approach, he got five Krauts and a machine gun with three grenades before a sniper shot him in the head. Though wounded, Mutschler ordered his men forward and when he tossed a grenade through a first-floor window, 41 Krauts came out and resigned. In a revenge duel with Kraut snipers who had picked off three of our aid men, Pvt. Lawrence J. Cunningham of Long Beach, California, turned his machine gun over to a buddy and stalked the snipers with a rifle. He killed four snipers in reprisal for the death of the aid men. He was killed that night while investigating noises to the right of his gun position.

The 349th, shortly after taking over from 1st Battalion, 351st, on Della Tombe, continued its attack but was unable to advance beyond the crest of the mountain. Severe fighting ensued and resistance mounted steadily. The enemy, funneling replacements to his line outfits and with an excellent supply of ammo and food, was determined to check this drive and to avoid a breakthrough into the Po Valley at this point. Enemy artillery was stepped up throughout the Division area as the Germans harassed supply lines and rear areas. Located at Belvedere, the Division rear echelon got a taste of what the doughboys endured as routine. Firing from the right flank in the vicinity of the Tossignano gun area, enemy artillery dumped shells in and near the town almost daily for a week. "Rear" suffered no casualties in its first time under fire. Some men gained a deeper appreciation for the line troops but others merely complained at what a tough life the rear was living. But they were living! During one barrage, Major Harvey R. Cook of Evansville, Indiana, Special Service Officer, won the Bronze Star for heroic achievement when he went out alone under fire to rescue a wounded Italian mule skinner. A few of the loudest critics, who also heard the cries for help, never left the safety of their respective cellars. A regiment of the 91st Infantry Division, sent up to help out on the right flank, proved to be no help at all when it bivouacked—despite advice to the contrary—too close to a swollen stream and lost half of its vehicles and supplies during a flash flood in the night. Supply roads in the Division area were nothing but quagmires and night blackout driving was a hazardous proposition. To aid the drivers, and also to furnish some help to attacking doughfeet, "artificial moonlight" was invented. This consisted of searchlight batteries focused on low-hanging clouds. The reflected light enabled drivers and infantrymen to get a faint idea of where they were going. The Germans adopted the artificial moonlight also but neither side bothered much about trying to knock out each other's lights.

When two assault platoons of E Company, 349th, were held up by cross-fire from machine guns near the crest of Della Tombe, Sgt. Henry A. Kochis of Clarksburg, West Virginia, led a squad through shell fire to the right flank. Kochis ran ahead of his men and with his tommy gun picked off four Krauts as he wiped out two of the nests. Then, as Kraut fire chopped down members of his squad, Kochis charged the third nest and smashed the gun after he killed the crew. With the fierce fire now lifted, the assault platoons moved up and drove the enemy from the hill. Service elements of the regiments did what they could to aid the forward doughboys as they packed rations and supplies over flooding streams. Mule trains slipped and slid along muddy trails as their skinners fought to get them through. At one point, two loaded mules slipped into a stream. T/5 Harold A. Gagnon of Winslow, Maine, dove into water after the supplies, stripped the rations from the floundering mules and then reloaded the beasts after he'd led them ashore. Later as the train neared the company CP, a mortar barrage broke up the column. Gagnon, although

An American soldier buried in debris during a bombing is freed by comrades.

badly wounded, refused medical aid until he managed to rally the mule-skinners and got the supplies unloaded and delivered.

American planes added to the division casualty list when they bombed the command post of the 1st Battalion, 351st, situated on Hill 471, near La Mores on October 11. Four planes bombed and strafed the CP shortly before noon. One of the buildings housing the command group personnel received a direct hit which killed four and wounded 14 of the occupants. As the planes circled for another run, Chaplain Elmer B. Hoover grabbed some white cloth, ran to an open spot near the wrecked building and laid out a ground signal for the planes. This quick action caused the planes to hold their fire and remaining bombs. Meanwhile, German SP's began laying in on the area but despite the barrage Chaplain Hoover organized a group of men to extricate the dead and wounded from the building. Although under fire, the chaplain's rescue squad removed the survivors from the rubble. The air raid was attributed to a case of mistaken identity.

Although the drive obviously was beginning to slow and units were losing men faster than they could be replaced, orders still came down from Army and Corps to push on. There were no reserves; all Fifth Army units had been committed, and the Apennines campaign now had developed into a grinding tug-of-war in the mud. No one of the fighting men really expected to break through to the Po Valley. With the terrain just one mountain after another, many really doubted that there was any such flat land as the Po Valley, or any such city as Bologna, which they

154

An 81mm mortar crew in the Mt. Grande area.

had been trying so desperately to reach. Unit commanders warned higher headquarters that the morale of their men was sinking steadily, that the men were nearing the point of absolute physical and mental exhaustion. But the orders still came down to "get that hill!" And they kept trying, and succeeding.

On the 17th, the Krautkillers took San Clemente, established a roadblock east of town and placed troops on Hill 435 to the northeast. Since the enemy made every possible attempt to stop the advance from this point it became apparent that Mt. Grande was the key to the entire enemy defensive line. Time was growing short. If Mt. Grande was to be taken at all it would have to be done before the Germans had an opportunity to reinforce it with fresh troops and organize for a last-ditch stand. On the night of October 19, the 1st and 2d Battalions, 349th, were poised to attack. The preliminary objectives already had been occupied.

The 1st Battalion objective was Mt. Cerrere; the 2d had the mission of driving through Del Chin, across Di Sotto and Di Sopra to the crest of Grande. The operation had to be completed by dawn to succeed. It meant calling on the last ounce of strength and guts in each doughboy. Each man knew that the long weeks of bloody fighting across rugged mountains in rain and mud—on a front which he had come to think was a front forgotten by everyone but the Germans—would be capped with failure if Grande was not taken. The 1st Battalion mission, to seize Mt. Cerrere, was of vital importance to the entire plan. Cerrere, 1,000 yards

155

southeast of Grande, was a prime point on the exposed right flank. To hold Grande without first taking Cerrere would be impossible since the troops would be open to fire from the right rear and to the possibility of being completely cut off.

At 2200 hours, October 19, the 1st Battalion pushed off with A Company, commanded by Lt. John Ernser, in the lead. Leaving Hill 450, the troops struggled through deep mud, advancing slowly in the darkness and a driving rain. Climbing up the rocky slope, Lieutenant Ernser led his men to the crest of the mountain, meeting no resistance and only slight artillery fire. A large building on the highest point was surrounded and 11 Krauts captured there. B and C Companies moved to the hilltop, joined A, and Mt. Cerrere was organized for defense. Once again the Krauts had underestimated the 88th and had been caught napping. Meanwhile, 2d Battalion was driving through the night to reach Grande itself before dawn. At 2130 hours G Company, commanded by 1st Lt. Robert Kelly, jumped off for Del Chin and took it without much trouble. Di Sotto was occupied next and halfway to Di Sopra the company drew fire from Krauts dug in around a large house. Deploying his lead platoon, Kelly paced the men in a smashing assault; killed four, wounded three, captured six and drove off the remnants of a full company. Less than an hour later the Germans hit back. First Lt. Frederick Cummings and his platoon took the brunt of the attack. Pfc. Charles Gilland cut down five with his BAR before his position was overrun. With his tommy gun blazing, Sgt. Erwin Baker rounded a corner of the building, pulled up short as a dozen Germans came at him. With his back to the wall he killed four; fire from the house dropped three more and the Krauts broke. Stumbling back down the hillside they left 15 dead and wounded behind them.

Pushing on to the north, G Company occupied Hill 581. At 0300 hours, F and E Companies passed over Hill 581 and started up the slopes of Grande. A devastating artillery preparation softened the objective as our troops advanced and heavy concentrations were dumped on possible Kraut reinforcement routes. In the first murky light of dawn, 2d Lt. Frank Parker with the 1st Platoon of F Company reached the highest point, the top of Mt. Grande. The rest of F moved up and occupied the northern part of the hill while E Company dug in on the reverse slope. Less than thirty minutes later, the Krauts attacked but were beaten off. The Krautkillers were on the knob to stay. At 1100 hours on the 20th, the 350th reported it had captured Mt. Cuccoli to complete the seizure of the entire Mt. Grande hill mass, the most strategic height along the entire Fifth Army front at the time and one which commanded on a clear day a view of the Po Valley and Highway 9 to Bologna. To the 349th went commendations from General Keyes and General Kendall. To the regimental CP went General Clark with congratulations to Colonel Crawford and the 349th for the taking of Grande and reminders of the grave necessity of holding it against all comers.

In action near Grande, S/Sgt. Delvin V. Sample of Muscatine, Iowa, and the 351st, was wounded twice as he knocked out two machine guns in haystacks and drew fire from an enemy house, diverting the Krauts' attention until his men took that objective with 28 prisoners. On the 22d, near Mt. Dogano, pint-sized Pfc. MacDonald Coleman of San Francisco, California, and the 349th, staged a one-man war and killed 6, wounded 1 and captured 15 of a group of Germans attempting to prevent the establishment of a roadblock. During a counterattack in the vicinity of Grande, Pfc. Andrew Tell, Jr., of Akron, Ohio, and M Company, 351st, broke up the party with his machine gun. Tell swung into action after his assistant gunner and 30 out of 35 riflemen were wounded. Before he stopped firing, Tell had killed 15 and wounded 35. The enemy withdrew. An artilleryman, Capt. Albert A. Nettles of the 338th Field and Beatrice, Alabama, won the Silver Star during the advance on Grande when he voluntarily moved forward with advance infantry elements to insure the maximum artillery support. At one point, he purposely exposed himself to draw fire, then called in support artillery on the Krauts who had given themselves away. Nettles was wounded after more than five hours of this performance but refused evacuation until spotter and communications replacements were sent up to take over his job.

The attack meanwhile ground on, with Farnetto falling to the 350th and Frasinetto to the 349th. The stone wall came at Vedriano where, with "stand and die" orders, the Germans beat off every attempt by the 351st to take the town. Through rain and ankle-deep mud the 3rd Battalion fought its way to the top of Montecalderaro on October 23, while Company G attacked Vedriano with considerable initial success. Coming around behind the town and hill at Vedriano, the men of Company G surprised and captured a column of 40 Germans and after a short fight took the town itself. The German commanders were quick to recognize the potential danger of this threatening attack and they committed their finest troops in a counterattack.

As Companies E and F battled heavy resistance on October 24 in an attempt to reach Company G, now surrounded and fighting desperately, a radio intercept picked up the following message from the 1st Parachute Regiment to the 1st Battalion, 4th Parachute Regiment: "Attack Vedriano. Vedriano is decisive!" Men of the 1st and 3rd Battalions, 351st, themselves locked in battle against German counterattacks, noticed the

Lt. Gen. Mark W. Clark, Fifth Army commander, and Lt. Col. Joseph B. Crawford, CO of the 349th, discuss the tactical plan.

rattle of small arms fire coming through the mist from Vedriano. In the afternoon the sounds of firing faded away and a short time later another German radio message was intercepted: "Vedriano retaken and 80 Americans captured." Company G was gone. Although they were overwhelmed and could not hold Vedriano against an attack of near-regiment strength, the men of Company G had approached closer to the Po Valley than any unit in the entire Fifth Army. It was less than 9,000 yards to Highway 9, the main lateral road for the German forces facing both the Fifth and Eighth Armies.

Vedriano, the closest point to the Po Valley yet assaulted by any unit of the Fifth Army, remained in enemy hands. It couldn't be taken, yet orders continued to come down to get it.

By now, all units of the 88th were in sorry shape. The constant driving, the mud and rain, heavy casualties which had cut some companies to as little as twenty men, the nervous exhaustion and low morale, all were danger signals that a crackup was coming. Commanders hated to order their weary men out—some platoon leaders risked court-martial by refusing to lead their exhausted remnants in any more assaults. Chaplains and doctors warned that any further attempts to advance would be dangerous, if not disastrous. Both the strength and the will of the troops to go on were fast slipping toward complete breakdown. One fresh division might have been enough punch to get the Fifth Army through to the Po—one fresh regiment assigned to the 88th might have taken the Division through Vedriano and on to Highyway 9. There were no fresh troops and the weary men who had taken the battle for more than six weeks had had just about enough. But the orders still came down to "get that hill"—orders for a hill when one unit commander said he couldn't even order his men to take a house.

Rising casualty reports sent back to Fifth Army and general information received by that headquarters finally led to an informal survey of front-line conditions in the 88th. Once at the front, Fifth Army officials were convinced that the reports were well founded and that the recommendation to dig in and rest the troops was the only possible solution; anything else would have been suicide. That's where, and how, the drive through the Apennines was stopped. Orders went out to all units to hold where they were and dig in for the winter. If the 88th, one of Fifth Army's crack units and the spearhead for most of the Apennines campaign, said it couldn't be done without rest and help, then it couldn't be done. With glazed eyes and unbelieving ears, the doughboys heard that the push was over and that they were going back for rest.

The 88th left its youth up there in those Apennines—left more than 6,000 dead and wounded on those bleak mountains—scrawled its mark in blood over every foot of that hellish terrain as it wrote a glowing page in Fifth Army history. For once and for all, it proved to its own satisfaction and to the satisfaction of everyone who could read the story told starkly on battle maps and in casualty reports, that the 88th could take it, and dish it back twice as hard. And somehow in the give-and-take, the Division members had lost the last of their doubts and acquired a fierce, new pride in their outfit.

Gill Robb Wilson told about this new pride in a dispatch to the New York *Herald Tribune*. Wilson reported how one evening "in the dusk I stopped to sit down beside a wounded boy waiting his turn for evacuation. He had a bullet in the hip. 'What paper you from, buddy?' he asked. I told him. 'Give us a boost, will you?' he said. I can't mention the name of a wounded man until his folks are notified, I told him. 'Ah, hell,' he said, 'I don't mean me, I mean the outfit.' So I promised, and here is the boost.

"If I belonged to the 88th Division, the first draftee division to hit the enemy and at it consistently from below Anzio to the Rubicon, I would be as proud of the outfit as the boys in it are. I would forget the dark and cold and mud to root for the gang just like that kid was doing. I would be cussing the wound that took me out of action and association with the 88th even as that draftee civilian soldier did. I am even proud to have been among them a bit," Wilson concluded.

A combat correspondent with the Division sent home a story on the relief, a story whose theme was "when doughboys march back from hell—that's a real parade!"

"We watched a parade tonight," he wrote. "It probably wasn't much of a parade by civilian standards. It wasn't like the one we have down Main Street on Memorial Day. It was nothing like the one we'll probably have on Victory Day. You civilians never have seen one like it. You probably never will.

"There was no reviewing stand. There were no bands. There were no flags. There were no crowds lining the route.

"The air was raw—not exactly ideal weather for a parade. It was raining—a cold, driving, stinging rain that soaked through clothes and made wet feet seem wetter.

"The route was a hub-deep mud path dignified by being called a road. The rain added more liquid mud to the six inches or more which slopped from bank to bank.

"There were no bands—but there were sound effects. Periodically, there was the shuddering crash of medium artillery pieces firing from a roadside grove. In answer was the whistle and crunch of an incoming shell—not near enough to bother ducking. Faintly on the downwind came the chatter and cough of machine guns.

"It was uncomfortable, physically, watching that parade. But mentally and emotionally it was thrilling, an experience almost impossible to describe but one that was absolutely unforgettable. It was the paraders who aroused that feeling. The paraders were infantrymen—doughboys who had been through all the hell the enemy could devise. They had taken it; lived through it. They were on the way back now for a rest, on the way back to dry clothes, hot food, sleep, amusement, to all the things which are part of your daily routine but which had been denied to them for so long. They were on their way back to a place where there would be 'freedom from fear.'

"They were tired men, exhausted men. They'd been up in the lines for 44 days and nights, for more than six weeks of rain and mud and cold and pain and sudden death.

"They'd fought in these hills and mountains for 44 days and nights. They'd attacked, and battled, and won. They'd rooted and hunted and blasted the Germans out of hills and caves and strongpoints that were believed impregnable.

"They'd pushed the American lines farther north—they'd crept and crawled and fought over terrain supposed to be impassable. They'd heard and read, maybe even thought, that what they were supposed to do was 'impossible.' But somehow, they'd done it anyway—they'd performed the

Exhausted doughboys going back for a rest.

'impossible.' And done it with no bugles or fanfare or newsreel cameras
—with nothing but courage and persistence and maybe prayer, which are
the only important things.

"Not all of them were coming back. There were a lot of faces missing
from the ranks of that parade. There were men who remained up in those
hills and mountains. They were dead men. They were privates and sergeants and lieutenants and majors and colonels—rank didn't matter. They
were all dead. They'd done their job too and done it magnificently. They
already had reached their rest area.

"The men riding those trucks had none of the polish and brass of the
usual parade. They were unshaven, gaunt, haggard. They were wet and
covered with mud and their uniforms were filthy and ragged. But no one
minded or cared much about their appearance. Those were the marks of
combat men, of infantrymen, and they were marks and badges of honor
and distinction.

"They were quiet men. Some of them slept, leaning on a buddy's
shoulder with a wet blanket thrown over huddled heads and shoulders. A
few talked—one or two waved in recognition. But most of them just sat
there, staring straight ahead with apparently unseeing eyes. The hell they
had lived in, and through, was still too close.

"Later, farther down the road, some of them might sing or yell at a
signorina in some tiny village as the convoy rumbled through. Still later,
and farther back, there would be arguments and kidding and loud,
friendly bull sessions. And memories would soften. And hot food and
sleep and relaxation undisturbed by bullets or shells or alarms would

161

bring weight and color to their bodies and faces. But all that was still to come, and they hadn't reached it yet. They were still on the way back and quite unknowingly were making the finest and most thrilling parade that anyone ever could be privileged to see.

"I was happy to see it, this parade of men coming out of the lines for a rest. They didn't know, and would be sore if they were called it, but they were magnificent. As magnificent as the infantry always is. And it made you humble to realize just how much you owed to these front-line doughboys. It's too bad you couldn't have seen it. A lot of civilians should have seen that parade. It might make them understand things a little better. It might make them value things a little more. It might make them give thanks—to God, and to the front-line doughboys, for keeping the war from them."

As the doughs headed back for Montecatini-Terme for rest, another correspondent, Milton Bracker, cabled a review of draftee outfits to *The New York Times*. Based on a year's observation of the 88th, Bracker wrote that "these men have forgotten that but a year ago they were called draftees. The important thing is that these men, whether they live or die, will have shared in one of the important accomplishments in American military history; the establishment of proof that the peoples' army called into being by the Selective Service Act of 1940 had what it took."

Our patrols were active . . .

FIFTH ARMY COMMUNIQUÉ

THE WINTER LINE

The switch from foxholes in the Apennines to feather-beds in Monte-catini-Terme hotels and resorts was like a quick trip from hell to heaven for doughboys of the 88th. Montecatini, the Italian counterpart of America's Saratoga Springs, had been taken over completely and suddenly by the Fifth Army as a rest center for the troops when it became evident that the drive through the Apennines was at an end. Located about 40 kilometers west of Florence, the town became the winter playground for the 88th's gods of thunder. It was strictly a fighting man's town.

"This place is nice and exclusive," said Sgt. Ralph Singer of Rochester, New York, a platoon sergeant. "We raise all the hell we want and we don't have to worry about offending civilians, This is 'Boys' Town' with champagne." A succint comment was offered by Cpl. Harold Lafferty of Long Island City, New York, a rifleman, who said: "I wish they'd bomb this town with beer bottles and put a head on every street." The bombers never came with that kind of load but the MPs were kept busy enough handling other loads moving through its streets.

The first visit of the 88th to Montecatini was a short one. All units of of the Fifth Army were in tough shape and needed rest. As the first one out of the line, the 88th also had to be the first one back in so that doughs of other outfits could get a crack at rest and relaxation. The first Blue Devils into town could hardly believe that such a comparative paradise existed so close to the mud they had lived in so long. Several days of rest and showers and clean clothes helped to erase some of the more awful combat memories and the casualty-stunned Division began to come alive again. All units were quartered in what had once been the top tourist hotels. Sulphur and health baths were available for those desiring them. Movies, plays, dances, skating rinks, tennis courts and all the other attractions of a rest center were theirs for the asking. The Division Band played from hotel to hotel for unit dances and parties and the local *signorinas* turned out in force, with or without the usual bunch of family and chaperons, including Italian boy friends.

But the chief occupation in Montecatini, after training hours, was the bar bull session where old battles were refought and sometimes, new battles were begun. The Blue Devils were proud of their combat record, and in the fire of the Gothic Line had gained a fierce and new pride in their nickname. For the first time since they had hit Italy, they felt as good as, or better than, any other outfit. Arrival of several new divisions with less combat time than the 88th—the 91st, which had come in at the Arno River in late July, and the 10th Mountain, which just had arrived—lifted the 88th out of the freshman class of Fifth Army and the Blue Devils were taking a back seat to nobody. This new pride in outfit resulted in a

Hot showers were available and appreciated at the shower and clothing exchange unit set up close behind the lines.

mass chip-on-the-shoulder attitude—the men weren't braggarts but they didn't intend to stand idly by while some newcomer described how his outfit had won the war. The 88th had been in there punching since Cassino and it angered the men to listen to some late arrival describe his month, or less, of combat time. Or tell his bar audience how tough his division had had it the previous summer in the States in desert training, or the previous winter in the mountains practicing ski runs. It might have been tough, 88th men agreed, but at least the heat and the cold and the training had been accomplished without the accompaniment of Kraut rifle, machine-gun and artillery fire. And while those new outfits had been enduring the rigors of the United States, the doughs of the 88th had been climbing and fighting in Italy, always under fire and with sudden death riding the enemy's gunsights and trigger fingers. More recently, the 88th had left a lot of its oldest members up in the Apennines; every survivor had a buddy who no longer was with him. Arguments in every bar and bull session raged long and loudly. If Highway 65 was tough, then Mt. Capello was no picnic. If Livernagno was hot, how about Sassoleone, and Castel del Rio? If Hill 701 was hard to take and hold, Mt. Battaglia was no daisy chain. Every step of the long haul through the Apennines was

165

Engineers patching up a trail in the Mt. Grande area.

fought and refought, and when words ran out or arguments were no longer satisfactory, fists swung and the battles were fought again before a smaller and more partial audience. Blue Devils and Red Bulls and Pine Trees tangled all over town until MPs managed to get in and slap on the brakes. Montecatini was a fighting man's town.

Favorite rallying point for all troops was the Trianon Theater which was converted into a huge night club. Here the crowds gathered about 1,000 strong for two performances a day. There were 189 small tables on the main floor and a balcony upstairs where a couple of hundred more customers could be served. A long bar was staffed by 8 Italian bartenders while 37 waiters hopped the tables. Drinks were thirty cents apiece for rum, whiskey and cognac—with or without pimento in the bottle—and a sparkling beverage, called champagne, was sold by the bottle. Even if they couldn't enjoy the beverage the champagne bottle corks made excellent ammunition for popping friends at nearby tables. As the night and excitement wore on, the popped corks generally went astray, temperatures rose and in no time the main floor of the Trianon looked like the assault on a blockhouse. Combat technique was employed to good advantage by the participants and Lord help the rear-echelon GI who wandered into the fray. Although the officer in charge of the Trianon was an old 88th man, Lt. William Hearne of Greensboro, North Carolina, a former rifle platoon leader, the Blue Devils were chucked out just as impartially and enthusiastically as the rest.

166

Montecatini was where the civilian population had lived before the war on the free-spending tourists of all nations who came there for the health baths. Mussolini had a villa on the outskirts of town. Montecatini, during the GI occupation, was where the civilians existed by taking in GI washing, working for the military in its hotels or dining rooms, or working on the military—free-spending tourists of another era—by selling souvenirs, knick-knacks, *vino* or roast chestnuts, the latter at a fantastic price for *castagna*. As usual, the *signorinas* and GIs got along very well despite language barriers and several-score marriages resulted from the fraternizing. Mussolini's villa was taken over by CIC detachments. The GI tourist boom was bigger, and richer, than anything the splendid town had seen in peace days. The Fifth Army Red Cross unit known formerly as "The Tent Club" set up in Montecatini and soon had one of the best clubs operating in all Italy. An unofficial queen of jitterbugs, known to thousands of GIs by no other name than Mississippi—her real name was Ann Jenkins of Alabama—was one of the nightly attractions in the ballroom, while Helena Day, Margo, Rosemarie, Eleanor Bailey, Lolo and Bob Smith worked overtime to make the club, and the BTO Room, a terrific success.

"We're Off Again" was the current stage hit in town, and the show name became the 88th's motto in a matter of weeks as orders came to move back into the lines. The Division took over the sector to the east of Highway 65 and settled down to a routine of patrolling and active defense of the sector. Kraut artillery was murderous and reserve as well as front-line areas were subjected to fierce barrages. A scheduled line straightening attack was called off when it became evident from increased enemy activity that our plans were known to him. Christmas in the line was a bleak one. "Peace on earth" was a bit hard to believe but the doughboys looked to the New Year with hope. Again in January, units of the 88th began shuttling back to Montecatini for rest.

There had been changes in command during the months following the Apennines slowdown, chief of which sent Brig. Gen. Guy O. Kurtz to command of Fifth Army Artillery. Brig. Gen. Thomas E. Lewis, former Fifth Army Artillery head, succeeded General Kurtz. From the 34th Division came Brig. Gen. Harry B. Sherman to replace Brigadier General Ramey as Assistant Division Commander. In the 349th, Col. Percy E. LeStourgeon was named to succeed Colonel Crawford, rotated to the United States. Col. Franklin P. Miller assumed command of the 351st when Colonel Champeny was ordered to the States for a new assignment. At the top, General Kendall made his second star, and the Fifth Army

Troops returning to bivouac area after working on secondary defense positions.

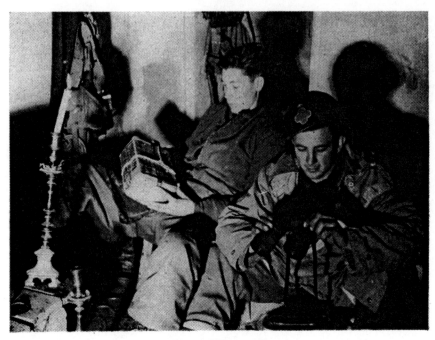

"Merry Christmas!"

command was taken over by Lt. Gen. Lucian K. Truscott, Jr. as Lt.
Gen. Mark W. Clark moved to command the 15th Army Group.

From the States came word that an 88th man had been honored by
Notre Dame. During his junior and senior years at Notre Dame, John M.
Hennessey, Jr. of Louisville, Kentucky, had often mentioned to one of
his teachers, a Father Leahy, that some day he hoped to merit from his
schoolmates the honored Irish yell: "He's a man! Who's a man! He's a
Notre Dame man!" In 1941, Hennessey graduated with honors—but not
that one. On July 14, 1944, Hennessey, then a field artillery captain with
the 88th, was killed in action. During a pre-game football rally in the fall
of 1944, Father Leahy got up and told the students about Hennessey's
death and his unsatisfied ambition. Father Leahy's last words were
drowned out by a terrific clamor for: "Yell, yell, yell!" and every Irish
throat roared forth in a wall-quaking: "He's a man! Who's a man! He's
a Notre Dame man! Hennessey! Hennessey! Hennessey!"

On the 17th of January in the rest area, some of the 88th's old battles
and heroes were remembered, and honored with formal presentation
ceremonies. Top award was a Medal of Honor to 2nd Lt. Charles W.
Shea of The Bronx, New York and the 350th, for his performance in
his first forty minutes of combat action on Mt. Damiano during the first
hours of the May 1944 pushoff. The 3d Battalion, 351st, and the 2d
Battalion, 350th, were awarded the Distinguished Unit Citation for ac-

170

Familiar road signs make their appearance as German long-range artillery starts reaching back.

tions at Laiatico and Mt. Battaglia, respectively. To Major Erwin B. Jones, 350th, T/Sgt. Manuel Mendoza, 350th, and Capt. John J. King, 349th, went the Distinguished Service Cross for their valorous deeds during the drive through the Apennines.

Because Rome trips and the Florence Army Rest Center could accommodate, at best, only a comparative few of the 88th, the Division opened its own rest center in Montecatini. Three hotels were taken over by the Division, a housekeeping cadre went to work and in less than a week, combat-weary 88th men were relaxing in the Blue Devil Rest Center. A dance orchestra from the Division Band played nightly at dinner and several nights a week for rest center dances. Considered a model of its kind, the 88th Rest Center won praise as a morale factor from higher headquarters and the idea soon was adopted by all other units of the Fifth Army.

Back into the lines again and the 88th took the sector astride Highway 65. For the first time since the May 1944 jumpoff, the Division was in an area where a fair network of roads was available and transportation could move without bogging down in the morass that had passed for roads in previous sectors under Division control. With the battles in Germany and the Pacific reaching a series of dramatic climaxes, the static front of the Italian campaign was not headline news—not even in Italy. The war settled down to what was basically an infantry war, a struggle of man against man, patrol against patrol, mortar against mortar. The

171

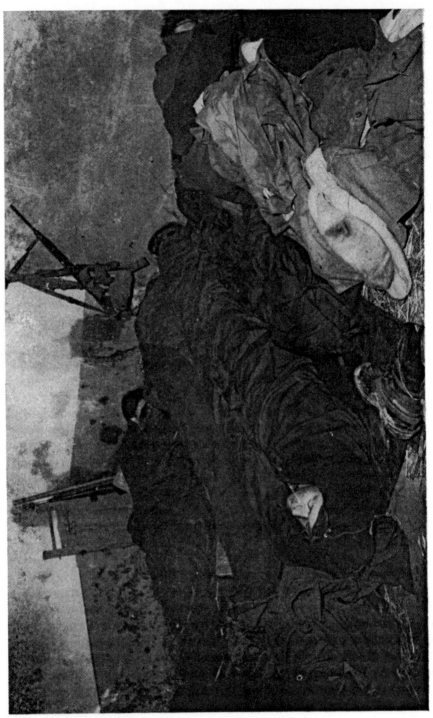

Sacked in.

Final briefing before checking out on a daylight patrol.

spectacular news and communiqués of the drive from below Rome to the Gothic Line were out. Since the Gothic Line the chief job had been to pin down the 26 German divisions in northern Italy so that they could not be used elsewhere. Despite predictions from experts in the United States, the enemy showed no signs of withdrawing and became, in the understatement that is military parlance, "increasingly sensitive to our patrols."

The fierceness of the fire fights mentioned so briefly in the daily Italian front communiqués could best be illustrated by an action involving a platoon leader of the 350th, who killed 4 Krauts and captured 16 while breaking up an enemy strongpoint opposing his platoon's advance. Hearing German voices from the reverse slope of a hill, Lt. Frederick L. Griffiths of Shaker Heights, Ohio, ran several times to the crest, hurled hand grenades into the Kraut trenches and then ducked below the brow of the hill to escape heavy return fire. After Griffiths had exhausted his supply of grenades, 16 Krauts came up the hill with their hands above their heads and 4 were found dead in their positions.

In the 351st, a special volunteer group of fighters was organized into a hard-hitting unit. They called themselves the Ranger Platoon, and were led by Lt. Ralph Decker of Los Angeles, California. And Decker really led the way. On one patrol against a suspected enemy strongpoint, Decker and his men were held up by two Kraut machine guns. Decker rushed the

Patrol members plot route as coffee comes to a boil.

emplacement and forced the surrender of the crew. While searching the house, Decker found a dugout occupied by several Krauts. They refused to come out. Decker tossed two grenades into the dugout, then planted 60 pounds of explosives on top and blew it up. He then covered the withdrawal of his patrol.

Another patrol, led by Lt. Linnsey L. Wheeler of Addy, Washington, furnished a line for a communiqué. But the story behind the line was much more interesting. Wheeler was leading a five-man patrol when they were challenged by a sentry. Wheeler got him with a tommy burst, then stormed the building. In a brief duel he mowed down one Kraut coming out of the door with a machine gun in his arms. In a hand-to-hand struggle, he took care of another Kraut. As the patrol moved back, one man was wounded by a mine. Wheeler sent the patrol in and remained with the wounded man to protect him until help arrived.

No wonder the enemy became increasingly sensitive to our patrols. Those patrols weren't out just for the walk.

Freezing cold and snow covered the front, and Highway 65 was like a skating rink. Most of the war correspondents holed up for the winter in Florence and Rome, but a few of the old faithful like Sid Feder of the Associated Press, Jack Foisie, Stan Swinton, Bob Fleischer of *Stars and Stripes* came up front to cover the winter war. There were stories to get, if the correspondents wanted to come up and dig for them. Stories like the artillerymen of the 338th who combined comfort with business and

174

A signalman tracing a broken field wire in a maze of communication lines.

set up their guns under pyramidal tents. The artillerymen, whose personal problems about keeping dry were thus solved, were enthusiastic about the idea, and 1st Sgt. Al Scotti of Long Island, New York, said, "It keeps the boys happy and the Krauts confused. Nice combination." A lad named Pfc. William N. Zane of Camden, New Jersey, and an ammo carrier in a mortar squad of the 349th, achieved passing fame when he was labeled as the best-dressed man in Fifth Army, even in combat, by *Stars and Stripes*. Then there was Lt. Mauricio Aragon of Avondale, Arizona, who showed up one day at the 349th CP, told them he was very glad to have been awarded the Bronze Star but that he would be much happier if the citation did not read "Posthumous Award." "When the shrapnel hit my wrist on Hill 499 I told the platoon sergeant I was going back to the hospital," he related. Regimental Headquarters was a bit reluctant until field-commissioned Lieutenant Aragon appeared to convince one and all that the report of his death was slightly exaggerated. Pvt. John Drews of Portchester, New York, hit the mail jackpot when he raked in 175 letters and seven packages from a 349th mail orderly. Drews asked for—and got —a three-day pass so he could read them. A chap named Sgt. Paul Revere of Braintree, Massachusetts, turned up as a forward artillery observer with the 350th. A descendant of the American Revolutionary war hero, Revere was not very clear on his relationship except that it "had something to do with my great-great-grandmother."

An inquisitive artilleryman, Cpl. James Nolan of Brooklyn, New

175

Battle-weary.

A rear QM ration depot.

York, had a long-standing curiosity satisfied when he went on a patrol with the infantry. On the way up the boot, Nolan had had his adventures. During the march on Rome he returned from a wire-laying job to discover that he'd been in German territory. Later, near the Arno, a *Teller* mine destroyed his six-by-six but miraculously blew him clear. Yet Nolan wasn't satisfied. He kept wondering how tough it really was for infantrymen on patrol and finally asked if he could go alone on a company-strength infantry raid. The answer was, "Yes, but you're crazy." They gave him a carbine and two grenades, both of the latter being lost on the way out through the taped minefields. At 2100 hours the patrol reached an objective. One doughboy claimed they were only six miles from Bologna but no one was exactly sure. Machine guns and mortars opened up. For seven and a half hours Nolan crouched against the hard ground. At last the word came to pull back. There had been casualties and no prisoners had been taken. Once back, Nolan lost his curiosity for patrol work.

There were tragic stories too. A detail from Company B, 313th Engineers, was working with mines in preparation for the installation of a defensive minefield. The mines, about 200 in all, were loaded on a truck and the men were beginning to open the boxes when the mines exploded. Fourteen men were killed and 18 were wounded. Two trucks were demolished and the house in which the engineers had been living was blown down by the force of the explosion.

177

Livergnano.

Although it was a defensive war, in this winter of 1945, it was a bitter war. Our patrols probed enemy defenses nightly—our artillery pumped shells at his guns and supply dumps—our planes and his strafed and bombed highways on both sides of the lines. The cold and ice and snow made life miserable for the doughboys. And there always was the ever-present threat of death. Staff sections of the Division, after study of all available information, formulated new plans for defense of the area and new plans for attack as well, for in answer to rumors that the Krauts might try a drive similar to the Ardennes push in France, General Kendall passed the word along that "the 88th will not retreat an inch."

Back in the States, communiqués from the Italian front were brief and almost perfunctory in their description of "heavy patroling constituted the only activity" on the Fifth Army front. All press and civilian eyes seemed to be on the battle fronts of France and Germany and the Italian front came to be known bitterly among the men who fought and died on it as "the forgotten front." What the press and public did not realize was that some 26 enemy divisions were tied down on the Italian front by the Fifth and Eighth Armies—enemy divisions which, if able to be transferred from Italy, might have been used to good advantage on the Eastern or Western Fronts. Civilian military analysts brushed off the Italian front as though it never existed, or if they bothered to mention it at all, dismissed it casually by saying that they had information which indicated that the bulk of the German armies was withdrawing from Italy. The

178

Sweeping for enemy mines.

doughboys up in the lines wondered, as they fought off patrol raids, who had supplied that erroneous information to the analysts. It could be called a quiet war. There were many who compared it to the months of static warfare along the Garigliano front. Without headlines or fanfare, men were wounded there, died there. Relatives at home, who read the newspapers, wrote their sons in the firing line "how glad I am that you are in Italy, where there is no fighting." That was the hardest blow of all. That was really tough to take after coming in off a difficult patrol or sweating out an artillery barrage.

"We're getting letters from home now telling us that we're all coming home soon, that we'll be there in a month or so at the most," said S/Sgt. Mitchell Jasinski of New Bedford, Massachusetts. "They talk like they know more than we do about the war. Those letters about coming home are bad. They get us all excited over nothing. They shouldn't write that stuff."

In mid-February, Gen. George C. Marshall, Chief of Staff of the U.S. Army, visited the Italian front. His 88th tour included lunch at the Division CP after which he inspected the 2d Battalion, 350th, in a sunlit field over which whistled outgoing shells. He awarded the DSC to Lt. Steven M. Kosmyna of Perth Amboy, New Jersey, and all the assorted generals present praised the combat records of the 350th and the 88th. Later General Marshall inspected installations of the 338th Field Artillery. What he saw during his tour was "very reassuring," he said in an

Chow line.

official statement. "The difficulties of the mountainous country, with few roads and winter conditions, are very real. The strength of the enemy's positions in such a country is equally apparent. Under these conditions, our U.S. troops and those of our Allies have done a splendid job and made a great contribution to the war. A large German force has been held in Italy and prevented from bolstering the enemy's hard-pressed troops on the Eastern and Western fronts." General Marshall, who was met at the 15th Army Group CP by a guard of honor composed of military representatives of twelve nationalities of the Fifth and Eighth Armies, had high praise for the teamwork displayed in Italy by the United Nations. The mixed guard of honor was commanded by Major Erwin B. Jones of the 350th.

During the days and nights in the Winter Line, several thousand replacements had been funneled up to the 88th. In order to prevent what had happened during the Apennines drive, regimental replacement pool training areas were instituted and the new men were given several weeks of indoctrination and battle training before they were assigned to units. Officers and selected noncoms from the units to which they were to be assigned were sent back to the replacement pools to help train the new men. The newcomers were glad to have the advice and experience of the combat veterans made available to them.

On its first battle anniversary, March 5, 1945, its rounding out of

Regimental commanders: Col. Franklin P. Miller, 351st; Col. James C. Fry, 350th; Col. Percy E. LeStourgeon, 349th.

twelve months in combat, the 88th knew it no longer was a young division, "a new outfit." Its men had long since forgotten that they had been called draftees, had comprised the first all-Selective Service infantry division to go into combat on any front in this war. During those twelve months, the Division had piled up 317 days of combat time. Individual honors won in this period included two awards of the Medal of Honor, one Distinguished Service Medal, 22 Distinguished Service Cross, 50 Legion of Merit, 321 Silver Star and clusters, 1,313 Bronze Star and clusters, 7 Soldier's Medal, 12,000 Purple Heart and more than 14,000 of the Combat Infantryman Badge. Overall casualty lists showed 11,285 names: with 2,137 killed, 8,248 wounded, 521 missing in action, and 379 captured during the year. It had left its youth at Santa Maria Infante, Cianelli, Mt. Bracchi, Itri, Fondi, Rome, Laiatico, Bloody Ridge, Volterra, San Miniato, Mt. Acuto, Gesso, Mt. Capello, Mt. Grande, Mt. Battaglia, and a score or more of other towns and villages—on every mountain that it fought up and over—had met and conquered 12 German divisions—had scrawled its proud Cloverleaf across mile after mile of mud and blood and battle. It knew, as it held in the Winter Line that its battle path still had many more miles to be trod, and fought, on that road home.

Clare Boothe Luce talks with a group of 351st "Rangers."

In an effort to find out, if possibe, the reasons which motivated a soldier going into battle, the 349th I&E Office sponsored an essay contest, open only to rifle companies, on "Why I Fight." The judges were three NCOs chosen from the battalions with instructions to "pick what you think best expresses the feeling of most of the men, not something flowery you think the colonel might like." The judges' choice was a letter written by Pvt. Edward C. White of Worcester, Massachusetts, a rifleman in I Company.

White's letter said, "You would be surprised how many there are who couldn't answer that [Why I Fight] without deliberating a few minutes and still be vague. Even as I write, I am prone to stop and take a few puffs from a cigarette, thinking it over more carefully. There are millions of good reasons why I or any man fights. There is the reason ballyhooed by patriotic citizens, 'Fight for life, liberty and pursuit of happiness. Fight for your country.' One can also fight for his loved ones, his home and security, his job, kept open for him by a grateful employer—all of these are good reasons. I fight for all of these, of course, but I also have other, more intimate reasons.

"I'd like to go out and walk along the streets in 'civvies' without a pass or an 'Off Limits' sign to mar my pleasure. I'd like to have a key on my keyring for my own door of my own home, to be able to sit comfortably

182

Brigadier General Thomas C. Lewis
He took over the Redlegs in January 1945.

before the radio and listen to Bob Hope. There are thousands of other little things, like: Sipping malteds at Scotty's or playing the latest hit tunes on the jukebox. Bowling a few strings at the Bowling Green, or buying the latest Dorsey or James recordings and having the gang over to the house for an evening and cleaning up the mess after they leave. It's all those little things put together that makes me want to fight. Those are

183

the things that make life colorful, lend zest to the art of living. Without those little things—which you never appreciate until they're not there any more—all the big reasons wouldn't mean much," White concluded.

The winter, and the lull, were beginning to break. Early in March, the 88th was pulled out of the line and sent to a combination rest and specialized training area near Florence. There was more training than rest and with the snows disappearing under the impact of an early spring sun, the 88th worked hard to get in shape for the drive it had long expected, the drive which would take it those final few miles through the Apennines, the few miles it had not been able to make in the fall of 1944 and which had rankled in Division memory ever since. Command changes moved Colonel Fry to the post of Assistant Division Commander and Col. Avery M. Cochran took over the 350th. On March 31, in a full Division review at the Florence airport, the 88th demonstrated its readiness to the top commanders who came to see it perform.

Once we identified the United States 88th Division we knew where the main effort would be . . .

MAJOR GENERAL VON SCHELLWITZ
CG, GERMAN 305TH INFANTRY DIVISION

THE PO VALLEY

The Po Valley drive was the nearest to a Victory Parade the 88th Division ever got. Except for the first three days before the breakthrough, the drive was more of a footrace with all Fifth Army divisions bouncing around in each other's sectors like chickens in a neighbor's back yard, and scrambling off in task forces to capture big cities whenever and wherever they pleased. The Krauts, completely disorganized, surrendered by regiments, fought among themselves or tried frantically to get off the flat land and up into the mountains of the Inner Fortress.

Fighting under what was politely called a "military security blackout," the 88th shot like an arrow out of a taut bow and spearheaded from the Apennines to the Brenner Pass. Because of a strange, and at times unfair, Army policy of deleting all mention of the 88th from official communiqués in the early days of the push, the Blue Devils got scant press credit for their achievements. But if they failed to get the headlines, they got something vastly more important in the long run—they got Krauts and territory and the thrill of smashing the enemy into final surrender high in the Tyrolean Alps. There was no stopping the Division on the ground.

Once into that flat and long-promised land of the Po Valley after cutting through two Nazi divisions and practically fighting through two American divisions which had left their sectors and angled across our line of advance, the 88th broke through to the Po River, crossed it, flanked a prepared defense line and clawed its way through the highest mountains in Italy to a junction at the Brenner Pass with the Seventh Army and the European front. On their final rampage the Blue Devils destroyed three Nazi divisions, partially destroyed three more, badly mauled six others and bagged 38,000 prisoners before the Krauts called it a day and a war and surrendered.

Although fighting men of neither side knew it, the war in Italy was on its last legs before the final push ever got started. It was over and won, and all that remained to be done was the fighting. German and Allied representatives were holding preliminary peace talks in Italy and Switzerland as the doughs began preparations for the final assault. The fighting men didn't know this, but they could sense that the end was near. The news from Europe was so good that they had no desire for another push against the fanatical Krauts who held Italy. In their opinion it would be better to sit tight along the Italian line and let it fall with the expected capitulation of German forces in Europe. But Allied commanders, although already dickering for peace terms, had other ideas and figured that one more heave would do the trick.

Since the Krauts knew the strength and disposition of all Allied front-

Monterumici, taken by the 349th and 350th in some of the toughest fighting in the drive to the Po Valley.

line units in Italy from long association and the long patrolling in the stagnant winter line—just as we knew his units—the necessary deception and hiding of the main assault direction was hard to achieve. To accomplish it insofar as possible, the "scramble" plan was devised. Briefly, this plan called for a shuffling of divisions along the entire front with portions of divisions showing up in the line at scattered and unexpected places both to confuse enemy agents behind our lines and patrols from enemy front-line units. Another part of the plan called for a "whipsaw" strategy of attack—jumping off on different days in widely divergent sectors so as to keep the enemy off balance, keep him shifting forces to meet each new attack and confused until the very end as to the location and direction of the main assault. During the winter everything had been built up for this final drive and the Allies had everything in their favor. Nothing had been overlooked; this time the Po Valley would be reached.

Immediately after the Division review at the Florence airport, the 88th Division was placed under a security blackout and on paper, at least, it ceased to exist. All identifying markers were painted off trucks and vehicles, shoulder insignia vanished, road signs were encoded, and all troops were instructed not to identify themselves or their units to anyone, even friends or other Allied troops. Then the scramble plan went into operation. The 350th Combat Team moved to an area near the mouth of the Arno River for intensive river-crossing training. Battalions of the 349th were split up between the 34th and 91st Divisions, while the 351st and the artillery units remained in the training area near Florence. In a few days the plan was shuffled again. The 351st went to Pisa, the 350th to Pietramala, and the 349th took over the 34th Division sector. Artillery units went to calibration areas near the Arno and then began moving into silent positions in a sector west of Highway 65. One provisional battalion was sent to Forli and attached to Eighth Army, providing new specula-

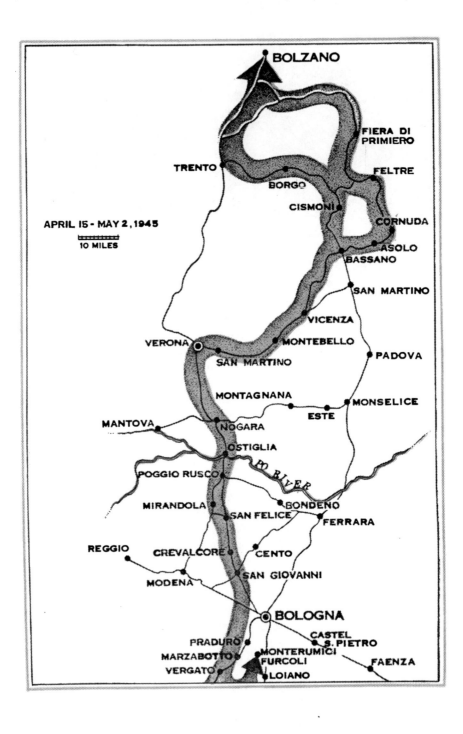

INTO THE PO VALLEY

In early April 1945 the armies in Italy were alerted for what everyone knew was the final campaign of the war; Victory was in the air.

II Corps of the Fifth Army had the most difficult task, and the Blue Devils were given the main effort. The 88th Division faced the enemy along Furcoli Ridge and opposite Monterumici. The 91st Division was on the right and the South Africans immediately to the left.

The story of the campaign consists of an all-out slugging contest which eventually broke the enemy line. Then came the swift pursuit through the Po Valley where 38,000 prisoners of war were sent to the rear from the Blue Devils' zone of action.

A double hope for the future.

tion for enemy agents who were trying to ascertain just where the 88th would be committed. With our regiments spread from Pisa almost to Bologna and with advance details in Forli, this policy did succeed in confusing the enemy—he expected us at any one of a half dozen different points, except at the point where we finally hit him.

While maintaining screening forces and normal patrols in their old sectors, the 91st moved astride Highway 65, the 34th went to the right of the 91st. On the left or west of 65 was the 88th and on its left flank the 6th South African Armored Division. The buildup continued during the early part of April with attacks in the Eighth Army sector near the Adriatic while the 92d Infantry Division jumped off for Massa in Western Italy. Further deception was practiced in the II Corps zone with sudden crescendos of massed artillery fire on selected areas across the Corps front, followed by probing infantry patrols to simulate attacks. On the 9th of April, the Eighth Army jumped off in its major effort to cross the Senio River. The 88th continued moving into silent positions. On April 14 the air support for the IV Corps attack commenced, followed by the jump-off of the U.S. 10th Mountain Division, the Brazilian Expeditionary Force and the U.S. 1st Armored Division. On the left of IV Corps, the 92d Division in Massa identified a new German division on its front, showing that Kraut reserves were being shifted and committed. The plan was working. On the Eighth Army front the British crossed the Reno River to make the main effort on the north and in the south the fall of Imola marked the rapid progress of the Polish Corps. The entire II Corps front remained ominously quiet but contrary to our hopes, the Kraut there showed no signs of withdrawing or shifting. He still intended to defend Bologna and that approach to the Po Valley with all he had.

Main objective for the 88th was, as usual, a tough nut. For six months the Kraut had dug his defenses into the caves, smashed buildings and ridges of the jagged mountains which faced the II Corps and the 88th. Before the assault the 88th Division was under the foot and around the leg of a boot-shaped ridge running north and south from Mt. Adone at the top of the boot to Monterumici at the ankle end, with caves and gullies of Furcoli as the war-vulcanized heel, thence west to the key hills of 427, 403 and 375 along the boot sole and finally to the narrow toe in the Setta River. The crack German 8th Mountain Division, defending this boot during the winter, had fought off patrols of three American divisions and had learned to cover every possible avenue of approach. Its importance to the Germans was emphasized by Major General Schricker, commander of the enemy 8th Mountain Division, who told his troops that "Monteru-

Krauts holed up in caves like this on Monterumici and stood off the 88th for three days.

mici at this time is the most vital sector of the entire division. I have no doubt that the enemy will make every effort to take possession of the Monterumici feature in order to obtain a basis for a large-scale attack." In the early morning of the 15th the screening elements of the 34th and 91st withdrew through our lines and the 88th Division, reinforced, prepared to continue the attack to destroy the German organization in Italy.

The 15th of April was a clear, warm day and in the morning the first planes came over. There were 765 heavy bombers and 200 medium bombers with assigned missions along Highways 65 and 64. Rover Pete flew close-support missions and at 1630 hours the dive bombers blitzed Mt. Sole in the South African sector with fire bombs and rockets. Then at 2230 hours the artillery erupted in 30,000 rounds of supporting fire for the infantrymen who were commencing the advance into the enemy defenses. At 2230 hours the last great assault of the Allied armies in Italy began with the 349th and 350th Infantry Regiments jumping off on time. Almost immediately the enemy proved his intentions to defend his winter positions to the last round and by midnight our assault battalions hardly had reached the main line of resistance. By 0120 hours the 6th South Africans had attacked up bomb-scorched Mt. Sole to entrench two companies on the peak despite heavy casualties and at 0300 hours the 91st and 34th Divisions jumped off in their attack zones against stiff resistance.

192

Daylight found our regiments in exposed positions. The 3d Battalion, 349th Infantry, was stopped by the cliffs and defensive fires at K-12; while the 1st Battalion had scarcely reached the outskirts of Furcoli. The 350th Infantry had reached the ridge beneath the towering walls of enemy-occupied Mt. Adone, but neither La Torre on the south of the saddle nor Santa Lucia on the north was in our hands. A platoon of medium tanks was detached from the 350th Infantry and given to the 349th to assist in clearing the caves and strongpoints of Furcoli. And a directive was addressed to the Commanding Officer, 349th Infantry: "Continue the attack during daylight hours, 16 April, employing armor . . . Renew attack 2100B, passing 2d Battalion through 1st Battalion to capture objectives in zone . . ."

In the assault lines the fight continued. Reports trickled in.

1120B. Captain Honeycutt, 349th Infantry, by telephone. "Have people on top of Furcoli ridge. They seem to hold west half of ridge. Are working up on 403. Are trying to get tanks and TDs in position to support. People are receiving heavy mortar fire. Have only cleared west half of Furcoli."

1125B. Telephone from 350th. "Are now coming out of Di Sotto and heading toward cemetery in Di Sopra."

1225B. 349th called. "A little hot time right now. Di Sopra is still directing fire on our people on Furcoli ridge and has forced some people to draw back . . . Have committed A Company which is moving up to reinforce B Company.

1315B. Call from 350th. "Company I is on top of Monterumici [Hill 578]. Not in village of Di Sotto . . . All around and above it . . . working on cemetery." (The enemy had allowed an entire company to pass through Di Sotto before opening fire on the following troops, E Company, splitting and disorganizing it by surprise fire.)

1615B. Phoned from 350th. "Forming up to go into Di Sotto again."

1805B. 350th Infantry. "Are temporarily out of contact with one company near the cemetery . . . Krauts are dug in on top of highest point . . . Troops never got quite into Di Sotto . . . Going to put in two companies of Red tonight . . . One to take Sopra, the other to help out on Sotto."

1810B. 349th called. "Three tanks are up in Furcoli. A Company started up on the hill to go west but is now stopped at the road junction in Furcoli."

1835B. Colonel Cochran, CO, 350th, called General Kendall. "We have just shot some Krauts off the top of the hill with TDs and I am getting ready to get my 1st Battalion up tonight." The General replied, "You may have to move the 2d Battalion in towards Monterumici. We've got to get that mountain tonight."

1945B. S-3, 349th Infantry. "B Company sits almost at the top of Hill 497 [above Furcoli]. Can't get over top. A Company has joined B. Is to cut left north of road and clear rest of Furcoli ridge to 427. Want to get C Company to 403 . . . G Company to follow A Company to Il Poggiale and 379 and Le Braine. A stops to hold 427. The 2d Battalion drives to K-12 and Vado. Difficulty with K-12 is limited room for maneuver . . ."

2010B. II Corps sent a TWX. "In order to obtain maximum results from blows already struck and to prevent regrouping and reorganization of the enemy, commanders of all echelons will continue the present drive without pause and with maximum energy until a breakthrough is forced."

At 2150B, the Division Commander called his regimental commanders. "The Division has had light casualties—fewer than a hundred—and has taken no prisoners . . . we must go where the Kraut is and take our objective."

The South Africans on our left flank were winning a magnificent success as they seized the tri-cornered features, Mt. Cappana, Mt. Sole and Mt. Abelie. But the 88th seemed to make no gains, and C Company, 349th Infantry, hit on the flanks by a counterattack, fell back to its H-hour positions, twenty-four hours after the jump-off. The 351st Infantry moved to close reserve positions in Trasasso.

April 17th was the hardest day of fighting.

0245B. 349th on the phone. "Company A beginning to move on Hill 403. The 2d Battalion with F Company going to Le Braine, G Company in rear of F Company headed for Poggiale. L Company got as far as K-12 along with two tanks. One tank was hit by some kind of a shell or bazooka. They received a counterattack and had to pull back with remaining tank to Ca Valla."

0600B. The first good news of the day from the 350th. "The 1st Battalion definitely has Di Sopra and are having a terrific fire fight." And by 0835B they could report, "Company A attacking highest point on hill now . . . K Company has a platoon in the cemetery . . . 2d Battalion is in good shape . . . 3d Battalion will garrison the hill after reorganization."

And General Kendall replied on this day of agonized inching into the stubborn Kraut defenses, "the whole situation is going to loosen."

By 0910, there were four companies on Monterumici, the first Division objective to be captured since the grim autumn days of Monte Grande. The situation seemed to improve even for the 349th Infantry as

C Company pushed well forward into Il Poggiale with F Company holding the rim of a bowl above Le Braine.

But by midnight the 349th Infantry had to report: "Company A still trying for Hill 427 . . . Tank to support them hit a mine west of Furcoli . . . G Company is pretty well pocketed now." The 350th Infantry, though claiming Monterumici, was fighting hard under Mt. Adone with the 2d Battalion and was painfully moving the 1st Battalion off the ridge onto the western slopes, while the 3d Battalion on top of Monterumici was unable to make patrol contact with the 349th Infantry directly below them in Furcoli.

Reserve power was given the 349th Infantry by the 88th Reconnaissance Troop which relieved the 3d Battalion (0300) and allowed it to attack through the 1st Battalion at daylight; but the picture remained black. After 55 hours of steady fighting, the breakthrough seemed as far distant as ever. The 350th Infantry reported, "It looks as if we are about stopped for the time being . . . 2d Battalion can't make much progress . . ." The 349th added at 0610B, "We don't know whether or not G Company has been captured . . . E Company in Poggiale couldn't find them . . . F Company unable to make progress towards Le Braine."

Then at 0955 Colonel Fry called from E Company field phone that the 3d Battalion had cleared Hill 427 and was calling for tank support, and stated, "Things are breaking. Must put the heat on."

But already the black picture had reached higher headquarters, and at 1025B, exactly one-half hour after our own breakthrough began, the 88th Division received verbal orders to move to exploit the IV Corps penetration: "The 351st Regiment is to move into the Vergato area . . . prepare to attack 21 April under operational control IV Corps . . . The remainder of Division will follow . . . Mt. Adone has fallen to the 361st."

No journal reports could tell the story of the men who, though not wanting to fight and risk possible wounds or death so near to the probable end of the war, nevertheless went into action and with savage fury rooted the Germans out of those caves which for months had frowned down on 88th lines and made life miserable for the doughs who had spent the long winter months crouched before them, hardly daring to move. The stories of men like Sgt. Niel F. Luckie of Artesia, New Mexico, and the 349th, who set up his machine gun on a bare knoll and knocked out three Kraut machine guns as his B Company struggled toward Furcoli. And Capt. Robert E. Richard of Newark, New Jersey, the commanding officer of B, who lost a foot in a minefield after he'd brought his men up but nevertheless dragged himself to a tank, clung to the side of it and directed tank fire on Jerry machine guns until they quit firing. And S/Sgt. Billy J.

From this height German defenders had perfec

servation on troops pushing toward the Po Valley.

Blue Devils advance past wrecked tank after the breakthrough at Monterumici.

Edmundson of Linneus, Missouri, who was leading his squad in an attack on machine-gun nests when he stepped on a mine and was wounded seriously. Edmundson lay there in the minefield shouting instructions to his squad, pointing out targets and firing rifle grenades with such accuracy that he killed four and wounded five Kraut gunners. Or T/5 Albert C. Burke of Rochester, New York, who got seven men and two flamethrowers to within two hundred yards of their destination when enemy mortars wounded all of them. Burke brought the wounded back to an aid station then returned to the spot, picked up both flamethrowers and delivered them personally.

What real chance had the Krauts when GIs like Pfc. Orville G. Warren of Belleville City, Illinois, and K Company, 350th, started after them? Warren crawled through a minefield to flank Kraut riflemen who were holding up his squad's advance. He killed three with rifle shots, then accounted for two more with a delayed grenade; stayed out there blazing away until his company moved up. Or S/Sgt. Ernest C. Hardesty of Tulsa, Oklahoma, who got his trapped squad out of a minefield by calmly working under mortar and machine-gun fire until he had disarmed enough of the mines to clear a path, then went back in and carried out the wounded. In an early morning counterattack against G Company, 350th, 1st Lt. George Fumich, Jr., of Pursglove, West Virginia, showed the Krauts what manner of men was coming at them. Fumich dashed to the top of a hill and in full view of the enemy he began tossing hand grenades, pulling the pin, holding the grenade a few seconds then lobbing it into the air so it burst like an air bomb. Fumich disposed of a box of grenades in this manner, and a score or more of enemy soldiers. Lt. Col. Donald A. Yongue of Summerville, North Carolina, won the nickname "Bare Fist Colonel" when he surprised a Kraut with a machine pistol and knocked out the startled gunner with two staggering blows.

The medics, as usual, were calmly heroic, and got sore if they were called that. Pfc. Henry Perkins of Philadelphia, worked like a Trojan taking care of K Company wounded. A GI tripped a mine on a steep slope and fell seriously wounded. Perkins rushed into the minefield, staked the wounded man into a position to keep him from sliding and then reset both his legs in the middle of a barrage that drove others to cover. Perkins treated three more mine casualties and then aided litter bearers in moving the wounded over minestrewn trails to the aid station. Another outstanding medic was Pfc. Marshall R. Weigott, Jr., of Cincinnati, Ohio, and attached to B Company, 350th. Weigott, in the midst of a hail of fire, treated and helped evacuate twenty wounded. He worked until he collapsed but next day was back on the job.

Krauts captured in the Po Valley drive at the 88th PW cage in Poggio Rusco.

One of the strangest medic tales to come out of the war unfolded when Pvt. Theodore Weiss of Brooklyn, New York, and eight other medics got trapped behind enemy lines, then bargained their way to freedom. Weiss and eight litter-bearers went behind the lines to pick up two of our wounded. On the way back they were captured and taken to a German dugout, Weiss acting as spokesman. Weiss said he spent the next hours trying to swing a deal for their freedom but the German officer in charge insisted the only deal that could be made was a swap. The night before,

A medical battalion convoy crossing the Po over a ponton bridge.

An 88th patrol at the Po River bridge at Ostiglia.

the Kraut said, they had captured two of our aid men but released them to go back to G Company with four Kraut medics to treat the wounded. The Krauts had not returned. The swap, therefore, was to be the four German medics, plus the two previously captured aid men and two wounded men in exchange for our nine litter-bearers. Weiss shaded the deal to eliminate turning over the two aid men and got permission to go back to G Company CP. At the CP 1st Lt. Peter P. Mazur was against giving up the wounded and Weiss persuaded him to come back over on

Doughboys ride Alligators in the Po crossing.
201

Blue Devils dash for cover after establishing a bridgehead on the north bank of the Po.

the German side and argue it out. The argument lasted a couple of hours but the bargain finally was struck and carried out—nine litter bearers and two aid men for the four German medics.

One of the 88th's best known officers and once part of a unique father-son combination was killed on Monterumici. He was Capt. Charles P. Lynch, Jr., of Atlanta, Georgia, son of the former commanding officer of the 350th. Lynch went ahead as lead scout for his company which was to seize Monterumici ridge. He successfully directed an attack which resulted in capture of Di Sopra, encouraged his men to hold during two counterattacks and then led the men in the final assault on the ridge. He was killed when within ten yards of the top.

Major Edwin H. Marks, Jr., of Cincinnati, Ohio, and the 351st, won the Silver Star for his dangerous volunteer trip across 2,000 yards of fire-swept terrain to call off friendly artillery fire which was falling on our troops by mistake. At the 600-yard mark he was forced into a ditch by a Kraut machine gun; he crawled out of the line of fire and continued on. About four hundred yards more and he again was pinned, this time by an artillery barrage and fifteen enemy riflemen. Marks dodged this threat, and still later another Kraut machine gun. Finally he reached the artillery observer and got him to change direction of fire.

Although there was plenty of rough stuff ahead, the resistance of the Krauts at Monterumici was about the last organized resistance they were able to make against the 88th in Italy. Monterumici and Mt. Adone com-

Dressed to kill, Corporal Gregory Perez awaits the order to cross the Po.

prised their last real mountain defenses. On the other side of those heights the terrain sloped down to the Po Valley with its flat terrain and network of main and secondary roads. The Krauts had gambled everything on the mountains—and lost, finally. In the Po Valley they had little in the way of organized defenses and the campaign on those flatlands rapidly turned into a chase.

Leaving the 350th to continue north to assist the 91st Division, the 349th and 351st Combat Teams swung over to Highway 64, already clogged with the traffic of three divisions, to resume the attack. The 351st was ordered to jump off followed by the 349th, moving on Division order. All plans were thrown away, however as the 10th Mountain Division, racing diagonally to the right across the IV Corps front and far out of its sector, forced the 85th Division to conform to this diagonal. The tactics of both these divisions tended to pinch out the 88th. This resulted in a nightmare maneuver as the 351st attacked north through all enemy or

Antitank guns joined heavier artillery in furnishing support for troops crossing the Po River.

friendly units in its path; while the 350th, coming out of the hills at Praduro, had to cut through three divisions in order to come into Division reserve at Gesso. The 88th was the bottom of a gigantic T trying to punch through a top which was the 10th and 85th.

Such confusion might sound funny to some but to the doughs who were harassed by left-flank enemy pockets bypassed by other units and left for them to clean up, the sight of other American units deliberately and with no apparent reason cutting across their path, was a stupid and maddening procedure. No one benefited by the cowboy maneuver except the fleeing Krauts who gained precious hours to put valuable distance between themselves and the American divisions milling about in the last foothills before the Po. Front-line unit commanders were choleric as they attempted to unsnarl the tangle.

The mess finally was straightened out when it was agreed that 88th units would relieve in place all 85th units as they were overtaken. The original battle order was resumed and the 351st poured down out of the mountains and met only slight resistance on the plain. To the right Bologna had fallen to the 34th Division. To the left the 10th had cut Highway 9. The Kraut was on the run and orders came from Corps to utilize every possible means to move doughboys forward to press the pursuit and attack. Moving up on line the 349th and 351st pushed off abreast and headed due north. San Giovanni fell on the 21st to the spearhead, and both regiments doubletimed on to the Panaro River.

Moving to Crevalcore, the Division CP followed the infantry into town with surprised headquarters personnel rounding up a couple of equally surprised Krauts in the CP itself. Definitely annoyed at what he considered rear-echelon stuff, Colonel Miller of the 351st departed hastily

A tank of the 752d Tank Battalion which supported the attack on Vicenza, with a dead man at the controls, half demolishes a building.

from Crevalcore when the first headquarters trucks rolled in. Never before in any push had the Division CP tailed the infantry so closely. Kraut snipers in the fields wounded the Division Artillery Commander and one artillery battalion commanding officer was stranded for hours by German artillery which lay in between him and his outfit. A member of a billeting party flushed six Kraut snipers from a building he'd selected as a CP site. Crevalcore was a slightly confused town, but no more so than the rest of what the correspondents called "a fluid front."

By now the Krauts were surrendering in droves. Their supply lines snapped by fast-moving task forces and armored patrols, their transport wrecked by air bombardment, their spirits broken by the swift and relentless surge of American units across the Po plain, the Krauts had had more than enough and wanted to give up. PW cages in the 88th overflowed and they still kept coming in. Entire companies surrendered to advance scouts. Kraut columns on the roads were blocking our own units and front-line commanders began waving them into the fields, not wanting to bother to stop and take any more prisoners. PWs became a drug on the market as they tried desperately to surrender to somebody, anybody. The 88th's PW total swelled to 12,000 in three days.

Our doughs were tired but with the end now in sight, they forgot their weariness and kept punching on. Nothing is so heady as the wine of victory and the doughs wanted more of it. This was the kind of war

Wounded in the battle for Vicenza, a Blue Devil is carried to an aid station.

they'd read about, seen in the movies, and this was the kind of war they wanted to end as quickly as possible. Everything was on the move. The front had been smashed wide open and the 88th surged on to shatter what was left of the pieces. New objectives were taken and passed even before formal orders were issued designating them as objectives. In the rear heavy-tank units and bridging equipment struggled to keep pace with the high-stepping infantrymen.

Not all the Krauts surrendered. Snipers and isolated enemy pockets, often supported by tanks and self-propelled guns, fought on in hopeless, desperate delaying attempts. The attempts, and the Krauts who made them, were short-lived, thanks to GIs like Pfc. Stephen S. Lowicki of Bristol, Connecticut, and F Company, 351st. Lowicki put two machine guns out of action, killed one and captured twenty as he wiped out one pocket. And Sgt. Richard A. Robbins of Binghamton, New York, and the Recon Troop. When a company of Krauts cut off the jeep section of the 3d Platoon and bottled them up in a house, Robbins moved his armored car up to support the trapped group. In the open and wounded twice, Robbins kept his car firing until all of the platoon returned. Lt. Charles C. Haynes of Durham, North Carolina, and the 349th, led his men in a bayonet charge against a group which had forced them off their

206

supporting tanks. Haynes got six himself and his platoon overran the attackers, capturing 70 of them. Not all of our men lived to remember what they'd done. One who didn't was T/5 Bernard Smach of Binghamton, New York, a radio operator with a forward OP of the 913th Field. Smach took position in the top floor of a house to adjust artillery fire on a Kraut roadblock which had stopped the 351st near Crevalcore. Although an enemy mortar barrage partially wrecked the house. Smach stayed there more than a half hour until he'd brought the artillery in perfectly and broken up the roadblock. He then ran with his radio to another house to repeat the performance but a Kraut machine gun got him at the door.

The two assault regiments, alternating their battalions in line, continued their tireless, exhilarating pursuit. Crossing the Panaro River over a bridge captured intact, they raced on toward the Po. The 350th passed through the 351st on April 23 and by midnight that night, Colonel Fry and the motorized forces of the 2d Battalion, 350th, washed their hands in the Po River at Bonizzo. To our left in the IV Corps sector the 10th Mountain and 85th Divisions already were across the river heading north with a 36-hour start. Bridging equipment for the 88th was late in coming up and Corps orders were to cross in whatever manner possible. Wrecked and abandoned German equipment littered the south bank of the river, especially in the shambles that had been the town of Revere. Scrounging was excellent and the doughboys, waiting for orders to move across, filled in spare time by salvaging Kraut horses and vehicles and staging impromptu rodeos. II Corps MPs, humorless as usual, broke up the Wild West shows by impounding all Kraut vehicles.

By the time the Po River was reached the 88th had bagged 15,000 prisoners with the 349th accounting for more than 9,000 of the total. Prize catch was Major General Von Schellwitz, 305th Infantry Division commander, taken along with his headquarters staff by the 349th as it drove through Magnacavallo. The doughs who captured the Kraut "brass" were Pfc. Taylor Abercrombie of Hollywood, Calif., and Pfc. Joseph Wells of Weippe, Idaho. His division all but wiped out, General Von Schellwitz paid the Blue Devils one of their brightest compliments when he told interrogators that "as soon as I saw where the 88th Division was being committed I realized where the main effort would be—they have always spearheaded Fifth Army drives."

Shortly after noon on the 24th, the 351st Infantry's Ranger Platoon climbed across the struts of the smashed Ostiglia railroad bridge to establish the first 88th bridgehead on the north bank of the Po. Captain Charles D. Edmondson led the picked group. He and his men crawled

Street fighting in Vicenza.

along the railroad trestle to the broken span. Every Kraut on the north bank opened up on Edmondson as he swung down into the water at the end of a rope and struggled across the 100-foot gap to tie the final knot in the improvised hand bridge. Wounded, Edmondson climbed the ladder to the railbed and continued to lead his men in three hours of savage fighting before the bridgehead was secured. An engineer, S/Sgt. Robert J. McConlogue of Hollis, New York, accompanied the first 10-man patrol across, on a mission to determine if the bridge could be repaired for large bodies of troops. Expert spotting and directing of support artillery by Capt. John L. Corcoran of Chicago, silenced Kraut machine guns near Ostiglia which had attempted to stop the Rangers

On the double into Vicenza.

crossing. When the Rangers made it to the opposite bank, Corcoran used artillery and chemical mortars for a protective smoke screen to cover the infantry battalions which crossed in amphtracs and assault boats.

Once across the formidable barrier of the Po River, the race to Verona got under way. Verona, a key rail and communications center, was the Fifth Army objective. Driving for the city with a 36-hour head start were the 10th Mountain and 85th Divisions. It looked like a hopeless race as far as the 88th was concerned. But to the Blue Devils there was no such word as hopeless. Doughboys of the 351st in their seventh day of continuous marching, passed the 85th, drew parallel to the 10th, and after a record sprint of 35 miles entered Verona by midnight of the 25th, the

209

88th troops surge past the bodies of dead Germans to enter the key city of Verona.

first Allied troops in the city. The Spearhead lived up to its name. The 351st took Verona after chopping through 1st and 4th Parachute Division strongpoints along Highway 12. The 10th Mountain took the Villafranca airport and entered Verona from the west and was preparing to issue press releases on its capture when it learned, to the extreme annoyance and amazement of its staff officers, that troops of the 88th had beaten the 10th into the city.

Also amazed was an officer PW of the 4th Parachute Division who told his captors he considered it "absolutely impossible for you people to reach Verona in such a short space of time—how do you do it?" The footsore doughboys had no time to stop and tell him or to celebrate their achievement of taking a city whose fall split the German forces in the Po Valley and cut off the main escape route through the Brenner Pass.

The march to Verona was no ballet dance as many doughs could testify, including Pfc. Marvin A. Noll of Reading, Pennsylvania, and E Company, 351st. Noll, a member of a platoon about ten miles ahead of the battalion engaged in clearing secondary roads to Verona, took a jeep about two miles ahead of the platoon and found a group of 97 Krauts. Though he knew discovery meant instant death, Noll reconnoitered the setup and then returned to lead his platoon to a position from which all 97 were taken without firing a shot. Later when the platoon was attacked on the flank by a motorized unit, Noll stood his ground in a cross-fire of machine guns and bazookas and killed four, wounded three and captured eight. Pfc. Rodolpho Sanchez of Boise, Idaho, a lead scout for his squad, suddenly was surrounded by a group of Krauts who demanded that he surrender. Knowing that his squad would fall into the ambush if he didn't warn them, Sanchez answered by firing his rifle grenade into the pavement at their feet. That shot killed three Germans and wounded seven as well as Sanchez himself. Warned by his signal, however, the squad came up and captured the 30 survivors. Three strongly defended roadblocks at Buttapietra, Magnano and Verona were broken by S/Sgt. Erwin H. Bender of Hamilton, Ohio, and his squad of E Company. First Lt. William F. Brennan of Maspeth, Long Island, New York, and his platoon from C Company, 349th, had a busy session near Oppeano. Maspeth and his men attacked a group of houses from which small arms and an 88 had opened up on the battalion column. The Germans outnumbered the Krautkillers and Maspeth sent for reinforcements. Before help could come up the battle was over, Maspeth picking off the crew and destroying the 88 with six killed and seven wounded.

Near Verona occurred one of those unexplainable and tragic incidents of war, an incident which took some of the glory out of the capture. A small task force of the 351st had stopped at a crossroads to check maps and take a ten-minute break. Two American planes buzzed the column which was clearly marked with air identification panels. The planes buzzed a second time while the air-ground radio operator attempted to raise the ships' radios. He never made contact, for suddenly the planes dove and strafed the column, killing the radio crew and destroying the gasoline supplies.

The treadway ponton bridge across the Po River was not completed until four hours after the foot troops had reached Verona but when it opened, all the transportation in the Corps rolled northward. The 88th Division CP moved to San Giovanni Lupato, south of Verona, and the entire Division prepared to cross the next water barrier, the Adige River, and seize the communications center of Vicenza, another main Fifth Army objective. The 3d Battalion, 350th Infantry, was first to cross the Adige on the 26th and established a firm bridgehead on the north bank. A railroad bridge in Verona was repaired to carry tanks and TDs and by 0700 hours on the 27th, the three regiments and the armor were driving east on Highway 11 for Vicenza. Something new was added to tactics in Italy when a "bicycle battalion" of the 350th Infantry—the 2d Battalion —pedaled from Nogara to San Martino to make the most novel "liberation" ever recorded in the Italian campaign. The novelty was rather short-lived, however, for higher headquarters ordered the bikes returned to their Italian owners and the doughboys were back in their old, familiar, footsore element—picking 'em up and laying 'em down. In a 24-hour dash along Highway 11, troops of the 1st Battalion, 350th, rode armor of the 752d Tank Battalion and the 805th Tank Destroyer Battalion to take Vicenza. Bitter house-to-house fighting raged here before the city was taken and this lightning move east trapped thousands of Germans from more than six divisions.

Crossing of the Adige River and the swift flanking movement to Vicenza rendered absolutely useless the strong Adige Line on which the Germans had counted to delay Allied forces before the Alps. The 88th had moved so fast that the Krauts were unable to withdraw to their Adige Line positions and hundreds of emplacements—with guns in place and pointed south—were unoccupied and far to the rear of the spearheading 88th. Artillery units of the Division were hard-pressed to keep pace with the rush of the Infantry. The redlegs kept so far forward that the cannoneers were taking a good percentage of the Krauts. At one point the 337th Field captured the bulk of a German artillery battalion. Surrender of entire enemy units to the Blue Devils was not uncommon. Among outfits taken intact were three German field hospitals, an ordnance dump, an

Artillery loading for the crossing of the Adige River.

engineer bridge dump, a battalion of Georgians and a full company of Czech troops. The latter unit insisted first on being allowed to join the 88th's fight against the Krauts and then, when that was impossible, demanded that they be permitted to stage a formal surrender parade. About this point in the proceedings, the Ranger Platoon of the 351st, which had made the original capture, began manifesting itchy trigger fingers and the Czech colonel decided that a live surrender would be better than a dead one. They quit arguing and turned in their arms.

Thousands of fleeing Krauts, surging up on the 40-mile open right flank of the 88th, found their escape route to the north blocked by our capture of Highway 11. The highway represented a thin line of 88th territory running from Verona to Vicenza through solid enemy territory. Thousands of troops to the north of the highway still manifested fight as they withdrew slowly into the foothills of the Italian Alps. For several days, that highway was a nightmare. Krauts coming up from the south halted at the thinly held road line. Krauts north of the road, in sudden forays, cut the road in several places long enough for hundreds of their brethren to get across. They'd hold the road open until 88th troops could make it back from points near Vicenza and clear up the roadblocks. Many

213

The attack moved swiftly through Bassano.

truckloads of Krauts, fleeing across northern Italy from one Allied unit, blundered into 88th convoys rolling from Verona to Vicenza. The leader of one 350th convoy was startled one night to discover that his original convoy had suddenly been increased by five trucks. Checking, he discovered the trucks were loaded with Krauts who thought, in the darkness, that they had joined one of their own units. The Krauts were equally startled and many were suddenly dead when 88th doughs opened up on them from leading and trailing vehicles. As had happened twice previously in the offensive the Division CP convoyed into Vicenza while a tank battle still raged. Sniper fire continued for several hours and headquarters personnel helped round up the Kraut marksmen. Even Division Rear got in the ball game with a "task force" of cooks and bakers led by Capt. John E. Boothe of Washington, D. C., accepting surrender of 66 Krauts, 30 Fascists and the entire Lightning Battalion of the Italian Fascist 10th Flotilla, for a total bag of 322 at then un-liberated Schio. The "fluid front" as described in the official communiqués set a new high in understatement. Italian Partisan troops, who had done such stellar work in the Po Valley behind the German lines prior to the Allied offensive and had paved the way for many American triumphs, joined the 88th as it steamrollered through town after town. Italian civilians, a more intelligent and energetic type than their southern brothers, hung white flags out the windows of their houses and gave the troops a minor edition of a "Rome welcome" when they came through.

An MP, Pvt. Henry Perchalski of Hightstown, New Jersey, made the most important arrest of his career when he tagged a Kraut truck which sped through his traffic post. The truck was loaded with about thirty Krauts who sprayed soldiers and civilians with rifle and machine-gun fire. Perchalski fired into the truck then took up the chase, firing tommy-gun bursts at the careening vehicle until its occupants surrendered. Lt. Thomas A. White of Clarksburg, West Virginia, damaged his carbine as he sprinted for a machine gun located in a house. White engaged the two Krauts in a hand-to-hand battle and took the decision after he killed one of them with a shovel. A medic, Lt. Earl C. Winter of Hepburn, Iowa, drove an ambulance into the midst of a fire fight, carefully loaded the wounded and then wheeled the ambulance through the flying lead to the rear. When another ambulance loaded with blood plasma was cut off by an enemy flank attack, 1st Sgt. Roy H. Lusk of Miami, Florida, commandeered a tank and went to the rescue. Lusk directed the tank fire and succeeded in driving the enemy away from the cargo of blood plasma which then was rushed forward to where it was most needed. A weapons-carrier driver, Pfc. Harold L. Fick of Allentown, Pennsylvania, volunteered to go after a Kraut bazookaman when the entrenched enemy opened up on a column of 350th vehicles. Fick got the bazookaman and killed six more before he calmed down.

Pfc. George W. Boykin of Lufkin, Texas, outsmarted the enemy with a handful of GIs and partisans. Boykin volunteered to clear out a Kraut strongpoint which was harassing a 351st column. While working his tiny band in a skirmish line toward the house Boykin was wounded. He rushed forward, killed two in a machine-gun nest and then the Krauts, who thought they were surrounded, gave up. Boykin supervised the evacuation of sixty PWs before he submitted to treatment. Artillerymen joined the assault when Kraut paratroopers infiltrated battery positions. Lt. Lawrence E. Sommers of Dallas, Texas, organized twenty "redlegs" armed with bazookas and carbines and led them in an attack on the Germans' positions, killing or capturing the entire enemy force with his small crew. Lt. George E. Meadows of Lake Wales, Florida, personally picked off three bazookamen who were working on our tanks, then led his men against the bulk of an enemy convoy. When the scrap was over 30 Jerries were dead, 50 were PWs. An advance scout, Pfc. Harold F. Elmore of Crisfield, Maryland, cleared the way for his squad when he killed four with bayonet and grenades, then followed an enemy trench to a dugout where he captured ten and had them disarmed when his comrades arrived.

While leading a five-man reconnaissance patrol, Lt. Edward E. Walsh, of New York City, met intense fire. He dispatched two men to bring up

Troops of the 350th on the road to Feltre.

PWs taken during the Po drive march back to a PW cage.

the platoon and while waiting stood off the Krauts who started to close in on him. When the platoon came up, Walsh formed two squads in a fire base and led the third to the rear of the enemy. Surprised by the sudden fire from front and rear, a total of 143 Krauts called it quits. T/5 Homer C. Powell of Kirkland, Texas, rescued two men from a Recon Troop armored car which had been knocked out by an antitank gun. Powell accomplished the rescue despite the loss of a foot. Covering fire was provided by T/5 John Johnson of Jeffries, Wisconsin, the car's gunner. Although he had lost one leg and been badly wounded in the other by the shot which crippled the vehicle, Johnson, unable to stand and barely able to hold himself in his seat, continued to fire his 37mm at the enemy. His heroic act enabled the crew of a second car to escape.

Three of the most heartbroken Blue Devils were the riflemen who captured a $50,000 Nazi payroll and then gave it all away. The trio—Pfc. Carl M. Miloslavitch of San Francisco, Webb Garnett of Richmond, Virginia, and James Ford of Glendale, California—were clearing a building at Cento when they discovered a large wooden box. In the box they found $50,000 of German-printed Italian money. The men did not believe the money usable and passed most of it to others as souvenirs. Miloslavitch gave away his entire share; Ford kept $10 and Garnett, the luckiest, retained $850. Later, the trio learned to its sorrow that the money was

Vehicles of the 88th roll up the steep passes of the Italian Alps as the Blue Devils chase the Krauts into final surrender.

acceptable as a medium of exchange and that they'd given away a small fortune.

After battling to reach the flat land of the Po Valley for more than a year, 88th troops suddenly awoke to the fact that in less than two weeks they'd traversed all the flat country in Italy and once again were faced with the old, familiar mountains. From Vicenza the troops had hoped to continue on east to Venice and then a junction with Yugoslav forces. That was the hope, and the rumor. The fact was a rude awakening when the Division turned and drove northeast into the mountains, the highest mountains in all Italy. The enemy resistance increased as the I Parachute Corps, withdrawing into the mountains, fought to slow the 88th's advance. The Kraut had his back to the last wall. At 1250 hours

218

on the 29th, the 351st Infantry secured the bank of the Brenta River at Bassano and made a crossing in strength on the 30th, cleaning the town of Bassano and opening the gateway to the so-called Inner Fortress or Inner Redoubt, the area in which Hitler had been expected to make his last stand with picked SS troops.

Winter clothing and shoepacs were issued to the troops as the regiments crunched north through the snow and Dolomite Alps. The 351st took Fonzaso and 2d Battalion, 349th, captured Feltre on May 1. Later that day the 351st moved on to Borgo and took that town by 1200 hours May 2 while the 349th advanced to Fiera di Primiero. New orders went out to all units of the Division listing Innsbrück, Austria, as the next big objective to be reached via the Brenner Pass. Both the Italian and European fronts were crumbling rapidly but still the Krauts seemed willing to resist indefinitely, a resistance which was more than futile as peace terms already had been signed at Caserta and the war in Italy was over. We learned of its end from the Germans.

First news of the surrender was given the 88th by three officers of the German 1st Paratroop Division who entered our lines at 1600 hours May 2 under a white flag and informed the 351st Infantry that the war in Italy was over, that an unconditional surrender had been signed and in effect since 1400 hours and that both sides were to remain in place until further orders had been received. Unable to raise Division by radio for confirmation, Colonel Miller, fearing a trick, told the Krauts they could have one hour to surrender their own unit. If this was not done, Miller said his troops would continue the attack. Shortly before expiration of the hour, a second German party entered our lines with the same story. Miller gave this group fifteen minutes to surrender and then, despite warnings that the Germans would resist any attempt to advance, Miller ordered his regiment forward. The Germans fought back, and in the short scrap four men were killed and six wounded.

Back at Division CP, out of radio touch with all units, the first official word came from Corps shortly after 1800 hours—four hours after the surrender had gone into effect—that hostilities had ceased in Italy but that the advance would continue. A news broadcast over BBC from London a few minutes before Corps orders were received actually was the first complete news that the 88th CP had on the end of the war. While G-3 was preparing new battle plans, the radio in the G-2 office blared out the cheerful news from London that "joy was unconfined among front-line troops in Italy tonight as they celebrated the end of a long and bitter campaign." It was a nice thought, that celebration, but rather an inaccurate description of events in the 88th sector where the war continued to rock grimly along.

German soldiers who defended Brenner Pass walk unguarded to a PW cage after surrendering unconditionally.

Motorcycle messengers were sent to all units by General Kendall and at 2100 hours May 2 orders finally came from Corps that all units were to halt in place. It was early on May 3 before all units were notified. Although the war had ended at 1400 hours May 2, it had taken more than twelve hours to halt the fighting in the 88th sector even though the Germans themselves, advised of the peace terms long before they went into effect, had tried to halt the battle on schedule.

In the 88th, it was prolonged more than four hours before the first official word came through. The German soldiers knew it on time, the BBC radio in London thousands of miles from the tragic little drama being shot out in the Dolomite Alps, and even the press in America knew that the end had come long before the fighting troops.

While the regiments instituted security measures in their sectors, the 349th Infantry, motorized, took off for the Brenner Pass. Moving more than sixty miles through the beaten enemy and racing the 85th Division, which also had the same objective, advance patrols of the 349th were the first elements of the Allied armies in Italy to make junction with forces moving south from Germany. At 1051 hours May 4 the European and Mediterranean fronts became one unbroken line when the 349th made contact with patrols from the 103d Division, VI Corps, Seventh Army, a few miles south of the Brenner Pass. In the lead contact jeep were Lt.

GIs of two divisions guard the Brenner Pass.

Col. Ralph E. Haines and Pfc. Barney Beadle, both of the 349th, and Major Gerald Munn of the G-3 Office. The 88th had scored another, and a notable first. The history-making event was recorded on the spot by Division and Seventh Army radio correspondents and the story of the junction was broadcast to the United States and the world over the NBC Army Hour. It had been a glorious eighteen days, a smashing finish to almost fourteen months of combat. From the jumpoff against cave-studded Monterumici on the heights before Bologna, the 88th had cracked through the final mountain defense line and raced more than 305 combat miles in 18 days, destroyed six Nazi divisions, bagged 38,000 prisoners, wrung unconditional surrender from the battered Krauts high in the Alps and then went on to make the linkup with SHAEF forces. Speaking for the men who should know, better than any, of the 88th's fighting ability, captured Major General Schulz of the 1st Parachute Division, the pride of the Wehrmacht, told his interrogators "the 88th Division is the best division we have ever fought against—we fought you on Mt. Battaglia, Mt. Grande and in this action now completed."

The battle history of the 88th was finished. And the men of the 88th knew, as they waited for further orders, that they had done their part, and magnificently, in winning a war. No one claimed that the Division had won the war itself but all knew that it had played a stellar role in the Italian campaign. All knew that it had been one of the best American divisions in Italy. In fact, the Germans had rated it as the best. A captured document which was an enemy appraisal of American units facing the Germans in Italy said the 88th was "a very good division with excellent fighting material." After departure of the U.S. VI Corps for southern France the 88th "was rated as the best U.S. division in Italy. Very good leadership." That excellent fighting material and good leadership had teamed since the first days at Minturno to produce the Blue Devils. And the men of the 88th knew, as they speculated on future moves, that they had kept the pledge made for them on a dusty Oklahoma plain almost two years before. They knew that the torch burned undimmed—the colors were unsullied. They had made good all the advance predictions. And the price of victory had not been cheap—the 88th had left more than 15,000 dead and wounded on the long trail from Minturno to the Brenner Pass.

Despite the glowing accounts of the BBC radio, there was no wild celebrating in the 88th sector when the war finally ground to a halt. The news was almost too good to be true even though the doughs had been expecting it for days. There was joy at news of the end but it was a quiet joy, a joy which was expressed in calm fashion as a feeling of intense relief and deep gratitude swept the lines. "What can you say about a thing like this?" reflected one soldier. "It's too big. All you can do is say 'Thanks, God,' for He's the only One Who can understand how a guy really feels now." Some of the men just sat and stared at each other in the strange silence, taking turns saying in a dazed voice: "It's over—it's over!" But neither one actually listening and each busy with his own thoughts for which there were no words. "All I know is that my men won't get shot at any more and that's all I give a damn about," said one junior officer.

The war was over. The silence was loud.

Our policy is one of just plain being tough!

BRIG. GEN J. C. FRY

Brigadier General James C. Fry
He commanded the 88th during its POW Command and early occupation days.

"The world will be better for the enthusiasm and earnestness with which the Blue Devils performed every phase of their duty. It was a great privilege to have been numbered among their ranks. Those who died or suffered grievous wounds for their country did so in the earnest belief that they were fighting in a worthy cause. We must never forget the sacrifices that were made or cease our efforts to make certain that they were not made in vain."

THE POW COMMAND

For several days after war's end, it was a bit difficult to tell the victor from the vanquished.

German units facing the 88th far outnumbered the Blue Devils and despite their unconditional surrender, they roamed the countryside pretty much at will. Some commanders even had the effrontery to tell 88th officials that they, and their units, would like to enlist with the Allies to fight the Japanese. The section of Italy occupied by the 88th had been Austrian territory until the end of World War I when it had been awarded to Italy. A majority of the population was Austrian, had never considered themselves as Italians and consequently were sympathetic to the Germans. There was no wild welcome for 88th troops. For the most part they were looked upon as invaders instead of liberators and their arrival in cities and towns throughout the area was greeted with cold stares and gestures of disapproval. Kraut soldiers were cocky, even in defeat, and refused to admit that they had lost a war. In addition to the cool, and in places hostile, attitude of the people, the area was filled with thousands of fugitives and suspected war criminals who had fled there from all over Europe. The situation was potentially explosive.

In Bolzano the situation bordered on the fantastic. During the war, Bolzano had been headquarters for the Commander-in-Chief, German Southwestern Command and also for the SS troops. Commanding the SS, toughest of all German troops, was General Karl Wolff who bossed the SS in Italy and was a top henchman to Heinrich Himmler. Wolff kept his luxurious headquarters establishment and his SS troops maintained their roadblocks, MP control and swanky office buildings and quarters. They really had found a home in Bolzano and hated to give it up. When the 88th Division CP moved to Bolzano on May 6, the advance quartering party was confronted by SS troops who refused to move out of buildings selected as CP sites. The Krauts cited terms of the surrender agreement which they claimed guaranteed their continued occupancy of present buildings until other "suitable" quarters could be provided. A CP building for the 88th finally was obtained after General Wolff ordered one of his sub-offices to move out and he granted permission to the 88th to move in. For several days, SS troops roamed the streets of Bolzano on foot or in military vehicles with their German and Austrian girl friends, frequented bars and cafes, ignored 88th vehicles and troops arriving in town and behaved pretty much as though all their past horrors were to be forgiven with little more than a figurative slap on the wrist. GIs wondered "who the hell won this war?" as they watched groups of Nazi troops parading through Bolzano streets singing "Hitler is My Führer" or the "Horst Wessel" song. Elsewhere throughout the Division area, the per-

225

German soldiers roll a heavy steel keg of stolen Italian gold reserve bullion out of its cache in the Brenner Pass.

formance was the same. In the 349th sector, one German colonel went so far as to stage a formal medal presentation ceremony with his regiment drawn up in full formation. Two American noncoms nearly touched off a riot when they broke up the party by arresting the colonel and ordering the regiment to quarters. GIs and officers grumbled openly at the apparent hands-off and easy-peace policy in regard to the Germans. But orders from outside the Division said not to provoke the Germans. The Germans were provoked anyway, being Germans, and four days after the war ended, they blew up a building in Bressanone which had been selected as an 88th barracks. No one was injured at Bressanone but at Colle Isarco, a time bomb left in the cellar by Germans moving out, wounded 22 members of the 349th Infantry and burned down the battalion CP.

Brig. Gen. Thomas Lewis, Division Artillery Commander, established the City Command Section of Bolzano and, employing the 339th Field Artillery Battalion, enforced the surrender terms in that town. Throughout the regimental areas, local city commands also were established with an 88th officer in charge as local provost marshal. Instructions were issued to the German commanders in regard to the assembly of all German units within the Division area for disarmament and administration. The Division area extended generally from the north shores of Lake Garda north

CP of the 1st Battalion, 349th at Colle Isarco. The building was wrecked and burned by the explosion of a German bomb left in the cellar.

to the Brenner Pass and in a zone approximately 100 kilometers wide and 140 kilometers long. There were about 150,000 enemy personnel in the area when the 88th took over. The general plan was to permit the Krauts to administer for themselves temporarily and to locate and collect their badly disorganized forces so that they could be evacuated by units. The easy days were over. All enemy troops were ordered restricted to their barracks or bivouac areas with only those engaged in administrative duties permitted the use of the roads. All enemy transport and equipment was collected in huge supply dumps.

Official news of the unconditional surrender of enemy forces in Europe was broadcast on May 9 and VE-day was celebrated throughout the

227

Captured SS men after the raid on SS headquarters in Bolzano.

Germans turning in their arms and equipment to members of the 339th Field Artillery at Bolzano.

Division area. Thanksgiving services were held in the Division but the troops were reminded that peace had not been restored completely to the world, that bitter fighting continued in the Pacific Theater, and that the 88th must be prepared to continue the struggle. The hottest rumor in the Division was that the 88th would return to the States for a Victory Parade on July 4 and after further training would be sent to the Pacific.

The honeymoon in Bolzano was ended by Col. James C. Fry within a matter of hours after he took over as town commander. After securing identifications of all SS units in the area, Colonel Fry led a raiding party of artillerymen and Recon troopers against the headquarters of SS General Karl Wolff. Ironically enough, the raid was staged on Wolff's birthday and Colonel Fry was the top unwelcome guest. A private little birthday party was in progress when he entered the room and ordered the arrest of General Wolff and Wehrmacht General Heinrich von Vietinghoff-Scheel, German commander in northern Italy. Frau Wolff was indignant at what she called high-handed procedure and threatened Colonel Fry with disciplinary action over what she called "the breaking of an agreement with Army higher-ups." She was arrested also. In all, the raid on Wolff's headquarters and barracks yielded 2,000 SS personnel, valuable

229

documents, $8,000,000 and the private and priceless coin collection of King Victor Emanuel of Italy. The birthday feast, including some delicious squab and champagne, was sent across the street to General Kendall's headquarters with the raiders' compliments. By now, the Germans and the Austrian civilian population were beginning to see that they really had lost a war and that the 88th meant business. The slapping-down of the arrogant SS was a clear sign.

Throughout the Division area, the separate units staged raids of their own, cleaning up subordinate SS concentrations and rounding up stubborn Krauts who had refused previously to comply with Division directives regarding the turning in of their weapons. German soldiers in civilian clothes, false discharge papers, healthy Krauts hiding in hospitals and the portion of the Austrian civilian population who were willing to hide SS personnel were factors which complicated the roundup. Special raiding patrols and search parties were sent out from all units to bag top Nazis. A CIC detachment under Capt. Harry Riback, of Chicago, picked up Frau Heinrich Himmler and daughter Margaret in a chalet hideout only 15 miles from Bolzano. Himmler himself had stayed there for a short time before the war ended and then moved to Gestapo headquarters at Colle Isarco where he remained until his return to Germany. Corinne Luchaire, one-time French screen star, and her father, the former Vichy Minister of Information and Propaganda, were arrested in Merano. Also taken into custody in Merano by the 349th was the entire crew of the Nazi Radio Propaganda section in Italy but Axis Sally, the No. 1 star of the show, managed to elude capture at that time. Most of the suspected war criminals gave up quietly. One who tried to fight it out was Major Mario Carita, head of the Italian SS and Italy's Public Enemy No. 1. Carita was killed in his mountain hideout near Siusi by Cpl. James Dodaro of Chicago and the 350th. Carita fired at the raiders as they broke into his room. Dodaro was wounded in the stomach but cut down Carita with his tommy gun.

Caves and underground tunnels yielded huge quantities of Nazi loot sent there from all parts of Europe for storage. More than 23 tons of gold, worth about $25,000,000, were collected in Bolzano and at the Fortezza fort, near the Brenner Pass. Priceless paintings, rugs, tapestries, silks, furniture, jewelry and trinkets were uncovered by searchers of the 88th. Also found stored in the caverns were supplies of war, large caches of food and ammunition and gasoline, which the Nazis had tucked away to be used in the defense of the Inner Fortress.

Life in the Bolzano–Merano area was like something out of the movies for the victorious GIs. Resort hotels were taken over by platoons. Infantry companies vied with each other in establishing elaborate messhalls with civilian waiters and dance bands. Unit bars sprang up overnight. The noncoms emulated the officers and started a variety of clubs restricted to the first-three-graders, then sergeants and corporals. This club breakdown ended when Pfcs. and privates in the 349th opened a club in Merano and barred all noncoms from the premises. With the Krauts now behind bars or in detention cages, the local *signorinas* switched uniforms and the unit dances were well stocked with pretty partners. Though work continued, the Blue Devils found plenty of time for play in this beautiful resort area. Truly, more than one GI found that home he had been looking for in the Army.

The assembly of German surrendered units within the Division area continued for several days. At the same time the regiments and their attachments thoroughly familiarized themselves with the units in their areas to facilitate their evacuation when orders for such movement were received. An additional area was added to each regimental zone of responsibility when the 88th took over the former 10th Mountain Division sector. The evacuation of surrendered units began on May 14 when all SS troops within the Division area were moved to the Modena PW inclosure. Thereafter, evacuation of certain special units continued and on May 17 mass evacuation began. The 88th Division moved surrendered enemy forces, the bulk of which were the German Fourteenth Army and Tyrolean Army, to concentration and staging areas at Bassano and Ghedi.

A disagreement between the Allies and Marshal Tito over the disposition of Trieste made necessary the moving of II Corps to strengthen Allied forces in that area. The 88th was relieved from II Corps, placed directly under Fifth Army control and took over evacuation of surrendered enemy personnel in the former II Corps sector. The 85th Division and the Bassano PW Staging Area were placed under operational control of the 88th.

The evacuation of German surrendered units continued until May 29 at which time the Division area was cleared of all surrendered forces except those units specifically retained on orders of higher headquarters. These included railroad, signal, *Todt* and hospital units. A total of 110,118 surrendered individuals was evacuated from the Division area to PW staging areas during the period; 27,151 being evacuated in one day, May 22. Highway 12 was clogged daily with long convoys of defeated Nazis rolling south. Interspersed in the convoys were hundreds of vehicles from Europe carrying Italians who had been slave laborers in Germany or occupied countries and thousands more refugees who were taking the long road home, on foot.

Bivouac area of the surrendered German Fourteenth Army at Ghedi airport.

The commander of the Italian Folgore Group accepts command of the Bolzano-Merano area at formal relief ceremonies before the Italian war memorial in Bolzano.

The 88th's evacuation job had been done. More tasks lay ahead. On May 31, in a colorful ceremony at Bolzano's War Memorial, the 88th turned over command of its sector to the Italian Folgore Group. Both commanding generals bestowed pretty compliments on the fighting records of each other's divisions, the Italians cheered their native troops but the Austrians looked on glumly at the ceremony which to them meant nothing. The Austrians disliked intensely the substitution of Italian for American troops. The animosity was so open in certain quarters that it was decided not to move the entire 88th Division but to leave behind enough troops to act as a buffer between the Italians and Austrians. The 349th Infantry Regiment was detailed to remain in the area with the rest of the Division moving to Lake Garda.

No Vacations

To soldiers who had looked for a long vacation after combat ended, the mission assigned the 88th in June 1945 was not a pleasant prospect. With its job of evacuation finished, the 88th was assigned to guard, control and administer some 300,000 PWs in concentration areas stretching from Naples to the Brenner Pass. The job itself was difficult enough but

234

Soldiers of the 349th cross a mountain stream as they patrol the Italian-Austrian border to prevent escape of German deserters.

with redeployment steadily depleting Division ranks, the accelerated I&E study program and the opening of numerous rest camps and leave areas, the PW mission rapidly became a nightmare.

The Division CP was established in Desenzano on Lake Garda. Units of the Division bivouacked for a short time near Desenzano, then fanned out throughout Italy to take over their guard roles. A special POW Command section was set up to handle the Krauts. The command included five separate areas: Merano–Bolzano, Ghedi, Modena–Verona, Aversa–Bari, and Leghorn–Pisa–Florence sub-commands. (See pages 359–360 for outline of POW Command activities.) The POW command was charged with administering the Krauts under its control and allocating German units to all Allied commands in Italy which requested them for work purposes. In the first weeks, the prime idea was that the

235

Krauts would be put to work in mine-clearing, road-building and reconstruction projects in sections of Italy which had been hard hit by the war. Krauts also were furnished to base and rear-area units for manual labor tasks, KP and other onerous details so that GIs might finally get a break.

CIC and Intelligence Sections of the Division screened the PWs at each cage to weed out the wanted war criminals, SS personnel and other enemy agents. Master lists of war criminals and wanted personnel were sent down from USFET Headquarters to augment the theater lists. Guard details for the cages and work parties were supplied by 88th units and Blue Devils were spread all over Italy as they worked their charges.

Col. James C. Fry, Assistant Division Commander, was named to head the MTOUSA POW Command. His plan was simple: "Our policy is one of just plain being tough. They'll get nothing from us but groceries and work." And he carried it out, offsetting home-front stories and fears of laxity and pampering in the postwar quarantine of the men who killed for Adolf Hitler. Largest of the concentration areas was Ghedi Airport, where 68,247 Germans and 642 Fascists learned who won the war.

After the surrender in Italy, the survivors of five German divisions were ordered to Ghedi. Troops of the 351st Regiment and the 442nd Regimental Combat Team handled the processing. The PWs piled in at the rate of 20,000 daily. Fire-arms were confiscated from the few who still retained them. Every German was stripped. A mountain of loot—radios, clothing, bicycles, even women's silken underwear—was taken from them for eventual disposition by AMG. The Krauts were taken aback by the strict impartiality of their treatment. One enemy officer came up to a processing team to complain that he had been forced to wait three hours before his turn came. "That's all right," a Blue Devil replied. "We've had to wait five years to get you here." All the Germans lived in a two-and-a-half-mile area of puptents, with everyone sleeping two to a tent, from colonels on down. The surrendered forces were fed captured German rations, supplemented by American canned rations and fresh bread baked in their own field kitchens. There was no tobacco or candy ration and only essential items, such as shaving equipment, were given the PWs. Crisp military discipline was insisted upon and the work day lasted from 0600 hours to 1630 hours. There was no organized recreational program except what their own special service companies could set up. "They're out there, and if they want to play tiddleywinks it's OK," said Colonel Fry. "If they don't, that's OK too." Except for a few recalcitrants, who quickly were weeded out and placed in special punishment areas, the Germans were easy to handle after they got the idea that the 88th wasn't kidding. Straight down the line, from the commander to

Maj. Gen. Paul W. Kendall bids farewell to members of his command before leaving Ghedi for a new assignment in the States.

riflemen, the motto at Ghedi—and all other PW concentration camps— was "Be tough!" Colonel Fry was determined that the men of the nation which started two wars in a lifetime would learn that this time the democratic world would not be fooled into forgiving and forgetting. On June 18, after holding the job for three months, Colonel Fry received the rank to which he was entitled as Assistant Division Commander. The single star of his new rank was pinned on by his orderly, Cpl. Rocco Calderone of Trenton, New Jersey, and the new general paid tribute to the thousands of nameless men who had fought under his command up the Italian boot. "I elected to have Corporal Calderone pin on the star which represents my promotion," General Fry said, "because he is a former member of the 350th and it is to the fighting qualities of that regiment, to the courageous men—living and dead—who served under my command while I was its regimental commander, that I owe my promotion more than anything else."

Undertaking to destroy the so-called "Nazi Religion," a by-product of National Socialism, Chaplain Wallace M. Hale set about to bring a rebirth of Christian religion to the German prisoners under 88th control. Chaplain Hale organized and directed his assistant chaplains, representing several faiths, in screening former German chaplains and ministers from the ranks of the PWs. Religious essentials of equipment were borrowed or improvised and when the screening was completed, a Chaplains Corps

237

was set up and functioning in the remnants of the German Army for the first time since 1942 when the Nazis virtually had abolished the office.

The German sick and wounded were collected in the hospital zone of Merano, where the 349th administered the sector, sent patrols into the hills to search for refugees and deserters, guarded the Brenner Pass and the Swiss and Austrian borders, and kept peace between the Italian and Austrian elements of the civilian population. The Modena and Verona cages were handled by the 350th and the Recon Troop. Artillery units were sent to Pisa, Leghorn, Bari, Aversa and Caserta to handle Krauts in those places. The 88th lost its second commander in July 1945. General Kendall, in late June, was ordered to the States to take part in a victory tour and celebration. On the day before he reported back to the 88th CP at Desenzano, War Department orders arrived which relieved him from command of the 88th and assigned him to command of Camp Roberts, California. General Kendall left Ghedi by plane on July 21, with an honor guard of Blue Devils lined up to see him off. Command of the Division was assumed by Brigadier General Fry.

In July, orders came from USFET directing that repatriation of Kraut prisoners begin at once. A clearing cage was set up at Verona and 88th men, themselves ineligible for discharge under the point system, took on the job of escorting former battle enemies back to their homeland. Trains were sent daily from Verona via the Brenner Pass to Innsbrück where USFET officials and guards took over. First shipments made included some 4,000 German WACs, nurses and camp followers. The PWs traveled 30 to a boxcar with one 88th guard assigned to each car. The trip took three days. After the first round-trip, one battalion commander volunteered his battalion for the permanent guard detail. He told his superiors that the guard assignment was a "wonderful morale-builder for the men."

During the month of July, 78,743 surrendered enemy personnel were repatriated and transported to USFET; 3,377 surrendered enemy personnel were released and discharged in Italy; 9,569 Czechs were transported to USFET at Pilsen; and 7,171 Russians were sent to a repatriation camp in Brück, Austria. The home-bound trains were no joyous caravans for the Krauts knew they were going back to destruction and misery in their own land. They were going back in disgrace; the once-proud and mighty Wehrmacht was straggling back in defeat. For some of the PWs, there was no road home. They took the quick way out by suicide. Not all who tried this route were successful at it. One who failed was Lt. Gen. Herbert Schmull, one-time head of the Nazi Transportation Corps, whose identity was discovered when he slashed his wrists with a

C-ration can at Verona. As a group, the White Russians were the most difficult to move. Partners of the Nazis during the war, the Russians told their Allied guards that certain death awaited them on their return to their homeland. They were herded aboard boxcars at gun point.

Early in August, the MTOUSA POW Command was ordered to reduce its responsibilities by guarding and administering only those German service units working for the Army Air Forces, Mediterranean Theater of Operations, the University Training Command at Florence and the Military Railway Service. The responsibility for guarding and administering all other German service units passed to the major commands for whom these units were working. The original mission remained, however, of guarding and administering POWs and surrendered enemy personnel in cages and hospitals, and repatriating POWs and surrendered enemy personnel. Also, the Merano hospital area and the city command of Merano remained the responsibility of the POW command. Special MP patrols continued to scour the hills in the Merano area for Nazi criminals and deserters. Repatriation trains rolled northward and during the month some 45,734 surrendered enemy personnel were transported to USFET and 2,381 were discharged in Italy. By month's end, the eventual breakup of the MTOUSA POW Command was in sight. The Modena–Verona sub-command was inactivated and the Merano–Bolzano sub-command discontinued all roadblocks in the area and operation of the city command of Merano. Various non-division units were relieved from attachment to the 88th and the Blue Devils prepared to wind up their POW mission.

REDEPLOYMENT

When news of the Army's point system was announced in the summer of 1945 the GIs of the 88th reserved judgment until the point values and total necessary for discharge were fixed. When the discharge requirement of 85 points was announced in May 1945, the expressions of disgust were long and loud. The Division average was 67 points. Only a scattered handful could make the grade for home and civilian life.

Army statements said that the point system—so many points allowed for Army service, overseas time, decorations, and dependents—had been developed after interviews with thousands of soldiers in all theaters of war. The only theater to which interview teams were not sent was the Italian theater. But the doughs didn't know that. In many respects, the point system was unfair. No special credit was given for combat time and rear-echelon clerks with battle stars frequently had as many points as front-line riflemen. Many Air Forces ground-crew men with less than one

Some called it black market, others gray market. It was the same money in any case.

year overseas and service at rear bases far removed from combat areas were able to compile enough points for a quick trip home via the battle-star route. After some fourteen months of combat, the prospects for the Blue Devils under the point system were grim. The war in the Pacific still was raging and all indications were that the earlier promises of the Division going to "Rome, Berlin and Tokyo," would come true. At best, all that even the most optimistic GI could hope for was a trip to the Pacific via the States, a short furlough at home before further combat. There were plenty of rumors, but few actual facts.

Early redeployment plans called for the 88th to be shipped to the States on completion of its PW mission, re-trained, re-equipped and held in reserve for possible use in the Pacific. The tentative sailing date was set for September 1945. This plan suddenly was changed and early in June the 88th was listed as a Class IV unit, to be inactivated in the U. S. Before sailing however, the Division was to be stripped of its low point personnel, filled up with high-point men from other units and sent home as a carrier division. The men who had made the 88th Infantry Division a crack outfit were slated for redeployment as casuals and further service in other outfits. The point system had no sentiment; a war in the Pacific was still to be won.

Redeployment of the 88th began simultaneously with the PW mission. The Division was handed a staggering job of guarding and administering Krauts while redeployment calls stripped hundreds, then thousands, from its ranks. An already difficult PW mission was made all the more difficult by the constant drain on manpower. This drain began as a trickle, soon swelled to a flood. Division and unit personnel sections were frantic as they struggled to check records of outgoing thousands. Periodically during the summer, thousands of high-pointers were shipped to the 88th, remained a few days or a week, then were shipped out again. Protesting and cursing—even some of the toughest doughs shed a few tears when they had to take off their blue shoulder patches—the Blue Devils started on the road home, alone.

In combat a man grows to love his buddies and to develop a fierce pride in his outfit. The combat fraternity is a close-knit and an exclusive organization. An outsider, a non-combat soldier, never could understand the comradeship and fraternity existing among the fighting troops. To the doughboy, there is only one good squad—his. The platoon of which his squad is a part is, to him, the best in the company ; his company is the best in the battalion, and so on up the line to division which in its turn, becomes the best in the Army. He'll grumble and criticize his outfit among his buddies but will take nothing from outsiders. In general Army planning, the breakup of the 88th was necessary. In terms of the individual soldier—infantryman, artilleryman or special trooper—the breakup was a cruel and heartless thing. Friendship ties forged in combat, loyalties born out of sweat and blood and fear, love of unit come out of hate and death, all these could not be changed by mere transfer orders. Blue Devils they had been christened—Blue Devils they remained even though transferred to other units.

Artillerymen dropped trails on their howitzers for the last time in Ordnance parks—signalmen spliced their last wires—engineers knew they had set their last fire in the hole!

By late June 1945, the "effectiveness of the 88th as a fighting unit was so reduced that it would take six months to bring the Division back to fighting strength," General Kendall said. The crack 88th which had steamrollered through the Po Valley was by now little more than a number. The drain on manpower continued. Regiments shrank to battalion size; companies were cut to platoon strength. Some companies went out of existence altogether and units were combined for the sake of better control. The medical battalion stood reveille one morning with one officer, four enlisted men and a dog present for duty.

Deprived of the chance to go home with the Division they had made famous, men of the 88th sweated out transfer orders as divisions with less combat time than the 88th sailed for home, intact. First to leave was the 10th Mountain, followed by the 91st Infantry and the 85th Infantry

Divisions. Even though they were scheduled for the Pacific, they were returning to the States as divisions and 88th doughs envied them.

As the 88th shrank in size, it became apparent that by sailing date there wouldn't be enough left to fill one Liberty ship. Since high- as well as low-pointers were constantly being transferred out, the conviction grew that the 88th probably would be inactivated in Italy. There never was anything official on this, but the 88th probably would have gone out of existence in that fashion except for a later change in plans which gave it a new lease on life.

Reduction of the discharge total to 75 points in September whittled Division ranks still lower and by the middle of the month there were but 1,200 officers and men left in the 88th. Some 13,800 Blue Devils had been redeployed. The 88th existed in name only.

INFORMATION AND EDUCATION

Born during combat as pretty much of an unwanted stepchild, the Information and Education Section came into its own in the first few weeks of peace. Shoved aside during the previous Winter "because we are fighting a seven-day war," I&E under Major Fred V. Harris at Division level went into high gear at war's end.

Ambitious programs calling for establishment of unit schools, vocational training courses and orientation of soldiers for their eventual return to civilian life were mapped by I&E Officers. Backed enthusiastically by General Fry, the large-scale programs were hampered by the PW mission and redeployment. There was great interest in the unit schools among the men and the most successful were the schools in the 349th Infantry and the 313th Medical Battalion. This latter was so successful that it operated itself out of business when a visiting staff officer ordered a return to daily training programs "since the men seem to have so much time to sit around in classrooms." In addition to unit schools, large groups of men were enrolled at the University of Florence for college-level work.

Every unit had its own newspaper. Most of the papers were mimeographed but some few were printed. The Division Press-Radio Section, which during the war had written and sent 60,000 news and feature stories to Stateside newspapers, published the first Division newspaper in June 1945. Printed in Milan, the paper was a four-page tabloid called *The Blue Devil*. This paper celebrated the Division's third anniversary in July 1945, with the publication of a special eight-page anniversary edition. Convinced of the paper's value to the Division, General Fry directed that *The Blue Devil* continue publication "until the last man steps on the boat for home."

Two of the adopted Blue Devils—the Misses Fannye Beatty and Rosamond Myers—of the ARC Clubmobile unit.

Unit recreation programs also were set up on a grand scale. Some units operated bus and plane tours of old 88th battlefields. Special Service sections organized unit talent contests and booked in touring USO shows and plays. PX rations were increased. Unit Red Cross staffs were augmented and additional snack bars were opened throughout the Division area. A Division Rest Center Hotel was opened in Milan. Day passes were granted to Milan and Venice, and large quotas left daily for rest centers in Rome, Florence, Venice, Lake Como, Capri, and Genoa. Seven-day tours of Switzerland were inaugurated and thousands took advantage of the opportunity to visit this beautiful country. Units fortunate enough to be stationed in or near large towns built swank billets and messes. Life in the Merano area was so pleasant that one GI forsook the Fifth Army Rest Center at Lake Como to "go back to the outfit where I've really got

French General Henri Doyen decorates the colors of the 88th with citation streamers representing the award of the Croix de Guerre in a ceremony at Nice, France.

it made." Except for some few isolated cases, life in Italy that summer of 1945 was more of a vacation than anything else for GIs of the 88th. They'd fought hard to win a war and while they could, they enjoyed some of the fruits of victory.

The beginning of the end of the Pacific war was seen with the dropping of the first atomic bomb. Though no one knew exactly what the bomb could do, the general reaction was that "it must be pretty terrific" and "the war can't last much longer." Announcement of the second atomic bomb convinced even the most skeptical and when the final word on the surrender of Japan was released, it was almost anticlimactic. There was no general roaring hilarity but rather a quiet acceptance of the fact that the global conflict had ended. Point scores no longer mattered since redeployment now was only in one direction—home. A few more weeks or months overseas were not hard to take since there no longer was the prospect of further action. Each man began making his own personal plans for establishing a beachhead at New York and a D-day at home.

Early in September, 88th units were ordered to cut supplies and equipment to the bone preparatory to winding up operations in Italy. Its postwar job was judged about 75 per cent complete. Since taking control of PW inclosures in Italy units of the Division had repatriated 151,141 Germans, Austrians, Czechs, Russians, Italians and other nationals. During September the last of the prisoners, some 62,000, were screened and placed aboard trains for home.

Old combat days were recalled on September 18 when the 88th Division was awarded the Croix de Guerre by the French Government for the "support and assistance" it had furnished French troops in action from the Gustav Line to the Arno River. A picked detail of Blue Devils was sent to Nice, France, by plane and truck for the formal presentation ceremony. French General Henri Doyen awarded the Division citation to General Fry, 88th acting commander, and French and American troops paraded along the Riviera following the ceremony. Award of the Croix de Guerre to the 88th was a signal honor. Only one other division in the Mediterranean Theater, the 34th Infantry Division, had merited such an award.

All guesses and rumors on the 88th's future were upset on September 25 when it was announced that the 88th had been selected for the occupation mission at Trieste, then under control of the 34th. All Blue Devils with more than 70 points were transferred to the 34th which was to be sent home as a carrier unit. Low-point members of the 34th were transferred to the 88th. Turning over its PW mission to the British, the 88th moved to Trieste late in September and by October 5 had completed relief of the 34th.

That was the last move of what was left of the old combat 88th. The 88th which started at Gruber was finished. It was the 88th in name only. Only a comparative handful of original Blue Devils was left in its ranks. Majority of the replacements were from the 34th Division, men who were low on points and who simply swapped Red Bull patches for the Cloverleaf.

As the 88th began its occupation mission, units of the 34th closed in at the Bagnoli Staging Area in Naples. More than 1,200 Blue Devils joined it there for the trip home. Although officially transferred to the 34th, the Blue Devils were accorded a special privilege by the 34th's Commanding General. They were not required to wear the 34th patches and were permitted to continue wearing their 88th insignia "because of the great, and true, pride you men have in what was a great outfit. You left the States wearing its colors—you deserve to wear them back."

Our job is to produce peace.

GENERAL DWIGHT D. EISENHOWER

Major General Bryant E. Moore
Veteran of both the Pacific and European fronts, he bossed the 88th in its occupation
mission.

OCCUPATION

Control of the American sector of the Morgan Line and the American responsibilities in Venezia Giulia were taken over by the 88th Division at noon on October 3, 1945. The closing in of the units by the Division and the actual handling of their predecessors' jobs had been going on for the week previous. Originally located at Cividale, the Division CP soon moved to Gorizia for better control.

Two new units were attached and then later assigned to the 88th for its occupation mission. These were the 752nd Tank Battalion and the 15th Field Hospital which some months later was reorganized and redesignated the 391st Station Hospital.

The Division continued to be under MTOUSA for normal command functions, but it also was under the operational control of the British 13 Corps commanded by Lt. Gen. Sir John Harding. And the 88th Division and the 13 Corps were to prove again to the world that British and American troops can work side by side, under British Command, without friction.

Fought over by various nations and factions since about 800 A.D., the territory comprising the Venezia Giulia Peninsula became part of the Austro-Hungarian Empire early in the 19th Century. Austria developed the already-flourishing port of Trieste as its main outlet to the sea and by the outbreak of World War I, Trieste had become one of the greatest seaports of the world. As part of the price for entering the first World War on the side of the Allies, Italy was given Venezia Giulia, less Fiume. An Italian coup in 1922, led by D'Annunzio, seized Fiume by force of arms while the then weak and newly created Jugoslavia could only watch. Thus was sown the final seed which engendered the continuous controversies between Italy and Jugoslavia.

In May, 1945, Marshal Tito's Partisan forces established control, as hostilities ceased, over the greater part of the area. British troops entered Trieste itself and forced the surrender of the remaining German forces on May 2 and 3. A provisional government was set up by Tito's armed Partisans. Tito was warned by Field Marshal Alexander that control of the area must be decided by the Peace Conference. Agreements were drawn up whereby Allied Military Government would govern part of the territory and the Jugoslav Government the remainder. It was necessary to keep open Allied lines of communication with American and British forces in Austria and the line which was to become known as the "Morgan Line" was drawn. West of the Morgan Line was Zone "A," under AMG control, and east of it was Zone "B," under the Jugoslav Government. The Morgan Line was named for Lt. Gen. Sir W. D.

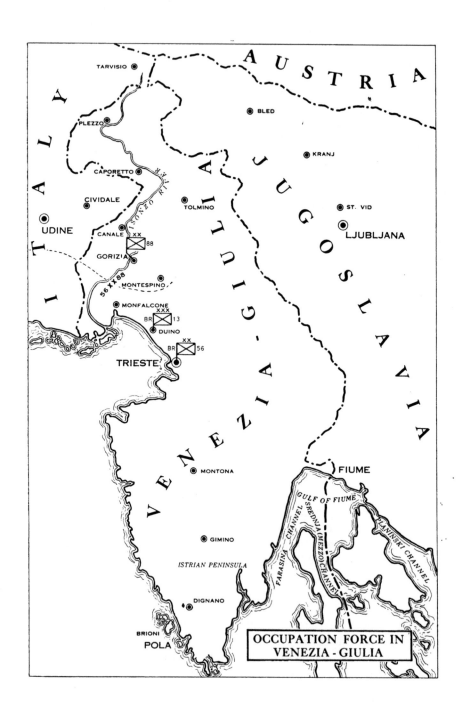

OCCUPATION FORCE IN
VENEZIA - GIULIA

OCCUPATION

After fighting so long to attain peace the Blue Devils were given the task of occupying turbulent Venezia-Giulia. This area had been transferred to Italy from Austria after World War I and was the focal point of distrust and un-rest between Jugoslavia and Italy. Following in the foot-steps of former occupational troops—Germans, Cossacks, Partisans, Fascists, Jugoslavs, New Zealanders, South Africans and British—the 88th was constantly on parade. As representatives of American Democracy in this troubled land, soldiers of the Division "Diable Bleu" were a potent force for understanding and goodwill between America and Italy. The peaceful occupational role was carried out with the same high spirit that served the Di-vision so well in combat.

Leading units of the 349th pass the Division CP in Gorizia during the 1946 Army Day Parade.

High in the mountains in the occupation zone of Venezia-Giulia, two 88th soldiers scan the Yugoslav village and railroad station of Ratece.

Morgan, Supreme Allied Commander, Mediterranean, who worked it out in detail.

As AMG took over in June, 1945, it found that the Jugoslavs had left behind them a complete system of regional government. By early August, AMG came to the conclusion that the administrative bodies left behind did not represent the population fairly and were not efficient. Local government was established under AMG and cooperation of the Slovene elements ceased. From then on the area was a political hot spot with Jugoslavs and Italians vying for control. The Americans and British were in the middle.

Thus the AMG of 13 Corps, of which the 88th Division was a part, entered into the trusteeship of its zone in Venezia Giulia. Its task was to administer the area with complete impartiality and hasten its rehabilitation; to establish law and order; to permit a free press and free expression of political opinion, and to encourage a rapprochement between Italians and Slovenes who would have to live together whatever the final decision

253

Trieste was a hot spot with 88th troops constantly on the alert to prevent trouble.

MPs remove a rioter from the scene of action at Gorizia.

of the Peace Conference. The mission of the military was to support the Allied Military Government.

Replacing personnel was the 88th's first major problem as it took over its occupation duties. Only 1,145 "Blue Devils" were on hand. They were augmented by transfers of 329 officers and 6,617 enlisted men from the 34th Division. Shortly after the switch, more than 6,000 replacements fresh from the United States arrived on the transport *Wakefield*. The replacements, or "Wakefield Commandos" as they were called, were processed and routed to their units by personnel section members under a new system worked out by Lt. Col. Martin H. Burckes, Adjutant General.

The expected change in command came on November 6, 1945, when Maj. Gen. Bryant E. Moore arrived at Udine to take over the 88th from Brig. Gen. James C. Fry. General Moore was a veteran of service in both major theatres of war. He led the 164th Infantry of the Americal Di-

255

Blue Devils and Red Cross girls on leave in Venice feed the pigeons in Piazza San Marco.

vision in Guadalcanal for six months. Promoted to brigadier general following his work in the Pacific, he became assistant division commander of the 104th Division and participated in the campaign for Antwerp. Later he was assigned to command the 8th Division in the Ruhr campaign. The 8th was in process of deactivation at Fort Leonard Wood, Mo., when General Moore was ordered to fly to Italy to command of the 88th.

The first few weeks the Division was in Venezia Giulia were quiet ones from the standpoint of civilian demonstrations. This calm was not to last long. On the first Sunday in November, the Division MPs and part of the 349th got their first in a long series of experiences in handling excited civilians whose principal aim seemed to be mutual assault, pro-Italians on one side and pro-Jugoslavs on the other. Occasion for the first outburst was the anniversary of the Armistice Day marking the Italian-Austrian peace treaty of 1918. This particular demonstration was in

256

Gorizia and was rather quickly and easily handled by the inexperienced American forces. The riot technique of the mobs was to improve as time went on. The local civilians soon learned that the Americans didn't want to hurt them and would not shoot them down in cold blood in order to control them. They began to take advantage of this kindness and to become more difficult.

As a result of the large number of high point men who had been sent home and of the integration into the 88th Division of low point men from dozens of different outfits there was little left of the Blue Devils' proud record of discipline and efficiency. On General Moore's first day of command he supplemented the Division program with a firm directive to forge the Division into an integrated fighting unit capable of performing efficiently any mission in connection with the operational role. The work already underway was accelerated by his fine leadership and background of combat command. Sensible training programs were established and a non-commissioned officers' school was started at the Lido in Venice.

While the Division received for the month of November 2,259 enlisted replacements, it lost 4,645 through redeployment. December was worse since the Division received only 294 replacements as against a loss of 2,394.

December was a month of stormy weather, and some stormy demonstrations, but as Christmas approached, and it appeared that the combat veterans of the 88th were to have their first peaceful Yuletide in several years, it was ruined for them by the murder of an American soldier on Christmas Eve.

On December 23, all units of the 88th were hosts to civilians and children in the towns throughout the area. In Gorizia's Piazza Vittoria, thousands of children swarmed about General Moore as he distributed candy and gifts and the general was beseiged by the youngsters. Headquarters Company personnel helped to ease the crowd by setting up additional candy distribution points.

Pfc. William Shinn of the 349th never saw Christmas that year. He was ambushed by suspected Jugoslav assailants on Christmas Eve as he fixed a broken field wire near the CP of E Company, 349th. Shinn died in a Battalion Aid Station shortly after he was picked up on the highway. His death hasn't been forgotten.

Training in January was more vigorous and more rigorous than ever. All ranks displayed a new interest in knowing how to shoot straight, in how to cover each other and in how to prevent surprise. By the month's end the 88th was earning the plaudits of visiting correspondents who wrote home about the fine combat division the United States had in

Venezia Giulia. Division Artillery had received a new commander during the month. He was Brig. Gen. Eric S. Molitor.

Recreation programs were stepped up. Probably the biggest morale booster was the inauguration of trans-Atlantic phone service to the States. The redeployment trend finally was reversed with 3,043 replacements joining while only 764 men were transferred out. Strength of the Division was stabilized in February for the first time in the five months since it had started its new mission. No replacements were received and only 188 enlisted men were shipped out.

A major regrouping of the Division was effected during February in order to rotate battalions doing Morgan Line outpost duty. The regrouping put the three infantry regiments abreast, each having one battalion on the line. K Company of the 349th went to Rome to perform garrison duties there. This Rome assignment continued for several months being rotated among top-notch companies of the Division.

A campaign for the "March of Dimes," sponsored by the Division Radio Station, was concluded with over $11,000 being raised by voluntary contributions. The Division newspaper, *The Blue Devil,* had a project of its own. An eight-year-old Italian boy, Giuliano Cabbia of Feltre, had been blinded by the kick of a German horse during Nazi occupation of his town. Divisionites contributed more than $3,000 to send Giuliano to the States for an eye operation. Doctors at Johns Hopkins Hospital in Baltimore, Md., did what they could for him, refusing payment, and the blind boy returned to Italy with Pfc. Howard Gorgas of the 349th who had been caring for him for months. Balance of the fund was turned over to the American Consul at Florence to be used for Giuliano's education.

The long-awaited Foreign Ministers' Delegation for studying the Italian–Jugoslav boundary question finally arrived in Trieste on 7 March. On 10 March two civilians were killed and several wounded in Servola, a suburb of Trieste, as a result of disorders arising from an attempt on the part of the Venezia Giulia Civil Police (who were trained by and continued under the supervision and control of the 13th Corps) to remove a flag illegally flown from a church steeple. A strike of Trieste workers was called, and a huge orderly demonstration of about 100,000 participants formed for the funeral of the victims. The next day the pro-Italian population turned out twice as many for a demonstration of their own to impress the Ministers' Delegation. On 15 March a Jugoslav major of the War Booty Commission was wounded by unknown assailants in Trieste, inciting further charges against the Civil Police and Allied Military Government. The return of the boundary delegation to Zone "A" after

Giuliano Cabbia, blind Italian boy who was adopted by the 88th and sent to America for treatment, back home with his parents in Feltre.

visiting Zone "B" touched off a series of demonstrations throughout the area, especially in Gorizia and Trieste. In Gorizia, both factions demonstrated simultaneously in front of AMG Headquarters, where the Delegation was meeting, while a path wide enough for a jeep separated them. Less than 100 men from the Division Military Police and a company of the 349th Infantry effected this separation of the two hostile mobs. It was an example of perfect discipline exemplified by the troops as they quietly went about their jobs, with not one person being injured or even arrested. Its effect on the civilians themselves was enormous, and increased their respect for the now well trained 88th Division.

On the 23d, Brig. Gen. Ridgely Gaither arrived to become Assistant Division Commander. General Gaither was soon to make his presence felt throughout the Infantry units, as he started a realistic battle school up in the mountains near Tarvisio, where every doughboy of the Division took combined training with artillery and tank units taking part.

As the month drew to a close, bitter criticism of AMG and the Venezia Giulia Civil Police began to be expressed in some of the local press and in radio broadcasts from Belgrade, the capital of Jugoslavia. At the same time, Jugoslav troop reinforcements behind the Iron Curtain of the Morgan Line began to be apparent, and were announced as "defensive." The time for a firm stand had arrived, and General Morgan, the Allied Commander in the Mediterranean, made it without hesitation in the following official statement. General Morgan said:

Recent troop movements have occurred in the area of Venezia Giulia under Jugoslav military administration. At the same time, there has been renewed and unwarranted criticism from abroad of Allied Military Government in Zone "A." Attempts have been made to create incidents detrimental to public order in Allied Military Government territory and to undermine the authority of public security agencies in Venezia Giulia. There should be no question as to what attitude the Allies will take in the circumstances.

The Allied Military Government authorities will continue, as in the past, to administer the territory in Zone "A" in the interest of peace and security and to uphold the authority of the Civil Police.

The troop reinforcements in the Jugoslav zone have been described as defensive in character. But the only claimant to this area with armed forces in Zone "A" is Jugoslavia itself. Defensive measures are obviously not necessary against the only other forces in Zone "A," the British and American Forces . . . stationed there to maintain order pending the peace settlement.

The representatives of the Soviet Union, France, the United States and Great Britain are now at work preparing a just and fair peace settlement. Until this settlement is achieved our obligations and our responsibilities are clear. Public order will be enforced with justice, and in our zone we shall tolerate no attempt to prejudice in any way the final disposition of the territory. To this end the American and British governments have authorized me to declare it is the firm intention to maintain their present position in Venezia Giulia until an agreed settlement of the territory dispute has been reached and put into effect.

During March, the already close and friendly relations with the 56th London Division were cemented even more firmly by the inauguration of officer exchanges between them and ourselves. Exchange officers served in their opposite number's jobs for two week periods. This policy was continued through the Spring, including exchanges with the British 6th Armored Division.

In sports, the Division's All-Star Basketball Team easily won the MTO championship and the MTOUSA Ski Team, a majority of which came from the 88th, triumphed over the ETO team in the Alps. Baseball and softball practice was started, aided by a touch of Spring in the air. New

Red Cross clubs were opened, and the PX opened a gift shop in Gorizia. Train 88, a new institution in Italy, ran daily from Naples to Udine, and daily trains started south from Udine. Later, this service was extended to Gorizia, and finally to Trieste. It eased the supply situation and made more certain the regular receipt of fresh rations. Plenty was going on besides controlling crowds and manning lonely Morgan Line outposts.

April's high spot was easily the Army Day parade in Gorizia on the 6th. All units of the Division participated, including the 752nd Tank Battalion, with its complements of medium and light tanks. The parade lasted for two hours and was concluded by units of the Desert Air Force flying in salute overhead. The ceremony was witnessed by the entire population of the surrounding area, who were visibly impressed by the display of power and precision of the "Diavoli Blu."

Now that the 88th was becoming better known in the States, a steady stream of reporters, movie cameramen, feature writers and finally newspaper executives came to look at the "Blue Devils." They went away properly impressed. One of them, Julius Ochs Adler of *The New York Times,* who had been a DSC winning Infantry company commander in World War I and a brigadier general, assistant commander of an infantry division in the Pacific Theater in World War II, had this to say: "I had a chance to see a group of soldiers on the Morgan Line today, and as a former soldier myself, I can honestly say that I've never seen a finer group anywhere, either here or in the Pacific." This was on April 25 and the unit he saw that day was L Company of the 349th Infantry.

The 88th Recon Troop was mighty busy during the month, doing constant patrolling of a lonely hilly area known as the "Collio," northeast of Cormons, and now and then uncovering caches of hidden arms. Stray shots in the night continued to greet men on Morgan Line outposts and patrol duty. None was hit, and investigation always wound up in one of two ways: Either someone was feeling happy at a wedding celebration in Zone "B" and decided to show his enthusiasm by firing a few rounds from the tommy gun he had used in Partisan warfare, or "We have no knowledge of any shooting. If there were any, it must have been directed toward what we thought were suspicious characters trying to sneak across the line from Zone 'A' into Zone 'B.'"

Toward the end of the month, all sorts of rumors, obviously inspired for terroristic reasons, began to percolate throughout the area, particularly among the civilian elements. Most of them had to do with supposed seizure of power on or just preceding May Day. Precautionary measures were taken, since the Division took neither rumors nor their denials for granted. May Day, 1946, passed very quietly, however, with well con-

Maj. Gen. Bryant E. Moore points out the boundaries of Venezia-Giulia on a map to a group of visiting publishers and executives.

trolled demonstrations by pro-Jugoslav elements. The crowds were large, but generally held comfortably in check by the combined efforts of the Venezia Giulia Civil Police, the MPs of the 56th London Division and 88th MPs. In Trieste, men of the 349th Infantry were MPs as well as infantrymen. There the camera of a U. S. Army Pictorial Service photographer was snatched from his jeep as it passed through a crowd of 500 Slovene demonstrators. It was smashed before he could jump out to recover it.

The Division Signal Company continued on at the same terriffic pace it had been maintaining for the past six months. The Signalmen were maintaining communications over a front wider than that generally set up for an army. They were running a radio operators' school and a radio repair school. During April alone, they installed 110 miles of wire. Their radio repair shop repaired over 300 radio sets, tactical and Special Service sets combined. Their LEGION switchboard handled over 500 calls an hour over 62 extensions and 47 trunks. The teletype system sent 501 messages and received 443. The Message Center handled 11,852 messages, and approximately as many miles were driven by its motor messengers.

May was a month of activity. Many plans formulated during the early Spring were pushed to fruition. Among these were the use of the Cortina

Ordnance takes on a major repair job.

and Lido Rest Center areas by complete units, with training in the morning and recreation in the afternoon. This turned out to be one of the most popular moves made for the comfort of personnel during the entire first year of occupation. Units were rotated in and out of these rest centers every two weeks.

During May, families began to arrive in the Division. On the 21st, 39 wives and 34 children came in on the *Vulcania* at Naples, and were met by a reception committee and all of the husbands concerned. This was the beginning of an influx that was to continue in steadily mounting numbers from then on. The new arrivals were initially quartered at Lido, which had been prepared for them, but as the number of families increased, the need for more accommodations found families spread from one end of the Division area to the other, and in Cortina, the Division's winter sports playground.

Freight was arriving by the Division's daily "Train 88" at the rate of 110 tons per day. Over 40 carloads were received during the month for Army Exchange Service alone. The Ordnance shops, augmented by German maintenance companies, completed the repair of 749 major and minor units, while the Ordnance Supply Platoon received a 45 carload shipment of vehicles from PBS. Ordnance repaired 131 weapons, large and small. The instrument section repaired 59 fire control instruments and 40 watches. One thousand two hundred and seventy-seven long tons of ammunition were received and distributed, while the reserve at the dumps was held intact. Special Service received enough athletic equipment to supply the needs of the Division for the entire summer. Meanwhile they concentrated, in conjunction with the technical services, on plans for opening and improving the nearby Grado Rest Center.

Two rifle battalions, the Recon Troop, two tank companies, an honor guard from the 351st Infantry and heavy equipment units participated in a great Victory Day Parade with 13 Corps in Trieste, commemorating the anniversary of the German surrender in Italy. This was a tremendous show of force and armed might, taking three hours to pass in review. The movement of units to the Trieste area in preparation for it, and the impact of the parade itself, probably did much to prevent any excess May Day ardor, in a way that was probably more effective than trying to stop it after it had been started.

Civilian demonstrations were an old story to the Division by this time. If they were authorized, and they generally were, the Division pitched in on its share of seeing to it that the paraders were themselves orderly and that they were protected from any elements who had opposite feelings. Practice alerts were held at intervals and personnel took their appointed stations promptly. The "firm intention" of the Allied Commander was being carried out by men fully capable and determined. Prior to 15 May, the meeting of the Big Four Foreign Ministers in Paris was awaited with reasonably quiet anticipation by all political groups, each confident that its side would prevail. When the meetings adjourned with no settlement having been reached, there was a resurgence of open unrest, manifested by inflammatory articles in the press of both sides, and by overt acts of violence in Trieste. Anniversaries of all sorts continued to be seized upon for display of flags and for parades attended by mutual revilement and brawls. Tito's birthday on May 25 passed without serious incident, however.

The strength of the Division remained near T/O strength, although there was an excess of 579 in those going out over those coming in. Twelve platoons of the Division participated in Memorial Day exercises throughout the MTO, going to Rome, Naples and Leghorn. They went to and fro by motor, conducting short ceremonies in towns and villages en route, including cities on the east coast of Italy. Memorial Day services within the Division Area included those at Trieste, Tarvisio, Plezzo, Volzana, Cormons, Cividale, Buttrio and Gorizia.

June 1946 was a difficult period for the Allied Occupation Forces in Venezia Giulia, and the 88th Division had its share of the difficulties. The calm discipline of the troops and the intensive training they had been taking in the previous six months paid off and successfully prevented serious trouble. A regrouping of the Division gave additional strength in depth to the center of its position. More of its reserve strength, particularly the 350th Infantry, moved southeastward, and gave the Division Commander additional trained units almost within voice distance of his busy CP in Gorizia.

On June 2, the Italian people had their election of representatives to their newborn kingless government. There was voting in Udine province, where the Engineers, the Medics, the hospital, the Ordnance, the Quartermaster and parts of the 350th and 351st were billeted. No voting was conducted in the disputed territory of Venezia Giulia. All units in the voting areas stayed in that day, and the next, so that there might be no semblance of Allied control of the election and of the possible disputes growing out of it. It was a most orderly election, conducted on democratic principles, and the Italian people may well be proud of the peaceful way in which it was held.

The 1st Battalion of the 349th, in Trieste, was extremely busy in June. The opposing political factions' tempers had been shortened by the long wait for the decisions on the boundaries, and flare-ups between them were frequent. These culminated in a riot on the last day of the month in which seven Americans and two British were wounded.

The disorders on that day started at the boundary of Venezia Giulia and worked in toward the center. Competitors in an Italian bicycle race were stoned near Pieris, about 40 kilometers from Trieste, and word of it soon reached the city. The Italian elements in Trieste had been growing more vociferous and more confident in recent weeks, and roving bands of them began to attack Slovene and Communist installations throughout the port city. The Venezia Giulia Civil Police called out their reserves to cope with the rioters, but there were too many places and too many people for their force to handle. They were quickly joined by British and American units kept in Trieste for just such a purpose. One of the more serious outbreaks occurred at the printing plant of *Il Lavoratore,* a Communist newspaper. There the mobs seized the papers as they came out of the building for afternoon delivery and burned them.

By midnight of that day, Allied flying squads had broken up the incipient mobs, but the disorders resumed again the following morning with further attacks by pro-Italians against Communist offices and by infiltration of Slovenes into the city for the purpose of finding their political opponents and engaging in pitched street battles with them. Again, shots were fired at the police, and paving bricks torn from the street to hurl at them. When late afternoon saw the authorities in complete control again,

A new Italo-American alliance at Gorizia.

the casualty list of the two days included one civilian and one VG police-man killed, 7 American and two British wounded, and at least 100 civilians wounded or injured. To some, these riots seemed to be the signal for a general uprising or the movement of Jugoslav troops to Trieste "to restore order." No such attempts were made, and perhaps they were never thought of. If they had been, the evident firm determination of the com-bined Allied Force to prevent illegal seizure of power discouraged them. On the 27th the USS *Fargo*, a first-class cruiser, joined two American destroyers and several British craft in Trieste harbor on a visit to the Queen City of the Adriatic.

The month of June cleared the calendar with the 88th Division "Blue Devils" tactical as in combat; alert to their responsibilities; with a mutual feeling of confidence among officers and enlisted men; topping the theater in recruiting; low in the theater in motor accidents, VD rate and AWOLs; still putting on a first-class sports program; bringing coffee and doughnuts to infantrymen and tankers and artillery observers at mountain-top OPs; redeploying men with a groan; discharging their duties in a key position in the occupation of Zone "A" of Venezia Giulia —an area under the eyes of the entire world. As a reporter for the *Chicago Tribune* who visited us that month said, we were "at peak form" and "razor sharp."

On July 3, the Big Four Ministers' meeting in Paris finally came to a decision on Trieste. Their inability, for months previous, to come to an understanding, had been the indirect but none the less primary cause of most of the riots in and near Trieste in recent months. But, curiously enough, their decision to internationalize the port city, making it a free state whose integrity would be assured by the United Nations Organization, only touched off a new series of disorders. The Italians were not satisfied. They felt they had been robbed of a city which for hundreds of years had been populated by Italians more than any other nationality, regardless of which flag had flown over it. The Jugoslavs were not satisfied. They felt that the fact that the hinterland of Trieste is predominantly Slav in character gave them the right to control the port which served the area. Most of the inhabitants of Trieste were not satisfied, since they felt that a clear-cut decision to give the city and its environs to one country or the other might have stilled, after a year or so, the claims of the other. Now they foresaw years of wrangling ahead, with both Italy and Jugoslavia attempting to infiltrate outsiders into Trieste, for the purpose of controlling elections and ultimately setting up another claim to it. They looked at the example of Fiume, at the other end of the Istrian Peninsula, which had been set up as a free port by the Versailles Treaty following World War I. In 1922, Italy, figuratively thumbing its nose at the League of Nations, had seized and kept Fiume. Now the inhabitants of Trieste wondered if, after the American and British forces had been withdrawn, Jugoslavia would attempt a similar coup. They were buoyed up by the knowledge that the UNO was far stronger than the old League of Nations, and in addition had the full partnership of the United States, but this only slightly diminished their fears. Meanwhile, both Italy and Jugoslavia stated they would refuse to sign a treaty based on the compromise plan that had been reached.

The month was marked by a series of general strikes, demonstrations, bomb throwing and shooting incidents. An unauthorized parade in Gorizia, protesting against the decisions in Paris, was dispersed by 88th MPs without serious incident. Partially successful strikes throughout the area until the 12th were highlighted by a number of acts of intimidation, principally grenade and bomb throwing at houses and business places of non-sympathizers during the hours of darkness.

Up north of Caporetto there is a little village called Ursina. It is in Zone "A," close to the Morgan Line. After the decisions reached by the Big Four have been signed and implemented, it will become part of Jugoslavia. But on July 12, 1946, and for a long while thereafter, it was in the occupation zone protected by American forces against any unpeaceful means of settling its future destiny. Investigating the presence of a group of men near Ursina, Lt. Edmund Downer of L Company, 351st Infantry, and his patrol of seven men were fired upon. They were still in Zone "A," as were their assailants. The fire was returned, and in the ensuing fire fight, two Jugoslav soldiers were killed. No Americans were killed or wounded. The American patrol was outnumbered, but the training they had been receiving paid off.

Diplomatic representations by Jugoslavia to the U. S. immediately followed, but these soon ceased as it became evident from the circumstances that the fire fight must have occurred on the American side of the line.

Only four days later an American soldier was murdered near the Division's southern boundary. Pfc. Walter L. Kagawa of Miresses, Pennsylvania, had joined the Division a few days before when his old outfit, the famous Nisei 442d Combat Team, was broken up. He was killed in ambush near Trieste.

The Division had celebrated its fourth anniversary the day before Walter Kagawa was murdered on the lonely road from Trieste. Birthday greetings had been received from Generals Eisenhower, Clark, Lee, Devers, McNarney, Keyes, and Jaynes, and quite naturally, from former 88th commanders, Generals Sloan, Kendall and Fry. Lt. Gen. Sir John Harding sent a message in which he recalled the magnificent name the 88th Division had made for itself in battle and in its equally difficult present occupational task. He said he was "extremely proud and happy to have the famous Blue Devils" under his command. All of these greetings were published in the July 15 issue of the *Blue Devil*, which was then mailed to every former member of the Division for whom a mailing address could be found. An evening military and sports carnival, which included everything from exhibitions by Spitfires and motorcycle trick riders to bathing beauty and jitterbug contests, was planned for Gorizia's "Campo Sportivio." It was rained out on the evening of the 15th but was held on the 16th under clear skies. Many thousands of GIs and an equal number of civilians attended and enjoyed themselves to the utmost. Special Service served free beer. The Red Cross passed out coffee and snacks. The whole enterprise was planned under the personal control of Colonel Robert J. McBride, the Chief of Staff, one of the fast-thinning ranks of the originals from Gruber who had been with the Division in the four years since activation. Colonel McBride left for the States for an assignment in Washington, by the end of the month. He was temporarily succeeded by Lt. Col. William J. McDonnell, who had come to the Division shortly before as Assistant to Colonel McBride.

August, the eleventh month of the 88th Division's job as the U. S. Occupational Force in Venezia Giulia found troop dispositions generally unchanged as continued emphasis was placed on the operation and inspection of roadposts along the Morgan Line. Several incidents of international importance, including the shooting down by Jugoslav forces of two Army passenger-carrying planes, kept the Division on the alert, even though the incidents themselves did not directly affect the peace and security within the Division's assigned area, with the possible exception of an incident in Gorizia on August 9. This incident resulted in the banishment of a Jugoslav officer from the 88th's area.

A pro-Italian faction was holding a memorial service to the men of Gorizia who fell in World War I. During the ceremony in a public park two hand grenades were thrown into the crowd. Six policemen and 28 civilians were wounded. Just as the wounded were being taken away, a Jugoslav Army car with two officers and their driver drove past the monument. The Italians, infuriated at the bombing and in their excitement blaming the Jugoslavs, gathered about the car and attempted to punch its occupants. Division MP's escorted the vehicle from the scene and during a search found three grenades and a pistol, contrary to orders that arms would not be carried outside the area in which the Jugoslav detachment was located. The trio was taken into custody and the matter reported to General Moore.

The senior of the two officers was Major Vlado Despot, who had been for many months the Political Commissar of the local Jugoslav detachment. When called before General Moore the Jugoslav officer was extremely dictatorial and insulting. An official inquiry board heard Major Despot deny prior knowledge of the weapons and admit that but for the intervention of American MP's he would have been injured seriously by the angry civilians. Major Despot, for his conduct and breach of orders, later was banished from Zone "A."

Two days later, an American Red Cross jeep was fired on in daylight. On the 22d, the Division Mobile Library truck, on its way to bring a bit of relaxation to a Morgan Line outpost, was fired upon on the main highway north of Gorizia. The driver, Pfc. Wade Tarnglee, realizing that his top-heavy vehicle was not built for a race, quickly dismounted and returned the fire with his semi-automatic carbine. The assailants apparently took off.

During this first half of the month, the firm Allied determination to protect the area from instigators of trouble was high-lighted by several surprise raids for hidden arms. One of these used four battalions of troops—two from the British 56th London Division and two from the

Lt. Gen. John C. H. Lee, MTOUSA commander, presents the Distinguished Unit Citation streamer to the 2d Battalion, 351st.

349th Infantry. Liaison planes of our Division Artillery worked in close cooperation with the ground troops in that one.

Meanwhile, plans which had begun early in July for a Division Review to honor the 2d Battalion of the 351st Infantry at Gorizia on August 20 were brought to completion. The taut international situation provided no reason for it, nor to postpone it. The review came off as scheduled, and the colors of the 2d Battalion of the 351st were decorated with the Distinguished Unit Citation Streamer by Lt. Gen. John C. H. Lee, MTO-USA Commander, during a most impressive ceremony on a windswept field under sunny skies. Many newspapermen who failed to ask enough questions assumed the review was solely to show off our power to the Jugoslavs, who could see it from the hillsides of Zone "B" a few miles away. No doubt they were properly impressed by the giant review of almost three-quarters of the Division's strength, because it was an event to be remembered by those who saw it, as an outstanding presentation of American troops and guns at their best.

The Distinguished Unit Citation of the 2d Battalion, 351st, was for its outstanding job of wresting Mt. Cappello from a determined and numerically superior German force, and then holding it despite wave after wave of bitter counterattack, during the period September 27–October 1, 1944. Also decorated on that day was Lt. Col. D. E. Townsend, assistant to General Gaither in the battle training program carried out all summer in the Julian Alps. Colonel Townsend had recently joined the Division, and his award was the Distinguished Service Cross, for the extraordinary heroism he had displayed in action with the 10th Mountain Division in the bitter fighting to open the Po Valley.

The Division Review occurred almost at the same moment that the Tito Government was handed the demand of the US, that the personnel of the two C–47s forced down by Jugoslav planes after they had gone a few miles out of their way in crossing the Alps, be returned within forty-eight hours. The living were returned well within the time limit, at 9:50 P.M., August 22, at famous outpost 36 on the Morgan Line. They had been fourteen days without American food, and their first demand was for coffee from Lt. Donald A. Paulson of F Company, 349th, who met them at the roadpost. Six days later, the bodies of the five men who had been killed when the second of our planes was shot down were brought into Zone "A" through the same outpost. There they were turned over to General Moore by US Ambassador to Jugoslavia Richard C. Patterson, and placed in waiting ambulances, temporarily serving as hearses. Ambassador Patterson said, "I have talked to Marshal Tito about this incident and he has assured me that there will be no repetition of the incident."

Religious and medical officers escort the bodies of five American airmen shot down in Jugoslavia across the Morgan Line into 88th territory for shipment to the States.

The Ursina incident of the previous month had been by now thoroughly investigated, and it appeared to be time for an official statement. General Morgan, the Supreme Allied Commander, gave it out, and simultaneously refuted in terms unmistakable by anyone, the statements in the Jugoslav press. He stated that results of "detailed investigations of the incident have proved that these statements were entirely false." He then went over the incident step by step, using the expression "definitely not true" time after time as he discussed the statement in the Belgrade newspapers. He completed his remarks by saying, "the results of the inquiry show that the statements made in the Belgrade press were utterly false and were apparently intended to divert attention from the illegal presence of Jugoslav troops in Zone 'A.'" Meanwhile, our own State Department made public a note delivered to the Jugoslav Government on August 16 in which it stated that the US "emphatically" rejected the Jugoslav protest regarding the Ursina incident. The note went on to say that the Jugoslav protest was "apparently based on the distortion of evidence."

The redeployment of fathers during August, which took away most of the senior, more mature NCOs, and the transshipment to the States of 311 officers due for discharge, seriously cut into the supply of trained leaders. Unit commanders tightened their belts, said, "Here we go again," and started training leaders all over again.

It was apparent that the coming winter would probably find the 88th still on occupation duty in Venezia Giulia, so in July preparations were made, and supplies requisitioned, for the cold months to come. They started arriving in August. Eight thousand eight hundred and fifty-four tons of freight came in, in addition to 237 carloads of coal, which was only the beginning. Despite strict economy in the use of gasoline, the Division's operational job over one thousand square miles of territory made necessary the issuance of 335,216 gallons of 72-octane gas and 20,232 gallons of 80-octane gas in that month. The latter was for the L-5 planes and for the tanks.

Twenty-three American reporters visited the Division in September, its twelfth month of occupation duty. One of them, Daniel Jacino of the Associated Press photography staff, was wounded in Trieste on September 8, when seven men from K Company of the 351st Infantry also were wounded. The 8th of September is a famous date in Italy. Political connections before the "Otto Settembre" are generally kept quiet, if possible, by those who were supporters of the old Mussolini regime. If they are pinned down, they say with a supposed disarming smile, "Oh, yes, but that was before the 8th of September!" What they mean, and the hearer is supposed to know by some telepathy that they mean it, is that after September 8, 1943, they were strong supporters of the Allied cause, but that before that date, when Italy accepted the terms of unconditional surrender, they conformed to the government line.

Since September 8, 1946, was to be the third anniversary of the surrender to the Allies, it provided an opportunity for the so-called anti-Fascist groups in Venezia Giulia to ask AMG for permission to hold a celebration. AMG refused on the ground that it would lead to public disorder. During the month, many requests for political manifestations were refused for the same reason. Nevertheless, in the San Giacomo district of Trieste, which had always been a trouble spot, an estimated seven thousand persons gathered with flags, banners and placards in one of the carefully planned "spontaneous demonstrations of the will of the people" which this area sees frequently.

The Civil Police, together with men of the 3d Battalion, 351st Infantry, all of whom wore MP designations on their helmet liners, moved in to break up the threat to public order and to uphold the AMG order forbidding the demonstration. It had been found, by experience, that looking on such disregard of Allied Military Government orders with a kindly eye only led to riots and to a feeling among the populace that the Allies were too weak or too indulgent to uphold their own orders.

As the men of K Company kept the crowds moving, meanwhile

breaking the big groups into smaller ones, the grenade was thrown. In addition to the AP photographer, seven men of the company were slightly wounded by the fragments.

In the Division, the month was notable for the honors and ceremonies extended, and the visits of dignitaries who congratulated its commander on the manner of performance of duty. They saw the results of constant training of the large numbers of enlisted men and officers received during this and the preceding month, so that the stress on attaining and preserving high operational efficiency would be realized. Training was not only for individuals, but also for the larger-scaled development of closely-knit combat teams in which the technique of interrelated units was kept up to the standard necessary for the only Division in the American Army at full strength and operationally fit, in the Fall of 1946.

On September 9 an incident occurred at Trieste which had international implications. This followed by less than twenty-four hours the wounding of seven 88th-men in that port city. The following communiqué, issued by AFHQ a week later, after it had gathered all of the facts in the case, tells the story.

CASERTA, Sept. 17 (UNN).—In order to correct certain misapprehensions due to a certain erroneous statement made in recent Jugoslav press releases, a spokesman for AFHQ issued the following statement of facts today:

On 8 September, seven military policemen were wounded by a hand grenade in Trieste.

At about 0300 hours on 9 September, a large explosion occurred in Trieste. A mobile patrol of the American police was sent to investigate. Near the scene, this patrol encountered a weapons carrier in which were six Jugoslav soldiers. After a pursuit of more than a mile, this vehicle was stopped and its occupants taken into custody. The six Jugoslav soldiers were taken to the US Military Police station in Trieste. The Provost Marshal's office was notified, and it was directed that the Jugoslavs be turned over to the VG Police. This was done. When a careful search of their persons was made, it was found that five of them had hand grenades.

Approximately one hour later on the morning of 9 September, S/Sgt. Robert C. Webb, of the 88th Division was still on duty in charge of the US Military Police Station in Trieste. He heard the sound of marching feet and when he looked out of the door he saw a detachment of five Jugoslav soldiers approaching the station. One of these soldiers was a Capt. Anton Segota, commanding officer of the guard company, Jugoslav detachment for UNRRA in Trieste.

Captain Segota entered the police station and advanced on Sergeant Webb. The sergeant said that he felt he was being surrounded and, remembering that seven police had been wounded on the previous day and that an hour earlier six Jugoslavs had been arrested while carrying concealed hand grenades, he became alarmed, drew his pistol and covered the Jugoslavs.

In a subsequent protest to 13 Corps Headquarters Captain Segota claimed that he had asked Sergeant Webb the whereabouts of the six Jugoslav soldiers who had previously been arrested. Captain Segota charged that after Sergeant Webb drew the pistol, he lined up the five Jugoslav soldiers, including Captain Segota, called for help from a rear room, searched the Jugoslavs, found no arms on them, used abusive language toward them, kept them at pistol point until an officer arrived.

An American investigation was instituted on 12 September.

Testimony showed, according to findings of the Board, that Captain Segota and his detachment of four Jugoslav soldiers had, in fact, called at the US Military Police Station to request the release of the Jugoslav soldiers previously apprehended.

The Board found that the acts of the Military Police would have been improper under normal conditions, but the background of hand grenades, explosion, time of night, the inability to understand each other, and other circumstances, justified the detention under armed guard of Captain Segota and his party.

It is pointed out that investigations show that the six Jugoslavs, who were detained as a result of having grenades on their possession, had no connection with the explosion the morning of 9 September. These six men were turned over to the Headquarters of the Jugoslav detachment by 13 Corps on 11 September with instructions that they be sent across the Morgan Line out of Zone "A," as a result of their failure to obey orders forbidding the carrying of weapons. (end of AFHQ Communiqué)

Some idea of the magnitude of the training task during these first twelve months of occupation duty may be gleaned by a look at the figures showing the turnover of personnel during that year. Not only was there a terrific job for G-1 and the AG in making sure that the right people went home at the right time, and that the incoming men were properly classified and allotted to units according to need and authorized strength, but there developed upon G-3 a terrific task of training and retraining from the ground up, month after month. Under G-3 also came the I & E Section, with its duty of setting up proper indoctrination and orientation of not only the replacements as they came in, but also the necessity of keeping the personnel of the Division informed. *The Blue Devil* newspaper and the American Expeditionary Radio Station were important adjuncts of the Troop Information Program handled by the I & E Section in this connection. During most of the year, Lt. Col. James E. Tyler held down the G-3 post, succeeding Lt. Col. Ralph E. Haines when the latter went up to the 350th to assume command early in the year.

In just one year, the Division received 1,329 officers and 28,177 enlisted men. In that same year there were shipped out 1,149 officers and 17,005 enlisted men. And this wasn't a replacement training center which normally operates on a turnover scale of such proportions but was a combat division, operationally ready for any task that an American combat division must be ready to undertake upon order.

As the first year of occupation duty was drawing to a close the hope began to rise that General of the Army Dwight D. Eisenhower would visit the Division. When hope had been all but abandoned, General Eisenhower arrived by train early on the morning of October 16 up in the northeast corner of the Division area where the 351st Infantry maintains contact with British forces in Austria and looks across the pre-war Italo–Jugoslav border at the soldiers with the Red Star on their headgear. General Eisenhower was greeted there by top-ranking Division and Mediterranean Theater officials.

Starting in Tarvisio, General Eisenhower made a day-long tour of all units in the Division. After formal inspections of units, he would gather the personnel about him for informal discussions, quizzes and reports from home. He told all the men that it was the job of the Armies of Occupation to "produce peace." The formal inspection tour was completed at the Campoformido airfield outside Udine and there General Eisenhower found an Allied Guard of Honor drawn up for him. This, he said, symbolized "a perpetuation of that great unity which through those long and bitter months of warfare brought about the greatest and most complete victory of all time."

The letter which the Division Commander promptly sent to the personnel of the Division that evening is a fitting close for this history, for it not only reflected his feelings, but the feelings of each "Blue Devil."

Headquarters 88th Infantry Division
United States Army
APO 88

17 Oct. 1946

Subject : General Eisenhower's Visit
To   :   The Officers and Men of the 88th Division

The visit of General Eisenhower was truly a great occasion for every one of us. Everybody that could possibly be turned out had a chance to see him and hear him, and feel his sympathy and sincere regard and understanding for all. To those whose duties did not enable them to see him, General Eisenhower sends his greetings.

General Eisenhower planned and commanded the greatest military operation in the history of the world. Millions of soldiers have served under his command. It was therefore a great honor to have him visit our Division from one end of it to the other, and to express himself so cordially and so admiringly toward us. You made a splendid impression on him. As your commanding general, I am naturally very proud of you.

Every one of you must feel great pride in belonging to an outfit like this, so well known to the people of our country, and with such an important and worthwhile mission.

Every one of us must resolve to do his part to make the Division better. From General Eisenhower's faith in us we must take new strength as soldiers, and work together to improve our mess, our living conditions, our motors, our field efficiency.

Let us each be better representatives of our great nation; let us do everything we can to improve ourselves, and to make the "Blue Devil" Division the greatest outfit in the world.

General Lee, our theater commander, joins in thanks to you for your labors and for your accomplishments.

BRYANT E. MOORE
Major General, Commanding

The 88th, in peace as well as in war, had "a job to do." And did it.

WHITE CROSSES. And beneath white crosses in military cemeteries at Carano, Follonica, Castelfiorentino, Pietramala and Mirandola, Italy, lie the Blue Devils who never came back. They fought and died, for us. We remember them. This is the 88th's Honor Roll.

BATTLE CASUALTIES

Please God, silence the scheming and the stupid in our Government and let the honest and strong lead us to right. Otherwise we fight in vain. If we cannot correct ourselves, how can we lead others from their chaos?

FROM THE DIARY OF PVT. MORGAN J. QUINN, 88TH CAVALRY RECONNAISSANCE TROOP, KILLED IN ACTION AT CARPANE, ITALY, APRIL 30, 1945.

Abreu, Joe M., Sgt, 350th Inf
Adams, Alfred D., Pfc, 913th Fa Bn
Adams, Charles E., Pfc, 349th Inf
Adams, Edward D., Pfc, 350th Inf
Adams, Lafayette B., 1st Lt, 350th Inf
Adams, Woodrow W., Pvt, 351st Inf
Adams, Edward J., Pvt, 349th Inf
Adkins, Albert B., S/Sgt, 349th Inf
Adler, Richard C., S/Sgt, 349th Inf
Aebig, Clement E., Pfc, 351st Inf
Affannato, George C., Pvt, 350th Inf
Aiken, Charles L., T/Sgt, 351st Inf
Ainsworth, Chester L., Cpl, 913th Fa Bn
Ajamian, Armen S., Pvt, 350th Inf
Albarado, Antonio, Pfc, 350th Inf
Albarella, James J., Pfc, 351st Inf
Alessi, Dominick J., S/Sgt, 351st Inf
Alfaro, Antonio P., Pvt, 350th Inf
Alldredge, James J., Pvt, 330th Fa Bn
Allegra, Joseph A., S/Sgt, 350th Inf
Allen, Calvin O., 2nd Lt, 350th Inf
Allen, George W., S/Sgt, 350th Inf
Allen, John J., Jr., Pvt, 350th Inf
Allen, Robert H., Pvt, 351st Inf
Allen, Robert L., Pfc, 351st Inf
Allison, Fred W., Pfc, 349th Inf
Allison, Wilmoth W., Pfc, 350th Inf
Alonso, Ernesto, Capt, 351st Inf
Alperstein, Ernest, Pvt, 313th Med Bn
Altschuler, Nathaniel C., Pvt, 351st Inf
Ament, John W., Pfc, 349th Inf
Amos, William O., Pfc, 349th Inf
Andersen, Roy F., Pfc, 351st Inf
Andersen, William E., Sgt, 349th Inf
Anderson, Floyd O., Pfc, 351st Inf
Anderson, Fred, Jr., Pfc, 350th Inf
Anderson, Roy L., S/Sgt, 349th Inf
Anderson, Theodore E., Pvt, 349th Inf
Anderson, William R., Pvt, 350th Inf
Anderson, Willie C., Pvt, 351st Inf
Andrews, Hollis E., Cpl, 339th Fa Bn
Andrews, William K., Pvt, 351st Inf
Angle, Roy S., S/Sgt, 350th Inf
Alvarez, Tony J., Pvt, 351st Inf
Apts, Willie B., Pfc, 351st Inf
Anttila, Eugene W., Pfc, 349th Inf
Arbuszeski, Thomas A., Pfc, 350th Inf
Arechiga, Manuel, Pfc, 349th Inf
Arends, Harold L., Pfc, 350th Inf
Argentati, Merico E., Pfc, 349th Inf
Arias, Alfredo B., Pvt, 349th Inf
Arispe, Gregorio, Pvt, 351st Inf
Arkow, David, Pvt, 350th Inf
Armer, Elmer, Pfc, 350th Inf
Armstrong, Rex G., Pvt, 349th Inf
Army, Henry L., S/Sgt, 350th Inf
Arnett, Ray F., Pvt, 350th Inf
Arnett, Winford, Pfc, 350th Inf
Arrowsmith, James K., Pfc, 351st Inf
Ashcraft, Farrell F., Pfc, 349th Inf.
Ashenden, James H., Pvt, 350th Inf
Asher, Lyle E., Pvt, 350th Inf
Ashton, Edward M., Pfc, 350th Inf
Asselin, Albert L., Pfc, 351st Inf
Aston, Reese V., Capt, 350th Inf
Atchison, John C., Pvt, 350th Inf
Atkins, Isaac V., Pfc, 351st Inf

Attara, Joseph A., Pfc, 351st Inf
Attenberger, Harold L., Pfc, 350th Inf
Auclair, Joseph J., Pvt, 349th Inf
Auger, Paul E., Pvt, 351st Inf
Avril, Howard C., Pvt, 349th Inf
Axelrod, Seymour, Pic, 351st Inf
Ayala, Roberto R., Pvt 349th Inf
Back, Harvey J., Pvt, 349th Inf
Backlund, Edgar W., Pvt, 350th Inf
Badt, Alexander B., Pvt, 350th Inf
Baehr, Conrad F., Pvt, 350th Inf
Baer, John S., 2nd Lt, 350th Inf
Baeza, Diego, Pfc, 351st Inf
Baggett, Harry E., Pfc, 351st Inf
Bagley, Charlie A., Pfc, 349th Inf
Bailey, Harvey, Pfc, 349th Inf
Baish, Earl R., Pfc, 351st Inf
Baker, Carl F., Sgt, 350th Inf
Baker, Joe E., T/5, 349th Inf
Baker, Marion H., Pfc, 350th Inf
Baker, Wayne C., Pvt, 349th Inf
Baldridge, Norman S., Pvt, 351st Inf
Baldyga, Joseph, Pfc, 351st Inf
Ball, Homer, Pvt, 349th Inf
Ball, Kenneth E., Pvt, 351st Inf
Ballinger, Gerald K., Pvt, 351st Inf
Banko, John J., Pfc, 349th Inf
Banks, Charlie, Pfc, 350th Inf
Barbeau, Bernard E., Pfc, 351st Inf
Barber, Dale C., Pvt, 350th Inf
Barber, Virgil R., Pvt, 349th Inf
Barker, Harold H., S/Sgt, 350th Inf
Barker, Warren A., Pvt, 351st Inf
Barnard, Clarence R., Pfc, 349th Inf
Barnes, Billie B., Pfc, 349th Inf
Barnes, David A., Pfc, 351st Inf
Barnette, Garneth W., Pfc, 349th Inf
Barney, Merrill E., Pvt, 351st Inf
Baron, Edwin T., T/4, 349th Inf
Barrett, Charles E., Pvt, 351st Inf
Barron, Earl, Pvt, 351st Inf
Barron, James V., Pvt, 351st Inf
Bartholomew, Keith B., Sgt, 351st Inf
Bartlett, Francis W., Pvt, 350th Inf
Bartlett, George E., Pvt, 350th Inf
Bartlett, Louis J., T/Sgt, 351st Inf
Bartley, Frank P., S/Sgt, 349th Inf
Bartoshnik, Samuel B., Cpl, 349th Inf
Bartush, Edward, Pvt, 350th Inf
Bashinski, Pete P., Pfc, 349th Inf
Basile, Joseph M., Pvt, 350th Inf
Basirico, Vito, Pfc, 350th Inf
Bass, Thomas H., Pfc, 351st Inf
Batchelor, Jesse J., Pvt, 350th Inf
Bathke, Norbert H., Pvt, 349th Inf
Bathory, Alex J., Pfc, 349th Inf
Baynard, William W., Pfc, 351st Inf
Beasley, Thomas J., Pvt, 349th Inf
Becker, Raymond, S/Sgt, 349th Inf
Beckly, Arthur R., Pfc, 350th Inf
Beidinger, Frank J., Jr., Pfc, 349th Inf
Beighley, Charles N., Pvt, 350th Inf
Belben, Clayton E., Pvt, 351st Inf
Belkin, Philip, Pvt, 349th Inf
Bellei, Edmund D., Pvt, 349th Inf
Bellesheim, George N., Pfc, 351st Inf
Belmonte, Daniel J., Pvt, 351st Inf

Belt, Charles A., Pvt, 351st Inf
Benak, Steve J., Pfc, 349th Inf
Bence, Billie E., 2nd Lt, 350th Inf
Bender Henry, Pvt, 351st Inf
Bennett, Frederick J., T/Sgt, 351st Inf
Bennett, Paul R., Pvt, 349th Inf
Bentley, Harold J., Pfc, 350th Inf
Benton, John W., Pfc, 350th Inf
Bergeron, Emile C., Jr., Pvt, 349th Inf
Berk, Ernest I., 2nd Lt, 351st Inf
Bernard, James W., Pvt, 349th Inf
Bernardinelli, John, Pvt, 349th Inf
Bernhard, Stephen V., S/Sgt, 313th Engr Bn
Berns, William N., Jr., Pvt, 351st Inf
Berretta, Lawrence, Pvt, 349th Inf
Berry, Charlie W., Pvt, 350th Inf
Berry, Daniel F., Pfc, 351st Inf
Berry, William P., Pfc, 351st Inf
Biancamano, John J., Pvt, 351st Inf
Biancamano, Michael N., S/Sgt, 349th Inf
Bible, Harry J., Pfc, 351st Inf
Bielema, Bennett, Pfc, 350th Inf
Bielusiak, Steve J., Pvt, 351st Inf
Biernat, Thomas F., Sgt, 351st Inf
Bigley, Milton R., T/5, 913th Fa Bn
Bilotto, Anthony, Cpl, 351st Inf
Binde, Irving, Pfc, 351st Inf
Birchfield, Tom, Pfc, 351st Inf
Bishop, Edward J., Pfc, 339th Fa Bn
Bivins, Robert L., Pfc, 349th Inf
Black, Ivan D., Pfc, 351st Inf
Black, James O., Cpl, 349th Inf
Blair, Howard R., Sgt, 350th Inf
Blaisdell, Royal F., Pfc, 351st Inf
Blanchette, Emile J., Pvt, 349th Inf
Blankenship, Braxter A., Pfc, 349th Inf
Blanckenship, Henry W., Pvt, 351st Inf
Blish, Delwin G., Sgt, 351st Inf
Block, Thomas J., T/5, 338th Fa Bn
Bluck, Henry A., Pfc, 351st Inf
Boardman, Eugene T., Pfc, 351st Inf
Bobbs, Leonard, Pvt, 350th Inf
Bobrowski, Theodore S., Sgt, 350th Inf
Bochenski, Nathew, Pfc, 351st Inf
Bock, Kenneth H., Pvt, 350th Inf
Bodvar, Carl O., Pfc, 351st Inf
Boettger, Roy A., S/Sgt, 351st Inf
Boisclair, Philip J., Cpl, 351st Inf
Boissenin, Emil J., Pvt, 351st Inf
Boisvert, George A., Jr., Pfc, 349th Inf
Boisvert, Robert R., T/Sgt, 349th Inf
Bolin, Ed, Cpl, 351st Inf
Bolt, William C., Pfc, 351st Inf
Bonosoro, Americo, Pfc, 351st Inf
Bonshock, Edward J., Pvt, 351st Inf
Borden, Raymond D., Pfc, 351st Inf
Boston, Robert M., Pfc, 351st Inf
Botelho, Eugene V., Pvt, 350th Inf
Boucher, Robert E., Pfc, 350th Inf
Boudreau, Joseph F., S/Sgt, 349th Inf
Bordovsky, Robert E., Pvt, 351st Inf
Boursaw, James M., Pvt, 349th Inf
Bowen, Henry M. L., Pvt, 350th Inf
Bowen, Thomas S., Cpl, 351st Inf
Bowen, William, Pvt, 350th Inf
Bowersock, Glenn, Pfc, 350th Inf
Bowles, Harry J., Pfc, 350th Inf
Bowley, Raleigh, 2nd Lt, 351st Inf
Bowman, James W., Pvt, 351st Inf
Bowman, Thomas E., S/Sgt, 350th Inf
Bowsh, John, Pvt, 313th Engr Bn
Boyer, Joseph J., Pvt, 351st Inf
Boyer, Raymond K., Pfc, 350th Inf
Boysen, Frederick O., 2nd Lt, 350th Inf
Braccilli, Richard J., Pfc, 88th Cav Ren Tr
Brackett, Felix D., Pvt, 351st Inf
Bradley, Andrew F., Jr., Pvt, 349th Inf
Bradshaw, Herbert L., Cpl, 350th Inf
Bradshaw, James M., Pvt, 350th Inf
Brady, Jacob L., Pfc, 350th Inf
Braen, Arthur H., S/Sgt, 351st Inf
Brandon, Glenn G., Pfc, 351st Inf

Bradstaetter, Frank R., Sgt, 349th Inf
Brandt, John H., Sgt, 349th Inf
Brannigar, James, Jr., T/5, 351st Inf
Bray, Raymond A., Sr., Pvt, 349th Inf
Brazauskas, Raymond J., Pvt, 350th Inf
Brazinski, John, Pvt, 913th Fa Bn
Brenner, Franz J., Pvt, 349th Inf
Breshinger, Arthur P., Pvt, 913th Fa Bn
Brewer, Paul U., Pfc, 349th Inf
Briggs, Alwin F., Cpl, 338th Fa Bn
Broad, George E., Sgt, 351st Inf
Brooker, Arnold L., Pvt, 313th Engr Bn
Brooks, Ezra, Pvt, 349th Inf
Brooks, Oscar B., Pvt, 349th Inf
Brouillard ,Joseph A., T/5, 351st Inf
Brown, Floyd G., Pfc, 350th Inf
Brown, George W., S/Sgt, 350th Inf
Brown, Harold Nac Y., Maj, 351st Inf
Brown, Joseph E., S/Sgt, 350th Inf
Brown, Kenneth L., Pfc, 349th Inf
Brown, Raymond L., 2nd Lt, 349th Inf
Brown, Robert L., 1st Lt, 349th Inf
Brown, Stanley R., Pfc, 350th Inf
Brown, Thomas D., Pvt, 350th Inf
Brown, William H., Pfc, 350th Inf
Bruckner, Curt A., Pvt, 351st Inf
Bruno, Dominic J., Pvt, 349th Inf
Bruton, Jess C., Pvt, 350th Inf
Bryson, Loren F., 1st Lt, 349th Inf
Bryson, Denver T., Pvt, 351st Inf
Brzezinski, Chester, Pfc, 349th Inf
Buchanan, Eldred H., Jr., Cpl, 351st Inf
Buck, Neil, Pfc, 349th Inf
Buckley, Daniel, Pfc, 350th Inf
Budo, Calvin B., Sgt, 350th Inf
Buff, Charlie E., Pfc, 351st Inf
Bunch, Billy L., Pvt, 350th Inf
Bunch, Roy L., Pvt, 349th Inf
Buonanno, Anthony R., Pvt, 350th Inf
Burey, Arthut L., S/Sgt, 349th Inf
Burch, Foster C., 1st Lt, 351st Inf
Burdick, Valerian F., Pvt, 351st Inf
Burford, John G., Pfc, 350th Inf
Burg, Elmer J., 2nd Lt, 349th Inf
Burgess, Frank E., Pfc, 349th Inf
Burke, Pearle Clair, S/Sgt, 313th Engr Bn
Burkett, Edward J., Sgt, 351st Inf
Burkett, Warren H., Pvt, 351st Inf
Burkholder, Wilbur C., Pfc, 350th Inf
Burnett, Stanley H., Pvt, 350th Inf
Burns, John R., Jr., 1st Lt, 351st Inf
Burrows, Edward L., S/Sgt, 349th Inf
Burton, James B., Jr., Pfc, 349th Inf
Burton, William F., Pvt, 350th Inf
Bush, Donald W., Pvt, 350th Inf
Bystraan, Corwin, Pvt, 349th Inf
Butler, Forrest O., Pfc, 351st Inf
Byrne, Neil W., Pfc, 349th Inf
Cabarrubia, Trinidad, Jr., Pfc, 350th Inf
Caccavallo, John, Pfc, 351st Inf
Calabrese, Vincent, Cpl, 349th Inf
Caldwell, Robert A., Pvt, 350th Inf
Caldwell, Robert A., Sgt, 349th Inf
Caldwell, Robert R., Pfc, 351st Inf
Caldwell, William H., Pfc, 350th Inf ,
Callaway, Glen, T/4, 350th Inf
Callow, William J., Pfc, 350th Inf
Cama, Paul J., Pvt, 351st Inf
Camarra, Albert, T/5, 313th Med Bn
Cambron, Glenn R., Sgt, 349th Inf
Camp, Max W., Sgt, 350th Inf
Camps, William S., Pvt, 349th Inf
Campano, Frank A., Jr., Pfc, 350th Inf
Campbell, Andrew M., 1st Lt, 349th Inf
Campbell, John E., Sgt, 350th Inf
Campbell, Mark V., Pfc, 350th Inf
Campbell, Robert, Pfc, 351st Inf
Campbell, Spencer S., Pfc, 351st Inf
Campise, Sam, Pvt, 350th Inf
Canterbury, Barnabas, T/Sgt, 350th Inf
Capolingua, Carlw, Pvt, 350th Inf
Capozzi, Frank D., Pfc, 351st Inf

Cappillo, Victor A., Pfc, 350th Inf
Caprio, Nicholas, Pfc, 351st Inf
Caputo, Anthony F., Pvt, 351st Inf
Carden, Wade H., Jr., Pfc, 350th Inf
Cargill, Jessie L., S/Sgt, 349th Inf
Carley, George L., Pvt, 349th Inf
Carnagio, James J., Pvt, 350th Inf
Carolan, Wendell P., T/4, 351st Inf
Carozza, Joseph P., Pvt, 351st Inf
Carpenter, George H., 1st Lt, 350th Inf
Carpenter, Gordon W., Cpl, 349th Inf
Carpenter, Robert J., Pvt, 351st Inf
Carpentier, Rene L., Sgt, 350th Inf
Carr, Thomas J., Jr., Pvt, 351st Inf
Carraro, Dante, Pvt, 350th Inf
Carrier, William R., Pvt, 351st Inf
Carrigg, Paul R., Capt, 313th Engr Bn
Carter, Charles C., Pfc, 350th Inf
Carter, Hiram C., Cpl, 351st Inf
Carter, Johnnie W., Pfc, 351st Inf
Casale, Ralph, S/Sgt, 349th Inf
Caskey, Garlen R., Sgt, 351st Inf
Cassady, Henry C., Pvt, 349th Inf
Cassell, Ernest E., Pfc, 351st Inf
Castilloux, Harry, Pvt, 350th Inf
Castle, Lafayette C., Pfc, 349th Inf
Castro, Jesus R., Pfc, 349th Inf
Catalamo, Morris E., Pvt, 351st Inf
Caufield, Arthur E., Pvt, 349th Inf
Cervy, Larry A., Pvt, 349th Inf
Chaffins, Fred, Pvt, 350th Inf
Challoner, Wallace R., Pvt, 350th Inf
Chamberlain, Lyndon R., Pfc, 350th Inf
Champagne, Laurie N., Pvt, 349th Inf
Chanovich, Samuel, Jr., Pvt, 349th Inf
Chapman, R. C., Pvt, 350th Inf
Charlier, John, Pfc, 351st Inf
Chase, James P., S/Sgt, 350th Inf
Cheeseman, Elwood, Pfc, 337th Fa Bn
Chernoff, Eugene V., Pvt, 349th Inf
Chess, Phillip S., Jr., 1st Lt, 349th Inf
Chew, William, Pfc, 350th Inf
Childress, Louis C., Jr., Pfc, 350th Inf
Chilik, Nestor M., Pvt, 349th Inf
Chiribel, Pablo, Pvt, 350th Inf
Chong, Richard, Pvt, 350th Inf
Christensen, Ralph E., Pfc, 351st Inf
Chu, Che Y., Pfc, 349th Inf
Chudoba, John, Pfc, 351st Inf
Chupak, Milton, S/Sgt, 349th Inf
Church, Edward J., Capt, 351st Inf
Ciallelo, John M., Pvt, 350th Inf
Ciarletto, Alfred J., Pfc, 350th Inf
Ciattoni, Vincent, Pfc, 350th Inf
Cimini, Frank J., Pfc, 351st Inf
Cioffi, William A., S/Sgt, 350th Inf
Cipriano, Angelo M., Pvt, 351st Inf
Ciresi, Frank A., Pfc, 350th Inf
Clancy, John C., Jr., 1st Lt, 351st Inf
Clark, Charles C., Cpl, 351st Inf
Clark, Foy M., S/Sgt, 351st Inf
Clark, Richard W., Sgt, 351st Inf
Clement, Louis, Pfc, 350th Inf
Cline, George E., S/Sgt, 349th Inf
Coad, Walter W., Pfc, 349th Inf
Cobb, Fred E., Pvt, 350th Inf
Cobb, Wesley L., Pfc, 350th Inf
Coble, Roy W., Pvt, 350th Inf
Cohen, Donald M., Pvt, 351st Inf
Cohen, Maurice, Pvt, 351st Inf
Cohen, Max, Pvt, 351st Inf
Cohen, Morris A., Pfc, 313th Med Bn
Colbert, Ovis E., Pfc, 351st Inf
Cole, Emery L., Pvt, 350th Inf
Coleman, Andrew S., Pvt, 349th Inf
Coleman, Charles M., S/Sgt, 349th Inf
Colemano, David F., Pvt, 350th Inf
Coleman, Richard I., Pvt, 349th Inf
Coles, Ralph L., Pfc, 349th Inf
Coletti, Carlo A., Pvt, 350th Inf
Colgrove, John E., Pvt, 313th Engr Bn
Collier, Albert L., T/5, 313th Med Bn

Collin, Albert, Pfc, 350th Inf
Collins, Albert, Pvt, 350th Inf
Collins, Herman N., Pvt, 350th Inf
Collins, James R., Pfc, 351st Inf
Collins, John H., T/5, 350th Inf
Colpitts, Clarence C., Pvt, 350th Inf
Coltrain, Marvin W., Pfc, 351st Inf
Comer, Overton L., Pfc, 350th Inf
Comfort, Bobby E., Pvt, 351st Inf
Commander, Walter F., 2nd Lt, 337th Inf
Conklin, Robert E., Pvt, 350th Inf
Conley, Hill F., Pfc, 351st Inf
Conlon, Thomas P., Jr., Cpl, 350th Inf
Connell, John D., Pfc, 349th Inf
Connell, Joseph F., Pfc, 351st Inf
Consiglio, Guido, Pfc, 349th Inf
Conyers, Harry D., 2nd Lt, 313th Engr Bn
Cook, Claude J., Jr., Pfc, 350th Inf
Cook, Eugene K., Pvt, 350th Inf
Cook, James C., Pfc, 349th Inf
Cook, James F., Pfc, 349th Inf
Cook, Lauren G., Sgt, 350th Inf
Cook, Luther H., Pvt, 351st Inf
Cooke, Arnold F., Pfc, 350th Inf
Cooper, Ephraim C., Pvt, 350th Inf
Cooper, Lacy T., Pvt, 351st Inf
Coppedge, Donald C., Pfc, 349th Inf
Corbe, Joseph T., Pvt, 351st Inf
Corcoran, Stephen M., Pfc, 351st Inf
Cordeau, Harold, Pfc, 349th Inf
Cornelson, Lester, Pfc, 349th Inf
Cornett, Leonardo R., Pvt, 350th Inf
Corso, Leon A., Pvt, 349th Inf
Cory, Lewis E., Sgt, 349th Inf
Cosby, Ray H., 2nd Lt, 351st Inf
Costa, Virgil, T/5, 349th Inf
Costello, Frank R., Pfc, 349th Inf
Cotinola, Lorenzo, Jr., Pvt, 351st Inf
Coulter, Floyd W., Pfc, 350th Inf
Courtmanche, Nelson A., Sgt, 349th Inf
Cowger, Francis M., Pvt, 350th Inf
Cox, George C., T/Sgt, 351st Inf
Cox, William H., Pvt, 350th Inf
Craft, John D., Pfc, 349th Inf
Craft, Stanley L., Pfc, 349th Inf
Crafton, Willie V., Pvt, 350th Inf
Crain, Everett E., Cpl, 313th Engr Bn
Crawford, Charles F., Pvt, 350th Inf
Crawford, Gainard E., Pvt, 350th Inf
Crawford, Graham W., Pfc, 349th Inf
Critelli, Thomas D., Pfc, 350th Inf
Crooker, Robert E., Pfc, 351st Inf
Crosby, Brown L., Pvt, 350th Inf
Cross, James I., Pvt, 351st Inf
Cross, Stanley J., Pfc, 349th Inf
Croteau, Armand, Pfc, 350th Inf
Crox, Alfred D., Pfc, 351st Inf
Crumpton, Elmer L., Pvt, 349th Inf
Cruz, Richard, Pfc, 349th Inf
Csomay, Joseph F., T/5, 351st Inf
Culler, Egbert H., Pfc, 349th Inf
Cumby, Rubin M., Pfc, 350th Inf
Cunningham, Lawrence J., Pvt, 351st Inf
Cuomo, Patey J., Sgt, 350th Inf
Curci, Aldo F., Pfc, 350th Inf
Curow, William H., S/Sgt, 350th Inf
Curran, Thomas G., Sgt, 349th Inf
Curry, Elmer E., Pfc, 350th Inf
Curson, Clarence W., Jr., Pfc, 349th Inf
Curtis, Boyd A., Pfc, 350th Inf
Curtis, Frank, Pfc, 349th Inf
Curtis, George, Pvt, 349th Inf
Custer, Charles L., Pvt, 351st Inf
Cutillo, Louis J., Sgt, 349th Inf
Cutter, Derald D., Pfc, 351st Inf
Cutting, Percy, Pfc, 349th Inf
Cyr, Leonard H., Sgt, 350th Inf
Dangel, John J., Pvt, 351st Inf
Danielson, Edward A., Pfc, 349th Inf
Danilowicz, B. J., Pvt, 338th Fa Bn
Darby, Estill E., Pvt, 351st Inf
Darby, George B., 2nd Lt, 350th Inf

Dasse, Edward R., Pvt, 349th Inf
Daugherty, David L., Pvt, 350th Inf
Daum, Lloyd C., T/3, 788th Ord Lm Co
Davern, John J., T/4, 388th Fa Bn
Davies, Gilbert A., Pfc, 349th Inf
Davies, Vernon, Pfc, 349th Inf
Davila, Esidro V., Pfc, 349th Inf
Davis, Buford, Pvt, 351st Inf
Davis, Buford A., Pvt, 350th Inf
Davis, Cecil W., Cpl, 88th Ren Tr
Davis, Early E., Ptc, 351st Inf
Davis, Elmer, Pfc, 349th Inf
Davis, George W., Pfc, 349th Inf
Davis, James, Pfc, 351st Inf
Davis, John F., Pfc, 351st Inf
Davis, Kenneth H., Pvt, 350th Inf
Davis, Nathan H., Pvt, 351st Inf
Davis, Oliver M., Pfc, 349th Inf
Davis, Raymond F., Pvt, 349th Inf
Davis, Robert A., Pfc, 349th Inf
Davis, Robert L., Pvt, 351st Inf
Davis, Samuel G., 2nd Lt, 349th Inf
Dawson, Robert P., Pfc, 913th Fa Bn
Di Benedetto Martin, 1st Lt, 350th Inf
Dean, Charles E., Pfc, 349th Inf
De Angelis, George J., Pvt, 351st Inf
De Avila, Francesco, Pvt, 351st Inf
Deay, Walter D., Pfc, 351st Inf
De Barry, Releford L., Pfc, 350th Inf
De Dominick, Frank J., Pvt, 349th Inf
De Ford, Rufus R., Pvt, 350th Inf
De Franco, Serafino, Pfc, 350th Inf
De Gregorio, Vincent, T/Sgt, 351st Inf
De Grio, Emil R., T/5, 788th Ord Lm Co
Deimler, Herman, Pvt, 351st Inf
Deinlein, Leonard, Cpl, 350th Inf
Deising, Earl J., Sr., Pvt, 351st Inf
Delalla, Attilio J., Pvt, 349th Inf
De La Rosa, Roque F., Sgt, 349th Inf
D'Elia, Peter E., Pvt, 351st Inf
Dell'Ova, Joseph C., S/Sgt, 349th Inf
Delmore, Thomas J., Pvt, 313th Engr Bn
Delwo, Elmer E., Pfc, 350th Inf
De Maggio, Steve, S/Sgt, 349th Inf
De Menil, Richard N., Pvt, 350th Inf
De Monte, Michael A., Pvt, 350th Inf
De Muth, William G., Pfc, 339th Fa Bn
Demyanovich, William G., Pfc, 339th Fa Bn
Demyanovich, Charles, Pvt, 351st Inf
Denney, Richard E., Pvt, 350th Inf
Dennis, Deforest R., 2nd Lt, 351st Inf
Dennis, John H., Pfc, 350th Inf
Dennis, Orren E., Pvt, 350th Inf
Denton, Sam S., Pfc, 351st Inf
De Ridder, Robert J., Pfc, 351st Inf
Derosby, Louis J., S/Sgt, 350th Inf
Derrick, Charles R., Pfc, 349th Inf
De Salvo, Charles, S/Sgt, 349th Inf
Desiderio, Ernesto M., 1st Lt, 350th Inf
De Silvey, Barnett J., Pfc, 351st Inf
Deske, William D., Sgt, 350th Inf
Desper, Jennings A., Pvt, 349th Inf
Dessaint, Eugene A., Pvt, 350th Inf
Detz, Stanley, Pvt, 349th Inf
Deuso, Edward C., Pvt, 350th Inf
Devereaux, Russell W., Pfc, 351st Inf
Devins, William J., Pfc, 349th Inf
De Vito, Anthony, S/Sgt, 349th Inf
De Vito, Frank D., S/Sgt, 349th Inf
De Viveiros, Bento C., Sgt, 351st Inf
De Wald, William H., Pvt, 350th Inf
Dial, Clifford O., Pvt, 351st Inf
Dial, James C., T/5, 351st Inf
Dickinson, Caluf A., Pfc, 351st Inf
Dickson, Jewell E., Pvt, 337th Fa Bn
Didio, Angelo J., Pvt, 351st Inf
Diffley, Harry S., Pfc, 349th Inf
Dimitrakis, John C., Pfc, 351st Inf
Dininger, George R., Cpl, 351st Inf
Dionne, Claude E., Pvt, 349th Inf
Dionne, Joseph T., T/5, 338th Fa Bn
Dionne, Paul E., T/4, 313th Engr Bn
Di Primo, Joseph, Pvt, 350th Inf

Di Silvio, Samuel A., Pvt, 350th Inf
Disney, Edison J., Pvt, 351st Inf
Dittman, Albert E., Pfc, 350th Inf
Dixon, Argonne C., 1st Lt, 351st Inf
Dixon, Ray A., Pvt, 351st Inf
Dixon, Stanley B., Pfc, 350th Inf
Dixon, Stanley R., Pvt, 349th Inf
Dizmang, Adrian L., 1st Lt, 350th Inf
Doak, Earlie, Pfc, 350th Inf
Dobak, John L., 1st Lt, 351st Inf
Dobbs, Earnie, Pvt, 351st Inf
Dobson, George F., Ptc, 351st Inf
Dodies, Norman, Pfc, 350th Inf
Doggett, Don M., Pvt, 350th Inf
Dolan, Edward L., 2nd Lt, 351st Inf
Donato, Ernest J., S/Sgt, 350th Inf
Donnelly, Hugh A., 2nd Lt, 351st Inf
Dopp, Merle L., Pvt, 351st Inf
Doran, James E., Pfc, 351st Inf
Dornak, Alvin N., Pfc, 349th Inf
Doss, Kenneth J., Pfc, 349th Inf
Dossett, L. D., Pfc, 350th Inf
Doty, Raymond W., Pvt, 351st Inf
Dougherty, Vincent R., Pvt, 351st Inf
Douglas, Irving M., Sgt, 351st Inf
Dowell, Jesse L., Pfc, 349th Inf
Downing, Cornelius J., M/Sgt, 351st Inf
Doyle, Richard L., Pfc, 349th Inf
Drake, George W., Pvt, 349th Inf
Draper, Ernest C., Pfc, 351st Int
Drapp, Andrew M., Pfc, 349th Inf
Draschil, Nicholas M., Pfc, 350th Inf
Dreslik, Michael J., Pfc, 351st Inf
Drino, Nick A., S/Sgt, 349th Inf
Drumheller, Calvin E., Pfc, 350th Inf
Drury, Ervin L., Pvt, 351st Inf
Duckworth, Clark L., Pfc, 351st Inf
Duclos, Rudolph E., Pfc, 350th Inf
Dudek, William S., Pfc, 351st Inf
Dudley, Clifford, Pfc, 351st Inf
Duguay, Arsene, Pfc, 350th Inf
Duich, Joseph K., Pfc, 350th Inf
Dusmenil, Freddie J., Pfc, 350th Inf
Duncan, Elmer W., Pfc, 350th Inf
Dunlap, Alfred R., Pvt, 350th Inf
Durfee, Orin K., Pfc, 349th Inf
Durkes, Wilfred J., Pvt, 350th Inf
Durniak, Paul, Pvt, 349th Inf
Durocher, Wilbert J., T/Sgt, 351st Inf
Dye, Albert, Pfc, 351st Inf
Dyer, Porter H., Pfc, 349th Inf

Ealum, Harmon W., Cpl, 351st Inf
Earles, Warren C., Pfc, 351st Inf
Eason, Amos L., Pvt, 338th Fa Bn
Easton, Raymond R., Pfc, 349th Inf
Eberhard, Richard L., T/4, 350th Inf
Ecay, Elmer S., Pvt, 349th Inf
Echman, Charles E., Pvt, 349th Inf
Edick, Richard T., Pfc, 351st Inf
Edmundson, Billy J., S/Sgt, 349th Inf
Egglestom, Clay D., Pfc, 351st Inf
Eggleston, Thomas A., 2nd Lt, 349th Inf
Eickholt, Clarence L., Pfc, 351st Inf
Eiland, Madison C., Pvt, 351st Inf
Einecker, James, S/Sgt, 350th Inf
Eji, William K., Sgt, 349th Inf
Eison, Coley B., Pfc, 350th Inf
Ellig, William E., S/Sgt, 350th Inf
Elliott, John A., Pvt, 350th Inf
Ellis, Harry F., Jr., Pvt, 349th Inf
Ellis, Harry G., Pvt, 351st Inf
Ellis, Morton, Pvt, 350th Inf
Ellis, Norman D., T/Sgt, 351st Inf
Elmore, Frank S., T/Sgt, 350th Inf
Elms, William J., Jr., Sgt, 349th Inf
Elzweig, Max M., Pvt, 351st Inf
Engling, Herbert A., Pfc, 350th Inf
Ennis, John R., Pfc, 350th Inf
Enright, Paul E., Pfc, 350th Inf
Erickson, Bill M., Pfc, 351st Inf
Erickson, Curtis C., Pvt, 350th Inf
Erickson, Glen H., Capt, 351st Inf

Ermann, Gustav, Pvt, 350th Inf
Erthum, Thomas J., Pfc, 350th Inf
Espinoza, Julio, Pfc, 350th Inf
Estell, Roscoe F., Pvt, 351st Inf
Evans, Roger L., Pvt, 351st Inf
Fagan, Norman, Pvt, 350th Inf
Fagerlee, Sigerd O., 2nd Lt, 351st Inf
Fairley, David, Pfc, 349th Inf
Falk, Henry, Pvt, 349th Inf
Fallon, Jack W., Pvt, 351st Inf
Falotico, Pasquale J., Pvt, 351st Inf
Famichetti, Rocco, T/5, 350th Inf
Fanelli, John J., Pfc, 350th Inf
Farrell, James J., Pvt, 351st Inf
Farrell, Thomas O., Pfc, 349th Inf
Faust, Frederick, War Correspondent, Civilian,
    Attached 351st Inf
Favate, Louis A., Pfc, 349th Inf
Favors, Smity W., Pfc, 350th Inf
Fay, John M., Pfc, 351st Inf
Feather, Howard L., Pfc, 350th Inf
Feazelle, Charles A., Pvt, 350th Inf
Fechter, Harold E., Sgt, 350th Inf
Fehnel, Charles P., Pvt, 351st Inf
Feiter, Jacob G., Pvt, 350th Inf
Felder, Harry, Pfc, 349th Inf
Fenimore, Daniel J., Sgt, 349th Inf
Ferguson, James A., Pfc, 349th Inf
Feriola, Joseph S., Pfc, 349th Inf
Fernandez, Carlos S., Pvt, 350th Inf
Ferragamo, Christy, Pfc, 350th Inf
Ferraiuolo, Julius V., S/Sgt, 349th Inf
Fiala, Stanley, Pvt, 350th Inf
Fickless, Neil M., Pfc, 350th Inf
Fiechter, Charles D., S/Sgt, 349th Inf
Fifer, Russell P., Sgt, 349th Inf
Fillingness, Oliver A., Pfc, 351st Inf
Finch, John W., Pfc, 351st Inf
Finn, Robert I., Pfc, 349th Inf
Fisher, John L., Pfc, 351st Inf
Fisher, William J., Pvt, 351st Inf
Fitzmaurice, William J., Sgt, 349th Inf
Flak, Frank A., Sgt, 351st Inf
Flamini, Anthony E., Pfc, 351st Inf
Flannery, Willis J., Jr., Pvt, 351st Inf
Fleischman, Daniel, Pvt, 349th Inf
Fleming, Duane W., Pvt, 350th Inf
Flood, Leo T., Pfc, 349th Inf
Flores, Basilio, Pvt, 350th Inf
Flores, Reyes, Jr., Pfc, 350th Inf
Forbes, Cecil D., Pvt, 350th Inf
Forbes, Lee, Jr., 1st Lt, 349th Inf
Ford, Edward C., Pfc, 349th Inf
Ford, Russell H., Pfc, 350th Inf
Ford, Thomas F., Pvt, 350th Inf
Forquer, Wallace P., Pfc, 351st Inf
Fosner, Albert C., T/5, 350th Inf
Foss, Forrest T., 2nd Lt, 349th Inf
Fossa, Alfred, Sgt, 913th Fa Bn
Foster, James H., Sgt, 350th Inf
Foster, Marvin E., Pfc, 351st Inf
Fournier, Robert J., Cpl, 349th Inf
Fowler, Albert D., Pfc, 349th Inf
Fox, Elwood C., Pvt, 349th Inf
Fox, Albert L., Pfc, 349th Inf
Fox, James C., Pfc, 351st Inf
Fragale, Frank, Pvt, 350th Inf
Fragozo, John, Pfc, 350th Inf
Francavilla, Anthony V., Pfc, 351st Inf
Frankel, Irving, Pfc, 350th Inf
Frankum, Cecil F., Pfc, 351st Inf
Frazier, Calvin M., Jr., Pvt, 350th Inf
Freitag, Albert W., Pvt, 349th Inf
Frew, George, Pvt, 349th Inf
Fricke, Albert R., S/Sgt, 349th Inf
Froehlich, William L., Pfc, 349th Inf
Frohn, Gerry A., Pfc, 349th Inf
Froncak, Charles N., Pvt, 350th Inf
Fruchtnicht, Paul, Pfc, 349th Inf
Fulbright, Leonard E., Pvt, 351st Inf
Fulgham, Marshall E., Pfc, 913th Fa Bn
Fullington, Fred S., Pfc, 349th Inf

Fultz, Ralph M., Pvt, 351st Inf
Furr, Charles P., Lt Col, 351st Inf
Furrow, Chelsea I., Pfc, 349th Inf
Furtak, Walter, Pvt, 351st Inf
Furtick, Mack N., S/Sgt, 351st Inf
Gabriel, Evan T., Pfc, 349th Inf
Gaffke, Clarence W., Pvt, 349th Inf
Gaffney, Stiles B., 2nd Lt, 350th Inf
Gaglione, Samuel R., Pvt, 351st Inf
Gahn, Alfred E., Pvt, 351st Inf
Gaitanis, James, Sgt, 351st Inf
Gale, Herbert F., Pfc, 350th Inf
Gall, Edward G., Cpl, 351st Inf
Gallamore, John E., Pfc, 350th Inf
Gallant, Edward, S/Sgt, 351st Inf
Galliard, Fred C., 1st Lt, 349th Inf
Gamble, John L., Pvt, 351st Inf
Ganschow, Adolph H., Pvt, 349th Inf
Ganun, Harol W., T/4, 88th Inf Div Band
Garbarino, Charles F., Pvt, 349th Inf
Garcia, Abram M., Pfc, 350th Inf
Garczewski, Edward S., Pvt, 350th Inf
Gardner, Richard W., Pfc, 350th Inf
Garland, Lewis H., Pfc, 349th Inf
Garnett, Archie T., Pfc, 351st Inf
Garrard, Wilber S., Pvt, 351st Inf
Garrett, Johnnie L., Pfc, 350th Inf
Garris, John I., Pvt, 351st Inf
Garris, Claude D., Pfc, 350th Inf
Gaudette, Ernest J., Pvt, Hq & Hq Btry Div
    Arty
Gaulke, Robert A., Pfc, 313th Med Bn
Gauthreaux, Gilbert C., Pfc, 350th Inf
Gavreledes, Peter G., Pvt, 351st Inf
Gazerro, Eugene, Pvt, 913th Fa Bn
Gbur, Michael, Pfc, 351st Inf
Gell, James, Pfc, 351st Inf
Gendron, Albert E., 1st Sgt, 349th Inf
Geniotto, Thomas C., Pfc, 351st Inf
Genovese, Joseph, Pvt, 349th Inf
Genta, John, Pvt, 351st Inf
George, Harold C., Pfc, 349th Inf
Germanski, Theodore, Pfc, 350th Inf
Gerngross, Donald C., Pvt, 351st Inf
Giannino, Joseph C., Pfc, 350th Inf
Gabson, Fred E., Pfc, 351st Inf
Gieter, Albert, T/5, 349th Inf
Gilbert, Herbert K., 2nd Lt, 350th Inf
Gilchrest, Harold J., Pfc, 313th Med Bn
Gilland, Charles W., Pvt, 349th Inf
Gilliland, Romaine E., 1st Sgt, 351st Inf
Gilmore, Joseph A., Capt, 313th Med Bn
Ginn, Oliver, 2nd Lt, 351st Inf
Gionet, Leon L., Pvt, 351st Inf
Girard, Ferdinand R., Cpl, 350th Inf
Giunta, Joseph J., Pvt, 351st Inf
Glasscock, Robert J., Jr., Pvt, 349th Inf
Glawe, Harvey H., Pvt, 351st Inf
Glendinning, Warren A., Pfc, 349th Inf
Glover, Benjamin J., Pvt, 351st Inf
Glovka, Edward G., 2nd Lt, 339th Fa Bn
Glynn, Emmett D., Pvt, 349th Inf
Gobeil, George A., Pfc, 351st Inf
Godalla, Nick J., Pfc, 351st Inf
Godin, Florian A., S/Sgt, 349th Inf
Goetz, Harold C., Pvt, 350th Inf
Goldblatt, Stanley, Pvt, 350th Inf
Goldner, William R., Pvt, 337th Fa Bn
Goldman, Herbert G., Pfc, 350th Inf
Goldsmith, Lee O., Pvt, 350th Inf
Goldstein, Albert, Pvt, 349th Inf
Goldstein, Bernard H., 1st Lt, 349th Inf
Gomez, Elio M., Pfc, 350th Inf
Gonzales, Rafael F., T/4 338th Fa Bn
Gonsalves, Francis C., T/Sgt, 350th Inf
Good, Everett L., Pvt, 351st Inf
Goodick, Douglas E., Cpl, 350th Inf
Goodman, George M., Pfc, 351st Inf
Goolsby, Ira G., Pvt, 350th Inf
Goodrich, Gordon M., Pfc, 351st Inf
Goral, William P., Pfc, 351st Inf
Gordon, Leo, Pfc, 349th Inf

Gormley, Thomas M., T/5, 313th Engr Bn
Gould, Byron K., Jr., Pfc, 313th Engr Bn
Goyette, Edward W., Pvt, 350th Inf
Grabiec, Stanley J., Pvt, 350th Inf
Grabowski, Stephen P., Pvt, 349th Inf
Graham, Donald J., Pfc, 350th Inf
Graham, Joel R., Pfc, 351st Inf
Graham, Thomas P., T/Sgt, 351st Inf
Grando, Benedict M., Cpl, 337th Fa Bn
Grant, Charles H., Pvt, 350th Inf
Grape, Robert E., S/Sgt, 350th Inf
Grass, Raymond W., S/Sgt, 350th Inf
Gray, Daniel E., Pvt, 351st Inf
Gray, Robert L., Pfc, 349th Inf
Green, Arie C., Pfc, 350th Inf
Green, Harold L., Pvt, 349th Inf
Green, Grover C., Pvt, 351st Inf
Green, Hugh T., Jr., Pfc, 351st Inf
Green, Joseph, Pvt, 351st Inf
Green, Paul W., 1st Lt, 350th Inf
Green, Roy G., Pvt, 350th Inf
Greenberger, Solomon, Pfc, 351st Inf
Greenlaw, Alonzo H., S/Sgt, 350th Inf
Greenlaw, Berton L., Sgt, 349th Inf
Gregor, Edward J., T/4, 350th Inf
Greiner, Elbert E., T/Sgt, 351st Inf
Gribbin, Edward S., 2nd Lt, 350th Inf
Griego, Leopoldo, Pvt, 350th Inf
Griesing, William H., Sgt, 350th Inf
Griffin, Henry J., Pvt, 350th Inf
Grill, Winthrop D., Pfc, 350th Inf
Grochowski, Anthony P., T/Sgt, 350th Inf
Grogro, Arthur A., 1st Sgt, 351st Inf
Grohman, Charles, Jr., Pfc, 350th Inf
Gronko, Charles P., Pfc, 349th Inf
Groome, William, Pfc, 351st Inf
Grose, Eugene C., Pfc, 350th Inf
Grosco, Carmine J., Pvt, 313th Engr Bn
Grubar, Joseph R., Pvt, 351st Inf
Grubb, Alfred C., Pvt, 351st Inf
Grzbouski, Theodore V., Pfc, 351st Inf
Guariglia, Peter J., Pfc, 349th Inf
Guarisco, Charles L., Pvt, 349th Inf
Gudger, James D., Pvt, 349th Inf
Guenther, John R., Cpl, 350th Inf
Guerra, Santos, Pvt, 350th Inf
Guerrette, Reno L., Pfc, 350th Inf
Guevara, Noe, Pfc, 337th Fa Bn
Guglielmone, Matteo B., Pfc, 351st Inf
Guilin, Salvator, Pvt, 349th Inf
Guise, John G., Pfc, 351st Inf
Gursky, Peter, Sgt, 351st Inf
Gutkowski, Erwin J., Pfc, 313th Engr Bn
Haas, Alphone A., T/4, 349th Inf
Hacker, Harry I., Pvt, 350th Inf
Hadley, Blaine E., Pfc, 349th Inf
Haefner, Thomas R., Pfc, 349th Inf
Hagenburg, Charles S., Pvt, 349th Inf
Hairell, Vernon E., Sgt, 350th Inf
Haley, Floyd B., Cpl, 349th Inf
Hall, Alonzo L., Pvt, 350th Inf
Halme, Richard A., Pvt, 350th Inf
Halow, George B., Pfc, 350th Inf
Hamilton, Edward R., Pvt, 350th Inf
Hamilton, John V., Pfc, 351st Inf
Hamilton, Robert W., Pvt, 350th Inf
Hammonds, Lomax, Pfc, 351st Inf
Hammonds, Timothy W., Pfc, 349th Inf
Hampton, Leonard C., Pfc, 350th Inf
Hanckock, Charles H., S/Sgt, 349th Inf
Hancock, Walter S., Pvt, 351st Inf
Haney, Roy W., Jr., Pfc, 350th Inf
Hankins, William T. L., Pvt, 349th Inf
Hanlon, Edmund F., Pfc, 349th Inf
Hanmer, Donald R., Pvt, 351st Inf
Hannappel, Henry C., Pfc, 350th Inf
Hansler, Edgar C., Pfc, 349th Inf
Hanson, Charles H., Pfc, 350th Inf
Harder, Roland, S/Sgt, 88th Sig Co
Hargis, Ernest C., Pfc, 351st Inf
Harknett, Richard F., Pvt, 349th Inf
Harless, Orville W., S/Sgt, 350th Inf

Harmon, Lloyd R., Pvt, 351st Inf
Harms, Emil J., Pvt, 349th Inf
Harper, William F., 1st Lt, 351st Inf
Harrington, Donald L., Pfc, 350th Inf
Harris, John R., Jr., Pfc, 350th Inf
Harris, Robert N., Pvt, 349th Inf
Harris, Wilburn, Pvt, 349th Inf
Harrison, George W., Pfc, 351st Inf
Harsh, Earl E., Pvt, 349th Inf
Hart, Edwin R., Pvt, 350th Inf
Hartman, Emil W., Jr., 1st Lt, 349th Inf
Hartman, Henry A., Pfc, 349th Inf
Hartman, Sheldon, Cpl, 351st Inf
Hartman, Louis J., Pfc, 351st Inf
Harvey, David D., Pfc, 350th Inf
Harvey, John, Pvt, 349th Inf
Haskins, Luther D., Pfc, 350th Inf
Hastey, Errold, Pfc, 350th Inf
Hastings, Henry G., Pfc, 350th Inf
Hastings, John J., Jr., S/Sgt, 350th Inf
Hatem, Anise, Sgt, 788th Ord LM Co
Haugen, Paul R., Pfc, 350th Inf
Haun, Alfred L., Pfc, 349th Inf
Hauser, George H., Pfc, 350th Inf
Hawes, William S., Pvt, 350th Inf
Hawkins, Isaac, Sgt, 351st Inf
Hawkins, John I., Cpl, 313th Med Bn
Hayes, Herman M., Pfc, 351st Inf
Haynes, Leonard B., Pvt, 349th Inf
Hearon, William E., Pfc, 349th Inf
Hecker, Kenneth R., Pfc, 349th Inf
Heitzman, Lloyd J., Pfc, 350th Inf
Hejka, Clarence J., Pvt, 350th Inf
Held, Keith J., Sr., Pfc, 351st Inf
Helfrich, Lewis, Pvt, 351st Inf
Hemstreet, Thomas C., Pvt, 350th Inf
Hench, Roger W., Pfc, 351st Inf
Hendrix, Charley W., Pfc, 351st Inf
Henkel, William K. W., Pfc, 351st Inf
Hennessy, John M., Capt, 337th Fa Bn
Hennessy, Philip, Pfc, 351st Inf
Hennigan, Edward M., Pvt, 349th Inf
Henningson, Warren J., Pfc, 350th Inf
Hensel, Hugh A., Pvt, 350th Inf
Hensley, James W., Pfc, 350th Inf
Hentges, Clifford W., Pvt, 349th Inf
Herdman, Dencil C., Pfc, 349th Inf
Herman, Richard J., S/Sgt, 350th Inf
Hernandez, Joe A., Pvt, 313th Engr Bn
Hernandez, Vicente Y., S/Sgt, 349th Inf
Herzog, Virgil F., 1st Lt, 349th Inf
Heyer, William R., Jr., Pvt, 351st Inf
Hibbs, Cecil V., Pvt, 351st Inf
Hickling, Floyd L., S/Sgt, 350th Inf
Hicks, Gilbert F., Pvt, 350th Inf
Hiddleson, Harvey J., Pfc, 350th Inf
Hill, Earnest A., Pvt, 350th Inf
Hill, Harry H., Pfc, 913th Fa Bn
Hill, Kaleryo T., Pfc, 351st Inf
Hill, Thomas E., T/Sgt, 351st Inf
Himes, Everett, Pvt, 351st Inf
Hinkle, Victor, Pfc, 350th Inf
Hinton, Henry, Pvt, 351st Inf
Hinton, Harry L., Pvt, 349th Inf
Hitchcock, Lenzie B., Pvt, 351st Inf
Hnatek, Edward F., S/Sgt, 349th Inf
Hoagland, Lewis H., Pvt, 349th Inf
Hobart, Harris, Pvt, 351st Inf
Hobgood, Robert J., Pvt, 349th Inf
Hocutt, Robert O., Pfc, 350th Inf
Hoda, Joseph R., Cpl, 351st Inf
Hodge, Charles R., Pvt, 350th Inf
Hodges, John W., Pvt, 351st Inf
Hodgetts, Ernest L., Pvt, 349th Inf
Hodgson, Martin L., Pvt, 349th Inf
Hodson, Leroy S., Jr., Pfc, 350th Inf
Hoffer, Clarence G., Pvt, 351st Inf
Hoffine, Newton, Pfc, 351st Inf
Hoke, James B., Sgt, 350th Inf
Holbrook, Henry L., Jr., Pvt, 349th Inf
Holladay, Henry C., Pvt, 349th Inf
Holland, Ace W., Sgt, 349th Inf

Holland, Alfred F., S/Sgt, 349th Inf
Holland, Joseph L., Pvt, 351st Inf
Hollingsworth, Marvin C., Pfc, 350th Inf
Holmes, David E., S/Sgt, 350th Inf
Homa, Steve L., Pvt, 349th Inf
Holmes, Samuel C., Jr., Pvt, 350th Inf
Honeycutt, Leftredge W., Capt, 349th Inf
Hood, Ralph R., Pfc, 349th Inf
Hopkins, Raymond F., Pvt, 350th Inf
Horn, Benjamin A., Sgt, 350th Inf
Horne, Lamar E., Pfc, 350th Inf
Horton, Charles O., Pfc, 351st Inf
Horwath, Stephen E., Pvt, 351st Inf
Hoskins, Raymond, Pvt, 349th Inf
Houck, Marvin K., T/4, 349th Inf
Houston, Dan, Pfc, 351st Inf
Howard, Ernest L., Pvt, 351st Inf
Howard, Norman L., Pfc, 350th Inf
Howard, Thomas G., Cpl, 351st Inf
Howe, George L., Sgt, 349th Inf
Hoyda, Chester V., S/Sgt, 350th Inf
Hrabovsky, Laddie J., Pfc, 349th Inf
Hubert, Daniel W., Pvt, 351st Inf
Hudak, Eugene S., Pvt, 351st Inf
Hudelson, Ralph F., Pvt, 351st Inf
Hudgins, Glen H., Pfc, 349th Inf
Hudon, Louis J., Pfc, 349th Inf
Huerta, Pedro, Pvt, 349th Inf
Huffman, Ambrose F., Pfc, 351st Inf
Huffman, Gerald M., Sgt, 349th Inf
Huffstetler, R. C., Pfc, 351st Inf
Huggins, William M., S/Sgt, 349th Inf
Hughes, Charles F., Pvt, 350th Inf
Hughes, Jerry W., Pvt, 350th Inf
Hughes, Jessy W., Pfc, 349th Inf
Hughes, John L., Pvt, 351st Inf
Hughes, William G., Pfc, 351st Inf
Humphrey, Harold B., 1st Lt, 350th Inf
Hunt, Edward R., Pvt, 350th Inf
Hunt, Howard, Sgt, 351st Inf
Hurley, Edward T., T/Sgt, 349th Inf
Hutchinson, Millard J., Pvt, 313th Med Bn
Hyche, James V., T/5, 350th Inf
Iannelli, George O., Cpl, 350th Inf
Ignasiak, Sylvester J., Pvt, 351st Inf
Imbro, Michael A., Cpl, 350th Inf
Imotichey, Charles W., Pfc, 350th Inf
Indursky, Jacob D., Pvt, 349th Inf
Inger, Samuel, Pfc, 351st Inf
Irwin, Donald C., Pvt, 350th Inf
Jablenski, Wilbert F., Pvt, 351st Inf
Jabonski, Paul I., Pfc, 349th Inf
Jackson, Arvo J., Pfc, 349th Inf
Jackson, Henry J., 1st Lt, 349th Inf
Jackson, John T., Pvt, 351st Inf
Jackson, Lambert W., Pfc, 350th Inf
Jacob, Rene J., Pfc, 350th Inf
Jacobson, Richard W., Pvt, 351st Inf
Jadatz, Edward A., Pfc, 351st Inf
Jajko, Bernard J., Pfc, 350th Inf
James, Leonard L., Pfc, 350th Inf
Janke, Edwin R., Pfc, 351st Inf
Jaramillo, Leonor, Pfc, 351st Inf
Jaskott, Joseph, Pfc, 351st Inf
Jatko, Stephen J., S/Sgt, 349th Inf
Jedlicka, Lawrence L., T/4, 349th Inf
Jeffcoat, James, Pfc, 351st Inf
Jenkins, Prince D., Pfc, 349th Inf
Jenkins, Robert M., Pfc, 351st Inf
Jenney, John T., Jr., Pfc, 351st Inf
Jensen, Henry W., T/5, 349th Inf
Jensen, Knud, Pvt, 351st Inf
Jeresek, David L., Pfc, 349th Inf
Jeske, Ernest P., Pvt, 350th Inf
Jevelekian, Myron L., Pvt, 350th Inf
Jimenez, David, S/Sgt, 349th Inf
Johnson, Bruce, T/4, 351st Inf
Johnson, Burl, Pfc, 350th Inf
Johnson, Charles R., T/5, 349th Inf
Johnson, Eino E., Pfc, 351st Inf
Johnson, George T., Cpl, 351st Inf
Johnson, Howard B., T/5, 349th Inf

Johnson, James T., Pvt, 351st Inf
Johnson, John O., T/5, 88th Rcn Tr
Johnson, Johnnie P., Pfc, 350th Inf
Johnson, Richard, Pfc, 351st Inf
Johnson, Roy A., Pfc, 351st Inf
Johnson, Roy A., Jr., Pvt, 351st Inf
Johnson, Walter W., Pvt, 349th Inf
Jolly, Rome A., Pvt, 351st Inf
Jones, Clair L., Pfc, 351st Inf
Jones, Columbus D., Cpl, 913th Fa Bn
Jones, Glenn, Pvt, 351st Inf
Jones, Wyman C., Pvt, 349th Inf
Jordan, Francis A., Pfc, 349th Inf
Jordan, John O., Pvt, 350th Inf
Joyce, Thomas P., Pfc, 351st Inf
Judd, Charles G., Jr., Pvt, 351st Inf
Julian, John B., Pvt, 351st Inf
Juris, Tony J., Pvt, 351st Inf
Kaczka, Edward, Cpl, 351st Inf
Kader, Warren G., S/Sgt, 350th Inf
Kaleka, Walter, Pfc, 350th Inf
Kalem, Louis, Capt, 350th Inf
Kameg, Theodore J., Sgt, 350th Inf
Kaminski. Albert S., Pfc, 349th Inf
Kanaskie, James J., T/4, 313th Engr Bn
Kannberg, Milton, Pfc, 351st Inf
Kanopka, Stanley J., Cpl, 350th Inf
Kaplan, Lawrence N., Pfc, 350th Inf
Karjolic, Walter E., Pvt, 349th Inf
Karnis, Edward H., Pvt, 351st Inf
Karr, Alfred E., Pfc, 351st Inf
Kearney, Matthew W., 1st Lt, 349th Inf
Kearney, Robert K., Pvt, 349th Inf
Kearsing, Donald R., 2nd Lt, 350th Inf
Kedzuh, John, Pvt, 351st Inf
Keenan, James F., Pvt, 349th Inf
Keene, Willie, Pvt, 350th Inf
Kees, Thomas E., 2nd Lt, 350th Inf
Keilty, Joseph C., Pvt, 349th Inf
Kelch, Vernon, Pfc, 350th Inf
Kellenberger, Edward L., Pvt, 350th Inf
Kellen, William H., Cpl, 351st Inf
Kelley, Francis G., Pvt, 351st Inf
Kelley, Fred J., Pfc, 349th Inf
Kelley, Miley J., Pfc, 351st Inf
Kelly, Carl B., Pvt, 350th Inf
Kelly, Keith M., Pvt, 349th Inf
Kelly, Leo M., T/5, 349th Inf
Kelly, Patrick C., Pfc, 349th Inf
Kelly, Robert C., Capt, 349th Inf
Kelly, William H., Cpl, 351st Inf
Kelnhofer, Raymond J., Pvt, 349th Inf
Kemmerling, George A., Pfc, 349th Inf
Kemper, Emory A., Capt, 351st Inf
Kendall, Raymond E., Lt Col, 351st Inf
Kennedy, Charles L., 2nd Lt, 351st Inf
Kennedy, Ellesworth C., S/Sgt, 349th Inf
Kenney, Edward M., Pfc, 351st Inf
Kenwell, Philip E., Pfc, 351st Inf
Kerr, William H., Jr., Pfc, 350th Inf
Keyser, Charles G., Sgt, 351st Inf
Kidd, Melvin J., Pfc, 349th Inf
Kildahl, Paul H., Pfc, 351st Inf
Kiley, William J., Pfc, 350th Inf
Kilgore, Louis B., Pvt, 351st Inf
Killiam, Reuben L., Pvt, 350th Inf
Kindred, Harold C., 1st Sgt, 349th Inf
Kimple, Eugene F., 2nd Lt, 350th Inf
King, Buster, Pfc, 349th Inf
King, Charles W., Pvt, 350th Inf
King, Frank W., Pvt, 350th Inf
King, Hubert H., Pvt, 351st Inf
King, Mont V., Pvt, 351st Inf
King, Theodore R., Pfc, 349th Inf
Kingston, Clayton G., Pvt, 351st Inf
Kinne, Herbert M., Sgt, 338th Fa Bn
Kinne, Roy E., Pvt, 350th Inf
Kinsella, Arthur J., Pfc, 351st Inf
Kinsey, Arthur M., T/5, 913th Fa Bn
Kirchgessner, G. J., S/Sgt, 349th Inf
Kirkland, Ollie B., Pfc, 351st Inf
Kiser, Robert L., Pvt, 351st Inf

Klaustermeyer, Ernest H. W., Pfc, 349th Inf
Klee, John R., Pvt, 350th Inf
Klein, Ronald, Pfc, 351st Inf
Klimek, Joseph, Jr., Pfc, 349th Inf
Klinzing, Allan D., Pvt, 350th Inf
Klotz, Marvin H., Pfc, 351st Inf
Klunk, Richard J., Pfc, 350th Inf
Klushank, John, 2nd Lt, 351st Inf
Klushmeier, Victor H. E., S/Sgt, 349th Inf
Knapp, Francis W., Pvt, 350th Inf
Knapp, Rudolph H., Pfc, 351st Inf
Knapp, Stewart D., Pvt, 349th Inf
Knoch, Merle D., Pvt, 349th Inf
Knott, Adrian E., Pvt, 351st Inf
Knox, John E., Pfc, 349th Inf
Knutson, Arthur S., S/Sgt, 338th Fa Bn
Koepka, Wallace A., Pvt, 351st Inf
Koerner, Harry, 2nd Lt, 349th Inf
Koizumi, Utaka, Pvt, 349th Inf
Kolias, Peter, Pfc, 350th Inf
Kolovich, Joseph, Pfc, 351st Inf
Kolyno, Burdett K., Pvt, 351st Inf
Kopacz, Edward F., Pvt, 349th Inf
Koropchak, John, Sgt, 350th Inf
Kosack, Stephen W., Sgt, 349th Inf
Kosko, Anthony, Pfc, 349th Inf
Koszykowski, Alex, Pvt, 349th Inf
Kottler, Donald D., Cpl, 351st Inf
Kotzelnick, Robert F., Pvt, 349th Inf
Kovalchuck, John, Pvt, 351st Inf
Kovis, John, Pvt, 351st Inf
Koziol, Frank A., Pvt, 351st Inf
Kozlowski, Zigismund P., Pfc, 350th Inf
Kozluk, Steve, Pfc, 351st Inf
Kramarczyk, Thaddeus J., Pvt, 351st Inf
Kramer, Raymond A., Pvt, 350th Inf
Kramer, Thomas, Pvt, 350th Inf
Kramer, Wilbert M., Pfc, 350th Inf
Krasnow, William, Pvt, 349th Inf
Krauleidis, Walter M., Pfc, 350th Inf
Kraus, John A., T/Sgt, 351st Inf
Kreiser, Russell E., Pvt, 351st Inf
Kreismer, Robert F., Pvt, 349th Inf
Kreismas, Stephen J., Pfc, 351st Inf
Kreklow, Walter W., 1st Lt, 349th Inf
Krider, Charley L., Pfc, 349th Inf
Kriete, Howard W., Pvt, 351st Inf
Krucks, Kenneth E., 1st Lt, 349th Inf
Krueger, William M., Sgt, 350th Inf
Kryszczuk, Charles A., 2nd Lt, 351st Inf
Kugelman, Daniel, Pvt, 349th Inf
Kunicki, Michael, Pvt, 351st Inf
Kunis, James H., Pfc, 351st Inf
Kuntz, Donald C., Pfc, 313th Engr Bn
Kuropatkin, Charles W., Pvt, 349th Inf
Kurzawa, Harry B., Pfc, 350th Inf
Kutz, Robert F., Pfc, 351st Inf
Kyle, Samuel J., Pvt, 349th Inf
La Fave, Frederick D., Pvt, 351st Inf
Lahey, Louis E., Cpl, 350th Inf
Lahre, Carl J., Pvt, 350th Inf
LaMar, John R., S/Sgt, 351st Inf
Lambersky, George W., Pfc, 349th Inf
Lambert, Norman J., Cpl, 351st Inf
Lamoureux, Neil E., Sgt, 351st Inf
Lampman, Henry W., Pvt, 349th Inf
Landes, Howard M., Jr., Pfc, 351st Inf
Landon, Edward A., Pvt, 351st Inf
Landers, Edward, Pfc, 350th Inf
Landry, Jeffrey C., Pfc, 351st Inf
Landry, Joseph L., Pfc, 350th Inf
Lane, Lawrence E., S/Sgt, 349th Inf
Lane, Park, T/4, 88th Cav Rcn Tr
Lane, Raymond E., Pfc, 350th Inf
Lang, Paul L., Pfc, 351st Inf
La Porta, Louis, Pfc, 349th Inf
Larson, Nils G., Pfc, 349th Inf
La Rue, John A., Pfc, 351st Inf
Lasyone, Clayten E., Pvt, 351st Inf
Lavallee, Walter, Sgt, 349th Inf
Lavender, Clyde F., Pfc, 351st Inf
Lavender, Fred W., Pvt, 351st Inf

Lawler, Joseph C., Pvt, 351st Inf
Lawrence, Archie F., Pfc, 349th Inf
Lawrence, James R., Pvt, 351st Inf
Lawson, Wyle M., Pfc, 351st Inf
Layman, Alexander D., S/Sgt, 349th Inf
Layton, Clyde Stormes, Sgt, 313th Engr Bn
Leatherwood, Y. J., Pvt, 350th Inf
Lebeuf, William, Pvt, 350th Inf
Le Boy, Cecil, 2nd Lt, 349th Inf
Lee, Francis X. J., 1st Lt, 350th Inf
Lee, John S., Pfc, 351st Inf
Leekya, Peter, Pvt, 351st Inf
Leesley, Edwin, Cpl, 351st Inf
Legano, John R., Pfc, 350th Inf
Legler, Robert H., Pvt, 351st Inf
Lehman, James B., Pvt, 350th Inf
Leichty, Leonard H., Pfc, 350th Inf
Leinonen, Sulo M., Pfc, 349th Inf
LeMunyan, Charles B., Pfc, 350th Inf
Lenerville, Lowell K., Pfc, 351st Inf
Lenett, David B., Cpl, 351st Inf
Leo, Frank J., Pfc, 349th Inf
Leon, George H., Jr., Pfc, 338th Fa Bn
Leonti, Joseph, Pfc, 349th Inf
Lercher, Robert J., Pvt, 351st Inf
Lerner, Charles, Cpl, 351st Inf
Lester, Charles N., Pvt, 313th Engr Bn
Lester, Orland D., Pfc, 349th Inf
Leveille, Henry, S/Sgt, 349th Inf
Levie, Raymond C., Jr., T/5, 337th Fa Bn
Levin, Donald A., Pfc, 350th Inf
Levine, Melvin M., Pvt, 351st Inf
Levitt, Harold F., Pfc, 349th Inf
Levy, Harry, T/4, 350th Inf
Levy, Irving, Pvt, 351st Inf
Lewis, Jack H., 1st Sgt, 338th Fa Bn
Lewis, William A., Cpl, 349th Inf
L'Homme, Leonel, Pfc, 349th Inf
Lainza, Joseph, Pfc, 350th Inf
Licari, Joseph L., Pvt, 349th Inf
Lidsky, Kalman, Pvt, 350th Inf
Lickert, Donald H., Pvt, 351st Inf
Liggett, Clarence, Pfc, M P Platoon 88th Inf
Light, Roy E., Pfc, 351st Inf
Lindberg, Raymond G., Pfc, 351st Inf
Likowski, Henry, Pfc, 351st Inf
Lindsey, Robert R., Pfc, 349th Inf
Lindauer, Leon, Pfc, 351st Inf
Line, George H., Pfc, 351st Inf
Lininger, Henry C., Pfc, 351st Inf
Linn, Robert J., Pvt, 350th Inf
Lione, Ralph, Cpl, 351st Inf
LiPuma, Peter J., Cpl, 351st Inf
Lis, John A., Pfc, 350th Inf
Lis, Walter J., Pvt, 350th Inf
Lissi, Alfred J., Pvt, 350th Inf
Little, George I., Sgt, 351st Inf
Lloyd, Edwin W., Pfc, 351st Inf
Locarriera, Luke J., Pfc, 349th Inf
Locke, Joseph T., S/Sgt, 350th Inf
Lodyga, Frederick W., Pvt, 351st Inf
Loewenthal, John, T/4, Div Hq Co
Loftis, Edward T., Pfc, 349th Inf
Lombard, Perley W., Jr., Pfc, 351st Inf
Lonergan, James E., Pfc, 349th Inf
Long, Johnnie F., Pvt, 351st Inf
Long, Marvin V., Pfc, 349th Inf
Loos, Rudolph V., Pfc, 351st Inf
Lopez, Edward L., Sgt, 349th Inf
Lorance, Ernest J., Pvt, 338th Fa Bn
Lord, Harold L., Pvt, 351st Inf
Lorenz, Henry D., Pvt, 351st Inf
Lorusso, Michael J., Pvt, 349th Inf
Louderback, Thomas L., Pfc, 350th Inf
Loughin, Patrick T., Pvt, 351st Inf
Lovelace, Paul H., 1st Lt, 350th Inf
Lovel, Howard L., Pvt, 351st Inf
Lovette, Oliver C., Pfc, 351st Inf
Loving, Benjamin N., Pfc, 349th Inf
Lowhorn, Cecil C., Pfc, 349th Inf
Loyd, Grant, Pfc, 350th Inf
Lucas, Dominick, F., Cpl, 350th Inf

Lucero, Amado, Cpl, 351st Inf
Lucero, Antonio, Pfc, 349th Inf
Luera, Rejies L., Pfc, 350th Inf
Lujan, Jesus, Pfc, 349th Inf
Lukacovic, August J., Pfc, 351st Inf
Lukes, Richard M., Pvt, 349th Inf
Lunn, Odber F., Pfc, 349th Inf
Lusk, Joseph W., Pvt, 350th Inf
Luther, John, Pvt, 351st Inf
Lynch, Charles P., Jr., Capt, 350th Inf
Lynch, Donald E., Pfc, 349th Inf
Lynch, Frederick N., T/5, 349th Inf
Lyons, Harold E., Pfc, 349th Inf
Lyons, Robert I., 1st Lt, 349th Inf
MacDonald, Leo M., 1st Lt, 351st Inf
MacDonald, Paul C., S/Sgt, 350th Inf
MacDonald, Robert A., Pvt, 349th Inf
MacDonald, Robert C., Pfc, 349th Inf
MacDougall, William D., Pvt, 350th Inf
Macejka, Joseph P., Pvt, 351st Inf
Machan, James A., Pvt, 351st Inf
Machi, Mario L., Pvt, 349th Inf
Macias, Manuel E., Pfc, 313th Engr Bn
Maciolek, Stanley, Pfc, 350th Inf
Mack, Kenneth R., Pvt, 350th Inf
Mac Kenzie, James S., Pfc, 351st Inf
Mackey, Patrik A., S/Sgt, 349th Inf
Madden, Jerry A., 2nd Lt, 350th Inf
Madden, William F., Pvt, 349th Inf
Madison, Martin L., Pvt, 351st Inf
Madrid, Jose P., Pfc, 349th Inf
Madritsch, Herbert A., Pfc, 349th Inf
Magnani, Armido, Pfc, 351st Inf
Magnusin, Walter E., 1st Lt, 913th Fa Bn
Mahder, William C., Pvt, 350th Inf
Maher, Edmund R. D., 1st Lt, 350th Inf
Mahmde, Charles L., Pvt, 351st Inf
Maiocco, James, Pvt, 350th Inf
Malczak, Edward T., Pvt, 350th Inf
Malin, Howard, Pvt, 349th Inf
Mamrot, Walter E., Pvt, 349th Inf
Manchine, Herbert J., S/Sgt, 349th Inf
Mandel, Max, Pvt, 351st Inf
Manders, William H., Pfc, 350th Inf
Manley, Clyde H., Pfc, 350th Inf
Manning, John, Pfc, 349th Inf
Manning, Raymond A., T/5, 351st Inf
Manning, Raymond R., Sgt, 350th Inf
Mantia, Sam J., Pfc, 349th Inf
Maracini, Albert J., Sgt, 350th Inf
Marchekewitz, Vincent, T/Sgt, 349th Inf
Marcinow, Leon, Sgt, 350th Inf
Marcisewski, Joseph J., Cpl, 350th Inf
Margulies, Murray, Pvt, 351st Inf
Marion, George A., Jr., T/5, 350th Inf
Markel, Hyman, 2nd Lt, 351st Inf
Markham, James H., 1st Lt, 351st Inf
Marquez, Francisco A., Sgt, 349th Inf
Marsh, Harold L., Pvt, 349th Inf
Marsh, Odis D., Pvt, 350th Inf
Marshall, Walter J., Pvt, 349th Inf
Martin, Carl W., Jr., Pvt, 349th Inf
Martin, Cecil, S/Sgt, 350th Inf
Martin, Edgar, Sgt, 351st Inf
Martin, John Jr., Pfc, 349th Inf
Martin, Thomas H., Pvt, 350th Inf
Martinez, Alejo, Pvt, 350th Inf
Martinez, Zacairo M., Pvt, 913th Fa Bn
Martz, Frank Jr., Pvt, 350th Inf
Marysyk, Frank J., T/4, 313th Engr Bn
Marze, Johnnie L., Jr., Sgt, 350th Inf
Masek, Roy R., Pvt, 351st Inf
Masi, Frank V., Pvt, 349th Inf
Maskiewicz, Edward, Pfc, 351st Inf
Mason, Frank W., Pfc, 351st Inf
Mason, Robert E., Pvt, 349th Inf
Mason, Robert W., Pvt, 350th Inf
Masson, Robert B., Pfc, 349th Inf
Materek, Edward J., S/Sgt, 349th Inf
Mathews, Marvin C., T/Sgt, 349th Inf
Mathis, Loren L., Pfc, 351st Inf
Matlock, Boyd W., Pfc, 350th Inf

Matney, Marion M., Pfc, 349th Inf
Matuszewski, Frank E., Pfc, 350th Inf
Matzker, Frederick, T/5, 351st Inf
Maupin, Harris G., Pvt, 351st Inf
Mazza, John, Sgt, 351st Inf
McBrayer, George W., Pfc, 350th Inf
McCallum, Donald E., Pvt, 350th Inf
McCarty, Edward H., Pfc, 350th Inf
McCaskey, Patrick K., 1st Lt, 351st Inf
McClung, Guy A., Cpl, 351st Inf
McCauley, John J., Pfc, 349th Inf
McClure, Trevelyan L., 1st Lt, 351st Inf
McCollom, Oliver G., 2nd Lt, 349th Inf
McCombe, John H., Pfc, 350th Inf
McCorkle, John C., Pfc, 351st Inf
McCormick, Frank W., T/Sgt, 351st Inf
McCormik, Michael, Pfc, 349th Inf
McCoy, Orville E., Pvt, 349th Inf
McDaniel, Billy R., Pvt, 351st Inf
McDonagh, Thomas P., Jr., Cpl, 351st Inf
McDonald, Louis A., Jr., Pvt, 350th Inf
Mc Donald, William H., Pfc, 351st Inf
McDonald, Willie G., Pfc, 349th Inf
McDonnell, Lester M., Pfc, 351st Inf
McElhone, Joseph V., Pfc, 349th Inf
McElligott, Lawrence J., Pfc, 350th Inf
McElwee, George J., Pvt, 88th Rcn Tr
McFadden, John J., Pvt, 351st Inf
McGehee, William R., Pvt, 351st Inf
McGill, Theodore S., 1st Lt, 337th Fa Bn
McGinn, Edward A., Pfc, 350th Inf
McGinnis, John M., Pfc, 350th Inf
McGonis, Albert J., Pfc, 350th Inf
McGuire, Dan J., 2nd Lt, 338th Fa Bn
McGuire, Harley, T/4, 351st Inf
McHale, James B., Pvt, 349th Inf
McHale, William J., Pvt, 350th Inf
McHugh, Stephen J., Pvt, 349th Inf
McIlwain, Harold J., Pvt, 349th Inf
McIntosh, Benjamin F., Sgt, 349th Inf
McKinsey, Henry R., T/Sgt, 351st Inf
McLaughlin, Joseph P., Pvt, 349th Inf
McLeod, Albert R., Sgt, 350th Inf
McMahon, Jack J., Pvt, 349th Inf
McMahon, James G., Lt, 351st Inf
McMicken, James E., Pfc, 351st Inf
McNally Robert C., Cpl, 338th Inf
McNamara, Ed W., Pfc, 349th Inf
McNeely, Loyd C., Pfc, 349th Inf
McNeil, Paul J., Pvt, 350th Inf
McNutt, Opie L., Pvt, 349th Inf
McPhee, John H., Sgt, 349th Inf
McQuaig, Russell J., Pfc, 350th Inf
McVey, James J., Pvt, 351st Inf
Meade, Walter, Pvt, 350th Inf
Meadows, Leo, Pvt, 351st Inf
Meadows, Samuel S., Sgt, 350th Inf
Means, Robert C., 1st Lt, 349th Inf
Meckenberg, Arnold, Pvt, 350th Inf
Mecsey, Joseph, Pvt, 350th Inf
Medina, Ernest, Sgt, 350th Inf
Meeks, Clarence R., Capt, 351st Inf
Meeks, Ray B., Pfc, 351st Inf
Meenach, Clarence L., Pfc, 349th Inf
Megaro, Herman V., Pvt, 351st Inf
Meier, Robert H., Cpl, 349th Inf
Mendez, Serafino O., Pvt, 351st Inf
Mercier, George E., Pfc, 351st Inf
Meskimen, Joseph E., Jr., Sgt, 351st Inf
Messer, Ben H., Pfc, 350th Inf
Mestas, Felix B., Jr., Pfc, 350th Inf
Metcalfe, Andrew R., S/Sgt, 349th Inf
Meurer, Fred P., Sgt, 351st Inf
Meyer, Edgar A., T/Sgt, 349th Inf
Meyer, William H., 1st Lt, 349th Inf
Mezera, Joseph, Jr., Pvt, 349th Inf
Michaels, Edward J., Cpl, 351st Inf
Micucci, Joseph A., Pfc, 349th Inf
Middleton, Willis R., Pfc, 350th Inf
Mielke, Frederick H., S/Sgt, 351st Inf
Mike, Drew, S/Sgt, 350th Inf
Mikeska, Joe E., Pfc, 350th Inf

Milano, Amerigo P., Pvt, 349th Inf
Milewska, Edward J., Pfc, 351st Inf
Millbeck, Richard L., Pfc, 349th Inf
Miller, Charles R., Pfc, 350th Inf
Miller, Estin, Pfc, 350th Inf
Miller, Everett, Pfc, 351st Inf
Miller, Francis J., Pfc, 350th Inf
Miller, George, Pfc, 351st Inf
Miller, Harold E., S/Sgt, 350th Inf
Miller, James E., S/Sgt, 350th Inf
Miller, Raymond L., T/Sgt, 351st Inf
Miller, Robert G., Pfc, 350th Inf
Miller, William, Pfc, 350th Inf
Mills, Frederick S., Pfc, 313th Med Bn
Mills, James L., T/4, 349th Inf
Mills, Joseph, T/Sgt, 351st Inf
Millspaugh, Robert C., 1st Lt, 350th Inf
Milner, Kenneth W., Pfc, 351st Inf
Milton, Harold F., Pvt, 351st Inf
Milvet, Joseph A., Pfc, 350th Inf
Ming, James T., Pfc, 313th Engr Bn
Minick, Harry M., Pfc, 351st Inf
Mink, Arvel E., Pfc, 349th Inf
Minolaio, Carmen L., T/Sgt, 349th Inf
Minor, Franklin J., Cpl, 350th Inf
Mirowitz, Edward C., Pfc, 350th Inf
Mitchell, Albert L., Pfc, 349th Inf
Mitchell, Irving S., Pfc, 350th Inf
Mitchell, Murray M., Pvt, 350th Inf
Mittelstedt, William, Pvt, 350th Inf
Mix, Albert, Pvt, 351st Inf
Mizer, Dorman C., Pvt, 350th Inf
Moats, Ralph W., Pvt, 350th Inf
Mock, Robert S., S/Sgt, 313th Engr Bn
Mokay, Alexander, Pvt, 350th Inf
Moline, Harold F., Pvt, 351st Inf
Monismith, John R., Pvt, 350th Inf
Monocchio, Herman A., T/5, 351st Inf
Montague, Richard J., Pfc, 351st Inf
Montagro, Alfred C., Pfc, 349th Inf
Montauk, Harvey, Pvt, 351st Inf
Montamajor, Manuel, Pfc, 349th Inf
Montes, Joaquin A., Jr., Pfc, 349th Inf
Montes, Jose S., Pvt, 349th Inf
Montgomery, Charles F., Pfc, 350th Inf
Montoya, Jake T., S/Sgt, 350th Inf
Montoya, Leonardo, Pfc, 350th Inf
Moore, Garvin B., Sgt, 349th Inf
Moore, James H., S/Sgt, 349th Inf
Moore, R. D., Pfc, 350th Inf
Moore, Richard H., Pvt, 349th Inf
Moore, Vern C., Pfc, 349th Inf
Moorefield, Charlie C., Pfc, 350th Inf
Mora, Marciano V., Pfc, 349th Inf
Mordecai, John T., Pfc, 350th Inf
Morefield, James W., Pvt, 913th Fa Bn
Morgan, Chester, Pfc, 349th Inf
Morgan, Herman G., Pfc, 351st Inf
Morgan, William P., Jr., T/5, 351st Inf
Morin, Lucien A., S/Sgt, 349th Inf
Morris, Jesse T., Jr., Pvt, 350th Inf
Morris, Robert L., Pfc, 351st Inf
Morrison, James H., Pfc, 350th Inf
Morse, Lyde B., Sgt, 349th Inf
Morse, Edgar L., Pfc, 349th Inf
Morse, Herbert W., Pvt, 351st Inf
Morse, Raymond W., Pvt, 351st Inf
Morse, Stanley M., Lt, 350th Inf
Mortensen, Lawrence, S/Sgt, 350th Inf
Mortimore, Bruce C., Cpl, 337th Fa Bn
Mortko, Chester J., Pfc, 349th Inf
Morton, Thomas W., Pvt, 351st Inf
Moscato, Anthony, Pvt, 349th Inf
Mosteller, William J., Pfc, 351st Inf
Motil, Louis, S/Sgt, 351st Inf
Mowatt, Clarence S., Pfc, 351st Inf
Moynahan, Bernard W., 1st Lt, 351st Inf
Mueller, William F., Pvt, 349th Inf
Muholland, Thomas, Pvt, 913th Fa Bn
Muller, Herman F., Pvt, 351st Inf
Mullins, Gilmer, Pfc, 351st Inf
Mullins, Homer, Pfc, 351st Inf

Mullins, James P., 2nd Lt, 349th Inf
Munroe, William R., T/5, 350th Inf
Munsey, Joe R., Pfc, 349th Inf
Murchison, Edgar R., Pfc, 351st Inf
Murphy, Clifford P., Pvt, 351st Inf
Murphy, Francis T., Pvt, 338th Fa Bn
Murphy, Francis W., Pvt, 351st Inf
Murphy, John J., Pvt, 349th Inf
Murphy, John J., Pvt, 351st Inf
Murphy, John O., Cpl, 351st Inf
Murphy, Paul G., S/Sgt, 349th Inf
Murphy, Robert J., 1st Lt, 351st Inf
Murphy, Thomas F., Pfc, 350th Inf
Murray, Elmer C., S/Sgt, 349th Inf
Murzynowski, Walter, Pvt, 351st Inf
Mussett, Alfred, Pfc, 350th Inf
Myers, Ralph C., Pvt, 349th Inf
Nagle, Eugene J., Pvt, 349th Inf
Nalback, Peter P., 1st Lt, 350th Inf
Naples, Samuel F., Pvt, 350th Inf
Narvaez, Manuel Z., Pvt, 350th Inf
Nastrucci, Harry G., Pfc, 351st Inf
Natale, John V., Pvt, 350th Inf
Nations, Hildon H., 1st Sgt, 350th Inf
Naylor, George M., S/Sgt, 349th Inf
Neddenriep, Kermit H., Pvt, 351st Inf
Neddo, Frederick, Sgt, 351st Inf
Neely, James D., Pvt, 350th Inf
Neely, John H., Pvt, 350th Inf
Neglia, Wilfred, Pfc, 351st Inf
Neimi, Richard U., Pvt, 349th Inf
Neivelt, Sam, Pvt, 349th Inf
Nelson, Dewey J., Pvt, 350th Inf
Nelson, Earl, Pfc, 350th Inf
Nelson, Edward A., Pvt, 350th Inf
Nelson, Filmore, Pvt, 349th Inf
Nelson, Lee, Pvt, 351st Inf
Nelson, Robert C., Pvt, 350th Inf
Newell, James J., Pfc, 351st Inf
Newman, Otis, Cpl, 351st Inf
Newton, Garrett L., S/Sgt, 337th Fa Bn
Nichola, Jesse W., Pfc, 349th Inf
Nichols, Norman A., Pfc, 349th Inf
Nicholson, Artie B., Jr., Pvt, 349th Inf
Nickell, Charles E., Pfc, 350th Inf
Nickles, Ralph G., Pvt, 88th Sig Co
Niedzwiecki, Edward J., Pfc, 351st Inf
Niekamp, Robert E., Pfc, 351st Inf
Nierenz, Arvid E., Pfc, 349th Inf
Nigro, Rocco P., Pfc, 351st Inf
Noble, Beryl S., Pfc, 351st Inf
Noble, Walter E., Pfc, 350th Inf
Nolan, James W., S/Sgt, 351st Inf
Nolan, John F., Pvt, 350th Inf
Nolen, Amos F., Pvt, 350th Inf
Noonan, John A., Pvt, 351st Inf
Nordrum, Ingman J., Sgt, 351st Inf
Norman, James W., Pvt, 350th Inf
Norris, Ether T., Jr., Pfc, 350th Inf
North, Charles L., Pvt, 351st Inf
Norton, Herman G., Pvt, 350th Inf
Norton, John J., Pvt, 351st Inf
Norton, Lewis, T/Sgt, 350th Inf
Norton, Ralph L., Pvt, 350th Inf
Noto, Carl J., Pfc, 349th Inf
Novick, Max, Pvt, 350th Inf
Noyes, James F., Sgt, 351st Inf
Noyes, Richard F., Pfc, 351st Inf
O'Connor, Charles H., Sgt, 349th Inf
O'Donnell, Edward F., Jr., Pvt, 349th Inf
Oertel, George C., Jr., 2nd Lt, 350th Inf
O'Haier, William A., Pvt, 350th Inf
Ohne, Herman W., Lt Col, 351st Inf
Oldfield, John P., Pfc, 349th Inf
Olejar, Frank W., Pfc, 351st Inf
Oles, Vincent, Pfc, 351st Inf
Olguin, Louis M., Pfc, 349th Inf
Oliver, Fred T., Jr., Pvt, 350th Inf
Olsen, Robert G., Pvt, 350th Inf
Olson, Richard W., Pvt, 351st Inf
Ondrey, Robert G., Pfc, 349th Inf
Oneal, Melvin F., Pfc, 351st Inf

O'Neil, Charles T., Pvt, 350th Inf
O'Neil, Gerald A., Pfc, 349th Inf
Orcutt, Woodford A., Pvt, 351st Inf
Oreskovich, Mike J., Maj, 350th Inf
Orloski, Myron S., Pvt, 350th Inf
Orlowski, Sidney P., Pvt, 350th Inf
Ormsbee, John R., Pvt, 351st Inf
Ortendahl, Robert L., Pvt, 351st Inf
Orth, Donald W., Pvt, 351st Inf
Ortiz, Louis R., Pfc, 351st Inf
Osajda, Edward F., Pfc, 351st Inf
Osborn, Ralston G., Jr., Pvt., 350th Inf
Osisek, Peter J., 2nd Lt, 350th Inf
Ostune, John, Pvt, 351st Inf
Otremha, Stephen J., Sgt, 349th Inf
Ott, Robert J., Pfc, 349th Inf
Ott, William P., Capt, 350th Inf
Outten, John W., Jr., Pvt, 349th Inf
Overstreet, James R., Lt, 350th Inf
Owcarz, Frank M., Pfc, 351st Inf
Owens, James J., Pfc, 349th Inf
Owens, Lee J., Pvt, 351st Inf
Oxford, Edwin B., Sgt, 351st Inf
Oyler, Edward D., Sgt, 351st Inf
Pacely, Lowell E., Pfc, 313th Fa Bn
Page, Minor B., Pvt, 350th Inf
Page, Orin L., Jr., Pfc, 349th Inf
Painter, Earl F., Cpl, 350th Inf
Painter, Harry V., Pvt, 350th Inf
Paiva, George, Pfc, 351st Inf
Paladino, Frank J., Pvt, 350th Inf
Palmer, Robert W., Pfc, 351st Inf
Paluch, Joseph E., Pvt, 350th Inf
Palumberi, Rosario F., Sgt, 350th Inf
Pando, George S., Pfc, 351st Inf
Pankey, Gordon W., Pfc, 349th Inf
Pany, Sylvester J., Pfc, 351st Inf
Pape, Elmer J., S/Sgt, 351st Inf
Pappas, Leon L., Lt, 351st Inf
Parish, Roy F., Pvt, 349th Inf
Parker, Albert C., S/Sgt, 350th Inf
Parker, Elmer C., Pvt, 351st Inf
Parker, Jack S., 2nd Lt, 349th Inf
Parker, Judson S., S/Sgt, 349th Inf
Parker, Raphael B., Pfc, 351st Inf
Parkinson, Roy H., Pvt, 350th Inf
Parla, Samuel P., Pvt, 351st Inf
Parrish, Harless, Pfc, 351st Inf
Parrott, Donald R., Pvt, 351st Inf
Parrotte, Jules V., T/5, 313th Engr Bn
Patrick, William S., Pfc, 349th Inf
Patti, Joseph J., Pvt, 350th Inf
Pattison, George B., Pfc, 351st Inf
Patton, Edward L., Cpl, 351st Inf
Patton, Robert M., Pvt, 350th Inf
Paul, Alfred C., Pfc, 351st Inf
Paul, Leon A. J., Pfc, 351st Inf
Payer, Frank W., Lt, 350th Inf
Payne, Estes E., Pvt, 351st Inf
Payne, Howard J., Pfc, 350th Inf
Pearlman, Morton J., Pvt, 350th Inf
Pecor, Leonard L., Pvt, 350th Inf
Peeler, Frank, Pvt, 350th Inf
Pekins, Robert E., Pfc, 313th Engr Bn
Pelham, Adam G., Pvt, 350th Inf
Pellerin, Gerard A., Pfc, 349th Inf
Penney, John A., Pfc, 349th Inf
Pennington, Willie E., Pfc, 349th Inf
Pentico, William H., Pvt, 351st Inf
Pentz, Walker H., Cpl, 349th Inf
Pepe, Pasquale, Pfc, 351st Inf
Pepin, Raoul A., Pvt, 351st Inf
Pepper, Kenneth, S/Sgt, 350th Inf
Peralta, Louis, Pfc, 350th Inf
Perciavalle, Anthony P., Pvt, 351st Inf
Pereira, Louis, Pvt, 349th Inf
Perfetti, Louis, Pvt, 350th Inf
Perich, Marijan M., Pvt, 349th Inf
Perillo, Salvatore, Pvt, 350th Inf
Perreault, Louis N., Pfc, 351st Inf
Perry, Ralph E., Sgt, 313th Engr Bn
Perry, Walter F., Pfc, 350th Inf

Pescod, Dennis N., Pfc, 350th Int
Peskie, Frank C., Pvt, 350th Inf
Peters, Fred, Jr., Pfc, 351st Inf
Peters, Herbert E., Pfc, 350th Inf
Peters, James H., Pfc, 351st Inf
Petersen, Ervin E., Pvt, 349th Inf
Petersen, William J., Pvt, 88th Rcn Tr
Peterson, Charles M., Pvt, 349th Inf
Petoff, Soi, Pvt, 351st Inf
Petracco, Victor J., Sgt, 350th Inf
Petrak, Eugene J., Cpl, 350th Inf
Petrie, Willard F., Jr., Pvt, 349th Inf
Petrillo, Joseph P., Cpl, 337th Fa Bn
Petrucci, Pasquale A., Pvt, 349th Inf
Pettey, Ernest F., Jr., Pfc, 351st Inf
Peverstorf, Ronald A., Pfc, 350th Inf
Peveto, Ira L., Pvt, 351st Inf
Pfaff, Herman, 1st Lt, 313th Engr Bn
Pfalzer, George C., T/5, 349th Inf
Pharo, Glenn W., Pfc, 351st Inf
Phelan, Earsal D., Pvt, 350th Inf
Phillips, Arthur K., S/Sgt, 349th Inf
Phillips, Avner J., Pfc, 349th Inf
Phillips, Charles O., Pfc, 351st Inf
Phillips, Ellis L., Cpl, 351st Inf
Phillips, Gerald E., Sgt, 913th Fa Bn
Phillips, Wilson A., Pvt, 351st Inf
Phillis, Robert G., Pfc, 350th Inf
Phipps, William M., Pfc, 351st Inf
Piantino, Bernard F., Pvt, 350th Inf
Piatek, Victor J., Cpl, 349th Inf
Piazza, Joseph F., Pfc, 351st Inf
Picciotti, Nicholas, Pfc, 350th Inf
Pickul, Michael F., Sgt, 350th Inf
Pieczynski, Arnold W., Pfc, 350th Inf
Pienta, Edward F., Pfc, 351st Inf
Pierce, Herman B., Pfc, 350th Inf
Pierce, William E., Pfc, 351st Inf
Pierce, William L., Lt, 349th Inf
Pilichowski, Henry J., Pfc, 349th Inf
Piontek, Joseph J., Pfc, 350th Inf
Piperata, Alexander, Pvt, 350th Inf
Pippi, Angelo W., Pfc, 350th Inf
Pirri, Santo, S/Sgt, 338th Fa Bn
Piscitelli, Michael J., Pvt, 351st Inf
Plank, Roger E., 1st Sgt, 350th Inf
Plate, William C., Pvt, 349th Inf
Platt, George E., Pvt, 349th Inf
Pleau, Ernest J., Sgt, 350th Inf
Ploettner, Frank W., Pfc, 350th Inf
Plumb, Robert L., Pfc, 350th Inf
Podoll, Robert F., Pvt, 350th Inf
Polcari, Angelo M., 2nd Lt, 350th Inf
Pollack, Harry M., Sgt, 349th Inf
Poole, Earnest E., Sgt, 350th Inf
Pooler, Howard E., Pvt, 351st Inf
Porter, Ernest C., Jr., Pvt, 350th Inf
Porter, Wallace K., Cpl, 913th Fa Bn
Portera, Frank P., Pvt, 351st Inf
Portschy, Walter J., Pvt, 350th Inf
Porton, Willie E., Pfc, 349th Inf
Potenberg, Raymond W., Pfc, 350th Inf
Potrykus, Jerome F., Pvt, 351st Inf
Potter, Ralph L., Pvt, 350th Inf
Poturica, Anthony, Pfc, 350th Inf
Poucher, Kenneth S., Pfc, 351st Inf
Poush, Carlos L., Pvt, 350th Inf
Powell, Eddie H., Pvt, 351st Inf
Prarizzi, Angelo R., Pfc, 350th Inf
Prather, John H., Pfc, 349th Inf
Pratt, Russell J., Sgt, 351st Inf
Preciado, Luciano S., Pvt, 349th Inf
Presson, Howard, Pfc, 351st Inf
Prewett, Clay W., Pfc, 349th Inf
Price, Melvin A., Pvt, 338th Fa Bn
Price, Mercer B., Pvt, 349th Inf
Priest, Omer L., Pvt, 338th Fa Bn
Proctor, Donald V., T/3, 349th Inf
Proctor, Elwin G., Pvt, 351st Inf
Proulx, Henry J., Pfc, 349th Inf
Pucci, Alexander C., Pvt, 351st Inf
Pucci, Vinitius J., Sgt, 350th Inf

Puckett, Lewie D., Sr., Pvt, 350th Inf
Pudleiner, Raymond T., Pfc, 350th Inf
Pulling, Robert H., Pvt, 313th Engr Bn
Purkiss, Kenneth M., Cpl, 351st Inf
Putman, Eugene N., Pvt, 350th Inf
Puz, Anthony, Jr., Cpl, 351st Inf
Pyenta, Peter P., S/Sgt, 351st Inf
Pyrce, Stanley T., Pvt, 350th Inf
Quick, Irvin, Pvt, 351st Inf
Quillin, Sydney L., Pfc, 349th Inf
Quinn, Morgan J., Pvt, 88th Rcn Tr
Rab, Adolph E., Pfc, 338th Fa Bn
Racine, Arthur L., Pvt, 351st Inf
Racinski, Alfred J., Pfc, 350th Inf
Rackley, Malvin F., S/Sgt, 351st Inf
Radaskiewicz, William J., Pfc, 350th Inf
Rader, Harvey W., Pfc, 350th Inf
Radics, Joseph G., S/Sgt, 351st Inf
Radlo, Carl B., 1st Lt, 351st Inf
Radocy, Louis, S/Sgt, 349th Inf
Rafferty, Jack B., Pfc, 350th Inf
Ragon, Carl W., Pfc, 351st Inf
Rahilly, Donald F., T/Sgt, 350th Inf
Rainwater, John M., Pvt, 350th Inf
Rakowski, William H., Pvt, 351st Inf
Raley, Amos C., 2nd Lt, 351st Inf
Rambo, Leo J., Pvt, 349th Inf
Ramirez, David A., Pvt, 349th Inf
Ramirez, Guarinez, Pfc, 351st Inf
Ramirez, Romeo M., T/Sgt, 349th Inf
Ramirez, Thomas F., Pvt, 351st Inf
Ramsey, George W., Pfc, 350th Inf
Ramsey, Henry J., Pvt, 350th Inf
Ramsey, Lloyd M., Pfc, 350th Inf
Randall, John, Jr., Pvt, 351st Inf
Randall, Robert F., Pvt, 351st Inf
Rankin, Junior R., S/Sgt, 351st Inf
Ransom, Leroy D., Pvt, 349th Inf
Ransom, Samuel W., Pvt, 350th Inf
Ratajczak, Norman S., Pvt, 351st Inf
Ratay, Stanley V., Sgt, 350th Inf
Ray, Joseph A., Pfc, 351st Inf
Raymond, Chester O., Pfc, 350th Inf
Reda, Michael, Pvt, 350th Inf
Redish, Mike, Pfc, 351st Inf
Reed, Albert M., Pvt, 351st Inf
Reed, Edgar T., Pfc, 350th Inf
Reed, Gifford D., 2nd Lt, 313th Med Bn
Reed, Walter, Pvt, 351st Inf
Reedy, Carl F., Pfc, 350th Inf
Reef, Ray W., Pvt, 349th Inf
Reedell, Axel S., Pfc, 351st Inf
Reek, William O., Pfc, 351st Inf
Rees, Lloyd G., Cpl, 351st Inf
Reid, Cecil L., Pvt, 350th Inf
Reid, Chester W., 2nd Lt, 351st Inf
Reihs, Robert R., Pfc, 351st Inf
Reilly, Henry D., Pfc, 349th Inf
Reilly, John F., Pvt, 350th Inf
Reilly, Richard F., Pvt, 351st Inf
Reitmaier, Robert E., Pfc, 351st Inf
Reitz, William F., Pvt, 350th Inf
Rensel, William A., Jr., Pfc, 350th Inf
Reshel, Andrew P., Pfc, 350th Inf
Ressler, James D., Pfc, 349th Inf
Reyes, Jose P., Pfc, 349th Inf
Reyes, Refugio, Pvt, 351st Inf
Reynolds, Everett, Pfc, 349th Inf
Rezendes, Alfred L., Pfc, 349th Inf
Resendez, John D., Pfc, 350th Inf
Rhatigan, Thomas M., Cpl, 351st Inf
Rheaume, Leo J., Pfc, 350th Inf
Rhodes, Arthur D., 1st Lt, 351st Inf
Rhodes, James E., T/Sgt, 349th Inf
Rhodes, Leo D., Pvt, 350th Inf
Ricard, Edward J., Pvt, 350th Inf
Rice, Lawrence M., Sgt, 350th Inf
Rice, Paul B., Pfc, 351st Inf
Rice, Ross A., Pvt, 351st Inf
Richardson, Charles, Pfc, 351st Inf
Richardson, Lawrence C., Pfc, 350th Inf

Richardson, Marion E., Pfc, 349th Inf
Richardson, William J., Pfc, 351st Inf
Richens, Marion L., Pfc, 351st Inf
Richerson, Stanton, Pfc, 349th Inf
Rickett, John F., Pvt, 349th Inf
Ricketts, Harry E., T/Sgt, 350th Inf
Rickey, George T., Pvt, 349th Inf
Rider, Irving F., Pvt, 349th Inf
Rielly, John J., T/5, 88th Cav Rcn Tr
Ries, Grover K., 1st Lt, 350th Inf
Ries, Walter E., Pvt, 350th Inf
Rife, A. G. H., Pvt, 351st Inf
Riga, Alvin V., Capt, 351st Inf
Riley, William M., Sgt, 350th Inf
Rinaldi, Sebastiano R., Pfc, 351st Inf
Riordan, James F., Cpl, 350th Inf
Riordan, William F., Pfc, 350th Inf
Ripley, Samuel E., T/Sgt, 349th Inf
Riquier, Gerard E., Pfc, 351st Inf
Ritter, Chester W., Pfc, 351st Inf
Ritter, Henry R., Pvt, 351st Inf
Ritter, Loyal G., Pfc, 349th Inf
Roache, Michael J., Pvt, 350th Inf
Roark, Donald E., Pfc, 350th Inf
Roberts, Wilbert L., Pvt, 350th Inf
Roberts, William A., Pvt, 313th Engr Bn
Robinson, Amos, Pvt, 349th Inf
Robinson, Herbert A., Pvt, 350th Inf
Robinson, John S., Pfc, 349th Inf
Robinson, Lawrence M., Pvt, 350th Inf
Robles, Bernardo, Pfc, 349th Inf
Rochira, John, Pfc, 351st Inf
Rocke, Donalds S., Lt, 351st Inf
Rodes, Walter L., Jr., Pvt, 351st Inf
Rodman, Earl K., Pfc, 350th Inf
Rodriguez, Hendrick F., Pvt, 351st Inf
Rodriguez, Fernand J., Pfc, 350th Inf
Roe, David P., 1st Lt, 350th Inf
Roedel, Bernard J., Pvt, 350th Inf
Roeder, Robert E., Capt, 350th Inf
Rogers, Francis J., Pfc, 351st Inf
Rogers, Raymond F., Pfc, 349th Inf
Rogers, Thomas F., Pfc, 351st Inf
Rogolewich, Michael P., Pvt, 351st Inf
Romanowski, Anthony E., T/Sgt, 349th Inf
Romans, Arlen W., Pfc, 350th Inf
Romeo, Carmen M., Pfc, 349th Inf
Romine, Ralph M., Sgt, 349th Inf
Romualdi, Ciro, Pvt, 350th Inf
Rook, Thayes E., Pfc, 350th Inf
Rose, Alexander G., Pfc, 351st Inf
Rose, Arnold E., Pfc, 351st Inf
Rose, Earl B., Jr., 2nd Lt, 351st Inf
Roselli, Luciano P., Pvt, 351st Inf
Rosemblum, David A., Pvt, 351st Inf
Rosensteel, Carl C., Pvt, 350th Inf
Rosner, Sheldon, Pvt, 351st Inf
Ross, Florry B., Pvt, 351st Inf
Ross, Frederick M., Pvt, 350th Inf
Rossi, Ernest C., Pfc, 349th Inf
Rota, Joseph J., Pfc, 351st Inf
Roth, Joseph A., Pfc, 350th Inf
Rotunda, Augustine, Pvt, 349th Inf
Rouker, Mathew J., Pfc, 350th Inf
Rowe, George P. L., Pfc, 350th Inf
Rowland, Jesses W., Pvt, 350th Inf
Roy, Lucien A., Sgt, 351st Inf
Rucureto, Patsy, Pfc, 351st Inf
Rudd, Louis L., Pfc, 349th Inf
Ruedel, Robert, Pvt, 350th Inf
Runyon, Charles R., Pfc, 351st Inf
Runyon, Clyde W., Pvt, 350th Inf
Russell, Rex O., Pvt, 351st Inf
Russell, Scott, S/Sgt, 350th Inf
Russo, Joshua, Pvt, 351st Inf
Russo, Peter, Pvt, 351st Inf
Rutherford, Clayton H., Jr., Pvt, 350th Inf
Rutland, Archie N., Pvt, 349th Inf
Ryan, Harold A., Pvt, 351st Inf
Ryan, James G., 1st Lt, 337th Fa Bn
Ryder, James F., Pvt, 349th Inf

Saar, Frederick A., Pvt, 351st Inf
Sabo, Ernest G., S/Sgt, 349th Inf
Sadlek, Francis J., Pfc, 350th Inf
Saienni, Biagio J., Pvt, 351st Inf
Salazar, Filomon, Pfc, 351st Inf
Sale, Clyde R., Pfc, 350th Inf
Saliers, Claude B., Pfc, 350th Inf
Sallstrom, Edwin M., Pvt, 350th Inf
Salvio, Jerry J., Pfc, 351st Inf
Salzwedel, Gustav A., Pfc, 350th Inf
Sample, Edward L., Pfc, 350th Inf
Sampolske, Joseph J., S/Sgt, 349th Inf
Sandaine, Albert J., T/5, 351st Inf
Sanders, Frank E., Pfc, 350th Inf
Sanders, Henry S., Cpl, 349th Inf
Saporito, Thomas A., Pfc, 349th Inf
Sarno, Carmine F., Cpl, 351st Inf
Sarofsky, Simon, Pfc, 350th Inf
Saviano, Henry, Pvt, 351st Inf
Saylor, John D., Pfc, 349th Inf
Schaffer, George D., Capt, 351st Inf
Schaible, Thomas F., Pfc, 350th Inf
Scharf, George A., Pvt, 350th Inf
Schermann, Walter C., Pfc, 351st Inf
Scherrer, Alphonse J., S/Sgt, 351st Inf
Schick, Arthur C., S/Sgt, 351st Inf
Schimpf, George A., Pfc, 349th Inf
Schlachter, Francis M., Sgt, 349th Inf
Schlesinger, Klauber, Pvt, 351st Inf
Schneider, John E., T/Sgt, 351st Inf
Schilling, Edward C., Pvt, 349th Inf
Schokman, Luke O., Lt, 349th Inf
Schults, Vainard O., Pfc, 349th Inf
Schuster, Edward B., T/5, 351st Inf
Schwartzman, George F., Pfc, 88th Rcn Tr
Scocozza, Alfred, Pvt, 351st Inf
Scott, David L., Pfc, 351st Inf
Scott, Jesse W., Pvt, 350th Inf
Scott, Walter W., Capt, 350th Inf
Scoville, Donald A., Pvt, 350th Inf
Scytkowski, Frank A., Pvt, 351st Inf
Seaburn, Harry J., Jr., Cpl, 351st Inf
Sears, Milton L., 1st Lt, 351st Inf
Seckinger, Richard C., Pvt, 913th Fa Bn
Secrest, Edward, Pfc, 351st Inf
Sedlak, Joseph J., S/Sgt, 350th Inf
Sedman, Leonard L., Pvt, 349th Inf
Seely, George G., Pfc, 350th Inf
Seger, John F., Jr., Pvt, 349th Inf
Sellitti, Julius W., Sgt, 350th Inf
Seneta, Eugene J., Pfc, 351st Inf
Sepsis, George P., Pfc, 351st Inf
Serdar, George R., S/Sgt, 350th Inf
Serrata, Rodolfo, Pvt, 349th Inf
Sesselmann, George F., 2nd Lt, 351st Inf
Shaddan, Clarence W., Pvt, 351st Inf
Shaffer, Raymond E., Pvt, 349th Inf
Shane, Ralph, Pvt, 350th Inf
Shannon, Alton N., Pvt, 351st Inf
Sharos, James L., Sgt, 351st Inf
Shaw, Bill D., Pfc, 351st Inf
Shaw, Everett E., T/Sgt, 350th Inf
Shaw, Richard J., Sgt, 351st Inf
Shaw, Thomas L., Pvt, 349th Inf
Shawanokasic, Raymond J., Pfc, 349th Inf
Shea, William N., Pvt, 349th Inf
Sheenan, John T., Pvt, 351st Inf
Sheerer, Whitman, Cpl, 351st Inf
Shemela, Warren K., 1st Lt, 351st Inf
Shepard, Joseph F., Pvt, 350th Inf
Sheperd, Nobart, Pfc, 350th Inf
Sheridan, Alfred W., Pfc, 350th Inf
Sheridan, Joseph M., Pfc, 350th Inf
Sherwin, Stanley L., Pfc, 350th Inf
Shields, Thomas L., T/5, 351st Inf
Shilling, John R., Cpl, 351st Inf
Shirley, Virgil W., Pfc, 351st Inf
Shoemaker, Herbert D., Capt, 351st Inf
Shortercarrier, Ralph E., Sgt, 350th Inf
Shortt, Stephen J., Pvt, 351st Inf
Shreve, Edward C., Pvt, 350th Inf
Shuler, Cleo N., Pfc, 351st Inf

Shuler, John E., S/Sgt, 349th Inf
Shumaker, James L., Pfc, 351st Inf
Shutter, Robert H., Cpl, 351st Inf
Shy, Burnell R., 1st Lt, 349th Inf
Siemsen, Duane M., Pfc, 349th Inf
Siewenie, Elmer G., Pvt, 351st Inf
Sigbicny, Lloyd T., Pfc, 351st Inf
Silva, Manuel J., Jr., Pvt, 351st Inf
Simer, Alfred C., S/Sgt, 350th Inf
Simon, Eli, Pvt, 351st Inf
Simon, Herman S., Sgt, 337th Fa Bn
Simon, Julius, Pvt, 350th Inf
Simpson, Harold P., Pfc, 351st Inf
Simpson, Theodore L., Pvt, 351st Inf
Sims, Roy, Pvt, 351st Inf
Sinclair, Francis R., Pfc, 351st Inf
Sirchia, Philip J., S/Sgt, 351st Inf
Sisam, Darrell H., Pvt, 351st Inf
Sitarz, Mithell R., Pfc, 350th Inf
Sitzman, Frederick J., Pfc, 351st Inf
Sjoblom, Verner R., Pfc, 350th Inf
Skalby, Clifford M., Capt, 350th Inf
Skarupincki, Leo J., Pvt, 351st Inf
Skene, Willard R., Capt, 313th Engr Bn
Skinner, Fay, Pvt, 351st Inf
Skrycki, Joseph A., Pfc, 350th Inf
Slater, Gilbert V., Pfc, 350th Inf
Sledjick, Bernard, Sgt, 351st Inf
Smach, Bernard, T/5, 913th Fa Bn
Smaligo, Paul, Pvt, 351st Inf
Small, Lester E., Pvt, 351st Inf
Smith, Arnold B., Pvt, 351st Inf
Smith, Corris H., Sgt, 337th Fa Bn
Smith Donald O., S/Sgt, 350th Inf
Smith, Edward G., Pfc, 351st Inf
Smith, Frank L., Pfc, 350th Inf
Smith, George C., Jr., Pfc, 351st Inf
Smith, Harry W., Pfc, 351st Inf
Smith, James G., Pfc, 350th Inf
Smith, James O., Pvt, 351st Inf
Smith, Luther A., 2nd Lt, 313th Engr Bn
Smith, Matthew P., Jr., Pvt, 350th Inf
Smith, Oklay J., Pfc, 351st Inf
Smith, Randolph, Pvt, 349th Inf
Smith, Winfield O., S/Sgt, 349th Inf
Smullen, Albert G., Pfc, 351st Inf
Smythers, Lyman M., Pvt, 350th Inf
Sneed, Lloyd J., Cpl, 351st Inf
Snyder, Grant L., Pfc, 350th Inf
Snyder, James E., Pfc, 350th Inf
Snyder, Kenneth H., Pfc, 350th Inf
Solana, Paco, Pfc, 350th Inf
Solomon, Jack, Pvt, 351st Inf
Soltys, Anthony J., Pfc, 351st Inf
Sommers, Leo, Pfc, 350th Inf
Sorci, Alberto A., Pfc, 351st Inf
Soriano, Sidney, Sgt, 351st Inf
Sorrell, Robert D., Pfc, 350th Inf
Souhrada, Richard C., Pfc, 350th Inf
Sousan, George J., Pvt, 351st Inf
Southard, Elmer, Pvt, 349th Inf
Southern, Carl E., Pvt, 350th Inf
Sowell, Arnold B., Pfc, 350th Inf
Spangenburg, Jack B., 2nd Lt, 351st Inf
Sparling, Clifford, Cpl, 339th Fa Bn
Spatt, Joseph, Pfc, 350th Inf
Spears, Earl, Pvt, 349th Inf
Spehler, Paul V., Pfc, 351st Inf
Spellicy, Richard N., T/4, 338th Fa Bn
Spencer, James A., Pfc, 350th Inf
Spence, Leslie L., Pfc, 349th Inf
Spens, Charles W., Pvt, 350th Inf
Spero, Lernard M., Pvt, 349th Inf
Spero, Michael J., Pvt, 350th Inf
Sperry, Eugene T., Pvt, 351st Inf
Spierson, George J., Pvt, 350th Inf
Spiezio, James S., Pfc, 313th Engr Bn
Spindler, Robert H., Pvt, 351st Inf
Spradling, Donald L., Pvt, 351st Inf
Sprague, Amos, Pfc, 351st Inf
Sprague, Earl W., Pfc, 349th Inf
Spudich, Steve J., Pvt, 350th Inf

Spurling, Roy F., Pvt, 349th Inf
Stahl, Elmer W., Pfc, 350th Inf
Stahl, Harold B., Pvt, 349th Inf
Stanbrough, Herman L., Pfc, 351st Inf
Stanczyk, Henry P., Pfc, 351st Inf
Standen, Thomas J., Pfc, 350th Inf
Stanfield, Garnet L., Pvt, 350th Inf
Stange, Henry L., Pvt, 350th Inf
Stankowich, John, Pvt, 351st Inf
Stanley, Harvey V., Pfc, 351st Inf
Stark, Robert S., T/5, 337th Fa Bn
Starch, Raymond J., Pfc, 351st Inf
Stark, Woodrow W., Pvt, 351st Inf
Stasis, Anthony P., Pvt, 350th Inf
Steadman, Paul F., Pvt, 349th Inf
Stec, Theodore J., Sgt, 351st Inf
Steele, Aulton, Pfc, 351st Inf
Steinbach, Dennis J., Pvt, 351st Inf
Steiner, Emile A., S/Sgt, 349th Inf
Steinhart, Vernon G., Pfc, 350th Inf
Steinmann, Henry G., Cpl, 351st Inf
Steltz, Lester E., Pvt, 351st Inf
Sterle, Edward P., T/5, 350th Inf
Stevens, A. C., Pfc, 351st Inf
Stevens, James G., Pvt, 350th Inf
Stevens, Walter T., Jr., Pvt, 350th Inf
Stewart, Charles E., Pfc, 351st Inf
Stewart, Harry R., S/Sgt, 351st Inf
St. Holmes, Downing L., Pfc, 351st Inf
Stines, Stanford, Pfc, 351st Inf
Stipa, Dino F., T/5, 351st Inf
Stitt, George R., Sgt, 349th Inf
Stoddard, William H., Pvt, 351st Inf
Stoffer, Ray A., Pvt, 350th Inf
Stone, Robert K., S/Sgt, 349th Inf
Stone, Saul, S/Sgt, 351st Inf
Storer, Lendell P., S/Sgt, 349th Inf
Stout, Lyle L., Pfc, 349th Inf
Strathmann, Carl B. W., Pfc, 349th Inf
Strayer, Joseph M., Pfc, 350th Inf
Street, Arnold Leroy, Cpl, 313th Engr Bn
Streuli, William A., Sgt, 339th Fa Bn
Striar, Bernard, Pfc, 350th Inf
Stroud, J. C., Cpl, 338th Fa Bn
Strouss, Alfred R., Pvt, 349th Inf
Struble, Chancy C., Pfc, 351st Inf
Stuart, Morris, Pfc, 350th Inf
Studer, Eugene J., Pvt, 349th Inf
Succa, Renzo, Pvt, 349th Inf
Suchier, Hugh C., Pfc, 351st Inf
Sudecz, James A., Pvt, 350th Inf
Sullivan, Eugene T., Jr., Pfc, 351st Inf
Sullivan, John W., Cpl, 351st Inf
Sumakis, Andrew G., T/5, 88th Div Hq Co
Summer, James S., Pfc, 351st Inf
Summers, Raymond W., Pfc, 351st Inf
Summer, Neal E., T/Sgt, 350th Inf
Sundberg, Edwin A., Pvt, 349th Inf
Sutker, Victor J., 2nd Lt, 351st Inf
Sutton, Ralph A., Pvt, 350th Inf
Svacha, Walter A., Pfc, 350th Inf
Swanson, Arthur C., Sgt, 349th Inf
Swanson, Walter E., Pvt, 351st Inf
Swarm, Marion W., Pfc, 349th Inf
Swart, John M., Pvt, 349th Inf
Swart, Theodore N., Pvt, 349th Inf
Swartz, Russell F., Jr., Pfc, 350th Inf
Sweat, John R., Pvt, 351st Inf
Sweeney, Malcolm E., Pfc, 351st Inf
Sweetin, Jerry C., Pvt, 349th Inf
Swisz, Arthur P., Pfc, 350th Inf
Szafranski, Chester E., Pfc, 349th Inf
Tacke, Alfred E., T/3, 351st Inf
Taikowski, Edmund L., Pvt, 351st Inf
Talley, Blair A., S/Sgt, 349th Inf
Tankersley, James W., Pvt, 351st Inf
Targett, Bish E., Pvt, 350th Inf
Tarlton, George W., Pfc, 351st Inf
Tarquinio, Anthony J., Pvt, 351st Inf
Tarrant, Marvin K., Pfc, 349th Inf
Tassey, James A., Pfc, 350th Inf
Tavares, Benjamin, T/4, 337th Fa Bn

Taylor, Chester, Pvt, 351st Inf
Taylor, Curtis E., Pvt, 350th Inf
Taylor, Donald G., Pfc, 351st Inf
Taylor, Earl E., Pfc, 349th Inf
Taylor, Floyd, S/Sgt, 350th Inf
Taylor, Frank J., S/Sgt, 350th Inf
Taylor, Leonard W., Sgt, 351st Inf
Taylor, Richard N., Pfc, 350th Inf
Taylor, Van D., Pvt, 351st Inf
Tays, Mack, Pfc, 350th Inf
Teabo, Robert M., Pfc, 350th Inf
Telep, Joseph S., Pfc, 351st Inf
Teller, Harold R., Pfc, 350th Inf
Tennyson, Howard W., Pfc, 349th Inf
Terry, Cecil C., Pvt, 351st Inf
Terry, Leslie E., Pvt, 350th Inf
Tetreault, Gordon H., Pfc, 351st Inf
Tetting, Charles A., Pfc, 350th Inf
Teuber, Frank H., Pfc, 349th Inf
Theakston, Garnet D., Pvt, 351st Inf
Theobald, Charles R., Sgt, 349th Inf
Theobald, Harold E., 1st Lt, 350th Inf
Theriault, Rudolph J., Pfc, 350th Inf
Thibault, Charles J., Pfc, 350th Inf
Thibodeau, Rieul E., Pfc, 351st Inf
Thomas, Harry E., Pfc, 351st Inf
Thomas, Raymond E., Pvt, 350th Inf
Thomas, William L., Pfc, 351st Inf
Thompson, Clifford L., Pfc, 351st Inf
Thompson, Daniel E., Jr., 2nd Lt, 351st Inf
Thompson, James H., Pfc, 349th Inf
Thompson, Travis E., 2nd Lt, 349th Inf
Thompson, Wilburn R., Pvt, 349th Inf
Thompson, William S., 2nd Lt, 350th Inf
Thompson, George A., Jr., Pvt, 349th Inf
Thompson, Gerald W., Pfc, 349th Inf
Thorman, Carl G., Pvt, 350th Inf
Thorne, Norman B., Pfc, 349th Inf
Thornhill, Milton C., Pvt, 349th Inf
Thornton, Charles T., Capt, 349th Inf
Thrasher, Andrew L. R., S/Sgt, 351st Inf
Tiedemann, Harold W., Pvt, 351st Inf
Tigirena, Pedro B., Pfc, 349th Inf
Tillberg, George R., Pvt, 351st Inf
Tiseo, Victor R., Pvt, 349th Inf
Todd, Leonard W., Pvt, 350th Inf
Tomacchio, Rosario A., Pvt, 349th Inf
Tome, Walter L., Pvt, 349th Inf
Tomlinson, William V., Sgt, 350th Inf
Tonseth, Norman E., Cpl, 350th Inf
Torok, Louis, Pfc, 351st Inf
Torok, Louis G., Pfc, 349th Inf
Torre, Amedeo A., Pfc, 350th Inf
Torres, Rudolfo C., Pvt, 350th Inf
Tortorice, Anthony J., T/4, 351st Inf
Tortherow, Garland, Pfc, 350th Inf
Tovar, Felipe G., Pfc, 351st Inf
Townsend, Fayette E., Pfc, 351st Inf
Tracy, Francis J., Pfc, 351st Inf
Tracy, Leonard B., Pfc, 350th Inf
Trame, Robert E., Pvt, 351st Inf
Trammell, Travis, Pvt, 349th Inf
Trapp, Edward O., Pfc, 349th Inf
Treuter, Werner, Sr., Pfc, 350th Inf
Trevino, Joe, Pfc, 350th Inf
Trilone, Anthony, T/Sgt, 350th Inf
Trimble, Jimmie L., Pvt, 350th Inf
Trousdell, John E., T/5, 350th Inf
Troxell, George W., Pvt, 349th Inf
Troy, James A., Pfc, 351st Inf
Trubenbach, Alfred C. E., 1st Lt, 351st Inf
Trusler, Melvin W., Jr., Pvt, 351st Inf
Tubbs, Horace E., Pvt, 350th Inf
Tucker, Edward E., Jr., 1st Lt, 351st Inf
Tucker, John T., Pvt, 351st Inf
Tully, Frank J., Pvt, 349th Inf
Tunk, Robert F., Jr., Pvt, 349th Inf
Tuozzola, Frank W., Pvt, 349th Inf
Turczynski, Ralph T., Pfc, 349th Inf
Turner, Alton D., Pvt, 351st Inf
Turner, Cloyce M., Pfc, 351st Inf
Turner, Letch, Pfc, 351st Inf

Turner, William E., Pfc, 349th Inf
Twardy, Alfred F., Pvt, 351st Inf
Tyler, Robert F., Cpl, 351st Inf
Typrowicz, Walter S., Pvt, 350th Inf
Tyson, L. C., S/Sgt, 351st Inf
Uhler, Delman, S/Sgt, 350th Inf
Ulin, Dean G., Pvt, 351st Inf
Upchurch, Jodie J., Pvt, 349th Inf
Updike, Robert L., Pfc, 349th Inf
Urban, Andrew, Pvt, 351st Inf
Urbanski, Raymond, Pfc, 351st Inf
Urton, William W., Pfc, 349th Inf
Usborne, Robert T., S/Sgt, 350th Inf
Vacca, Anthony A., Sgt, 351st Inf
Vail, Allan R., Capt, 351st Inf
Valcourt, Oscar G., Pvt, 351st Inf
Valenti, Joseph A., Pfc, 351st Inf
Valeri, Anthony, Pvt, 350th Inf
Vallarelli, Anthony J., Pvt, 350th Inf
Vamos, George J., Sgt, 313th Med Bn
Vanacora, Dominick J., Pvt, 349th Inf
Vanacore, Michael T., Pvt, 351st Inf
Van Bergen, John F., Sgt, 351st Inf
Vander Molen, Julius J., Pvt, 350th Inf
Van Effen, J., Jr., Pvt, 350th Inf
Van Etten, Charles E., Pvt, 349th Inf
Van Hine, Frank, Sgt, 350th Inf
Van Iderstine, Joseph E., T/4, 913th Fa Bn
Vartabedian, George G., Pfc, 350th Inf
Vasconcellos, Alfred V., Pvt, 351st Inf
Vasholz, Alfred H., 2nd Lt, 349th Inf
Vasquez, Lupe R., Pvt, 351st Inf
Vasquez, Rosalio M., Pfc, 349th Inf
Vaughn, Alfred, Pfc, 350th Inf
Vaughn, Warren F., T/5, 350th Inf
Veale, Leroy W., Pfc, 349th Inf
Vecchio, Anthony, Pfc, 350th Inf
Veith, Louis M., T/5, 351st Inf
Venter, Robert M., T/Sgt, 349th Inf
Venturella, Joseph B., Pvt, 351st Inf
Vera, Armando, Cpl, 351st Inf
Vesce, Joseph H., Pfc, 351st Inf
Vick, Jack W., Jr., Capt, 338th Fa Bn
Viggers, Eugene A., Pfc, 350th Inf
Vigil, Flavio, Pfc, 349th Inf
Villarreal, Valentin G., Pfc, 349th Inf
Vingis, Daniel, Pvt, 350th Inf
Voiles, Loren J., Pfc, 350th Inf
Von Borstel, Carsten A., Pvt, 351st Inf
Vonderlieth, Henry E., S/Sgt, 913th Fa Bn
Voss, Raymond G., Pvt, 350th Inf
Vranesic, William G., Pfc, 350th Inf
Vroeginday, Peter, Sgt, 349th Inf
Vyvial, Edward J., Pvt, 349th Inf
Wachus, Stanley J., T/Sgt, 351st Inf
Wade, Erbie, Pvt, 350th Inf
Wade, Lyle A., Pfc, 350th Inf
Wagner, William J., S/Sgt, 350th Inf
Walden, George F., Pvt, 351st Inf
Waldhart, Carl J., Pfc, 351st Inf
Waldron, Austin, Pvt, 350th Inf
Walker, Elmer F., Pfc, 349th Inf
Walker, George J., 2nd Lt, 349th Inf
Walker, Lee R., Pfc, 349th Inf
Walker, Richard P., 1st Lt, 349th Inf
Walker, William J., Pfc, 350th Inf
Waller, Jack L., Pvt, 350th Inf
Walsh, David P., Pfc, 351st Inf
Walsh, John J., Pvt, 349th Inf
Walter, Joseph P., Capt, 349th Inf
Walters, Charles H., Sr., Pvt, 349th Inf
Walters, George J., Pfc, 349th Inf
Walters, Oliver B., Pfc, 351st Inf
Walton, Carroll L., Pvt, 351st Inf
Ward, Christopher C., Jr., Pvt, 350th Inf
Ward, Fred E., Pvt, 351st Inf
Ward, James B., Pfc, 350th Inf
Warkentien ,Milton K., T/5, 351st Inf
Warming, Eric W., Pfc, 350th Inf
Warner, Henry L., Pfc, 350th Inf
Warren, Edwin W., Jr., Pvt, 351st Inf
Warren, Robert D., Pfc, 350th Inf

Warrick, Joseph B., Pfc, 351st Inf
Warszewicz, Walter J., Pvt, 313th Engr Bn
Waselnak, Nicholas, Pvt, 350th Inf
Waslaski, Richard, Pfc, 349th Inf
Wassdorf, Petrus J., 1st Lt, 349th Inf
Wasson, Oran L., Pvt, 351st Inf
Watkins, Richard D., Pvt, 350th Inf
Watson, Donald S., S/Sgt, 350th Inf
Watson, William C. G., 1st Lt, 350th Inf
Watt, Thomas G., S/Sgt, 349th Inf
Wattu, Eino O., S/Sgt, 350th Inf
Webb, Charles E., Pvt, 349th Inf
Webb, Clarence, S/Sgt, 349th Inf
Webb, Edward L., Pfc, 351st Inf
Weber, Louis N., Pvt, 351st Inf
Weik, William C., Jr., Pfc, 350th Inf
Weinbrenner, John E., Pvt, 349th Inf
Weiner, Abraham S., Pvt, 350th Inf
Weinstein, Seymour, Pfc, 349th Inf
Weintraub, Sigmund, Pfc, 350th Inf
Weisbecker, William H., Pvt, 350th Inf
Weiss, Leslie, Pfc, 350th Inf
Weisser, Albert G., Pfc, 351st Inf
Weissman, Joseph, Sgt, 349th Inf
Welch, Earl M., Pfc, 349th Inf
Welch, Wallace H., 1st Lt, 349th Inf
Welenc, James I., Sgt, 351st Inf
Wells, Harry O., S/Sgt, 350th Inf
Wendelin, Paul A., S/Sgt, 350th Inf
Wennerberg, Alvar H., Sgt, 349th Inf
Wenning, Marvin R., Pvt, 313th Med Bn
Wesson, Alfred E., Pvt, 350th Inf
West, James R., Pvt, 350th Inf
Whalen, Richard K., Pfc, 349th Inf
Wheat, Doyle, Pfc, 349th Inf
Wheeler, Homer F., Pvt, 349th Inf
Whelpley, Donald C., Pvt, 351st Inf
Whimert, Frederick S., Pfc, 351st Inf
Whitaker, Wayne D., Pvt, 351st Inf
White, Claude O., Pfc, 350th Inf
White, Horace C., Pfc, 350th Inf
White, Jack D., 2nd Lt, 350th Inf
White, John O., Pvt, 349th Inf
White, Julius, Pvt, 350th Inf
White, Roland G., Jr., Pvt, 350th Inf
Whitt, Charles M., Sgt, 351st Inf
Whitt, Ervin C., Pvt, 351st Inf
Wichrowski, Chester J., T/Sgt, 351st Inf
Wick, Frank J., Pvt, 350th Inf
Wickham, Donald E., Pvt, 351st Inf
Wieland, Clemence E., Pfc, 88th Cav Rcn Tr
Wildung, Edward J., Jr., Pvt, 351st Inf
Wiley, James R., Pvt, 349th Inf
Wilkins, Lyle H., Pvt, 351st Inf
Willard, Earl B., 2nd Lt, 339th Fa Bn
Willard, Herbert C., Pvt, 350th Inf
Willet, Raymond E., Pfc, 351st Inf
Willey, Henry O., S/Sgt, 351st Inf
Williams, Arthur W., Sgt, 349th Inf
Williams, Carlton, T/4, 351st Inf
Williams, David D., Pfc, 351st Inf
Williams, Ralph L., S/Sgt, 350th Inf
Williams, Ray R., Pvt, 350th Inf
Williams, Wilmot J., Pfc, 351st Inf
Williamson, Howard C., Pvt, 351st Inf
Willis, Henry F., Pvt, 349th Inf
Willis, John F., Pvt, 349th Inf
Willis, Thomas, 2nd Lt, 338th Fa Bn
Wilson, Donald J., Pfc, 350th Inf
Wilson, James F., Pfc, 349th Inf
Wilson, Robert H., Pvt, 349th Inf
Wilson, Virgil L., Pfc, 351st Inf
Wilson, William K., 2nd Lt, 350th Inf
Wilson, Wilmer W., Cpl, 350th Inf
Windhalz, Julius J., Pvt, 350th Inf
Winesett, Louis E., Jr., Pfc, 350th Inf
Winkel, Raymond J., Pfc, 350th Inf
Winter, Martin H., Pvt, 349th Inf
Winters, Paul D., T/3, 351st Inf
Wireman, George D., Pvt, 349th Inf
Witt, Clifford E., Pvt, 350th Inf
Wogan, Patrick J., Pfc, 350th Inf

Wojewoda, John A., Pvt, 351st Inf
Wolbrink, Raymond H., Pfc, 350th Inf
Wolf, Paul L., 1st Lt, 351st Inf
Wolfe, Earlie L., 2nd Lt, 349th Inf
Wolff, Albert, Pfc, 351st Inf
Wolfgang, Luther C., Pfc, 349th Inf
Womack, Carl L., Pvt, 350th Inf
Womack, Hardy T., Pvt, 350th Inf
Wood Bertram, Pvt, 350th Inf
Wood, Edgar G., Pfc, 349th Inf
Wood, Edgar W., Pvt, 349th Inf
Wood, Lee E., Pvt, 349th Inf
Woodall, Herman S., Pvt, 351st Inf
Woods, Opal L., Pfc, 349th Inf
Woodyard, Darrell B., Pvt, 351st Inf
Wooten, Jackson H., Pfc, 349th Inf
Worthington, Kenneth C., Pfc, 349th Inf
Wright, Edward W., Pvt, 350th Inf
Wright, George D., Pvt, 349th Inf
Wright, J. D., T/5, 337th Fa Bn
Wright, James L., Pfc, 351st Inf
Wright, Paul A., S/Sgt, 351st Inf

Wyre, Ellis A., Pfc, 351st Inf
Yager, Walter B., Pvt, 349th Inf
Yanez, Joe P., Pvt, 350th Inf
Yannucci, Samuel E., Pfc, 349th Inf
Ybarra, Guillermo O., Pvt, 350th Inf
Yliliemi, Arthur E., Pfc, 349th Inf
Yohannan, Paul, Pfc, 350th Inf
Young, Arthur, Pfc, 350th Inf
Young, Clarence C., Pfc, 350th Inf
Young, Gerald L., Pvt, 351st Inf
Young, Guy E., Pvt, 351st Inf
Young, James V., Sgt, 313th Engr Bn
Zamora, Gustavo, Pvt, 351st Inf
Zelinsky, George E., Sgt, 349th Inf
Zeuschner, Werner G., Pfc, 351st Inf
Ziegler, Frank J., S/Sgt, 351st Inf
Zifchak, Andrew R., Pvt, 351st Inf
Zimmer, Raymond E., Pfc, 349th Inf
Zola, Earl M., Pfc, 349th Inf
Zuchowski, Benjamin T., Cpl, 351st Inf
Zuena, Ernest V., Pvt, 351st Inf
Zumpetta, Peter A., Pvt, 351st Inf

DECORATIONS AND AWARDS

In their combat time officers and men of the 88th earned their awards and decorations the hard way. On succeeding pages are the names of men who were decorated for heroic or meritorious service with the 88th Division from its entry into combat until the lists were closed out in September 1945. Personnel officers of each unit compiled the lists at the direction of the Division Commander and unit commanding officers certified each list as official. Insofar as possible the lists have been checked to reduce errors to a minimum. If errors do occur they are unavoidable and apologies are extended to those whose names may not appear in this section.

KEY

BSM	Bronze Star	SS	Silver Star
DFC	Distinguished Flying Cross	AM	Air Medal
DSC	Distinguished Service Cross	SM	Soldier's Medal
DSM	Distinguished Service Medal	MIA	Missing in Action
LM	Legion of Merit	MF	Medal of Freedom
MH	Medal of Honor	Post	Posthumous award

* Oak Leaf Cluster

Captain *Robert E. Roeder,* 01285307, Infantry, Army of the United States. For conspicuous gallantry and intrepidity at the risk of his life above and beyond the call of duty on 27 and 28 September 1944 on Mt. Battaglia, Italy. Captain *Roeder* commanded his company in defense of the strategic Mt. Battaglia. Shortly after the company had occupied the hill, the Germans launched the first of a series of determined counterattacks to regain this dominating height. Completely exposed to ceaseless enemy artillery and small-arms fire, Captain *Roeder* constantly circulated among his men, encouraging them and directing their defense against the persistent enemy. During the sixth counterattack, the enemy using flame throwers and taking advantage of the fog, succeeded in overrunning the position. Captain *Roeder* led his men in a fierce battle at close quarters to repulse the attack with heavy losses to the Germans. The following morning, while the company was engaged in repulsing an enemy counterattack in force, Captain *Roeder* was seriously wounded and rendered unconscious by shell fragments. He was carried to the company command post where he regained consciousness. Refusing medical treatment, he insisted on rejoining his men. Although in a weakened condition, Captain *Roeder* dragged himself to the door of the command post and, picking up a rifle, braced himself in a sitting position. He began firing his weapon, shouted words of encouragement, and issued orders to his men. He personally killed two Germans before he was killed instantly by an exploding shell. Through Captain *Roeder's* able and intrepid leadership his men held Mt. Battaglia against the aggressive and fanatical enemy attempts to retake this important and strategic height. His valorous performance is exemplary of the fighting spirit of the Army of the United States. (*General Orders No. 31, War Department, 17 April 1945*)

Second Lieutenant *Charles W. Shea,* 01540616 (then technical sergeant), Company F, 350th Infantry Regiment, United States Army. For conspicuous gallantry and intrepidity at the risk of his life above and beyond the call of duty on 12 May 1944 near Mount Damiano, Italy. As Sergeant *Shea* and his company were advancing toward a hill occupied by the enemy, three enemy machine guns suddenly opened fire inflicting heavy casualties upon the company and halting its advance. Sergeant *Shea* immediately moved forward to eliminate these machine-gun nests in order to enable his company to continue its attack. The deadly hail of machine-gun fire at first pinned him down but boldly continuing his advance Sergeant *Shea* crept up to the first nest. Throwing several hand grenades, he forced the four enemy soldiers manning this position to surrender, and disarming them he sent them to the rear. He then crawled to the second machine-gun position and after a short fire fight forced two more German soldiers to surrender. At this time the third machine gun fired at him, and while deadly small-arms fire pitted the earth around him Sergeant *Shea* crawled toward the nest. Suddenly he stood up and rushed the emplacement and with well-directed fire from his rifle he killed all three of the enemy machine gunners. Sergeant *Shea's* display of personal valor was an inspiration to the officers and men of his company. (*General Orders No. 4, War Department, 12 January 1945*)

DISTINGUISHED SERVICE CROSS

Major Harold B. Ayres .... 351st Infantry
Sgt. Lee H. Beddow .... 350th Infantry
2nd Lt. John H. Bishop .... 350th Infantry
Major Frank W. Carmon, Jr. .... 351st Infantry
Col. Arthur S. Champeny* .... 351st Infantry
1st Lt. Perry J. Cheeney .... 351st Infantry
Pfc. Macdonald Coleman .... 349th Infantry
1st Lt. Pat G. Combs .... 913th Field Artillery
Capt. Thomas L. Cussans .... 350th Infantry
1st Lt. Ralph Decker, Jr. .... 351st Infantry
1st Lt. John E. Ebel .... 351st Infantry
1st Sgt. Paul N. Eddy .... 351st Infantry
Pfc. Walter C. Ellsworth .... 351st Infantry
Col. James C. Fry .... 350th Infantry
Pfc. Herbert G. Goldman (Post) .... 350th Infantry
1st Lt. Kenneth W. Gray .... 349th Infantry
Pfc. Dencil Herdman (Post) .... 349th Infantry
T/5 John O. Johnson (Post) .... Reconnaissance Troop
Major Erwin B. Jones .... 350th Infantry
Capt. Robert C. Kelley (Post) .... 349th Infantry
Lt. Col. Raymond E. Kendall (Post) .... 351st Infantry
Capt. John J. King .... 349th Infantry
2nd Lt. Steven M. Kosmyna .... 350th Infantry
2nd Lt. John T. Lamb .... 351st Infantry
2nd Lt. John A. Liebenstein (MIA) .... 349th Infantry
Capt. Charles P. Lynch, Jr. (Post) .... 350th Infantry
1st Lt. Trevelyn L. McClure (Post) .... 351st Infantry
S/Sgt. Sam McGowan .... 351st Infantry
T/Sgt. Manuel V. Mendoza .... 350th Infantry
1st Lt. Donald E. Muston .... 350th Infantry
Capt. Theodore W. Noon, Jr. .... 351st Infantry
2nd Lt. Charles W. Pierce .... 351st Infantry
T/Sgt. Romeo M. Ramirez (Post) .... 349th Infantry
S/Sgt. Aubrey B. Sally .... 349th Infantry
S/Sgt. Delvin V. Sample .... 351st Infantry
1st Lt. William B. Sandlin, Jr. .... 351st Infantry
1st Lt. Walter W. Scott .... 350th Infantry
1st Lt. Richard P. Walker (Post) .... 349th Infantry
2nd Lt. Linnsey L. Wheeler .... 351st Infantry
Major Charles D. Edmondson .... 351st Infantry

DISTINGUISHED SERVICE MEDAL

Maj. Gen. John E. Sloan   Maj. Gen. Paul W. Kendall

HEADQUARTERS AND HEADQUARTERS COMPANY

Allen, Court P., T/4, BSM
Allen, Donald F., Pfc, BSM
Bausher, Robert D., Capt, BSM
Bedolli, Albert J., S/Sgt, BSM
Belden, Donald T., T/4, BSM
Beggs, Elmore D., Lt Col, BSM, LM
Blum, Milton, Capt, BSM*
Brauer, Robert J., Maj, BSM
Brown, Horace M., Maj, BSM
Brown, Kenneth D., 1st Lt, BSM
Brown, Herbert D., Capt, BSM
Brown, Thorburn K., Brig Gen, BSM
Brown, William C., Capt, BSM
Burckes, Martin H., Lt Col, BSM
Buttenberg, Donald J., T/4, BSM
Calderone, Rocco, T/5, BSM, PH
Calsetta, Edwin H., Sgt, BSM
Carlough, Louis A., S/Sgt, BSM
Casterline, James I., Maj, BSM
Conrad, Alvin L., WOJG, BSM
Cook, Harvey J., Maj, BSM
Coulter, Malcolm W., S/Sgt, BSM
Daly, Arthur P., Sgt, BSM
Davidson, James R., Lt Col, BSM
Delaney, John P., T/Sgt, BSM, LM
Demey, Cornelius, Pvt, PH
Deutchman, Henry J., T/Sgt, BSM
Dougherty, Thomas E., Lt Col, LM
Douglas, Chester L., T/5, BSM, PH
Dow, William G., T/4, BSM
Draudt, Charles F., M/Sgt, LM
Drocco, Joseph E., T/4, BSM
Dupras, Paul A., Cpl, BSM
Eggerding, Howard H., M/Sgt, BSM
Estrada, Anthony B., Sgt, BSM
Fein, Rolf A., T/Sgt, BSM
Feith, Edward F., WOJG, BSM
Flanagan, James A., Maj, BSM*
Flynn, Harold D., T/4, BSM
Foley, Edward W., 1st Sgt, BSM
Foner, Henry J., CWO, LM
Freemon, William G., T/5, BSM
Fry, James C., Brig Gen, SS, DSC, LM, BSM, PH***
Gottlieb, Irving, T/5, BSM
Graham, William T., T/4, BSM
Gross, Dean C., T/4, BSM
Hale, Wallace M., Lt Col, BSM
Harris, Frederick V., Maj, BSM
Heiser, Clement F., T/3, BSM
Hemphill, Raymond E., T/5, BSM
Hilliard, Irvin R., T/Sgt, BSM
Hobbs, Frank C., Capt, BSM, PH
Holtfreter, William M., T/4, BSM
Hough, Edgar A., T/3, BSM
Hunter, Glen L., 1st Lt, BSM
Jackson, William A., 1st Lt, BSM
Johnson, Russell L., Sgt, BSM
Karrer, Robert J., Lt Col, BSM
Kahler, Henry V., M/Sgt, BSM
Kane, Maurice M., Lt Col, BSM

Keller, Neil, Capt, BSM*
Kelly, John F., 2d Lt, BSM
Kendall, Paul W., Maj Gen, BSM, LM**, SS, PH, DSM
Kennedy, Harold W., T/4, BSM
Kouba, Loumir, M/Sgt, BSM
Lambeth, Hubert G., S/Sgt, BSM
LaMotte, Frank W., Lt Col, BSM, LM
Lee, Hubert, Capt, BSM
Lehmann Wolfgang J., 1st Lt, BSM
Long, Frank T., S/Sgt, BSM
Martinez, Manuel, WOJG, BSM
Mazur, Edmund A., T/5, BSM
McBride, Robert J., Col, BSM, LM*
McGrath, Arthur F., T/4, BSM
McMellon, Frank, Sgt, BSM
Miller, Jack C., Maj, BSM
Modaffari, John A., CWO, BSM
Moss, Leonard G., 1st Lt, BSM
Moulton, George H., Maj, BSM
Murphy, Elton T., 1st Lt, LM
Myers, Frank R., Capt, BSM*
Nardi, Anthony J., T/4, BSM
Palmer, Roland E., Capt, BSM
Patterson, William T., 1st Lt, PH
Post, Harold W., T/Sgt, BSM
Quinn, John R., Pvt, PH
Rohme, Joseph J., T/5, BSM
Roth, Harold, M/Sgt, BSM
Rothhammer, Robert C., Capt, BSM
Ruhmor, Robert K., 1st Lt, BSM
Sample, Arthur N., Lt Col, BSM
Sappington, Homer A., Lt Col, BSM
Sayles, Franklin N., T/4, BSM, PH
Schenck, Harry J., M/Sgt, BSM
Schoch, Herbert C., Jr., T/Sgt, BSM
Skorepa, Louis F., Sgt, BSM
Sloan, John E., Maj Gen, SS, DSM
Slutzky, Joseph, Maj, BSM
Smelser, Hugo D., Sgt, BSM
Smith, John D., Sgt, BSM
Snow, Jerrold D., Maj, BSM*, LM
Stone, Jack M., T/4, BSM
Stutesman, John H., Capt, BSM
Sullenberger, John W., M/Sgt, BSM
Sullivan, George D., Capt, BSM
Topic, Peter L., Lt Col, BSM, LM
Treseder, Donald W., Lt Col, BSM
Turner, Thomas F., WOJG, BSM
Twait, Henry O., M/Sgt, BSM
Van Iderstine, Arthur P., Sgt, BSM
Vokoun, Joseph F., 1st Lt, BSM
Walker, George L., Maj, BSM, LM
Walls, Ward L., S/Sgt, BSM
Ward, Newell J., Capt, BSM
Wehr, Joseph H., Pfc, BSM
Werts, Day B., Maj, BSM
Williamson, Ira, Pvt, PH
Wist, Theodore A., T/Sgt, BSM
Zerger, Waldo J., Maj, BSM

349TH INFANTRY REGIMENT

Abbott, James E., Pvt, PH
Abercrombie, C (i.o.) W., Pvt, PH
Abercrombie, James R., 1st Lt, PH
Abercrombie, Kenneth, Pvt, BSM
Aberte, Charles W., Pvt, PH
Aborn, Edward S., Pfc, PH, BSM
Abshier, Ewell C., T/4, PH, BSM*
Ackman, Stewart C., 1st Lt, BSM
Adler, Richard C., S/Sgt, PH*
Adkins, Albert B., S/Sgt, PH*
Adams, Edward J., Pvt, PH*
Adkins, Kenneth R., Pvt, PH

Addison, John J., Sgt, PH
Adams, Columbus, Pfc, PH
Adams, Elmer, Pvt, PH
Adams, Wilbur H., Pfc, PH
Adams, Charles E., Pfc, PH, SM
Adams, James T., Pfc, PH
Adams, Rexford, Pfc, PH
Adkisson, Forrest O., Sgt, PH
Adamczewski, Raymond T., Pfc, PH
Adams, George C., Sgt, PH
Adams, Dallas C., 1st Lt, PH
Adams, Eugene J., Maj, PH, BSM

Adams, Harold H., Pfc, BSM
Adams, Raymond, Pfc, BSM
Agala, Roberto R., Pvt, PH
Agidio, Joseph, Pfc, PH
Aguiler, Benedict J., Pfc, PH
Aileo, Edward J., Maj, BSM
Aiello, John, Pfc, BSM
Alvarez, Marcelo A., Pvt, PH
Alvino, Henry A., Pfc, PH
Albert, Joe, Pfc, PH
Alo, Alfred E., Pfc, PH*
Allen, Erwin P., Pvt, PH
Allbrooks, James M., Pvt, PH
Alley, Rufus G., Pvt, PH
Aldridge, James E., Pvt, PH
Alejandro, Nunez, Sgt, PH
Allen, Kenneth E., Pvt, PH
Allen, Charles E., 1st Lt, PH
Alexander, Erwin R., Pfc, PH
Aliperti, Louis, Pfc, PH
Allen, Kenneth E., Pfc, PH*
Alves, Antonio, Pfc, PH
Alsteraum, Charles W., 1st Lt, PH
Almarez, Joe R., Sgt, PH, SS
Alvarez, Joseph, Sgt, PH
Alves, Llewellyn, Pfc, PH
Alramowitz, Joseph, Sgt, PH
Albert, Joseph, Pfc, PH
Allison, Fred W., Pfc, PH
Albert, Norman G., Pfc, BSM
Alldaffer, Robert C., S/Sgt, BSM
Allenbaugh, William E., Pvt, BSM
Allington, Earl J., Pfc, BSM
Alt, Russell F., Pfc, BSM
Amerson, Carl W., Pvt, PH*
Amos, William O., Pvt, PH*
Ament, John W., Pfc, PH
Anderson, Harold E., T/Sgt, PH
Andruk, Joseph, Pfc, PH
Anderson, Stewart P., Pvt, PH
Antill, William L., Pfc, PH
Anderson, Henry V., 1st Sgt, PH
Anastassiou, Thomas P., 1st Lt, PH
Andrews, William, Pvt, PH
Anttile, Eugene, Pfc, PH*
Andrews, Orville E., Pfc, PH, SS
Anderson, Alton O., Pvt, PH
Anders, George F., Pvt, PH
Anderson, Roy L., S/Sgt, PH, BSM, SS
Anderson, William E., Sgt, PH
Anderson, Theodore E., Pvt, PH
Anderson, Lester W., 1st Lt, PH
Andrews, Harry A., S/Sgt, SS
Andreotta, Donald V., T/Sgt, BSM
Aparicio, Raul R., Pfc, PH*
Aquilera, Sam A., Pfc, PH
Argrew, George M., Pvt, PH
Arntfield, Francis J., Pvt, PH*
Arter, Everett W., Pvt, PH, BSM
Arnoldin, Joseph A., Jr., Pfc, PH
Arellano, Jose M., Pfc, PH
Areano, Louis, S/Sgt, PH
Aronld, Royce, Pfc, PH
Arnold, Robert, Pfc, PH
Aragon, Mauricio M., 1st Lt, PH***, BSM
Arevaale, Luis S., S/Sgt, PH
Armstrong, Jimmie D., Pfc, PH*
Arrington, Earl W., Pvt, PH, BSM
Arnold, James W., Sgt, PH
Arechiga, Manuel, Pfc, PH
Argentati, Merico E., Pfc, PH
Arias, Afredo B., Pvt, PH
Armstrong, Rey G., Pvt, PH
Armato, Joseph P., Capt, BSM
Arndt, Robert E., Pfc, SM
Arnett, Cecil C., T/5, BSM
Ashcraft, Farrell F., Pfc, PH
Asselin, Albert L., Pfc, PH
Ashekian, Manick J., Pfc, BSM
Athey, Sherman H., Pvt, PH

Atherton, James L., Pvt, BSM
Auclair, Joseph J., Pfc, PH*
Austin, John D., 1st Lt, SS
Avril, Howard C., Pvt, PH
Ayala, Jose T., Cpl, PH

Baker, Douglas R., Pvt, PH
Barratt, Roy R., T/5, PH, BSM
Balentine, Carl E., Pvt, PH
Bates, Merril O., Sgt, PH
Bass, Claud E., Pfc, PH
Baak, Clifford N., Pvt, PH
Bancroft, Hollis A., Pfc, PH
Barnett, Don C., Pvt, PH
Baltazar, Ramirez P., T/Sgt, PH
Balyeat, Earl L., Pvt, PH
Bailey, Orville W., Pvt, PH
Ball, Homer, Pvt, PH
Bartenstein, Laverne F., Pfc, PH
Baluvelt, Robert H., Pvt, PH
Bartley, Frank P., S/Sgt, PH
Barns, Billie B., Pfc, PH
Baird, Joseph, Pvt, PH
Bartoshnik, Samuel B., Cpl, PH
Barber, Virgil H., Pvt, PH
Bagley, Charlie A., Sr., Pfc, PH
Barn, Edurn T., T/4, PH
Bashinski, Pete P., Pfc, PH
Bailey, Harvey, Pfc, PH
Bathory, Alex J., Pfc, PH, BSM
Back, Harvey J., Pvt, PH
Baker, Wayne C., Pvt, PH
Banke, John J., Pfc, PH
Barnard, Clarence R., Pfc, PH
Ball, Homer, Pvt, PH
Barnette, Carneth W., Pfc, PH
Bathke, Norbert H., Pvt, PH
Banch, Roy L., Pvt, PH
Barber, Noel M., Pvt, PH
Barak, Bernard, Pfc, PH
Bayne, Lee H., Pfc, PH*
Bahr, Herbert E., 1st Sgt, PH
Baggett, Judson E., Pvt, PH
Barry, Frederick J., Pfc, PH
Barthell, Milton A., Pvt, PH, BSM
Baskin, Alvin, Pfc, PH
Barnes, George R., Sgt, PH
Barnett, William, Pfc, PH
Baggett, James H., Pvt, PH
Bagley, Robert N., Pvt, PH
Bailley, Grady L., Pvt, PH
Baltrus, John, Pvt, PH
Baker, Ralph A., Pfc, PH
Baker, Francis L., Sgt, PH
Bargent, Walter E., Pfc, PH
Bailey, Oscar R., Pfc, PH
Baker, Joe F., T/5, PH
Ballin, William, S/Sgt, PH, BSM
Barson, Harry, S/Sgt, PH, BSM
Barth, Leonard, Pvt, PH, BSM
Bancroft, Hollis, Pvt, PH
Ballentine, R. E., Pvt, PH
Balcerzak, Clements, Sgt, PH
Baker, Robert A., Pfc, PH
Baltrusch, Carl R., Pvt, PH
Barsh, Bernard, Pvt, PH
Batson, Joe G., Pvt, PH, BSM
Bareitzman, Marion E., Pfc, PH
Ballard, Ira, Pvt, PH
Barron, John J., Pfc, PH*, SS
Bates, Merril O., Pfc, PH, BSM
Barbera, Michael, Pfc, PH
Bayde, William, Pfc, PH
Barnett, Warren A., Pfc, PH
Bartow, Albert, Pfc, PH
Bach, Herman L., Cpl, PH
Barrilleaux, Rolland J., Pvt, PH
Bass, Claude E., Pvt, PH
Baker, Irwin E., Sgt, PH, BSM, SS
Badman, Robert P., Pfc, BSM

Baehner, Charles H., 1st Lt, PH, SS
Bales, Emery J., T/4, BSM
Ballard, Roy V., T/5, PH, BSM
Banasz, Raymond C., T/5, BSM
Banasawiecz, Edward F., S/Sgt, BSM
Banko, John T., Pfc, SS
Banks, Joseph R., Pfc, BSM
Barker, John P., 2nd Lt, PH*, SS
Barnett, John R., Pfc, BSM
Batiste, George A., Pfc, SS
Battiston, Armand J., Sgt, PH
Bauder, Donald A., 1st Sgt, BSM
Beach, John S., Jr., Pvt, BSM
Bedell, Lester L., Pfc, PH
Berry, Francis I., Pfc, PH, BSM
Beasley, Trot E., Pfc, PH
Beasley, Robert W., S/Sgt, PH
Beidinger, Frank, Pfc, PH
Becker, Raymond, S/Sgt, PH
Berry, Joe L., Pvt, PH
Bettis, James H., Pfc, PH*
Belles, Selestinio, Pvt, PH
Belcher, James R., Pfc, PH, BSM
Benoit, Norman R., Pvt, PH
Bernard, James W., Pvt, PH
Bernardinelli, John, Pvt, PH, SS
Beck, Charles T., Sgt, PH
Belleie, Edmund D., Pvt, PH
Benak, Steve J., Pfc, PH
Bennett, Paul R., Pvt, PH, SS
Bergeron, Emile C., Jr., Pvt, PH
Berretta, Lawrence, Pvt, PH*
Belkin, Philip, Pvt, PH
Becker, Richard W., Pfc, PH
Bernard, William A., Pfc, PH*
Bennett, William A., Pfc, PH
Berndt, Louis L., Cpl, PH
Bench, Elvin C., Pfc, PH
Bowman, George W., Pfc, PH
Berbary, Joseph, Sgt, PH
Becker, Morris, Pvt, PH
Bellmont, Ted L., Capt, PH, BSM, SS
Bell, Cecil W., Pfc, PH
Benlehr, George A., Pvt, PH
Bell, Cornelius W., Pfc, PH
Berning, John H., Pvt, PH*, BSM
Benton, Evans J., Pvt, PH
Belsanti, Mario, Pfc, PH*
Benz, Carl, Capt, PH
Berg, Robert B., Pvt, PH
Bengel, Clifford A., T/4, PH
Bettencourt, Ralph L., Pfc, PH
Benoit, Forris P., S/Sgt, PH
Becker, Martin W., 2nd Lt, PH
Bedinsky, Albert J., Pvt, PH
Bergstrom, Albert S., Pvt, PH
Berías, Bernard B., Sgt, PH
Belcher, J. D., Pvt, PH, BSM
Beukema, Gerali, Pfc, PH
Bennett, Michael E., Sgt, PH
Besurck, Joseph N., S/Sgt, PH
Bergstrom, Robert W., Pvt, PH
Bergquist, Carl W., Pfc, PH
Bernett, Willie, Pvt, PH
Best, John J., Pvt, PH
Benincosa, Salvatore J., S/Sgt, PH
Bergeron, Raoul J., Pfc, PH, BSM
Beckham, Ralph, Pvt, PH
Behnke, Paul R., Capt, PH, SS
Beil, Thomas H., Pfc, BSM
Belson, Wallace C., Pfc, BSM
Bennett, Walter T., Pfc, BSM
Bergman, Hyman, Sgt, SS
Bernhardt, Irving F., S/Sgt, BSM
Best, Larry S., 1st Lt, BSM
Biancamano, Michael N., S/Sgt, PH
Bivins, Robert L., Pfc, PH
Bittner, James J., Pfc, PH
Bittman, Herbert W., T/4, PH, BSM
Biehl, Boyd C., Pvt, PH

Biesiadecki, Patrick W., Sgt, PH
Bialli, Anthony M., Pfc, PH
Billings, Gordon, Pvt, PH
Bittle, Jimmie W., Pfc, PH
Bird, Albert, Pvt, PH, BSM
Bielusiak, Joe J., Pfc, BSM
Biggins, Walter F., T/5, BSM
Bisciglia, Carl M., 1st Lt, BSM
Black, Kenneth C., Pfc, PH
Blair, Odell, Pvt, PH
Black, James O., Cpl, PH
Blankenship, Broxter A., Pfc, PH
Black, Emil O., Pvt, PH
Blanchette, Emile J., Pvt, PH
Bledsoe, Earl G., Pfc, PH
Blass, Joseph, Pfc, PH
Blue, William O., Pvt, PH, BSM
Blakeslee, Ronal D., T/5, PH
Blauser, Melvin H., Pfc, PH
Blackwood, Osso C., Pfc, PH
Blanton, Walter O., Pfc, PH
Black, John W., Pfc, BSM
Bluedorn, Samuel, Jr., Pfc, BSM
Blackwell, Olen, Pfc, BSM
Bowman, Odus A., Pfc, PH*
Bowden, Ralph L., Pvt, PH
Bowes, George P., Pvt, PH
Bowen, W. C., Pvt, PH
Boyd, Johnny C., Pfc, PH*
Bowan, Arlie W., S/Sgt, PH
Bowan, Harry R., Pfc, PH
Boisvert, Robert R., T/Sgt, PH
Boudreau, Joseph F., S/Sgt, PH
Boursaw, James M., Pvt, PH
Boisvert, George A., Jr., Pfc, PH
Boyd, Orris E., Pvt, PH
Boyd, Marvin E., S/Sgt, PH*, SS
Booker, Amos G., Pfc, PH
Bousman, Thomas I., Jr., Pvt, PH
Bosley, Chester R., Pfc, PH
Bonilla, Julio, Pvt, PH
Boicourt, Arvel, Pvt, PH
Borke, James A., S/Sgt, PH
Bogner, Virgil B., 2nd Lt, PH
Bosman, Myron J., Sgt, PH
Boulanger, Charles H., S/Sgt, PH, BSM
Bowman, Henry, Pfc, PH
Bomerno, Joe, Pfc, PH
Boyland, John I., S/Sgt, PH
Bonner, Neil R., S/Sgt, PH, BSM
Bowen, Harry, Pfc, PH
Bolks, Stanley, Pvt, PH
Bobo, Herman M., Pfc, PH
Borresen, Roy, Pvt, PH
Boyletn, Edward J., Pvt, PH
Bolden, Glen D., Pvt, PH
Bosch, Jay O., Pvt, PH
Boersen, Herman, Pfc, PH
Bodenbach, Raleigh J., Pfc, BSM
Bohn, Eugene E., Sgt, BSM
Borg, Charles J., Sgt., BSM*
Boyd, Donald J., Pfc, BSM
Boykin, Henry, S/Sgt, BSM
Brunner, Carl, Pfc, PH
Brown, Edward E., Pfc, PH, BSM
Braccia, Anthone E., S/Sgt, PH
Brewer, Hugh C., Pvt, PH
Brytherch, Benjamin, Pfc, PH
Breasheare, Luther, Pvt, PH
Broffman, Louis, Pfc, PH
Brown, Noel, Pfc, PH
Brown, Webster E., Pvt, PH
Brooks, Ezera, Pvt, PH
Brzizinski, Chester A., Pfc, PH
Brooks, Oscar B., Pvt, PH
Bruno, Dominic J., Pvt, PH
Bradley, Andrew F., Jr., Pvt, PH
Brown, Raymond L., 2nd Lt, PH, SS
Bray, Raymond A., Sr., Pvt, PH
Brandstatter, Frank R., Sgt, PH

Brewer, Paul U., Pvt, PH*
Brown, Robert L., 1st Lt, PH, BSM*
Brenner, Franz J., Pvt, PH
Bryson, Loren F., 1st Lt, PH, SS
Brandt, John H., Sgt, PH
Brand, William R., Pvt, PH*, BSM
Brown, George F., T/Sgt, PH, BSM
Bridges, Roy N., Pvt, PH
Bradsher, Flint N., Pvt, PH
Brazil, Louis S., Pvt, PH
Brooks, Francis A., Pvt, PH
Braswell, Dewey R., Pfc, PH
Brickel, Paula A., Pfc, PH
Breedon, Edward E., Pfc, PH**, BSM
Braglia, Geno E., Pfc, PH
Brown, Thurmon, Pvt, PH
Brooks, Agee, Cpl, PH
Brennan, George J., Sgt, PH
Brazowski, Willis, Pfc, PH
Brown, Kenneth D., Pfc, PH
Braccia, Anthony, Pfc, PH
Brinker, Burton L., Pfc, PH
Brittingham, Forest E., Pfc, PH
Broskie, Thomas G., 1st Lt, PH
Brown, Montsaul F., Pvt, PH, BSM
Brentlinger, Arthur L., Pfc, PH
Bright, Howard N., Sgt, PH, BSM
Brenum, Soliro E., Pvt, PH
Bringle, Riley S., Sgt, PH
Broz, Frank J., Pfc, PH
Brosig, Irwin, Pfc, PH
Brooks, Francis A., Pvt, PH
Branigan, Jean F., Pvt, PH
Brunkhorst, Harold W., Pvt, PH
Bradley, Gerald A., Pvt, PH
Brady, Francis J., Sgt, BSM
Brandli, Edwin E., S/Sgt, BSM
Bray, James H., Pvt, BSM*
Breheny, George R., WOJG, BSM
Brennan, William F., 1st Lt, PH, SS
Bristow, Robert L., Sgt, BSM
Broehert, Frank, Jr., Pfc, BSM
Brondyke, Harry J., Jr., Pfc, SS
Brooker, Walter E., Capt, PH, BSM
Brown, William E., Pfc, BSM
Browning, James A., Capt, BSM
Bruce, James D., 1st Lt, PH
Bryson, William F., 1st Sgt, BSM
Butkofski, Wilfred J., T/5, PH*, BSM
Burden, Charles, Pfc, PH
Buckner, William F., Pvt, PH
Buhl, Louis S., Pvt, PH
Burris, Edward W., Pfc, PH*
Bucholz, William, Pfc, PH*
Bukocsik, John S., Pvt, PH
Bustraam, Corun, Pvt, PH
Burby, Arthur L., S/Sgt, PH
Burg, Elmer J., 2nd Lt, PH
Buck, Neil, Pfc, PH
Burton, James B., Pfc, PH
Burgess, Frank E., Pfc, PH
Burrows, Edward L., S/Sgt, PH, BSM
Bunse, Marvin C., 1st Lt, PH*
Butfiloski, Frank, S/Sgt, PH*
Burgess, Clarence A., Pvt, PH
Burns, Edward J., 1st Lt, PH, BSM
Bultema, Howard, Pfc, PH
Buck, Theodore, Pfc, PH
Bullen, Otis O., Pvt, PH
Burnell, William, Pvt, PH*
Buis, George, Cpl, PH
Burkett, Ray W., Pfc, PH
Burbee, John, Pvt, PH
Bull, Jesse D., Pfc, PH
Buchanan, Arthur J., Pvt, PH
Busby, Herman D., Pfc, PH
Bush, Donald C., Pvt, PH
Bullock, Harold R., Pfc, PH
Burnett, Noel, Pfc, PH
Butler, William C., Pvt, PH

Burchfield, Paul L., Pvt, PH
Bubb, Harold J., Pfc, PH
Burford, Gerald J., Pvt, PH
Buchina, Michael, T/Sgt, PH
Buchanan, Harry E., Pfc, PH
Burby, Gordon F., Sgt, PH
Burke, Charles J., Pvt, PH
Bullock, Robert L., 1st Lt, PH, BSM*
Buono, Leo P., T/5, BSM
Burgan, Oscar D., S/Sgt, BSM
Byrne, Neil W., Pfc, PH
Byrgu, Elmar, Pvt, PH
Byrd, Charles D., Pfc, BSM

Canestrino, Arthur, Pfc, PH
Carrion, Edward, Pfc, PH
Caldwell, Franklin, S/Sgt, PH, BSM
Caine, Harold T., Pfc, PH
Capardino, William, Pvt, PH
Case, Ivan C., Jr., S/Sgt, PH, BSM
Castonguay, Paul R., Pfc, PH
Campazaro, Joseph L., Pfc, PH
Capranica, Vincent J., S/Sgt, PH
Caranci Pasco R., Pfc, PH
Carrell, Douglas S., T/Sgt, PH, BSM
Carrocceho, Charles S., Pvt, PH
Carter, John H., 1st Lt, PH**, SS
Cape, Richard R., Pfc, PH*
Carrion, Edward A., Pfc, PH
Campbell, Douglas S., Pfc, PH
Casaccia, Louis P., Pvt, PH
Carr, Francis J., Pvt, PH
Camp, William G., Pvt, PH**
Callaugher, William, Pvt, PH
Carver, Melvin, Pvt, PH*
Campbell, Aaron, Pvt, PH
Canady, Buster, Pvt, PH
Castonguay, Paul R., Pvt, PH
Canup, Elbert D. F., Pfc, PH
Calhoun, Thomas W., Pvt, PH
Campbell, Ernest E., Pvt, PH
Caulford, Robert, Pfc, PH, BSM
Candelaria, B. J., Pvt, PH
Cargill, Jesse L., S/Sgt, PH*, BSM
Caruso, Frank, Pfc, PH, BSM
Cander, Clarence E., Pfc, PH
Carpenter, Robert, Sgt, PH
Callahan, Edgar C., 2nd Lt, PH*
Carlich, Edward, Pvt, PH
Capuana, Ernest J., Pvt, PH
Culver, Edward, Pfc, PH
Cate, Oliver P., Pfc, PH
Castillo, Manuel T., Pvt, PH
Calabrese, Vincent, Cpl, PH
Cassidy, Henry O., Pvt, PH
Carpenter, Gordon W., Cpl, PH
Caldwell, Robert A., Sgt, PH
Campbell, Andrew M., 1st Lt, PH, SS
Casale, Ralph, S/Sgt, PH
Canfield, Arthur E., Pvt, PH
Cambron, Glenn R., Sgt, PH
Castro, Jesus R., Pfc, PH
Castle, Lafayette C., Pfc, PH
Camann, Herbert A., Pfc, PH
Capp, Heil S., 1st Lt, PH
Carnell, William L., T/Sgt, PH
Casby, Walter S., Pfc, PH
Calver, Cecil R., Pfc, PH
Carroll, John H., Pfc, PH
Cassidy, Daniel N., T/5, PH
Capps, Oden A., T/3, PH, BSM
Callison, Robert A., S/Sgt, PH, BSM*
Carr, George A., 1st Lt, PH
Calcaterra, Charlie J., Pfc, BSM
Cammarano, Dominick N., T/5, BSM
Campos, Joe M., Pfc, BSM
Cannillo, Dominic, Pfc, BSM
Carille, Anthony J., T/4, BSM
Carroll, Dexter, Pvt, PH
Carroll, Thomas E., T/3, BSM

Carruth, Claude W., Jr., S/Sgt, BSM
Castellano, Louis A., S/Sgt, BSM
Castillo, Quadalupe, Pvt, PH
Cedrone, Louis, Pfc, PH*, BSM
Cervi, Larry A., Pvt, PH, BSM
Ceverly, Alvin A., S/Sgt, PH
Cerini, Gregory A., Pfc, PH, BSM
Chrusciel, Walter J., Cpl, PH
Chimento, Joseph, Sgt, PH
Chilik, Nester N., Pvt, PH
Christie, Harold M., Pfc, PH
Christensen, Robert H., Pvt, PH
Checota, William E., Pvt, PH
Choate, Richard T., Pfc, PH*
Chickan, Peter, Pfc, PH
Chajkowski, Philip J., Pvt, PH
Chilik, Nestor M., Pvt, PH
Chu, Che Y, Pfc, PH
Champagne, Laurie N., Pvt, PH
Chernoff, Eugene V., Pvt, PH
Chess, Philip S., 1st Lt, PH
Chupak, Milton, S/Sgt, PH
Chanowich, Samuel, Jr., Pvt, PH
Chack, Andrew, Pvt, PH
Christaldi, Carmin C., Pvt, PH
Christie, Donald J., Pvt, PH
Chambers, Charles R., 1st Lt, PH
Champion, Henry T., Pvt, PH
Christ, Leo F., Pfc, PH
Chalakee, John, Jr., Pfc, BSM
Chmielinski, John S., Sgt, BSM
Chaphs, Glenn J., Pvt, PH
Chickan, Peter, Pfc, PH
Chalfin, Melvin H., Pvt, PH
Ciccioli, Louis, T/5, PH
Cimato, Ralph V., Pfc, PH
Cirri, Raphael, Pvt, PH
Ciplu, Nicholas L., S/Sgt, PH
Cippola, Frank J., Pvt, PH
Cirillo, Anthony P., Pfc, BSM
Clark, Robert L., Pfc, PH*
Cline, Charles O., Pfc, PH*
Clutters, William E., Pvt, PH
Clark, Oscar E., Pfc, PH
Clemente, Guido, T/5, PH, BSM
Clevenger, Merrela D., Pfc, PH
Cline, George E., S/Sgt, PH
Clarke, Francis J., Pfc, PH
Clements, Earl W., Pfc, PH
Claelin, Fred L., Pfc, PH
Clanton, Richard L., Sgt, BSM
Clark, Jefferson W., Sgt, BSM
Cleveland, Albert H., Sgt, BSM
Clough, James, T/Sgt, BSM
Collins, Phillip F., Pfc, PH
Coulston, Jose E., S/Sgt, PH
Collison, George L., Pfc, PH
Cochran, Robert D., Pfc, PH
Cohen, Philip, Pfc, PH
Cole, Ralph C., 1st Lt, PH
Cormier, Lewis A., Pfc, PH, BSM
Cook, James, Pvt, PH
Corcoran, Ruben E., Pfc, PH*
Colbert, Clarence F., Pfc, PH
Cole, Ted, Sgt, PH
Collins, Elick, Pfc, PH*
Cohter, Charles R., Pvt, PH
Colasanto, Arthur, Pfc, PH
Conyers, John R., Pvt, PH
Coppedge, Donald C., Pfc, PH
Coutu, Peter D., Pfc, PH
Cooper, John T., Pfc, PH
Cole, Lester A., Pfc, PH
Connelly, Michael F., Pvt, PH
Coomes, Joseph R., Sgt, PH
Corrigan, Eugene, Pfc, PH
Corle, Robert, Pvt, PH
Connell, John D., Pfc, PH*
Coles, Harold J., 1st Lt, PH
Coleman, James C., Pfc, PH
Corwin, Hamilton S., Sgt, PH

Cox, Earnest C., Pfc, PH
Coaker, John T., Jr., Pvt, PH
Contriras, Ralph J., Pvt, PH*
Conley, Ollie, Pvt, PH
Cohent, Philip, Pvt, PH
Connell, Roland L., Pvt, PH
Connors, Joseph, T/5, PH
Cornelson, Lester I., Pfc, PH
Cook, James C., Pvt, PH*
Conner, William H., Pvt, PH
Coleman, Leonard B., Pvt, PH
Corley, George L., Pvt, PH
Coleman, Richard I., Pvt, PH
Coppedge, Donald C., Pfc, PH
Cory, Lewis E., Sgt, PH
Costa, Virgil, T/5, PH
Consiglio, Guido, Pfc, PH
Courtemanche, Nelson A., Sgt, PH
Costello, Frank R., Pfc, PH
Coles, Ralph L., Pfc, PH
Coad, Walter W., Pfc, PH
Cordeau, Harold, Pfc, PH
Cornlson, Lester L., Pfc, PH
Corso, Leon A., Pvt, PH
Coleman, Andrew S., Pvt, PH
Coleman, Charles M., S/Sgt, PH
Cook, James F., Pfc, PH
Cotton, Joseph W., Pfc, PH
Coutts, Harold, Pfc, PH, BSM*
Coker, Martin A., Capt, PH, BSM
Corain, Hamilton S., S/Sgt, PH
Cooper, Francis J., Pfc, PH
Converse, Floyd E., 1st Lt, PH
Coulston, Joe R., S/Sgt, PH, BSM
Coffey, Charles H., S/Sgt, BSM
Coleman, MacDonald, Pvt, DSC
Congelio, Alphonse B., S/Sgt, BSM
Cook, Lawrence E., Sgt, BSM
Cooper, Donald G., Pvt, BSM
Coppola, Anthony M., Pfc, BSM
Cornelson, Lester L., Pfc, PH
Costa, Anthony, S/Sgt, SS
Cox, Johnnie H., Cpl, BSM
Cox, Thomas E., Pfc, BSM
Crisp, Eugene W., Pfc, PH, BSM
Crane, Donald N., Pvt, PH
Crabtree, Carl D., Pfc, PH
Crawford, Robert D., Sgt, PH
Cromen, Richard T., Pvt, PH
Crawford, John W., Pvt, PH
Crawford, Walter, Pfc, PH
Crawford, William H., Cpl, PH
Crosby, DeVon, Pvt, PH
Cross, Donald S., Pvt, PH
Cross, Stanley J., Pfc, PH
Cruz, Richard, Pfc, PH
Craft, Stanley L., Pfc, PH
Croft, John D., Pfc, PH
Crawford, Graham W., Pfc, PH
Crumpton, Elmer L., Pvt, PH
Crawford, Winfred C., Pfc, PH
Cruz, Thomas, Pvt, PH
Crawford, Edward E., Pfc, PH
Crater, William R., T/3, BSM
Crawford, Joseph B., Col, LM*
Croft, J. S., Pfc, BSM
Crowley, Leo J., Capt, PH, BSM
Cruz, Henry, Pfc, BSM
Cunady, Buster, Pfc, PH
Cutright, Ray H., 1st Lt, PH*, BSM
Curson, Clarence, Pfc, PH
Cunningham, Carl E., Pvt, PH
Cuda, Anthony, Pvt, PH
Curtis, Gerald N., Pvt, PH
Cutting, Percy, Pfc, PH
Curtis, Frank, Pfc, PH
Culler, Egbert H., Pfc, PH
Curran, Thomas G., Sgt, PH, BSM
Curtis, George, Pvt, PH
Cutillo, Louis J., Sgt, PH, BSM
Cure, Eugene L., Pfc, PH

Cundrle, George L., Pfc, PH
Cunningham, Daniel E., T/Sgt, PH, BSM
Cuddy, John E., Sgt, BSM
Cummings, Frederick E., 1st Lt, PH, SS
Curren, Ralph F., Pfc, BSM
Cusmano, Anthony, T/5, BSM
Cyech, Theodore, Pvt, PH
Czito, Charles, Sgt, BSM
Czaplicki, Andrew J., Pvt, PH
Celli, Vincent, Pvt, PH

Davis, Wendell W., Pfc, PH
Davey, Edward J., 2d Lt, PH*
Danish, John F., Pfc, PH
Davey, Robert C., T/Sgt, PH
Davis, Chester W., Sgt, PH
Davison, Arnold J., Pvt, PH
De Francesco, Michael J., Pvt, PH
Davidson, Harold F., Pfc, PH
Davis, Ozie W., Pfc, PH
Daster, Richard O., Pfc, PH
Dawson, Harold T., Pfc, PH
Davies, Vernon, Pfc, PH*
Darden, Frank C., Sgt, PH
Day, Willam M., Pvt, PH
Dampier, Dan B., Pfc, PH
Dalebouit, Martin J., Pfc, PH
Daly, Louis G., S/Sgt, PH
Davis, Elmer, Pfc, PH
Davis, Samuel G., 2d Lt, PH
Davis, Oliver M., Pfc, PH
Davies, Gilbert A., Pfc, PH
Danielson, Edward A., Pfc, PH
Davies, George W., Pfc, PH
Davila, Esidro V., Pfc, PH
Davis, Raymond F., Pvt, PH
Dasse, Edward R., Pvt, PH
D'Angelo, Peter, S/Sgt, PH, BSM
Daibon, William V., Pfc, BSM
Danzi, Kenneth J., T/Sgt, BSM
Davey, Edward J., T/Sgt, BSM
Davis, Bernard F., S/Sgt, BSM
Davis, Clyde M., Capt, BSM
Davis, Merle, Pvt, PH
Dayhoff, Marion B., Pvt, BSM
Demes, Garmine A., S/Sgt, PH
DeFazio, Anthony V., T/Sgt, PH, BSM
Desmaris, Maurice G., Pfc, PH
Deutman, George M., 1st Lt, PH, BSM*
Dallas, Jim, Pvt, PH
Dearing, Samuel J., Pvt, PH
Demann, Edwin K., Pfc, PH
Deleary, Fredrick, Pvt, PH, BSM
Delfaco, Carmon, Pfc, PH
Dehoff, Robert F., Pvt, PH
Decker, Roy J., Pvt, PH
Demono, Ralph, Pvt, PH
De Vito, Frank D., S/Sgt, PH, BSM
Devens, William J., Pfc, PH
Devrics, John J., Pvt, PH
Detamble, Howard M., 2d Lt, PH
Denham, Joe B., Pvt, PH
Desrosiers, Garman, Pvt, PH, BSM
Devall, Earl J., 1st Sgt, PH
Decker, Richard L., Pfc, PH
Dezelle, Carl F., Pfc, PH
Detz, Stanley, Pvt, PH
Dentman, George M., 2nd Lt, PH
Defen Baught, Elton G., Pvt, PH
Desbrow, William E., Pvt, PH
DeGrace, Lawrence J., Pvt, PH
Del'Ova, Joseph C., Pfc, PH*, BSM
DeWitt, Thomas, Pfc, PH
Demmers, Frank, Pvt, PH
Denny, William W., 1st Lt, PH, BSM
De Salvo, Charles, Sgt, PH
De Domenick, Frank J., Pvt, PH
De Lalla, Attillio J., Pvt, PH
De Mazzio, Steve, S/Sgt, PH, SS
Dean, Charles E., Pfc, PH
Despar, Jennings A., Pvt, PH
Detz, Stanley, Pvt, PH

Derrick, Charles R., Pfc, PH
De Angelis, Louis C., Pvt, PH
Decker, Herbert C., S/Sgt, PH, BSM
DeCost, Norman J., Jr., S/Sgt, BSM
DeCostraus, Thomas, Pfc, BSM
Deen, Samuel G., Pfc, BSM
Delay, Ercel C., Pvt, BSM
Denys, Alex W., 2d Lt, BSM*
Dest, William, 1st Lt, BSM
DeVoe, Albert H., Pfc, BSM
Dick, Gordon W., Pfc, PH*
Diamond, Benjamin W., Pfc, PH
Dickson, Denslow A., Sgt, PH*, SS
Ditta, Joseph J., Sgt, PH
Diepold, John H., Pvt, PH
Dickman, Herman B., Pvt, PH
Didie, Anthony, Pfc, PH
Diaz, Santos F., Pfc, PH
Dittmar, Francis, S/Sgt, PH, BSM
Dillard, Raymond L., Pfc, PH
Dillard, George W., Sgt, PH
Dimberil, Thomas, Sgt, PH
De La Rosa, Rogue, Sgt, PH
Diffley, Harry S., Pfc, PH
Dionne, Claud E., Pvt, PH
Diaz, Bernard, Pvt, BSM
Dillman, Morris W., Pvt, PH
Doan, Francis M., Pfc, BSM
Doud, Verdon J., T/5, PH, BSM
Dow, Seldon, Pfc, PH
Donner, Robert V., Pfc, PH
Dowdy, Glenn H., Sgt, PH
Dorson, Cecil O., Pvt, PH
Dokka, Arthur W., Sgt, PH, BSM
Dobbins, George J., Pvt, PH
Dodd, Loyd R., Pfc, PH
Downs, Wallace G., Pvt, PH
Donback, Howard M., Pvt, PH
Domiano, Felix, S/Sgt, PH
Doenah, Elvin H., Pvt, PH
Dodson, Raymond L., Pvt, PH
Duncan, Alfred, Pvt.
Dollar, B. F., Pvt, PH, BSM
Dornak, Alvin H, Pvt, PH
Downs, Kenneth R, Sgt, PH, BSM
Downing, Russell J, Pfc, PH
Dowell, Jesse L., Pfc, PH
Doyle, Richard F., Pfc, PH
Doss, Kenneth J., Pfc, PH
Dobbins, Daniel R., Pfc, PH
Donnelly, William J., Sgt, BSM
Doorbos, Louis, Pfc, BSM
Dorker, Bernard E., S/Sgt, SM, SS
Dorman, Thomas J., 2d Lt, BSM, SS
Dripps, Lloyd E., Pfc, PH
Drazdowski, Henry A., Pvt, PH
Drake, Donald H., Sgt, PH
Drapp, Andrew M., Pfc, PH
Drino, Nick A., S/Sgt, PH
Dunn, George A., Pfc, PH, BSM
Dupray, Clarence E., Pfc, PH, BSM
Dusky, Raymond A., Pfc, PH
Ducharme, Joseph A., Pvt, PH
Durfee, Owen, Pfc, PH
Dustman, Donald V., Pvt, PH
Durnerin, Robert L., Capt, PH
Dunn, D. E., Sgt, PH
Duffy, Robert R., 1st Lt, PH, BSM
Durance, Howard A., Pvt, PH
Duncan, Alfred, Pvt, PH
Duke, Thomas B., S/Sgt, PH
Dyer, Porter H., Pfc, PH
Durnick, Paul, Pvt, PH
Dudiak, Daniel, Sgt, LM
Duehing, Clarence A., Pvt, SS
Duncan, James T., Sgt, SS
Duryea, George F., Pfc, BSM
Dzeawgue, Benjamin J., Pvt
Dzewiecki, Raymond A., Pvt, PH

Earhardt, Arthur J., Sgt, PH
Earls, Leophas, Pvt, PH

Eastman, Raymond R., Pfc, PH
Easen, Kenelan H., 1st Lt, BSM, SS
Eberhart, Willard G., Pfc, PH
Ecklund, Loren F., Pvt, PH
Echman, Charles E., Pvt, PH
Ecay, Elmer S., Pvt, PH
Edmonds, Arvel, Pfc, PH
Edmundson, Billy, Sgt, PH, BSM, SS
Edwards, Lowell L., T/5, PH
Edwards, Charles W., Pvt, PH
Edwards, Grady B., Pvt, PH
Egreschitz, Joseph M., S/Sgt, PH, BSM
Eggleston, Thomas A., 2d Lt, PH
Eisenimmer, John, T/4, BSM
Eji, William K., Sgt, PH
Elkins, Kenneth E., Pvt, PH
Elis, Paul, Pfc, PH
Elliot. Colin C., Sgt, PH
Ellison, James L., Pfc, PH
Evenfejicht, George G., Sgt, PH
Ell, Alfred, Pfc, PH
Ellis, Harry F., Pvt, PH
Elms, William J., Jr., Sgt, PH, SS
Emond, Joseph T., T/Sgt, PH, SS
Emeraon, John E., 1st Lt, BSM
Enencker, Harold J., Pfc, PH
Engelan, Eugelan, Pfc, BSM
Erwin, Allen P., Pvt, PH
Ernser, John J., 2d Lt, BSM
Erskine, Robert H., Pvt, PH
Erford, Lawrence, Pvt, PH
Ervin, John W., Pfc, PH
Ernest, Jack R., Pvt, PH
Esquibel, Trinidad, Pvt, PH
Esty, Clayton N., S/Sgt, PH
Espinesa, Frank C., Sgt, PH
Espinola, Anthony F., Pvt, PH
Esty, Edward P., Pvt, PH
Espasito, Salvadore, Pvt, PH
Eter, Roy G., Pfc, PH, BSM
Evans, Ketrell, Pvt, PH
Evans, Parry B., Pvt, PH
Ewing, Walter A., Pfc, PH, BSM
Eyer, Leon S., Pfc, PH
Eygnor, Carl G., Pfc, BSM
Ezyk, Walter D., Pvt, PH
Ezersky, John E., Pvt, PH

Fairley, David, Pfc, PH*, BSM
Farrell, Thomas O., Pfc, PH
Favata, Louis A., Pfc, PH
Falk, Henry, Pvt, PH
Farber, Jack, Cpl, PH
Farline, Domenick, Pvt, PH
Faulkner, Cecil R., Pvt, PH
Fadden, Ernest, T/Sgt, PH
Fantasia, Eli O., Pvt, PH
Farrara, Nicholas A., Sgt, PH*
Farley, Joe H., Pfc, PH
Fadden, Ernest J., S/Sgt, PH
Fazzano, Anthony R., Pvt, PH
Fastuca, Joseph N., Pvt, PH
Farrington, Arthur W., T/4, PH
Felder, Harry, Pfc, PH
Ferraiuolo, Julius V., S/Sgt, PH
Ferguson, James, Pfc, PH
Fenimor, Daniel J., Sgt, PH
Feriola, Joseph S., Pfc, PH
Fellers, Earnest, Pfc, PH
Ferraro, Michael, Pfc, PH*
Fenske, Gerald P., Sgt, PH
Fejes, Paul G., Pfc, PH
Fedeury, Eldred K., T/Sgt, PH
Ferguson, Walter T., Cpl, PH
Ferland, Gerard, Sgt, PH, BSM
Fentheringill, Bert J., Pfc, PH
Fetterer, Ernest, Pfc, PH
Feldpausch, Lewis G., Pfc, PH
Feast, Edward G., Sgt, PH
Fellipelli, Fellipo L., Sgt, PH
Felice, Dominick A., Cpl, PH
Feldman, Sol, Pvt, PH

Felt, Clifton A., Pfc, PH
Ferrell, William T., Pfc, PH
Feeney, Luke J., Pvt, PH
Fetters, William E., Sgt, PH
Ferline, Domenick, Pvt, PH
Ferrera, Charles, T/5, BSM
Ferries, William R., Pfc, BSM
Fertig, Hyman, T/3, BSM
Fiechter, Charles D., S/Sgt, PH
Fifer, Russell P., Sgt, PH
Fitzmaurice, William J., Sgt, PH
Finn, Robert I., Pfc, PH
Fiorillo, Dominick A., Pvt, PH
Fisher, Marvin L., Pvt, PH
Fissel, Paul L., Pfc, PH
Fitzpatrick, John J., Pfc, PH
Fish, Roy J., Pvt, PH
Field, Harold S., Pvt, PH
Field, Cecil P., Pfc, PH
Filek, John A., Pvt, PH
Filipek, Walter, T/5, BSM
Fish, Leonard R., Pfc, BSM
Flores, John, Cpl, PH, BSM
Flores, Genaro A., Pvt, PH
Floyd, Olin, Pfc, PH
Flores, Gilbert, Pfc, PH
Fletcher, John T., Sgt, PH, BSM
Flood, Leo T., Pfc, PH, SS
Flores, Hector M., S/Sgt, PH*, SS
Fleischman, Daniel, Pvt, PH
Fleazer, Joseph T., Pfc, PH
Flores, Juan; Pfc, PH
Fleet, Clyde R., Pvt, PH
Flournoi, Charles A., Pvt, PH
Flavin, Stanley F., Sgt, PH
Fox, Elwood C., Pvt, PH*
Fox, Albert L., Pfc, PH
Forbes, Lee, Jr., 1st Lt, PH
Fowler, Albert D., Pfc, PH
Foss, Forrest T., 2d Lt, PH
Fournier, Robert J., Cpl, PH
Fontanez, Fernando, Pvt, PH*
Foos, Clarence W., S/Sgt, PH, BSM
Foreman, Ralph, Pfc, PH, SS
Foust, Homer L., Pvt, PH
Fowler, Norris R., Maj, PH, BSM
Foley, Cyril J., S/Sgt, PH
Fontaine, Roland A., S/Sgt, BSM
Foster, John F., Sgt, SS
Frohn, Jerry A., Pfc, PH
Friedgen, Frank R., Pfc, PH
Franklin, Philip W., S/Sgt, PH*
Fromuth, Wilfred D., S/Sgt, PH
Frew, George, Pvt, PH, BSM
Froehlich, William L, Pfc, PH
Fretag, Albert W., Pvt, PH
Fricks, Albert R., S/Sgt, PH
Francolino, Peter P., Pvt, PH
Frost, Lloyd A., Sgt, PH
Fruchtnicht, Paul, Pfc, PH
Fries, Paul J., S/Sgt, PH
Frischkorn, John E., Pfc, PH
Francisose, Dominick J., Pfc, PH
Fragale, Dominick, S/Sgt, PH
Franklin, Willard, Pvt, PH
France, Roby, Pfc, PH
Franklin, Howard M., 1st Lt, LM
Fray, Ralph L., T/5, BSM
Frazier, Ernest R., S/Sgt, SS
Frisillo, Albert L., Pvt, BSM
Frey, Clifford R., T/4, PH, BSM
Fries, Paul J., S/Sgt, BSM
Funehar, Edward H., Pfc, BSM
Fuson, Norman L., S/Sgt, BSM
Fuell, Walter E., Pvt, PH
Fullington, Fred S., Pfc, PH
Fuszver, Vernon J., Pfc, PH
Fulton, Cecil M., Pvt, PH
Fulton, Thomas, Pfc, PH
Furr, Ira C., S/Sgt, PH
Furrol, Chelsea J., Pfc, PH

Gaffke, Clarence W., Pfc, PH
Gashwyterva, Ivan, Pvt, PH
Gamboni, Emanuel, Sgt, PH, BSM
Gates, Willis W., S/Sgt, PH
Gardner, Buron W., Sgt, PH, BSM
Gay, Bud, Pfc, PH, BSM
Grahm, Edward W., Pvt, PH
Gardin, William K., Pvt, PH
Garcia, Gabriel, Pfc, PH
Gaffenn, Thomas T., Pvt, PH
Gale, Joseph D., Pfc, PH
Gabriel, Evan T., Pfc, PH
Galliart, Fred C., 1st Lt, PH, SS
Garbarine, Charles I., Pvt, PH
Garland, Lewis H., Pfc, PH
Garris, John J., Pvt, PH
Ganschow, Adolf H., Pvt, PH
Garcia, Manuel, T/4, PH
Garcia, Louis G., Pfc, PH
Gallado, Reuben G., Pfc, PH
Gassensmith, Paul W., Pfc, PH
Gaetano, Angelo M., Pvt, PH
Gardner, Harold L., Pvt, PH
Gayle, Joseph B., Pfc, PH
Gallagher, Russell, Pfc, PH
Garris. John I., Pvt, PH
Garcia, Luciano, Pfc, PH
Garbarino, Charles F., Pvt, PH
Gashwytema, Ivan S., Pvt, PH
Gallardo, Lazaro, Sgt, BSM
Gamelin, Albert L., Pfc, BSM
Garlick, Evans W., Pvt, BSM
Gardund, Victor, Cpl, BSM
Garner, Herbert L., Pfc, BSM
Gatey, George T., T/5, BSM
Gavin, John T., Sgt, BSM
Gennace, Emmanuel, Pfc, BSM
Goodman, Michael J., Pfc, PH
Gembrowski, Frank J., Pfc, PH
George, Henry, Cpl, PH
Genovese, Joseph, Pfc, PH
Gendron, Albert G., 1st Sgt, PH
George, Harold C., Pfc, PH, SS
Getsy, Albert C., Pvt, PH
Gestor, Charles T., Pvt, PH
Geis, Martin M., Pfc, BSM
Gellina, Alfred A., S/Sgt, PH
Garambia, Michael J., Cpl, BSM
Gerome, William P., Pfc, PH
Gillispie, John J., Sgt, PH
Giltner, Robert N., Cpl, PH
Gieia, James, Pvt, PH
Gilland, Charles W., Pvt, PH, SS
Gieter, Albert, T/5, PH
Gilliam, Bascon J., Jr., Pfc, PH
Girard, Paul H., Pfc, PH, BSM
Girard, Aldo G., Pfc, PH
Gillen, Oscar D., Pvt, PH
Gilkey, William T., Pfc, PH, BSM
Gillette, Perry, Pfc, PH
Gifford, Wayne E., Pfc, PH
Gildatrick, Frank W., T/5, BSM*
Ginter, John T., Pfc, BSM
Gipson, Eston, T/4, BSM
Gloyd, Clarence H., Pvt, PH
Glasscock, Robert J., Pvt, PH
Glynn, Emmet B., Pvt, PH
Glendenning, Warren A., Pfc, PH
Glynn, Richard J., Pvt, PH
Gleaton, Dorsey W., Sgt, PH
Goldtrap, William H., Pvt, PH
Goess, Clement G., Pfc, PH
Goodman, Bernard G., Pfc, PH, SS
Gonnalla, Thomas J., Pvt, PH
Gorman, Glen R., Pvt, PH
Goodwin, Travia M., Sgt, PH, BSM
Gordon, Albert, Cpl, PH
Gould, Earl A., Pfc, PH, BSM
Gomez, Thomas M., Pvt, PH
Gordon, Leo, Pfc, PH
Goldstein, Bernard H., 1st Lt, PH
Goldstein, Albert, Pvt, PH

Goodin, Florian A., S/Sgt, PH
Goolsby, John T., Pfc, PH
Gayatte, Alfred, Pvt, PH
Goch, Seymour C., T/Sgt, PH
Golder, Irance J., Sgt, PH
Gotowald, Stanley P., Pfc, PH
Goodwin, Irving, Pvt, PH
Gosselin, Lionel J., Pfc, PH
Goebel, Milton C., Pvt, PH
Gollaher, Oliver A., Pfc, PH
Gordon, William J., S/Sgt, PH
Gonsolaz, Ramon V., Sgt, PH
Goldfarb, Abe, Pvt, PH
Goggin, Hubert B., Pvt, PH
Golosborouch, Harold F., Pvt, SS
Gulembiewski, Henry F., Pfc, BSM
Gonnella, Thomas J., Pfc, BSM
Gonzales, Aletandro G., Pfc, BSM
Green, John R., S/Sgt, PH
Green, Leonard, Sgt, BSM
Gregory, Horace G., Pfc, PH
Gray, Woodrow W., Pfc, PH
Green, Harry A., Pfc, PH, BSM
Gronowski, Matthew J., Pfc, PH, BSM
Grounds, Wayman R., Pfc, PH
Grubstein, Canvil, Pvt, PH
Gray, Kenneth W., 1st Lt, PH*, BSM, SS, DSC
Gregg, Clyde, Pvt, PH
Grahm, James W., Pvt, PH
Grisson, Donald L., Pvt, PH
Groover, Robert L., Pfc, PH
Green, Harold L., Pvt, PH
Grabowski, Alexander, S/Sgt, PH
Grabrowski, Stephen P., Pvt, PH
Gronke, Charles P., Pfc, PH
Greenlaw, Burton L., Sgt, PH
Greembine, Charles W., Pfc, PH
Grant, Sigmond J., Pvt, PH
Gray, Ralph D., Pvt, PH
Gruckalak, Steve A., S/Sgt, PH
Gray, Robert L., Pfc, PH
Graves, James U., Pfc, PH
Greco, Joseph F., Pfc, PH
Gresco, Michael A., Pfc, PH
Greene, James P., Pfc, PH
Groen, Clement, Pvt, PH
Grady, Dennis A., Pfc, BSM
Grant, Norvol C., S/Sgt, BSM
Green. Foster, Pfc, BSM
Grennwalt, Frank E., Pfc, BSM*
Griffth, Sidney P., Pfc, BSM
Gromatski, Charles H., T/4, BSM
Groans, Bernard P., Pfc, BSM
Guillen, Francisco R., Pfc, PH
Guajardo, Pedro, Sgt, PH, SS
Guidarelli, Elio J., Pvt, PH
Gudger, James D., Pvt, PH
Guarisco, Charles L., Pvt, PH
Guillemette, Andre J., Pfc, PH
Guntharp, Walter A., Capt, PH, SS
Guzman, Jose E., Capt, PH
Gulley, Alvis, Pfc, PH, SS
Gurney, Joseph, Pvt, PH
Guariglia, Peter J., Pfc, SS
Guarino, Anthony C., T/Sgt, BSM
Guido, James A., Pvt, PH
Guyer, Francesco T., T/Sgt, BSM

Hannon, Francis W., Pvt, PH, BSM
Hanscom, George R., Pvt, PH
Haaven, Henry T., Pfc, PH, BSM
Hager, Edwin A., Pfc, PH*
Haaf, Fred W., Pvt, PH
Haselbauer, Edwin A., Sgt, PH
Hashkowitz, Benjamin L., Pfc, PH
Halliday, Charles P., Sgt, PH*
Hartman, Henry A., Pfc, PH*
Hart, Joseph J., Pfc, PH*, BSM
Hammontree, Earl J., Pvt, PH, BSM
Hart, George H., Pfc, PH
Havila, Esidio, Pfc, PH

Hagemann, Donald H., Pfc, PH
Hamrick, Wilmer R., Pfc, PH
Hagstrom, Paul J., Pvt, PH
Hartley, Ernest O., Pfc, PH
Harvey, William P., Sgt, PH*, BSM
Hall, James W., Pfc, PH, BSM
Hammel, Robert W., Pvt, PH
Harris, John E., Pvt, PH*
Hashkowitz, Benjamin W., Pfc, PH
Harris, Samuel R., T/4, PH
Hasse, Quinton B., Pvt, PH
Halprin, William F., 2d Lt, PH
Harris, William S., Pfc, PH
Hall, Jay, Sgt, PH
Hamrick, Travis, Cpl, PH
Harding, Harman L., Pvt, PH
Hardy, Raymond M., Pfc, PH
Hagenburg, Charles S., Pvt, PH
Hay, Walter M., Pvt, PH
Harriss, John, Pfc, PH
Hartley, Ernest, Pfc, PH
Hamrick, James H., Pvt, PH, BSM
Hall, Donald, Pfc, PH
Harvey, Roland H., Sgt, PH
Hayes, Lawrence T., Pfc, PH
Haber, Benjamin, Pvt, PH
Hahn, Herbert S., S/Sgt, PH
Harper, Kenneth R., Pvt, PH
Harrell, Calvin C., Pfc, PH
Harrington, Peter F., Pfc, PH
Harvey, John, Pvt, PH**
Hatridge, Lawrence E., Pfc, PH
Hapworth, Ivan, Pfc, PH
Hadley, Charles R., Pfc, PH
Hampton, William H., Pfc, PH
Hammond, George E., S/Sgt, PH, BSM
Hamilton, Richard O., 2d Lt, PH
Hatchell, Earl W., Pvt, PH
Hanson, Vernald R., Pvt, PH, BSM
Harrison, Harry S., Pfc, PH
Hazlett, John C., Cpl, PH
Hailes, Francis E., Pvt, PH
Hampltin, William N., Pvt, PH
Haddix, Harlan W., Pfc, PH
Hans, Philip, Cpl, PH
Hanzey, Harry H., Sgt, PH, SS
Harrison, Weslie W., Pvt, PH
Haerta, Pedro, Pvt, PH
Hain, Walter, Pvt, PH
Hamilton, Howard L., S/Sgt, PH, BSM
Hammontree, William A., S/Sgt, PH
Hauser, Albert A., Pfc, PH
Haynes, Charles C., Jr., 1st Lt, PH, SS
Hackworth, George R., Pvt, PH
Hand, Carlton H., T/Sgt, PH, SS
Haggland, Ray, Pvt, PH
Harvey, Nelson M., Pvt, PH
Hates, Carl E., Pvt, PH
Harrington, Peter E., Pfc, PH
Habas, Stanley A., Pvt, PH, BSM
Harris, Bruce M., T/Sgt, PH
Hankins, William T. L., Pvt, PH
Haas, Alphonse A., T/4, PH
Harris, Robert N., Pvt, PH
Haaron, William E., Pfc, PH
Hartman, Emil W., 1st Lt, PH, SS
Haynes, Leonard B., Pvt, PH
Haley, Floyd B., Cpl, PH
Haefner, Thomas R., Pfc, PH, BSM
Harris, Wilbur, Pvt, PH
Hansler, Edgar C., Pfc, PH
Hancock, Charles H., T/Sgt, PH, BSM, SS
Harknett, Richard F., Pvt, PH
Harms, Emil J., Pvt, PH, BSM
Hadley, Blaine E., Pfc, PH
Hammonds, Timothy W., Pfc, PH
Harsh, Earl E., Pvt, PH
Hackett, Francis J., 1st Sgt, PH, BSM
Haeser, Peter G., 1st Sgt, BSM
Hall, Edward L., Pfc, SS
Hall, Jack B., Cpl, BSM
Hamel, Willis W., M/Sgt, LM

Hanke, Harley E., S/Sgt, BSM
Hansen, Alvin A., 1st Lt, BSM
Hanson, Lloyd R., T/4, BSM
Harshbarger, Robert C., Pfc, BSM
Hauser, R. D., Pfc, PH
Hayes, Beverly B., 1st Lt, PH
Hays, Earl C., Jr., Capt, BSM
Hegg, Wayne E., T/Sgt, PH*
Heller, Hjalmer H., Pvt, PH
Heintz, Peter, Jr., Pvt, PH
Herrera, Relles, Pvt, PH
Hentsch, Charles P., Pvt, PH
Hert, James D., Pvt, PH
Healy, Charles F., Pfc, PH*, BSM
Hebert, Warren E., Pfc, PH
Henderson, James E., Lt Col, PH, BSM, LM
Henes, William J., Pvt, PH
Hendershott, George B., Pfc, PH
Heron, Thomas A., T/Sgt, PH
Hensley, Robert E., Pfc, PH
Hearon, William E., Pfc, PH
Hetrick, William A., Pfc, PH
Heaven, Henry A., Sgt, PH
Herston, Warren W., Pvt, PH
Hernanies, Visente, Sgt, PH
Heyes, Pedro, Pfc, PH
Henderson, Harold H., Pvt, PH
Hernandez, Pablo, Pvt, PH
Henry, Redman R., Pvt, PH
Hentges, Clifford D., Pvt, PH*, SS
Henne, Franklin, Pvt, PH
Hess, Alfred W., Lt Col, PH
Heberle, Thomas, Pfc, PH, BSM
Herman, Lawrence, Pvt, PH, BM
Hendricks, George B., Pvt, PH
Hester, Boyce, Pvt, PH
Henrichsen, Roy H., Pvt, PH, BSM
Hedgas, William L., Sgt, PH
Hefferman, Thomas P., S/Sgt, PH, BSM
Heis, Harold G., Pvt, PH
Henderson, Arthur P., Pvt, PH
Herdman, Dencil C., Pvt, PH, DSC
Herandez, Visente Y., S/Sgt, PH
Hecker, Kenneth R., Pfc,
Hefner, John B., Sgt, BSM
Helberg, Ruben, Cpl, BSM
Henes, Paul D., Pvt, SS
Hernandez, Ceaser T., Pvt, BSM
Herrera, Relles, Pfc, BSM
Hickman, Bain M., 1st Lt, PH*
Higgins, Frank P., S/Sgt, PH
Hinojos, Justino, Pvt, PH
Himis, Timothy L., Pfc, PH
Higgins, Frank, T/Sgt, PH
Hildum, Richard L., Pvt, PH
Hill, Raymond H., Pfc, PH
Higgins, Thomas E., Sgt, PH, BSM
Hilderbrand, Howard F., Pvt, PH
Hirsch, Robert B., Pvt, PH
Hinatek, Edward F., S/Sgt, PH
Hinton, Harry L., Pvt, PH
Higgins, William S., Sgt, PH
Hill, Boyd L., Pvt, PH
Hill, Irving H., Pfc, BSM
Hinkle, Earl A., Sgt, BSM
Hoff, William H., Cpl, PH
Hoffman, Edward H., Pvt, PH
Hoffer, Aaron S., Pvt, PH
Howard, Claude M., Lt Col, PH
Hoy, Leo J., Jr., T/Sgt, PH
Hollis, James R., 1st Lt, PH, SS
Hoover, Leroy E., Pvt, PH
Howison, Jack W., S/Sgt, PH
Howaniec, Chester B., Pfc, PH
Hoptman, Julian, Pvt, PH
Holt, Coolidge, Pfc, PH, BSM
Holtz, Grant, Pfc, PH
Howard, Robert S., Pfc, PH, BSM
Howarth, Harold, Pvt, PH
Honeycutt, Leftredge W., Capt, PH*, BSM*
Hoiges, Paschall L., Pvt, PH
Hoyt, Glenwood, Pvt, PH, BSM

Hohl, Joseph F., S/Sgt, PH, BSM
Holley, Mitchell C., Pfc, PH
Howard, Harvey, Pvt, PH
Hofer, Wesley D., Pfc, PH
Holtman, Carl C., Pfc, PH
Holsappe, Franklin E., Pfc, PH
Howells, Donald S., S/Sgt, PH
Hoose, Robert A., Pvt, PH
Houseman, Donald R., 2d Lt, PH
Holzworth, Reuben H., Pfc, PH
Holliday, Roy C., T/Sgt, PH
Howard, James E., Pvt, PH
Howarth, Harold, Pvt, PH
Howells, Don T., Cpl, PH
Hofman, Charles H., Pvt, PH, BSM
Holt, Victor R., 2d Lt, PH
Holt, James E., Sgt, PH
Horgan, James F., Sgt, PH
Holland, Alfred F., S/Sgt, PH, SS
Hood, Andrew J., Pvt, PH
Hodgetts, Ernest L., Pvt, PH
Houck, Marvin K., T/4, PH
Hood, Ralph R., Pfc, PH
Hoagland, Lewis H., Pvt, PH
Hodgson, Martin L., Pvt, PH
Hoskins, Raymond, Pvt, PH
Homa, Steve L., Pvt. PH
Holland, Ace W., Sgt, PH
Holbrook, Henry L., Pvt, PH, BSM
Holladay, Henry C., Pvt, PH
Howe, George L., Sgt, PH
Hobgood, Robert J., Pvt, PH
Hofer, Wesley D., Pvt, BSM*
Hofmann, George J., Pfc, BSM
Hoffner, Earl V., Pfc, BSM
Hohman, Elmer P., Major, BSM
Holman, William D., Pvt, PH
Homesley, Ralph, 1st Sgt, SS
Hoover, Herbert E., S/Sgt, PH
Hope, James L., S/Sgt, BSM
Housley, Otis T., 1st Lt, BSM, SS*
Howard, Henry L., Pfc, BSM
Howard, Richard, T/5, BSM
Howe, Robert C., Capt, PH
Hrobak, Valentine, Pfc, PH
Hrodsky, Louis, Sgt, PH
Hrabousky, Laddie J., Pfc, PH
Hughes, Bruce, Pvt, PH
Hughes, Jesse W., Pfc, PH, BSM
Hughson, Samuel J., Pfc, PH
Humphries, J. D., Jr., Pfc, PH
Huckaby, Meddian J., Pvt, PH
Huber, William, Pfc, PH
Hutchins, Charles E., Pvt, PH
Huerta, Vincente F., Pfc, PH
Hughes, Amel B., Pfc, PH
Hurst, Henry N., Pvt, PH
Hurley, William E., Pfc, PH
Hudon, Roger J., Pfc, PH
Hurchman, Robert, Pvt, PH
Hulitt, Charles, Pvt, PH
Huffnagle, Joseph D., S/Sgt, PH, BSM
Hunt, Otis L., Pfc, PH
Hunter, Raymond, Pfc, PH
Hughes, Edward R., Pvt, PH*
Hurchman, Robert, Pvt, PH
Huggins, William M., S/Sgt, PH, BSM
Hudon, Louis J., Pfc, PH
Hudgins, Glen H., Pfc, PH, SS
Hurley, Edward T., T/Sgt, PH, BSM
Hurzog, Virgil F., 1st Lt, PH
Huffman, Gerald M., Sgt, PH
Hymes, George S., Pfc, PH
Hubert, George H., Sgt, BSM
Huebner, Klaus H., Capt, BSM
Hughes, James J., Jr., Sgt, BSM
Hultz, Grant E., Pfc, PH
Hunt, Sidney C., WOJG, BSM
Hunter, Arthur T., Pfc, BSM

Ianndi, Chester A., Pvt, PH
Igniaro, Joseph, Pvt, PH

Ihnat, Michael, Pvt, PH
Irwin, George C., Pvt, PH, BSM
Irwing, John E., 1st Lt, PH*
Islowitz, lwring H., Pvt, PH
Ivers, Andrew C., Pvt, PH
Izydorczak, Edmund, S/Sgt, BSM

Jacobs, Stanley A., Pfc, PH
Jaiko, Eugene, Pfc, PH
Jaynes, Harold E., Sgt, PH
Jacobson, Roy, Pvt, PH
Jauger, Raymond B., Pvt, PH
Jackson, Henry J., 1st Lt, PH
Jatko, Stephen J., S/Sgt, PH
Jackson, Arvo, J., Pfc, PH
Jabonski, Paul I., Pfc, PH
Johnson, Claude W., Pvt, PH
Jarke, Robert, Pfc, PH
Jarvell, Rembert L., 1st Lt, PH
Jasiniski, Mitchell S., Sgt, PH
James, Whaley O., Pfc, PH
Jahn, Franklyn A., Pvt, PH
Jared, Edebert, Pfc, PH
James, Thomas H., Pfc, PH
Jaramillo, Secoro N., Pfc, PH
Jackson, Brance, T/Sgt, SS
Jagger, Howard M., S/Sgt, BSM
Jasinski, Mitchell S., S/Sgt, BSM
Javins, Rexford P., Capt, BSM
Jenkins, Reese E., Pfc, PH
Jensen, Robert G., Pfc, PH
Jensen, Henry W., T/5, PH
Jeresek, David R., Pfc, PH
Jedlicka, Lawrence L., T/4, PH
Jennings, Ralph N., Pvt, PH
Jervello, Anthony J., Pvt, PH
Jensen, Charles J., 1st Lt, PH
Jeannette, Louis, S/Sgt, PH*
Jenkins, Lonzo R., Pfc, PH
Jenkins, William E., 1st Lt, PH*, BSM
Jensen, James J., S/Sgt, PH
Jicie, David, Pfc, PH
Jimenez, Leo A., S/Sgt, PH
Johnson, Raymond M., Pfc, PH
Johnston, George, Pfc, PH
Jones, Wyley, Pfc, PH
Joyner, William W., Pfc, PH
Jones, James D., Sgt, PH
Jones, Norman P., Pvt, PH
Jones, Maurice T., Pfc, PH
Jonetski, Kenneth J., S/Sgt, PH
Jones, Russell, Pfc, PH
Johnson, William M., Pfc, PH
Johnson, James, Pvt, PH
Johnson, Charles A., T/5, PH
Johnson, Howard B., T/5, PH, SS
Jones, Wyman C., Pvt, PH
Jordan, Francis A., Pfc, PH
Johnson, Kenneth W., Pfc, PH
Joyce, William E., Jr., 1st Lt, PH, SS
Johnston, Joseph A., Pvt, PH
Jones, Herman H., Sgt, PH, BSM
Johnson, Ray, Pvt, PH
Johnston, Grover C., Pvt, PH
Johnson, Walter W., Pvt, PH
Johnson, Dorsey R., Pvt, PH, BSM
Johnson, Harry J., Pvt, PH
Johnson, Roy P., Sgt, PH
Jones, John E., Pfc, PH
Johnson, William O., Pfc, PH, BSM
Johnson, Kenneth M., Pvt, PH
Jones, Lawrence E., Pfc, BSM
Jones, Robert H., Sgt, BSM
Jones, Thomas K., Pfc, BSM
Jones, William H., Pfc, BSM
Jonkman, Norman, T/5, BSM
Jones, William M., Pfc, BSM
Johnson, Albert L., S/Sgt, BSM
Johnson, Clarence G., T/4, BSM
Johnson, Ralph W., T/5. BSM
Johnson, William T., Pfc, BSM
Johnson, Jewel J., Pfc, BSM

Johnston, Robert C., T/Sgt, BSM
Jorgenson, Raymond J., T/Sgt, BSM
Jovanovich, Martin, S/Sgt, BSM
Joyner, Dewey M., Pfc, BSM
Jubb, Robert W. A., 1st Lt, PH
Junkala, Carl J., Pvt, PH
Justice, Everett W., Pvt, PH
Juliano, Nick, Pfc, PH
Jumper, Lester, Pfc, PH
Julliard, Albert J., Pfc, PH
Jusxzynski, Joseph J., Pvt, PH
Jurkowski, John J., Sgt, PH, BSM

Kallerup, John U., Pfc, PH
Kaminski, Albert S., Pfc, PH
Kosqykowski, Alex, Pvt, PH
Kay, James, Jr., Pfc, PH
Kahl, James H., Pvt, PH
Kauffman, Howard P., Pvt, PH
Kasper, John F., Pfc, PH
Karijolic, Walter E., Pvt, PH
Kaplan, Martin, Pfc, PH
Kain, Vincent, Pvt, PH
Karibian, Norman, S/Sgt, PH
Karseras, Demetrias H., Pvt, PH
Karkanon, Leo A., Cpl, PH
Kadrovach, Peter, Pfc, PH
Kaczmarek, Peter, Pfc, PH
Kaull, Ralph W., Pfc, PH
Karbmam, William H., Pvt, PH
Kane, Vincent J., 2d Lt, PH, BSM*
Kable, Amos B., Pfc, BSM
Kalel, George F., 1st Sgt, BSM
Kalkstein, Elliot M., 1st Sgt, BSM
Kaltwasser, Richard F., Pfc, BSM
Kaplan, Arthur, T/Sgt, BSM
Kemmerlin, George A., Pfc, PH
Kelley, Fred J., Pfc, PH
Keilty, Joseph C., Pvt, PH
Kearney, Matthew W., 1st Lt, PH
Kearney, Robert K., Pvt, PH
Kelnhofer, Raymond J., Pvt, PH
Kelly, Robert C., Capt, PH*, BSM, SS, DSC
Kennedy, Ellesworth C., S/Sgt, PH, BSM
Kelly, Patrick C., Pfc, PH
Kelly, Leo M., T/5, PH*
Kelly, Keith M., Pvt, PH
Kelly, Earl J., Capt, PH
Kennedy, John F., Pfc, PH*
Kelly, Philip P., Pvt, PH
Kettke, Frederick, T/Sgt, PH
Kempesty, Joseph, Pvt, PH
Kelley, Wilbur, Pvt. PH
Kelley, Joseph S., Pfc, PH
Kelly. Jack S., Pfc, PH
Kenny, John W., Pvt, PH
Kerber, James L., Pvt, PH
Keen, Elvin L., S/Sgt, PH
Kemsey, Roy J., Pvt, PH
Kelly, Stephen F., Sgt, PH
Keslowitz, Joseph, Pfc, PH
Ketner, Robert V., Pvt, PH
Key, Herchell E., Pvt, PH
Keithly, Raymond N., Sgt, PH
Kellar, Anson, Pfc, PH
Kendall, George P., 1st Lt, PH
Kenniff, Joseph, Pfc, PH
Kettering, William T., 1st Lt, PH, SS
Kearney, John T., 2d Lt, PH
Keeler, Owen H., Pfc, BSM
Kehoe, Edward A., Pfc, BSM
Kelly, Henry A., Sgt, BSM
Kelley, Martin J., T/5, BSM
Kepchar, George F., Sgt, BSM
Kesterson, Millard M., Jr., Pvt, BSM
Kennard, Hubert B., Pvt, PH
Kidd, Melvin J., Pfc, PH, SS
Kirchgessner, Gerald J., S/Sgt, PH
King, Buster, Pfc, PH, SS
King, Theodore R., Pfc, PH*
Kindred, Harold C., 1st Sgt, PH
Kinzel, Thomas J., Pfc, PH

King, Olin L., Pfc, PH
King, Frank E., 1st Sgt, PH*, BSM
Kingston, Lincoln L., Pfc, PH
Kilmer, Kenneth L., 2d Lt, PH
King, Herman, Jr., Pfc, PH, BSM
King, Earl W., S/Sgt, PH, BSM
King, George E., Pfc, PH
King, John J., Capt, PH, SS, DSC
Kitchen, Oscar G., Pvt, PH
Kielty, Joseph A., Lt Col, SS
Kierman, Alfred, S/Sgt, BSM
Kijek, Edward R., Pfc, BSM
Kim, Frank, Cpl, BSM
Klusmeier, Victor H. E., S/Sgt, PH
Klaustermeyer, Ernest H. W., Pfc, PH
Klimek, Joseph, Jr., Pfc, PH
Kluntt, Elmer, Pfc, PH
Klein, Arthur, Pvt, PH
Klardie, George G., T/Sgt, PH, BSM
Klepp, Leonard H., Cpl, PH
Klaf, Herbert, Pvt, PH
Klein, Nicholas J., T/5, BSM
Knapp, Stewart D., Pvt, PH
Knox, John E., Pfc, PH
Knoch, Merle D., Pvt, PH
Kneupper, Leroy, Pfc, PH
Knowles, Charles C., Pfc, PH*
Knuska, Charles J., Pvt, PH
Knapp, Carl M., 2nd Lt, PH, BSM
Knox, Robert L., Major, BSM
Korzumi, Eltika, Pvt, PH
Kotzelnick, Robert F., Pvt, PH
Koerner, Harry, 2nd Lt, PH
Koshe, Anthony, Pfc, PH
Kosack, Stephen W., Sgt, PH
Korbelic, Frank M., Pvt, PH
Koine, Frank F., Pvt, PH
Koonce, Herbert R., Cpl, PH
Kopke, Thomas L., PH
Konczak, Paul P., Pvt, PH
Kolockovsky, John T., Pvt, PH
Koirona, Anthony, T/5, PH
Koumou, Chris T., S/Sgt, PH
Korzenowski, John V., Pvt, PH
Kofel, Michael, Jr., Pvt, PH
Kovatz, Andrew F., Sgt, PH
Konopke, Peter P., Pvt, PH*
Kohler, Vern, T/5, PH
Kochis, Henry A., S/Sgt, PH, SS
Konze, William K., 1st Lt, PH
Kozlowski, Walter A., Pfc, PH
Kohlenbeck, Roger B., Pfc, PH
Kopacz, Edward F., Pvt, PH
Korchach, Andrew, Pvt, PH
Koffroth, Raymond R., Pvt, PH, BSM
Koch, Stanley O., 1st Lt, PH
Koenig, Reinhold A., Pfc, BSM
Krider, Charley L., Pfc, PH
Kruks, Kenneth E., 1st Lt, PH
Kreisner, Robert F., Pvt, PH*
Kreklow, Walter W., 1st Lt, PH*
Krasnow, William, Pvt, PH
Krase, Fred C., Pfc, PH
Kraus, George, Pvt, PH
Kruciak, Jerome, Pfc, PH
Kruithof, Arthur D., S/Sgt, PH*
Kruszewski, Ray F., Pfc, PH
Krug, Matirice R., Pfc, PH
Kreisler, Elmer J., Pfc, PH
Kroska, Andrew F., Pfc, PH
Kraus, Arthur J., Pvt, PH
Kraus, Arthur, Pvt, PH
Kugelman, Daniel, Pvt, PH
Kuropatkin, Charles N., Pvt, PH
Kusey, Samuel F., Pfc, PH
Kurvanowicz, Frank, Pvt, PH
Kulik, Joseph S., Pfc, PH
Kuipstein, Willie L., Pvt, PH
Kubla, Anthony, Pfc, PH
Kussman, George W., T/Sgt, PH
Kuppersmith, Alex, Pfc, PH
Kunze, John H., 1st Lt, BSM

Kuhlenschmist, Wilbur E., T/5, BSM
Kuhlman, Arthur L., 2nd Lt, SS
Kulick, Henry L., Pvt, BSM
Kurzawski, Raymond J., T/Sgt, BSM
Kyle, Samuel J., Pfc, PH*
Kostecki, Edward J., S/Sgt, BSM
Kovacks, Philip A., 2nd Lt, BSM
Krasley, Paul A., Pfc, BSM

LaRocke, Clifton M., Pfc, PH
Layman, Alexander, S/Sgt, PH
Laguardia, Daniel, Pfc, PH
Larson, Edward D., Pfc, PH
Laskowski, Edward J., Pfc, PH
Lavallee, Walter, Sgt, PH
Lachen, Hubert J., Pvt, PH
Larsen, William H., Pfc, PH
Lazration, Russell, Pfc, PH
Lagesse, Joseph E., Sgt, PH, BSM
Laux, Richard, Pfc, PH, BSM
Lane, George J., Pvt, PH
Laurate, Salvatore, Sgt, PH
LaBozeta, William C., 2nd Lt, PH
Lawson, Joseph A., Pvt, PH
Lamanno, Vito J., Pvt, PH
Landau, Murray J., Pvt, PH
Lambert, Juriem F., Pvt, PH
Larkin, John F., Pfc, PH, BSM
Lackey, Ira, T/Sgt, PH, BSM
Lazaro, Nicholas J., Pvt, PH
Larkins, Wilfred L., S/Sgt, PH, SS
LaPorte, Laronee S., Pvt, PH
Lauson, Earl A., Cpl, PH
Lane, Carl T., Pfc, PH
Lawson, George M., Pvt, PH
Langley, Charles A., Pfc, PH
Law, Dewy W., Pfc, PH
Langenberger, Julius O., Pfc, PH
LaBlank, Albert J., Pfc, PH
Larson, Nils G., Pfc, PH, SS
Lavender, Fred W., Pvt, PH
Lane, Lawrence E., S/Sgt, PH
Lambersky, George W., Pfc, PH
Lawrence, Archie F., Pfc, PH
Layman, Alexander D., S/Sgt, PH
Lamb, Bruce E., Pfc, BSM
Lane, Charles, Pfc, BSM
Lane, George E., T/5, BSM
Lang, Melvin F., S/Sgt, PH, BSM
Lapham, Francis A., T/Sgt, BSM
Lapore, Kenneth F., Pfc, PH
Lara, Joe S., Pfc, SS
Larocke, Clifton M., Pfc, BSM
Levitt, Harold F., Pfc, PH
Leo, Frank J., Pfc, PH
Lewis, William A., Cpl, PH
Levesque, Charles W., S/Sgt, PH, BSM
Lessing, Donald, Pfc, PH
Lewis, William A., Cpl, PH
Leach, John W., Pfc, PH
Lee, Curtis R., 2nd Lt, PH
Lenzi, Victor, Pvt, PH
Lee, James W., Pvt, PH
LePage, Kenneth F., Pfc, PH, BSM
Lepsevich, John J., Pfc, PH
Levine, Jules, Pvt, PH*, SS
LePenna, Gerald T., Pfc, PH
Lee, John P., Sgt, PH, BSM
Lecaha, George, Pfc, PH
Lesage, Peter D., Pfc, PH
Leslie, Wayne D., Pfc, PH
Lecroy, Harold, Pvt, PH
Lesley, Billie, Pvt, PH
Leppirt, Lloyd H., Pvt, PH
Lester, Orland D., Pfc, PH
Leveille, Henry, S/Sgt, PH
LeBoy, Cecil, 2nd Lt, PH
Leinonen, Sulo M., Pfc, PH
Leonti, Joseph, Pfc, PH
LeBlanc, Albert J., Pfc, BSM
LeBlanc, Euclid T., Pfc, BSM
LeClaire, Fred J., S/Sgt, BSM

Leggio, Anthony J., T/Sgt, BSM
Leimback, Alvin L., Pfc, BSM
Leiski, Joseph M., Pfc, BSM
Lemaster, Elroy H., 1st Lt, SS
Lepisto, Carl W., Pvt, BSM
Lesher, Herman I., Sgt, BSM
LeStourgeon, Percy E., Colonel, LM
Levins, Arthur J., Pfc, PH
Levitsky, Michael, 1st Lt, PH, SS
L'Heureux, Walter L., Pfc, PH
Lindsey, Robert R., Pfc, PH·
Lister, Carl L., Pvt, PH
Lindsley, Robert J., Pfc, PH
Limon, Manuel V., S/Sgt, PH
Little, Jack C., Pvt, PH
Lindsley, Chester, Pfc, PH
Linkous, Arthur, Pvt, PH
Linjille, George D., Pvt, PH
Livermian, John K., Pfc, PH
Lignori, Thomas J., Pfc, PH
Lincks, Edward M., Pfc, PH
Linton, Thomas, Pfc, PH
Lindsay, Chester M., Sgt, PH
Litteral, Edward, Pfc, PH
Listak, Edward J., Pvt, PH
Lindahl, Anferd B., T/5, PH
Linton, Thomas, Pvt, PH
Licari, Joseph L., Pvt, PH
Liebenstein, John A., 2nd Lt, DSC
Lienhard, Paul E., S/Sgt, BSM
Lindahl, Sven C., Capt, BSM
Linville, George D., Pfc, BSM
Livingston, Frank, T/Sgt, BSM
Long, Marvin V., Pfc, PH
Loving, Benjamin N., Pfc, PH
Lorusso, Michael J., Pvt, PH
Locarriera, Luke J., Pfc, PH
Lopez, Edward L., Sgt, PH, BSM
Lowhorn, Cecil C., Pfc, PH
Lonergan, James C., Pfc, PH, SS
Loftes, Edward T., Pfc, PH
Lopez, Alfonso A., Pvt, PH
Lord, Roland E., Pvt
Lotterhos, William E., Major, PH, BSM, LM
Logan, Charles A., Pfc, PH
Lovell, Robert E., Pfc, PH
Loughridge, Glenn E., Pfc, PH*, BSM
Long, Irwin, Pfc, PH
Lowell, Frank J., 2nd Lt, PH
Loeffler, Elgin, Pfc, PH
Lopez, Andres, Pvt, PH
Lotti, Benedetto, Pfc, PH
Loud, Stuart L., Pfc, PH
Lozano, Fabian R., Pfc, PH
Lonozak, Edward A., Pvt, PH, BSM
Locke, Charles F., Pvt, BSM
Locke, Roy A., Jr., Pvt, BSM
Lockey, Ford L., Pvt, BSM
Lockhart, Samuel V., S/Sgt, PH
Lohmar, Frederick J., T/3, BSM*
Lombardi, Cesaro L., S/Sgt, BSM, SS
Lovell, Arthur A., S/Sgt, BSM
Lunn, Odber F., Pfc, PH
Lujan, Enrique, Pvt, PH
Lucci, Louis J., Pfc, PH
Lucas, William N., Pvt, PH
Luster, Clyde, Pvt, PH
Lute, Dalmar G., Pvt, PH
Lumbert, Harland R., Sgt, PH
Ludwig, Joseph W., Pfc, PH
Lucia, Frank J., Pfc, PH
Lund, Eugene L., Pvt, PH
Lucero, Antonio, Pfc, PH
Lujan, Jesus, Pfc, PH
Lukes, Richard M., Pvt, PH
Luckie, Niel F., Sgt, SS
Lyons, Harold E., Pfc, PH
Lynch, Donald E., Pfc, PH
Lyons, Robert I., 1st Lt, PH
Lynch, Frederick N., T/5, PH
Lyon, John W., Lt Col, PH, SS**, LM
Lyons, Heaton B., Pfc, PH, BSM

Lyon, Claire L., Pfc, PH, BSM
Lyon, Laurin A.. 1st Lt, PH
Lynch, Bernard F., 1st Lt, PH, BSM, SS*
Lynn, John, 1st Lt, BSM
Lyons, Charles J., Pfc, BSM
Lyons, James P., Major, BSM SS*

Manie, Mike, Pvt, PH
Manning, Lawrence L., Pfc, PH
Mabry, Clifford. Pfc, PH
Malkewski, Dan L., Pfc, PH
Martin, Gus H., Pvt, PH
Marchelewitz, Vincent, S/Sgt, PH
Maruszewski, George R., Pvt, PH
Mattson, Henry N., Pvt, PH
Marimacci, Joseph E., Pfc, PH
Marques, Francisco A., Sgt, PH
Mallette, Stanford R., Pvt, PH
Maclva, Smith L., Pvt, PH
Macklroy, John J., Pvt, PH
Magnani, Joseph E., Pvt, PH
Mahoney, Billie A., Pfc, PH
Martin, Thomas J., Pvt, PH
Malin, Howard. Pvt, PH
Matney, Cecil A., Capt, PH, SS
Maculey, Irving, 2nd Lt, PH
Mallar, Russel J., Pvt, PH
Marcsek, Alexander T., Cpl, PH
Marchinski, Joseph, Pfc, PH
Martinez, Louis S., Pfc, PH
Mactenosh, Benjamin, Sgt, PH
Mahan, John B., Pfc, PH
Matchett, Marion K., S/Sgt, PH
Maibli, Glen L.. Pfc, PH
Mayberry, Stuart A., Pvt, PH
MacSwain, Albert B., T/Sgt, PH, BSM
Machodo, Joe J., Pvt, PH
Maniscalio, Emanuel, Pvt, PH
Mathis, Otis C., Pfc, PH
Mayne, Woodrow, Pvt, PH
Maynard, Joseph R., Pfc, PH
Martin, John E., 2nd Lt, PH
Mathez, Mike J., Sgt, PH
Massey, Laverne C., Pvt, PH
Mathew, Marvin C., T/Sgt, PH
Manchine, Herbert J., Sgt, PH
Malmquist, Clarence O., T/4, PH
Matney, Marion. Pfc, PH
Marchand, John D., Pvt, PH
May, Eugene, Pvt, PH
Marschall, John L., Capt, PH, BSM
Madino, Margarito L., Sgt, PH
Magruier, Dersance L., Sgt, PH
Marino, Patsy, Sgt, PH
Martin, Vernon R. Pvt, PH, BSM
Manuel, Carajas. Pfc, PH
Martinez, Gonzalo E., Pfc, PH
Marek, Richard D., 1st Lt, PH
Manroel, Samuel, Pvt, PH
Marinez, Luis S., Pvt, PH
Maroney, Jack J., Pvt, PH
Mayhew, William C., Pvt, PH
Malynn, Anthony, Cpl, PH
Makiez, John J.. Pfc, PH
Mather, Alden R., S/Sgt, PH
Maxwell, Oliver M., Pfc, PH
Mahoney, Harry E., Pvt, PH
Makey, Patrick A., S/Sgt, PH
Mazza, Joseph L., Pvt, PH
Maddox, L. B., Pfc, PH
Mathis, Wendell A., Pfc, PH
Maniai, Sam, Pvt, PH
Maine, Everett C., Pvt, PH
Maxwell, Lloyd C., Pvt, PH, BSM
Mason, Earl W., Sgt, PH
Matke, Joseph, S/Sgt, PH
Manwarren, Joseph, Pfc, PH
Mason, Robert B.. Pfc, PH
Madritach, Herbert A., Pfc, PH
Mason, Robert E., Pvt, PH
Marsh, Harold L., Pvt, PH
Manchine, Herbert J., S/Sgt, PH, BSM

Madrid, Jose P., Pfc, PH
Marshall, Walter J., Pvt, PH
Machi, Mario L.. Pvt, PH
Masi, Frank V., Pvt, PH, BSM
Manning, John, Pfc, PH
Mamrot, Walter E., Pvt, PH
Mantia, Sam J., Pfc, PH
Martin, Carl W.. Pvt, PH
Madden, William F., Pvt, PH
Materek, Edward J., S/Sgt, PH
Martin, John J., Pfc, PH
MacDonald, Robert C., Pfc, PH
MacFarland, George S., Pvt, BSM
Madison, Eugene G., Pfc, BSM
Manney, Robert J., 1st Lt, BSM
Mahr, Harry E.. 2nd Lt, BSM
Mahlun, Oscar. Pfc, BSM
Mamon, John V.. 1st Sgt, BSM
Mangano, Ignatius T., Sgt, BSM
Maniscaleo, Emanuel A., Pvt, SS
Marcean, Roger R., T/3, BSM
Marek, Clement H., Pfc, BSM
Marquardt, Wallace H., T/5, BSM
Marshall, Ervin P.. T/Sgt, BSM
Marstra, Chester L., Pfc, PH, BSM*
Martin, Resbert R., 1st Lt, PH*, BSM
Martin Manuel, Pvt, PH
Martinez, Adolph P., T/5, BSM
Masi, Edward J., T/5, BSM
Mason, Concaro L., Pfc, BSM
Mast, John D., Sgt, BSM
Maxam, Douglas C., Cpl, BSM
May, Thomas J., Pfc, BSM
Mayor, Reginald D., 1st Lt, BSM
Mazur, Louis A.. S/Sgt, BSM
Mazur, Peter P., 1st Lt, SS
McCleod, Henry R., Pfc, PH
McClean, Eldon B., Pfc, PH
McCay, Elvin B., Pfc, PH
McAlary, Ralph, Pfc, PH
Mceowen, John W., Pfc, PH
McAda, Thomas A., Pvt, PH
McGarrity, Douglas H., Pvt, PH
McHale, James B., Pvt, PH
McCarthy, Hubert J., Pfc, PH
McCoy, Paul J., 2nd Lt, PH
McCain, Ralph, Pfc, PH
McCarthy, Leathel, Pfc, PH
McQue, Martin G., T/Sgt, PH
McGurick, Patrick W., Sgt, PH, SS
McCray, Howard, Pvt, PH
McDowell, Arnold, Pvt, PH
McCleod, Walter H., Pfc, PH
McLaughlin, Alvin S., Pfc, PH
McAbie, Joel J.. Pvt, PH
McKenna, Robert E., Pvt, PH
McCann, Joseph, Sgt, PH, BSM
McNamara, William, Pfc, PH
McWilliams, Robert B., Pfc, PH
McCauley, John T.. Pvt, PH
McNeil, Raymond E., Pfc, PH
McHugh, Stephen J., Pvt, PH
McFarland, Gerald S., Pvt, PH
McAbie, Filmore W., Capt, PH*, BSM
McIlwain, Harold J., Pvt, PH
McElhon, Joseph V., Pfc, PH
McCormick, Michael, Pfc, PH
McRhee, John H., Sgt, PH
McMahon, Jack J., Pvt, PH
McNutt, Opie L.. Pvt, PH
McIntosh, Benjamin F., Sgt, PH
McDonald, Willie C., Pfc, PH
McNeely, Lloyd O., Pfc, PH
McCollom, Oliver G., 2nd Lt, PH
McAlenter, Herman W., T/5, BSM
McAtamnry, James G., T/Sgt, SS
McBratney, John G., Pvt, BSM
McLovich, Andrew. 2nd Lt, PH
McFalrand, Richard D., 1st Lt, BSM
McGuire, Philip J., Pfc, BSM
McIlroy, John F.. Pfc, BSM
McKay, Walter J., Pvt, BSM

McLaron, Walter W., 1st Lt, BSM
McMahan, Charley C., S/Sgt, BSM
McManus, James E., S/Sgt, BSM
McGurdie, Dale M., S/Sgt, BSM
Meek, James P., Pfc, PH
Meirdirko, Robert F., 2nd Lt, PH
Menzemer, Cecil L., Pfc, PH
Meguiar, George J., Pvt, PH
Menton, Ernest, Pfc, PH
Mercer, Ernest, Pfc, PH
Mendez, Pablo, Sgt, PH
Merritt, Harold, Pfc, PH
Meyers, Edgar A., T/Sgt, PH
Merklein, Orville H., T/5, PH
Mester, Howard W., Pvt, PH
Meeks, Loyce C., Pvt, PH
Mestdagh, Joseph H., Pvt, PH
Meslaw, Harley O., Pfc, PH
Meyers, Lester J., Pfc, PH
Meyers, Ralph C., Pvt, PH
Meyers, Wallace H., 1st Lt, PH
Meenach, Clarence L., Pfc, PH
Means, Robert C., 1st Lt, PH
Mezera, Joseph L., Pvt, PH
Metcalf, Andrew B., S/Sgt, PH
Meir, Robert H., Cpl, PH
Melchan, Albert, 1st Lt, BSM
Mell, Elmer L., Cpl, BSM
Melisano, Joseph L., Pvt, BSM
Merrill, Buell, Pvt, PH
Meservier, Joffre, S/Sgt, BSM
Metcalf, Andrew N., S/Sgt, SS
Miller, Earl H., Pvt, PH
Mills, Gay, T/4, PH, BSM
Miller, Charles L., Sgt, PH
Milleron, Lloyd H., Pfc, PH
Mitrovic, Paul R., Pfc, PH
Miller, James H., Pvt, PH
Miller, Alvin H., Pfc, PH
Militell, Joseph J., Pvt, PH
Milshoe, Clifford D., Pvt, PH
Miller, Edward O., Pvt, PH
Miller, Edward P., Pvt, PH
Michael, Raymond N., Pfc, PH
Mielke, Wesley D., Pvt, PH
Mitchell, Maurice E., Pvt, PH
Miller, John H., Pfc, PH
Miller, Woodrow A., Pfc, PH
Miller, Harry M., Pvt, PH, BSM
Mirands, Nibbs S., Pvt, PH
Michel, Virgil L., Pfc, PH
Mitrovich, Sam K., S/Sgt, PH
Milligan, John R., Pvt, PH
Minelaio, Carmen L., S/Sgt, PH
Miller, Wallace C., Sgt, PH
Millbick, Richard L., Pfc, PH
Miller, Stanley J., Pvt, PH
Michailo, Edward, Pvt, PH
Miller, Carl H., Pvt, PH
Mikishas, George R., S/Sgt, PH, BSM
Miller, Doughlas W., Pvt, PH
Miller, George D., Pvt, PH
Micucci, Joseph A., Pfc, PH
Milano, Americo P., Pvt, PH
Mink, Arvle E., Pfc, PH
Mitchell, Albert L., Pfc, PH
Michalowski, Charles W., S/Sgt, BSM
Michalski, Ferdinand J., Pfc, BSM
Michaud, Albert A., Pfc, BSM
Michel, Raymond N., Pfc, BSM
Middleton, William A., Sgt, SS
Millane, William G., S/Sgt, BSM
Miller, Harry A., T/5, BSM
Miller, Joseph H., S/Sgt, BSM
Milligan, Everett, S/Sgt, PH
Minetti, Douglas, Pfc, BSM
Mirhanda, Elba S., Pfc, BSM
Mitchell, John L., Pvt, PH
Montes, Joaquin A., Jr., Pfc, PH
Mowery, Sherman M., Pfc, PH
Morgan, Frank D., Pvt, PH
Montalto, Leonard, Pfc, PH

Moore, Claude J., Sgt, PH
Moltalbono, Jasepe C., Pfc, PH
Mosay, Frank J., Cpl, PH
Mora, Marciano V., Pfc, PH
Morgan, Frank D., Pvt, PH
Moire, Granville M., Pvt, PH
Montgommery, Wescott, Pvt, PH
Mooney, Daniel, S/Sgt, PH, SS
Moriniti, Les A., Pfc, PH
Morgan, James M., Pvt, PH
Molner, Robert J., Pvt, PH
Morgan, Chester, Pvt, PH
Moreno, David, Pvt, PH
Morris, Robert L., Pfc, PH
Moran, John J., Pvt, PH
Mora, Morcianov, Pvt, PH
Morales, Samuel R., Pfc, PH, BSM
Motos, Kempton E., Pfc, PH, BSM*
Moriasett, Homer L., 1st Lt, PH, BSM
Molinoro, John V., S/Sgt, PH
Mondragon, Selso J., Pvt, PH
Moffith, Chester R., Pfc, PH
Molnar, Steve, Pvt, PH
Montagro, Alfred C., Pfc, PH
Morth, Chester J., Pvt, PH
Moore, Garen B., Sgt, PH
Morin, Lucien A., S/Sgt, PH
Moscato, Anthony, Pvt, PH
Morse, Edgar L., Pfc, PH
Moore, James J., S/Sgt, PH
Montes, Jose A., Pfc, PH
Morris, Clyde B., Sgt, PH
Montemayer, Manuel, Pfc, PH
Moore, Richard H., Pvt, PH
Moore, Vern C., Pfc, PH
Mol, Arthur W., S/Sgt, PH, BSM
Molinaro, Joan V., T/Sgt, PH, BSM, SS
Moore, Donald B., Pfc, BSM
Moreno, Adam N., Pfc, BSM
Morrow, Robert P., Major, LM
Morton, Lawrence J., Pfc, BSM
Munsey, Joel R., Pfc, PH
Musselman, Russell L., Pfc, PH
Mueller, Edgar A., Pvt, PH
Muicla, John K., Pvt, PH
Muldzianowski, Joseph, Pfc, PH
Murchie, John H., T/5, PH, BSM
Murray, Bernars A., Sgt, PH, BSM
Munser, Robert E., Pvt, PH
Murry, John C., Pvt, PH
Murphy, Frank J., Pfc, PH
Murphy, Walter E., Pfc, PH
Murray, Harry M., Pvt, PH
Mudge, Phillip G., S/Sgt, PH
Munch, Paul O., Jr., S/Sgt, PH
Murray, Evans M., Pfc, PH
Mulligan, Patrick J., S/Sgt, PH
Murphy, James, Pfc, PH
Muskus, Michael S., S/Sgt, PH
Munson, Martin B., Pfc, PH
Mullin, George L., Pfc, PH, BSM
Murphy, Charley J., S/Sgt, PH
Murphy, John J., Pvt, PH
Munsey, Joe R., Pfc, PH
Mullen, James P., 2nd Lt, PH
Murphy, Paul G., S/Sgt, PH
Mullen, George T., Pfc, BSM
Mullin, Richard T., T/5, BSM
Munn, Jerald H., Major, BSM*
Mungo, Joseph M., S/Sgt, BSM
Muntz, Neil M., Pfc, BSM
Murzittrogd, Arthur, S/Sgt, BSM
Murphy, Charles J., 1st Lt., BSM
Murphy, James W., Sgt, SS
Moskus, Michael S., S/Sgt, BSM
Murphy, William G., Pvt, BSM
Myers, Louis, S/Sgt, PH
Myers, Horace L., Pvt, PH
Mylott, Nil M., Sgt, BSM

Naylor, George M., S/Sgt, PH, BSM
Naigle, Eugene A., Pvt, PH

Nagy, Frank, Pfc, PH
Naranio, Fraylan, Pvt, PH
Nardona, Angelo, Pfc, PH
Nakashian, Arshag, Pvt, PH*
Norris, Kenneth L., Pfc, PH
Napolitano, Anthony, Pfc, PH
Nava, Joe V., Pfc, PH
Nash, George E., Pvt, PH
Nakola, Louis, Pfc, PH
Nadler, Harold, Pvt, PH
Namiak, Michael J., S/Sgt, PH
Nazarowitz, Eugene, Pfc, SS*
Nelson, Filmore, Pvt, PH
Neivelt, Sam, Pvt, PH
Neimi, Richard U., Pvt, PH
Neiman, John E., Pvt, PH
Needle, Norris, Pvt, PH
Nelson, Norman R., Sgt, PH, BSM
Neunert, Robert E., Pvt, PH
Needham, Frank J., 1st Sgt, PH
Ness, Julius B., Capt, PH
Nelson, Robert T., Cpl, PH
Nelson, Earl R., Pvt, PH
Nelson, Willard S., Pfc, PH
Nezza, John J., Pvt, PH
Neff, Clifford M., Pvt, PH
Neisen, Louis M., Pfc, PH
Newson, Matthew, Pvt, PH
Neill, Glenn O., T/4, BSM
Nelson, Clifford N., T/Sgt, BSM
Nelson, Raymond N., Jr., Capt, BSM
Newman, Daniel F., 1st Lt, BSM
Newnam, Alonzo R., 1st Lt, BSM, SS
Nichols, Norman A., Pfc, PH
Nicholson, Artie B., Jr., Pvt, PH
Nichols, Jesse N., Pfc, PH
Nierenz, Arvid E., Pfc, PH
Nichols, Harold A., Sgt, PH
Niver, Joseph, Pvt, PH
Nicolson, Merle A., Pvt, PH
Nishaus, William C., PH
Niedopytalski, Casimir J., S/Sgt, BSM
Niford, Chester R., 1st Lt, BSM
Noto, Carl J., Pfc, PH
Noll, Andrew C., Pvt, PH
Novak, Lawrence J., 2nd Lt, PH, BSM
Normand, Camille A., Sgt, BSM
Novak, John R., Pfc, PH
Noonan, Roger F., Pfc, PH
Norton, Edward T., Pvt, PH
Norris, Edward J., Pvt, PH
Nowiski, Ore A., Cpl, PH
Northrop, John I., Cpl, PH, BSM
Nobb, George W., Pvt, PH
Noble, James G. P., Pvt, PH
Novak, John A., Pvt, PH
Norton, Irving C., Pfc, PH
Nowaczeski, Stanley L., Pfc, PH
Nycz, Julius S., Pvt, PH
Nush, John, Pvt, PH
Newberry, Gerald B., Pvt, PH

Oamanski, Vincent, T/Sgt, PH
Oatsvall, Lester P., Pfc, PH
O'Brien, Thomas E., Pvt, PH
O'Connor, William J., Pfc, PH
O'Connor, John C., Pfc, PH
O'Connor, Daniel J., Pfc, PH
O'Connor, Charles H., Sgt, PH, BSM
O'Connell, Raymond A., Pfc, BSM
Odiorne, William L., Pfc, PH
O'Donnell, Edward F. Jr., Pvt, PH
Ochsanfeld, Joseph E., Pvt, PH
Olson, Lee C., T/5, PH
Olsen, Arthur W., Pvt, PH
Olivere, Anivo, Pvt, PH
Olsen, Harold H., Pfc, PH
Olshove, Tony, Pfc, PH
Olshakoski, Michael, Pfc, PH
Olivarez, Alferedo D., Cpl, PH
Olson, Burton L., Sgt, PH
Olguin, Louis M., Pfc, PH
Oldfield, John P., Pfc, PH

O'Neill, William H., Sgt, PH
O'Neill, Arthur S., Pfc, PH
Ondrey, Robert G., Pfc, PH
O'Neil, Gerald, Pfc, PH
O'Dohrty, Robert C., Pfc, PH
Orr, David, Pvt, PH, BSM
Orrick, Junior F., Pvt, BSM
Ortiz, Jose R., S/Sgt, BSM
Ortiz, Nicholas, S/Sgt, BSM
Ortig, Sam G., Sgt, PH
Orders, Eldin R., Pfc, PH
Orkowski, Ledwig, Sgt, PH
Ortega, Blas R., Pfc, PH
Orlando, Daniel J., Pfc, PH
Ortz, Sam G., Sgt, PH
Ositten, John W., Jr., Pvt, PH
Ott, Robert, J., Pfc, PH
Otramba, Stephen J., Sgt, PH
Otero, Ray J., Cpl, BSM
Ott, Aaron E., Pfc, PH
Ourada, Rudy P., Sgt, PH
Overstreet, Vigil D., Pfc, PH
Owen, Edward R., Pfc, PH, BSM
Owens, James J., Pfc, PH

Parent, Frank H., Pvt, PH*, BSM
Pallette, Sanford, Pfc, PH
Page, King, Pfc, PH
Paul, John, Pfc, PH*, BSM
Payer, Raymond H., Pfc, PH
Payne, Peter W., S/Sgt, PH
Parker, Frances N., Pvt, PH
Pacci, John G., Pvt, PH
Pann, Louis M., Pvt, PH
Parks, Martin E., Pfc, PH
Pahl, Kenneth M., Pvt, PH
Pagluiso, Dominic, Pfc, PH, BSM
Parkman, Lorence, Pvt, PH
Passiales, John J., Sgt, PH
Pace, Louis V., T/5, PH
Parker, Clinton E., T/Sgt, PH*
Patton, Commodore N., Pvt, PH
Parish, Roy F., Pvt, PH
Page, Orin L., Jr., Pfc, PH
Parker, Jack S., 2nd Lt, PH, SS
Panke, Gordon W., Pfc, PH
Patrick, Willis S., Pfc, PH
Parker, Judson S., S/Sgt, PH
Pare, Herve, Pvt, PH
Patton, Hearld, Pvt, PH
Panskey, Gordon W., Pfc, PH
Parkey, Donald K., Pvt, PH
Payne, Joseph W., Pfc, PH*
Pavia, Otto, S/Sgt, PH
Page, Lloyd, Pfc, PH
Palma, Frank, Pfc, PH
Padilla, Esquipula, Pvt, PH
Parras, Juan C., Pvt, PH*
Panone, Robert L., Pvt, PH
Patrick, Melvin, Pfc, PH
Paytherch, Benjamin, Pvt, PH
Panter, Leighton H., Pfc, PH
Pardi, Amdio E., Pfc, PH
Pace, Patrick J., T/3, BSM
Padilla, E. C., Pfc, PH
Petrouski, Edward, Pfc, PH
Pearce, Clarence O., S/Sgt, PH
Perry, Thomas J., Pfc, PH
Petroni, Alfred, Pvt, PH
Petry, Gerald J., Pfc, PH
Pedrotti, Wallace L., Pfc, PH
Peters, Frank E., Pvt, PH
Peters, Myron C., Pfc, PH
Pennington, William H., Pfc, PH, BSM
Perry, Harry, 2nd Lt., PH
Peuschel, Ernest H., Cpl, PH
Peninegar, James, Pvt, PH
Peterson, Marvin R., Pvt, PH
Petroni, Alfred, Pvt, PH
Pelletier, Leo R., Pfc, PH
Peterson, Thomas, Pvt, PH
Perich, Margan, Pvt, PH
Petrie, Willard F., Pvt, PH

Penny, John A., Pfc, PH
Petrucci, Pasquale A., Pvt, PH
Pereira, Louis, Pvt, PH
Pentz, Walker H., Cpl, PH
Peterson, Erwin E., Pvt, PH
Perez, Salvador C., Pfc, PH
Pellek, Isadore W., Pvt, PH
Pennington, Willy E., Pfc, PH
Peterson, John P., 2nd Lt, PH, BSM
Petrowski, Edward, Pvt, PH
Pellerin, Jerald, Pfc, PH
Perreault, Edward T., Pfc, PH
Perkins, Talmadge, Sgt, PH, BSM
Peterson, Earl, Pfc, PH
Peck, Wallace L., Sgt, PH, BSM
Pell, Russell, A., 1st Sgt, GSM
Pennington, Joseph T., Pvt, PH
Penttinen, Oliver J., Pfc, BSM
Perham, Stanton J., Sgt, BSM
Peterson, Dwight W., Capt, BSM
Petterson, Donald O., Capt, BSM
Phillips, Arthur K., S/Sgt, PH, SS
Pfalzer, George C., T/5, PH
Phillips, Avner, J., Pfc, PH*
Pheils, Floyd, Pvt, PH
Phaiah, Arthur J., T/5, BSM
Phillips, Louis, T/5, BSM
Phipps, Robert E., Pfc, BSM
Pickerell, Frank, S/Sgt, PH*, BSM
Piper, Henry G., Pfc, PH
Pickett, Donald, Sgt, PH
Pierog, Julius R., Cpl, PH
Pilipowics, Joseph F., Pvt, PH
Pine, Leroy N., Cpl, PH
Pirie, Frederick D., Sgt, PH
Pico, Joseph, Sgt, PH
Pintes, John, Pvt, PH
Pilichowski, Henry J., Pfc, PH
Pierce, William L., 2nd Lt, PH, SS
Piatek, Victor J., Cpl, PH
Pisano, Alfred, Pvt, PH
Pincus, Lawrence, Pvt, PH
Pilling, Glenn D., Pvt, PH
Piscatello, Frank J., Pfc, PH, BSM
Pierce, Wilfred F., Pfc, PH
Piper, William C., Jr., Pfc, SM
Platt, Leon, Sgt, PH
Plonko, Walter, Pfc, PH
Plagens, Raymond C., Pvt, PH
Plutt, Waran C., Pfc, PH
Plate, William C., Pvt, PH
Platt, George E., Pvt, PH
Platzer, Kenneth, Pfc, PH
Plant, Oliver L., Pvt, PH
Plath, Richard I., 2nd Lt, PH
Plagens, Raymond, Pvt, PH
Plante, Raymond L., 2nd Lt, BSM
Posner, Marvin D., T/4, PH
Poniatowski, John S., Pvt, PH
Posner, Martin, Pvt, PH
Pokorski, Harry S., Pfc, PH
Pohnert, Carl N., Pvt, PH
Poti, Russell R., Pfc, PH
Popkin, Jess W., Pvt, PH
Porter, William C., Pfc, PH
Pollack, Harry M., Sgt, PH
Poston, Willie E., Pfc, PH
Pollino, Vincent A., Pvt, PH
Powaser, Frank E., Pvt, PH
Pompeii, Louie P., Pvt, PH
Pope, Micheal F., Pfc, PH
Pool, John D., Pvt, PH
Post, Thomas B., Pfc, PH
Powell, James L., Pvt, PH
Poskey, Lee, Jr., Sgt, BSM
Potter, Beryl W., Capt, BSM
Povondra, Ray F., Pvt, PH
Prosser, James T., Pfc, PH
Proctor, Leon, Pfc, PH
Przonek, John S., Pfc, PH
Price, Bernard C., Pfc, PH
Pratt, Charles L., Pvt, PH

Price, Mercer B., Pvt, PH
Preciado, Luciano S., Pvt, PH
Pritts, Harold C., Pfc, PH
Prother, John H., Pfc, PH
Proctor, Donald V., T/3, PH, BSM
Pruett, Clay W., Pfc, PH
Price, LeVerne N., S/Sgt, PH, BSM
Price, Marar, Pvt, PH
Pridham, Sherman, S/Sgt, PH
Prunty, Olen, Pvt, PH
Prince, Golden C., Pfc, PH
Pritchett, Grover L., T/Sgt, PH, BSM
Provensano, Joseph, Sgt, BSM
Ptak, Joseph A., Pvt, PH
Pucci, Raymond, Pfc, PH
Purtill, William M., T/Sgt, PH, BSM
Puckett, Billy, Pvt, PH*
Pugh, James F., Pvt, PH
Purgason, Aubrey B., Pfc, PH
Pullin, Aubrey B., Pfc, PH

Quillin, Sydney L., Pfc, PH
Quintana, Frank E., T/4, PH
Quinn, Leo F., Pvt, PH
Quinlisk, William R., Pfc, PH, SS
Quinn, James P., Cpl, PH
Quendag, Verne, Pvt, PH
Quick, Milton E., T/5, PH
Quigley, Hugh E., Lt Col, BSM, SS, LM
Quiroz, David E., S/Sgt, PH, SS

Raymond, William F., Pvt, PH
Rawbottom, Walter G., Pfc, PH
Rasmussen, Curtiss A., Pvt, PH
Randolph, Oscar L., Pvt, PH
Ramonowski, Anthony F., T/Sgt, PH
Rancourt, Donald V., Pfc, PH
Rajecki, Alex A., Pvt, PH
Ravaijis, Bernard A., S/Sgt, PH
Randall, Glenn H., Sgt, PH
Ramirez, Rueben L., Pvt, PH
Rabinson, Ruben L., Pfc, PH
Rabless, Bernardo, Pfc, PH
Ramer, Otis, Pfc, PH
Rabe, Walter L., Sgt, PH
Ravitz, Abraham, Pvt, PH
Rawson, Howard W., Pvt, PH
Randall, Clinton F., Pvt, PH
Ramirez, David A., Pvt, PH
Ramirez, Romeo M., T/Sgt, PH, DSC
Radocy, Louis, S/Sgt, PH
Ransom, Leroy D., Pvt, PH
Rangal, Adolph H., Pvt, PH
Rathbum, Vearl R., Pvt, PH
Ramsey, Robert L., Pvt, PH
Ramsey, Roy L., Pfc, PH
Rapoza, John, Pfc, PH
Racioppi, Nicholas D., Sgt, PH
Radzanoski, Thaddeus, Pvt, PH
Ray, William L., Pvt, PH
Raichard, Elmer, Pfc, PH
Ral, Augustin, Pfc, SS
Ratt, Carl A., S/Sgt, BSM
Ramirez, Baltasar P., S/Sgt, PH, BSM
Rasbach, Harry C., Jr., T/4, BSM
Rayner, Louis, Pvt, PH
Reilly, Joseph E., Capt, PH, SS
Reyes, Jose P., Pfc, PH
Restivo, Angelo C., Pfc, PH
Reid, Thomas R., Pvt, PH
Renraud, Robert M., Pfc, PH
Rendez, Frank, Pfc, PH
Realry, John B., Sgt, PH
Renels, Thomas D., 2nd Lt, PH
Reyes, Pedro, Pfc, PH
Redfield, George W., Pfc, PH
Repke, Charles E., Pfc, PH
Reed, Dale R., Pvt, PH, BSM
Regleski, Albert F., Pvt, PH
Ressler, James D., Pfc, PH
Reef, Roy W., Pvt, PH
Reynolds, Everett, Pfc, PH, BSM

Rezendis, Alfred L., Pfc, PH
Reilly, Henry D., Pfc, PH
Rench, Walter, Pfc, PH
Reedy, Oscar R., S/Sgt, PH
Redfield, Lynn C., 1st Lt, BSM
Reece, William C., Pfc, BSM
Reintobn, Oscar H., Capt, BSM*
Rezendez, John A., Cpl, BSM
Rhoades, James E., T/Sgt, PH
Rheinschmidt, Walter E., Pfc, PH, BSM
Rhodes, James E.. T/Sgt, PH
Rhoades, Clarence A., Pfc, BSM
Rigley, Joseph W., Pfc, PH
Richetts, Kenneth W., Sgt, PH
Richards, Basil J., Jr., Pvt, PH, BSM
Riece, William C.. Pfc, PH
Riviar, Victor E., Sgt, PH
Ritter, Wallace M., Pvt, PH
Richardson, Marion E., Pfc, PH
Ringling, Harry A., Pfc, PH
Rider, Irving F., Pvt, PH
Rickay, George T., Pvt, PH
Ripley, Samuel E., T/Sgt, PH, BSM, SS
Ritter, Loyal G., Pfc, PH
Rickett, John F.. Pvt, PH
Richarson, Stanton, Pfc, PH
Rio, Mauel F., Sgt, PH
Rice, Harry L., Pfc, BSM
Rice, Joseph C., Capt, BSM
Richard, Robert E., Capt, PH*, BSM*, SS
Richardson, Omar D., T/Sgt, SS
Riddle, Charles, T/Sgt, BSM
Rinker, Albert E.. 1st Lt, BSM
Rogers, Lannon C., Pfc, PH
Robinson, Carl, Pvt, PH
Rondon, Frank I., Pfc, PH
Rodriguez, John P., Pfc, PH
Roberts, William E., Pvt, PH, BSM
Rosa, James D. Jr., Pvt, PH
Rocha, Harry M., Sgt, PH
Rode, Ralph R., Pfc, PH
Rogers, Raymond B., Pvt, PH, BSM
Rossi, Earnest C., Pvt, PH
Rosecrans, Elmer C., Cpl, PH, BSM
Romine, Ralph N., Sgt, PH
Rounier, Raymond J., S/Sgt, PH
Robless, Manuel, Pfc, PH
Rodriguez, Macario, Pfc, PH
Rowe, Robert W., S/Sgt, LM
Robertson, Homer J., Pvt, PH, BSM
Ropirham, Stanton F., Sgt, PH
Roberts, Marion, Pvt, PH
Rossi, William J., Pfc, PH
Rohrer, John A., Sgt, PH
Ridriguez, Diego, S/Sgt, PH
Rowen, Arlie W., S/Sgt, PH
Rohman, Bertram, Pvt, PH
Rosenberger, Harry C., Pvt, PH
Roberson, Horace, Pfc, PH
Rowe, Calvin D., Pfc, PH
Robertson, Warren L., Sgt, PH, BSM
Rotunda, Augustine, Pvt, PH
Robison, Amos, Pvt, PH
Romeo, Carmen N., Pfc, PH
Roberts, Fred E., Pvt, PH
Robbins, Nelson E., Pvt, PH
Robertson, Durman B., Pfc, SS
Rodgers, Edson R., Capt, BSM, SS
Rogers, Walter F., T/5, BSM
Ronaldo, Henry P., Cpl, BSM
Ronninges, John D., Capt, BSM
Rosall, Charles O., Pfc, PH
Rosa, Perry L., Pfc, BSM
Rose, Richard L., Sgt, BSM*
Rose, Murrell S.. CWO, PH
Rosner, Lewis, Pfc, PH
Rouler, Raymond L., S/Sgt, PH
Ruzich, George P.. Pvt, PH
Rusby, David R., Pfc, PH
Rudhoff, Frances L., 2nd Lt, PH
Ruttard, Archie N., Pvt, PH
Rudd, Louis L., Pfc, PH

Rude, Robert, Pfc, PH
Rueff, Alfred R., T/5, BSM
Rupp, Joseph J., Capt, PH, BSM, LM
Russo, Joseph D., Pfc, BSM
Rybak, William L., Pfc, PH
Ryan, Leonard R., Pvt, PH
Ryan, William C., Sgt, PH

Sally, Aubrey B., S/Sgt, PH*, DSC
Samuels, Sam, Pvt, PH*, BSM
Sarna, Frank A.. Pfc, PH
Sanchez, Albert. Pvt, PH
Sanders, Henry S., Cpl, PH*
Santos, Refugio G., Pfc, PH
Sasvedra, Ygnacio, Pfc, PH
Savich, William, 1st Lt, PH**, SS
Sabo, Carl E., 1st Sgt, PH, BSM
Sabo, Michael, Sgt, PH
Saldana, Faustino, Pfc, PH
Sarlls, Glenn B., T/5, PH
Saari, Fred A., Pfc, PH
Saxton, Warren J., Pvt, PH
Sayre, Evans R., Pvt, PH
Sampson, Everett G., Cpl, PH
Sapinski, Frank, T/5, PH
Salvador, Guilan, Pvt, PH
Saborwitz, Rubin I., Pvt, PH
Sabella, Joseph J., Pvt, PH*
Salpas, Komas J., S/Sgt, PH
Sabatini, Norman L., 1st Lt, PH
Sassi, Dante, S/Sgt, PH
Saporite, Thomas A., Pfc, PH
Sanchez, Joe P.. Pvt, PH
Sabo, Ernest G., S/Sgt, PH
Sampolska, Joseph J., S/Sgt, PH
Saborwitz, R. T., Pvt, PH
Samorajczyk, Zigmont, Pfc, PH
Sanchez, Benito, Pfc, PH
Sanders, Roy L., Sgt, BSM
Saylor, John D.. Pfc, PH
Schade, Joseph N., S/Sgt, PH
Schneider, Joseph W., S/Sgt, PH*
Schultz, Oscar, Pfc, PH*
Schwartz, Herbert, Pfc, PH
Schaefer, John F.. Cpl, PH
Schriever, Roy, Pfc, PH
Scalcione, Peter, S/Sgt, PH*
Schroeder, Raymond O., S/Sgt, PH
Scott, Vincent B., Pfc, PH
Schultz, Norman A., Pfc, PH
Scott, Theodore R.. Pfc, PH*
Schaffer, Raymond E., Pfc, PH
Schmidt, Bernard J., Pfc, PH
Schaeffer, Duwaya, Pfc, PH
Schweitzer, Charles, T/5, PH
Schmitt, Joseph P., Pvt, PH
Schockman, Luke O., 1st Lt, PH, BSM
Schultz, William B., Capt, PH, BSM
Schultz, Harla G., Pvt, PH
Scianna, Thomas M., Pfc, PH
Scott, Arthur J., Pvt, PH
Schilling, Edward, Pvt, PH
Schultz, Vainard O., Pfc, PH
Schimps, George A., Pfc, PH
Schill, Clifford D., T/5, BSM
Schmidt, Paul E., Pfc, BSM
Schrader, Frederick S., 1st Lt, BSM
Schuelke, Mitchell A., J., T/5, BSM
Schwartz, Morris. T/4, BSM
Seibeh, Henry, Pfc, PH
Seehye, Andrew F., Sgt, PH
Sewell, George S., 1st Lt, PH, BSM
Sears, Howard L.. Pfc, PH*
Seubert, Joseph L., Pfc, PH
Sexton, Patrick J., 2nd Lt, PH
Sesman, William H., T/Sgt, PH
Seitz, Clifford F., Pvt, PH
Sesso, Sam A., Pvt, PH
Seidenfeld, Jacob, S/Sgt, PH*, SS
Selig, Raymond N., Pfc, PH
Seymour, Clarence R., Pvt, PH
Sentz, John M., Pvt, PH

Sechan, Edward, Pfc, PH
Sears, Oscar, Pfc, PH
Seymour, Carroll, Pvt, PH
Sewell, Arnold B., Pvt, PH
Sedman, Leonard L., Pvt, PH
Serrata, Rudolfe, Pvt, PH
Seleway, John, Sgt, BSM
Short, Adron L., Pfc, PH
Shumansky, Leonard, Pvt, BSM
Shackleford, Leonard, Pvt, PH
Shaw, Thomas L., Pvt, PH
Shoulders, Thomas W., Pfc, PH
Short, Fred E., Pfc, PH
Shea, George W., Pfc, PH*
Shelton, Vaughn, Cpl, Ph
Sheppard, Donald E., T/5, PH
Shelly, Herbert W., Pfc, PH
Shea, Leo F., Pvt, PH*
Shissios, Constant, Pfc, PH
Shatto, James, Pfc, PH
Shrout, Ricardo C., Pvt, PH
Shaffer, Lyle G., Sgt, PH
Shipman, Paul K., Pvt, PH
Shepherd, Herbert, Pvt, PH
Shepherd, Charles H., 2nd Lt, PH**, SS
Shupinus, John R., Pvt, PH
Sherry, John W., S/Sgt, PH
Sheldon, Kenneth, S/Sgt, PH, BSM
Steinbeck, Percy A., Pfc, PH
Shipe, Clarence J., Pfc, PH
Shiffletti, Ralph, Pfc, PH
Shissias, Constant, Pfc, PH
Short, Adren L., Pfc, PH
Shawkett, Murray E., Pfc, PH
Shaffer, Raymond E., Pfc, PH
Schwanokasic, Raymond J., Pfc, PH, BSM
Shy, Burnell R., 1st Lt, PH
Shea, William N., Pvt, PH
Shuler, John E., S/Sgt, PH
Shabronsky, Edward, Pfc, BSM
Shaffer, Raymond D., Pvt, PH
Shaver, Bernell W., Pfc, BSM
Shepherd, Cecil E., T/5, BSM
Sheets, Richard B., Sgt, BSM
Sherman, Wayne E., T/5, BSM
Shuey, Harold E., Major, PH
Shuss, J. Logan, 1st Lt, PH
Sikich, Alexander A., Pfc, PH
Simkouski, Stanley J., S/Sgt, PH
Siwik, Stanley P., Pfc, PH
Siemsen, Duane, Pvt, PH
Simkowski, Stanley, S/Sgt, PH
Sims, Henry F. H., 1st Lt, PH*
Singer, Seymour, Pvt, PH
Silva, Andres, Pvt, PH
Sirois, Victor J., Cpl, PH
Silverstein, Jack, 1st Lt, PH* SS
Sharpe, Grant, Sgt, PH
Sievers, Fred U., 1st Lt, PH, BSM
Sims, Jack, Pfc, PH
Siira, Clarence W., S/Sgt, PH
Siemsen, Duane M., Pfc, PH
Siger, John F., Jr., Pvt, PH
Simoncek, Walter C., Sgt, LM
Simonsen, Carol E., Pfc, BSM
Singer, Seymour, Pvt, BSM
Sink, John E., T/4, BSM
Sirois, Victor, Cpl, PH
Siwek, Stanley P., Pfc, BSM
Simpson, Darryll L., Pvt, PH
Sears, Archie W., Pfc, BSM
Skeen, Rolin C., Pfc, PH
Skoglund, Richard E., Pvt, PH
Skrunds, Alfred V., Pfc, PH
Skelest, William, Pfc, PH
Slayton, Maynard L., Pfc, PH, BSM
Slezak, William E., Capt, LM
Smith, Charles R., T/Sgt, PH
Smith, Harry E., Pvt, PH
Smith, Horace, Pvt, PH
Smarsh, Micheal, Pfc, PH
Smith, Scott E., S/Sgt, PH*

Smalls, Edwin J., Pvt, PH
Smith, Kenneth J., Pvt, PH
Smith, Norman L., Pvt, PH
Smith, Charles C., Pfc, PH
Smith, Stanley, T/4, PH
Smith, Douglas, Pfc, PH
Smith, Arnold K., Pfc, PH
Smolenski, Frank, Pfc, PH*
Smith, R. V., Pvt, PH
Smith, Dessie, T/Sgt, PH*
Smith, Albert B., Pvt, PH
Smith, William N., Pfc, PH
Smith, Leland E., Pfc, PH
Smith, Robert C., Pvt, PH
Smitak, Stanford, Pfc, PH
Smull, Francis W., Cpl, PH
Smith, Randolph, Pvt, PH
Small, Claude W., S/Sgt, PH
Smith, Arden L., Pfc, PH
Smith, Winifred O., S/Sgt, PH
Smith, Clayton E., Pvt, BSM
Smith, Edward C., T/4, BSM
Smith, Eugene C., Pfc, BSM
Smith, Francis A., Jr., Cpl, BSM
Smith, Jesse J., 1st Lt, BSM
Smith, John R., Sgt, BSM
Smith, Preston L., 1st Sgt, BSM
Smith, Russell J., Pvt, PH
Snyder, Richard B., Pfc, PH
Snow, Jerrold D., Major, PH
Snead, Earnest D., Pfc, PH, BSM
Snider, Richard S., 1st Lt, PH*
Sniffin, Charles R., 1st Lt, PH, BSM
Sosa, Joseph B., Pfc, PH
Sosis, Leon, Pfc, PH, BSM
Soland, Martin C., Pfc, PH
Sobo, Micheal J., Pvt, PH
Souza, William T., Pvt, PH
Southard, Elmer, Pvt, PH
Skeen, Victor L., 2nd Lt, PH
Solon, Arnold, Sgt, BSM
Sonneschein, Marcus, T/4, BSM
Sortino, Joseph A., Sgt, BSM
Speck, William R., S/Sgt, PH
Sosinski, Anthony, Pvt, PH
Spilios, William, Sgt, PH
Spurlin, Roy F., Pvt, PH
Spero, Bernard M., Pvt, PH
Spears, Earl, Pvt, PH
Spence, Leslie L., Pfc, PH
Sprague, Earl W., Pfc, PH
Spencer, Calvin B., Pvt, PH
Spitz, Joseph, Pvt, PH
Spencer, Chubby L., T/5, PH*, BSM*
Spangler, Phelix, Pvt, PH
Speck, William R., T/Sgt, PH, BSM
Spires, Jack, Pvt, PH
Spies, Stanley H., Pfc, PH
Spano, Carlo J., Pfc, BSM
Sparks, Gorman N., S/Sgt, BSM
Spicer, William E., Pfc, BSM*
Squier, Ralph J., Pfc, PH
Stone, Hugh M., Pfc, PH
Stoyanoff, John, Pfc, PH
Strickland, Harley E., S/Sgt, PH
Sternaman, Donald E., T/Sgt, PH
Stephenson, Harry J., Pfc, PH, BSM
Stephens, Walter E., Pfc, PH
Strouse, William, Pfc, PH
Statler, F., Pfc, PH
Street, Albert E., Pfc, PH*
Storck, Norman H., Pfc, PH
Strzmieczny, Walter S., Pfc, PH
Strathmann, Carl B. W., Pfc, PH, SS
Storer, Lendell P., S/Sgt, PH
Steadman, Paul F., Pfc, PH
Studer, Eugene K., Pvt, PH
Stitt, George R., Sgt, PH
Stahl, Harold B., Pvt, PH
Stout, Lyle L., Pfc, PH
Stone, Robert K., S/Sgt, PH
Steiner, Emile A., S/Sgt, PH

Stedingh, Kurt W., 2d Lt, PH*
Stinson, James I., Pvt, PH
Steen, Samuel, Pvt, PH
Stevens, James T., Pvt, PH
Steenlage, John C.,, PH
Stevenson, Dennis, Pfc, PH
Steed,, Robert T., Pvt, PH
Stevens, Francis W., 1st/Sgt, PH
Streigl, Francis A., 1st/Sgt, PH, BSM*
Steelnack, William E., S/Sgt, PH, BSM
Straus, Louis H., Sgt, PH
Stover, Charles R., Pfc, PH
Stewart, George, Pfc, PH
Strecher, Peter A., Pvt, PH
Stong, Albert, Pvt, PH
Stachurski, Ray F., T/Sgt, PH
Stone, Hugh M., Sgt, PH
Storey, Fred C., Pfc, PH
Stallings, Shelly M., Pfc, PH
Stephens, C. L., Pfc, PH
Stair, Russell G., Pfc, PH
Staggs, Floyd F., Pvt, PH
Stanford, Allen G., Pfc, PH
Steffa, Ronalo, Pfc, PH
Stanton, Paul A., Pvt, PH
Staggs, Ben H., Pfc, PH
Stewart, Glenn, Pfc, PH
Strukel, Frank, Pvt, PH
Steinback, LeRoy A., Pfc, PH
Still, Albert C., Pvt, PH
Stiles, Eugene, Pvt, PH
Strong, Albert, Pvt, PH
Stuck, Benjamin F., Pvt, PH
Strand, Helmar C., Pvt, PH
Steward, Vernon A., Pfc, PH
Stroop, Sidney R., Pvt, PH
Stine, Floyd M., Pvt, PH
Stewart, John L., Pvt, PH
Strzverke, Rastoro, Pvt, PH
Sullivan, John T., Pvt, PH, BSM*
Stajek, Joseph P., Pfc, PH
Stromberg, William H., Pfc, PH
Stryznski, Henry B., Pvt, PH
Swisher, Calvin C., Pfc, PH
Steineck, Wayne C., Capt, PH
Stewart, George R., Jr., Pfc, BSM
Stirzaker, James F., Sgt, BSM
Storck, Norman H., Pfc, BSM
Stiefel, Alfred, Sgt, BSM
Subanski, Walter, Pvt, PH
Sulger, Victor B., Pfc, PH
Sunday, Albert F., Pfc, PH
Sullivan, Jeremiah P., T/Sgt, PH, BSM
Supak, Emil, Pvt, PH
Sullo, John J., Pfc, PH
Succa, Rengo, Pvt, PH
Sulak, Abdon A., Pfc, BSM
Suss, Alexander M., Pfc, BSM
Swegles, James, Pvt, PH
Swanson, Alfred J., Pvt, PH
Swackhammer, Floyd G., S/Sgt, PH
Sweet, Richard K., Pvt, PH
Swires, James H., Pfc, PH
Swanson, Arthur C., Sgt, PH
Swart, Theodore N., Pvt, PH
Sweetin, Jerry C., Pvt, PH
Swart, John N., Pvt, PH
Swarm, Marion W., Pfc, PH
Swan, Philip L., Pfc, PH, BSM
Swanson, Irving R., Pvt, PH
Symonds, Donald E., Pvt, PH
Sylvester, Clifford A., Pvt, PH
Syth, Arthur A., Pvt, PH
Szramczewski, Chester F., Pvt, PH
Szurpicki, John J., S/Sgt, PH*
Szafranski, Chester E., Pvt, PH*
Szczepaniak, Leo W., Pvt, PH
Szortek, Jerome, Pfc, PH

Taylor, Robert J., Pvt, PH
Tankeraly, Allen W., Pfc, PH
Tackett, Orville, Pvt, PH

Tavaralo, Carmine, 2nd Lt, PH, SS
Taylor, John W., Pvt, PH
Taub, Phillip, Pvt, PH
Taggette, Norman, Pfc, PH*
Talaski, Victor J., Sgt, PH*
Tarrant, Marvin K., Pfc, PH*
Talley, John D., Pvt, PH
Taylor, Arthur, Pfc, PH
Taylor, Arthur J., Pfc, PH
Taylor, Ernest D., Pfc, PH
Taylor, John L., Sgt, PH, BSM
Taylor, Earl E., Pfc, PH
Tally, Blair A., S/Sgt, PH
Tapia, Ambrosio V., Pfc, BSM
Teague, William R., Pvt, PH
Tertrault, Ernest A., Pvt, PH
Tedford, Theodore, Pvt, PH
Templeman, Carmin, Pvt, PH
Tezzi, Harry, Pvt, PH
Teska, James, S/Sgt, PH
Tetter, Max I., Pfc, PH*, SS
Tester, Willie, Pvt, PH
Tessier, Joseph J., T/Sgt, PH, BSM
Teuber, Frank H., Pfc, PH
Tennyson, Howard W., Pfc, PH
Terrell, Richard M., T/5, PH
Thompson, Thomas J., Pfc, PH
Thiele, Henry, S/Sgt, PH
Theobald, Charles R., Sgt, PH
Therialt, Alphonse J., Pfc, PH
Therkildsen, Oliver J., Pvt, PH
Thornbrough, Robert A., Sgt, PH
Thomas, Fred A., Pfc, PH
Thornbill, Milton C., Pvt, PH
Thaxton, Howard D., Pfc, PH, SS
Thorton, Charles T., Capt, PH
Thiebud, Charles P., Pvt, PH
Thomas, Andrew J., Pvt, PH
Thompson, Edgar, Pvt, PH
Thomas, Isle, Pvt, PH
Thompson, Cody E., Pfc, PH, BSM
Thompson, Walter J., Pvt, PH
Thorsen, Raymond K., Pfc, PH, SS
Thermos, Hick, Pvt, PH
Thompson, James H., Pvt, PH
Thorne, Robert C., Pvt, PH
Thompson, Charles, 2nd Lt, PH
Thomas, Willard J., 1st Lt, PH
Thillet, Veriglio, Pvt, PH
Thomson, Gerald W., Pfc, PH
Thompson, Wilburn R., Pvt, PH
Thomson, George A., Jr., Pvt, PH
Thorne, Norman B., Pfc, PH
Thomas, Albert I., 1st Lt, BSM, SS
Thomas, Lawrence, Pfc, BSM
Thompson, Allen E., Pvt, BSM
Thompson, Robert W., Pfc, BSM
Tigirena, Pedro B., Pfc, PH
Tiel, Francis L., Pfc, BSM
Tine, John D., Pfc, PH
Tibrio, James, Pvt, PH
Timony, James F., Pfc, PH
Tino, Frank J., Pfc, PH
Tittle, Chester, Pvt, PH
Timmerman, Lucas, Pvt, PH
Tiseo, Victor, Pvt, PH
Tinelli, Micheal, Pvt, PH
Tomlin, Julius R., Pvt, PH
Tolan, Fred G., T/5, PH
Tonkin, Donald S., Sgt, PH
Tofanelli, Joseph C., Pvt, PH
Toole, John D., Pfc, PH, BSM
Townsend, Benjamin R., 1st Lt, PH
Toner, Thomas J., Pfc, PH
Toconita, John, Pvt, PH
Townsend, Herbert L., Pvt, PH
Tolley, Marvin J., Pvt, PH
Tondera, Frank W., Pfc, PH
Tolbert, Ralph D., Pfc, PH, BSM
Torok, Louis G., Pfc, PH, SS
Tome, Walter L., Pvt, PH
Tomacchio, Rosario A., Pvt, PH

Tobin, Harold F., S/Sgt, BSM
Tomes, Earl L., Pfc, BSM
Torres, Daniel, Cpl, BSM
Torres, Frank, S/Sgt, BSM*
Torres, Sam F., Pvt, BSM
Toy, Alfred R., S/Sgt, BSM
Trivisonne, Pasquale, Pfc, PH
Trapp, Edward O., Pfc, PH
Traumell, B. R., Pvt, PH
Tritle, Daniel B., Pvt, PH
Tronga, Angelo G., Pfc, PH
Trosheim, Harry J., Pfc, PH
Trogan, Walter P., S/Sgt, PH
Trangolo, Carl, Pfc, PH
Tracy, Zeb B., Pfc, PH
Trepasco, Frank A., Cpl, PH
Tracy, William J., S/Sgt, PH, BSM
Troxell, George W., Pvt, PH
Tracey, William F., 1st Lt, BSM
Turner, Wilbert E., Pfc, PH
Tucker, Edgar A., Pvt, PH
Tunk, Robert F., Jr., Pvt, PH
Turczynski, Ralph T., Pfc, PH
Tully, Frank J., Pvt, PH
Turner, William E., Pfc, PH
Tuozzola, Frank W., Pvt, PH
Tubbs, Horace E., Pvt, PH
Tucker, Herman, Pfc, BSM
Tuminski, Stephen R., T/Sgt, PH, SS
Turek, William B., S/Sgt, BSM
Turich, Frank P., Sgt, BSM
Turton, William F., T/4, BSM
Tweed, Joseph F., Pfc, BSM
Tyrell, Jay H., Pvt, PH

Uliano, Peter A., Pvt, PH
Unrien, Louis C., 1st Lt, PH, BSM
Ullman, Leo M., Pfc, BSM
Unger, William, Pvt, PH
Updike, Clifford E., Pfc, PH
Upchzwcki, Joseph J., Pvt, PH
Updike, Robert L., Pfc, PH
Urvena, Jesus S., Pfc, PH
Urton, William W., Pfc, PH
Urban, Joseph G., Cpl, BSM
Urgo, Michael, Cpl, BSM

Valerio, Eugene, Pfc, PH, BSM
Vail, Robert E., Capt, PH
Vasholz, Alfred H., 2nd Lt, PH
Vanacora, Dominick J., Pvt, PH
Vasquez, Robert M., Pfc, PH
Van Etten, Charles E., Pvt, PH
Van DeVentur, Jack G., Pfc, BSM
Vandries, Afons J., T/4, BSM
Vanuygriff, Thomas W., Pfc, BSM
Vanek, William R., Sgt, BSM
Vecchio, Anthony, Pfc, PH
Vercher, Nicholas L., Pvt, PH
Vergano, Ottavio R., Pvt, PH
Vestimiglia, Andrew J., Pvt, PH
Venchos, Michael, Pvt, PH
Ventura, Arthur C., Pfc, PH
Vergano, Ottevio R., Pfc, PH
Venetianer, Harry, Pvt, PH
Verduzco, Frank, S/Sgt, PH
Veale, Leroy W., Pfc, PH
Vyvial, Edward J., Pvt, PH
Venter, Robert E., T/Sgt, PH, SS
Vecchio, Salvatore M., Pvt, BSM*
Vega, Jesse R., Pfc, SS
Viehlant, Ray W., Pfc, PH
Vincher, William, Sgt, PH
Vincent, Lowell R., Pfc, PH
Vittorio, Joseph, Pfc, PH, BSM
Victirine, Robert E. T., 2nd Lt, PH
Vitales, Prooper A., Pfc, PH
Villareal, Gilbert H., S/Sgt, PH
Virgil, Flario, Pfc, PH
Villarreal, Valentin G., Pfc, PH
Vieira, Americo, Pfc, BSM
Virira, Louis J., Pfc, BSM

Villa, Joseph V., Pfc, BSM
Vincent, Earl T., Pfc, BSM
Vlacaneich, Joseph A., M/Sgt, LM
Voyiatzis, Louis, Pfc, PH
Voyd, Douglas E., Pfc, PH
Von Weldon, Eugene, Pfc, PH
Voreginday, Peter, Sgt, PH
Vockel, Elmer E., Sgt, BSM
Vollmer, Elbert J., S/Sgt, BSM
Vyvial, Edward J., Pvt, PH

Walton, Cecil L., Pfc, PH
Wall, William G., Sgt, PH
Walsh, Thomas A., 1st Lt, PH, SS
Waterman, Walter H., Pfc, PH
Warfield, Everett, Pfc, PH
Wallace, Rounts, Pfc, PH
Watson, Otha O., Pvt, PH
Wazelle, Robert W., Pvt, PH
Warren, James H., Pvt, PH
Warner, Robert E., Pvt, PH
Waters, Hollis E., Pvt, PH
Walls, Parry L., Sgt, PH
Wang, Wat K., Pfc, PH
Wallace, Francis J., Pvt, PH
Wallace, Joseph T., Pfc, PH
Walker, Edmond T., Pvt, PH
Walker, Elmer F., Pvt, PH
Wassdorf, Peter J., 1st Lt, PH
Walters, George J., Pfc, PH
Walsh, John J., Pvt, PH
Waslaski, Richard, Pfc, PH
Walker, George J., 2nd Lt, PH
Walters, Charles H., Sr., Pvt, PH
Walker, Lee R., Pfc, PH
Walker, Richard P., 1st Lt, PH, DSC
Watt, Thomas G., S/Sgt, PH
Walter, Joseph P., Capt, PH
Wacaster, Howard B., T/4, BSM
Walker, H. D., Sgt, BSM
Walker, William R., T/4, BSM
Walkiewiez, John J., Pvt, SS
Wallace, George T., Pfc, BSM
Wallace, Jesse A., Pfc, PH
Wallenstein, Henry, T/5, PH
Walske, Robert F., Sgt, BSM
Warren, Gerald, T/Sgt, BSM
Waskel, Walter F., Pfc, BSM
Watkins, Alfred E., Pfc, BSM
Watkins, Luther D., Pfc, BSM
Wells, Edgar L., Pfc, PH
Wells, Joseph L., Pfc, PH
Westfall, William A., Pvt, PH
Wells, Ralph C., Pfc, PH
Wesselive, Morris J., Pvt, PH
Welch, Wallace H., 2nd Lt, PH
Westead, William H., S/Sgt, PH
Weidman, Frank C., Pvt, PH
Weber, Francis C., Pvt, PH
Webster, Bruce G., Pvt, PH
Wellman, John J., Pvt, PH
Wechmanewski, Henry A., Pfc, PH
Weaver, Herman L., Pvt, PH
Weslow, Leo, Pvt, PH
Werts, Abraham J., Pvt, PH
Welshmier, Daonald J., Pfc, PH
Weygand, Fred T., Cpl, PH
Wells, Edgar L., Pfc, PH
Weiberg, Meyer, Pvt, PH
Webb, Charles E., Pvt, PH
Weinstein, Seymour, Pfc, PH
Wireman, George D., Pfc, PH
Weissman, Joseph, Sgt, PH, BSM
Webb, Clarence, S/Sgt, PH, BSM, SS
Wellis, John F., Pvt, PH
Weinbranner, John E., Pvt, PH
Weikum, Lester F., Pfc, BSM
Weinch, Michael, Pfc, PH
Welch, Leroy L., 1st Lt, PH, BSM
Werner, Luther F., Pfc, BSM
Werner, Paul D., Pvt, BSM
Werner, Walter F., M/Sgt, BSM

Wexler, Harry, S/Sgt, BSM
Whitlock, Lawrence B., Pfc, PH
White, Henry J., Pfc, PH
Whitmore, Jewell W., Pvt, PH
White, Milas L., Pvt, PH
White, Paul J., Pfc, PH
White, Raymond R., T/5, PH, BSM
White, John O., Pvt, PH
Willey, Albert N., Pfc, PH
Whiteaker, Earl H., S/Sgt, PH
Whiley, Jack, Pvt, PH
White, Edward C., Jr., Pfc, BSM
White, Harry M., Pvt, BSM
Whiteaker, Earl L., 2d Lt, PH, SS
Williams, Donald L., Pvt, PH
Wilson, William H., Pvt, PH
Wilson, Melvin T., Pfc, PH
Wise, John F., Pvt, PH
Wilson, James R., S/Sgt, PH, BSM
Winget, Clifford O., Pvt, PH
Weitzner, Charles, Pvt, PH
Wildman, Robert G., Pfc, PH
Wiser, Douglas E., Pvt, PH
Wijton, Clayton M., T/5, PH
Willis, Henry F., PH
Williams, Arthur W., Sgt, PH
Winter, Martin H., Pvt, PH
Wituski, Virgil G., S/Sgt, PH, SS
Wilkiti, Burley A., Pfc, PH
Wilson, Morin O., Pvt, PH
Williams, Emery F., S/Sgt, BSM
Williams, Leo A., S/Sgt, BSM
Wilson, Doyle H., Pfc, BSM
Wilson, Paul A., S/Sgt, BSM
Wilson, Ralph D., S/Sgt, BSM
Winebranner, Arthur W., T/Sgt, BSM
Wing, Charles G., S/Sgt, BSM
Whitham, Henry C., Pvt, BSM
Wnuk, Steven, Sgt, PH
Woods, Lorina R., Pfc, PH
Wolney, Elmer, Pfc, PH
Wolfe, Quentin, Pvt, PH
Woltz, Louis P., S/Sgt, PH
Woodson, Eugene W., Pvt, PH
Wood, Donald O., Pvt, PH
Wolfe, Everett G., Pfc, PH
Wolfe, Earlie L., 2d Lt, PH
Woltinger, Russell, Pvt, PH
Worman, William D., Pvt, PH
Wong, Kim Y., Pfc, PH
Wolf, Truman R., Sgt, PH
Woodzel, Roy J., Pvt, PH
Wojcikiewicz, Frank J., Pfc, PH
Wood, Marion E., Pvt, PH
Woods, Edwin J., Pfc, PH
Wood, Lee E., Pvt, PH
Wothington, Kenneth C., Pfc, PH
Woods, Opal L., Pfc, PH
Wolfgang, Luther C., Pfc, PH
Wooten, Jackson H., Pfc, PH
Wojcik, Chester R., Pfc, SS
Woods, Donald F., S/Sgt, BSM
Woodman, Robert F., Pfc, BSM

Woods, Barber, Pfc, BSM
Woods, D. W., Pvt, PH
Worta, John, Jr., S/Sgt, BSM
Wright, Dale J., Pvt, PH
Wright, Claude O., Pvt, PH
Wright, George D., Pvt, PH
Wyman, Philip, Pvt, PH, BSM
Wyatt, Floyd, Pfc, BSM
Wyekoff, Fred L., Pvt, BSM
Wyman, Vernon L., Pfc, BSM

Yaeger, Walter B., Pvt, PH
Yannacci, Samuel E., Pfc, PH
Yates, James W., Pfc, PH, BSM
Yates, Thomas, S/Sgt, PH
Yanez, Salome, Pfc, PH*
Yearly, Lester, S/Sgt, PH
Yeager, Walter G., Lt Col, SS
Yecny, Eddie, Pfc, BSM
Yliniemi, Arthur E., Pfc, PH
Young, Robert L., Pvt, PH
Youmuni, Thomas H., Pvt, PH
Youngquist, Berger A., Pfc, PH
Youdar, Claude H., Pvt, PH
Young, Ralph F., 1st Lt, PH
York, Melvin A., Pfc, PH
Younis, Lloyd, S/Sgt, PH
Young, Gordon S., Pvt, PH
Young, Robert B., Pfc, PH
Yongue, Donald, Capt, PH
Young, Jack, Pvt, PH
Young, Alonzo W., Pfc, BSM
Young, Ross E., 1st Lt, PH*
Yudhan, Abraham, Pvt, PH
Yustwan, Robert, Pvt, PH

Zarafine, Murphy J., Pvt, PH*
Zagorsky, John, Pfc, PH
Zaurla, Edward R., Pfc, PH, BSM
Zaremski, Edward T., Cpl, PH*
Zani, Joseph P., Pvt, PH
Zaccarios, Martinova, Pfc, PH
Zabawa, Joseph J., S/Sgt, BSM
Zampicienie, Joseph, Pfc, BSM
Zeiders, Kenneth E., Pvt, PH*
Zelinski, Thomas F., Pvt, PH
Zeneski, Stanley A., Sgt, PH
Zelcovitz, Alfred, Pvt, PH
Zelinsky, George E., Sgt, PH, BSM
Zigo, Henry, Sgt, PH
Zichittella, Joe M., Pvt, PH
Ziellechouski, Walter, Sgt, PH
Zimmer, Raymond E., Pfc, PH
Zimmerman, Joseph A., Pvt, PH
Zielinski, William, Pfc, PH
Ziomek, Alexander, Pfc, PH
Zischav, Robert E., Pfc, PH*
Ziegfield, William S., Sgt, PH, BSM
Zielinski, Alfred J., Pfc, BSM
Zlostik, Peter T., Pfc, PH
Zmrtrewicz, Stanley J., S/Sgt, PH*, BSM
Zradicka, Micheal J., Pvt, PH, BSM
Zuckouski, Lee J., Pvt, PH

350TH INFANTRY REGIMENT

Abbot, Jesse E., Pvt, PH
Abernathy, Ora W., S/Sgt, BSM
Acerbi, Louis F., Sgt, PH
Ackerman, Arlan W., Pfc, PH
Acquaviva, Chester, Sgt, PH*
Adalio, Albert, Pvt, PH*
Adams, Armand A., Sgt, BSM
Adams, Elmer B., 2nd Lt, PH
Adams, Jewel L., Pvt, PH
Adams, Joseph J., Pfc, PH
Adams, Lafayette B., 1st Lt, PH
Adams, Robert M., Pvt, PH
Adams, Warren G., Pfc, BSM
Adams, William D., Pfc, PH
Aguilar, Andres T., Sgt, SS, PH*

Aguilera, John P., Sgt, PH
Ahrens, Harold, Jr., S/Sgt, PH
Akers, George, Jr., S/Sgt, PH
Albarado, Antonio, Pfc, PH
Alberte, Charles W., Pfc, PH
Ahn, Andrew, Pfc, BSM
Albertson, Gerald W., T/5, BSM, PH
Albright, Robert H., Cpl, BSM
Alexander, Lealon A., Pfc, BSM
Alfaro, Antonio P., Pvt, PH
Alfieri, Salvatore, Pfc, PH
Allanbrook, Douglas P., S/Sgt, BSM
Allen, Alcott A., Pfc, PH
Allen, Calvin O., 2nd Lt, SS (Post)
Allen, Earl D., Pfc, PH

Allen, George W., S/Sgt, SS (Post), PH
Allen, James H., Pfc, PH
Allen, Maynard F., Pfc, PH
Allen, Richard H., Pfc, PH
Allen, Walter D., Sgt, PH
Allogio, Carmen T., Sgt, BSM
Altieri, Eugene V., Cpl, BSM
Alves, Antonio J., Pvt, PH
Alves, Joseph S., Pfc, PH*
Alvillar, Ignacio B., Pfc, PH
Amick, Jesse W., T/5, BSM, PH
Amos, Robert N., Pfc, BSM
Anderson, Alvin R., S/Sgt, PH*
Anderson, Charles R., Sgt, BSM
Anderson, Fred, Jr., Pfc, SS (Post)
Anderson, Harold S., Pfc, PH*
Anderson, James L., Pfc, PH
Anderson, Lealand H., Sgt, PH
Anderson, Warren E., Pvt, PH
Anderson, William L., Pfc, PH
Andros, William, Pfc, PH
Andrzejewski, Theodore E., Pvt, PH
Angelo, Fred F., Pfc, PH**
Ankney, Donald E., Pvt, PH
Annicchiarico, Joseph, Pvt, SS
Anthony, Charles T., Cpl, BSM
Anthony, Luther L., Jr., Pfc, PH
Anthony, Michael L., 1st Lt, PH
Antonelli, Mario, Pfc, PH*
Arata, Edward S., Pfc, PH
Archambeault, Malcolm E., Pvt, PH
Arias, Bruno, Pfc, PH
Arias, Henry, Cpl, PH
Armstrong, Boyd H., T/5, BSM
Arnett, Winford, Pfc, PH
Arnette, Thomas R., Pfc, PH*
Arnold, Sanford, 1st Lt, PH*
Artcliff, Warren D., Pfc, PH
Arthur, Leon L., Jr., Pfc, PH*
Ashby, Goldie R., Pvt, PH
Ashe, Robert N., Pfc, PH*
Ashton, Edward M., Pfc, PH
Ashton, Roy G., Sgt, BSM
Aston, Reese V., Capt, SS (Post), BSM
Atkinson, Loren E., Sgt, BSM
Ault, William H., Pfc, BSM
Aument, Donald P., Pvt, PH
Ausborne, Roland C., Pfc, PH
Austerman, Floyd H., Pfc, BSM
Austin, John F., T/5, BSM
Austin, Russell, Pfc, BSM, PH*
Avila, Samuel R., Pvt, PH
Awtry, Howard F., Pfc, BSM
Ayers, Ellis W., Pvt, PH

Babec, John J., Pfc, PH
Babcock, Stanley G., Pfc, PH
Babeno, Charles J., Pfc, PH
Backherms, Hubert F., Sgt, PH
Baeli, Frank, Cpl, PH
Bagwell, E. J., Pvt, PH
Bailer, Donald B., Sgt, SS, BSM
Bailey, Leo F., Jr., Pfc, PH
Bailey, William, Pvt, PH
Bair, Thomas E., 1st Lt, BSM*
Baise, Joseph E., Pfc, BSM, PH*
Bakalian, John R., T/Sgt, SS, PH
Baker, Calvin D., Cpl, PH
Baker, Harry, Pvt, PH
Baker, James J., 1st Lt, BSM
Baker, Roy C., Pfc, PH
Baker, William F. P., Pfc, PH
Baker, Willie F., Pfc, PH
Baldivia, Refugio C., Pfc, SS, PH
Baldwin, Wayne C., Pvt, SS
Ball, Michael J., Pfc, PH
Ballard, Clem L., 1st Lt, BSM
Ballard, J. W., Pfc, BSM
Banas, Andrew J., T/5, BSM
Banyai, Martin, Pfc, BSM
Baranoski, Felix J., Sgt, PH
Baratoo, Henry, Pfc, PH

Barba, Ralph A., Pfc, BSM, PH
Barber, Dale C., Pvt, PH
Barbieri, Aldo, Pvt, PH
Barcus, Delbert L., 2nd Lt, PH
Bare, Walter E., Lt Col, SS
Barker, Carl O., Pvt, PH
Barkowosky, Alexander, T/4, BSM
Barlage, Leroy J., Sgt, PH
Barna, Steven, T/Sgt, BSM
Barnes, Michael J., Pfc, PH
Barnett, Frank E., T/5, PH
Barnett, Stephen J., S/Sgt, BSM
Barnhard, Charles R., Pfc, BSM
Barnoski, Peter, 1st Sgt, BSM
Barnum, Leroy G., Sgt, PH
Barone, Frank F., T/Sgt, SS, PH
Barrell, Percival R., Pvt, BSM, PH
Barrett, Broadus C., Sgt, PH
Barrette, Louis F., S/Sgt, BSM
Barron, Orville F., Pfc, SS
Barone, John J., T/4, PH
Barry, Jerome P., Pfc, PH*
Barta, Andrew, T/Sgt, BSM
Bartholomay, Kenneth J., Sgt, PH
Bartkowiak, Henry F., S/Sgt, PH
Bartkus, Francis C., Sgt, PH
Bartlett, Emry, Jr., Pfc, BSM
Bartley, Eldon E., T/5, BSM, PH
Bartman, Edward B., Pvt, PH
Bartoli, Sergio J., Pfc, PH
Barwick, Chester C., Pfc, PH
Basha, Frank L., M/Sgt, BSM
Basha, Roger, Pvt, PH
Basielewski, Stanley, Pvt, PH
Basom, Merle D., 1st Lt, LM
Bartoli, George J., Pfc, BSM
Bates, James A., Pvt, BSM
Bates, John, Pvt, PH
Bates, John C., Pvt, PH
Bates, Lonnie L., Pvt, PH
Bator, Arthur O., S/Sgt, PH
Battafarano, Leonard A., Capt, BSM
Bauer, Rudolph, Pfc, BSM
Baumann, Ernest W., Jr., Capt, BSM
Bavasi, Emil J., S/Sgt, PH
Bavisotto, Philip P., S/Sgt, PH
Baxter, Marvin D., Sgt, PH*
Beam, Winthrop M., Pfc, PH
Bean, Lawrence A., Pfc, PH
Bear, Norman, Pvt, PH*
Becerra, Osvaldo, Pvt, SS, PH
Beck, Lewis G., Pfc, PH
Beckerdite, Bobbie E., Pvt, PH
Bedall, George H., T/Sgt, BSM
Beddow, Lee H., Sgt, DSC, PH****
Bednarz, Benedict, Cpl, PH
Beeler, Lester E., Pfc, BSM
Beers, Duncan H., T/Sgt, BSM*
Beers, Wollington P., Pvt, PH
Behrens, Ralph C., Pvt, PH
Beko, Kalman J., Pfc, PH
Belcher, R. L., T/5, PH
Belcher, William W., Pvt, PH
Belisle, Theodore G., Pfc, PH*
Bell, Clarence A., S/Sgt, BSM, PH*
Bell, Donald W., Pfc, PH
Bell, Elgie, Pvt, PH
Bell, William G., 1st Lt, BSM*
Belue, John T., Jr., Pvt, BSM
Benavidez, William B., S/Sgt, PH
Bendel, Laverne L., Pfc, PH
Bends, Lon F., 1st Lt, PH
Benham, Harold I., Pvt, PH
Benjamin, Harold V., S/Sgt, PH
Benner, Robert J., Jr., Pfc, BSM
Bennett, Carl J., Pfc, PH
Benson, Charles H., Jr., Pvt, PH
Benson, George, S/Sgt, BSM, PH*
Benson, Kenneth E., Sgt, PH*
Benty, Lewie C., Pfc, PH
Benway, Albert L., S/Sgt, BSM
Benzel, Richard D., Pfc, BSM

Berkley, William H., Pfc, PH
Bernal, Juan, Pfc, PH
Bernier, Eugene E., Pfc, PH
Bernier, Henry N., T/Sgt, BSM
Bernstein, Louis, Cpl, BSM
Berry, Lester F., Pvt, PH
Bertzos, Michael E., Pvt, PH
Berube, Wilfred, Pvt, PH
Besterda, Carl J., S/Sgt, PH*
Bewalder, Charles J., S/Sgt, BSM
Bianchi, Arnold W., T/Sgt, BSM
Bielawski, Veneeslaus M., T/Sgt, PH
Biettkoff, William, Pfc, PH
Birchler, Paul R., Pvt, PH*
Bishop, John H., 2nd Lt, DSC
Bishop, William R., Cpl, BSM, PH*
Bjorkman, Edward R., Sgt, PH
Black, Ephraim D., Jr., Pvt, PH
Blackstone, Joseph E., Jr., Pvt, PH
Blackwell, Roy L., Pfc, BSM, PH
Blake, Leon, Pfc, PH
Blanchard, Lucius, Pfc, BSM
Blankenship, Lester B., Pfc, PH
Blanks, Charles J., Pfc, BSM, PH
Blayer, Benjamin, Pvt, PH
Blazek, George T., 1st Lt, PH
Blazinicic, Steve K., Pvt, PH
Bleau, Floyd J., Cpl, BSM, PH
Bledsoe, Clyde E., Pfc, PH*
Boatner, Mark M., III, 1st Lt, BSM
Boback, Joseph, T/Sgt, BSM, PH
Bobik, George D., T/Sgt, BSM*
Bobrowski, Theodore S., Sgt, PH
Bock, Robert P., Pfc, PH
Bocock, Edward F., Sgt, PH
Boden, Ray C., Pfc, PH*
Bogardus, King J., Jr., Capt, BSM*, LM
Bolander, Clarence R., Pvt, PH   .
Bolland, Clarence M., Pvt, PH
Bollman, Marvin J., Pfc, PH*
Bonar, Vernon A., Pvt, PH
Bond, Romio S., Pfc, PH
Bongiovi, Louis V., T/4, BSM
Bonnell, George C., Pvt, PH
Booher, Obert D., T/Sgt, PH
Boone, Otho J., Pfc, SS, PH
Bootle, Mack C., Pvt, SS, PH
Borquist, Sterling A., Capt, SS, PH
Bosquez, Rafael, Pfc, PH
Bossong, Robert J., Pfc, PH
Bost, Joseph E., 1st Lt, BSM
Boston, Charles T., Pvt, PH
Boston, Ralph A., Pfc, PH
Bostwick, Lynn R., Pvt, PH
Boudreaux, Andrew A., Pfc, PH
Bourbeau, Paul H., Pfc, PH
Bourne, John J., Pfc, PH
Bouroue, Odilon J., S/Sgt, PH*
Boverssaa, Blanchard D., Pfc, PH
Bowersock, Glenn L., Pfc, BSM (Post)
Bowman, Edgar E., 1st Lt, PH
Bowman, Gerard J., Pvt, PH
Bowman, Thomas E., S/Sgt, BSM (Post)
Boyd, Robert D., Sgt, BSM, PH
Boyd, Oran L., Pfc, PH
Boyer, Raymond K., Sgt, PH
Boyle, Joseph F., T/Sgt, BSM
Boysen, Frederick O., 2nd Lt, BSM (Post), SS (Post), PH
Boxberger, George H., Pvt, PH
Brackett, Leroy R., Pfc, PH*
Bradshaw, Albert H., Pvt, PH
Bradshaw, Herbert L., Pvt, BSM
Brady, Chester W., S/Sgt, BSM
Brady, Jacob L., Pfc, PH
Bralczyk, Edward, T/5, PH
Bramante, Domenic J., Cpl, PH*
Brand, John S., 1st Lt, PH
Brandow, William C., Pfc, PH
Brask, Bernhard S., Capt, BSM
Braswell, Carl M., Pvt, PH
Brazauskas, Raymond J., Pvt, PH

Brecht, Joseph C., Pfc, PH
Bredon, Pat M., Jr., Sgt, BSM
Breen, John W., Pfc, PH*
Brennan, John T., Sgt, BSM
Breucker, August, Jr., Pfc, PH
Briar, Jack R., Pvt, PH
Briggs, Seth B., Pvt, PH*
Brighton, Senator, Pfc, PH
Briley, Felix H., Pfc, BSM
Briones, Ambrosio, Pfc, PH
Brooks, George H., S/Sgt, BSM
Brooks, Nicholas R., Capt, PH*
Brookman, Nathan, Pvt, PH
Brophy, John R., Pvt, PH*
Brown, G. W., Pfc, PH
Brown, George W., S/Sgt, PH, BSM (Post)
Brown, Joseph, S/Sgt, SS (Post)
Brown, Kenneth D., 1st Lt, PH
Brown, Monte A., Jr., T/3, BSM
Brown, Otha J., Jr., Pvt, PH*
Brown, Robert E., Pfc, PH
Brown, Robert P., Pfc, PH
Brown, Russell W., Pvt, BSM
Brown, William H., Pfc, BSM (Post)
Browne, Richard J., T/5, PH
Bruce, Robert J., 1st Lt, PH
Brucks, Charles J., Pvt, PH
Brunelle, Arthur J., Pfc, PH*
Bruning, Clyde E., Pvt, PH
Bruscini, Thomas C., Pfc, PH**
Bruton, Glenn H., Cpl, BSM
Bryan, Alvin C., Pfc, PH
Bryant, Harold L., Pfc, PH
Bryant, James A., Pfc, PH
Bryant, Kermit E., Pvt, BSM
Bryson, Loren F., 1st Lt, BSM*, PH
Bryant, James A., Pfc, BSM
Buccelli, Jerry A., Pvt, PH
Bocchicchio, Anthony L., Pvt, PH
Buchanan, Donald L., Pfc, BSM, PH
Buchanan, Robert L., Pvt, PH
Buchmeyer, Raymond H., Pvt, PH
Buckholz, Fritz E., Pvt, PH*
Buchy, Francis X., S/Sgt, PH
Buckley, Daniel, Pfc, BSM (Post)
Buckner, Louis R., 1st Lt, BSM*, PH*
Buisson, Guimault L., Pfc, PH
Bukowski, Joe F., Pfc, PH*
Bullard, William H., Pfc, BSM
Bullock, James L., S/Sgt, SS
Bullock, Odis W., S/Sgt, PH
Bultman, Lester, Pvt, PH
Bunch, George W., Pvt, PH
Buonanno, Anthony R., Pvt, PH
Burall, John C., Pfc, PH**
Burge, Tracy C., S/Sgt, PH*
Burgess, Roland A., Sgt, SS, BSM*, PH
Burgio, Carmelo C., S/Sgt, BSM
Burke, Albert C., T/5, SS
Burke, Francis V., Cpl, BSM
Burnett, L. C., Pfc, PH
Burnette, Mose G., S/Sgt, PH
Burnham, Robert A., S/Sgt, BSM, PH
Burns, Albert W., Sgt, PH**
Burns, Elliot J., T/Sgt, BSM, PH
Burns, Harry, Pfc, BSM, PH
Burns, John J., S/Sgt, BSM, PH
Burns, Raymond E., Pfc, PH
Burton, Milfred T., Pfc, PH
Burton, Robert L., 1st Sgt, PH*
Bush, Harry J., Pvt, PH*
Businger, James G., Pvt, PH
Bussiere, Hugh, Pvt, PH
Bussman, Rudolph F., Pfc, BSM
Butcher, Clarence E., S/Sgt, PH
Buth, Herbert W., Pvt, PH*
Butler, George B., Pfc, PH
Butler, Harwell J., Pvt, PH
Butsch, Thomas C., Maj, LM, BSM
Butz, Donald M., Pfc, PH
Buxbaum, Sanford M., Pvt, PH
Buxton, John, Sgt, SS, PH

Buzzard, Arthur F., Pfc, PH
Byers, Francis L., Pfc, BSM
Byers, Leonard C., Pfc, PH*
Byloo, Raymond J., T/5, BSM
Byrd, Gilliam R., Pfc, PH***
Byrne, William F., Pvt, BSM

Cabarrubia, Trinidad, Jr., Pfc, PH
Cacciatore, Frank J., Cpl, BSM, PH
Cacko, Arthur A., Sgt, BSM, PH
Cadena, Caledonio B., Pfc, PH, BSM
Cafaro, Philip J., S/Sgt, PH
Cafritz, William N., Pfc, PH
Cain, Alfred, Pfc, PH
Caldwell, Earl R., Jr., Pfc, PH
Cahill, Louis G., Pfc, PH
Calagna, Pasquale, Pfc, BSM
Calderone, Rocco A., T/5, PH
Calhoun, Ray G., Pfc, PH*
Caliendo, Anthony A., T/4, BSM
Caligiuri, Anthony P., 1st Lt, BSM
Callahan, Francis J., S/Sgt, PH
Calzaretta, Omar A., Pfc, PH*
Cambelbeek, George P., S/Sgt, PH
Campano, Frank A., Jr., Pfc, PH
Campbell, Bernard, 1st Lt, PH
Campbell, Curtis P., Pfc, BSM
Campbell, Edward E., Pvt, PH
Campbell, Elton F., Pfc, SS
Campbell, Robert S., Sgt, PH
Cambell, William P., Pvt, PH
Campos, Jose B., Sgt, PH
Canfield, Raymond P., Pfc, BSM, PH
Canto, Adam F., S/Sgt, PH
Capano, Vincent A., Pfc, PH
Capece, Francis, Sgt, SS
Capellupo, John P., Pfc, PH
Capobianco, Anthony J., Pfc, PH*
Carbonneau, Lionel J., T/5, BSM
Cardinali, Joseph, Pvt, PH
Carey, George E., S/Sgt, BSM
Carrillo, Frank, Pfc, PH
Carlisle, David B., WOJG, BSM
Carlson, Robert F., Pfc, PH
Carmichael, James P., 2nd Lt, PH**
Carmickle, Charles I., Pvt, PH
Carmody, Thomas H., T/Sgt, BSM
Carpenter, Buford C., Pvt, PH
Carpenter, George H., 1st Lt, SS (Post)
Carrington, David L., T/5, BSM
Carrino, John A., T/5, BSM
Carrizales, Paul, Pfc, PH
Carter, Clifford F., Sgt, PH
Carter, Harry B., Pfc, PH
Carter, Henry C., Sgt, PH
Carter, Robert F., Pfc, BSM
Carter, Robert R., Sgt, PH*
Carter, Willis H., Pvt, PH
Cartwright, Pearl R., Pfc, PH
Cassata, Roland J., Pfc, PH
Cassese, Gerard A., Pfc, PH
Cassidy, Alfred E., Sgt, SS, PH*
Casteel, John K., T/5, PH
Castelvetere, Frank A., Pfc, PH
Castillo, Antonio G., Pfc, PH*
Castilloux, Harry, Pvt, SS (Post)
Cataldo, Paul V., Pfc, PH
Catanzaro, Frank, Sgt, BSM
Catapano, Dominick C., Pvt, PH
Catauro, Alexander, Pvt, PH
Catone, Patsy J., S/Sgt, PH
Caulder, James A., T/Sgt, PH*
Cavanaugh, Archie J., Pfc, PH
Cekus, Walter E., Pfc, PH
Celaya, Simon, Pfc, PH*
Chabek, Lawrence, S/Sgt, BSM
Chadwick, Dawn A., Pfc, BSM, PH
Chagnon, Joseph F., Pvt, PH*
Chalich, Mellan, Pvt, PH
Chambers, Opal, Pfc, BSM
Chandler, Hardy R., T/4, BSM
Chandler, Isaac, Pfc, PH

Chaney, William R., Pvt, PH
Chapman, Robert P., Pfc, BSM
Charbonnet, Laurent A., Capt, PH
Chase, James P., S/Sgt, BSM (Post)
Chase, Louis E., Pfc, PH
Chavez, Rosendo, Pfc, PH
Chester, David N., Cpl, BSM**
Chew, William, Pfc, BSM (Post)
Chidyllo, Nicholas, Pfc, PH
Chieco, Anthony M., Sgt, PH
Childers, Lewis J., Pfc, PH
Childress, Louie C., Jr., Pfc, PH
Childres, Thomas J., Pfc, SS
Chilman, Arthur D., Pvt, PH
Chipps, Nelson L., Jr., Pfc, PH
Chittendon, Lawrence D., Pvt, PH
Chizinski, Leo J., Pfc, PH
Chowansky, Joseph, Pvt, BSM
Choy, Henry, Pfc, PH*
Chrestman, Matelon E., Pvt, PH
Christian, Leon G., T/5, BSM
Christiansen, Allan P., Pvt, PH
Christie, Charles J., Pvt, PH
Chumchal, Richard C., Pfc, PH
Church, Milton W., Cpl, PH
Church, Thomas E., Pfc, PH
Churchill, Leo J., Jr., Pfc, SS
Ciaramitaro, Samuel, Pfc, PH
Ciattoni, Vincent, Pfc, PH
Cilfone, Joseph G., Sgt, PH
Cinpinski, Burton A., Pvt, PH
Cintas, Bernaxe, Pvt, PH
Cioffi, William A., S/Sgt, PH
Cipriani, Henry B., Pvt, PH
Clapper, Joe, Pfc, PH
Clark, Francis E., Pfc, PH
Clark, Ralph J., S/Sgt, PH
Clauss, Alfred E., 1st Lt, BSM
Cleaver, Charles D., Pfc, BSM, PH*
Clement, Frank, Pfc, BSM*
Clemente, Joseph A., Pfc, PH
Clements, Raymond P., Pvt, PH
Clemmer, Lewis M., 2nd Lt, BSM, PH
Clevenger, Paul B., Sgt, PH
Clever, Russell K., Pvt, PH
Cline, Isaac S., Jr., Pfc, PH*
Cline, Robert C., T/Sgt, SS, SM, BSM
Clininger, Charles M., Pfc, PH**
Close, Raymond, Pfc, BSM
Clute, Neil O., Cpl, BSM
Coats, Herman L., S/Sgt, PH*
Cobbs, Willie C., Pfc, PH
Coble, Roy W., Pvt, PH
Cochran, Avery M., Col, LM, BSM, PH*
Cody, Robert L., Pfc, BSM
Coello, Amedio A., Pfc, PH
Coen, Dean B., 1st Lt, BSM
Cogan, John, S/Sgt, BSM, PH
Colanzo, Thomas, Pfc, PH
Cole, Raymond N., Pvt, PH
Coleman, Sam L., Pvt, PH*
Colla, Louis J., Pfc, PH
Coletta, Joseph, Pfc, PH
Colley, Edward W., Pvt, PH
Collier, Louis A., Maj, BSM
Colling, William G., Pvt, PH
Collins, Benjamin P., Jr., S/Sgt, PH
Collins, Grover J., T/Sgt, LM, PH*
Collum, Manus W., Pfc, PH
Collum, William, Pfc, BSM, PH
Colpitts, Clarence C., Pvt, BSM (Post)
Columbus, James F., Pvt, PH
Combest, Wayne, Sgt, BSM
Combe, Roy, Pfc, PH
Comella, Ercolino A., S/Sgt, PH
Comstock, Herbert I., Pvt, PH
Coniglio, Joe J., Pvt, PH
Conkwright, Joseph E., S/Sgt, PH
Conmy, John H., S/Sgt, PH
Connolly, Bernard, 1st Lt, PH
Constant, Raymond L., Sgt, PH
Conti, Americus, M/Sgt, BSM

Cook, Calvin C., Pvt, PH
Cook, Claude J., Jr., Pfc, PH
Cook, Lauren G., Sgt, SS (Post), PH
Cook, Levi J., Pfc, PH
Cook, Lloyd A., Pvt, PH
Cook, Oris, Pvt, PH**
Cooper, Corble L., Sgt, PH
Cooper, Ernest J., S/Sgt, PH
Cooper, John B., T/5, BSM
Cootware, William H., Pfc, PH
Coplin, Myer, Pvt, PH
Coppolo, Leonard, Sgt, PH
Corbin, Ralph P., Pfc, SS
Corcoran, Daniel, Pfc, PH
Corcoran, Harold T., Pvt, PH
Cordero, Frank G., Cpl, PH
Cordes, William F., Sgt, BSM
Cordiner, Duane N., 1st Lt, SS
Cordova, Adrian P., Sgt, PH
Cordova, Robert, Pfc, BSM
Cormier, John E., Pfc, PH
Cornelius, James S., Pfc, PH*
Corr, Lawrence L., Pfc, PH
Corso, Vincent J., T/Sgt, PH*
Cosgrove, Joseph J., Pfc, PH
Cospito, John J., Pfc, PH
Costa, Alfred, Pvt, PH
Costa, Anthony, Pvt, PH
Costello, Edward B., Sgt, PH
Costello, Francis P., M/Sgt, BSM
Coss, Walter L., Sgt, PH
Cote, Herbert, Jr., Pfc, PH
Cotoia, Rocco, T/Sgt, PH
Cousino, Adrian A., Cpl, PH
Covalsky, George E., Pfc, PH
Cowan, Charles E., Pvt, PH
Cox, C. W., Pfc, PH
Cox, Charles M., Pfc, PH
Cox, Crockett B., Sgt, BSM
Cox, George H., Pfc, PH
Cox, James B., Jr., Capt, PH
Cox, Wilbur, Pfc, PH
Cozzi, Patrick J., Pvt, PH
Crane, Robert E., T/4, BSM
Cranson, Harold S., Pvt, PH
Crawford, James J., Pvt, PH
Crawford, Maurice W., Pvt, PH
Creedon, Dan P., Pfc, PH
Crisler, Robert M., 2nd Lt, PH*
Criswell, William H., Pfc, PH
Cronin, James F., Sgt, PH
Cross, John W., Pfc, PH
Crosson, Herbert H., T/5, BSM
Croteau, Armand, Pfc, PH
Crugnola, Eugene J., T/5 BSM
Crutchfield, Lee A., Pfc, PH
Culbertson, Everett A., Sgt, BSM
Culp, Benjamin B., 1st Lt, BSM, PH
Culver, Pet E., Pfc, SS, PH
Cummings, Ellsworth M., Pvt, PH
Cummings, Paul A., Pvt, PH
Cunningham, George H., Pfc, BSM
Curlee, Thomas B., 1st Lt, BSM, PH*
Curren, Dan, S/Sgt, BSM
Curtis, Boyd A., Pfc, PH
Cussans, Thomas L., Maj, DSC, BSM*, PH
Custer, Robert J., Sgt, BSM

Daigle, Joseph B., Pfc, PH
Daily, Ira, S/Sgt, PH
Dailey, Joseph, S/Sgt, PH
Dale, Lucian G., Jr., 1st Lt, SS, BSM, PH*
Dale, Richard C., Pvt, PH
Dalessio, Russell J., S/Sgt, BSM, PH
D'Ambrosio, Ralph L., Pfc, PH
D'Amico, Joseph A., Pfc, PH
Daneli, Itale, Pfc, PH
Daniel, Clifford E., Cpl, PH
Daniels, John M., S/Sgt, BSM, PH
Danker, Henry F., Pfc, PH
Danley, Earl E., Capt, SS, BSM, PH
Dann, Francis E., Pvt, PH

Darnell, Jesse F., 1st Lt, BSM
Daspit, John A., Cpl, BSM, PH
Davidson, Daniel, Cpl, BSM
Davidson, Merwin R., Pfc, PH*
Davis, Abe, Pvt, PH
Davis, Avery C., Pvt, BSM, PH
Davis, Odell J., Pvt, PH
Davis, James W., Capt, BSM, PH
Davis, Millard Q., Capt, SS, PH
Davis, Raymond E., Pfc, PH*
Davis, Richard M., Capt, BSM
Davis, Robert A., Pfc, PH
Davis, Robert E., Sgt, BSM, PH*
Davis, Robert H., Pvt, PH
Davis, Robert S., Pfc, PH
Davis, Roger M., Pfc, PH
Davis, Thomas L., Sr., Pvt, PH
Davis, Victor M., Pfc, PH
Davis, William F., Cpl, PH
Dawkins, Harold J., Pfc, PH
Dawson, Earl B., Sgt, PH
Day, Bobbie H., Cpl, PH
Day, Daryl W., Pvt, PH
Dean, Jeffery D., S/Sgt, PH
DeAndrea, William, Sgt, PH
Debus, Carl P., Pfc, PH
DeCelles, Dominick D., Pfc, BSM, PH*
Deck, William W., Pfc, PH*
Decker, Richard F., Capt, BSM, PH*
Deem, Harry R., Pfc, PH
DeFazio, Ernest J., Cpl, PH
DeFilippis, Fugh A., S/Sgt, BSM
DeFloria, John J., Pfc, PH
DeFranco, Sorafino L., Pvt, PH
DeGlandon, Birk, Cpl, BSM
Deinlein, Leonard, Cpl, SS (Post)
Delacerda, Joseph A., Pfc, PH
Delancey, George S., Pfc, PH
Delaney, Walter, Pfc, PH
Delbene, Albert, Pfc, PH
Delbianco, Savino, S/Sgt, SS, PH
DeLena, Jerry J., Pfc, PH*
Deleone, Leonardo G., Pfc, PH
Delk, Gardner, Pfc, BSM, PH*
Delong, James C., Pfc, BSM, PH*
Deluca, Anthony, T/5, BSM
Delmont, Nicholas, Pfc, PH
Demartini, Adolph G., S/Sgt, BSM
DeMatei, Thomas L., Pfc, PH
DeMay, Cornelius, Pvt, PH
Demmi, Anthony, T/5, BSM
DeMondi, Peter A., Sgt, PH
Denoen, Walter E., Sgt, BSM, PH
Denis, Francis J., S/Sgt, PH**
Dent, William F., S/Sgt, PH
DeOlivera, Marcelino J., Pfc, PH
DiPetrillo, Alfred, Pvt, PH*
DeRenzo, William, Pfc, PH
Derosby, Louis J., S/Sgt, BSM, PH
Derosz, Joseph J., Pfc, BSM
DeSantis, Edward A., Pfc, BSM, PH
Deshon, George B., Lt Col, PH
Desolier, Edward, M/Sgt, BSM
D'Esopo, Dominick F., Pfc, PH
Desrosiers, Armand L., S/Sgt, PH
Dessaint, Eugene A., Pvt, PH
Devins, John, Cpl, PH
DeVito, Salvatore A., Pfc, PH*
DeWald, William H., Pvt, PH
Dewberry, Daniel A., Jr., Pfc, PH*
DeZwaan, Glenn, Pfc, BSM
Diakomis, George J., Pfc, PH
Dicey, Paul C., Pvt, PH
DeChiara, Generso R., Sgt, BSM
Dietrich, Edward J., Sgt, BSM, PH*
Diggs, Benjamin T., Pvt, PH*
DeGiacinto, Marco J., Pvt, BSM, PH
Dillinger, Stephen F., Pvt, PH
Dillner, Norman E., Pfc, PH
DiMatteo, Dominic R., Pfc, PH*
DiMatteo, Rocco J., Pvt, PH
Dimeo, Nick, Jr., Pfc, PH

Dimond, Carroll B., Pfc, PH
Dion, Norman A., S/Sgt, PH*
Dionne, Lawrence W., Pvt, PH
DiStefano, Damiano P., Pfc, BSM, PH
Dively, Dlair, Pfc, PH
Dixson, Walter H., T/Sgt, BSM
Dodaro, James, Cpl, SS, PH
Dodge, Arthur B., Jr., 2nd Lt, PH*
Donoghue, Edward J., Cpl, PH
Donato, Ernest K., S/Sgt, BSM
Donovan, Bertie A., Sgt, PH
Dondero, Charles A., S/Sgt, BSM
Donnell, Holland D., Sgt, PH
Dooner, Bernard T., Sgt, BSM
Dornacker, Charles H., Capt, BSM*
Douet, Jean A., Sgt, BSM
Douglas, Raymond F., Pfc, BSM, PH
Dove, George H., Pfc, PH
Dowdy, Gerald B., T/4, BSM
Dowell, George E., Pfc, BSM
Driscoll, Richard J., S/Sgt, PH
Driver, Rayford, Jr., Pfc, PH
Drogowski, Edward J., 2nd Lt, BSM
Duane, Francis K., 1st Lt, BSM, PH
Dubyak, George, Pfc, PH
Duddie, Andrew D., Pvt, PH
Duffy, George E., 2nd Lt, PH, BSM*, SS
Dugan, James C., Pvt, PH
Dugger, Virgil L., Pvt, PH
Duignan, John J., Pfc, PH
Dumesnil, Freddie J., Pfc, PH
Dumont, Cecil P., Pfc, BSM, PH
Dunaway, James E., Pvt, BSM
Duncan, Matthew I., Pfc, PH
Dunn, Oscar L., Pfc, PH
Dupree, Justin A., Pvt, PH
Dupuy, Elster J., Pfc, PH*
Durbin, Charles H., Pvt, PH
Dwy, Robert H., Pvt, PH
Dwyer, William S., S/Sgt, BSM
Dye, Shelby D., Pfc, BSM, PH*
Dyer, Charles H., Pfc, PH
Dykers, Lawrence H., 1st Lt, SS, BSM, PH
Dziadus, Toney, Pfc, PH

Earley, John H., Pfc, PH
East, Harry P., Pvt, PH*
Eastham, Kirby E., Pfc, PH
Eastridge, John E., T/Sgt, BSM
Ebarb, Herman, Pfc, PH*
Ebel, Edward G., Pfc, PH
Eberhard, Richard L., T/4, BSM (Post)
Eck, William J., Jr., Pfc, PH
Eckles, Van S., Pfc, BSM, PH
Edenhart, Thomas A., Sgt, PH**
Eder, John, Pfc, BSM
Edmunds, Richard D., Sgt, BSM
Edwards, William S., Pfc, PH
Eger, Henry F., T/5, BSM
Eggers, Charles A., 2d Lt, PH
Eimer, Frederick W., Pfc, PH
Eineker, James, S/Sgt, BSM (Post)
Eland, Michael L., Cpl, BSM
Elder, James L., Pvt, PH
Ellefson, Floyd S., Pfc, PH
Ellenberger, Edward, S/Sgt, BSM
Ellenwood, Roy D., Pfc, PH
Elliot, Irvin L., Pfc, PH
Elliot, Sam C., Pfc, PH
Ellison, John G., 1st Lt, PH
Elmore, Frank S., T/Sgt, SSM (Post), PH*
Elrod, James O., Pfc, PH
Else, Robert E., 2d Lt, BSM
Endress, Ernest, Pfc, PH*
Enger, Harold W., Pfc, PH
Englert, Francis J., Sgt, PH
Epperson, Robert E., Pvt, PH*
Eriksen, Norman G., 2d Lt, BSM, PH
Erickson, Norman R., Pvt, BSM, PH*
Ermacoff, Alec, Cpl, BSM
Erman, William J., S/Sgt, PH
Endicott, John E., Pfc, PH

Ennis, Clarence R., Pvt, PH
Erni, Michael J., Pfc, PH
Esparza, Ines, Pfc, BSM
Espinoza, Julio, Pfc, SS (Post)
Esposito, Victor A., Cpl, BSM
Esposito, Vincent J., Cpl, BSM
Evans, Melvin C., Pfc, PH
Evans, Norman T., Jr., Sgt, BSM
Evans, Rex R., Pfc, BSM, PH*
Ewel, George E., 1st Sgt, BSM, PH*

Faber, William A., Capt, BSM
Fagan, Norman, Pvt, SS (Post)
Fagerholm, Gustav H., Pvt, BSM
Fairechio, Carmine H., Pfc, PH
Falcon, Henry C., Sgt, PH
Fanelli, John J., Pfc, PH
Fanizzi, Antonio V., Cpl, BSM, PH
Farhar, Mose, Pfc, BSM, PH
Farmer, Bill C., Pfc, PH
Farmer, James D., T/5, BSM
Farmer, Norman D., Pfc, PH
Farne, William H., Pfc, PH
Farrara, Francis W., T/5, BSM
Farrell, James J., Pfc, PH
Farrell, Thomas F., Cpl, BSM
Farwell, George A., Pfc, SS
Faschan, Lawrence J., Pfc, PH
Faszold, Robert B., Pfc, PH
Faulkner, Henry W., Pvt, PH
Fay, Thomas F., T/5, BSM
Fay, Walter L., Pfc, PH
Fazzone, Ralph D., S/Sgt, PH*
Fegley, Walter E., Sgt, PH
Fetguson, Cecil H., Pfc, BSM
Ferguson, Everett C., 2d Lt, PH
Ferguson, Joseph V., S/Sgt, BSM*
Ferguson, Ralph W., Pfc, PH
Fernald, Phillip C., Pfc, BSM
Ferragamo, Christy, Pfc, PH
Ferrante, William V., S/Sgt, PH
Ferreira, Joseph F., Pvt, PH
Ferris, George W., Pfc, PH
Fiala, Stanley, Pvt, PH
Fick, Harold L., Pfc, SS
Fields, Corbett, S/Sgt, BSM
Fields, Richard E., Pvt, SS, PH*
Filipp, Joe F., Pvt, PH*
Findeisen, Alfred O., S/Sgt, BSM
Fingerhut, Walter C., Capt, BSM
Fingerman, Henry A., Pfc, BSM
Fink, Clayton F., Cpl, PH
Fink, Jacob F., 1st Sgt, BSM*, PH*
Fint, Joseph J., T/5, BSM, PH
Fiori, Ned H., Pvt, PH*
Fisher, Lloyd W., Capt, BSM
Fisher, Wayne C., Pvt, PH
Fitzgerald, Frank B., T/Sgt, PH
Fitzpatrick, Samuel W., Sgt, BSM, PH
Flannery, Benjamin F., Pfc, PH
Fleek, Fred A., Pvt, PH
Fleischer, Gilbert, Cpl, BSM
Fleming, Carl S., 2d Lt, PH*
Flynn, Edward E., Pfc, PH
Fodor, Barney, Pvt, SS, PH
Foegelle, Isidore L., Pfc, PH
Fogel, Isadore, Pfc, PH
Foley, John P., T/5, BSM
Folsom, Earl W., Jr., Cpl, BSM
Fonce, James, Pfc, PH
Fontella, Edmund, 1st Lt, PH
Forbes, Joseph W., T/Sgt, BSM
Ford, James T., Pvt, PH
Fore, Robert I., Pfc, SS, PH
Force, Herbert W., T/5, PH
Forsberg, Robert D., T/Sgt, PH*
Foster, Ernest E., Pfc, PH
Forsythe, Harry A., Pvt, PH
Fortune, Woodrow L., S/Sgt, BSM, PH
Foster, Harold C., 1st Lt, PH
Foster, Earnest P., S/Sgt, PH
Foster, Herbert L., T/4, BSM

Fowler, William M., Pvt, PH
Fox, Albert J., Pvt, PH
Fox, Dennis S., Sgt, PH
Fox, Lewis B., 2d Lt, PH
Foy, Haden F., Pfc, PH*
Fragman, Dominic B., Pvt, PH
Fragoso, Robert V., Pfc, PH*
Francito, Dominic A., Pfc, PH
Frank, Harold L., Pvt, PH
Frank, Louis M., Pfc, PH
Frank, Ruben E., Pfc, PH
Frankel, Herman, 1st Lt, PH
Frederick, Alpha, Jr., Cpl, PH
Freda, Carmine J., Cpl, PH
Freeland, Rex M., T/4, BSM
Freeman, Claude L., 2d Lt, PH
Freeman, James G., Pvt, PH*
Freeman, James M., Pfc, PH
Fregeau, Roland J., Pfc, BSM
Frentzel, Lloyd P., Pfc, PH
Frias, Jose G., Pfc, PH
Friedman, Arnold R., S/Sgt, PH*
Frising, William R., Pfc, PH
Fritzler, Theodore, Pfc, SS
Frye, Roy M., Pvt, PH, SS
Fucito, Dominick A., Pfc, PH
Fulginiti, Nicholas, Pvt, PH
Fullerton, John M., Pfc, PH
Fumich, George, Jr., 1st Lt, BSM
Furlo, Frank, A., 1st Lt, BSM

Gaffney, Edmund F., Pfc, PH
Gagliano, Thomas D., Pvt, PH*
Gaida, Theodore W., T/Sgt, BSM
Gaines, Bige, Pvt, PH*
Gaiser, Bernard J., Pfc, PH
Galetti, Albert L., Pvt, PH
Gallamore, John E., Pfc, PH
Gallant, Edward J., Pfc, SS
Gilligan, Thomas F., T/5, BSM
Gallinot, John F., Pfc, BSM
Gallo, Thomas, Pfc, BSM
Galow, Oscar G., T/Sgt, BSM
Galvin, William J., Pfc, BSM
Gambardella, Frank T., Pfc, PH
Garbacz, Stanley J., Sgt, PH
Garber, George, S/Sgt, PH
Garcia, Lino, Pfc, BSM
Garcaewski, Edward S., Pvt, PH
Gardenhire, William J., 1st Lt, PH
Gardner, Cecil J., Pvt, PH
Gatnett, Webb J., Pfc, BSM
Garren, Allard L., T/5, PH
Garreston, Donald E., Sgt, PH
Garrett, Ivan B., T/5, BSM
Garris, Delphia E., Pvt, PH
Garrison, Bradford T., 2d Lt, PH
Garza, Eliseo M., S/Sgt, BSM
Garza, Pedro G., Pfc, BSM, PH*
Gasier, Bernard J., Pfc, PH
Gathright, Johnnie, Pfc, SS
Gaul, Robert D., Pfc, BSM
Gaut, James V., 2d Lt, BSM*
Gauthreaux, Gilbert C., Pfc, PH
Gawlik, Edward S., S/Sgt, SS
Gendler, Albert A., Sgt, PH*
Gennell, Charles J., Sgt, SM, BSM
Gensel, Harry P., Pvt, PH
Gervino, Joseph, Sgt, SS, PH
Giandeini, Rodolfo, Pfc, PH
Giadone, Samuel A., Pvt, PH
Giannino, Joseph C., Pfc, PH
Gibaldi, Paul A., Pvt, PH
Gibson, Eugene I., Pvt, BSM
Gibson, James B., Pfc, PH
Gibson, William W., Cpl, BSM
Gierzak, Lucein V., T/Sgt, SS
Gilbert, John A., 1st Lt, PH
Gilbert, Richard J., Sgt, BSM
Gildea, Benedict J., Sgt, PH
Gill, John B., 1st Lt, BSM*
Gill, Robert E., Pfc, PH

Gillespie, Jack D., 1st Lt, BSM, PH
Gillette, Robert W., 1st Lt, PH
Gillis, Willie L., Pvt, PH
Gillum, Charles E., T/5, PH
Gilmore, Alexander R., S/Sgt, BSM
Gilmore, Gentry H., Pfc, PH
Ginsburg, Martin A., T/5, BSM, PH
Gioggia, Adolph E., Jr., Pfc, PH
Gladden, Howard W., Pfc, PH
Glahn, Leon, Pvt, PH
Glass, Alfred D., Pvt, PH
Glass, Dexter M., Pfc, PH
Glass, Raymond W., Sgt, PH
Glass, Russel P., Pvt, BSM
Glatz, John A., Jr., Pvt, PH
Godlewski, Charles T., T/5, BSM
Goertzen, Homer R., T/4, BSM, PH
Goethals, Ferdinand A., Cpl, PH
Goff, Vernon H., Cpl, PH
Golden, James, Sgt, BSM
Golden, Obie M., S/Sgt, PH*
Goldman, Herbert G., Pfc, DSC (Post)
Gombac, John J., Pfc, PH
Gomez, Alfonso M., Pfc, PH
Gomola, John, S/Sgt, PH*
Gonsalves, Francis C., T/Sgt, SS, BSM, (Post),
　PH
Gonzalez, Guadalupe, Sgt, PH
Gonzales, Tomas, Pfc, PH
Goodhart, John J., Pvt, PH
Goodick, Douglas E., Cpl, PH
Goodman, Charles B., Pfc, PH
Gossett, Weldon L., T/Sgt, BSM
Gostecnik, Joe, T/3, PH
Gottlieb, Irving, Pfc, BSM
Gottschling, Robert R., Pvt, PH
Goulet, George L., Pvt, PH
Gourley, Vincent E., Pfc, PH
Gower, Lewis N., Pvt, BSM
Grace, Donald J., Pfc, BSM
Graham, Donald J., Pfc, PH
Graham, James E., Pfc, PH
Granger, Jesse L., Pfc, PH
Grant, Garvin L., Pfc, BSM, PH
Grape, Robert E., S/Sgt, BSM (Post)
Grass, Raymond W., S/Sgt, SS (Post)
Grassel, Charles J., Pvt, PH
Grasty, Hampton, Pvt, PH
Graveley, Claude W., Pfc, PH
Gray, Dallas R., S/Sgt, SS, PH
Gray, Roy E., Capt, BSM*, PH
Greb, Paul T., Pvt, PH
Green, Charles E., Pfc, PH
Greenberg, Milton L., Pvt, PH
Greenbert, Milton L., Pvt, PH
Greene, Beacham F., Jr., Pfc, PH
Greene, Willard C., Pfc, PH
Gregory, Raymond O., Sgt, BSM, SS, PH*
Grenda, Joseph W., Sgt, BSM, PH
Grenier, Ernest M., Sgt, BSM, PH*
Greves, Nelson, Pfc, PH
Gribbon, Raymond T., Pfc, SS, PH
Grice, Joseph V., Pfc, PH
Griego, Leopoldo, Pvt, PH
Griffin, Dale H., Capt, BSM
Griffin, Martin J., Sgt, BSM
Griffith, Frederick T., 1st Lt, SS
Griffith, James W., Pvt, PH
Griffiths, Frederick T., 1st Lt, PH
Griffo, Peter P., Capt, BSM, PH
Grillo, Albert J., Pvt, BSM, PH
Grippo, Ralph N., T/Sgt, BSM*
Griscavage, John, S/Sgt, BSM
Grissinger, Charles J., Pfc, PH*
Grissom, Harold A., Pfc, BSM, PH
Griswold, Robert D., 1st Lt, BSM
Grochowski, Anthony P., T/Sgt, BSM (Post)
Groden, Linus J., S/Sgt, BSM
Grochowski, Anthony P., T/Sgt, PH
Grogan, Forest D., Sgt, PH
Grohman, Charles, Jr., Pfc, PH
Gromacki, Bruno L., Pfc, PH

Gruber, Noel H., T/4, BSM
Grunwald, Thomas F., Cpl, BSM
Guarino, Angelo C., Pfc, PH
Guarino, Adolph P., Pfc, PH
Guarriello, Salvatore J., Pvt, PH
Guerra, Joseph L., S/Sgt, BSM, PH**
Gulbranson, Leland R., Pvt, PH
Gurney, Robert A., T/Sgt, BSM, PH
Gutman, Aaron, T/Sgt, BSM, PH
Guttman, Howard S., Cpl, BSM
Guyton, Thomas L., Pfc, PH
Guzzardi, Raymond, Pfc, PH
Gwiscz, Frank S., Pvt, PH*

Haaff, Orval E., Jr., Pvt, PH
Haddad, Charles, Sgt, PH*
Haddix, Silas B., Pvt, PH
Haegstrom, Floyd A., Capt, BSM, LM
Hafferty, Floyd B., Pfc, PH
Hagmann, Jule C., Pfc, PH, SS
Hahn, Karl W., Cpl, PH
Hairell, Vernon E., Sgt, BSM (Post), PH
Halbert, Milo D., 1st Lt, BSM
Halcomb, Earl, Pvt, PH
Hale, Kenneth E., Pfc, BSM
Hale, Roy C., Pvt, PH
Haley, Roy R., Pfc, BSM
Hall, Alonzo L., Pvt, PH
Hall, Charles W., Pfc, PH
Hall, Cleveland, Pfc, PH
Hall, Eugene J., T/Sgt, PH
Hall, Hubert L., Pfc, PH
Hall, Jefferson E., Pfc, PH
Hall, Noel, S/Sgt, PH*
Hall, Lawrence R., Pfc, PH**
Hall, Robert W., Pvt, PH
Hall, Walter T., Jr., Sgt, BSM, PH*
Hallmark, James F., Pfc, BSM, PH
Halloran, Michael J., Pfc, BSM, PH
Halloway, Elmer, Pfc, PH
Halme, Richard A., Pvt, PH
Halstrom, Howard H., Pvt, PH
Hamilton, Vernon O., Pfc, PH
Hamlin, George, Jr., Pvt, PH
Hamm, Lewis R., S/Sgt, SS, PH
Hamm, Med L., Pfc, PH
Hammond, Donald J., WOJG, BSM
Hampton, Edward S., 1st Lt, PH
Hanan, Oliver M., T/5, PH**
Hand, Paul J., Pfc, BSM, PH
Handwerker, Hyme, Pvt, PH
Handzel, Clarence, Pvt, PH
Haney, Edgar, Pvt, PH
Hanger, Melvin A., S/Sgt, SS
Hankins, Earl M., Pfc, PH
Hanlon, Thomas P., Jr., Pfc, BSM
Hannah, Maurice L., Pfc, PH
Hanner, Howard E., Pfc, PH
Hanscom, Erald W., T/5, BSM
Hansen, Arthur, T/4, BSM
Hansen, Bill H., S/Sgt, PH*
Hanzel, Elmer J., Pfc, PH
Harber, Raymond C., Sgt, PH
Harciarek, Anthony J., Sgt, BSM
Hardesty, Ernest C., S/Sgt, SS
Harding, James K., Pfc, PH
Harland, Alger G., S/Sgt, BSM, PH
Harrington, Donald L., Pfc, BS (Post)
Harris, James P., Jr., Pfc, BSM
Hart, Barbee, Pfc, PH
Hart, Wayne A., Pfc, PH
Hartman, Charles H., Pfc, SS, PH
Hart, Dale A., Pfc, PH
Harver, Robert W., Pfc, PH
Harvey, William, Pfc, BSM
Harwood, Richard, Capt, SS, BSM*
Haselden, Tennyson K., T/Sgt, PH
Haskins, Donald R., Pfc, PH
Hatfield, Sam, Pvt, PH
Hatton, Elbert, S/Sgt, BSM, PH*
Haulk, Ralph, Pfc, PH
Haverty, Robert P., Pfc, PH

Hawkes, Melvin E., Sgt, BSM, PH**
Hawkins, Warren B., Cpl, BSM
Hawrylak, Walter, Pfc, PH
Hayes, Carl W., Pfc, PH
Hayes, James H., Pfc, PH
Haynes, Howard F., Pvt, PH
Hazzard, Donald R., Pfc, PH
Healey, Edward V., T/Sgt, BSM
Healy, George W., Pvt, PH
Healy, Percival I., Pfc, PH
Hearne, James M., Pfc, SS, PH
Hebel, Leonard J., 1st Lt, SS, PH
Heburt, Almos R., Pvt, PH
Heffner, Walter D., Pvt, PH
Heideman, Donald W., Sgt, PH
Heinbaugh, Dayton A., Pfc, PH
Heisler, Oscar G., Pvt, PH
Helmold, Alvin L., Pfc, PH
Henderson, Richard H., Pfc, SS
Hendrickson, Billy G., Sgt, BSM, PH*
Hendrickson, Richard B., Pfc, BSM
Hendrix, William E., Pvt, PH*
Hendrickson, Henry, Pvt, PH
Henry, Norman J., Sgt, PH
Henson, Dick H., Pfc, BSM
Henson, Gordon D., S/Sgt, BSM
Herbert, Charles E., 1st Lt, BSM
Herman, Morris M., Pfc, PH
Hearn, Thomas F., Pfc, PH
Hernandez, Anselmo, Pfc, PH*
Hernandez, Cruz, Pvt, PH
Hernandez, Mauro I., Pfc, BSM, PH
Hernandez, Raymundo, S/Sgt, PH
Herrie, James A., Pvt, PH
Herrigel, Fred, Pfc, BSM
Herrman, Raymond L., Pfc, BSM
Herron, Hugh J., Pfc, PH
Hesse, Burt L., Pfc, PH*
Hessler, Clarence W., WOJG, PH
Hertzog, Werner C., Pvt, PH
Hey, Gordon T., Pvt, PH
Heyman, Sidney, CWO, BSM*
Hicks, Allen E., Pfc, BSM
Hiffmeyer, Kenneth S., Pfc, PH
Higby, Charles, T/5, BSM
Higgins, Patrick J., Pfc, PH*
Hildesheim, Frederick, S/Sgt, BSM
Hill, John L., Pfc, PH
Hill, Ogden H., 1st Lt, BSM, PH*
Hill, William L., Cpl, BSM, PH
Hires, John D., S/Sgt, BSM
Hobbs, Adam, 2nd Lt, BSM
Hocking, George R., Pvt, PH*
Hodgkins, John D., Jr., S/Sgt, PH
Hodgkinson, Howard W., Pfc, PH
Hodgkinson, Melvin J., Pfc, BSM, PH
Hoefling, Norman F., T/4, BSM*
Hoey, Joseph P., Pfc, BSM
Hoff, Donald R., Pfc, PH
Hoffman, George W., Pfc, PH
Hoffman, Jonas V., Pfc, PH
Hofmeister, George R., Pfc, PH
Hogan, Clarence J., T/5, BSM
Hoke, James B., Sgt, PH
Holbeck, Howard, Sgt, PH
Holder, John H., Pfc, PH*
Holderman, Robert L., Pfc, PH
Holestin, Howard B., Pvt, PH
Holland, James G., Jr., Lt Col, BSM
Holland, Preston E., Pvt, PH
Hollenstein, Thomas J., Pfc, PH
Hollingsworth, Marvin C., Pfc, PH
Hollon, Maurice A., Jr., T/5, BSM
Holly, Pinkney H., S/Sgt, PH
Holman, Marlon A., Pfc, PH
Holstein, Curt E., Pvt, PH
Holton, Archie D., Maj, BSM
Homick, Nick, Pfc, PH
Hoobler, Robert E., 1st Lt, BSM
Hood, Oscar O., Pfc, PH
Hooker, Carl O., Pfc, PH
Hopel, Gilbert C., Pvt, PH

Hopkins, Erten O., Pfc, PH
Hopkins, Lyman R., Jr., 1st Lt, PH
Hopper, Charles H., Jr., Pvt, PH*
Hornbaker, Robert F., Pvt, PH*
Horne, Russell H., Pvt, PH
Horner, William L., Pvt, PH
Horowitz, Lawrence, S/Sgt, PH
Horowitz, Marvin C., Pvt, PH
Horvath, Stephen F., Cpl, BSM
Houck, Frederick L., Capt, BSM
Hougam, Donald K., Cpl, BSM
House, Fred, Pfc, BSM
House, Mike, Pfc, PH
Howard, Norman L., Pfc, SS
Hovatter, Duane A., Pfc, PH*
Howard, Thomas L., Pvt, PH
Howarth, William A., Pvt, PH
Howze, Robert M., Pfc, PH
Hoyda, Chester V., S/Sgt, BSM (Post)
Hubbard, J. B., Pfc, PH
Hudson, James R., Pfc, BSM
Huff, Verne R., Sgt, PH
Hughes, Earl B., Pfc, PH
Hughes, James J., Pfc, BSM
Hughes, Kenneth H., S/Sgt, SS, PH
Hughes, Robert E., Pfc, PH
Huizinga, Harold A., Sgt, PH
Hulbert, Max T., 1st Lt, BSM
Hull, Ralph J., Pfc, PH
Hull, Wiley G., Cpl, BSM
Hulshart, John A., Pfc, PH
Humphrey, Harold B., 2nd Lt, BSM*
Hundley, John P., 1st Lt, BSM
Hunsicker, John J., Pvt, PH
Hunt, Elmer L., Pvt, PH
Hunter, Walter L., 1st Lt, PH*
Hunter, William A., Cpl, PH
Huntley, Orrin H., Pfc, PH
Hupka, Nicholas, Sgt, BSM
Hurst, James E., Pfc, BSM
Hurst, William D., Pfc, PH
Hurst, Leon W., Pvt, PH
Hurt, Joseph R., Pfc, BSM, PH
Hutchison, Johnny P., Pvt, PH*
Hutson, Roy L., S/Sgt, BSM, PH
Hutton, Robert G., Pfc, PH
Hyche, James V., T/5, SS (Post)
Hyder, Richard R., Sgt, PH

Iannantuano, Joseph N., Pfc, PH
Iannelli, George O., Cpl, PH
Iannon, Louis J., Pfc, PH
Iatesta, James, Pfc, PH
Imbro, Michael A., Cpl, PH
Infanti, Salvatore, Pvt, PH
Iovanni, Frederico J., S/Sgt, BSM, PH
Isaac, Joseph C., Sgt, BSM
Isham, Fred E., T/5, PH
Isoldi, Frederick G., S/Sgt, BSM, PH
Ison, Willis, Pvt, PH

Jack, Richard, Pvt, PH
Jackson, Harry H., 1st Lt, SS*, BSM, PH
Jackson, James F., Cpl, PH
Jackson, Leonard, T/Sgt, BSM, PH
Jackson, Walter F., T/Sgt, PH
Jacob, Rene J., Pfc, PH
Jacobs, Hughbert J., Pvt, PH
Jacobs, Robert M., Pvt, PH
Jaffe, Filmore, 1st Lt, BSM, PH
Jajko, Bernard, Pfc, BSM
James, Virgil W., Sgt, BSM, PH
Jandreau, William J., Pvt, PH
Janecka, John, Pfc, PH*
Jasperson, David J., T/4, BSM
Jaswell, Nicholas, Pfc, BSM
Jaworek, Etelthed A., Pfc, PH
Jaynes, Frank A., Pfc, PH*
Jean, Gerard J., Sgt, BSM
Jefferson, Hamp, Pvt, PH
Jefferson, Richard M., Pfc, BSM
Jennings, James H., Pfc, BSM

Jennings, Walter D., 1st Lt, BSM
Jeppson, Martin I., Pfc, PH
Jornigan, Oliver L., Pfc, PH
Jewkins, Ellison J., Pfc, PH*
Johns, Myron W., Pfc, PH
Johns, Robert M., Pfc, PH
Johnson, Albert E., T/Sgt, BSM, PH*
Johnson, Alfred L., Pfc, PH
Johnson, Billy E., Pfc, PH*
Johnson, Howard L., 1st Sgt, PH
Johnson, James C., Cpl, PH
Johnson, Leory E., Pfc, BSM
Johnson, Melvin C., Pvt, PH
Johnson, Melvin L., Pvt, PH
Johnson, Millburn F., Pfc, PH
Johnson, Walter W., Cpl, PH
Johnson, Wayne E., S/Sgt, SS, BSM
Jones, Arthur J., Pfc, BSM, PH
Jones, Arthur L., Pfc, PH
Jones, Casey W., Pfc, PH
Jones, Charles A., Pfc, PH
Jones, Edward R., Pvt, PH
Jones, Erwin B., Maj, DSC, SS, BSM, PH
Jones, John W., Pfc, PH
Jones, Marshall W., Pvt, PH
Jones, Oliver D., 2nd Lt, BSM
Jones, Robert E., S/Sgt, BSM
Jones, William L., Sr., Pvt, PH
Jordan, Uhel F., Pvt, PH
Joslin, Ernest C., Sgt, PH
Jurena, Rudolph G., Sgt, PH
Juskaivicas, Henry A., Pfc, BSM
Jutkowitz, Joseph, S/Sgt, PH

Kadis, John J., Pfc, PH
Kahn, Arthur H., 1st Sgt, BSM, PH
Kaiser, Robert J., Pfc, PH
Kaiser, Rudolph W., Pfc, PH
Kalada, Joseph W., S/Sgt, BSM
Kaleka, Walter, Pfc, SS (Post)
Kalil, Edward R., Pfc, PH
Kamm, William K., Pvt, PH
Kapelczak, Leonard A., Pfc, PH
Karageorge, George K., Sgt, PH
Karcher, Howard W., S/Sgt, BSM
Kardisco, Joseph F., Pvt, PH
Karpinski, Edward T., Pvt, PH
Karpowicz, Joseph P., Pfc, PH
Kauffman, Charles G., Pfc, PH
Kavanagh, William T., 1st Lt, PH
Kaye, Julian, Pfc, PH
Kays, Roy F., Pfc, BSM
Kayser, Sam J., Jr., Pfc, PH
Keady, Joseph F., Pvt, PH
Kearsing, Donald R., 2nd Lt, BSM (Post)
Keckeisen, James, 2nd Lt, BSM
Keefer, Clarence L., S/Sgt, BSM, PH
Keel, Harlon B., Pfc, PH
Keen, Loren D., Pfc, BSM, PH
Keeton, William C., Sgt, PH
Keller, Neil, Capt, LM, BSM
Keller, Norman T., Pfc, PH
Kelley, Harry E., Pfc, PH
Kelley, Thomas W., Jr., Pfc, PH
Kellogg, Charles M., Pfc, BSM
Kemp, Homer B., Pfc, PH
Kemp, James F., S/Sgt, BSM
Keniston, Earlon A., Pvt, PH
Kennedy, Carl, Pvt, BSM, PH
Kennedy, Charles K., Sgt, PH
Kennedy, James H., Pfc, PH
Kennedy, Paul W., Pvt, PH
Kentzelman, Richard D., Sgt, PH*
Kephart, Ellsworth W., Pfc, BSM, PH
Kerrigan, Patrick J., S/Sgt, PH
Kerschke, Chester, T/5, BSM
Kertis, George, T/Sgt, BSM, PH
Keyer, Richard G., Pfc, PH
Kidd, Hurshel, T/Sgt, SS, PH
Kidder, Lawrence, Pfc, BSM, PH
Kiedanis, Olegardis, 1st Sgt, LM, PH*
Kierzek, Frank D., Cpl, BSM, PH**

Kiestlinger, Henry, Sgt, PH
Kilmer, Byarm T., Pvt, PH
Kimball, Brewster G., Pfc, PH*
Kincaid, Gilbert H., Pvt, BSM
King, Delmar C., Sgt, BSM, PH
King, Donald A., Pfc, BSM
King, Francis M., Capt, LM, BSM
King, Glenn S., Pfc, BSM
King, Lloyd D., S/Sgt, BSM, PH*
King, Luther L., Pfc, PH
Kinley, Joseph C., S/Sgt, PH
Kirgy, Adouff, 1st Sgt, PH
Kirchner, Robert W., Pfc, PH
Kirkham, Lavaughan, Sgt, PH*
Kitzmiller, Richard D., Pfc, PH
Klaassen, Henry, Jr., Pfc, PH*
Klarsch, Raymond L., Pfc, PH
Kleeman, Sidney, Pfc, PH
Klein, Robert R., Pfc, PH
Klein, Robert R., T/4, BSM, PH
Klein, Roman J., T/Sgt, PH
Kleinberg, Charles, 2nd Lt, PH
Kelement, Joseph R., T/Sgt, BSM
Klick, Walter R., S/Sgt, BSM, PH
Kliczewski, Edwin L., Pfc, PH
Klinge, William E., Pvt, PH
Knebel, Richard M., Pvt, PH
Kneiss, Michael, S/Sgt, BSM
Kneller, Russell C., Pfc, PH
Knight, Louis M., Pvt, PH
Knight, Stanley R., Pfc, BSM
Knop, Harry R., Pvt, PH
Knott, Eugene T., Pvt, PH
Knox, Thomas G., Pfc, PH*
Knudson, Bernard B., Pvt, PH
Knduson, Milton A., Pfc, SM
Koch, Frank J., Sgt, PH
Kochenour, Robert, Sgt, BSM
Kocjan, Frank J., 1st Sgt, BSM
Kodnia, William, S/Sgt, PH
Koenigsamen, Joseph P., Cpl, PH
Kolacki, William C., Pfc, PH
Komatinsky, Louis S., S/Sgt, PH
Konewal, Joseph S., Pvt, PH
Koonce, Richard J., Sgt, PH
Koopman, Bruce R., Sgt, BSM, PH*
Kosiba, Walter G., S/Sgt, BSM, PH
Kosinski, Edward J., Pfc, BSM
Kosko, Edward, Pvt, PH
Kosloski, William C., Pfc, PH
Kosmyna, Steven M., T/Sgt, DSC, SS, PH
Kottwitz, Earl A., Pfc, PH
Kovacek, Edward S., Pvt, PH
Kovaleski, Joseph S., S/Sgt, PH*
Krafton, Frederick W., Sgt, BSM, PH
Kramer, Linwood H., Pfc, PH*
Kranz, Dallas E., T/4, BSM
Krause, Kenneth A., Pvt, PH
Krek, Felix F., Pfc, PH
Krier, William H., Pfc, PH
Kroes, Robert H., S/Sgt, PH
Krueger, Roy E., Pfc, BSM
Kruger, Carl, S/Sgt, BSM
Kruger, John H., Pfc, PH
Kruse, Kenneth C., Pvt, PH
Kubek, Joseph, Jr., T/5, BSM
Kuhn, Jack R., Pfc, PH
Kuhr, Raymond C. F., Pvt, PH
Kulik, Stanley P., Pfc, BSM, PH
Kuntz, Harvey M., Pfc, PH*
Kunzelman, Edward G., Jr., 1st Lt, BSM
Kurczy, Michael, T/5, BSM, PH
Kurz, James R., 1st Lt, BSM, PH
Kurzawa, Harry B., Pfc, PH

LaBarr, James E., Pfc, PH
Lacroix, Fernand M., S/Sgt, SS
LaFlame, Loyal, Pvt, PH
La Fontaine, Alfred, Pfc, PH
LaFortune, John L., S/Sgt, BSM
Lagowski, Stanley, Sgt, PH
Lahey, Louis E., Cpl, PH

Lahti, Henry W., S/Sgt, BSM, PH
Laird, Robert L., Pvt, BSM
Lama, Joseph H., 2nd Lt, PH**
LaManna, Rocco P., S/Sgt, PH
La Matta, Vincent J., Pfc, BSM
Lambers, Harold N., 1st Lt, BSM, PH
Lambert, Robert G., Pvt, PH
Lamela, Herbert J., Sgt, PH
Lampe, Elmer F., 1st Sgt, PH*
Lamsa, John E., S/Sgt, BSM
Lancaster, Ibby J., Capt, PH**
Lancaster, Jerral E., S/Sgt, BSM
Landry, Allen E., 1st Lt, PH
Landry, Joseph L., Pvt, PH*
Lane, William W., Pfc, BSM, PH
Lang, Perley E., Jr., Pfc, PH
Langmier, Robert B., Pvt, SS
Langston, Willard L., Pfc, PH
Lanius, John C., Cpl, PH
Lanz, Robert D., Pfc, BSM
Lapiska, Steve, Pfc, PH
Larson, Walter E., Pfc, PH
Lassen, James P., Sgt, PH
Latva, Eino E., Pfc, BSM
Laufenberg, Mitchell M., S/Sgt, BSM
Laura, Rejies L., Pvt, PH
Laurence, Charles H., Cpl, PH
Law, John F., Pfc, PH
Law, Robert F., Pvt, BSM, PH
Lawes, Russell E., S/Sgt, BSM
Lawrence, Leo F., T/4, BSM
Lawson, Phillip, Pvt, PH
LeBrasseur, Leo J., Pvt, PH
Lee, Francis X. J., 1st Lt, BSM (Post)
Lee, Howard E., Capt, BSM, PH
Lee, King, Pfc, SS, PH*
Lee, Leland L., Sgt, BSM
Lee, William S., Pfc, PH*
Leeson, Clarence, Pfc, BSM
Lefevre, Everett J., Pvt, PH
Lehman, James J., Sgt, PH
Leick, Edward P., Pvt, PH
Leitzel, Arthur S., Pvt, PH
Lemaire, George A., Pfc, PH
LeMay, Gerald J., Sgt, BSM, PH
Lembke, Alfred L., Pfc, PH
Lemieux, Albert R., Pfc, PH
Lemon, Ralph J., Sgt, PH
Le Munyan, Charles B., Pfc, PH
Lenker, Arnold D., Pvt, PH
Lenker, Richard F., Pfc, PH
Lennon, Richard F., Sgt, PH*
Lents, William G., S/Sgt, PH
Leogrande, Martin C., T/4, BSM
Leonard, Arthur S., S/Sgt, BSM
Leone, Nickolas, Pfc, BSM
Lerma, Alejos, Sgt, PH*
Lerner, Irving, Pfc, PH
Lesnick, Charles E., 2nd Lt, SS, PH
Leszkowicz, Peter J., Pfc, PH
Levasseur, Roland A., Pvt, BSM
Leverett, Jasper N., Jr., Pfc, PH
Levesque, Ralph O., Pvt, PH
Levi, John E., Pvt, PH
Levin, Donald A., Pfc, PH
Levy, Harry, T/4, SS (Post), PH
Lewis, Arthur F., T/4, BSM
Lewis, Eugene C., T/Sgt, PH*
Lewis, James J., Pvt, PH
Leyman, John E., S/Sgt, PH
Libordi, Frank A., S/Sgt, BSM
Liddell, John W., Jr., Pfc, PH
Liller, Lemoine, Pvt, PH
Lin, Fook, Pvt, PH
Lindsey, V. H., Jr., Pfc, PH
Linthorn, Jack E., Pfc, PH
Lipps, Howard M., Pfc, PH
Lis, John A., Pfc, PH
Lissi, Alfred J., Pvt, PH
Lively, Leonard E., Pvt, PH
Livengood, Paul E., PH
Lloyd, Jack R., Pfc, PH

Locasto, Anthony C., Pvt, PH
Lockhart, Loney A., Pfc, PH
Loden, Dannie R., Pfc, PH*
Loeffler, Louis J., Pvt, PH
Lofquist, Stanley G., T/5, BSM
Loia, Louis S., Pfc, PH
Lombrana, Jose M. F., Cpl, BSM
Long, Julius V., S/Sgt, BSM, PH
Looney, Robert K., T/5, PH
Lopez, Desiderio, Pvt, PH
Lopez, Joe W., T/4, BSM
Lorenz, Donald R., Pvt, PH
Lott, Anthony B., Sgt, BSM
Loughlin, John J., Pvt, PH
Lowe, Bertram, Pfc, PH
Lowe, Willard B., Pfc, PH
Lozier, Bernard A., T/Sgt, PH
Lucca, Anthony L., S/Sgt, BSM, PH*
Ludtka, Bernard A., Cpl, BSM, PH*
Ludwig, Robert D., Pvt, SS
Lukasik, John P., Pfc, PH
Lundgren, Richard A., Pfc, PH
Lunsford, James V., S/Sgt, PH**
Lurz, Alfred E., Pfc, BSM
Lusk, Roy H., 1st Sgt, SS
Luttrell, Herman E., Pfc, BSM, PH
Lynch, Charles P., Col, BSM, PH
Lynch, Charles P., Jr., Capt, DSC (Post), BSM, PH
Lynch, Ralph R., Sgt, BSM, PH
Lynch, Robert J., Pfc, PH
Lyons, John J., Pvt, PH**
Lyons, Paul J., Sgt, PH

MacDonald, Augustine G., Capt, SS, BSM*, PH**
MacDonald, Francis J., T/Sgt, BSM*
MacDonald, Paul C., S/Sgt, SS (Post), PH
Mace, Lester, T/4, PH
MacIntosh, Norbert E., S/Sgt, BSM
MacIvor, Richard J., T/5, BSM
Mackin, John J., Pfc, BSM, PH
Madden, Oakley, S/Sgt, BSM
Madison, Emery C., Sgt, BSM, PH*
Madlock, Robert W., Pfc, BSM, PH
Madsen, Emil, Sgt, BSM
Maers, James J., T/5, BSM
Mager, Leonard S., Sgt, SS, PH
Maglione, Alfred J., Sgt, BSM
Mahaffey, William I., Pfc, PH
Maher, Edmund D., 1st Lt, SS (Post), PH*
Maher, Edward J., Capt, SS, PH*
Maher, Francis J., Pfc, BSM
Maher, Francis X., Pvt, BSM, PH
Mahoney, John B., T/5, BSM
Maiden, Clarence D., Cpl, PH
Maier, Fred W., Pfc, SS
Majeski, Frank A., Pfc, PH
Majewski, Edwin R., Pfc, PH
Majewski, Frank C., Cpl, PH
Major, Benjamin E., Pfc, BSM
Majure, Troy V., Capt, BSM, PH
Malec, Raymond J., Pfc, PH
Malley, Walter J., Pfc, PH*
Mallory, Delmar R., S/Sgt, PH
Malosky, Alex M., Pfc, PH
Mancuso, Pascuale A., Pfc, PH*
Manley, Clyde, Pfc, SS, PH
Mann, Glenn W., Pfc, PH
Manning, John E., Pfc, BSM
Manseau, Adelard J., Pfc, PH
Manson, Herbert C., T/Sgt, LM
Mansur, Kenneth J., Pfc, PH
Manville, Wilfred L., Pfc, PH
Manwaring, Robert S., Pvt, PH
Marashio, John J., Pvt, PH
Marcello, Antonio A., Pfc, PH
Marsh, Odis D., Pvt, PH
Marchese, Joseph B., Pfc, PH
Marek, Frank J., 1st Lt, BSM, PH
Marek, Frank J., S/Sgt, BSM, PH**
Marelli, Harry P., Sgt, BSM

Marino, Vincenzo, 1st Sgt, BSM, PH*
Markell, James L., Pfc, BSM
Markowitz, Jack, Pvt, PH
Marlow, Clarence, Pfc, PH
Marquez, Arthur M., Pfc, BSM
Marron, Samuel, Pfc, BSM, PH
Marsallo, Anthony A., Pfc, PH*
Marshall, George L., Pfc, PH
Marshall, William S., S/Sgt, PH
Martin, Cecil, S/Sgt, SS (Post)
Martin, Freddie L., S/Sgt, BSM
Martin, James J., Pfc, PH
Martin, John N., S/Sgt, BSM, PH
Martin, Joseph B., T/5, BSM, SS, PH*
Martin, Robert R., 1st Lt, PH
Martin, Robert L., S/Sgt, BSM, PH
Martinez, Joe A., Pvt, PH
Martinez, Joe R., Pvt, PH
Martinez, Paul, Pfc, PH
Martone, Joseph A., Pfc, PH
Martz, Charles E., Pfc, BSM
Martz, Frank, Jr., Pvt, PH
Marusak, Thomas B., Pvt, PH
Marusiak, Joseph S., Cpl, PH
Marzec, Steve J., Pvt, PH
Masella, James V., Pfc, PH
Mason, Charles, Pfc, BSM, PH
Massa, Shelia, D., Pfc, BSM
Massaro, John A., S/Sgt, PH
Massarone, Anthony, T/Sgt, PH
Massi, John J., Pfc, PH
Mathes, Ira A., Pvt, PH
Mathis, Acie M., Pvt, PH
Mattey, Frank J., 1st Lt, BSM*
Matthevys, Edward J., T/5, PH
Matthews, Milton A., Major, PH*, BSM
Matthias, James S., CWO, BSM
Matthews, Edward J., T/5, BSM
Matuyza, Edward J., Pfc, PH*
Mattoon, Edward S., Cpl, BSM
Maughan, Charles F., Pfc, PH
Maxa, Albert, Pfc, BSM, PH
Maxia, Robert R., Pfc, PH
Maxwell, Max R., Sgt, PH
Maxwell, William T., Pfc, BSM
May, Wayland, Pfc, BSM
Mayo, Sam, T/Sgt, SS
Mazzarella, Beni B., 2nd Lt, SS, PH*
McAllister, Lloyd A., Pfc, PH
Mc Ardle, John M., Pfc, SS, PH*
McArthur, John P., Pfc, PH
McBrayer, George M., Pfc, SS (Post), PH
Mc Burnie, Ernest F., Pvt, PH
Mc Cabe, Harry V., 1st Lt, BSM
McCarthy, Junior F., Pfc, PH
Mc Carthy, Walter F., S/Sgt, PH*
Mc Causland, Edwin L., Jr., Pvt, PH
Mc Clain, Robert M., Pfc, PH*
Mc Clanaghan, Robert, Pfc, BSM
Mc Collum, Vestal P., 1st Lt, BSM, SS, PH
Mc Combie, Alexander, Pfc, PH
Mc Conaghy, Thomas M., Pvt, PH
Mc Connell, John C., Pfc, PH
Mc Connaughey, Floyd J., Cpl, BSM
Mc Cormack, Terence P., Cpl, BSM
Mc Gough, Charles H., Pfc, PH
Mc Cuiston, John J., Pvt, PH
Mc Cuiston, Macon H., Pfc, PH
Mc Dade, Ralph R., Pfc, SS, PH
Mc Daniels, Alvin L., Pfc, BSM, PH*
Mc Dermott, Joseph M., Cpl, BSM
Mc Donald, Daniel J., Pvt, PH
Mc Donald, Horace J., Pvt, PH
Mc Donald, Leroy B., Pfc, PH
Mc Donald, Robert C., Pfc, PH
Mc Donald, Walter L., Pfc, BSM
Mc Duffee, Merle S., Pfc, PH
Mc Gettrick, Thomas F., Sgt, PH
Mc Gregor, Jay B., Pvt, PH
Mc Guinness, James J., Pvt, PH
Mc Kenna, Harold R., Pfc, BSM
Mc Kenzie, John W., Sgt, BSM, PH

Mc Keon, Bernard F., Pvt, PH
Mc Knight, Charles W., Pvt, PH
Mc Laughlin, Bernard L., Pvt, PH
Mc Laughlin, Timothy R., Pfc, BSM, PH
Mc Cluskey, Edward J., Pvt, PH
Mc Mahon, George E., T/5, BSM
Mc Mahon, Paul E., Pvt, PH
Mc Millan, Thomas, Pvt, PH*
Mc Mullen, Robert, Cpl, BSM
Mc Mullins, Marshall J., WOJG, BSM
Mc Nac, Walter, Pfc, PH
Mc Olphin, Dwight, Pvt, PH
Mc Omber, Benjamin F., S/Sgt, PH*
Mc Peters, George W., Pvt, PH
Mc Pherson, James T., Pvt, PH
Mc Quaig, Russell J., Pfc, PH
Mc Shane, Edward J., Pfc, PH
Mc Whorter, Julius B., Pfc, BSM
Mc Nelis, Anthony P., Pfc, PH
Meadows, George E., 1st Lt, BSM, SS, PH
Medynski, Rudolph, Cpl, PH
Meehan, Donald A., Pvt, BSM
Meehan, John F., Pfc, BSM, PH
Meisner, Frederick F., Pvt, PH
Mefford, Jack J., S/Sgt, SS
Meldrum, Wilmer J., S/Sgt, SS, PH***
Meledeo, Arthur A., Cpl, PH
Mendoza, Manuel V., T/Sgt, DSC
Mierzejewski, Casimir, Pfc, PH
Merrick, James J., Sgt, BSM
Mertzic, Paul P., Pfc, PH
Mesplie, Walter J., Pfc, PH*
Messer, George, Pvt, PH
Mestas, Felix B., Jr., Pfc, SS (Post)
Metrow, Edward L., Pfc, PH
Meverah, Joseph, Pfc, PH
Meyers, James C., S/Sgt, PH
Michael, Marshall P., Pvt, PH
Michetti, Joseph H., Pfc, SS, PH
Michelsson, Leo, Pvt, PH
Middendorf, Albert, Pfc, PH*
Middlebrook, Lawrence W., 1st Sgt, BSM
Mike, Drew S/Sgt SS (Post)
Miklos, George B., Pvt, PH
Miller, Albert J., T/4, BSM
Miller, Charles W., Pfc, PH
Miller, Claude L., Pfc, PH
Miller, Clifford, T/5, BSM, PH
Miller, Elwood L., Pfc, PH*
Miller, Francis M., 2nd Lt, PH
Miller, Frank W., Sgt, BSM
Miller, Harold E., S/Sgt, SS (Post)
Miller, Harold W., Pvt, PH
Miller, Howard, Pfc, SS
Miller, James E., S/Sgt, SS (Post)
Miller, Lawrence J., S/Sgt, BSM*
Miller, Luther R., Sgt, PH**
Miller, Michael J., S/Sgt, PH
Miller, Robert G., T/5, PH
Miller, Robert R., 1st Lt, PH*
Millet, Henry G., Pvt, PH*
Milliman, John R., Pfc, PH
Millington, Otis M., Pfc, PH
Mills, Vernon E., Pfc, PH*
Millspaugh, Robert C., 1st Lt, BSM, PH
Miloslavich, Carl M., Pfc, SS
Milot, Roger P., Sgt, BSM
Milstein, David, Pvt, PH*
Milvet, Joseph A., Pfc, PH*
Minnick, Joseph, Pfc, PH*
Minthorn, Jack E., Pfc, PH*
Minton, John W., Pvt, PH
Mioduszewski, Francis P., Pvt, PH
Miranda, Antonio, Sgt, PH*
Mis, Chester, S/Sgt, BSM, PH*
Miscavage, John E., Pvt, PH
Misicka, Jerome J., Pfc, PH*
Misitano, Vincent J., Sgt, PH
Miskinis, John J., 1st Lt, PH
Missaggia, Peter J., Pfc, BSM, PH*
Missey, Clifford L., Pfc, PH
Mitchell, George T., Pfc, BSM

Mitchell, James N., Pfc, BSM, PH
Mitchell, John B., S/Sgt, BSM
Mizzel, Clinton, Pvt, PH
Mockovak, John, Pfc, PH
Modlin, J. P., Pvt, PH
Moley, Edward R., Cpl, BSM
Molina, Jesus R., Pfc, PH
Moll, Luke E., Pvt, PH
Monaco, Gerald A., Pfc, PH
Monismith, John R., Pvt, PH
Moniz, Manuel J., Jr., S/Sgt, PH
Monk, Herman G., Sgt, BSM
Monsees, Walter L., Pvt, PH
Montano, Edward G., S/Sgt, BSM* PH
Montenelli, Benedice R., Pvt, PH
Montero, Andrew J., Pfc, PH
Montie, Floyd S., Pfc, PH*
Montoya, Jake T., S/Sgt, BSM (Post)
Mooradian, Egiso, Pfc, PH
Moore, Herbert E., Pfc, PH
Moore, Roy G., S/Sgt, BSM
Moran, Paul J., Sgt, PH*
Mordecai, John T., Pfc, SS, PH
Moreno, Francisco R., Sgt, PH
Morey, Joe V., Capt, BSM
Morgan, Elvin H., Pfc, PH
Morgan, Harry T., Pfc, PH
Morgan, Lawrence, Pvt, PH
Morgan, Milton, Pfc, PH
Morgan, Paul J., Sgt, PH
Morgan, Ross H., Pfc, SS, PH*
Morgan, Thomas O., Pvt, PH
Morgan, Wallace A., Pvt, PH
Morin, Hector G., Cpl, BSM
Morlan, John P., Pfc, BSM
Moroz, Edmund J., Pvt, PH
Morris, Francis X., Pvt, PH
Morris, James L., Pvt, BSM, PH
Morrison, Homer D., 1st Lt, BSM
Morrison, James H., Pfc, PH
Morse, Stanley M., 2nd Lt, PH
Mortimer, Leslie A., Pfc, PH*
Morton, Hirsh E., Pfc, BSM, PH
Moscaritolo, Rocco, Pfc, BSM
Mosier, Floyd L., Jr., Sgt, PH
Moskalik, Alvin L., Pfc, PH
Mosley, Hugh, S/Sgt, PH**
Moss, Robert, Pvt, PH
Mosso, Martin, Pvt, PH
Moszczynski, Theodore C., 2nd Lt, PH*
Motley, Halvin C., Pvt, PH
Mottola, Antonio F., T/4, BSM
Moulton, Olive, Pfc, PH
Mount, Johnnie, Sgt, PH
Moynihan, Cornelius, Pvt, PH
Mozingo, Roule C., 1st Lt, PH
Mudge, Lavern H., Pvt, PH
Mull, Allen L., Pfc, PH
Mulford, Herbert H., Pvt, PH
Mullins, George H., Pvt, PH
Mulvehill, Arthur P., T/5, BSM
Mundhenk, Henry W., T/5, BSM, PH*
Munsey, Jack S., Pfc, PH*
Murillo, Leslie, Pfc, BSM
Murphy, Charles E., Pvt, PH
Murphy, Gene A., Pvt, PH
Murphy, Joseph T., 2nd Lt, SS, PH
Murphy, Thomas B., Pvt, BSM, PH
Murphy, Thomas F., Pfc, PH
Murphy, Thomas J., Pvt, PH
Murillo, Peter, Pfc, PH
Musacchi, Louis, S/Sgt, PH*
Muscatello, William, T/5, PH
Mushman, Paul J., T/5, PH
Musnicki, Edward A., Sgt, PH
Moeller, Lester C., S/Sgt, BSM
Musolff, Richard C., S/Sgt, PH
Muston, Donald E., 1st Lt, DSC, PH*
Mutkala, Edwin V., Pfc, PH
Myer, Robert B., Pvt, PH
Myers, Harry S., Pfc, PH

Myers, Russell G., S/Sgt, PH
Myrshall, Henry J., Jr., S/Sgt, PH

Nagle, Charles J., Pfc, PH
Nalee, Raymond J., Pfc, PH
Napoli, Mendes L., Pfc, PH
Narhi, Donald L., Pfc, PH
Nash, Joseph S., 2nd Lt, BSM, PH
Navejar, Alejos, O., Pfc, PH*
Navin, Donald L., Pfc, BSM*
Neaton, Clair P., Pvt, PH*
Nedoroscik, Andrew T., 1st Sgt, BSM
Neely, Richard J., T/Sgt, SS
Nelson, Clarence C., Pfc, PH
Nelson, George K., Capt, BSM, PH
Nelson, Russell H., Pfc, PH
Nemergut, George J., Sgt, BSM
Nemeth, Lyle K., Pvt, BSM
Nesbitt, Robert J., Pfc, PH
Nessen, Henry G., Pvt, SS, PH
Neth, Marcus F., Pfc, PH
Netherland, Nelson, Pvt, PH
Nettles, Albert A., Capt, BSM (Post)
Neuman, Walter J., Sgt, BSM
Nevares, Juan A., Pvt, PH
Nevedal, Joseph S., Cpl, PH
Newman, Walter T., Capt, BSM
Nichols, Stanley E., Sgt, PH
Nicholson, Arthur A., Pfc, PH
Nicholson, Bill H., Sgt, BSM, PH
Nickerson, James D., Sgt, BSM
Niemi, Archie A., S/Sgt, SS, PH
Nimmo, Stuart F., Pfc, BSM
Nix, Claude D., Pvt, PH
Noga, Frank A., S/Sgt, BSM*
Nolan, Harold E., Pvt, PH
Noll, Marvin A., Pfc, SS, PH
Noonan, John J., T/Sgt, BSM
Norris, Farold R., Sgt, PH*
Norton, Lewis, T/Sgt, PH
Nosal, Albert G., Pvt, PH
Novak, Joseph, Pvt, PH
Novik, Arthur W., Pfc, PH
Nuessle, Marvin, Pvt, PH
Nugent, Thomas W., 1st Lt, BSM*
Nutt, Carl E., Pvt, PH
Nye, Francis E., Pvt, PH

Obarowski, Stephen V., T/5, BSM
O'Brien, Albert M., Pfc, PH
O'Brien, John P., Pfc, BSM
O'Byrne, Harold, Pvt, PH*
Occhipinti, Joseph W., Pfc, PH
Ochenkowski, Joseph J., T/Sgt, BSM*
O'Connell, Milton J., Sgt, BSM
O'Connor, John, Sgt, BSM
O'Connor, John R., T/Sgt, BSM, PH
O'Connor, John T., Sgt, BSM
Odell, Ervin, Pvt, PH
Odell, L. D., Pfc, BSM, PH*
Odelson, Oscar, Pfc, PH
Ofcharsky, John S., Pfc, PH
Oglesby, James A., Pfc, PH
O'Grady, Robert, Pfc, PH
O'Haier, William A., Pvt, PH
O'Hanlon, Owen, Cpl, BSM
O'Hara, Reece R., Pfc, PH*
Oldham, Junior A., T/Sgt, BSM
Olguin, Julian S., Pfc, PH
Oliphant, Roscoe A., T/4, PH
Oliver, Benjamin O., Pfc, PH
Olszewski, Harry, Pvt, PH
O'Malley, Vincent A., Pfc, PH*
Ordway, Arnold D., Pfc, PH
Orebaugh, Evert T., 2nd Lt, BSM*, PH
Oreskovich, Mike J., Major, BSM
O'Rielly, Thomas J., Pvt, PH
Orloff, Elmer W., Pvt, PH
Orosco, Onofre, C., Pvt, PH
O'Rourke, Phillip E., Pfc, PH
Orrell, Harold B., Cpl, PH
Orsak, Martin R., Pfc, PH

Orsini, Ransone J., Pvt, PH*
Ortegon, Mauro, Pfc, PH
Osborn, Donald E., Pvt, PH
Osborne, Joseph L., T/Sgt, LM, PH*
Osman, Gustave W., Pfc, PH
Ostaczeski, Michael L., Sgt, PH*
Ostrander, Albert S., 1st Lt, BSM, PH
Ott, William P., Capt, PH
Ovren, Randal M., Pfc, PH
Owens, Edward T., Pfc, BSM, PH
Oslust, Leo J., Pvt, PH

Pabilionis, John J., Pvt, PH
Pablo, Lopes, Pvt, PH
Pachniak, Edward, Pvt, PH
Paclawski, Walter J., 1st Lt, BSM
Paddick, Floyd L., T/5, SS, PH
Paddock, Sylvester M., T/Sgt, BSM, PH
Padilla, Fred E., Sgt, PH*
Page, Arley D., Pvt, PH
Page, Everett D., Pvt, PH
Page, Wallard D., Pvt, BSM
Paige, Murrell O., Pfc, PH
Painter, Harry V., Pvt, SS (Post)
Palazzi, Joseph A., Pfc, PH
Palestro, Salvatore, Pvt, PH
Palewitz, William, T/5, BSM, PH
Palladino, Ralph S., Pfc, PH
Palmer, Louis L., Pfc, PH
Palmer, Russell W., Pfc, PH
Palmer, Thomas F., T/5, BSM
Palmeri, Sebastian F., Pfc, PH
Panateri, Ernest J., Pfc, PH
Paniek, Stanley, Pvt, PH
Papa, Dominick C., T/Sgt, BSM*, PH*
Pappapetrou, George P., Pfc, BSM
Pappas, James O., Sgt, BSM, PH
Paradis, Arthur T., Pfc, BSM, PH*
Pardun, Laurence W., Pvt, PH
Parker, Albert C., S/Sgt, BSM (Post)
Parker, Edward F., Pvt, PH*
Parker, Philip D., Jr., Pfc, PH
Parks, Rupert C., S/Sgt, BSM
Parlin, Laurel E., Pfc, PH
Parnell, Donald L., Pvt, PH
Parr, Raymond W., Cpl, PH
Parrish, Frank W., Pfc, PH
Parsons, Archie L., S/Sgt, PH*
Parsons, Arvel C., Pfc, PH
Parsons, Clarence B., Pvt, PH
Parsons, Lawrence P., Pvt, PH
Partin, Clarence M., Pfc, PH
Partridge, Kenneth J., Pvt, PH
Paskvan, Cosmo D., Jr., Pfc, PH
Passalacqua, Salvatore, Pfc, PH
Passamonte, Anthony A., Sgt, PH
Passick, Joseph V., Pvt, PH
Pastina, Joseph C., Pfc, PH
Patrick, Arthur S., Pvt, PH
Patrow, Marvin A., Pvt, PH
Patterson, Edger L., Jr., Pvt, PH
Patterson, Joseph M., Jr., 1st Sgt, BSM, PH
Patuszynski, Chester, 1st Sgt, BSM
Patti, Anthony, 2nd Lt, SS
Paul, Stanley A., Pfc, PH
Pavese, Joseph M., Pvt, PH*
Pavlock, Theodore, Pvt, PH
Payer, Frank W., 1st Lt, PH
Paune, Clifford A., 1st Lt, BSM, PH**
Payne, John S., Pfc, PH
Payne, Preston H., Pfc, PH
Payton, Emmit C., Pfc, PH
Peach, Arthur E., Jr., S/Sgt, BSM
Pearce, Ralph A., Pfc, PH
Pedigo, Ralph J., Pvt, PH
Peek, Cleo, Pfc, SS*
Pelican, Otto J., Sgt, BSM
Pelkey, Robert H., T/5, BSM, PH
Pelletier, Joseph J., Pfc, BSM
Penberg, Jerome R., Pvt, BSM, PH*
Pennington, George W., Pfc, PH
Pennington, Ted I., Pvt, PH*

Pensel, Ralph A., 1st Lt, PH
Pepper, Kenneth, S/Sgt, BSM (Post), PH
Perchway, Melvin V., Pfc, PH
Perdue, Ira, Jr., Pfc, PH
Perez, Antonio B., S/Sgt, PH
Pergrem, Virgil, T/Sgt, PH
Perillo, Dominick, Pvt, PH
Perkins, Henry, Pfc, SS, BSM, PH
Perriman, William E., Pfc, BSM, PH
Perrin, Kermit F., Maj, PH
Perry, Edward, Pfc, BSM
Perry, Francis, Pfc, PH
Perry, Howard D., Pvt, PH
Pescod, Dennis N., Pfc, BSM
Pete, Patty, Pfc, PH
Peters, Leon J., Pfc, PH
Peters, Edward R., Pvt, PH
Peterson, Harry V., Pfc, PH
Peterson, Milo M., Pfc, PH
Petroacco, Victor J., Pvt, BSM
Petratuona, Joseph V., Pfc, PH
Petrilich, Michael J., S/Sgt, PH
Petrouski, Frank, Pfc, PH
Petrouski, Stanley, Pfc, PH*
Petruzzelli, Pasquale F., Pvt, PH
Pettegrow, Earl L., S/Sgt, PH
Peyron, John, Jr., Sgt, BSM
Phelps, Chester C., Pfc, PH
Phelps, Jesse F., Pfc, PH
Phenis, George M., Pvt, PH
Phillips, Donald O., Pfc, PH
Phillips, James T., Pvt, PH
Phillips, Noah A., Pfc, PH
Phillips, Robert C., Pfc, PH
Phillips, Wayne E., S/Sgt, BSM, PH
Phillips, Verner, Pvt, PH
Phillips, William J., Pfc, PH
Piazza, Austin T., Pvt, PH
Piazza, Nathan, Pvt, PH
Piecuch, Walter C., Pvt, PH
Pickard, Norman E., Pvt, PH
Pickens, Joe W., T/4, PH
Pickering, Curtis R., T/5, PH*
Pieniazek, Edward J., Pfc, PH
Pierce, Ralph E., Pfc, PH
Pietrowski, Charles S., Sgt, BSM
Pignotti, Egnazio V. Z., Pvt, PH
Pillard, Clarence L., Pfc, PH
Pingarelli, Nicholas J., Pvt, PH
Pinnick, Wallace A., S/Sgt, PH**
Pippi, Angelo W., Pfc, BSM, SS (Post)
Pires, Raymond, Pfc, PH
Pisarek, Chester J., Pfc, PH
Pittman, James N., Pvt, PH
Pitts, Edgar, T/5, BSM
Pitts, James B., S/Sgt, PH
Plank, Donald E., T/3, BSM*
Plank, Roger E., 1st Sgt, BSM*, PH
Plant, Norby D., Pvt, PH
Platt, Raymond E., Pfc, SS, PH
Plezia, Mike E., Pfc, BSM, PH
Plunkett, James E., Pfc, PH
Pochter, Sidney A., Pfc, PH
Polak, Frank J., Pfc, PH
Polewarczyk, Stanley A., Pvt, PH
Polinski, John, Jr., Cpl, PH
Politowski, Leo B., T/4, PH
Pollock, Robert J., Sgt, PH
Polly, Roy T., Pvt, PH*
Pontone, Enrico H., Pfc, BSM, PH*
Pope, Clyde F., Capt, BSM, PH*
Porta, Paschal G., Pfc, PH
Porter, Ernest C., Jr., Pvt, PH*
Porter, Ervin, Jr., Pfc, PH
Porter, George O., Pfc, SS, PH
Porter, George R., Jr., Pfc, PH
Portillo, William, Pvt, PH
Porto, Saturno, Sgt, PH
Poschke, William G., Pvt, PH
Posey, George R., Pvt, PH
Post, Walter W., Pfc, PH
Potratz, Arnold H., Pfc, PH

Powell, Hyrum R., Pfc, PH
Powell, Ira E., Pvt, PH
Powell, Maurice O., 1st Sgt, PH*
Powers, James C., 1st Lt, PH
Powers, James H., Pvt, PH
Powers, Joseph W., Pfc, PH
Powers, Ralph J., Capt, BSM
Powers, Thomas E., S/Sgt, SS, PH
Praegitzer, Walter, Pfc, PH
Prah, William F., Jr., 1st Sgt, BSM
Prater, William H., Sgt, BSM, PH
Prentice, Maurice C., Pfc, PH
Pressly, Henry E., Capt, BSM*
Preston, Carl, Pfc, PH
Prezlak, Maurice G., Pfc, PH
Price, Benjamin J., 1st Lt, BSM
Price, Elmer C., Pfc, SS, PH
Price, Thomas V., Pvt, PH
Pridemore, Marshall D., Pfc, PH
Priebe, Edward L., Pfc, PH
Priest, David C., Pfc, PH
Priestley, Norman, S/Sgt, PH
Primorose, John J., Pvt, PH*
Prior, Robert L., Pfc, BSM
Pritchard, James A., Pvt, PH
Proctor, John H., Jr., Pfc, PH
Proffitt, Lawrence H., Pvt, PH
Provencher, Philip L., T/5, BSM
Pruessing, Walter W., Pfc, PH
Pruitt, James E., Pvt, PH
Pruitt, Lawrence O., Pvt, PH
Pryor, Louis L., Pfc, PH*
Puckett, Lewie D., Sr., Pvt, PH
Puckett, Warren H., Pvt, PH
Pudleiner, Raymond J., Pfc, SS Post)
Pudsey, Frederic H., Sgt, PH*
Pupek, Frank, Jr., S/Sgt, PH*
Purtell, James J., Jr., Pfc, PH
Purvis, George F., T/Sgt, SS, BSM, PH
Putman, Berman J., Pvt, PH
Pyle, Merril E., 1st Lt, BSM
Pyne, Ernest E., Pfc, PH

Quesada, Alberto, Pvt, PH*
Quigley, Harold F., Pvt, BSM, PH
Quinn, Edward J., Pvt, PH
Quinn, Edward J., 1st Sgt, BSM
Quinn, Edward M., Pvt, PH
Quinn, Everett M., Pvt, PH

Rabeno, Charles J., Pfc, PH
Rademacher, George J., Pfc, PH
Rader, Charles E., T/Sgt, BSM, PH
Rader, Harvey W., Pfc, SS (Post), PH
Radolcin, Adam H., Cpl, PH
Rafas, Thomas J., Pvt, PH
Rafferty, Jack B., Pfc, PH
Raftery, James V., Pvt, PH*
Ragion, Edward F., S/Sgt, PH
Rainey, Thomas, T/5, BSM
Rahn, William J., Pfc, PH
Raines, Thomas, T/5, BSM
Rainville, Urgele, Pvt, PH
Raley, Donald A., Pfc, PH
Ralls, Benjamin R., Cpl, PH
Ramsey, McKinney H., Capt, PH
Ramsey, Stephen V., Pfc, PH
Raney, Stewart E., Pvt, PH
Ransom, Woodrow W., Pvt, PH
Rau, Robert R., Pfc, PH
Rayburn, Floyd C., Pfc, PH
Raymond, Winston A., Pfc, PH*
Reber, Walter J., Pvt, BSM, PH
Recklinghausen, William L., 1st Lt, PH
Rector, Jim, Pfc, BSM
Redfern, James H., Pfc, PH
Redfern, Russell W., T/5, SS, PH*
Redling, Albert H., T/4, BSM
Reece, Henry, Pfc, PH
Reed, Albert O., Pvt, PH
Reed, David W., S/Sgt, PH*
Reed, Franklin H., Pfc, BSM, PH

Reed, Milford, Pfc, PH
Reed, William W., Pfc, PH
Rees, Leroy H., Pfc, BSM
Regan, Myles L., Pvt, PH
Regoli, Mario J., Pfc, BSM
Reich, William T., S/Sgt, BSM, PH
Reid, Harold E., Capt, BSM
Reid, Robert E., 1st Lt, PH
Reid, Robert F., Jr., Pfc, BSM
Reilly, John E., Jr., Pfc, BSM
Reinhard, Samuel T., Jr., Pvt, PH
Reinhardt, Justin N., Pvt, PH
Reisinger, Glen E., Pfc, BSM
Reitzner, Lloyd J., Pfc, SS
Remish, John W., 1st Lt, BSM
Renda, Peter A., Pvt, PH**
Renda, Peter A., Pvt, PH**
Rensel, William A., Pfc, PH
Reo, Albert, Pfc, PH
Resh, Newton B., S/Sgt, BSM
Reynolds, Clyde R., Sgt, BSM, PH
Reynolds, Frank A., Pfc, SS, BSM, PH
Reynolds, Herbert H., Sgt, BSM
Rheaums, Leo J., Pfc, PH
Rhinehart, Homer C., Pvt, PH
Rhoades, Robert A., Pfc, PH
Ricardini, Remo R., Pvt, PH*
Ricciarelli, Joseph P., Sgt, PH
Riccio, Joseph L., Pfc, PH
Riccio, Robert, Sgt, BSM
Rice, Wendell K., Sgt, PH
Rich, Samuel J., Pfc, BSM, PH
Richards, Alfred O., Pfc, PH
Richards, Maurice E., Pfc, PH
Richards, Willard M., Cpl, PH
Richardson, Harold H., Pfc, PH
Richardson, Lloyd A., Pfc, PH
Richter, Sol, Pfc, PH
Ricketts, Harry E., T/Sgt, SS
Ricks, George A., Pvt, PH
Riegel, Fred R., Pfc, BSM
Rigby, Wayne J., Pvt, PH
Riley, Philip J., Pfc, PH
Riley, Samuel, Pvt, BSM, PH*
Rinella, Tony, Pfc, PH
Ritter, Frank, T/4, PH
Rivas, Saragosa, Pfc, PH
Riviers, Paul H., 1st Lt, SS*, PH*
Roach, Clovis J., T/4, BSM, PH
Roach, John D., Pvt, BSM
Roberson, George L., Pvt, PH
Roark, Donald E., Pfc, PH
Roark, Wilson M., Pfc, PH
Roberge, Leo G., Cpl, PH
Robbins, Jack L., Pfc, PH
Roberto, John M., Pfc, BSM
Roberts, A. C., Pfc, PH*
Roberts, Donald S., T/Sgt, BSM
Roberts, Wilbert L., Pvt, PH
Robertson, John W., Pfc, PH
Robidou, Wallace R., Sgt, PH
Rockhold, William J., Pfc, PH
Rockwell, Orley L., Pfc, PH
Rodhouse, Paul C., Pvt, PH
Rodrigues, Anthony J., S/Sgt, BSM
Rodier, Philip H., Pfc, PH
Rodriquez, Pablo M., Pfc, PH
Rodrique, Fernand J., Pfc, SS (Post), PH
Roeder, Robert E., Capt, CMH (Post)
Rogers, Basil E., Pfc, PH
Rogers, Charles E., Pvt, PH
Rogers, Elmer E., Pfc, PH
Rogers, Frederick D., Pfc, PH
Rogers, Joseph, Pfc, PH
Rogers, Wilford W., S/Sgt, PH
Roman, Andrew G., Pfc, PH*
Romano, Albert, Capt, PH
Romblad, Chester E., Pfc, BSM
Romero, Juan A., Pfc, PH
Romero, Luciano, Pfc, PH
Romero, Robert R., Pfc, PH
Root, Gerald S., T/5, BSM

Ropp, Ervin J., Pfc, BSM
Rores, George C., Pfc, PH
Rose, Bernard H., Pfc, BSM
Rose, Mc Cune J., Pfc, BSM
Rose, Rufus, Pvt, PH
Rose, Stanley B., S/Sgt, BSM, PH
Rosenfeld, Morris, Pfc, PH
Rosenfeld, Morris J., Pfc, BSM
Rosman, Alfred B., Pfc, BSM, PH
Ross, Cloyd E., Cpl, PH
Ross, William S., Jr., Pvt, PH
Roth, Fred W., 1st Lt, BSM*
Rothwell, Glen E., Pvt, PH
Rotroff, Philip M., Pvt, PH
Rouker, Mathew J., Pfc, PH
Rouleau, Frederick M., T/5, BSM
Rose, Oral A., Pvt, PH
Roseberry, Hudson, Pfc, PH
Rosenheim, Mercer D., Pfc, PH
Rossi, Frank A., Pfc, PH
Roark, Donald A., Pvt, PH
Rourke, John J., Pvt, PH
Rourke, Philip E., Pfc, PH
Rouse, Robert H., Pvt, PH
Rousses, Edward G., Pfc, PH
Raybal, Joe M., Pfc, PH
Ruben, Arthur P., T/Sgt, BSM
Ruben, Sam, T/3, BSM, PH*
Rubio, Sebastian R., Pfc, PH*
Rudy, Paul C., Sgt, BSM
Ruggiero, Pasquale, Pfc, PH
Rumanowski, Edward J., 1st Lt, BSM
Rupp, Ernest F., Pvt, PH
Ruppel, George M., T/5, BSM
Rusin, Albert, T/Sgt, BSM, PH
Russell, Henry L., S/Sgt, PH
Russell, John T., Sgt, PH*
Russell, Leory, Pfc, PH*
Russo, Alfred F., Pvt, PH
Russo, John, S/Sgt, BSM
Russo, Louis M., Pfc, PH
Russo, Peter P., Pvt, PH
Rutan, James F., Pvt, PH
Rutherford, Robert B., Pfc, PH
Rutledge, Claude W., Pfc, PH
Rutledge, Joseph G., Sgt, BSM, PH
Rutstein, Irving T., Pvt, BSM
Rutt, Warren W., Pvt, PH
Ryan, William J., T/4, BSM, PH
Ryle, Charles F., Pfc, PH

Sabo, John S., Pfc, PH
Sackman, Samuel B., Pfc, SS, PH
Sadlek, Francis J., Pfc, PH
Sadler, Gouye R., Pfc, PH
Sakach, Steven, S/Sgt, PH
Sakrison, George P., Sgt, SS, BSM, PH*
Saliers, Claude B., Pfc, SS
Sallee, Robert H., Jr., T/Sgt, SS, SM, PH
Sallemmi, Joseph T., Sgt, BSM
Salomune, Joseph, Pfc, PH
Salvina, Theodore F., Pvt, PH
Sampson, Joseph, S/Sgt, BSM, PH
Sanchez, Santiago, Jr., Pvt, PH
Sandaval, Jose D., Pfc, SS
Sandell, Uuno W., Pfc, PH
Sanders, Kenneth E., T/Sgt, SS (Post)
Sanders, Odell W., Pfc, PH
Sanderlin, Owen, Pvt, SS
Sanderson, Thomas, T/5, BSM
Sandgren, Howard C., Pvt, PH
Sandlier, Le Roy A., Pfc, SM
Sandiland, Lloyd W., Pfc, PH
Sanford, Robert H., 1st Lt, BSM
Sankowski, Henry J., Pfc, PH
Sanson, John D., T/5, SS
Santaella, Antonio L., T/Sgt, BSM
Santo, Alexander G., Pfc, PH
Sappington, James P., Pfc, PH
Satrappe, Frank J., Pvt, PH*
Saunders, Aubrey, Pfc, PH
Saunders, William J., T/Sgt, LM, PH

Saunderson, Kenneth A., T/4, BSM, PH
Saviano, Victor J., T/5, BSM
Sawicki, Joseph G., Pfc, PH
Sawyer, Thomas S., Sgt, PH
Saylock, Paul H., Pvt, PH
Scaglione, Gerald A., 1st Lt, PH
Scannel, Edward A., Pvt, PH
Scardino, Sam, Pfc, PH
Schaefer, Carl F., Pfc, BSM
Schaeffer, James E., Pfc, PH
Schar, Forrest H., Pfc, PH*
Schardt, Truman O., Pvt, PH
Schetzer, Henry G., Pfc, PH
Scheurman, Art E., S/Sgt, PH
Schickler, Arthur, Pfc, PH
Schieber, David W., Pfc, PH
Schiessler, Russell F., Capt, BSM*, PH*
Schihl, Allen A., Pvt, PH
Schilb, Andrew J., T/4, SS
Schlager, Walter, Pvt, PH
Schmidt, Eugene F., Pvt, PH*
Schmidt, Frank A., Pvt, PH
Schmidt, Milton L., S/Sgt, BSM
Schmidt, Richard R., S/Sgt, PH
Schmidt, Willard H., Pfc, PH
Schnepf, John E., Pfc, PH*
Schobitz, Anthony F., Pfc, PH
Schoeneman, Walter W., S/Sgt, BSM
Schreckendgust, Ben C., Pfc, PH
Schreier, Max, S/Sgt, SS
Schroeder, Donald F., 2nd Lt, PH
Schroer, Alfred, Pfc, PH
Schuko, Anthony J., Pfc, PH
Schuler, Royal S., 1st Lt, BSM
Schultz, John R., Pfc, PH
Schurick, Arthur D., S/Sgt, PH*
Schutte, Harvey, Pvt, PH
Schwartz, Harry E., Jr., Pfc, PH
Schwartz, Harry G., S/Sgt, BSM
Schwartz, Walter H., Pfc, BSM
Schwartz, Hyman H., T/Sgt, PH*
Schwarz, Henry O., S/Sgt, BSM, PH
Schwenk, John W., S/Sgt, PH
Sclafani, Gus D., Pfc, BSM
Sclafani, Joseph M., Pfc, PH
Scott, Arthur B., Cpl, BSM, PH
Scott, Jesse W., Pvt, SS (Post)
Scott, Walter W., Capt, DSC, BSM, PH, SS (Post)
Scovatti, Gabriel, Pvt, PH
Scrimo, John M., S/Sgt, BSM
Seagle, Garland F., Pfc, PH
Seaman, Lawrence B., Pfc, PH
Sebolt, Raymond E., T/Sgt, PH
Sebourn, Kenneth L., Sgt, BSM
Sedlak, Joseph J., S/Sgt, PH*
Seery, Frederick T., Pvt, PH
Segura, Robert D., Pfc, BSM
Seider, Frank, Pfc, PH
Seiter, Charles L., S/Sgt, BSM
Selbera, Manuel M., Pfc, BSM, PH
Serdar, George R., S/Sgt, PH (Post)
Sargent, Warren F., Capt, BSM, PH
Severson, John L., Pfc, PH
Sewell, Robert W., Sgt, BSM
Seymour, Clarence, Pvt, PH
Shabluk, Sam, Pvt, PH
Shackleford, Paul A., 1st Lt, PH
Shaddix, A. J., Pfc, PH
Shaffett, James T., S/Sgt, PH
Shambler, Stirling A., Pvt, PH
Sharman, Howard D., 2nd Lt, PH
Sharp, Leo E., Pfc, BSM
Sharpton, Willie P., Pfc, BSM, PH
Shaughnessy, James E., Sgt, BSM, PH*
Shaw, Ward M., 2nd Lt, PH
Shaw, Woodrow C., Sgt, BSM, PH
Shea, Charles W., T/Sgt, CMH
Shea, James D., T/4, BSM
Sheehan, Charles B., Pvt, PH
Sheldon, George H., Pvt, PH
Shelton, Claude S., Pfc, PH

Shepard, Joseph F., Pvt, PH
Shepherd, Hobart, Pfc, SS (Post)
Shopp, Clair M., Pfc, BSM, PH
Sheridan, Alfred, Pfc, BSM (Post)
Sheriff, Efrom C., Pvt, PH
Sheroda, Edward J., Pfc, PH
Sherwin, Stanley L., Pfc, BSM, (Post), PH
Shields, Charles V., Pfc, PH
Shipman, Hubert A., T/4, BSM
Shiro, Bernard C., S/Sgt, BSM
Short, George H., Pvt, PH
Short, William D., Pfc, PH
Shostak, Stanley M., Sgt, BSM, PH
Shuleski, Andrew P., Pfc, PH
Shuman, John O., Pfc, PH
Sides, Joseph N., Cpl, PH
Sides, Joseph N., Cpl, PH
Siegel, Eliezer, Sgt, PH
Siembak, Julius S., Pfc, PH
Siepietowski, Joseph A., T/Sgt, BSM, PH*
Sievers, Duane E., Sgt, PH
Sileo, Nicholas G., Pfc, PH
Silva, David E., Pfc, PH
Silva, Joseph E., T/4, SS
Silva, Joseph F., T/4, BSM
Silvey, Robert E., Cpl, PH
Sim, James R., Sgt, BSM
Simer, Alfred C., S/Sgt, BSM
Simon, Joseph P., S/Sgt, BSM
Simon, Richard, Pvt, PH
Simon, Ronald G., S/Sgt, PH
Simone, Carmine V., Pvt, PH
Simonson, Karl C., Pvt, PH
Simpson, Ray M., Capt, BSM
Sinclair, Charles A. S., Jr., S/Sgt, PH
Singer, Harry, Pfc, BSM
Singmaster, Lawrence, Capt, BSM, PH
Sinibaldi, Louis A., Pvt, PH
Sinkey, James R., Pfc, PH
Sipes, Harrold G., Pfc, PH
Sirois, Ernest A., Pfc, PH
Skaggs, Edward, Pfc, PH
Skalby, Clifford M., Capt, BSM, (Post)
Skelton, Charles L., Pvt, PH
Skiles, Jesse B., Pfc, PH*
Skinner, Ernestus F., Sgt, BSM
Skinner, Milton W., S/Sgt, PH*
Skogan, Donald E., T/Sgt, BSM
Skorb, Anthony, Pvt, PH*
Skubak, Mika A., Pvt, BSM, PH
Slack, Clayton H., S/Sgt, BSM, PH
Slade, Lewis, T/Sgt, BSM
Sloan, Douglas E., S/Sgt, SS
Sloan, Morris A., Pfc, PH
Sloan, Robert P., Pfc, PH
Slusher, Arbra B., Pfc, PH
Smarch, Michael, Pfc, PH
Smiley, George R., 1st Lt, PH
Smith, Arlon L., S/Sgt, BSM, PH*
Smith, Calvin A., T/5, PH
Smith, Clayton M., Cpl, BSM, PH
Smith, Earl P., Pfc, PH
Smith Edward E., Pfc, BSM
Smith, Edwin K., Pfc, BSM
Smith, Elmer G., Pfc, PH
Smith, Harold, Pfc, PH
Smith, Henry H., 2nd Lt, SS
Smith, Jessie H., Cpl, PH
Smith, Kenneth M., Pvt, PH
Smith, Olin E., 2nd Lt, BSM, PH
Smith, William L., 1st Lt, PH
Smith, Walter J., Pfc, PH*
Smith, William C., T/4, BSM
Smith, William H., Pfc, PH
Smith, Willard L., Pfc, PH*
Smoker, Lee, Pfc, PH
Snare, Amund H., Pfc, PH
Snitofsky, Harold, Pvt, PH
Snyder, James F., Pfc, SS (Post)
Snyder, Russell E., Pvt, PH
Snyder, Sherman, Pvt, PH
Sobieraj, Frank S., Pvt, PH

Sochat, Herbert, Pvt, PH
Sohanchak, John, Sgt, PH
Soja, Alexander J., 1st Sgt, BSM
Soldra, John J., S/Sgt, BSM
Solomon, William, Pfc, PH
Soloski, Joe, Pvt, SS, PH
Soltis, Joseph J., Jr., Pvt, PH
Soltwisch, Robert W., Pfc, PH
Soule, Glen C., Pfc, SS, PH
Souther, Francis W., Pfc, PH
Sowden, Everett E., S/Sgt, SS, PH
Spangler, William R., Pvt, PH
Spannagel, William V., S/Sgt, BSM
Spano, Emanuel T., 2nd Lt, LM, PH*
Spath, Carl F., T/4, BSM
Spence, Coy, Sgt, PH
Spencer, Ernest O., Pfc, PH
Spencer, George M., Pfc, BSM, PH
Spencer, Granville M., Pfc, PH
Spencer, Oscar F., Cpl, PH
Spencer, Parvin W., Pvt, PH
Sperling, Irving, Pvt, PH
Spikes, Tom, Pfc, PH
Spinosa, Joseph, Pvt, PH*
Spuler, Dean A., 1st Sgt, BSM
Spurling, William, 1st Lt, PH
Stacey, George W., Pvt, PH*
Stacks, Troy E., Pfc, BSM
Staheleck, Alfred S., Sgt, PH
Stahl, Elmer W., Pfc, PH
Staley, John P., Pfc, PH
Stallings, Donald E., S/Sgt, PH
Stamps, Hugh G., S/Sgt, BSM
Stanaback, Everett W., T/5, BSM
Staneika, John G., Sgt, BSM
Stange, Henry L., Pvt, PH
Stanley, Curtis R., Sgt, BSM
Staskowicz, Joseph, Pfc, PH
Steedman, James B., Cpl, PH
Stefanic, Stanley C., Sgt, PH
Steiner, Paul, S/Sgt, BSM
Stempkowski, Stanley A., Pfc, PH
Steffens, Ralph H., Pfc, PH
Stephens, Johnie, Pfc, BSM
Stephens, Thomas A., Pfc, PH
Stern, Henry W., 1st Lt, PH
Stern, Lionel, Pvt, PH
Stetson, Glendon G., Pvt, PH
Stevens, David L., Sgt, PH
Stevens, Roscoe A., T/5, BSM
Stevens, Walter T., Jr., Pvt, PH
Stevenson, John D., S/Sgt, BSM
Stillman, Charles J., Jr., Pfc, PH
Stewart, Lee A., Pfc, PH
Stock, Albert S., Pvt, PH
Stokas, Joseph V., Pfc, PH
Stone, Harry A., T/Sgt, PH
Stoner, Nolan R., Sgt, PH
Stoner, Willard C., Jr., Capt, BSM**
Stover, James R., S/Sgt, PH
Stowe, Stephen B., Pfc, PH
Strain, Kenneth L., Pvt, PH
Stratford, Eugene F., S/Sgt, PH
Stratman, Edward J., Maj, LM, SS, PH
Strayer, Joseph M., Pfc, BSM
Strazemski, Henry, Pvt, PH
Streich, Albert, Jr., S/Sgt, PH
Strickland, Elton C., Cpl, PH
Strickland, Richard R., T/Sgt, PH
Stricklin, Henry C., Sgt, BSM
Strong, Ed, T/5, PH
Strong, Kenneth, S/Sgt, PH
Stroup, Ray B., Capt, SS, PH
Studstill, Willie S., Pfc, BSM
Stueber, Louis A., Pvt, PH
Stumbo, Hamer S., Pfc, BSM
Stump, Charles J., T/Sgt, PH
Stwalley, Herbert J., T/Sgt, BSM
Suddeth, Ralph H., Pfc, PH*
Sukoneck, Jack, Pfc, PH
Sullivan, Bernard, Pfc, BSM, PH
Sullivan, Thomas J., Pfc, BSM

Sumner, Neal E., T/Sgt, PH
Suritz, Human, S/Sgt, BSM
Susnick, John J., T/5, BSM
Sutherland, Charles H., Pfc, PH
Sutterfield, Floyd E., T/Sgt, SS
Sutton, Arthur E., S/Sgt, PH
Swain, Richard E., Sgt, PH
Swatek, Robert C., Pfc, PH
Swayne, Floyd, Pvt, PH
Sweeney, William E., Pvt, PH
Sweet, George R., Pfc, PH
Swett, Daniel H., 1st Lt, SS, PH
Swift, Wilbur, Pvt, PH
Swim, Harlan R., Pfc, PH
Sylvia, Willard, T/Sgt, BSM*
Sylvia, William J., Pvt, PH
Szatmary, Eugene, Cpl, BSM
Szurek, Stanley J., Sgt, BSM

Taake, Raymond W., T/4, PH
Tabbert, Lawrence H., S/Sgt, PH
Tackett, Jesse L., Pvt, PH
Tafelski, Alexander, Pvt, PH
Taft, Harry W., S/Sgt, PH
Talach, Ralph, S/Sgt, PH*
Talbot, Edward J. G., Pfc, PH
Talley, Louis C., Jr., Capt, PH
Tapp, Richard T., Pfc, PH
Tarasiewicz, Roman V., Pfc, PH
Targus, Joseph P., Pfc, PH
Tavernia, Howard A., T/4, BSM
Taylor, Albert R., S/Sgt, BSM
Taylor, Curtis E., 2nd Lt, SS, PH*
Taylor, Edwin, Pfc, PH
Taylor, Frank J., Maj, BSM*
Taylor, Laverne R., Pfc, BSM, PH*
Taylor, Mark W., 2nd Lt, BSM
Taylor, Sammy L., Pvt, BSM
Teegarden, John T., Pfc, PH
Teitel, Milton, S/Sgt, PH
Teller, Harold R., Pfc, PH
Teleschow, Walter V., Jr., Pfc, PH
Tepfenhart, Steve A., Sgt, PH*
Terjesen, George M., Pfc, BSM
Terrell, Nathan, Pfc, BSM
Terrill, George, Pfc, PH
Terry, Henry N., Pfc, PH
Tessier, Joseph, Pfc, PH
Tetting, Charles L., Pfc, SS (Post)
Teves, Harold M., Pfc, PH
Theobald, Chester L., Pvt, PH
Theriault, Alban, T/Sgt, SS, PH
Thibault, Charles J., Pvt, BSM
Thiebedeau, Romeo E., Pfc, PH
Thomas, Alfred J., Pfc, PH
Thomas, Collins R., S/Sgt, BSM
Thomas, Donald B., Pfc, PH
Thomas, Frank, Pfc, PH
Thomas, Fred C., Pfc, PH*
Thomas, Jack, T/3, BSM, PH
Thomas, James H., T/5, BSM
Thomas, Murrel C., Pfc, PH
Thomas, Preston J., Pfc, PH
Thomas, Robert B., Pfc, PH
Thomas, William L., 1st Lt, PH
Thommes, Richard L., Pvt, BSM, PH*
Thompson, Albert F., Pfc, PH
Thompson, Cecil W., Pfc, BSM
Thompson, Eugene E., Pfc, PH*
Thompson, Harry S., Cpl, PH
Thompson, Joseph W., Pfc, BSM
Thompson, Melvin M., Pfc, BSM
Thompson, Paul W., Pvt, BSM
Thompson, W. S., 2nd Lt, PH
Thornhill, Roscoe W., Pfc, BSM
Thrift, Frederick W., Pvt, BSM
Throssell, Charles W., Capt, PH
Tibbels, John W., S/Sgt, BSM
Till, Wilbur L., Pvt, PH
Timcho, George M., Pvt, PH
Tittle, Robert A., Pvt, PH
Tobias, John B., Pfc, BSM

Toledo, Patrick T., Pfc, PH
Tomarazzo, Anthony D., S/Sgt, BSM*, PH
Toribio, Alphonse, Pfc, PH
Tooley, Willard, Pvt, PH
Tornetto, Alfred, Pfc, PH
Torraco, Mario, S/Sgt, PH
Torrez, Almundo R., Sgt, SS
Tortorelli, Frank P., Pvt, PH
Towner, Harvey D., 1st Lt, BSM
Towns, Milo E., Pfc, BSM
Townsend, Lonnie E., Jr., Pfc, PH*
Tremblay, Leon J., Pfc, BSM, PH
Trevino, Joe, Pvt, PH
Trilone, Antony, Sgt, SS (Post), BSM, PH
Trimm, Antolin, Pvt, PH*
Tringale, Angelo J., Pfc, PH
Troiani, Loredo, Pfc, BSM
Troiano, Constant A., Maj, PH
Trousdell, John E., T/5, BSM (Post)
Truesdell, Jesse N., Sgt, BSM
Truhett, Walter L., T/4, PH
Trujillo, Bimas, Pfc, PH*
Trzesczkowski, Thaddeus E., Pfc, PH
Tucci, Henry A., Pvt, PH
Tucciarone, Frank J., Pfc, SS, PH
Tucker, Clarence A., Sgt, PH
Tucker, Milton, Pvt, PH
Tupa, Charlie L., Pfc, PH*
Turlow, Dan J., Pfc, PH
Turner, Berry, Pfc, PH
Turner, Forrest E., S/Sgt, PH
Turner, Herbert O., T/5, PH
Turner, Raymond, Pvt, PH*
Turner, Ried H., Pvt, PH
Turner, Robert W., Sgt, BSM, PH*
Turner, Walter C., Jr., Pfc, PH
Turpin, Thomas J., Pvt, BSM
Turzo, Michael A., T/Sgt, PH
Tuttle, William P., 1st Lt, BSM
Tweedy, Graydon E., Pfc, PH
Twigg, Paul H., Pfc, BSM
Tyler, Millard D., Pfc, PH
Tyree, William H., Pvt, PH

Ucko, Paul M., S/Sgt, PH
Ulrich, George B., Pfc, PH
Underdown, Frank H., Pfc, PH
Urbanovsky, Bonnie E., Sgt, PH
Ure, Joseph A., 1st Lt, BSM, PH
Uriola, John, Pfc, BSM*
Urish, John J., Pvt, PH
Usborne, Robert T., S/Sgt, SS
Usher, Maurice L., Pfc, PH

Valdetero, Joseph W., 1st Sgt, PH
Valenzuela, Rosario A., Pfc, PH
Vallejo, Armando, Pfc, PH*
Van Asten, Gerald G., Pvt, PH
Vance, Kenneth E., T/3, BSM
Vanderback, Wilbur G., T/4, BSM
Vandergriff, James M., Pfc, PH
Vanderhoff, Arthur N., Pfc, PH
Van Duzee, Theodore J., Pfc, BSM
Van Dyke, Herman A., Pfc, BSM, PH
Van Es, Anton, Pvt, PH
Van Houten, John H., T/4, BSM
Van Kumpen, Gerrit, Pfc, PH
Van Matre, Teddie S., T/Sgt, BSM*
Vann, Lennie A., T/5, PH
Van Norman, Harry J., Jr., Pvt, PH
Van Remmen, Gordon G., Capt, BSM
Van Roy, Lambert J., Pfc, PH
Van Veizer, William F., T/5, BSM
Varanelli, Floyd E., Pfc, PH
Vargas, Albert R., Pvt, BSM, PH
Varsaci, Vincent J., S/Sgt, PH
Vasquez, Louis, Pfc, PH
Vaughn, James W., Pfc, PH
Vecerra, Jesus, Pfc, PH
Vedder, Ralph E., Pfc, PH
Veiga, John, Pvt, PH
Velasquez, Manuel M., Pfc, PH
Velez, Monserrate D., Pfc, PH

Verdugo, Santiago, Pfc, PH
Verenko, Victor, Pvt, BSM, PH
Verrello, Michael, T/4, BSM
Vetter, Lawrence C., Pfc, PH
Villarreal, Encarnasion C., Jr., Sgt, PH
Vincent, Chris R., Pfc, PH
Viner, Allen E., Sgt, BSM
Visco, Alfonso E., Cpl, PH*
Visconti, Samuel, S/Sgt, PH, BSM
Vogler, Rayjond E., Pfc, PH
Vonderkall, Herbert, Pvt, PH
Von Ohlen, Ronald R., Pfc, PH
Voortman, William C., Pfc, PH
Voris, Roger M., Pvt, PH
Vorm, Leslie S., Pfc, PH
Vranesic, William C., Pfc, BSM
Vukicevich, Alexander J., Pfc, PH

Walley, Robert P., T/Sgt, BSM
Wachob, Guy, Pfc, PH*
Wade, Grover L., Pfc, PH
Waddell, George W., Pfc, PH
Wade, Joseph A., 1st Lt, BSM
Wagner, Albert P., Pvt, PH
Wagner, Elmer P., Pfc, PH
Wagner, Floyd, Pfc, BSM
Wagner, Louis A., Sgt, BSM
Wagner, William J., S/Sgt, SS (Post)
Wagoner, Edward E., Pfc, PH
Wahl, Harry J., Pvt, PH
Waite, James C., S/Sgt, BSM
Wakefield, William H., Jr., Pvt, PH
Walaszek, Albin A., T/Sgt, PH
Waldron, Garrett A., Pfc, PH
Walker, John F., Pvt, BSM, PH
Walker, Lawrence E., Pvt, PH
Walker, Michael E., Pfc, PH
Walker, Steve A., Pfc, PH
Walker, William J., Pvt, PH
Wall, John C., Cpl, BSM
Wallace, Everette, 1st Sgt, PH
Wallace, John E., Pfc, BSM
Wallace, Voyd L., S/Sgt, PH
Wallaert, Marceil F., Cpl, PH
Walls, Carlus E., Pvt, PH
Walls, Clifton L., Pfc, PH
Walsh, James T., T/5, BSM
Walters, Rienhold E., Pfc, PH
Wangeman, Donald B., Pvt, PH
Warhainen, Hugo E., Pvt, PH
Ward, James, Pfc, BSM (Post)
Ward, Arthur Z., Pfc, PH
Ward, James F., Pfc, PH
Ward, John H., Sgt, PH
Ward, Morton E., Pvt, PH
Ward, William B., Jr., Pvt, PH
Ware, Robert W., Pfc, PH
Wargo, Henry A., Pfc, PH
Warner, Victor H., Jr., Pvt, PH
Warren, Orville G., Pfc, SS*, BSM, PH***
Warren, Robert D., Pfc, SS (Post), PH
Waseline, Steve, Pfc, PH
Wasilowski, Chester J., Sgt, BSM
Waters, Christopher J., Jr., Pvt, PH
Waterston, Colin C., Sgt, PH
Watson, Delbert J., Pvt, PH*
Watson, James E., S/Sgt, BSM, PH*
Watson, William C. G., 1st Lt, BSM (Post)
Wattu, Eino O., S/Sgt, BSM
Waybright, Joseph J., Pfc, PH
Weatherby, James R., T/5, PH
Weatherman, Grancis E., T/5, PH
Weatherman, Gene, Pfc, BSM
Weaver, Earl J., Capt, BSM*
Weaver, Edgar E., S/Sgt, PH
Weaver, Joseph M., Sgt, PH
Weaver, Raymond C., Pfc, PH
Webb, Erenst N., Pvt, PH
Webb, Roscoe A., T/Sgt, SS, PH*
Webster, Dan M., T/5, BSM
Weeks, David H., T/5, PH
Weeks, Kenneth, Pfc, PH

Wegiel, Stanley A., Pfc, PH
Weigott, Marshall R., Jr., Pfc, SS
Weih, George, T/Sgt, PH*
Weimer, Edward P., Sr., Pfc, BSM
Weintraub, Sigmund, Pfc, BSM (Post), PH
Weisbrot, Stanley, Pfc, PH
Weiss, Leslie, Pfc, PH
Welbron, Charles B., Pfc, PH
Welch, Joseph M., Pfc, BSM
Welch, Kenneth L., Pvt, PH
Welcher, Harold E., Pfc, PH
Weldon, Karl S., Sgt, PH
Welinsky, Valentine, Pfc, BSM
Welk, Anton, Pfc, PH
Wellard, Thomas C., Pfc, PH
Wells, Frank, Pfc, PH
Welsh, Ronald M., T/Sgt, PH*
Welty, Leory G., Pfc, PH
Wenge, Leslie E., S/Sgt, PH
Werkheiser, Norman H., Pvt, SS
Werley, Donald R., Pfc, PH
Westhoven, Jacob, Pfc, PH
Westphal, Chester W., Pfc, PH*
Wetz, Helmut A., Pfc, BSM, PH*
Weydig, Charles, Jr., Cpl, BSM
Weymer, William L., Pfc, PH
Wezyk, Edward F., Pvt, PH
Whalen, Michael D., S/Sgt, BSM
Wharton, Clifford L., Pvt, PH
Wharton, Jackson B., T/3, PH
Wheat, James E., T/Sgt, BSM, PH
Wheeler, Burton J., T/5, BSM
Wheeler, Daniel J., Pvt, PH
Wheeler, George R., Jr., 1st Lt, PH
Wheeler, John W., Pfc, PH
Whipple, William A., Pvt, PH
White, Clarence A., Pfc, BSM
White, Daniel, S/Sgt, BSM
White, Eugene B., Pfc, PH
White, Harold L., Pfc, PH
White, Howard F., Pfc, BSM
White, Isaac B., T/Sgt, LM, PH
White, Leslie, Pfc, PH
White, Norman A., Sgt, BSM*
White, Richard L., Pfc, PH
White, Roland D., T/5, BSM
White, Sydney, Pfc, PH
White, Virgil H., Pvt, PH
White Body, John, Pvt, PH
Whiting, Charles W., Pvt, PH
Whitley, James T., Sgt, BSM, PH*
Whitman, Byron H., 2nd Lt, PH
Whitney, George W., Pfc, BSM, PH
Whittle, Noah E., Pfc, BSM
Widdoss, Courtland, Pfc, PH
Widell, Albert H., Pfc, PH
Wieck, John L., S/Sgt, PH
Wieland, Warren R., Sgt, PH
Wiggins, Jefferson W., Jr., S/Sgt, PH
Wilber, Edward S., Pvt, SS
Wild, Bernard J., Sgt, SS
Wilhoite, Robert O., Pfc, BSM
Wilkerson, Arvil B., Sgt, BSM
Willey, Charles E., Pfc, SS, PH
Will, Jerome J., Pfc, BSM, PH*
Williams, Alton F., Pvt, PH
Williams, Benham E., Jr., Pvt, PH
Williams, David R., Pfc, BSM, PH
Williams, Donald F., 2nd Lt, BSM
Williams, Francis G., Pfc, PH
Williams, Frederick F., Pfc, PH
Williams, Irving L., Pfc, PH
Williams, Ralph L., S/Sgt, SS (Post)
Williams, Richard J., S/Sgt, PH*
Williamson, Corbett, Lt Col, SS
Williamson, Vance N., 1st Lt, BSM
Willie, Wayslow, Pfc, PH
Willis, Clifford C., Pvt, PH
Willis, Delma H., Pfc, PH
Willis, Marion H., Pfc, PH
Wilson, A. D., Pfc, PH
Wilson, Horace L., Pvt, PH

Wilson, Elmore J., Pfc, BSM
Wilson, Flavis C., T/Sgt, PH
Wilson, Fred W., Pfc, PH*
Wilson, Herman L., Pvt, PH
Wilson, James T., Cpl, BSM
Wilson, Lawrence A., Pvt, PH
Wilson, Odell, Pfc, PH
Wilson, Roswell G., Pfc, PH
Wilson, Warren H., Pfc, PH
Winchoba, Frank, Sgt, BSM
Winegar, Charles R., Pvt, PH
Winesett, Louis E., Jr., Pfc, SS (Post)
Winkel, Raymond J., Pfc, PH
Winking, Leo A., Pvt, PH
Winter, Earl C., 1st Lt, SS
Wirth, David K., 1st Lt, PH
Wise, Ernest G., Sgt, BSM
Wissel, Raymond C., T/5, BSM
Witt, Clifford E., Pvt, PH
Witt, William L., Pvt, PH
Witter, Vincent M., Lt Col, SS, BSM*, PH
Wiza, Anthony S., Pfc, PH
Wohlford, Donald E., Pvt, PH
Wolber, Fred J., Pfc, BSM, PH
Wold, Truman C., Sgt, PH
Wolf, John L., Pfc, PH
Wolnitz, Bernard B., T/5, BSM
Wolters, Joseph A., Pvt, PH**
Wood, Lewis L., Pvt, PH
Woodall, Claude W., Pvt, PH
Woodruff, Everett C., Pfc, PH*
Woolaver, James V., 1st Lt, BSM*
Worden, Clarence, Pvt, PH
Worrell, Harry W., Pvt, PH
Wright, Acie W., Pfc, BSM
Wright, Bernard D., T/Sgt, PH
Wright, Eldon M., Pfc, PH
Wright, Gordon V., Pfc, PH
Wurst, Charles P., Pfc, PH
Wyatt, Preston J., Pfc, PH

Yeager, John J., 1st Lt, BSM
Yebas, Joseph, Pfc, BSM
Yeary, Myrth M., Jr., Pfc, PH*
Yevoli, Rudolph J., M/Sgt, BSM
Yoder, Charles L., Pvt, PH
Yaloff, Jacob, Pvt, PH
Yonan, Joel E., Pfc, BSM, PH
Yongue, Donald A., Lt Col, SS, BSM*
York, Homer D., Pfc, PH
Young, J. A., Sgt, PH
Young, John T., Pfc, PH
York, Melvin A., Pfc, PH
Young, Lee J., Pfc, PH
Youngs, Richard, Pfc, BSM, PH
Young, Theodore F., Pvt, PH
Young, Wong Y., T/4, BSM

Zaccagnino, Emilio L., Cpl, PH
Zaccario, Nicholas F., Cpl, PH
Zachary, Paul M., Pvt, PH
Zacios, Walter J., Pfc, PH
Zakerski, Stanley A., S/Sgt, BSM
Zane, Samuel J., 1st Sgt, BSM
Zeck, Cyril D., Pvt, PH*
Zenga, Henry J., Pfc, PH*
Zerbe, John D., Jr., 1st Lt, BSM
Zibbell, Elmore, Jr., 2nd Lt, SS, BSM, PH
Zeiber, Charles G., Pfc, PH
Ziehn, Arthur, Pfc, BSM, PH
Ziemer, Herman F., Pfc, BSM, PH*
Zill, Lloyd C., Sgt, BSM
Zimmer, Lawrence J., T/5, BSM
Zimmerman, Thomas H., Pvt, BSM, PH
Zinkowicz, Joseph S., Pfc, PH
Zion, Joseph H., Pfc, BSM
Zippel, Richard, Pfc, PH
Zlotowski, Leo C., Sgt, BSM
Zoglman, Oscar M., 2nd Lt, PH
Zolla, James V., Sgt, BSM, PH*
Zujkowski, John P., Sgt, PH
Zweiback, William, Pfc, PH

351ST INFANTRY REGIMENT

Able, Claude L., Pfc, BSM
Abrams, William R., S/Sgt, BSM, LM
Ackerman, John R., Cpl, PH
Adair, Hollis W., Pfc, PH
Adams, Joseph W., T/Sgt, BSM, PH***
Adams, Lloyd E., Pfc, BSM, PH*
Adams, Sidney J., T/3, PH, BSM
Addington, Paul, Pfc, BSM, PH
Ader, Robert W., Pfc, PH
Adkinson, Fred W., Pfc, BSM
Adler, Joseph S., Pvt, BSM
Aehelski, Frederick J., T/4, BSM
Affenseller, Frank J., Sgt, BSM
Agostinucei, Louis A., T/5, BSM
Ahearn, Frank J., S/Sgt, BSM, PH
Ahern, James P., Pfc, PH
Ahern, Joseph G., Pfc, BSM, PH
Albro, Donald C., Pfc, PH
Alexander, William B., Pfc, BSM
Alford, James F., Pfc, PH*
Allen, Benjamin H., Pfc, BSM
Almendarez, Jesse G., Pvt, PH
Alonzo, Ernesto O., 1st Lt, BSM, PH*
Alperin, Seymour, S/Sgt, BSM
Alsen, Christian F., Pfc, PH*
Altwarg, Albert, T/4, BSM, PH
Anderson, Arthur G., Cpl, PH*
Anderson, Carie L., S/Sgt, PH
Anderson, Estil, Pfc, BSM
Anderson, George, T/Sgt, SS
Anderson, John E., S/Sgt, BSM
Anderson, John E., 2nd Lt, SS
Anderson, Maynard L., Pvt, PH
Anglin, Richard H., 1st Lt, BSM
Anthony, John C., Pfc, BSM
Archer, Eligah B., Pvt, PH
Armour, John F., T/4, PH
Arnold, Thomas D., S/Sgt, BSM
Askin, Henry W., 1st Lt, BSM
Attara, Joseph A., Pvt, PH
Autunno, Julius, Pfc, BSM
Ayers, Harold B., Major, BSM, DSC
Ayotte, Wallace, J., Cpl, BSM, PH*

Bach, Samuel M., Pvt, PH
Bachism, John, T/4, BSM
Baggett, Harry E., Pfc. SS (MIA)
Baggett, Judson E., Pfc, BSM
Balck, Ralph G., T/5, BSM
Balder, Paul H., Pvt, PH
Baldridge, Charles C., Pfc, PH
Baldwin, Foster A., Pvt, PH
Baljarevich, Milan D., Pvt, PH
Ball, George O., Pfc, BSM
Ballentine, George B., T/Sgt, PH
Ballos, Theodore, Pfc, PH
Baran, Joseph J., 1st Lt, SS, LM
Barbaccia, Frank J., T/5, BSM, PH
Bardo, Chester N., Pfc, PH
Barela, Benjamin, Pfc, BSM
Barkasy, Stephen, Pfc, PH*
Barrows, Richard A., T/5, BSM, PH
Barrs, Wilfred J., Pvt, PH
Basinski, Michael J., Sgt, BSM
Basta, Theodore, T/Sgt, BSM
Battafarano, Leonard A., 1st Lt, PH
Bauer, Charles J., Sgt, BSM, PH
Bauer, John, Pfc, PH
Baughman, Harry G., 1st Lt, SS, PH
Beak, Charles R., Sgt, PH
Becker, Henry, Cpl, BSM, PH
Beckett, Donald E., T/5, BSM
Becton, Edward J., Jr., PH
Bednarz, Edward T., Pfc, BSM
Belcher, Lloyd V., Pvt, BSM
Belcher, Paul, Cpl, BSM
Beli, Garlan T., Pfc, BSM
Belleshiem, George H., Pfc, BSM
Bender, Erwin H., S/Sgt, SS
Bengfort, Theodore J., T/4, PH

Berg, Ira L., Capt, BSM
Berky, Dezso, Pfc, PH
Bernstock, Nathan, S/Sgt, PH
Berring, Otis, T/5, PH
Berry, James E., Pfc, BSM
Beyenka, John T., 1st Lt, BSM
Bialkowski, William C., T/Sgt, BSM
Bible, Harry J., Pfc, BSM (Post)
Biernat, Stanley C., Pfc, PH
Billmaier, Bryce A., Pvt, PH
Binggeli, Fred G., Pfc, SS
Biondi, Pizzi A., Pfc, PH
Bizon, Henry, Pfc, PH
Black, Barney W., Pvt, BSM, PH*
Blais, Raymond E., Pvt, PH
Blanche, Frederick A., Jr., Capt, BSM*, PH*
Blank, Karl R., Pfc, PH
Blankenship, Dennis G., Pfc, PH***
Blazek, Stanley J., Pvt, PH
Bokie, Frederick E., Jr., 1st Lt, BSM
Boffio, John B., Cpl, PH
Bohn, Edward L., Pfc, BSM
Bohnert, Robert, Pfc, BSM
Boom, Henry C., Pfc, PH
Boone, Daniel D., 1st Sgt, BSM
Bonar, Alexander J., Sgt, BSM
Borelli, Frank J., Pfc, PH
Bosco, James C., Pvt, PH*
Boston, Charles F., Pvt, SS
Boston, Robert M., Pvt, BSM, SS (Post)
Bowchard, George J., Pvt, BSM
Bowers, Douglas H., Pfc, PH
Bowen, Thomas S., Cpl, PH, SS (Post)
Bowker, Robert E., 1st Lt, BSM
Bowles, Glenn R., Capt, PH, BSM
Bowler, James E., T/5, BSM
Boyd, Tillman, E., Lt Col, SS
Boykin, George W., Pfc, SS
Brady, Manley L., Pfc, PH
Braga, John, S/Sgt, BSM
Brainar, Donald R., Pfc, PH
Braithwaite, David, Pfc, PH
Branch, Clayton, Jr., CWO, BSM
Branningan, James, Jr., Pfc, BSM
Breen, John W., Pfc, PH
Beisner, Max, Cpl, BSM
Brendel, Ewald, Pvt, PH
Brennan, George H., Pvt, PH
Brennan, Robert F., T/5, BSM, PH
Brennan, Roger K., Pfc, PH
Brett, George C., S/Sgt, BSM
Brine, Richard G., S/Sgt, SS (MIA)
Briody, John J., Pfc, BSM, PH
Broco, George C., Pvt, PH
Broere, Howard W., Pfc, PH
Broff, George P., T/5, BSM
Broker, Edward J., Sgt, PH
Brook, Clifford, Pfc, PH*
Brooks, Charles M., Pfc, PH
Brooks, Stanley M., T/Sgt, PH*
Brooks, Willard D., Sgt, BSM, PH
Brown, Charles J., Pvt, PH
Brown, Elmer P., Pfc, BSM
Brown, Eyvind D., Pfc, PH
Brown, Harold Mac V., Major, BSM (Post)
Brown, Jack W., 1st Lt, BSM, PH
Brown, Maurice V., 2nd Lt, PH
Brown, Norman E., Sgt, BSM
Brown, Robert D., Capt, BSM
Brown, Roy W., T/4, PH
Brown, Rufus W., Pfc, PH
Bruce, George L., 1st Lt, BSM, PH
Bryan, Russell L., Pfc, BSM
Bubnis, John E., Pvt, PH
Buchanan, John H., Pfc, PH
Bukovesky, Nicholas, Sgt, BSM, PH**
Buonincontri, Alfred J., Cpl, BSM
Burch, Ace G., Pfc, PH
Burgert, Joseph H., Sgt, PH
Burkett, Alan L., Pfc, PH

Burkett, Warren M., Pvt, BSM (Post)
Burkholder, George N., T/Sgt, BSM
Burnham, Wayne, Pfc, BSM
Burns, George, Pfc, BSM*, PH
Burns, John F., S/Sgt, BSM
Burrell, Marion D., T/Sgt, BSM
Buzick, John W., Jr., 1st Lt, BSM
Byers, Eugene E., Pvt, BSM, PH*
Byrne, Gladin S., Jr., Pvt, PH
Byron, Raymond J., Major, BSM

Cacias, Joe V., Pfc, BSM
Cain, Michael J., Pvt, PH
Calp, Walter B., Pvt, PH
Camfferman, John, Pfc, PH*
Campbell, Edward, Pvt, PH
Campbell, James B., Pvt, PH
Campbell, John P., 1st Lt. BSM
Campbell, Paul H., Pvt, SS
Canada, Ralph, Pvt, PH**
Canty, Joseph M., Pfc, BSM
Cardone, John P., T/5, PH
Carlson, George T., Cpl, BSM
Carlstone, Robert K., Capt, BSM
Carmon, Frank W., Major, DSC, PH**
Carroll, Billy M., Pfc, BSM
Carsee, Roland A., 2nd Lt, BSM
Carver, Joseph A., Pfc, BSM
Case, Ernest L., Pfc, PH, BSM
Casper, Lewis J., T/4, BSM
Cassmassi, Joseph T., Capt, BSM
Cattle, Robert T., Jr., 1st Lt, BSM
Chadwick, Paul W., Pvt, PH
Chamberlain, Frank J., Pvt, PH
Chambers, Edward M., Pfc, PH
Chambers, Thomas T., Capt, BSM
Champeny, Arthur S., Col, DSC, BSM, PH**, SS
Chanez, Estanislado, Pfc, PH
Charles, Martin, Pfc, BSM
Charlier, John, Pvt, PH
Chartier, Arthur, Jr., S/Sgt, SS
Chavez, Jose D., Pfc, PH
Cheatham, Lawrence T., Jr., Pfc, PH
Cheeney, Perry J., 1st Lt, SS, DSC
Chmelynski, Joe, 1/Sgt, BSM
Chojnowski, Chester Z., Pvt, BSM
Christiansen, Lewis B., Capt, BSM
Christopher, Frank A., S/Sgt, SS
Christy, Raymond R., S/Sgt, BSM
Church, Fields H., T/Sgt, BSM, PH*
Clark, Jack, S/Sgt, PH
Clark, Nelson G., Pfc, SS
Clark, William H., Major, BSM
Clausen, Kenneth A., T/5, PH
Cleeves, Henry W., Cpl, SS
Cline, Virgil E., Pfc, PH
Clouse, Gilbert M., 2nd Lt, BSM
Clover, Richmond B., Pfc, PH
Cobb, Floyd E., Pvt, PH
Cobb, Laverne, Pfc, PH*, BSM
Coffey, John M., Pfc, PH
Cohen, Arthur, 1st Lt, PH*
Cohen, Menahem A., Pvt, PH
Cohn, Henry, T/5, BSM
Collins, Thomas C., Pfc, PH
Colannino, John, T/4, PH
Colbeck, Floyd C., Pfc, PH*
Colbin, Leon P., Cpl, BSM
Coleman, Loyal C., Sgt, PH
Collier, Calhoun C., 1st Lt, BSM, PH
Collins, Robert, S/Sgt, PH*
Collins, Robert L., Pvt, PH*
Combs, Milton, Sgt, BSM, PH
Comerford, Burke, Pfc, PH
Conner, Alva B., Pvt, PH
Connolly, Francis P., S/Sgt, PH
Conrad, Donald J., Pfc, PH
Conrad, Lawrence E., Pfc, BSM*, PH
Conti, Charles, Pfc, BSM
Cook, Isaac, Pfc, BSM, PH
Cooliver, Calvin C., T/Sgt, SS

Coombs, Charles F., Pfc, PH
Cooper, Bobbie E., Pvt, PH
Cooper, Saul, Pvt, PH
Cordero, Juan J., Pvt, PH
Corigliano, Philip A., Pvt, PH
Corrow, Harold J., Pfc, PH
Costello, Harry J., Pfc, BSM
Cowles, Henry W., Pfc, PH
Craw, James H., T/Sgt, BSM
Crawford, Robert C., 1st Lt, PH
Crimmins, Chester L., S/Sgt, BSM, PH, LM
Crites, Francis G., Pvt, PH
Crouse, Robert M., 1st Lt, BSM
Crox, Alfred D., Pfc, SS, BSM (Post)
Cruz, Joseph S., Pfc, BSM
Csomay, Joseph F., T/5, PH
Cueno, James F., Cpl, PH*
Culbertson, Paul L., 1st Lt, BSM
Cunningham, Lawrence J., Sgt, SS (Post)
Cunningham, James D., Sgt, BSM
Cunningham, William A., 2nd Lt, BSM
Cupit, Rufus M., Pfc, PH
Curiale, Salvatore L., T/4, BSM
Curran, Donald D., Pvt, PH
Curry, Earl S., S/Sgt, BSM
Curry, John F., 1st Lt, SS, PH
Curry, John T., Pvt, PH
Curry, Sol W., Pvt, BSM
Cusimano, Joseph, Pvt, PH

Daffner, Fred W., T/4, PH
Daily, Robert V., T/5, PH
Dall, George H., S/Sgt, BSM, SS
D'Andera, Tony, Pfc, BSM
D'Archangelo, Daniel J., Sgt, BSM
Daridson, Joseph G., Pvt, PH
Darling, Robert E., 1st Lt, BSM
Dattillio, Nicholas A., Pfc, BSM
Dau, Carl F., Pvt, PH
Davis, Buford, Pvt, PH
Davis, Early E., Pfc, PH
Davis, Paul D., 1st Lt, PH
Day, Carl O., 2nd Lt, PH
Day, Norman W., Pfc, BSM
Day, William J., Pvt, PH
Dean, George H., Pfc, PH
Deay, Walter D., Pfc, BSM (Post)
Deay, Walter E., Pfc, SS
Decker, Ralph, Jr., 1st Lt, PH
Decker, Raymond, Pvt, PH
Decugno, Yves L., S/Sgt, PH
Dedio, John J., Pfc, BSM, PH*
DeFranco, Phillip C., Pvt, PH*
Degnan, Frank A., T/4, PH
Degregorio, Henry, T/5, BSM, PH*
DeHoyos, Oswald, Sgt, SS
Delfiner, Henry, 2nd Lt, BSM
Delgato, Pablo, Pvt, SS
Delmar, Gordon, Pfc, PH
Delmasso, Fred L., Pvt, PH
DeLong, William D., Pfc, BSM
De Marco, John, S/Sgt, BSM
Demarco, John L., Sgt, PH*
DeMartyn, George A., Pfc, PH
Denicola, Ralph P., Pvt, PH
Depoda, Michael, Sgt, PH*
DeVore, Melvin V., Sgt, BSM
Dillon, Richard F., Pvt, BSM
Dincanson, James R., Pfc, PH
Dineen, Howard D., Pfc, BSM
Dininger, George R., Pfc, PH
Dionne, Marcel J., Pfc, BSM
Doerr, Wallace W., Pfc, BSM, PH
Doland, Edward L., 2nd Lt, PH
Dolde, Walter C., 2nd Lt, BSM
Dolkas, Tom P., Sgt, BSM
Domen, Harold R., T/4, BSM, PH
Donelson, Cavitt D., S/Sgt, PH*
Donelson, Henry M., 1st Lt, BSM, PH
Dougherty, Bernard H., Pfc, PH
Dowd, John R., Pfc, BSM
Dowell, Albert N., T/Sgt, BSM, PH**

Doyle, Jim S., Pfc, PH
Dozadousky, Michael, Pfc, PH*, BSM
Drake, James H., Lt Col, BSM, PH
Drozdowski, Edward M., Pfc, SS
Drozo, John J., Pvt, PH
Dryburgh, Walter F., Pfc, PH
Dubberly, Troy J., Pfc, PH
DuBois, Raymond L., Cpl, BSM
Duffy, Richard O., S/Sgt, BSM
Duggan, John J., T/Sgt, BSM
Duke, Paul P., Pfc, BSM
Dunkley, Wayne L., Pvt, PH
Duval, Lionel J., Pfc, BSM
Duzak, Andrew A., Pfc, PH
Dwyer, Howard J., Pfc, BSM

Eanes, Robert C., Pfc, BSM
Eaton, Robert R., Pfc, BSM
Ebel, John F., 2nd Lt, BSM, LM, PH
Ebersold, Clifford G., T/5, BSM, PH
Echard, Raymond E., S/Sgt, BSM
Eddy, Paul N., 1/Sgt, PH, DSC
Edmondson, Charles D., Capt, BSM*, PH*
Edwards, Chester H., Sgt, BSM
Edwards, Clarence W., 1st Lt, BSM, PH
Edwards, James H., T/Sgt, BSM
Edwards, Linton T., Pfc, PH
Eeck, David J., Pfc, BSM
Eichelberger, Paul, Pfc, BSM
Eichholz, Gerhard M., T/Sgt, BSM, PH, SS
Eisley, Anthony G., S/Sgt, PH
Ellis, Robert P., 2nd Lt, BSM
Ellis, Roy C., 1st Lt, SS
Elliott, Harmon C., Pfc, BSM
Ellsworth, Walter C., Pfc, DSC
Elmore, Harold F., Pfc, SS, PH
Emerick, Sherman W., Pvt, PH, BSM
Emery, Paul R., Sgt, BSM
Emmerthal, William G., S/Sgt, BSM
Endsley, Pete A., 1/Sgt, BSM, PH
Enger, David S., Pfc, PH
Engleson, Harold J., Pvt, BSM, PH*
Enochs, Jeff P., Capt, BSM, PH*
Epperley, Ivan E., Pfc, BSM
Erickson, Glen H., Capt, BSM (Post)
Errgong, John J., Sgt, BSM
Eschenback, Herman W., Pvt, PH*
Eulianc, John A., S/Sgt, BSM
Evans, John L., 1/Sgt, BSM, PH
Evans, Richard E., Pfc, PH
Evans, Robert B., 2nd Lt, PH

Fabrizio, Armand J., Cpl, BSM
Failla, Joseph S., Pfc, PH
Fairbanks, James M., T/Sgt, BSM
Falzerano, Gabriel, T/4, BSM, PH
Farmer, Asa E., Pfc, PH, SS (POW)
Faust, William H., Pfc, PH, SS
Felleman, John E., Jr., Pvt, PH
Ferguson, Clarence M., Cpl, SS
Ferguson, Lonnie G., Pfc, BSM, PH
Fernandez, Hector G., Pfc, BSM
Ferrara, Nicholas A., Sgt, PH*
Ferrington, Edmund P., Pfc, PH
Ficarra, Salvatore, Pfc, BSM
Fiegelist, Robert C., T/4, BSM
Field, Myer, Cpl, BSM*, PH
Fink, Russell H., Pfc, BSM
Finneran, Joseph M., Pfc, PH*
Finnerty, Frederick T., T/5, BSM
Fishburn, Kay H., Pfc, SS
Fisher, Dominick R., T/5, PH
Fisher, Ted E., Sgt, BSM
Fitzpatrick, John F., Cpl, BSM
Flannery, Charles R., Pfc, PH
Flatt, Floyd, Pfc, BSM
Flaum, Benjamin, S/Sgt, BSM
Flink, Leo A., Sgt, BSM
Flint, Ernest M., Pfc, BSM
Foley, William J., Pvt, PH
Foley, David W., T/4, BSM, PH
Fontaine, Arthur E., S/Sgt, BSM, PH

Forthoffer, Robert, Pfc, BSM
Foster, Donald W., Cpl, BSM
Fox, Carl E., S/Sgt, BSM
Fox, Roger H., T/Sgt, BSM
Frandsen, Earl F., 1st Lt, BSM
Frankel, Sol I., Major, BSM
Franklin, Benjamin J., PH
Franklin, Floyd E., S/Sgt, SS
Franklin, Gordie, Pfc, PH
Franks, William H., Pfc, BSM
Frazier, Otis L., S/Sgt, BSM, PH
Freeman, Claude H., T/5, BSM
Freeman, Olan R., Pfc, BSM
Fritschler, Edward, S/Sgt, PH
Froberg, William A., Pvt, PH
Fucci, James J., Sgt, BSM, PH
Furr, Charles P., Lt Col, BSM, LM
Fyhr, Carl I., T/5, BSM

Gable, Amos W., Pvt, PH
Gaeta, George, T/4, BSM
Gagnon, Harold A., T/5, PH
Galluccie, Paul A., Pvt, BSM
Gambold, Arol C., Pfc, BSM, PH
Garcia, Albert L., Pfc, PH*
Gasbarra, Amerigo, T/5, BSM
Gastonguay, Lyle D., Pvt, PH
Gaunt, John W., Pfc, PH
Gay, Howard R., Pfc, BSM
Geczi, William, 1/Sgt, PH*
Geelen, Leslie P., 2nd Lt, SS, BSM, PH
Gendron, Leo J., Pfc, PH
Genevay, Noel C, Pvt, PH
Gelston-Gelles, Robert H., 1st Lt, BSM
Gibbs, Marshall G., 1st Lt, BSM
Gibson, Frederick C., Pfc, BSM
Gilbert, R. L., Pvt, PH
Gilbert, William E., T/4, BSM
Gillen, Thomas J., 1st Lt, BSM
Gillespie, Howard A., Pvt, PH
Girard, Gerard L., Cpl, BSM
Glasgow, Lawrence J., Pfc, BSM
Glass, Russell P., Pvt, BSM
Gleason, Neil C., S/Sgt, PH
Glendening, Wm. A., 1st Lt, BSM
Glover, Benjamin J., Pfc, BSM, (Post)
Glune, Nevin A., Pfc, PH, BSM
Glynn, James T., S/Sgt, BSM
Godek, Edward J., T/5, BSM
Goffinet, Cahyle, T/4, BSM
Goffus, Joseph, Pvt, PH
Goldhagen, Raymond J., Pfc, PH*
Goldstein, Bernard, Cpl, BSM
Goldstein, Emanuel, S/Sgt, BSM
Goldstein, Milton H., Pfc, PH
Goldwag, Elias J., S/Sgt, BSM, PH
Gomes, Armand J., Pfc, PH
Gonzales, Augutin, Pvt, PH
Gonzalez, Julian G., Pvt, PH
Gonzales, Rodolfo, S/Sgt, SS, PH
Goodling, LeRoy C., Pfc, BSM
Gorman, John B., 2nd Lt, BSM
Gosa, George W., Pvt, BSM
Gosseen, David H., Pfc, BSM
Gotwalt, Daniel J., BSM, PH
Gould, Franklin L., S/Sgt, BSM
Grace, Thomas F., 1/Sgt, BSM, PH
Graham, Robert E., Pvt, PH
Gransow, George A., Pfc, BSM, PH
Grasser, Joseph L., T/4, PH
Greco, Raymond, Sgt, BSM
Green, Clarence B., Pvt, PH*
Green, Thomas S., Cpl, PH, BSM
Greer, James F., S/Sgt, BSM
Grefe, Raymond, S/Sgt, PH
Gregg, Ora, Cpl, PH
Gregory, Dewey R., Pfc, BSM
Gregory, George, T/5, PH
Greiner, Elbert E., T/Sgt, SS, PH
Grigsby, William C., Sgt, PH*
Grimsley, Marion K., Pvt, PH
Grippo, Vincent D., Sgt, BSM

Groesbeck, Byron, 1st Lt, PH*
Grzywacz, Edward J., Pfc, BSM
Guernsey, Charles R., Pfc, BSM
Guerrette, Reno L., Pfc, BSM
Guiles, Billie A., Pfc, BSM
Guinard, Walter J., Pfc, BSM
Guiterrez, Gabriel G., Pfc, BSM
Gulley, Frank, T/5, SS
Gursky, Peter, Cpl, PH
Gurule, Adolfo, Pfc, BSM, PH*
Guitierrez, Jack W., Pvt, PH

Hafer, Earl S., Pfc, BSM
Hager, William O., S/Sgt, PH, SS
Halka, Edward J., S/Sgt, BSM
Hall, Allen S., Pfc, BSM, PH*
Hall, James L., Pvt, PH
Hall, Richard G., T/5, SM, BSM
Hall, Vernon P., T/Sgt, BSM
Hamel, Gerard R., Pfc, PH
Hamilton, Grady R., Capt, BSM, PH*
Hamilton, Raymond, Pvt, BSM, PH*
Hammonds, Lomax, Pfc, BSM (Post)
Hamrysky, Charles J., T/Sgt, SS, PH
Haney, James M., Pfc, PH
Hansen, Walter A., Pfc, PH***
Hardy, John P., 1st Lt, PH*
Hargrove, James A., Cpl, BSM
Harper, Aubery C., Pfc, BSM, PH
Harpold, Robert D., Pfc, PH
Harrell, James P., Pfc, BSM, PH
Harris, Cecil P., Pfc, PH, BSM
Harris, Donald L., Cpl, PH
Harris, William H., S/Sgt, BSM
Harrison, Armstead, Pfc, BSM
Harrison, Edward A., Pvt, PH
Harrison, Harold A., Pvt, PH
Harrison, John L., Pfc, PH
Hartel, Harold H., T/4, PH, BSM
Hastings, Richard, Pfc, BSM
Hastings, Robert A., S/Sgt, BSM
Hawkins, Harold L., 2nd Lt, BSM
Hayduk, Andrew, Jr., T/Sgt, PH, BSM
Hayes, Chester W., Sgt, BSM
Hays, Orland W., Pfc, BSM
Hazen, Herman E., S/Sgt, BSM
Heath, Claude E., Pfc, BSM
Healey, Timothy W., 1st Lt, BSM, PH*
Hedrick, Samuel, Pfc, PH
Hedvall, Leonard A. J., Pfc, PH
Heeb, John, Pfc, BSM, PH*
Heffner, Robert E., Pfc, PH
Heeger, Robert B., Cpl, PH
Hege, Fred C., Cpl, PH
Heitman, Gilmer M., Jr., Capt, SS, PH
Henning, Robert F., Pfc, PH, BSM
Henderson, William C., Pfc, PH*, BSM
Hendrickson, Paul, Pfc, BSM
Henry, Andy F., 1st Lt, SS, PH**
Hensler, Eugene T., Pfc, PH
Henson, Thomas D., Pfc, BSM
Herrera, Jose E., Pfc, PH, BSM
Hess, Nicholas E., S/Sgt, BSM
Heuser, Robert W., 1st Lt, BSM*
Heyn, Kenneth E., Pvt, PH*
Hicks, Dan, Pvt, PH
Hiepler, Donald E., Pvt, PH
Higgins, William, Jr., S/Sgt, BSM
Hill, James, Pvt, BSM
Hinton, Woodrow, S/Sgt, BSM
Hobson, Victor W., Lt Col, SS, PH*, BSM, LM
Hodgdon, Charles F., Pvt, PH
Hodge, Dwayne, T/5, PH
Hodges, Dean B., Pfc, BSM, PH
Hoffman, Richard D., Sgt, SS
Hogan, Gerald R., S/Sgt, BSM
Hohenadel, William G., 1st Lt, BSM
Holas, Edward S., Pfc, PH
Holbein, Hans W., Cpl, BSM
Hollerman, Arthur C., Pfc, BSM
Holobeck, Kenneth C., Pfc, PH

Hoover, Elmer B., Capt, BSM, PH*
Hoover, James L., S/Sgt, PH
Hopkins, William L., T/4, BSM
Hornak, John G., Sgt, BSM
Houseman, Merle G., Pfc, BSM
Hovinga, Jacob, Pfc, BSM
Howard, Claude M., Lt Col, SS, BSM
Howard, Thomas E., T/4, PH, BSM
Howe, Arthur F., Sgt, PH
Howe, Richard O., Pfc, PH, BSM
Howell, Paul N., Pfc, PH
Hoyt, Warren G., Pvt, PH
Huffman, Harold E., Pfc, PH
Huffman, Truman M., Capt, BSM, PH
Hughes, Bradford, T/5, BSM
Hummel, Ray A., Pfc, BSM
Humpl, Frank J., Pfc, BSM
Huniznga, William, Pvt, PH*
Hunter, Benjamin J., 1st Lt, BSM
Hurd, Earl C., Pvt, PH
Huther, Lester R., Pfc, PH
Hutson, Alvin L., Pfc, BSM
Hyde, Alfred W., Pvt, PH
Hyde, Joseph T., Cpl, PH, BSM

Ignasiak, Sylvester J., Pvt, SS (Post)
Ison, Ronald P., Pvt, PH
Iverson, Donald J., Pfc, BSM

Jacobs, Charles R., Pfc, PH
Jacques, Horace H., Sgt, BSM
Jaime, Alfred C., 1st Lt, BSM
James, Hayden G., Pvt, PH
Jamrog, Stanley J., Pfc, PH, BSM
Janelle, Robert A., S/Sgt, BSM
Janowski, Raymond, Pfc, BSM
Jarvis, Edward, Pfc, BSM
Jaskolski, John A., Pfc, BSM
Jaskot, Joseph, Pvt, PH*
Jasper, William E., Pvt, PH
Javoroski, John J., Pfc, BSM
Jenkins, Robert M., Pvt, PH
Jenney, John T., Pvt, PH
Jerzak, Stanley, Pfc, PH
Jimenez, Abraham J., Pfc, PH, BSM
Jiminez, Frank A., Pfc, PH
Jollette, Gerard R., Pfc, PH*, BSM
Johnson, Adger H., Pfc, BSM
Johnson, Alden F., Pfc, SS
Johnson, Alfred R., Sgt, BSM
Johnson, Arthur, 1st Lt, PH, BSM
Johnson, Billy E., Pfc, PH
Johnson, Bruce J., Pfc, PH
Johnson, Carl W., T/4, BSM*
Johnson, David J., Pvt, PH
Johnson, Edward F., Sgt, BSM
Johnson, Elmer A., T/Sgt, BSM
Johnson, George H., Pfc, BSM
Johnson, Lyle E., Pfc, BSM
Johnson, Robert M., Pvt, PH
Johnston, Robert D., Pfc, PH
Joie, Joseph R., T/Sgt, PH, BSM
Jones, Charles C., Pfc, BSM
Jones, Ezrah H., Pfc, PH
Jones, Hewell P., Pvt, PH
Jones, William A., Sgt, BSM
John, William E., Cpl, PH
Jordan, Arnold J., Pfc, PH
Jurasz, Walter, S/Sgt, PH, BSM
Justice, James L., Pvt, BSM
Juuti, Oliva, Pvt, PH

Kane, Archie, S/Sgt, BSM, PH
Kane, John V., Pfc, PH
Kane, Joseph H., S/Sgt, BSM
Kann, Richard W., Pfc, PH
Karadimas, Constantine, Pvt, PH
Karras, Nicholas J., S/Sgt, BSM
Kasperitis, Martin W., Pfc, PH
Katz, Harold, Pfc, BSM
Kawa, Stephen C., T/5, BSM
Kaye, Lionel R., Capt, BSM

Keane, Henry, T/4, BSM
Kedzuh, John, Pvt, BSM (Post)
Keene, Jesse, Pvt, PH
Kees, Hobar E., Pfc, BSM
Keeton, Joseph, T/Sgt, BSM
Keil, William F., S/Sgt, BSM
Keller, Robert W., Pvt, BSM
Kendall, Raymond E., Lt Col, DSC
Kengerski, Stanley A., Pfc, PH*
Kennedy, William E., Pvt, PH
Kepley, John, S/Sgt, BSM, PH
Kerness, Leo J., S/Sgt, PH*, BSM
Kerouac, Edwin A., Pfc, BSM
Kessler, John D., 1st Lt, BSM
Key, Joseph, Pfc, BSM
Keys, Burlin, Pfc, BSM
Kildahl, Paul H., Pfc, PH
Kilgore, Louis B., Pvt, PH
Kimes, Edgar F., Pvt, BSM
King, Donald L., Pfc, SS
King, John J., Pfc, PH
King, Mont V., Pvt, PH
King, Walter G., Pfc, PH
Kirby, James A., S/Sgt, PH
Kirk, Morris E., T/5, PH
Kirkpatrick, Floyd J., Pfc, PH
Kistle, Oscar A., T/4, BSM
Klein, William H., Major, BSM, LM
Kler, Francis A., T/4, BSM
Knapp, Howard K., 2nd Lt, SS, SM
Knight, Charles W., T/5, BSM
Knight, Edward A., T/5, PH
Kobylinski, Casimer S., Pfc, BSM
Koczalka, Frank C., Pfc, PH
Koenig, Wilfred T., T/5, BSM, PH
Koncewicz, Joseph H., Pfc, PH
Konier, Peter J., T/5, BSM
Kornoelie, Frederick J., Pfc, BSM
Kotlarz, Walter A., Pfc, BSM
Kott, Louis, Pfc, PH
Kottyan, Eugene S., Pfc, PH
Kovach, John, Pfc, SS
Kowalski, Edward J., Pfc, PH
Kozik, Milo, Pfc, PH
Kozinski, John A., Sgt, BSM
Kraics, Frederick J., 2nd Lt, BSM
Krauack, Peter, Jr., Pfc, BSM
Kraus, Gilbert F., Sgt, BSM
Krause, George R., Pfc, PH
Kraus, John A., T/Sgt, BSM
Krauss, Fred K., Pvt, BSM*
Krejmas, Stephen J., Pfc, PH
Krolick, Edward J., Jr., S/Sgt, BSM
Krueger, Albert C., S/Sgt, SS
Kryszak, Anthony F., Pfc, PH*
Kuchta, John S., Sgt, PH
Kulka, Adam A., S/Sgt, BSM
Kura, Stephen, S/Sgt, PH

LaBlance, Elmer, Pvt, BSM
LaChance, Donald J., Pfc, PH
Lagnese, August, Pfc, BSM, PH
Lamar, John R., T/5, BSM (Post)
Lamb, John T., 2nd Lt, DSC, PH
Lambert, Hector R., Sgt, BSM
Lambert, John C., Pfc, BSM
Lanaham, Frank L., Pfc, PH*
Lance, John E., Pfc, BSM
Lancto, George E., S/Sgt, SS, PH**
Land, George, Pvt, PH
Landon, Harold F., Pvt, PH
Lanneville, Lionel, Pfc, PH
Lapp, Alfred F., Pfc, PH
Larson, Carl M., T/4, BSM
Lassiter, Jack R., S/Sgt, BSM
Laumen, Eugene W., S/Sgt, PH*
Lavin, Melvin M., Pfc, BSM
Lawson, Benjamin F., Pvt, BSM, PH
Leary, Charles A., Sgt, BSM
Lebek, Edward D., Pfc, BSM
Lebensorger, Frank H., 2nd Lt, PH
Lecomte, Greogoire J., Cpl, PH
Lee, Milton H., Sgt, BSM, PH

Leggett, Harry M., S/Sgt, BSM
Lehner, Paul, Capt, BSM
Lelko, Raymond S., Pvt, PH
Lemachko, John, Cpl, PH*
Lemire, Eugene E., Cpl, PH
Lenetti, Dominick, WOJG, PH, BSM
Leonard, Floyd K., Pvt, BSM, PH
Lerman, Jerome B., S/Sgt, BSM
Lester, Earl, T/4, BSM
Lester, Howard J., T/5, BSM
Lewandowski, Frank J., Pvt, BSM, PH
Lewandowski, William F., Pfc, PH
Lewis, Alfred, Pfc, PH
Lewis, Buren E., Pfc, BSM
Lewis, Irving A., Pfc, BSM
Lieberman, Harry A., 1st Lt, BSM
Liesner, Louis W., Pfc, BSM
Liffland, Sidney J., S/Sgt, PH
Lill, Leo T., T/4, BSM
Limbrunner, Frank E., T/Sgt, BSM
Limonik, John C., Pvt, PH*
Lindonen, Laurie, S/Sgt, PH**
Linville, Lamoin B., S/Sgt, BSM
Lisztwan, Joseph C., Pvt, PH
Little, John S., Pvt, PH
Little, Robert D., Pvt, BSM*
Loberg, Clifford O., Cpl, BSM
Lockear, Robert W., T/Sgt, PH
Locklin, Harvey E., S/Sgt, BSM
Lodesky, Robert F., Pvt, BSM
Logan, Hubert, Pfc, PH
Long, Aaron R., Pvt, PH
Lopez, Walker G., Pvt, BSM (MIA)
Lorenc, Theodore P., Pfc, BSM
Loterbaugh, Floyd P., T/Sgt, BSM*
Love, Garland D., Pfc, PH
Lowe, Roy, Pfc, PH*
Lowicki, Stephen S., Pfc, SS
Lown, Israel J., T/5, BSM
Lowry, Henry F., Pfc, BSM
Lubin, Leo, T/5, BSM
Lucas, Elmer, Pfc, BSM, PH**
Lukaes, William S., Pfc, PH
Lukaszewski, Chester M., Pfc, PH
Lumbard, George J., Pvt, BSM
Luna, David A., Pfc, BSM, PH
Lundquist, Norman L., Pfc, PH
Luther, Mark L., Pfc, BSM
Lyle, Emmet B., Capt, SS, PH
Lynch, David J., Pfc, BSM, PH
Lynch, William H., Pfc, BSM
Lynaugh, Quentin J., Pfc, PH
Lyons, Dock H., Cpl, BSM
Lytle, Joseph R., Pfc, PH

McAllister, James P., Pfc, PH
McAvoy, Arthur J., Pvt, BSM
McCafferty, Adrian, 1st Lt, PH
McCarthy, James, Jr., T/5, BSM, PH
McClay, Richard L., Pfc, BSM
McCormick, Frank W., T/Sgt, SS
McCraven, Philip, S/Sgt, PH
McCraw, Otha J., 2nd Lt, BSM, PH
McCulla, Verce R., Cpl, BSM
McDannald, Harold L., Sgt, PH**, SS
McDermott, Edward A., S/Sgt, BSM, PH
McDermott, William J., Sgt, BSM
McDonald, William C., WOJG, BSM
McDonnell, John J., Capt, SS
McDonough, Thomas F., 1/Sgt, BSM
McElyea, Truman E., Sgt, SS (MIA)
McEvoy, Andrew T., Pfc, BSM
McFarland, John C., Pfc, SS, PH
McGee, Lawrence W., Pvt, BSM
McGinty, James, Cpl, PH**
McGowan, Thomas F., S/Sgt, PH*, BSM
McGrann, Thomas A., 2nd Lt, PH, BSM
McGrath, John F., M/Sgt, LM
McKeage, Robert J., Pvt, PH
McKeever, James I., Pfc, PH
McKenna, Paul W., Pfc, BSM
McKinley, Russell, Pvt, BSM, PH
McKnabb, Edward L., Pfc, PH

McMahon, James F., T/4, PH, BSM
MacDonald, John M., Pvt, BSM
MacDonald, Lawrence J., Cpl, PH*
MacDonald, Leo M., 1st Lt, PH*
MacDonald, Lester F., 2nd Lt, PH, BSM
MacFaun, Ivan P., 2nd Lt, BSM
Machenry, Stanley, Pfc, PH*
Maciejewski, Leonard N., T/Sgt, SS
Magliaccio, Sam A., Pfc, PH
Mailander, Paul J., 1st Lt, BSM, LM
Majchrowicz, Walter S., 1/Sgt, PH, LM
Mallis, Joseph A., Pfc, PH*
Maloney, Patrick J., S/Sgt, PH, BSM
Mandia, Pat A., Pfc, PH*
Mancini, John F., T/Sgt, BSM
Mangan, Francis, Pfc, PH
Manning, John F., Pfc, BSM, PH
Maples, Lex V., T/Sgt, BSM
Marcus, Gordon K., 1st Lt, BSM
Maresco, Michael A., Pfc, PH
Mariano, Vincenzo, T/Sgt, BSM, PH
Marino, Vincent F., S/Sgt, PH
Markham, James H., 2nd Lt., PH
Marko, John, Cpl, PH
Marks, Edwin H., Jr., Major, SS, BSM
Marlowe, Walter J., 1st Lt, BSM
Martin, Eugene J., T/Sgt, SS
Martin, Frank, T/5, BSM
Martin, Lee, Pfc, BSM
Martinez, Benigno A., 1st Lt, BSM
Martinez, Lenardo L., Pfc, PH
Maryanovich, Walter, Pfc, PH
Mascera, Domninick, S/Sgt, BSM
Masin, Frank J., Pfc, BSM, PH
Mason, William T., Pvt, PH
Masone, James V., 1st Lt, PH*
Mattes, Albert, Sgt, PH
Matthews, John A., 1/Sgt, BSM, PH
Mattson, Walter J., Sgt, BSM
May, Dale R., S/Sgt, SS
Mayfield, Elton H., 1st Lt, BSM
Maynard, Carroll G., Pfc, PH
Mazetis, John J., Pfc, BSM
Mazza, Robert L., Cpl, PH
Meadows, Clifton A., Pfc, PH
Meeker, Charles L., Pfc, PH
Meeks, Clarence R., Capt, BSM (Post)
Meinel, George W., Pvt, PH*
Melillo, Nicholas, S/Sgt, BSM
Melton, Horace K., Pfc, BSM
Mercadante, Louis P., Pfc, PH
Mercer, Ernest J., Jr., S/Sgt, BSM*
Mericle, John A., S/Sgt, PH
Middelton, Joseph P., 2nd Lt, BSM
Migliaccio, Tony, Pfc, PH
Mikkelsen, Carleton R., 1st Lt, SS
Milam, Billy B., Pfc, BSM
Miller, Edgar R., Pfc, BSM
Miller, Howard E., Capt, PH
Miller, John C., T/5, BSM
Miller, Joseph F., Sgt, BSM
Miller, Philip, S/Sgt, BSM
Miller, Walter J., Cpl, SS, BSM
Miller, William L., Pvt, BSM
Milliken, John D., 2nd Lt, BSM
Mills, Joseph, Cpl, PH, SS
Minasian, Edward, Pfc, BSM
Minotte, Anthony R., Pfc, BSM, PH
Mincey, J. L., Pfc, BSM
Mishal, Harold M., Pfc, PH
Moats, Russell J., Pfc, PH
Moczmgemba, Daniel A., PH*, BSM
Moffat, Samuel S., Pfc, BSM
Moffett, Thomas F., Sgt, SS
Moll, Donald R., Pfc, PH*
Monroe, Gilbert H., T/5, BSM
Montague, Richard J., Pfc, SS (MIA)
Montoya, Ricardo, Jr., Pfc, PH
Moody, George R., M/Sgt, BSM
Moore, George J., Pfc, BSM
Moore, Henry C., Pvt, PH
Moore, Jay K., 1st Lt, BSM

Moore, Teddy A., Pvt, PH
Moore, William J., Jr., S/Sgt, PH
Moore, William V., Pfc, BSM
Moraitis, Elefterios J., Pfc, PH
Morawski, Leon, Pfc, BSM
Moreman, Percy J. Pfc, BSM
Moreschi, Harry T., Cpl, PH, BSM
Morford, Earl C., T/4, BSM
Moriarty Frances J., Cpl, PH**, BSM
Moriarty, John M., T/5, BSM
Morrison, James H., Pvt, PH
Morrison, Neil C., Pfc, PH
Mortensen, Edwin G., Pfc, BSM
Motguin, Bernard H., Pfc, PH
Mrowicki, Stanley J., S/Sgt, PH*
Mulcahy, Merlin M., 1st Lt, PH, BSM
Mullens, Ralph S., Pfc, PH
Mulligan, John J., T/Sgt, BSM
Mullins, Charles E., Pfc, PH
Mulvihill, Joseph A., Pvt, PH
Mundell, William R., S/Sgt, BSM
Munoz, Tidolo R., Pvt, BSM, PH
Murphy, Edward J., Sgt, BSM, PH
Murphy, John H., T/4, BSM
Murphy, Robert, 2nd Lt, BSM
Murray, Foster A., Pfc, BSM
Murray, Gerard F., 1st Lt, BSM
Murray Joseph A., Sgt, PH
Murrieta, Tony, T/4, PH, BSM
Mutschler, Herbert F., 1st Lt, SS, PH, BSM
Muvrin, Albert, 2nd Lt, SS
Myers, Harry S, Pfc, PH
Myers, Robert L., Pfc, BSM

Nall, Rogers C., Pvt, SS
Napolitano, John G., 2nd Lt, BSM
Neeley, John A., 1st Lt, SS
Nelson, Clifford T., Sgt, SS
Netzel, Richard G., Pfc, PH
Niditch, Sutart, T/5, PH*, BSM
Nierodzinski, Alex T., Cpl, PH
Nigro, Michael F., Pfc, PH
Nilsen, Henry E., 1st Lt, BSM
Nobile, Emil A., S/Sgt, PH, BSM
Noble, Beryl S., Pfc, BSM (Post)
Nolan, Loyal E., Pfc, PH
Noon, Theodore W., Jr., 1st Lt, DSC
Norkus, Alexander B., T/Sgt, BSM, PH
Norman, Ben H., Pfc, PH
Nosalo, Paul C., Pfc, PH
Novack, Tony A., Pfc, PH
Nowak, Walter F., S/Sgt, PH
Numrick, Herbert H., Pfc, BSM

Ober, Joseph A., Pvt, PH*
O'Brien, Edward T., S/Sgt, SS
O'Brien, Joseph W., Cpl, BSM
O'Brien, Matthew F., T/4, PH*
O'Hara, William, Pfc, PH
Ohme, Herman W., Lt Col, SS (Post)
Olas, Leon J., Pvt, PH*
Oldaker, Richard, S/Sgt, BSM
O'Leary, Curtis F., Pfc, PH
Olivas, Pablo R., Pfc, BSM
Olowieski, Stanley, Sgt, PH
Omerio, Frank L., Pvt, PH
O'Neal, Walter, Pvt, PH
Opyt, Edward F., Pfc, PH
Orloff, Peter, S/Sgt, BSM
Orona, Jose C., S/Sgt, PH, SS (Post)
Orton, Russell C., 1st Lt, SS
Osbourn, Warren E., Pfc, PH
Otten, John H., 1st Lt, BSM
Ouellette, Norman E., Pfc, BSM
Over, Ezra A., Pvt, PH

Paceley, Lowell E., Pfc, BSM (Post)
Padwe, Joseku, S/Sgt, BSM
Page, Amos F., Pfc, BSM
Page, Peat O., Pfc, BSM
Paianiuk, Natty, Pfc, BSM
Palazzolo, Daniel, Pvt, PH

Palermo, Sam F., Cpl, PH*
Pallett, Edward K., Pfc, BSM
Palm, Clifford A., Pfc, PH
Palmer, Robert H., T/5, BSM
Palmieri, James, Pfc, BSM
Pantha, Lloyd R., Sgt, PH*
Paoletti, Santo, Pfc, PH
Papp, Andy, Pfc, BSM
Parks, James D., Pfc, PH
Parks, Jasper D., 1st Lt, PH, BSM
Parks, Winifred D., Cpl, PH
Parker, Gerald J., Pfc, PH
Parker, Richard S., T/Sgt, BSM
Parnell, John C., Cpl, BSM
Parr, George L., Sgt, SS (Post)
Parsons, Ofa C., Pfc, BSM
Partin, Clarence M., Pfc, PH
Partridge, William F., 1st Lt, BSM, PH
Pashby, Douglas E., Pfc, PH*
Passick, Joseph H., Pfc, PH
Paterson, Thomas, Pvt, PH
Patton, Donald A., S/Sgt, BSM
Patukonis, John J., Pfc, SS, PH
Pavlinec, James F., Pvt, BSM, PH*
Pawelczak, Peter P., Sgt, BSM
Pawlik, John, Pfc, SS
Payne, William R., Pvt, PH
Pearson, Arnold H., S/Sgt, PH
Peck, Romeo O., Pfc, BSM
Peles, Nicholas, Sgt, BSM
Pelham, Richard C., Pfc, PH
Pelletier, Rene E., Pfc, PH
Pemberton, Harry H., Cpl, PH
Pent, William P., Pvt, PH
Penzell, Lawrence, T/5, BSM
Pepper, Abraham, Pfc, BSM
Pepperman, Harold A., 2nd Lt, BSM, PH
Perdains, Raymond E., 1/Sgt, BSM
Perez, Gergorio, Pfc, BSM*
Perkins, L. C., Sgt, PH
Perman, Calvin S., Pfc, PH
Perman, Galvin W., Pfc, BSM
Perry, Elbert M., Sgt, BSM
Perry, Ernest R., Pfc, BSM
Persson, Erik H., Pfc, BSM
Pesano, Edward J., 2nd Lt, SS
Peters, Eugene, Pfc, BSM
Peters, Fred, Jr., Pfc, PH
Peters, Victor, Pfc, BSM
Peterson, Edward E., S/Sgt, BSM
Peterson, John E., 2nd Lt, PH
Petro, John T., S/Sgt, SS
Petrosky, Francis A., T/5, PH, BSM
Pettit, Leon, T/5, PH, BSM
Petty, Lionel C., Pfc, PH*
Piela, George A., T/5, PH
Pierce, Charles W., 2nd Lt, BSM, DSC
Pillard, Clarence L., Sgt, BSM
Pinion, James E., Sgt, PH*
Piwonka, Fred L., 1/Sgt, BSM
Pizzi, Bionti A., Sgt, BSM, PH*
Pleau, Leo J., Pfc, PH
Plemmons, Thomas R., Sgt, PH
Podrasky, Andrew M., Sgt, BSM
Pointer, Marshall N., Pfc, PH
Polinsky, Alfred, Pfc, BSM
Poole, Charles E., 1/Sgt, BSM
Post, Chester A., M/Sgt, LM
Potocny, Ferdinand R., Cpl, PH*
Powe, Walker H., Jr., Capt, BSM, PH
Powell, James E., Pfc, PH
Powers, Reginald W., Sgt, BSM
Prange, John E., Pvt, PH, SS
Prater, Billy D., Sgt, BSM
Prather, Clayton, T/5, BSM, PH
Prather, Herbert E., S/Sgt, SS, BSM
Pratt, Howard, Pvt, BSM
Pratt, James H., Pfc, PH
Pratt, Russell J., Sgt, PH
Pratt, William L., S/Sgt, PH
Pressentin, Vernon F., 1st Lt, BSM
Price, Neel J., Capt, PH*, BSM*, LM

Printy, Richard L., Pvt, PH*
Proctor, Francis L., Pfc, BSM
Proffitt, James R., Pvt, BSM
Pruett, Henry R., Pvt, BSM
Prunty, Albert E., Pfc, BSM
Pucket, Howard E., T/5, BSM
Pulliam, Calvin A., 2nd Lt, SS
Purdy, Aubrey, Cpl, BSM
Pustejousky, Jerry J., Pfc, BSM

Quackenbush, Warren, Pfc, PH
Quarles, Herschel L., Sgt, BSM
Quayles, Harvey P., Pvt, BSM, PH
Quilty, Joseph J., Pvt, PH
Quinn, Raymond E., T/4, BSM, PH
Quinn, Terrance J., T/4, BSM, PH

Rabinowe, Albert W., Sgt, PH
Radosevich, Charles J., Capt, PH, BSM, SS, LM
Raduha, John J., Pfc, BSM
Ranalli, Joseph J., S/Sgt, BSM
Rankins, Junior R., S/Sgt, PH, BSM
Rapata, John E., Pvt, PH
Rapkin, Morris, Pfc, PH
Ratliff, Howard W., T/4, BSM
Ratoff, Robert R., S/Sgt, BSM
Rauch, Loren J., S/Sgt, SS
Red, Garland S., Pvt, BSM
Redfield, Herbert L., S/Sgt, SS
Reed, Ira J. T., Cpl, PH*, BSM
Regan, James C., Pvt, PH
Regula, George J., S/Sgt, PH
Reichardt, Frank O., Pfc, PH
Reichert, Donald H., Pfc, PH*
Reid, Chester W., 2nd Lt, BSM (Post)
Reid, John C., Capt, PH
Reilly, Richard F., T/5, PH
Reinwart, Albert F., Capt, SS, PH, BSM
Reppert, Luther G., Pfc, PH
Reynolds, Clarence W., Pvt, BSM
Rhees, James P., Pfc, PH
Rhodes, Charles E., Cpl, PH, BSM
Rhoten, Stephen W., Sgt, PH*, BSM
Rible, Lorraine J., S/Sgt, BSM, PH
Riccitelli, Arthur J., Pfc, PH
Richard, W. Wayne, Pfc, PH, SS
Richards, Lawrence W., Pfc, BSM
Richart, Stanton D., 1st Lt, PH*, SS
Rickenbach, Deloy, Cpl, SS
Rickman, Cecil L., Pfc, PH
Rielbasinski, Raymond, Pfc, PH*
Rife, Stanley S., 1st Lt, BSM
Riga, Alvin V., Capt, BSM, PH
Rigney, James C., Pfc, BSM
Riley, Eldon, Pfc, PH
Rita, Anthony J., Pfc, SS
Rivera, Harry, Pfc, BSM*, PH
Rizzuti, Eugene A., T/5, BSM
Roach, Richard W., Pfc, PH
Roberts, James W., Pvt, PH
Robeson, Albert D., 1st Lt, BSM
Robinson, Edward A., 2nd Lt, PH*, BSM
Robinson, John A., T/4, PH
Robinson, Robert R., Pvt, PH
Robuck, Billy C., S/Sgt, BSM
Rochira, John, Pfc, PH
Rodriguez, Benito H., Pvt, PH
Rodriguez, Fernando C., Pvt, PH
Rodriguez, Hendrick F., Pvt, SS (Post)
Rodriques, Louis A., Pfc, BSM
Roephke, John A., Cpl, BSM
Rogers, David C., 1st Lt, BSM, PH
Rogers, Duane O., Pvt, PH
Roginski, Charles H., Pvt, BSM
Rohlik, Arthur H., Pfc, BSM
Roland, LeRoy J., Pfc, PH
Rosamilia, Carl J., T/5, PH
Rose, James V., 2nd Lt, PH
Rose, Robert L., Pfc, PH*
Rosen, Joshua L., Cpl, BSM
Rosenblum, Irving, T/4, BSM

Rosenstein, Herman, 1st Lt, PH
Ross, Herbert C., Pvt, PH
Ross, Woodrow W., Pvt, PH
Rosenthal, Morris, T/5, BSM
Rossi, Anthony F., Cpl, BSM
Rossi, Arnold J., Cpl, BSM
Rossi, Carl L., Pfc, PH
Rotger, Anthony C., Pvt, BSM
Rowe, George E., Pfc, BSM
Roy, Lucien A., Sgt, PH
Rubino, Dominick, Pfc, PH
Rubino, George R., Sgt, SS, BSM
Runci, Richard A., Sgt, BSM
Ruocco, Adolph, S/Sgt, PH, BSM
Ruopp, Martin F., 1st Lt, BSM
Rutledge, A. J., Pvt, BSM
Russell, Charles R., Pvt, PH**
Russell, Howard C., Pfc, BSM
Russell, James, 2nd Lt, PH*
Rust, Lyle E., Pvt, SS
Rutledge, A. J., Pvt, BSM*
Ryan, Harold A., Pvt, BSM (Post)

Sabonis, Frank S., Pfc, BSM
Sabra, Budde P., T/5, PH
Sadler, David H., Major, PH*, BSM
Salberg, Edward, Pfc, BSM
Salinas, Victor O., Pfc, PH
Salmon, John W., Pvt, PH
Salo, Mitro L., Pfc, BSM
Salynski, Andrew, 2nd Lt, PH
Sample, Delvin V., S/Sgt, DSC
Sanchez, Rodolpho V., Pfc, SS
Sanders, Charlie W., Pvt, PH
Sandlin, William B., Jr., 1st Lt, DSC, PH, BSM
Sansouci, Aime, Pvt, PH
Sapko, Walter J., T/5, BSM
Saunders, Lester C., Pfc, BSM
Sautter, Edward G., 1st Lt, BSM, PH*
Sautter, Leo L., Capt, SS, PH
Schaefer, Hellmuth H., T/5, PH
Schaffer, George D., Capt, PH*
Schaller, Clyde R., T/Sgt, BSM
Scharfenberg, John D., Pfc, PH
Schechter, Joseph, Pvt, PH
Scheetz, Gilbert A., Pfc, BSM
Scheidecker, Frank, Pvt, PH
Schneider, Bertram O., Pfc, BSM
Schirlka, Lester J., Sgt, PH
Schmerghardt, Wendell, Pvt, PH
Schmidt, Robert C., T/5, BSM
Schmordus, William J., Sgt, PH*
Schmueser, Howard E., Pfc, PH
Schnabel, Jacob, Jr., Pfc, PH, BSM
Schneider, John E., S/Sgt, PH
Schnorbus, William J., Sgt, SS, PH
Schoeppner, John H., Cpl, BSM
Schutofsky, Joseph, Pvt, BSM
Schultz, Robert L., 1st Lt, BSM
Schweizer, William C., Pvt, PH
Scott, James B., Pfc, PH, BSM
Scott, James R., Pfc, BSM
Scott, William F., Jr., Pfc, SS
Scrivani, Edward A., Pfc, PH
Seiquist, Clayton H., Pvt, PH*
Sellers, Wilburn, Pfc, PH
Serbent, Warren F., Capt, BSM
Sergent, Malcolm P., Pfc, PH
Servitto, Edward A., S/Sgt, PH
Setina, John T., Pfc, BSM
Sexton, Carl, Pfc, BSM*, PH
Shafer, Carlyle S., Pvt, PH
Shaffer, George D., Capt, SS, PH* (Post)
Shaffer, Lee E., 2nd Lt, PH
Shaffer, Roy D., 2nd Lt, PH*
Shalata, Michael J., Pvt, BSM
Shapiro, Paul, Pfc, PH
Sharos, James L., Cpl, PH
Sharp, Earnes G., Pfc, PH
Shaw, Bill D., Pfc, SS, BSM (Post)
Shaw, Glen J., S/Sgt, BSM

Shaw, Lawrence L., S/Sgt, BSM
Shaw, Roy L., Jr., Pfc, BSM
Sheppa, George, Cpl, BSM
Sherlin, Joseph J., S/Sgt, BSM, PH
Sherman, Warren A., Pfc, SS
Shipley, Gerald S., Pvt, BSM*
Shoemaker, Clifton M., Pfc, PH
Shuler, Stephen E., Pfc, PH
Shull, Edwin L., Major, BSM, PH
Sibley, James E., 1st Lt, BSM
Siddall, Kenneth A., Pvt, PH
Siegel, Marvin C., T/5, BSM
Sigler, Raymond D., CWO, BSM
Simon, Clem T., T/Sgt, PH
Simon, Simon, S/Sgt, PH
Simmons, Lawrence E., Cpl, BSM
Simons, John, Pfc, PH*
Singerman, Arthur J., 1st Lt, PH
Sisenwein, Harry, Pvt, PH
Siswein, Harold I., Pfc, PH
Skalyo, George, Pfc, PH
Skowronski, Edward D., Pfc, PH
Skroubski, Bruno J., Pfc, PH
Slatcin, Meyer H., Capt, BSM
Smilewicz, Raymond J., Pvt, PH
Smith, Edward G., Pfc, PH
Smith, George, Pvt, PH
Smith, Robert A., T/Sgt, SS, PH
Smith, Russell G., T/5, BSM
Smoak, Francis M., Pvt, BSM
Smolinski, Raymond J., Pvt, PH**
Smullen, John H., T/Sgt, SS
Snowden, Jesse L., S/Sgt, PH*, BSM
Snyder, Richard D., T/4, BSM, PH*
Sobolewski, Stanley J., S/Sgt, BSM
Soellner, Frederick W., 2nd Lt, PH
Soileau, J. U., T/Sgt, BSM
Sokol, Eugene H., Pfc, PH
Solomon, Jerome I., T/5, BSM
Sopizak, Joseph S., Pfc, BSM
Sorber, Bert H., Cpl, PH
Sorensen, Horace, T/5, BSM
Sorrell, Herman H., Pvt, PH
Spayer, Joseph E., Sgt, PH
Spears, Albert, Pfc, PH
Spears, Harry A., S/Sgt, SS
Speranza, George J., Pfc, PH
Spicer, Charles M., T/Sgt, SS
Spinale, Phillip J., Pvt, BSM
Spires, William H., Pfc, PH
Sprague, Lester W., S/Sgt, BSM, PH
Sprague, William R., S/Sgt, BSM
Springer, Harry J., Cpl, BSM
Spurling, Stephen S., Sgt, BSM
Spurlock, James W., Pvt, PH
St. Hilaire, Brendan F., T/5, BSM
Stabb, John P., 2nd Lt, PH, BSM
Staley, Eddie W., Pvt, PH
Stamper, Melvin W., Pfc, BSM
Stancati, Rocco J., Pfc, PH
Stanley, Dennis P., Pfc, PH
Stapelton, Phillip N., Pvt, PH
Starling, William H., T/4, PH
Stec, Theodore J., Cpl, BSM (Post)
Steele, Aulton, Pfc, SS
Steele, William P., Pfc, PH
Steffens, Robert A., S/Sgt, PH
Steinacher, Norman W., Pfc, PH, BSM
Stellaway, Edgar G., Pfc, BSM
Stenquist, Donald G., Pfc, BSM*
Steranelli, Michael J., Cpl, BSM
Stickland, Cedric J., Pfc, PH
Stinnett, Wesley R., Pfc, PH*
Stockmal, Joseph C., Pfc, PH
Stone, Glen E., Pvt, PH
Stone, Joseph F., Sgt, BSM
Story, Thomas E., Pfc, PH
Stowell, Charles A., Jr., Pfc, PH
Stowell, Willard E., Pfc, BSM
Strausser, Richard K., T/5, BSM
Strickland, Ardis E., Pvt, BSM, PH
Stroika, Alvin M., S/Sgt, BSM

Stromer, Adolf F., T/4, BSM
Strong, Donald H., Pfc, PH, BSM
Strozzi, Joseph, S/Sgt, BSM, PH*
Stubbs, John D., Pfc, PH
Sturgis, Theodore F., Pfc, PH
Suhy, John A., T/5, BSM, PH
Sullivan, Thomas A., Sgt, BSM
Sunderland, William H., Pvt, PH
Surovoy, John D., Pfc, PH
Swafford, Henry L., T/4, PH
Swafford, William C., Sgt, BSM
Sweany, Harold V., T/Sgt, PH

Takach, John E., Pfc, SS
Tansey, Bernard P., Pfc, BSM, PH*
Tarala, Walter, Pfc, BSM, PH
Tardi, John A., Pfc, BSM
Targett, James S., Pvt, PH, BSM*
Tavennar, Jack D., Pvt, BSM*
Taylor, Donald, Pfc, SS (Post)
Taylor, Joseph, Pfc, PH
Taylor, Ray E., Pfc, PH
Taylor, Robert E., Pfc, BSM
Tell, Andrew, Jr., Pfc, SS
Terran, Vincent, Pvt, PH
Tessler, Ovila A., Pfc, BSM
Theiss, Gilbert A., Pfc, BSM
Theodoracopouios, John M., Cpl, PH
Thomson, George, Pvt, PH
Thom, Ian W., Cpl, BSM
Thompson, John W., Jr., S/Sgt, BSM, SS
Thompson, Robert E., Pfc, BSM
Thompson, William M., Capt, PH, BSM
Thorpe, Raymond L., Sgt, BSM
Tickle, John M., Pfc, PH
Tighe, Paul H., Cpl, PH, BSM
Tilton, John J., Pfc, BSM
Tinsley, Marvin H., Pvt, PH
Tipps, Jesse L., Pfc, BSM
Titus, Howard B., Pfc, PH
Tomaskovich, Joseph J., Pfc, PH*
Tomaszewski, Michael, S/Sgt, BSM
Toomey, Edward P., T/Sgt, BSM
Tosi, Arthur, Pfc, SS
Towne, Robert L., Pfc, BSM
Townsend, John C., Pvt, BSM
Tozer, Richard I., Pfc, PH
Tracy, Thomas C., Cpl, PH*
Tramel, Charles W., Pvt, PH
Trapp, W. A., S/Sgt, BSM
Tribble, Jesse L., Pvt, BSM
Trocchio, Andrew J., T/Sgt, BSM
Tropoano, Arthur G., Cpl, PH
Trumble, John W., 1st Lt, BSM
Trujillo, Juan E., Pfc, PH*
Tschida, Robert G., 2nd Lt, PH
Tucas, Harry P., Pfc, PH
Tuccilla, Peter L., Pfc, PH
Tuchapski, John, Pvt, PH
Tucker, John T., Pvt, PH*
Turner, James C., Sgt, BSM
Tyberg, George E., Pfc, SS
Tyler, John J., Pvt, PH
Tyler, John T., Pfc, BSM
Tynan, Stephen T., Cpl, PH*
Tyra, Louis, S/Sgt, BSM
Tyrrell, Wayne M., 2nd Lt, BSM

Unger, John, Pfc, PH
Urbanek, Daniel T., Pfc, PH*
Urbanovsky, Stephen J., Pfc, BSM
Uscio, Leo A., Pfc, BSM

Valent, William O., 1st Lt, BSM
VanAlstyne, Earl D., Lt Col, BSM, PH
Van Bergen, John F., Sgt, PH, SS (Post)
VanBrunt, Robert G., Pfc, BSM
Van Buren, Clifton C., Pvt, PH
Vance, Heber G., Capt, BSM
Vanderberg, William H., S/Sgt, SS
Van Horn, Cecil, Pvt, PH
Vanko, John, T/3, BSM, PH*

Van Riper, Wilber, Cpl, PH
Van Teslar, Stanley A., Pfc, BSM
Van Wickler, Daniel B., Pfc, PH*
Vasseur, Ellie, Pfc, PH
Vaughn, Clyde A., T/Sgt, SS
Veillon, Ardus, Pvt, BSM, PH
Venturella, Joseph B., Pvt, PH
Verdi, Joseph P., Pfc, SS
Verspoor, Edwin E., Sgt, BSM
Via, George E., Pfc, BSM
Vigorita, Carmine, Pvt, PH
Vincent, Jack W., Pvt, PH**
Violette, Leo J., Pvt, PH
Virgadula, Frank, Pvt, PH
Viscanti, Vicenzo, S/Sgt, PH
Vita, Joseph, S/Sgt, BSM
Vodacek, Thomas, Pfc, BSM, PH
Vosseler, Charles, Jr., Pvt, PH
Votaw, Charles, S/Sgt, BSM
Vrabel, Edward, Pvt, BSM

Wakefield, Audley, Pvt, PH
Walden, Lenward B., Pvt, PH
Walden, Leo, T/Sgt, BSM
Waldner, William A., T/5, BSM
Walker, Peter E., Pfc, PH
Wallace, Elmer, Pvt, PH
Wallenhorst, Urban R., Pvt, PH*, BSM
Walmer, William R., Pvt, PH
Walsh, Edward E., 1st Lt, BSM, SS, PH
Walsh, Gene L., S/Sgt, BSM
Walters, Raymond W., Pvt, PH
Ward, Samuel D., Pfc, BSM
Ward, Vernon L., Pfc, PH, SS
Ward, Vincent E., T/4, PH
Warf, Raymond, Pfc, BSM
Warf, Virgle J., Jr., Pfc, PH
Warner, Branch H., Pvt, PH
Warner, Robert L., Pvt, PH
Warren, Malcoln J., Sr., Pvt, PH
Waser, Werner F., T/Sgt, PH, BSM
Waszkiewicz, Thaddeus J., Sgt, BSM
Waters, Paul C., Cpl, BSM
Watroba, Andrew J., Pfc, BSM
Watts, Colman T., Pfc, BSM
Watts, William C., Cpl, SS, PH
Webb, John C., Pfc, PH
Webber, Harry, T/Sgt, PH, BSM
Weber, Arnold J., Sgt, BSM
Webster, Robert R., T/5, PH
Weiner, Sidney, Pvt, BSM
Weiss, Seymour, Pvt, BSM*
Wells, Elmer D., Pfc, PH
Wells, Lester E., Pvt, SS
Welsch, Franklin T., Pfc, PH
Wentworth, James W., Sgt, BSM
Weston, LeRoy E., Pvt, PH
Weyer, Charles T. A., Cpl, PH
Whalen, John R., T/5, BSM
Whetsel, Dwayne, Pvt, PH
White, Robert E., Cpl, BSM
White, Thomas A., 1st Lt, SS, BSM
Whittet, David S., S/Sgt, BSM
Wieters, Robert, Sgt, PH
Wilbur, Norman H., Pfc, PH*
Wilcox, Leo E., Pfc, BSM
Wilhelm, Robert P., Pfc, BSM
Wilhelm, Valentine, Pvt, PH
Wilkerson, John A., Pvt, PH
Wilkins, Lyle H., Pvt, BSM (Post)
Will, Jerome J., Pfc, PH
Willet, Raymond E., Pfc, BSM (Post)
Williams, Alfred A., Pfc, BSM
Williams, Billy D., Pfc, PH
Williams, Charlie L., Sgt, BSM
Williams, David D., Pfc, SS (Post)
Wilson, David G., Capt, BSM*
Williams, Ross E., Pfc, PH, BSM
Williams, Trevor E., Major, SS, BSM
Wilson, David A., Pfc, BSM
Wilson, Donald, S/Sgt, BSM
Wilson, Floyd M., Pvt, PH

Wilson, James B., 2nd Lt, BSM
Wilson, Thomas C., Pfc, SS
Wilson, Walter B., Pvt, PH
Wings, William F., Pvt, PH
Winters, Paul D., T/3, BSM (Post)
Winther, Peter E., Pfc, SS, BSM
Wise, John A., Pvt, PH
Wishart, John, Pvt, PH
Wojtawicz, Edward J., S/Sgt, BSM
Wolcott, Clifford R., 1st Lt, PH
Wolff, Albert, Pfc, PH
Wolfe, Raymond, Pvt, PH
Wolkowicz, Alfred, Cpl, BSM
Wong, Wing H., T/5, BSM
Wood, Kenneth M., Capt, BSM
Wood, Leonard O., Jr., Pvt, PH
Wood, Ralph C., Pfc, PH
Woodcock, Francis J., Sgt, BSM
Woodcock, Wilton A., Pfc, BSM
Woods, Archibald, T/4, BSM, PH
Woodside, William C., S/Sgt, SS
Woodward, J. B., Pfc, BSM

Workman, Minor S., S/Sgt, SS
Wright, Elmer W., Pfc, BSM
Wright, Eugene T/Sgt, BSM, PH
Wright, Preston S., 1st Lt, BSM
Wright, Wilbur H., T/Sgt, BSM
Wrobel, Walter J., Sgt, BSM
Wyman, Vernon L., Pfc, BSM
Wynkeep, Archie, S/Sgt, PH

Yanke, Albert G., Pfc, PH
Yankowski, Joseph A., Pfc, PH
Ybarra, Jesus P., Pfc, PH*
Yeager, Walter B., Lt Col, SS*, PH*, BSM
Yost, Gordon W., Pvt, PH
Young, Leonard T., Pvt, PH
Young, Raymond D., 1st Lt, BSM

Zawrotny, Joseph T., Pfc, PH
Zgabay, Edwin, Cpl, PH
Ziegler, Frank J., S/Sgt, SS (Post)
Zinsmerster, Willard T., S/Sgt, BSM
Zizi, John P., S/Sgt, PH, BSM

HEADQUARTERS BATTERY
DIVISION ARTILLERY

Bailey, Charles A., T/5, BSM
Beck, Rolland C., Capt, BSM
Brown, Horace M., Jr., Major, BSM
Burton, Edmond A., T/5, PH
Buysse, Leon, S/Sgt, BSM
Butler, Robert W., Capt, BSM
Champagny, Oliver T., M/Sgt, BSM
Chiarello, Nugent J., T/5, BSM
Dunford, Donald, Col, BSM
Evans, Ralph R., T/5, BSM
Fish, James L., Major, AM*****
Fisher, Henry W., S/Sgt, BSM
Fisher, Thomas A., T/4, BSM
Gtyr, Hrothr T., Jr., Major, BSM
Gallagher, Joseph, T/5, BSM
Gaudette, Ernest J., Pvt, PH
Henry, Eugene J., T/4, BSM
Hurt, Nathan, S/Sgt, BSM
Kennedy, Gregory R., Capt, BSM
Kowalik, Ernest E., 2nd Lt, AM*******
Kurtz, Guy O., Brig Gen, BSM, AM
Lewis, Thomas E., Brig Gen, BSM, PH*

Lockard, Valentine D., WOJG, BSM
Magnani, Robert S., Cpl, BSM
McHarg, Tom D., Capt, BSM, PH
Naramore, Vincent H., 1st Lt, BSM
Nixon, Victor M., 1st Lt, BSM
Pryor, Francis J., III, Capt, BSM
Quimby, Lloyd W., T/Sgt, BSM
Ritan, Andrew, Major, BSM
Reiss, Saul, 1st Lt, BSM
Rodrigo, Francis, Cpl, BSM
Rudnick, Joseph M., T/Sgt, BSM
Sawallis, Robert F., Capt, BSM
Schrock, Dalton E., T/5, BSM
Southall, Charles S., 1st/Sgt, BSM
Stutesman, John H., Jr., 1st Lt, BSM
Tauber, Richard A., M/Sgt, BSM
Vreeland, Elbert W., T/5, BSM
Wallis, Frank J., Jr., Major, LM
Williams, I. D., Cpl, BSM
Wilson, Arley J., Capt, AM*********
Winslow, John S., Lt Col, BSM
Powers, George T., Col, BSM

337TH FIELD ARTILLERY BATTALION

Bay, Ovid U., Capt, BSM
Bretschneider, Louis L., Capt, BSM, PH
Brooks, William S., Capt, BSM
Brown, Horace M., Jr., Major, BSM
Carty, Joseph, 2nd Lt, PH
Cooper, Edward P., 1st Lt, AM
Cunningham, John W., 1st Lt, AM
DeLuga, Sigmund S., 1st Lt, BSM
DeVaughn, James E., Capt, BSM
Fagerlie, Conrad I., 1st Lt, AM
Farrel, John J., 1st Lt, BSM, PH
Gandner, John J., 1st Lt, PH
Gold, Jerome, CWO, BSM
Hargreaves, Wilson, Lt Col, BSM, PH
Huyser, Henry, 1st Lt, BSM
Jackson, Donald W., Capt, BSM
Kennedy, Everett F., Capt, BSM
Koehler, Marvin L., Capt, BSM, PH
Lester, George H., Jr., Capt, BSM, PH
Lord, William G., 1st Lt, AM, PH
McDonald, Malcom B., Major, BSM
McNamara, Charles A., Jr., 1st Lt, BSM, AM
Messing, Victor D., 1st Lt, BSM
Morley, LeRoy B., Capt, BSM, PH
Munger, Robert S., 1st Lt, PH
Newman, Bernard J., 1st Lt, PH
Palmer, Roland E., Capt, BSM
Powers, George T., III, Col, LM, BSM

Pressly, David L., Capt, BSM
Rodgers, Carroll S., 2nd Lt, AM
Rosee, William H., 1st Lt, AM
Roudebush, George, Jr., 1st Lt, BSM, AM, **PH**
Sanders, James M., 1st Lt, BSM, PH
Shields, William F., 1st Lt, AM, PH
Tenzyk, Joseph J., 1st Lt, BSM
Adamowich, Stanley, T/5, PH
Alexander, Joe H., Pvt, PH
Atkins, Eugene A., Cpl, BSM
Armstrong, George P., Pvt, PH
Arnold, Williard A., T/4, PH
Arruda, George P., Pfc, PH
Avallone, Patrick J., Cpl, PH
Barton, James P., S/Sgt, PH
Baumann, Alvin P., Pfc, PH
Benson, Hjalmar, T/4, PH
Bianchetti, Gabriel, Pvt, PH
Blake, William F., Pfc, BSM
Board, Robert L., Pfc, PH
Bogacz, Fred, Sgt, BSM, PH
Bosher, George R., S/Sgt, BSM
Brassard, Oliver J., 1st/Sgt, BSM
Breault, Emery A., Cpl, PH
Bruff, Judd C., S/Sgt, PH
Carpenter, Douglas R., T/5, BSM
Chiravalli, Eugene E., S/Sgt, BSM
Ciccarelli, Anthony, Cpl, BSM

Clavette, Donat H., Pfc, PH
Cohn, Emil A., Jr., Pfc, PH
Combs, Bill, S/Sgt, BSM
Conklin, William J., T/4, BSM
Conners, Mathew J., Pvt, PH
Creasy, Hubert C., Pfc, PH
DeBellis, Elvido D., S/Sgt, BSM
Dickinson, Phineas W., Pvt, PH
D'Oria, Benjamin F., Pfc, PH
Downs, Wallace G., Pfc, PH
Dreiss, Charles G., S/Sgt, BSM
Duckro, Gerald B., Pvt, PH
Dunn, Arthur J., Sgt, BSM
Dyer, William G, Pvt, PH
Evans, James A., Sgt, BSM
Fair, John D., T/5, PH
Fennerty, Herbert S., T/5, PH
Field, Gilbert S., Cpl, BSM
Franklin, Neal A., S/Sgt, PH
Gervasi, Paul, Sgt, BSM
Getz, Fremont F., M/Sgt, BSM
Gillaspy, Vernie A., Pfc, PH
Girolamo, Allesandro, S/Sgt, PH
Goik, Arthur E., T/4, PH
Gormley, William A., Sgt, BSM
Griffin, Jimmie L., T/4, BSM
Guillemette, Andre J., Pfc, PH
Gustofson, Eino, T/4, PH
Gutierrez, Albert M., T/5, PH
Ghiorse, Angelo P., T/Sgt, BSM
Hapgood, Parker H., S/Sgt, PH
Harig, Gerald A., Pfc, BSM
Harrison, Skinner, Pvt, PH
Henson, Dalton T., T/4, BSM, PH
Hodges, Maurice D., T/5, PH
Idema, John J., Jr., T/3, BSM
Johnson, Neal N., Pfc, BSM
Kalmus, Frank H., Pfc, PH
Knox, Thomas L., Cpl, BSM
Krezelewski, Bernard J., S/Sgt, BSM
Lewis, James W., T/5, PH
Lucero, Louis, Pfc, PH
Lyons, William P., Cpl, BSM
MacKenzie, Frank R., Cpl, BSM, PH
Maxwell, George W., Cpl, BSM, PH
McDaniel, Robert H., T/4, PH
McDonald, Kenneth A., Sgt, PH
McDonald, Stanley E., Pvt, PH

McKeown, Daniel F., T/5, BSM
Meehan, Thomas A., T/Sgt, BSM
Mell, Joseph, Pvt, PH
Miller, Emmett A., T/Sgt, BSM
Mothes, Robert F., S/Sgt, BSM
Mousel, Raymond P., S/Sgt, PH
Mozingo, Milford J., T/5, BSM
O'Sullivan, Bernard, Pfc, PH
Paskal, William F., Pfc, BSM
Pavlovic, Edward G., T/5, BSM, PH
Petre, William E., T/5, BSM
Petrocine, Richard C., S/Sgt, BSM
Pilla, Andrew A., T/5, PH
Plank, Albert H., Pfc, PH
Pugliese, Anthony F., Pfc, BSM
Rakowski, John A., 1st/Sgt, BSM
Robbins, Joseph E., Pfc, PH
Roper, Robert O., T/4, BSM
Rosier, Anthony A., Pvt, PH
Rounds, Clifford H., Pfc, BSM, PH
Rowlands, George A., Sgt, PH
Russell, Fred J., Jr., Sgt, PH
Ruhl, John W., Cpl, PH
Salvucci, Charles, Pvt, PH
Schiewek, Ernest E., 1st/Sgt, BSM, PH
Santangelo, James, T/5, BSM
Schoppe, Alfonse L., S/Sgt, BSM
Scott, Levi F., Cpl, BSM, PH
Stapleton, Stacy L., S/Sgt, PH
Stewart, Eamon G., Pfc, PH
Stevens, Jesse E., Cpl, PH
Stoolman, Milton, Cpl, PH
Place, Paul R., Pvt, PH
Sterantino, Joseph J., Sgt, PH
Stone, William, Sgt, PH, BSM
Speights, Thomas H., T/5, PH, BSM
Stelline, Henry J., T/4, BSM
Tudor, Edward R., T/5, BSM
Thomason, Callie E., M/Sgt, BSM
Tomaselli, Fred N., S/Sgt, BSM
Vaughn, John H., T/3, BSM
Velez, John, Pfc, PH
Walenzinski, Joseph J., Pfc, PH
Walker, Dwight D., Cpl, PH, BSM
Warnecke, Henry A., Pfc, PH
Yates, Andrew, Pvt, PH
Dowling, Paul H., 1st/Sgt, LM

338TH FIELD ARTILLERY BATTALION

Abrigo, Edward, T/4, PH
Alldredge, James J., Pvt, PH*
Allen, William D., T/5, PH
Alu, Salvatore F., Pfc, BSM
Anderson, Horton F., Pfc, BSM
Antorino, Joseph T., Sgt, BSM
Arrisi, Angelo, T., Cpl, PH
Artish, Walter W., Pfc, PH
Asbrand, August R., Pvt, BSM
Bagdasarian, Eli D., S/Sgt, BSM, PH
Baldwin, Andrew, Pfc, PH
Barker, Arthur H., Pfc, PH
Barnett, Marshall D., Cpl, PH
Barnett, William C., T/5, PH
Barron, Fernand J., Sgt, BSM
Baytel, Louis, Jr., 2nd Lt, BSM, PH
Beard, Laurence C., 1st Lt, BSM
Beavers, Henry C., Pfc, PH
Berzinsky, William F., Jr., Capt, BSM, PH
Bidosky, John W., Sgt, BSM
Bielss, Leroy O., 1st Sgt, BSM
Blank, Irving, S/Sgt, BSM
Block, Thomas J., T/5, PH
Bludau, Alfred J., T/5, PH
Boling, Dale E., T/5, BSM
Boncompagni, Louis J., T/5, BSM
Born, Fred J., T/5, BSM
Boyarsky, Max, Pfc, PH
Boyle, William B., T/4, BSM, PH
Brand, Joseph G., Pfc, PH

Briggs, Alwin F., Cpl, BSM, PH*
Bruch, Ray K., Major, BSM
Bucior, Joseph F., S/Sgt, BSM
Bukala, Edmund P., Pvt, PH
Burlo, Wallace J., Pfc, PH
Campbell, William M., Cpl, BSM, PH
Carlson, Vincent H., Sgt, BSM
Candino, Michael, Pfc, BSM
Casey, Robert, Pfc, PH
Chaloux, Norman F., Pfc, PH
Chesnutt, Billy H., Cpl, BSM, PH
Cichy, William R., Pvt, PH
Clark, Lloyd D., Pfc, BSM, PH
Clements, Clarence F., Sgt, BSM
Coenen, Louis P., Sgt, BSM
Collins, Thomas E., Sgt, BSM
Cosentino, Nicholas, Pfc, PH
Cumberledge, Claude H., Pfc, PH
Danilowicz, Benjamin J., Pvt, PH*
Darcy, Leo F., Cpl, BSM
Davern, John J., T/4, BSM, PH
DeAngelis, Joseph, S/Sgt, PH
Delgado, James D., Sgt, BSM
Dettloff, Edwin T., T/5, PH
Dionne, Joseph T., T/5, PH
Drwiega, Theodore, Pfc, PH
Dufreche, Edward G., T/Sgt, BSM
Dunnington, Carl G., Pvt, PH*
Dvorscak, John I., Pfc, PH
Dzialuk, John M., 1st Lt, BSM, PH, AM

Eason, Amos L., Pvt, PH
Evon, John E., Jr., S/Sgt, BSM
Fava, Antonio A., Cpl, PH
Feinstein, Abraham H., Pfc, PH
Fowler, Donald L., Sgt, BSM
Freeman, Herbert C., Jr., Capt, BSM, PH
Florio, Frank J., Pfc, PH
Frasier, Russell G., Pfc, PH
Garland, Forrest A., Pfc, PH
Geller, Benjamin A., T/5, BSM
Giardinelli, Victor J., Pfc, PH
Giesey, Thomas F., Pvt, PH
Glunt, William J., Cpl, PH
Godwin, Ralph, Cpl, BSM
Godzik, Charles W., Pfc, PH
Golden, Morlton, T/5, PH
Gonzales, Rafael F., T/4, PH
Gossage, John H., Pfc, PH
Graham, William F., Pfc, PH
Gralla, Alex J., Cpl, PH
Gretz, Isadore P., S/Sgt, PH
Grothe, Harold N., Pfc, BSM
Gromek, Joseph J., Cpl, BSM
Gruner, William M., Cpl, BSM
Gullion, Billy B., Pfc, PH*
Hamilton, Forrest C., S/Sgt, PH
Hardcastle, Dallas C., Jr., Capt, BSM
Harris, Riley E., Pvt, BSM
Hazer, Kaleem, Capt, BSM*
Herbert, Kenneth C., Cpl, BSM
Hernandez, Jesus S., Pfc, PH
Hinshaw, Esper, 1st Lt, BSM*
Hess, Peter P., Cpl, PH
Holloway, Gerald F., Sgt, PH
Holmes, William R., T/Sgt, LM
Ingram, Noble C., Cpl, PH
Integlia, Angelo, S/Sgt, BSM
Jackson, Donald W., Capt, BSM, PH
Jacobs, Seymour B., 1st Lt, BSM
James, Edgar E., T/5, BSM, PH
Johnson, Andrew J., Pfc, PH
Jay, William B., Cpl, BSM
Jordan, William C., Pfc, PH
Kauffman, John H., 1st Lt, BSM, PH
King, Frank C., Pfc, PH
Kinne, Herbert M., Sgt, PH
Kloepper, Herman J., Sgt, BSM, PH
Knable, Bernard J., S/Sgt, BSM
Knox, John W., Pfc, PH
Knutson, Arthur S., S/Sgt, PH
Kram, Harold E., Pfc, BSM
Krebs, Conrad, Pvt, BSM
Kresge, Clinton F., T/5, BSM
Krizan, William R., 1st Lt, BSM*
Lackey, Wilfred J., Sgt, BSM
Lawrence, Richard L., Jr., Sgt, BSM
Lee, Howard A., T/5, BSM
Leon, George H., Jr., Pfc, BSM, PH
Lessa, Nicholas V., 1st Lt, BSM
Leus, August S., Pfc, PH
Lewis, Jack H., 1st/Sgt, BSM, PH
Linton, Fred M., Sgt, PH
Lively, Richard P., Lt Col, BSM*, PH*
Livingston, John H., 1st Lt, PH
Lorance, Ernest J., Pvt, PH
Lorfing, Lester A., Sgt, BSM, PH*
Lovell, Sidney E., 1st Lt, AM
Lovullo, Frank C., S/Sgt, BSM
Luttrell, John, S/Sgt, PH
Lugo, Anthony V., Pfc, PH
Lyons, Gene R., 1st Lt, AM*****
Lyttle, James, Cpl, PH
Macaulay, Donald K., Sgt, PH, BSM
Madden, Arthur W., S/Sgt, BSM
Mankowski, Eugene H., Cpl, PH
Mannix, Simon M., 1st Lt, BSM, PH
Marcela, Roland D. S., Pfc, PH
Marksfeld, Harry, Cpl, PH
Marsh, Wallace R., T/5, BSM, PH
Marshall, George W., Sgt, PH
Matisoff, Macey, T/Sgt, BSM
Matyjasik, Edward S., T/4, BSM, PH

McGowan, Raymond J., Cpl, BSM
McGuire, Dan J., 2nd Lt, BSM, PH*
McIntosh, Robert F., T/5, PH
McKee, Hugh H., 1st Lt, BSM, PH
McMahon, William J., Pfc, PH
McNally, Robert C., Cpl, PH*
McWhorter, Frank C., T/3, BSM
Merchant, Donald L., S/Sgt, BSM
Mesko, Paul, Sgt, BSM, PH
Meuer, William, Sgt, BSM
Milberger, Charlie J., Sgt, PH
Miller, Jerry F., 1st Lt, BSM
Millikin, Robert W., Pfc, BSM
Minogue, Francis X., S/Sgt, BSM
Missale, Joseph, Cpl, BSM
Mitchell, Billie N., 1st Lt, BSM*****, AM*****
Mitchell, Joseph C., S/Sgt, BSM, PH
Mleczko, William T., S/Sgt, BSM, PH
Monaco, Vito F., T/5, PH*
Morawski, Edward L., Pfc, PH
Morton, Joseph D., Capt, BSM, PH
Murphy, Francis M., CWO, BSM
Murphy, Francis T., Pvt, PH
Neilsen, Dan N., Sgt, PH
Nettles, Albert A., Capt, SS, BSM, PH
Nimphius, John J., Pfc, PH
O'Bryant, Virgil L., Pfc, SS, PH
O'Hara, Lewis B., Capt, SS, BSM*
Ochoa, Andrew, Sgt, BSM
Odom, Foy, T/5, BSM
O'Rear, James F., Pfc, BSM
Owens, Robert W., Pvt, BSM*
McPhail, Billie B., 1st Lt, AM*
Panek, Barney A., Sgt, PH
Parker, Alonzo C., Jr., Pvt, PH
Pazow, Lee, Capt, BSM
Perazzo, Emile G., 1st/Sgt, BSM
Peterson, Axel V., Pfc, BSM
Pollard, Ronald H., Pfc, BSM
Pone, Sidney, Capt, AM, BSM
Preece, Chester F., Pfc, PH, BSM
Praino, Frank S., Sgt, PH
Priest, Omer L., Pvt, PH
Pugsley, Robert E., T/5, PH
Purrott, Walter C., Cpl, BSM
Quinn, Arthur J., Sgt, BSM
Rab, Adolph E., Pfc, PH
Rankin, James B., Lt. Col, LM, BSM, PH
Revere, Paul, Sgt, BSM
Ricci, William A., T/4, BSM
Rigby, James A., Pfc, PH*
Riordan, John J., 1st Lt, BSM*, PH
Robertson, Robert L., Pfc, PH
Rohs, Fred S., Cpl, PH
Rom, Jack, Capt, BSM
Roman, John, Pfc, BSM
Ross, Robert W. P., T/5, BSM
Sadlowski, John, Pfc, BSM
Sanita, Albert A., Cpl, PH
Scalf, Eugene, Cpl, PH*
Schmitt, George R., Jr., T/3, BSM
Schavoni, Patrick J., Pvt, BSM
Schmitt, John H., T/4, BSM
Scotti, Alphonse V., 1st/Sgt, BSM
Seely, John F., Pvt, PH
Segura, Alberto, T/5, BSM
Selima, Walter S., Pfc, BSM, PH
Shannon, Richard W., Pfc, BSM, PH
Shenandoah, Fred A., Pvt, PH
Shimo, Paul J., T/5, BSM
Shirley, Melvin J., Pfc, PH
Sikora, Edmund, T/5, PH
Simpson, James H., Cpl, BSM, PH
Smallidge, Ralph M., Capt, BSM*
Smith, Allison J., Pvt, BSM, PH
Smith, Herbert R., Pvt, PH
Smith, Leslie D., S/Sgt, BSM*
Snyder, Gordon, Pfc, BSM, PH
Spahle, Frank X., Cpl, BSM, PH
Spann, Frederick C., Capt, BSM*
Spellicy, Richard N., T/4, BSM*, PH

Spring, Ernest A., Pfc, PH
Standish, Albert C., Capt, BSM**
Stein, David, 1st Lt, BSM*
Stein, Lawrence, T/4, BSM
Stearns, Walter, Pvt, PH
Stilwell, Melvyn S., Capt, BSM*, PH
Straka, Val A., Pvt, PH
Strong, William E., Pvt, PH
Stroud, J. C., Cpl, BSM*, PH*
Szuta, Eugene B., Sgt, BSM
Taranto, Anthony F., T/5, PH
Tarsa, Stanley J., T/4, PH
Tessier, Gerald J., T/5, PH
Thomas, Oscar E., 1st Lt, PH, BSM**
Thompson, Claude F., Cpl, PH, BSM*
Thompson, Willys C., Pfc, PH
Tillman, John G., Capt, PH, BSM
Timmons, George H., Pfc, PH
Turriglio, Frank R., Sgt, PH

Vassar, Everett L., Pvt, PH
Vergot, Nicholas M., 2nd Lt, SS, PH
Vick, Jack W., Jr., Capt, PH*
Walker, Frederick E., T/5, BSM
Weiss, Michael D., Pvt, PH
Wenger, Alvin P., T/5, BSM, PH*
Werher, Robert P., Sgt, BSM, PH
Weronowski, Stanley J., T/5, PH
Willis, Thomas, 2nd Lt, BSM*, PH*
White, Darrell, Pfc, PH
Wiggin, Donald G., T/5, PH
Wittbrodt, Casimer P., Sgt, BSM
Wood, Hershel J., Pfc, BSM, PH
Wright, Frank N., 1st Lt, BSM*
Wyatt, Riley E., Pfc, BSM
Wylie, Arthur L., Jr., Cpl, BSM
Yarzynski, Frank J., S/Sgt, BSM*
Zadik, Jacob W., Capt, BSM
Zimmerman, Eli J., Pfc, BSM

339TH FIELD ARTILLERY BATTALION

Ahern, Michael J., Jr., T/4, BSM
Alderson, Thomas V., T/5, BSM
Arcuri, John J., S/Sgt, BSM
Avery, Marion D., Lt. Col, LM
Ard, Jim R., Pvt, BSM
Arnold, Rufus, T/5, PH
Ashworth, Harry, Jr., Pvt, BSM
Baker, Oscar J., 1st Lt, LM
Barger, Herbert P., T/5, PH
Baumler, Michael C., Cpl, BSM
Bell, Shelia H., Pfc, BSM, PH
Bertoti, Julius C., T/5, PH
Biddle, James K., 1st Lt, BSM
Bisbee, Chester L., Pvt, PH
Blackburn, Ivan S., Pfc, BSM
Bland, John D., S/Sgt, BSM, PH
Bologna, Ciro L., Sgt, BSM, PH
Bonnette, Irley A., Capt, BSM
Borkowsky, Norman, Pfc, BSM
Bowen, Clarence A., Pvt, PH
Bowers, Chester O., Pfc, BSM
Braswell, Odell, 2nd Lt, AM
Bruns, Henry, 1st Lt, AM*****
Burgin, Earl T., S/Sgt, BSM
Bush, Everett D., Pvt, PH
Butler, Carl W., 1st Lt, BSM
Cabot, Stanley L., CWO, BSM
Cady, Earl C., 1st Lt, BSM
Cadley, Russell G., T/Sgt, BSM
Calabrese, Angelo C., T/4, BSM
Callison, Charles S., Cpl, PH
Cantone, Mario A., T/4, BSM
Carito, Anthony, S/Sgt, BSM
Casey, Arlie C., T/5, BSM
Cheron, Joseph J., Sgt, BSM
Chrusciel, Frank J., Pfc, BSM
Clifford, Francis J. P., CWO, BSM, PH
Cloutier, Gerard P., Pvt, PH
Cochran, Stanley A., Capt, BSM
Cole, Arthur L., Sgt, BSM
Collins, John A., Pfc, PH
Cordell, Woodrow W., Pfc, BSM
Cunningham, William T., Sgt, BSM, PH*
Currie, Roy F., T/4, PH
Dawson, John J., S/Sgt, BSM
Deatherage, Sterling R., Pfc, BSM
Decker, Kenneth J., 1st/Sgt, BSM
DeLeone, Marion M., Pfc, BSM
DePrima, Adolph C., Pvt, BSM
DeTurck, Roy S., Cpl, BSM
Divenuto, Salvatore J., PH
Dobish, Sidney, Sgt, PH
Dombrowski, Eugene J., Sgt, BSM
Donlin, Bernard P., Jr., Pfc, BSM
Druzbik, Chester V., Pvt, PH
Dull, Harry C., T/5, BSM
Dumesic, Anthony, 1st Lt, BSM
Edwards, Loyd W., Pfc, BSM
Eschen, Walter E., 1st Lt, BSM, AM

Faught, Jack W., T/5, BSM
Fittin, Daniel V., S/Sgt, BSM
Fortin, Gerard, T/5, BSM
Foster, Marvin W., Pfc, BSM
Fowler, John R., 1st Lt, BSM
Frazier, James L., Capt, BSM*
Frelin, Sheridan J., Cpl, BSM
Gauthier, Robert J., Cpl, BSM
Gibney, Thomas F., T/4, BSM
Gokee, Arlo G., S/Sgt, BSM, PH
Goldrich, Morris, Pfc, PH
Goodman, Abraham, T/5, BSM
Graham, Lewis G., T/5, PH
Griek, Walter W., T/5, BSM
Griffin, Raymond A., Jr., Cpl, BSM
Griffith, Edwin K., Cpl, BSM
Gromacki, Joseph, Cpl, BSM
Grosso, Nicholas A., T/Sgt, BSM
Groth, Walter W., Jr., Pfc, BSM
Guize, Michael A., Cpl, BSM
Gurnee, Earl R., Pfc, PH
Gutshall, Merlin J., Cpl, BSM
Hanson, Palmer, Maj, BSM
Harvey, Bailey O., T/5, BSM
Hastings, Paul J., T/5, BSM, SM
Havens, James H., T/5, BSM
Hayden, John T., 1st Lt, AM********
Heuston, Edward F., S/Sgt, BSM
Hoffman, John J., T/4, BSM
Innes, John R., Jr., T/4, BSM
Interrante, Charles S., Pvt, PH
Jaeke, Wayne A., 1st Lt, BSM, PH
Jankowsky, Peter J., Pvt, PH
Johnson, Manuel, Pfc, PH
Johnston, Charles W., S/Sgt, BSM
Kane, James E., 1st Lt, BSM
Kendra, Walter J., Pfc, PH
King, Roy E., Pvt, SM
King, William L., Pfc, BSM
Krause, Harry B., Cpl, BSM
Kutzer, Harold G., Cpl, PH
Lamonica, Sam, Pfc, BSM
Leen, Harold R., Pfc, PH
Leinker, Charles W., 1st Lt, BSM
Levis, Dale D., Capt, BSM
Liebowitz, Henry, S/Sgt, BSM
Linder, John C., T/5, BSM
Livingston, James E., T/4, PH
Liftin, Carl C., 1st/Sgt, BSM
Livett, Elton M., 1st Lt, BSM
Lowery, Frank D., Capt, BSM
Marcontell, Melvin, Pvt, PH
Martin, Kenneth L., T/4, PH
Masciantonio, Daniel R., T/5, BSM
Masterson, Willard H., T/5, BSM
McCabe, Joseph H., S/Sgt, BSM
McCaffity, Murph, Pfc, BSM
McElvany, Howard L., Cpl, PH
Merritt, Jewell L., Cpl, BSM

Michaud, Norman, Pvt, PH
Miller, Eugene H., Cpl, PH
Miller, Paul J., T/5, BSM
Mirabile, Frank, Cpl, BSM, PH
Misson, Fred, T/5, BSM
Mock, Edward H., T/4, BSM
Molzahn, Edwin L., 1st Lt, BSM
Moore, Francis R., 1st Lt, PH, AM*******
Muir, Robert J., Jr., S/Sgt, BSM
Mulligan, John H., M/Sgt, BSM
Munson, Milton G., S/Sgt, BSM
Napoleon, Francis J., Cpl, PH
Nye, Charlea A., III, Capt, BSM, PH
Olson, Eliot W., 1st/Sgt, BSM
Northrup, Dewey R., T/5, PH
Oppenheim, Allan J., Capt, BSM
Otterstrom, Albert E., T/5, BSM
Pappert, Alvin R., Cpl, BSM
Petrosky, Carl P., S/Sgt, PH
Phillips, Howard R., T/5, BSM
Pietroski, Stanley, Pfc, BSM
Potter, Johnnie C., Pfc, BSM
Prather, Clyde W., Pvt, PH
Prianti, John, Pvt, PH
Pulice, Frank L., Pfc, BSM
Ray, Jesse W., Cpl, PH
Raymond, Louis C., Pfc, PH
Reece, Paul E., T/3, BSM
Reed, Floyd R., 1st/Sgt, BSM
Reiley, Francis H., S/Sgt, BSM
Ricketts, Elwin T., 1st Lt, BSM, PH
Roginski, Stanley A., T/3, BSM
Roles, Charmer A., T/4, BSM
Romanski, William S., Cpl, BSM
Rommel, Oscar R., Pvt, PH
Rosales, Gilbert O., Pvt, PH
Rounds, Steuart B., T/4, BSM
Rowe, Troy G., Cpl, BSM
Rudesyle, John W., T/5, BSM
Ruggiero, John S., Cpl, BSM
Ruiz, Hilario B., Pvt, PH
Sabota, Thaddeus L., T/4, PH

Safford, John G., S/Sgt, BSM
Sails, Howard, 1st Lt, BSM
Sakara, Michael, Cpl, BSM
Schember, Joseph V., Sgt, BSM
Sennings, Raymond, Pvt, PH
Shugar, William, Pfc, PH
Siegrist, William H., T/4, BSM
Simon, Sidney, Cpl, BSM
Simpson, Harry B., Maj, BSM
Sienkiewicz, Henry J., T/5, BSM
Sloane, Edward N., Capt, BSM
Shee, John J., Cpl, BSM
Snodgrass, Marvin L., Pfc, BSM
Snow, Jack A., T/4, BSM
Snyder, Doyle M., Cpl, BSM, PH
Stanton, William J., T/4, PH
Stradley, Jay O., T/5, BSM
Strumer, Morris, Sgt, BSM
Sullivan, John M., S/Sgt, BSM
Terrell, Edgar A., Cpl, BSM
Terrell, Edmond, T/5, BSM
Tiso, Sebastian J., Sgt, BSM*
Tooles, John J., 1st/Sgt, BSM
Tucker, Earl C., S/Sgt, LM
Tucker, Rupert C., T/4, BSM
Urban, Walter J., Pvt, PH
Verdier, Mark L., T/4, BSM
Villanueva, Mateo R., Jr., Pvt, PH
Walk, Melvin E., S/Sgt, BSM, PH
Wall, Melvin E., S/Sgt, BSM
Wallace, Daniel H., S/Sgt, BSM
Walsh, Thomas D., Cpl, BSM*
Wargo, Michael, S/Sgt, BSM
Waters, Wallace E., 2nd Lt, BSM
Wattner, Alfred D., T/5, BSM
Weil, Joseph A., Cpl, PH
Weiss, Morton J., Sgt, BSM
Wiggin, Howard C., 1st Lt, AM******
Williams, Joseph A., Jr., Pvt, PH
Williams, Julio, Sgt, BSM
Wright, Lynford M., T/4, BSM
Yarian, Lowell A., Cpl, BSM, PH*

913TH FIELD ARTILLERY BATTALION

Alston, Frederick J., T/5, BSM
Andrews, James W., 1st Lt, BSM
Atkinson, Warren T., T/4, BSM
Avvenire, Mario A., Cpl, BSM
Bachmann, Herman R., T/5, BSM
Banulski, Joseph P., Pfc, BSM
Basinger, Howard E., Pvt, BSM
Bell, Russell O., Pvt, PH
Bendfeldt, Edward R., S/Sgt, BSM
Benefield, John C., T/Sgt, BSM, PH
Berkeley, Fred D., Lt, BSM
Bixler, David R., Pvt, BSM, PH
Black, Raymond F., Pvt, PH
Boone, Donald L., Cpl, BSM
Bossman, Paul R., Lt, BSM
Burroughs, Claude G., Pfc, PH
Caldwell, Joseph M., Capt, BSM, AM*
Cashman, Francis J., Pvt, PH
Casteneda, Ramon, Pfc, PH
Caylor, Joe L., Pfc, PH
Ceeley, Frederick F., Pvt, PH
Cheon, Ferdinand, Sgt, BSM
Cherrier, Richard H., Pfc, BSM
Chrzanowski, John J., T/Sgt, BSM
Chudy, Henry S., Pfc, PH
Clements, Jim, T/5, BSM**, PH
Clinton, Orville L., Pvt, PH
Combs, Pat G., Lt, DSC, PH
Compton, Waco D., S/Sgt, BSM
Coonrod, Roger A., Pfc, BSM
Cooper, William L., Pfc, PH
Corcoran, John L., Capt, SS, BSM*, PH**
Cornell, Charles H., 1st/Sgt, LM, BSM
Costanzo, Joseph A., Sgt, PH
Cox, George H., Pvt, PH
Creighton, Candell E., Sgt, BSM

Crider, Bower, S/Sgt, BSM
Culpepper, Olus L., Capt, BSM
Daniel, Cicero H., Maj, BSM
D'Augustino, Joseph D., Pvt, BSM
del Monte, Anthony J., S/Sgt, BSM, PH
DeStefano, Jerry J., T/5, BSM*
Dolinger, Milton B., Cpl, BSM
Dood, Cornelus F., Cpl, PH
Downing, Edwin L., Lt, SS, BSM*
Dunn, Charles F., Sgt, BSM
Dziuba, Leon, S/Sgt, BSM
Edgil, Earl T., Cpl, BSM, PH
Edmon, Cloyce G., Cpl, BSM
Eggenspiller, Francis X., Pfc, BSM
Eska, John J., Cpl, BSM*, PH
Evans, John H., Capt, BSM
Everett, Robert S., Sgt, BSM
Faulkner, Theodore W., M/Sgt, BSM
Feyock, Paul A., Pvt, PH
Filipone, Charles N., Pvt, PH
Finn, Thomas F., 1st Lt, BSM
Forrester, Leo J., Cpl, PH
Franklin, Richard D., Pvt, PH
Furnari, Benny S., Sgt, BSM*, PH
Glassman, Morton D., CWO, BSM
Grabelsky, Joseph, Sgt, BSM*
Graham, Ralph E., Cpl, PH
Grathwohl, John G., Capt, BSM
Gravette, Lewis T., Cpl, BSM
Gold, Oscar A., Sgt, BSM
Guiney, Edward D., Sgt, BSM
Habben, Ernest J., Pfc, PH
Hasiwar, Frank J., 1st Lt, BSM, AM
Healey, William R., 2nd Lt, BSM, PH
Helman, Earl W., Cpl, PH
Hight, Robert S., 1st Lt, BSM

Hopkins, George M., 1st Lt, BSM
Holakovsky, Joseph R., 1st Lt, AM*******
Houghton, Robert E., T/4, BSM
Humphreys, Marlin C., Cpl, PH
Hurst, Charles A., Jr., Sgt, BSM
Jablonski, Anthony, T/5, PH
Jennings, Joseph O., S/Sgt, BSM
Johnson, Ellis R., S/Sgt, BSM
Johnson, Harvey B., 1st Lt, BSM
Johnson, Robert P., Pfc, PH
Jones, Columbus D., Cpl, BSM*
Jones, Maxwell A., T/3, BSM
Jones, Wilford, Cpl, BSM*
Jordan, Garland C., Capt, BSM*, PH
Jorgensen, Harold G., Lt, SS, PH
Joslyn, Vernon A., Lt, BSM, PH
Kane, Joseph M., Pfc, BSM
Kennedy, James A., T/5, BSM
Kerestesy, John J., Pfc, PH
Kelymeer, William C., T/4, PH
Kolb, James E., T/5, BSM
LaRock, Anthony J., Cpl, BSM
Lattanzio, John, 1st/Sgt, BSM
LaVoie, Guy, T/5, BSM
Lawler, Thomas, T/5, BSM
Leach ,Melvin C., S/Sgt, BSM
Lee, Grady, 1st/Sgt, LM, BSM
Leies, Thomas M., Sgt, BSM, PH
Lindsey, Charles S., Pvt, BSM
Lott, Homer R., T/4, BSM
Lowell, Eddie R., Lt, BSM
Maki, Arnold P., S/Sgt, BSM
Manning, Edward W., Pvt, PH
Marcus, Roy, S/Sgt, BSM
Marcus, Sam, S/Sgt, BSM, PH
Martinez, Paul O., Pfc, BSM
Maschmann, James W., Lt, AM********, PH
Masdon, Earl C., Lt, AM*******
Mazza, Paul J., Jr., Pvt, PH
McClees, George D., T/4, BSM, PH*
McManus, Francis J., Jr., T/Sgt, BSM
McPhail, Arthur M., Lt, BSM
Mero, Bruce C., Cpl, BSM
Mesite, James E., Pfc, BSM, PH
Miller, Franklin P., Lt Col, BSM*, PH
Milley, Wallace A., M/Sgt, BSM
Moran, John A., T/5, BSM, PH*
Morehead, Jacob L., Capt, BSM*
Mulholland, Thomas, Pvt, BSM
Murray, Wilmur K., Cpl, BSM*
Murray, David S., Jr., T/5, PH
Myers, John W., Pfc, PH
Naab, Lawrence, Lt, BSM
Nowicki, Leonard J., T/4, BSM
Odom, J. B., Cpl, BSM
Olson, Earl M., Lt, BSM

Osborne, William G., Cpl, BSM
Patterson, James C., Cpl, BSM, PH
Penwell, Joseph, Sgt, BSM
Perrier, Henry R., T/5, BSM, PH
Petrey, James L., S/Sgt, BSM
Pettes, Frederick N., T/4, BSM
Pettys, Charles M., Capt, BSM
Phillips, David J., Capt, BSM, PH
Pinard, Germain, T/5, BSM
Potter, Maurice, Cpl, BSM
Radlo, Carl B., Lt, BSM*, PH
Rao, Albert, Pvt, PH
Rappaport, Abraham, Pfc, PH, BSM
Rathjens, Ralph E., T/5, PH
Register, Edgar C., Capt, BSM*
Reed, Jack C., Pvt, PH
Rhodes, Audley P., Sgt, BSM
Roman, Peter, Pfc, BSM
Rothman, Seymour, Capt, BSM
Rothwell, Carl W., Pfc, BSM
Ryan, John L., Cpl, BSM
Sadler, Earl W., Pvt, PH
Schilling, Richard E., WOJG, BSM
Schliessman, John, Sgt, BSM, PH
Schupp, Bobby J., Lt, AM
Sefton, Alfred B., S/Sgt, BSM, PH
Sewall, Robert L., Cpl, BSM
Sharp, David W., Pfc, PH
Sheremeta, Walter, Cpl, BSM, PH
Slone, Harry, Pvt, PH
Smach, Bernard, Pfc, PH, SS
Solis, Henry, Cpl, PH
Sommers, Lawrence E., Lt. Col, SS, BSM*
Sowers, Wade, Pfc, PH
Stafford, William W., T/5, BSM
Steele, Fayette, Pfc, BSM
Swart, Andrew J., T/5, BSM
Szczepaniak, Valentine S., Pfc, PH
Tamagni, Desidery, T/5, PH
Thomas, Vincent, Pvt, PH
Tocco, Salvatore V., Pfc, PH
Todd, Joe O., S/Sgt, BSM*
Trapp, Bernard, 1st/Sgt, SS, BSM
Trotter, Warren K., Lt, BSM
Umstead, Lawrence W., T/4, PH
Usher, Moses M., Cpl, BSM
Waitanek, Eugene S., T/4, BSM, PH
Wallace, Anthony R., T/4, BSM
Wicker, Idus Q., Lt, BSM
Wieczorek, Steve J., T/5, BSM
Wilburn, Otis L., Pfc, BSM
Worley, Norman L., S/Sgt, BSM
Wyman, Philip A., Capt, BSM, PH
Yetter, Robert C., Sgt, BSM
Young, Roy M., T/4, BSM
Zerba, Peter, Sgt, BSM, PH

HEADQUARTERS SPECIAL TROOPS

Humphries, Thomas J., Maj, BSM
Boothe, John E., Jr., Capt, BSM
Goldfarb, Harold, Capt, BSM
Feldman, Carl J., T/Sgt, BSM
Northam, Lindsay P., T/Sgt, BSM
Potter, John W., S/Sgt, BSM
Ratz, Robert P., T/3, PH

Shepherd, Dempsey J., Sgt, BSM
Harding, Fred W., Sgt, BSM
Simpson, George M., T/5, SS, PH
Kemp, Albert A., T/5, BSM, PH
Ragan, William M., T/5, BSM
Moses, Donald K., T/5, BSM
Thomas, Jessie J., Pfc, PH

Zarate, Ishmael, Jr., T/3, BSM

88TH CAVALRY RECONNAISSANCE TROOP

Acton, Robert W., Pfc, PH
Alvarado, Evaristo L., Pfc, PH
Baird, Samuel B., Jr., Pfc, BSM
Barrett, Orval, T/5, PH
Barter, Cecel E., Cpl, BSM
Bateman, John M., Sgt, BSM
Beales, Richard H., T/5, BSM
Bedard, Victor A., T/5, BSM
Bermingham, Thomas L., Pvt, PH
Blinn, Samuel F., T/4, PH

Boris, Alex, Pfc, BSM
Bowers, Lawrence J., 1st Lt, BSM, PH, SS
Bracilli, Richard J., Pfc, PH
Brown, Clinton A., S/Sgt, BSM
Brown, Nolan S., Pfc, PH, BSM
Brackett, Noah L., Pvt, PH
Ceder, John W., Pfc, BSM
Cunningham, John L., T/4, PH
Cutler, Roy T., Cpl, PH, BSM
Davis, Cecil W., Cpl, PH

Duffy, Thomas E., T/4, BSM
Drazba, John E., T/5, PH
Ernst, Frank, T/5, BSM
Finkelstein, Pincus, Cpl, PH, BSM
Finn, Dennis, Jr., Pfc, BSM
Fisher, Chester F., T/4, BSM
Fitzpatrick, Mathew J., Pfc, PH
Fulton, William H., Pfc, PH
Gass, Jacob C., T/5, BSM
Gaub, Edward W., T/5, BSM
George, Constantine L., Pfc, PH
Grimmett, Robert S., 1st Lt, PH*
Grohman, Leland C., T/5, PH, SS
Hallows, John H., T/5, BSM
Harmon, Ewin M., T/5, PH
Hatfield, George W., 1st/Sgt, BSM
Hill, William J., Pfc, PH
Holcomb, Billy L., T/5, PH
Horn, Homer M., Sgt, PH
Howard, Ernest M., Pfc, PH*
Hunt, John L., Pfc, PH, BSM
Hunt, Roscoe R., Sgt, BSM
Ivy, Willie J., S/Sgt, PH, BSM*
Jago, Kenneth S., T/4, BSM
Johnson, John O., T/5, PH, DSC
Kmetyk, John, Jr., Pvt, PH
Kuemin, Cassie W., Sgt, BSM
Lane, Park, T/4, PH
Lang, Harry A., Jr., Sgt, PH
Lindgren, Stanley R., Pfc, PH
Luke, Gregory J., T/4, BSM
Mahaffey, Robert A., Pfc, PH
Massey, Gabor, T/5, PH
Mazzetti, Emidio, Sgt, PH*
McElwee, George J., Pvt, PH
Medeiros, Morris C., Pfc, BSM
Miller, Adrian C., T/5, BSM
Miller, Frederick A., Cpl, BSM
Miller, Francis K., T/4, BSM
Mills, William W., Pfc, PH

Murphy, Kelly F., Pfc, PH, BSM
Nash, Norman G., Pfc, PH, BSM
Nelson, Elmer, Pfc, PH, BSM
Nordell, Carl A., Cpl, PH, BSM
Nowak, Richard J., T/5, BSM
Petersen, William J., Sgt, PH
Powell, Homer C., T/5, PH, BSM
Puffer, John R., 1st Lt, BSM
Purser, Ralph L., Pvt, PH
Quinn, Morgan J., Pvt, PH, BSM
Regan, Michael J., T/5, BSM
Richards, Richard E., Cpl, BSM
Rielly, John J., T/5, PH
Rielly, John T., 1st/Sgt, BSM*
Robbins, Richard A., Sgt, PH, BSM
Robisch, Gerald F., Cpl, BSM
Schwartzman, George F., Pfc, PH
Senn, Alan L., T/4, PH, BSM
Shaver, Howard D., 1st Lt, PH*, BSM
Shea, Roger M., 1st Lt, BSM
Smith, Lloyd D., 1st Lt, BSM
Smith, Otis A., Sgt, PH, BSM
Soper, Howard M., Capt, PH, BSM*
Spence, Richard W., T/5, PH
Speegle, Gordon W., T/5, PH
Starnes, Billy D., T/5, PH
Tucker, Samuel, Pfc, PH
Vass, Robert E., Pfc, PH, BSM
Wallace, Alexander P., 2nd Lt, PH, BSM
Wheaton, Sherman M., S/Sgt, BSM
Whitley, Herbert P., T/5, PH
Wieland, Clemence E., Pfc, PH
Wilkalis, John J., PH
Wood, Bernard L., T/5, PH
Wood, Royal R., T/4, PH
Yaruta, Frank J., T/4, BSM
Young, Charles E., T/5, BSM
Zajac, Joseph J., Pfc, BSM
Zaliagiris, Vito V., Cpl, PH, BSM

88TH SIGNAL COMPANY

Bailey, Charles A., T/Sgt, BSM
Beattie, Orrin H., T/5, BSM
Berberich, Sidney A., S/Sgt, BSM
Billingsley, William A., S/Sgt, BSM
Bixler, Raymond D., M/Sgt, BSM
Boland, William F., Pfc, BSM
Bradley, Edwin J., T/5, BSM
Brakefield, Morris H., Pfc, BSM
Brown, Bernard J., 1st Lt, BSM
Campbell, Deemer, Pfc, BSM
Carter, E. A., 1st Lt, BSM
Cohen, M. S., 1st Lt, BSM
Connolly, Robert D., Capt, BSM
Curtin, Michael F., 1st Lt, BSM
Collins, John, Pfc, BSM
Craythorne, John R., T/Sgt, BSM
Cunningham, John C., T/5, BSM
Dombrowski, William C., Sgt, BSM
Douglas, Stephen A., Sgt, BSM
Elner, Richard C., S/Sgt, BSM
Epstein, Bernard L., T/5, BSM
Feinstein, Sidney, T/4, BSM
Fitzpatrick, George J., S/Sgt, BSM
Fogarty, Lawrence F., WOJG, BSM
Gerlovich, Albert F., T/5, BSM
Goodmaster, Frank, S/Sgt, BSM
Goodwin, Harry S., Jr., T/4, BSM
Hageman, John H., Cpl, BSM
House, John M., S/Sgt, BSM
Huisman, James K., Pfc, BSM
Hunt, Clifton L., M/Sgt, BSM
Knox, Gaffrey C., T/5, BSM
Kotowski, Edward A., T/5, BSM
Krauth, Charles F., M/Sgt, BSM
Krenos, Julius, Jr., T/5, BSM
Lanandus, Milton F., Pfc, BSM
Lasko, Joseph S., T/5, BSM, PH

Lowrie, John M., T/4, BSM
Lucas, James B., T/5, BSM
Lyman, Jay O., T/3, BSM
Maurer, Roger W., 1st Lt, BSM
McCree, Charles H., T/3, BSM
McDaniel, Thomas H., T/3, BSM
Mesi, Michael S., S/Sgt, BSM
Morris, Robert P., T/3, BSM
Murray, Ernest L., T/4, BSM, PH
Nichols, John L., T/4, BSM
Olson, Marvin, Pfc, BSM
Payne, William H., T/5, BSM
Pinyan, Verbon, Pfc, BSM, PH
Picarella, Dominic F., T/Sgt, BSM
Pickett, Homer R., T/5, BSM
Reuter, Edward L., T/5, BSM
Roberson, Irvin E., Pfc, BSM
Rollins, Claburn J., T/5, BSM
Ruane, John J., T/4, BSM
Sanocki, Frank J., Pvt, BSM
Savage, Clayton J., T/4, BSM
Shaffer, Robert S., Cpl, BSM
Shurtleff, Carlyle H., Capt, BSM
Stewart, Robert W., Jr., WOJG, BSM
Stover, Sidney, Pfc, BSM
Stull, Bedford C., T/Sgt, BSM
Stockwell, Emerson K., T/5, BSM, PH
Torre, Andrew, CWO, BSM
Treseder, Donald W., Lt Col, BSM
Turek, Eddie A., T/4, BSM
Urich, William J., Pfc, BSM, PH
Unruh, Richard C., Sgt, BSM
Walz, Albert, T/5, BSM
Winn, Francis X., T/Sgt, BSM
Ware, Ray E., Pvt, PH
Wright, John J., T/5, PH

313TH ENGINEER COMBAT BATTALION

Alk, Alfred L., 1st Lt, BSM*
Armogida, Salvatore A., Lt Col, BSM
Bradley, Richard J., 1st Lt, BSM
Brierley, Allan G., Capt, BSM
Carrigg, Paul R., Capt, BSM
Conyers, Harry D., 2nd Lt, BSM
Curriden, Calvin F., 1st Lt, PH**, BSM*
Fallon, John J., WOJG, BSM
Feorene, Orlando J., Capt, BSM*
Ferguson, Thomas G., 1st Lt, PH*, BSM
Goofman, Sidney, Capt, BSM
Green, James H., Lt Col, PH*, BSM, SS
Huvane, James J., 1st Lt, PH
Johnsen, Sigurd S., WOJG, BSM
Jones, Willis C., 1st Lt, BSM*
Kunkel, George D., 2nd Lt, BSM
Lacroix, Robert C., Maj, PH*
Mathey, Charles W., 1st Lt, BSM
May, Martin M., Capt, SM
Oast, John W., III, Capt, BSM
Parkes, Colin G., Capt, PH
Purcell, Martin J., Maj, PH
Roesch, Maurice A., Capt, PH, BSM
Schupple, Henry L., Capt, BSM
Sidell, William T., Capt, PH
Shimunek, Frank A., 2nd Lt, PH
Snow, Jerrold D., Capt, PH, BSM*
St. Sauver, Richard T., 1st Lt, PH, BSM*, SS
Tucei, John P., 1st Lt, SS
Veligor, Anthony V., 2nd Lt, LM
Webber, Robert G., 1st Lt, PH, BSM
Dougherty, Thomas E., Lt Col, LM
Aleffi, Joseph J., T/5, BSM
Angurio, Joseph W., Pvt, PH
Arnott, Joseph R., Sgt, PH
Artino, Salvatore C., Pfc, BSM
Archer, John L., T/4, PH
Ashe, Raymond L., T/4, PH, SS
Aspy, Gerald L., Pvt, PH
Backos, Thomas, T/5, BSM
Barber, Casper J., S/Sgt, PH
Barnett, Laverne R., Cpl, BSM
Bartlett, Lehman, Pfc, PH
Barto, Edward W., Pfc, PH
Bayer, Martin J., Pfc, PH
Belnick, Joseph, Cpl, BSM
Betly, John V., T/5, BSM
Bodie, Sidney, Sgt, PH*
Bolioli, Fred J., Pfc, PH, BSM
Bombardier, Joseph E., Cpl, PH, BSM
Bones, Raymond E., T/4, BSM
Borrello, Anthony, Jr., T/5, PH
Bourscheid, Donald S., T/4, BSM
Bozzo, Victor A., Pfc, PH
Brown, Truman E., Pvt, PH*
Bruno, Kenneth D., Pfc, BSM
Burke, Pearle S., Sgt, PH, BSM
Burk, Walter L., Cpl, PH
Bush, Lawrence G., T/5, PH, BSM
Camp, James F., T/5, PH
Chastain, Eustace A., T/4, BSM
Chmiel, John F., Pvt, BSM
Cline, Clifford B., Pfc, PH, BSM
Cobb, Lawrence M., Pvt, PH
Cobb, Norman S., T/5, PH
Coletti, Rolondo, Pfc, BSM
Cooper, James B., Pfc, BSM
Cootware, Raymond S., 1st/Sgt, BSM
Costello, Jamie, Pfc, BSM
Cota, Armando F., Pvt, PH
Crandall, Colby L., T/4, PH, BSM
Darlack, Marian A., Pfc, PH
Davis, Melvin F., Pvt, PH
Davola, Phillip A., Pvt, PH, BSM
D'Bicari, Bresci, S/Sgt, PH, LM
DeMatteis, Vincent J., S/Sgt, BSM
Diamond, Lonnie V., Pvt, PH
Dickerson, Charles P., Pfc, PH
DiDomenico, Albert C., Sgt, PH

Donovan, Daniel E., Pvt, PH
Dupree, Paul V., T/5, SM
Eagan, William E., Sgt, PH
Eason, Homer L., T/5, BSM
Enos, George J., T/5, PH
Escanuelas, Fermin R., Pvt, BSM
Fick, James F., Pvt, PH
Fischer, William F., T/5, PH
Fisher, Joseph A., Jr., Pfc, BSM
Frazia, Renard, Pvt, PH, BSM
Fuller, Douglas R., T/5, BSM
Fulton, Francis J., Pvt, PH
Falkenbury, Weldon E., T/Sgt, PH*, BSM
Gadzinski, Stanley F., M/Sgt, PH
Garner, John J., Pvt, PH
Garramone, William, S/Sgt, BSM
Gates, Willard D., Pfc, BSM
Gaudreau, Maurice, T/4, BSM
Gehm, Maurice H., Cpl, BSM
Gervasio, Anthony J., T/4, PH
Gladstone, Samuel, T/5, PH
Glover, Cecil T., Pvt, PH
Goodman, Bernard, Pvt, BSM
Guertin, Robert W., Pvt, PH
Guboski, Frank, Pfc, PH
Gunter, Truman F., Pfc, PH
Haisler, Anton F., Sgt, BSM
Halderman, David W., Sgt, BSM
Hartley, John T., T/4, PH, BSM*
Hart, Francis R., T/Sgt, SS
Heller, Edward C., Pvt, BSM
Hermus, Francis A., Pfc, BSM
Hilbert, Valdemar N., T/4, PH
Hollis, Franklin L., T/5, PH
Horcsog, Stephen, Pfc, PH
Howard, Thomas D., Pvt, PH
Hubbard, Haldean W., Pfc, BSM
Hughes, Thomas D., Pfc, PH
Ickes, Donald B., Sgt, BSM
Jacoby, Reuben H., Sgt, BSM
Jameson, Avery C., Pvt, PH
Johnson, Sulo E., T/5, PH
Johnson, Price W., Pfc, PH, BSM
Johnson, Joseph F., Pfc, BSM
Jones, Oliver D., Pvt, PH*
Jones, Leslie N., T/5, PH
Kanaskie, James J., T/4, BSM
Kessler, John J., T/4, PH
Kinmore, Robert C., Pvt, PH
Kirby, Joseph H., Sgt, BSM
Klaus, Theodore, Pvt, BSM
Kochis, Adelbert G., Pvt, PH
Kolb, William J., S/Sgt, PH
Koznick, Peter, Pvt, BSMK
Kraus, Andrew J., Pvt, PH
Kuenze, Robert E., S/Sgt, BSM
Kunc, Edward, T/Sgt, PH
Lane, Albert C., Pvt, PH
LaPlante, Adrien H., T/5, PH
LaRosa, Stephen, T/5, PH
Leedham, Samuel H., Pfc, BSM
Lefko, Stanley, T/5, PH
Long, Jimmie E., Pfc, PH*
Lucyszyn, George, Pfc, BSM
Luzim, Louis, Pvt, BSM
Lydon, Ralph W., Cpl, BSM
Macias, Manuel E., Pfc, BSM
Maratea, Mauro A., Pvt, BSM
Mariano, Anthony A., S/Sgt, BSM*
Markowski, Walter G., T/5, BSM
Marsoli, Emelio, Sgt, PH, BSM
Martinez, Leonardo L., Cpl, BSM
Martorano, Tom, T/5, BSM
Mattheu, Robert F., Pvt, BSM
McAulay, David, T/5, PH
McConlogue, Robert J., S/Sgt, PH*, BSM
McFarland, John J., Pfc, PH
McKinney, Ota R., Cpl, PH
McLeod, Stanley N., S/Sgt, BSM

McNamara, Walter M., Pfc, PH
McPheters, Fank, Pvt, BSM
Meeks, Albert J., Jr., Cpl, BSM
Mellott, Augustus E., Pfc, PH
Miarmi, Sperindio P., T/5, PH
Mihaly, Alfred, Pvt, PH
Miller, Anthony, T/4, PH
Miller, William V., T/5, PH
Mitchell, George W., Pfc, BSM
Mobly, Grady J., Pvt, PH
Mock, Robert S., S/Sgt, BSM
Mooney, W. C., Pfc, BSM
Mott, Howard, T/5, PH
Mulyk, Walter P., T/4, PH
Murtagh, Andrew J., Pvt, SS
Mykytow, Milton, T/Sgt, BSM
Nania, Salvatore V., T/4, PH, BSM
Nawojski, Alfred F., Pfc, PH
Nyardy, Eugene, Jr., Pfc, PH, BSM
Ogden, James H., T/4, BSM
Olsen, Irving, Pfc, PH
Omslaer, James A., T/5, PH
Orosco, Ernest, Pfc, BSM
Palkovic, Henry A., M/Sgt, BSM
Paone, Tony S., Cpl, PH
Parker, Moody L., T/5, BSM*
Parker, William C., Pfc, BSM
Patano, Anthony J., Pfc, PH
Patasse, Anthony J., Pfc, PH
Pearson, Frank A., Pvt, PH
Pedro, Vincent, Pvt, BSM
Perecz, William B., T/4, PH
Perugia, Louis F., Pvt, PH
Porter, Galen L., T/5, PH
Post, Walter W., T/Sgt, BSM, PH
Poteete, John L., T/5, PH
Prisco, James, Pvt, PH
Pucher, Daniel N., T/5, PH
Purdy, James P., Pvt, PH*
Quinn, Garvis H., Pvt, PH*
Rayner, Charles H., Jr., Pfc, PH*
Reese, Wayne A., Pfc, PH*
Reeves, Cecil B., T/5, PH
Reid, Norman J., T/Sgt, PH, BSM*
Reyes, Jose M., Pvt, PH
Rodgers, Jerry L., T/5, BSM
Rodgers, John E., T/5, BSM
Ronhaar, John J., Sgt, PH
Ronquillo, Edward E., Cpl, PH
Rhoades, Robert F., T/5, PH
Rosicki, Chester J., Pfc, BSM
Rospierski, Frank, Sgt, PH
Rosato, Thomas A., Pfc, BSM
Salisbury, Herbert L., T/4, PH, BSM, SS
Santa, Victor, Sgt, BSM
Schafani, Charles, T/5, PH

Schatzberg, Barnet, Pvt, PH
Schneider, George S., Pfc, BSM
Schrenker, George A., Pfc, PH
Schroeder, Louis C., Cpl, PH
Schwartz, Wesley F., Pvt, PH
Shagawat, John P., Pvt, BSM
Sheffield, Herman G., Sgt, BSM
Sherman, Dale R., Sgt, BSM
Siegler, Louis J., Pvt, PH
Silva, Francis E., T/5, BSM
Simminger, Charles E., Pvt, PH
Singleton, Donald E., T/5, PH
Slifko, George T., Pvt, BSM
Smallidge, Victor G., T/5, BSM
Smith, Harold S., Pvt, PH
Smith, Phillip E., Pfc, PH
Smith, Carmel C., T/5, PH
Soriano, Refugio, Pvt, PH*
Stein, Jack M., Pfc, PH
Stewart, Donald B., Sgt, BSM
Stowitts, George C., S/Sgt, BSM
Studzniski, John W., T/4, BSM
Sullivan, Orval E., Cpl, BSM, SS
Tays, J. C., T/5, PH, BSM
Throckmorton, Henry C., T/3, PH
Totten, James W., T/Sgt, PH, SM
Tripoulas, Leo A., T/4, PH
Truckowski, Walter F., Pfc, PH, BSM
Trzaskes, John, Pvt, PH
Tuz, John, Pvt, PH
Vandewarker, William F., Jr., Pfc, PH
Varela, Candido S., Pfc, BSM
Vigilante, James J., T/5, PH*
Vogt, James R., Pfc, PH
Volpe, John, Pvt, PH*
Waite, Frank E., Cpl, PH
Walker, Howard D., Cpl, PH, BSM
Wall, Merrill B., Pfc, BSM
Webber, George A., Pfc, PH*
Wells, George P., Pfc, PH
Wells, Joseph O., M/Sgt, BSM
White, William H., Sgt, BSM
Whitney, Truman H., T/5, PH, BSM
Wilberts, Laurence, T/5, PH
Wilbur, Kenneth C., Pvt, PH, BSM
Wilkes, George H., T/5, BSM
Wippel, Ralph W., S/Sgt, BSM
Wisdom, Elmo L., Pfc, PH
Woods, John R., T/5, BSM
Woodward, Victor W., Pfc, BSM
Wright, Courtland J., T/4, PH*
Young, Gordon A., Pfc, PH
Young, Elvin J., Pvt, BSM
Zak, John H., T/5, PH
Zavistoski, Francis F., Sgt, BSM
Zeider, Irving, Pvt, PH

313TH MEDICAL BATTALION

Aguila, Calisto R., Pfc, BSM
Ahlen, Ralph J., 1st Lt, BSM
Anderson, Harry A. E., Pvt, BSM, PH*
Anthony, Kenneth W., Capt, BSM
Amos, Robert N., Pfc, BSM
Avirett, Wayne H., Pfc, BSM
Ayres, Thomas F., Pfc, PH
Bass, Jerome E., Jr., T/5, BSM
Baker, Russell W., T/5, BSM
Balter, Irving I., T/5, BSM
Barrack, Abraham S., T/4, BSM
Bates, Richard H., T/5, BSM
Beardsley, Russell J., Sgt, BSM
Boback, Charles J., Capt, BSM
Bork, Sam, Pvt, PH
Bounds, Frank, T/5, BSM, PH
Bragulia, William C., T/Sgt, BSM
Brooks, Robert W., Jr., Pvt, BSM
Brooks, Chester I., Pfc, BSM
Cahill, Thomas E., Jr., Pfc, BSM
Calverly, Buster, T/5, BSM
Carlson, Arthur I., T/5, BSM

Carroll, James G., Pfc, BSM
Carter, Roy E., T/5, BSM
Choate, John L., Pfc, BSM
Cleveland, Andrew B., Cpl, BSM
Conley, Robert L., Pfc, LM
Cooper, Benjamin F., Capt, BSM
Corden, Leo N., T/5, BSM
Cousins, Owen D., Capt, BSM
Crosby, Thomas M., Pfc, BSM, PH
Cummins, Herbert H., T/5, BSM
Curran, Robert L., Pfc, BSM
DiAurio, Thomas A., T/4, BSM
Doctor, Franklin D., Sgt, BSM
Dolan, Robert E., T/3, BSM
Egger, Luther W., Pfc, BSM
Evans, John R., Pvt, BSM
Evans, Ernest, S/Sgt, BSM
Evans, Dale O. R., Pfc, BSM
Fanning, Edward M., S/Sgt, BSM
Farley, Joseph A., Sgt, BSM
Ferguson, Harry S., Pfc, BSM
Ferri, Frank V., 1st Lt, BSM*

Fishel, Leo, Capt, BSM
Frank, Howard J., Sgt, BSM
Fry, Eugene, Pfc, BSM
Gasbarro, Armando R., T/5, BSM
Gilman, David C., S/Sgt, BSM
Goodwill, Richard F., Pfc, BSM
Greene, John H., T/4, BSM
Groeber, Edward O., Capt, BSM
Hamilton, Clarence T., T/Sgt, BSM
Hinckley, Ormond W., Pfc, BSM
Henderson, Alanda F., Pfc, BSM
Hughes, William F., Pvt, BSM*
Jacob, Zoltan, Pvt, BSM
Johnson, John W., Capt, LM
Johnson, Willie M., Cpl, BSM
Jones, Hermon, Pfc, BSM
Joslin, Emerson E., T/4, BSM
Kahn, Paul M., Sgt, BSM
Kessler, Ralph J., Capt, BSM
King, James P., Pvt, BSM
Knapp, Atlas D., Pfc, BSM
Kolb, John H., S/Sgt, BSM
Kopeloff, Arthur, T/5, BSM
Korpalski, Joseph S., Pfc, BSM
Kosoff, Marvin, T/5, BSM
Kowalik, Charles S., Sgt, BSM
Lackish, Peter P., T/5, BSM
LaForest, Joseph E., Sgt, BSM
LeBeau, Roland, 1st Lt, BSM
Lefebvre, Joseph G., Pvt, BSM
Lindsley, Harvey L., S/Sgt, BSM
Loeb, Roland A., Capt, BSM
Lopefsky, Samuel A., T/Sgt, BSM
Maricle, Elvin, Pfc, BSM
May, Martin M., Capt, BSM
McCartney, Rood P., Pvt, BSM, PH
McDonald, Walter L., Pfc, BSM
McKee, Robert J., Jr., 1st Lt, BSM
McWhorter, Robert E., CWO, BSM
Miles, William P., Cpl, BSM
Miller, Albert W., Pfc, BSM
Milliken, Irland, Pfc, BSM
Mills, Frederick S., Pfc, BSM
Mintz, Arthur E., 1st Lt, BSM
Morck, Clarence D., Pfc, BSM
Morton, James F., Capt, BSM
Mourhess, Lowell E., Pvt, BSM, PH
Myers, Harold E., S/Sgt, BSM
Nicholson, Raymond E., T/5, BSM
O'Brien, Edward, Sgt, BSM

O'Connor, Harry T., Pfc, BSM
Osborn, Gordon L., 1st/Sgt, BSM
Pacely, Lowell E., Pfc, BSM
Perry, James J., T/5, BSM
Phillips, Walter W., Pfc, BSM
Phillips, Vernon R., Capt, BSM
Phillips, Jio B., S/Sgt, BSM, PH
Pinckney, Kenneth M., Sgt, BSM
Polischuk, Wasyl J., Capt, BSM, PH
Posatko, Peter C., Capt, BSM
Pratt, Gerald J., 1st/Sgt, BSM
Ramos, Salvatore, Pfc, BSM
Ranson, John L., Capt, BSM
Regan, John J., Sgt, SS, PH
Riancavilla, John, T/5, BSM
Richmond, Paul C., Maj, BSM
Righter, Paul M., Pfc, BSM
Rivera, Hector G., T/5, BSM
Sayre, Lloyd S., 1st/Sgt, BSM
Schauff, Gerald J., Capt, BSM
Shortall, Thomas G., Sgt, BSM
Sisson, Milton M., Capt, BSM
Skinner, George W., S/Sgt, BSM
Sloane, Milton B., Lt Col, BSM
Slutzky, Joseph, Maj, BSM
Smith, Harvy L., WOJG, BSM
Smith, James C., S/Sgt, BSM
Sojda, Adam T., S/Sgt, BSM
Sokol, John P., Sgt, BSM
Sommer, Moses, Capt, BSM
Spreen, George E., S/Sgt, BSM
Stacy, Arthur W., Pfc, BSM
Stevenson, Robert G., T/4, BSM
Tinsley, Ernest G., Pfc, BSM
Teran, Carlos M., Capt, BSM
Tomlinson, Phillip F., Pfc, BSM
Trutt, Irving, Maj, BSM
Verrone, Carmine, T/4, BSM
Vest, James B., Pfc, BSM
Vosper, Bradley M., T/5, BSM
Williams, John R., T/3, BSM
Williams, Charlie L., Sgt, BSM
Wolfe, Howard W., Pvt, BSM
Woodson, John, M/Sgt, BSM
Yates, Darold F., Pvt, BSM
Young, Charles B., Sgt, BSM*
Zarr, John, Jr., Pfc, BSM
Zellefrow, Melvin L., T/5, BSM
Zill, Lloyd C., Sgt, BSM
Zumstein, Robert C., 1st Lt, BSM

88TH QUARTERMASTER COMPANY

Aiardo, Ignatzio E., S/Sgt, BSM
Bagley, John F., Sgt, BSM
Barone, Joseph T., Sgt, BSM
Beede, Noel E., Sgt, PH
Bialy, John J., Sgt, BSM
Bianco, Delmo J., Sgt, BSM
Brown, Bryan, Jr., T/5, BSM
Brown, Everett M., S/Sgt, BSM
Cleaves, John T., S/Sgt, BSM
Conitz, Irvin, T/5, BSM
Cramer, Frank W., S/Sgt, BSM
Crane, Ray T., 1st Lt, BSM
Cumbie, Orva P., Pvt, BSM
Curto, Rocco, T/5, BSM
Davisson, Lloyd D., Sgt, BSM
Ganch, John P., T/4, BSM
Gladfelter, Harold K., T/Sgt, LM
Hall, Karl S., Maj, BSM
Handrigan, Raymond F., S/Sgt, BSM
Hankins, Charles F., M/Sgt, BSM
Hart, LeeRoy J., 1st Lt, BSM

Kelly, Edward J., T/5, BSM
Kleger, Nathoniel, Sgt, BSM
McCarthy, George V., S/Sgt, BSM
Mello, Joao M., Pfc, BSM
Partin, William N., Capt, BSM
Polizzi, Anthony J., Sgt, BSM
Power, Joe E., 1st Lt, BSM
Rome, Howard J., Capt, BSM
Rutherford, Charles E., 1st Lt, BSM
Seaton, George E., Pfc, BSM*
Shoemaker, Verdett E., T/5, PH*
Silverman, Alvin L., 1st Lt, BSM
Smith, Denman T., Pfc, BSM
Sonner, Raymond E., Sgt, BSM
Thieman, Frederick J., S/Sgt, BSM
Turner, Gilbert C., T/Sgt, LM
Van Assen, Paul F., 1st/Sgt, BSM
Watson, James E., S/Sgt, BSM*
Wegge, Joseph A., T/4, BSM
Wilcox, John A., T/5, PH

788TH ORDNANCE (LM) COMPANY

Akin, Illey B., T/3, PH, BSM
Annotto, Joseph D., T/Sgt, BSM
Benson, George W., Jr., T/4, BSM

Burke, Patrick R., T/3, BSM
Brophy, Bernard M., 1st Lt, BSM
Canan, John W., Pfc, PH

Collins, William J., 1st/Sgt, PH, BSM
D'Alessandro, Anthony G., Sgt, BSM
Denes, Max I., WOJG, BSM
De Grio, Emil R., T/5, PH
Daum, Lloyd C., T/3, PH
Evans, Ronald M., Capt, PH
Fowler, John E., Pvt, PH, SS
Galland, Orris I., S/Sgt, BSM
Hoye, Francis M., T/5, PH
Hurst, Loren F., T/5, PH
Hatem, Anise, Sgt, PH
Hackman, Kenneth W., Pfc, PH
Ingebretson, Stanley A., S/Sgt, PH
Jacobs, Dana B., T/5, BSM
Jakad, Harold F., T/4, PH

Johnson, Robert B., Pvt, PH
Kopech, David P., T/3, PH
Lamer, Don O., T/4, PH
Louie, Harold K., T/5, PH
Leary, Oren H., S/Sgt, BSM
McGivern, Harry C., T/5, PH
Murphy, Joseph C., M/Sgt, LM
Prior, Harold F., Pfc, PH
Pascoe, James, 1st Lt, PH
Smith, John, Jr., Capt, BSM
Svilar, Matthew, 1st Lt, BSM
Snyder, John A., T/4, BSM
Schultz, Bernard L., S/Sgt, PH, BSM
Sheppe, Horace O., T/5, PH
Watt, John N., Capt, BSM

Wenger, John M., T/4, BSM

CIC DETACHMENT

Bai Rossi, Philip, Spec. Agent, BSM
Barnett, Lynn, Spec. Agent, BSM
Lucaire, William M., Spec. Agent, BSM
Lucid, Thomas A., Spec. Agent, BSM

Luongo, Joseph P., Spec. Agent, BSM
Morrison, Douglas J., Spec. Agent, BSM
Pascucci, Dominick J., Spec. Agent, BSM
Riback, Harry W., Spec. Agent, Capt, BSM

MILITARY POLICE PLATOON

Auwers, Joseph T., Jr., Cpl, BSM
Bates, Elisha L., Sgt, BSM
Boynton, John T., Pfc, PH
Callahan, Jack R., Pfc, PH
Carroll, John J., Pfc, PH
Castonguay, Lyle D., Pfc, PH
Chapman, Raymond F., Cpl, PH
Davis, George R., Sgt, BSM
Diakomis, George J., Pfc, BSM
Dibble, Lewis R., Pfc, PH
Glass, Walter R., 1st Lt, BSM
Godwin, Harry L., Sr., Pfc, PH
Gompper, John W., 1st Lt, BSM
Hamrick, Chester A., Cpl, PH
Hill, Joseph B., Jr., Pfc, BSM
Hobgood, Arthur C., 1st Lt, BSM, PH
Kimble, Arthur H., Pfc, PH

LaFrance, Arthur F., Sgt, BSM, PH*
LaVallie, Edgar J., S/Sgt, BSM
Lehmann, Earnest L., Cpl, BSM
Leonard, Leo B., 1st Lt, BSM
Littrell, George E., Pfc, BSM
Lyon, Samuel H., Major, BSM
Liggett, Clarence E., Pfc, PH
Murray, Julius E., T/4, PH
Perchalski, Henry C., Pfc, BSM, SS
Potts, George W., Pfc, PH
Robinson, Jack L., S/Sgt, BSM
Stalter, Robert A., 1st Lt, BSM
Terris, John B., Pfc, BSM
Traino, Joseph S., Pfc, PH
Tyler, Harold N., Jr., Sgt, BSM, PH
Vermillion, Kenneth R., Pfc, BSM
Westergren, Oscar A., Pfc, BSM

Winnicky, Henry V., Cpl, BSM

88TH DIVISION BAND

Menz, Alex D., WOJG, BSM
Cooper, Lester M., T/Sgt, BSM
Fehrle, Karl F., S/Sgt, BSM
Hamlin, Colin F., T/Sgt, BSM

Sharff, Albert J., S/Sgt, BSM
Cohen, Rubin, T/5, BSM
Pratt, Frederick F., T/5, BSM
Ochs, Clayton C., Pfc, BSM

AMERICAN RED CROSS

Archer, Elsie, MF
Beatty, Fannye, MF
Crawford, Virginia, MF

Myers, Rosamond, MF
Simmons, Sylvia, PH, MF
Smith, Faye, MF

BATTLE HONORS

WAR DEPARTMENT
Washington 25, D. C., 24 January 1945

As authorized by Executive Order No. 9396 (sec. I, Bul. 22, WD, 1943), superseding Executive Order No. 9075 (sec. III, Bul. 11, WD, 1942), citations of the following units in General Orders, No. 188, Headquarters Fifth Army, 20 December 1944, as approved by the Commanding General, Mediterranean Theater of Operations, are confirmed under the provisions of section IV, Circular No. 333, War Department, 1943, in the name of the President of the United States as public evidence of deserved honor and distinction. The citation reads as follows:

The *3d Battalion, 351st Infantry Regiment,* is cited for outstanding performance of duty in action during the period 9 to 13 July 1944 in the vicinity of Laiatico, Italy. During the attack on strongly fortified German positions in the vicinity of Laiatico, the *3d Battalion* occupied an advanced position devoid of cover and with both flanks exposed, and for 3 days withstood heavy enemy artillery and mortar bombardments as well as three vicious enemy counterattacks supported by tanks. Displaying courage, skill, and determined fighting spirit, the battalion frustrated all enemy efforts to defend the town and surrounding strategic positions. On the fourth day, the *3d Battalion* launched a night attack and penetrated the German stronghold from the flanks and rear. Aggressively exploiting its break-through, the battalion seized a German regimental command post after a savage hand-to-hand struggle in the darkness and cut the main escape route from the Laiatico hill mass. As a result of the *3d Battalion's* prodigious efforts, 425 prisoners were taken, 250 Germans were killed or wounded, and a large quantity of enemy weapons were captured which were promptly employed with telling effect against the battered German forces. The timely capture of this key enemy defensive position compelled the Germans to abandon a carefully prepared, strongly defended line and opened the route of advance to the Arno River. The fearlessness, heroic determination, and aggressive fighting spirit of the officers and men of the *3d Battalion, 351st Infantry Regiment,* resulted in a performance which brings honor to the armed forces of the United States.

By ORDER OF THE SECRETARY OF WAR:

G. C. MARSHALL
Chief of Staff

OFFICIAL:
J. A. ULIO
*Major General
The Adjutant General*

WAR DEPARTMENT
Washington 25, D. C., 22 February 1945

As authorized by Executive Order No. 9396 (sec. I, Bul. 22, WD, 1943), superseding Executive Order No. 9075 (sec. III, Bul. 11, WD, 1942), citations of the following units in General Orders, No. 8, Headquarters Fifth Army, 17 January 1945, as approved by the Commanding General, Mediterranean Theater of Operations, are confirmed under the provisions of section IV, Circular No. 333, War Department, 1943, in the name of the President of the United States as public evidence of deserved honor and distinction. The citation reads as follows:

The *2d Battalion, 350th Infantry Regiment,* is cited for outstanding performance of duty in action during the period 27 September to 3 October 1944 on Mt. Battaglia, Italy. The *2d Battalion* was assigned the mission of seizing and holding strategic Mt. Battaglia. For 7 days, in the face of incessant and violent counterattacks by powerful enemy forces which at times included elements of four divisions, this battalion clung tenaciously to its positions on the objective. Each attack was preceded by artillery and mortar barrages and climaxed by bitter fire fights, use of flame throwers by the enemy, hand-to-hand combat, bayonet charges, and grenade duels. The gallant officers and men of this battalion repulsed each attack with a marked display of fighting ability and teamwork. Evacuation of the wounded was extremely difficult because of the inclement weather conditions, the nature of the terrain, and the fact that the enemy artillery, firing from the front and both flanks, covered every route of approach to Mt. Battaglia with a hail of fire. Nevertheless, all casualties were promptly evacuated by teams of litter bearers who courageously transported the wounded for long distances through artillery barrages to a point in the rear where further evacuation could be carried on by ambulances. All supplies were brought to the battalion's positions by pack mules supplemented by carrying parties. On several occasions the ammunition supply became dangerously low, and when the men exhausted their hand grenades they resorted to throwing rocks at the oncoming enemy. Though fighting under the most adverse battle conditions, the officers and men of this battalion displayed an indomitable spirit that refused to waver under the fiercest enemy attacks. The outstanding fighting ability and magnificent courage displayed by the *2d Battalion, 350th Infantry Regiment,* are exemplary of the finest traditions of the Army of the United States.

By ORDER OF THE SECRETARY OF WAR:

OFFICIAL: G. C. MARSHALL
   J. A. ULIO   *Chief of Staff*
   Major General
   The Adjutant General

GENERAL ORDERS
No. 53   WAR DEPARTMENT
                         Washington 25, D. C., 11 June 1946
   As authorized by Executive Order 9396 (sec. I, WD Bul. 22, 1943), superseding Executive Order 9075 (sec. III, WD Bul. 11, 1942), citation of the following unit, as approved by the Commanding General, United States Army Forces, Mediterranean Theater, 29 April 1945, is confirmed under the provisions of section IV, WD Circular 333, 1943, in the name of the President of the United States as public evidence of deserved honor and distinction. The citation reads as follows:
   The *2d Battalion, 351st Infantry Regiment,* is cited for outstanding performance of duty in action during the period 27 September to 1 October 1944, near Mt. Capello, Italy. The 2d Battalion was assigned the mission of wresting the strategically important Mt. Capello from a determined and numerically superior German force. In the face of a withering hail of fire from all types of weapons, the *2d Battalion* launched its attack down the barren, forward slopes of Mt. Guasteto, Italy, eliminating a strong reverse slope German position in four violent assaults characterized by bitter fire fights and vicious hand-to-hand grenade duels. Although outnumbered, the soldiers of this organization maintained their captured position, despite ruthless enemy counterattacks preceded by intense artillery and mortar barrages. Although suffering from severe losses and confronted by fanatical enemy resistance, the courageous officers and men of the *2d Battalion* again resumed a full scale offensive and advancing by infiltration, neutralizing resistance by furious hand-to-hand fighting within the German positions, gained a foothold on the barren slopes of Mt. Capello. Setting a commendable example of coolness and efficiency in the face of great danger, the *2d Battalion* fought grimly, tenaciously maintaining its foothold, despite the murderous enemy fire and wave after wave of fresh enemy assault troops. In a notable display of combat skill, teamwork, and determination, the men of the *2d Battalion,* because of shortage of ammunition, resorted to captured German machine guns and German grenades to meet the enemy onslaughts. Utilizing personnel from battalion headquarters as riflemen, because of its heavily depleted effective strength, the battalion, in a final all-out assault, drove the enemy from Mt. Capello, retaining this strategic terrain feature, despite final desperate enemy counterattacks. The timely capture of this key enemy position frustrated violent enemy efforts to hold terrain of vital importance. A dangerous enemy penetration between the 351st Infantry Regiment and another hard-pressed infantry regiment on the right was averted by the heroic determination, self-sacrifice, and unfailing devotion to duty of the officers and men of the *2d Battalion, 351st Infantry Regiment.* The valorous performance of the *2d Battalion, 351st Infantry Regiment,* reflects great credit on the personnel of the regiment and upon the armed forces of the United States.
   By ORDER OF THE SECRETARY OF WAR:

                                DWIGHT D. EISENHOWER
OFFICIAL: *Chief of Staff*
   EDWARD F. WITSELL
   Major General
   The Adjutant General

OUTLINE OF POW COMMAND ACTIVITIES

The 88th Division assumed its twofold POW Command duties on 7 June 1945, to repatriate a minimum of 100,000 Germans and to form an estimated maximum of 120,000 of them into service units. POW strength figures at the time indicated that the 88th Division had approximately 295,000 Germans available to accomplish this dual mission. Later figures raised this total above 320,000 as Germans came in out of the hills, unguarded German service units were discovered and taken over, and responsibility for the Czech PWs was transferred from Fifth Army to the Division. The total included Italians, recalcitrants, wanted persons, field and general officers, friendly nationals and seriously sick and wounded.

The MTOUSA POW Command formulated, without precedent or guidance, policies for the treatment of PWs; organized and administered a command that was spread all over Italy (with over 600 miles between some elements of the division; guarded and administered more than 320,000 PWs in hundreds of cages and PW service units with little more than 12,000 available guards—all of this while the fluctuating demands of redeployment caused constant changes of key personnel to include more than a two hundred per cent turnover of the Division personnel during the three and one-half months life of the POW Command! Small wonder that lights burned far into the night, clerks tore their hair out; sentries met themselves coming off and going on guard; officers counted and inspected Krauts in their sleep; bulging Jerry-filled trains toiled up through the Brenner Pass and creaky convoys under Blue Devil supervision were seen in the remotest parts of Italy.

The MTOUSA POW Command was inactivated on orders of CG, MTOUSA as of 12:00, noon, 25 September 1945. During its existence, it had accomplished the following:

Repatriation of Germans or Austrians	135,893
Repatriation of Czechoslovakians	11,008
Repatriation of Russians	7,984
Repatriation of other friendly nationals	2,978
Discharged released in Italy (almost entirely South Tyrolean)	10,567
Turnover of Neo-Fascists to Italian Government	32,212
Turnover of PWs organized into service units to British	12,000
Organized into service units	112,000[1]
Total PWs disposed of	324,642

In commenting on this piece of work it seems permissible to boast that the 88th (Blue Devil) Division took more prisoners in active operations than any other division in the Italian Theater, evacuated by far the greatest number to the rear after VI-day; without a break, discharged the POW Command Mission with all its ramifications and then with smooth and quiet efficiency assumed the occupational role in Venezia–Giulia.

[1] This figure included general service units of Ordnance, Engineer, Chemical, Quartermaster, Signal, Medical, and Veterinary troops who were used to assist in moving dumps, loading ships and otherwise speeding the redeployment of American troops.

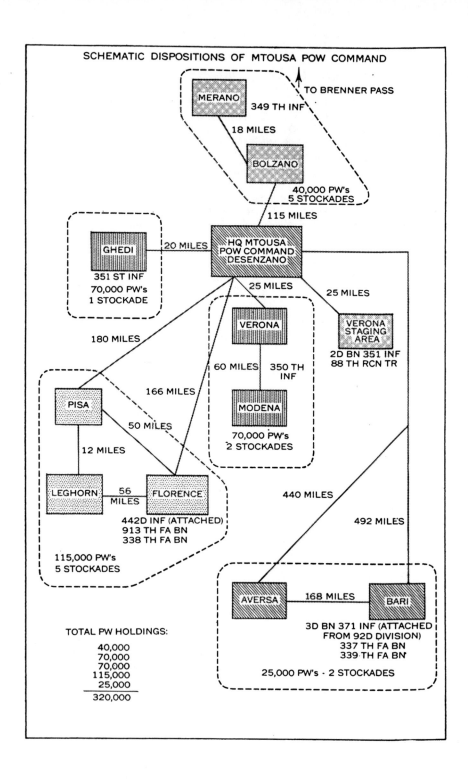

SCHEMATIC DISPOSITIONS OF MTOUSA POW COMMAND

TO BRENNER PASS

MERANO
349 TH INF

18 MILES

BOLZANO

40,000 PW's
5 STOCKADES

115 MILES

GHEDI ─ 20 MILES ─ HQ MTOUSA POW COMMAND DESENZANO

351 ST INF
70,000 PW's
1 STOCKADE

25 MILES

25 MILES

180 MILES

VERONA

VERONA STAGING AREA

2D BN 351 INF
88 TH RCN TR

60 MILES   350 TH INF

166 MILES

PISA

50 MILES

MODENA

70,000 PW's
2 STOCKADES

12 MILES

LEGHORN ─ 56 MILES ─ FLORENCE

442D INF (ATTACHED)
913 TH FA BN
338 TH FA BN

440 MILES

492 MILES

115,000 PW's
5 STOCKADES

AVERSA ─ 168 MILES ─ BARI

3D BN 371 INF (ATTACHED
FROM 92D DIVISION)
337 TH FA BN
339 TH FA BN

25,000 PW's · 2 STOCKADES

TOTAL PW HOLDINGS:

40,000
70,000
70,000
115,000
25,000
─────────
320,000

LaVergne, TN USA
16 December 2010
208997LV00007B/5/P